D0883291

HUMAN
GEOGRAPHY
People, Place, and Culture

HUMAN GEOGRAPHY
People, Place, and Culture
CANADIAN EDITION

ERIN H. FOUBERG
NORTHERN STATE UNIVERSITY

ALEXANDER B. MURPHY
UNIVERSITY OF OREGON

H. J. DE BLIJ
MICHIGAN STATE UNIVERSITY

CATHERINE J. NASH
BROCK UNIVERSITY

WILEY

JOHN WILEY & SONS CANADA, LTD.

Copyright © 2012 John Wiley & Sons Canada, Ltd.

All rights reserved. No part of this work covered by the copyrights herein may be reproduced or used in any form or by any means—graphic, electronic, or mechanical—without the prior written permission of the publisher.

Any request for photocopying, recording, taping, or inclusion in information storage and retrieval systems of any part of this book shall be directed to the Canadian copyright licensing agency, Access Copyright. For an Access Copyright licence, visit www.accesscopyright.ca or call toll-free, 1-800-893-5777.

Care has been taken to trace ownership of copyright material contained in this text. The publishers will gladly receive any information that will enable them to rectify any erroneous reference or credit line in subsequent editions.

Statistics Canada information is used with permission of the Minister of Industry, as Minister responsible for Statistics Canada. Information on the availability of the wide range of data from Statistics Canada can be obtained from Statistics Canada's Regional Offices, its website at http://www.statcan.ca, or its toll-free access number 1-800-263-1136.

Library and Archives Canada Cataloguing in Publication

Human geography: people, place, and culture/Erin H.
Fouberg ... [et al.].—Canadian ed.
Includes bibliographical references and index.
ISBN 978-0-470-15806-7 1. Human geography. I. Fouberg, Erin Hogan
GF41.H893 2011   304.2   C2010-907602-8

Production Credits
Acquisitions Editor: Rodney Burke
Vice President & Publisher: Veronica Visentin
Senior Marketing Manager: Patty Maher
Editorial Manager: Karen Staudinger
Production Manager: Tegan Wallace
Developmental Editor: Gail Brown
Media Editor: Channade Fenandoe
Editorial Assistant: Laura Hwee
Interior Design: Interrobang Graphic Design Inc.
Cover Design: Joanna Vieira
Cover Image: © Brownstock
Printing and Binding: Courier

Printed and bound in the United States of America
1 2 3 4 5 CC 16 15 14 13 12

WILEY

John Wiley & Sons Canada, Ltd.
6045 Freemont Blvd.
Mississauga, Ontario L5R 4J3
Visit our website at: www.wiley.ca

PREFACE

Welcome to the Canadian edition of *Human Geography: People, Place, and Culture*. The goal for this edition was to build on the strengths of the American text, while bringing a Canadian perspective to geographical issues. Understanding the importance of the geographical requires a global perspective while considering the intricate interrelationships between people and places across constantly shifting and multiple scales—the *human-environment* relationship. In creating a Canadian edition, it was important to ensure that a Canadian focus was maintained. This was achieved in three main ways:

- By using Canadian examples in conjunction with broader international and global illustrations to integrate a sense of the distinctive Canadian geographical circumstances within broader contexts. Most of these examples draw on well-known contemporary and historical events of interest to encourage attentiveness to Canadian histories and geographies.

- By highlighting the research and publications of top Canadian scholars influential in geographical scholarship in the various subdisciplines. These stand side-by-side with references to the leading work in the field, highlighting Canadians' contributions to international research and scholarship.

- By including in each chapter a field note authored by relatively new Canadian scholars commenting on how and why they came to do the work they do and a brief discussion of the nature of their research. These are designed to demonstrate the passion and personal commitment scholars bring to their careers and to encourage students to think about their own curiosities and interests.

The perspectives on the processes and impacts of globalization are highly contested but undeniable in both their presence and their influence. Canada occupies a particular (and mobile) place within these processes. Globalization is a set of processes that flow and pulsate across and through country boundaries—processes that have different outcomes in different places and across scales. The goals in writing the Canadian edition were first, to help students appreciate the role people play in shaping places and the way that places shape people; second, to provide a larger context so that students can better understand their world; third, to give students the tools to engage in the complexities of the debates about the political, social, and economic fallout of globalization; and fourth, to help students think geographically and critically about their world.

Most important, perhaps, students today are living in a world that is quite different from what any other generation has experienced; they are living, as geographer Andrew Kirby explains, "not in a world without boundaries or without limits, but simply a world." Today's students engage daily with the world, whether or not they are conscious of that fact. Students are part of the world, and many have a global identity. They need to make sense of themselves not just in their home, college or university, locality, nation, and region, but also beyond their world. Globalization means that people and places across the world are constantly interacting. For good or for ill, each of us is a part of that interaction. Each of us, therefore, must make sense of who we are and what our role is in this globalized world, and we each must think critically about how we can shape our world. With globalization, the way people make places and shape their identities has global, local, and individual implications. What people do today, whether making a pilgrimage to a river or buying a product, happens in a global context.

When students understand the role people play in making places, see the geographic context in which a major issue occurs, learn to think geographically and critically about the world, and appreciate the complexities of globalization, they become geographically literate and are better prepared to confront the challenges of the twenty-first century.

Features of the Canadian Edition

This Canadian edition integrates text, photos, and illustrations to help students understand the role people play in shaping the world, to provide geographic context to the issues we discuss, to teach students to think geographically and critically, and to explain the complexities of thinking geographically and what that actually means; that is, understanding that "place matters" and that who they are and their possibilities, limitations, and opportunities depend on *where* they are. For this reason, each chapter begins at the level of the personal, with examples and illustrations that will resonate with most students' experiences in their everyday lives.

The Canadian edition strives to cultivate a *spatial perspective* in students as they study a range of issues from political elections and urban shantytowns to gay urban neighbourhoods and farming life. While there are many possible ways to conceptualize the spatial, this edition uses five themes to organize students' thinking—location, region, place, landscape, and movement. Throughout the chapters, one or more of these themes is examined within the context of human-environment relations.

This edition uses Key Questions as the organizing principle for each chapter in the text. The Key Questions are listed after the opening field note of each chapter and serve as the outline for the chapter. At the end of each section, the reader is presented with a summary of Main Points that are the key concepts or ideas discussed in that section and that help to answer the Key Questions for that section. Students may use the Key Questions and the Main Points as a convenient summary of the information and for study purposes. Instructors may use the Key Questions and Main Points to prepare lectures, develop examination questions, or to generate class discussion.

Several features of the Canadian edition provide context and help students learn to think geographically. Each chapter in this edition includes one or more Field Note (including a chapter-opening field note), written by one of the authors, providing context for the particular author's experiences in the field and pulling students into the chapter. Each chapter also includes one or more Guest Field Note contributed by professionals and researchers in the field. The author field notes serve as models of how to think geographically and the guest field notes detail scholars' commitment to the discipline of geography through their specific research interests.

Chapter Organization

This text is organized around the main subdisciplines in geography. The chapter order reflects the desire to introduce students to geographical scholarship in a logical and intuitive order. The text begins with a discussion in the first two chapters about the processes and debates around the concept of globalization, which provides the wider context for the rest of the book. Chapter 3 introduces the subdiscipline of political geography, providing the pivotal historical background for understanding the current world order, including the political, economic, and social circumstances. We then consider the distribution of human populations over the surface of the earth by examining population geography in Chapter 4 and migration in Chapter 5. The human-environment relationship, the heart of geographical enquiry, is the focus of Chapter 6 as we survey the scholarship on nature, society, and the environment. Chapters 7 and 8 constitute an introduction to the subdisciplines of social and cultural geography, respectively. Chapter 9 focuses on agricultural development and the emergence of stable human settlements as well as rural life. In Chapter 10, we examine the process of urbanization, a central concern of geographers given that the majority of the world's people live in urban environments. We explore aspects of economic and development geographies in Chapter 11 and make important linkages with those themes of globalization introduced in Chapter 2. In Chapter 12, we examine the important field of transportation geographies, a timely topic given increasing global concerns about pollution, environmental degradation, and the problems of moving people and goods on a variety of scales. Chapter 13 concludes the text with a consideration of the geographies of industrialization and the service sector.

The Teaching and Learning Package

The Canadian edition of *Human Geography: People, Place, and Culture* is supported by a comprehensive supplements package that includes an extensive selection of resources.

RESOURCES THAT HELP TEACHERS TEACH

The *Human Geography: People, Place, and Culture* Canadian Edition Instructor Site www.wiley.com/go/fouberg. This website provides a wealth of resources for instructors to facilitate their teaching and course management and to help enhance their students' learning. The site includes:

On-Location Videos. This rich collection of original and relevant footage was taken during H. J. de Blij's travels. These videos, which are available on the instructor and student companion websites, cover a wide range of themes and locations.

A complete collection of **PowerPoint presentations**. These presentations are intended to enhance lecture presentations and serve as an effective overview and point-form summary of the key concepts of each chapter.

A comprehensive **Test Bank** with multiple-choice, fill-in, matching, and essay questions. The Test Bank is distributed via the secure instructor website and can be used in all major test application programs.

A comprehensive collection of **animations** and **additional resources**.

Wiley Faculty Network (WFN). This peer-to-peer network of faculty is ready to support your use of online course management tools and discipline-specific software/learning systems in the classroom. The WFN will help you apply innovative classroom techniques, implement software packages, tailor the technology experience to the needs of each individual class, and provide you with virtual training sessions led by faculty for faculty.

RESOURCES THAT HELP STUDENTS LEARN

Student Companion Website www.wiley.com/go/fouberg. This easy-to-use and student-focused website helps reinforce and illustrate key concepts from the text. It also provides interactive media content that helps students check their understanding and prepare for tests. This website provides additional resources to complement the textbook and enhance students' understanding of geography:

On-Location Videos provide a first-hand look at life in different locations around the world.

Action-Oriented Activities enable students to apply their knowledge and understanding of the chapter material.

Map Quizzes help students master the place-names that are crucial to their success in this course. Three game-formatted place-name activities are provided for each chapter.

GeoDiscoveries Modules allow students to explore key concepts in greater depth using videos, animations, and interactive exercises.

Chapter Self-Test Quizzes provide immediate feedback to true/false, multiple choice, and short-answer questions.

Web Links put useful electronic resources into context.

Acknowledgements

In preparing the Canadian edition of *Human Geography*, we benefited immensely from the advice and assistance of colleagues in geography who took the time to read and evaluate the draft manuscripts. We thank them for their insightful and invaluable feedback.

Mark Troy Burnett, *Mount Royal University*
Robert Dilley, *Lakehead University*
Sean Doherty, *Wilfrid Laurier University*
Michael Fox, *Mount Allison University*
Jason Grek-Martin, *Saint Mary's University*
Michael Imort, *Wilfrid Laurier University*
Daniel H. Olsen, *Brandon University*
Lucy M. Sportza, *University of Guelph*
Rosario Turvey, *Lakehead University*
Jon Unruh, *McGill University*

In the Canadian edition, a number of our colleagues in geography contributed guest field notes, which added a wonderful dimension to the text. We believe these guest field notes will help students to better appreciate the role of fieldwork in geographic research and we hope they will help to motivate students in their own research. We thank the following contributors.

Christopher Fullerton, *Brock University*
Sutama Ghosh, *Ryerson University*
Nicole Gombay, *University of Canterbury*

Jason Grek-Martin, *Saint Mary's University*
Marilyne Jollineau, *Brock University*
Sarah de Leeuw, *University of Northern British Columbia*
Heather Maguire, *York University*
Sarah Jane Meharg, *Royal Military College of Canada*
Robert Oliver, *Virginia Polytechnic Institute and State University*
Natalie Oswin, *McGill University*
Victoria Tasker, *Brock University*
Valerie Thomas, *Virginia Polytechnic Institute and State University*
Nicole Yantzi, *Laurentian University*

Thank you to the following team at Wiley for their commitment to excellence and their professionalism: Rodney Burke, Acquisitions Editor; Patty Maher, Marketing Manager; and Gail Brown, Developmental Editor. Thank you also to all those involved in the production of this textbook, in particular copy editor Audrey McClennan, proofreader Laurel Hyatt, and permissions and photo researchers Christina Beamish, Luisa Begani, Cynthia Howard, Mary Rose MacLachlan, and Julie Pratt. All the writing, producing, and marketing of this book would be wasted without an energetic and dedicated sales staff. We sincerely thank all the publishing representatives for their tireless efforts and energy. Sincerest thanks are also offered to all who worked on and contributed to the wide assortment of supplements and ancillaries for this textbook.

I am very grateful to family and friends who supported me in the writing of this textbook. Many thanks to my partner, Cindy Berry, and to my colleagues in the Department of Geography who contributed time and effort to the production of this text. A special thanks to Christopher Fullerton for bringing his expertise to this project and writing Chapter 9 (Agriculture), Chapter 11 (Development), and a chapter unique to the Canadian edition, Chapter 12 (Transportation). Another special thank you to Marilyne Jollineau, not only for contributing the Guest Field Note for Chapter 1, but for reviewing the section on remote sensing and the appendix on mapping. Finally, this text could not have been completed without the commitment, dedication, and expertise of Heather Maguire, research assistant *par excellence*.

Catherine Nash
St. Catharines, Ontario

January 2012

ABOUT THE AUTHORS

Erin H. Fouberg

Erin Hogan Fouberg grew up in eastern South Dakota. She moved to Washington, D.C. to attend Georgetown University's School of Foreign Service, where she took a class in Human Geography from Harm de Blij. At Georgetown, Erin found her International Relations classes lacking in context and discovered a passion for political geography. She earned her master's and Ph.D. at the University of Nebraska-Lincoln. After graduating, Dr. Fouberg taught for several years at the University of Mary Washington in Fredericksburg, Virginia, where the graduating class of 2001 bestowed on her the Mary Pinschmidt Award, given to the faculty member who made the biggest impact on their lives.

Professor Fouberg is Associate Professor of Geography at Northern State University (NSU) in Aberdeen, South Dakota. Her research and publications focus on the governance and sovereignty of American Indian tribes and on geographic education. Professor Fouberg served as Vice President of Publications and Products of the National Council for Geographic Education. She enjoys travelling, camping, exercising, golfing, and watching athletic and theatre events at NSU.

Alexander B. Murphy

Alec Murphy grew up in the western United States, but he spent several of his early years in Europe and Japan. He obtained his undergraduate degree at Yale University, studied law at the Columbia University School of Law, practised law for a short time in Chicago, and then pursued a doctoral degree in geography (Ph.D. University of Chicago, 1987). After graduating, Dr. Murphy joined the faculty of the University of Oregon, where he is now Professor of Geography and holder of the James F. and Shirley K. Rippey Chair in Liberal Arts and Sciences. Professor Murphy is a widely published scholar in the fields of political, cultural, and environmental geography, with a regional emphasis on Europe. His work has been supported by the National Science Foundation, the National Endowment for the Humanities, and the Fulbright-Hays foreign fellowship program.

Professor Murphy served as the President of the Association of American Geographers in 2003. He is also Vice President of the American Geographical Society. For 11 years he was one of the editors of *Progress in Human Geography*; he currently co-edits *Eurasian Geography and Economics*. In the late 1990s, he led the effort to add geography to the College Board's Advanced Placement Program. His interests include hiking, skiing, camping, music, and of course exploring the diverse places that make up our planet.

H. J. de Blij

Harm de Blij received his early schooling in Europe, his college education in Africa, and his higher degrees in the United States (Ph.D. Northwestern, 1959). He has published more than 30 books and over 100 articles, and has received five honorary degrees. Several of his books have been translated into foreign languages.

Dr. de Blij is Distinguished Professor of Geography at Michigan State University. He has held the George Landegger Chair at Georgetown University's School of Foreign Service and the John Deaver Drinko Chair of Geography at Marshall University, and has also taught at the Colorado School of Mines and the University of Miami. He was the Geography Editor on ABC-TV's "Good Morning America" program for seven years and later served as Geography Analyst for NBC News. He was for more than 20 years a member of the National Geographic Society's Committee for Research and Exploration and was the founding editor of its scholarly journal, *National Geographic Research*. He is an honorary lifetime member of the Society. Professor de Blij is a soccer fan, an avid wine collector, and an amateur violinist.

Catherine J. Nash

Catherine Jean Nash was born into a military (Navy) family and spent the first decade of her life moving from Victoria to Ottawa, Halifax, Montreal, and finally Ottawa again. She began her working life as a lawyer practising municipal law, expropriations, and land development. After eight years in private practice, she returned to university and completed a Masters in Regional and Urban Planning at Queen's University. It was there that Professor Nash took a third-year geography course, Gender and Geography, sparking her interest in the geographical. Professor Nash completed her Ph.D. at Queen's in 2004 and is currently an Associate Professor in the Department of Geography at Brock University in St. Catharines, Ontario.

BRIEF CONTENTS

CONTENTS

HUMAN
GEOGRAPHY
People, Place, and Culture

chapter 1

INTRODUCTION TO HUMAN GEOGRAPHY

The Geographical Imagination

IN APRIL 2007, the Canadian Broadcasting Corporation (CBC) launched the *Seven Wonders of Canada* event. The organizers challenged Canadians to nominate their choice for the top Canadian *wonder*. They defined a wonder as either a spectacular physical site or an amazing human creation. Contestants needed to demonstrate how their choice reflected an essential Canadian-ness. Submissions were judged on their uniqueness and originality, their historical significance, and their ability to inspire and to provoke emotion and pride in our Canadian places.

The event drew some 25,000 nominations and over one million votes. In on-line voting through the CBC website, six of the top seven wonders were Niagara Falls, the northern lights, the Cabot Trail, Nahanni National Park, the Rockies, and the Sleeping Giant. The top pick was the Bay of Fundy (Figure 1.1), with the highest tides in the world; spectacular marine, animal, and plant life; and distinctive tidal bores, mud flats, and marshes. Human creations were also showcased—Anne of Green Gables house, the Library of Parliament, the Spiral Tunnels of the Canadian Pacific Railway in British Columbia, Château Montebello, and the Vimy Memorial.

In formal judging, the final list was an eclectic mix of human-made and physical sites. Taking top spot was the canoe, arguably the quintessential Canadian icon and a truly inspired choice. It speaks of our colonial history of exploration and settlement and our connections with Canada's indigenous peoples and wilderness landscapes. Many of our well-known writers,

(a)

(b)

(c)

FIGURE 1.1 Wonders of Canada. (a) Bay of Fundy, New Brunswick; (b) Vimy Memorial, France; and (c) Niagara Falls, Ontario. (Mike Grandmaison/Corbis; Paul Thompson/Corbis; © Joe Fox/Alamy)

artists, and politicians—such as Bill Mason, E. Pauline Johnson, and Pierre Elliot Trudeau—sought inspiration, comfort, and solitude by canoeing our lakes and rivers. Today, no summer camp, cottage, or recreational area—from Canada's national parks to the Rideau Canal—is likely to be without a canoe (Figure 1.2).

The runners-up also reflected Canadians' connections with places of both natural beauty and architectural wonder—including the Rockies, Pier 21, Prairie skies, Niagara Falls, the igloo, and Old Quebec City. Even if we have never been to Niagara Falls, it is part of our imagined sense of Canada, giving us a collective sense of connection to well-known places, even if they are unseen. What it means to be Canadian is, for many of us, deeply attached to these everyday landscapes in which we live, be they urban or rural, natural or human built.

For a human geographer, the *Seven Wonders of Canada* competition illustrates the multiple interests of geographical studies—the political, the social, the economic, and the cultural. Human geography is about the ties that bind us to place and the emotions that drive us apart. It is about how we interact with our environment, how we change it, and how our landscapes have an impact on us. For human geographers, then, the relationship between the human and natural worlds is a constant preoccupation, providing us with never-ending possibilities for exploration and study.

Source: *Canadian Wonders*, www.cbc.ca/sevenwonders.

(a)

(b)

(c)

FIGURE 1.2 The Canoe in Canada. The canoe and canoeing is an intrinsic part of Canada. (a) Canadian Canoe Museum, Peterborough, Ontario. (b) Innu making canoes near Sheshatshiu, Newfoundland, ca. 1920. (c) Pierre Trudeau paddles a canoe in 1968, in the waters off Baffin Island's Clearwater Fiord. (© Canadian Canoe Museum; © photo by Fred C. Sears/Library and Archives Canada PA-148593; Peter Bregg/The Canadian Press)

KEY QUESTIONS FOR CHAPTER 1

1. What is human geography?
2. What are geographic questions?
3. Why do geographers use maps and what do maps tell us?
4. Why are geographers concerned with scale and connectedness?
5. What does it mean to "think geographically" and how do we do it?

1.1 What Is Human Geography?

It's not the land that has made our country what it is … it's the way we've shaped it and the things we've built on it, the monumental achievements of engineering and imagination in which we took a wilderness and forged it into a nation. (Christopher Hume, *Toronto Star*, June 9, 2008)

Human-environment The reciprocal relationship between humans and environment.

Human geography One of the two major divisions of geography; the spatial analysis of human population, its cultures, activities, and landscapes.

Physical geography One of the two major divisions of geography; the spatial analysis of the structure, processes, and location of the Earth's natural phenomena such as climate, soil, plants, animals, and topography.

Geographers study **human-environment** relationships. In this context, "environment" refers to both the natural world and the myriad places created or built by humans. The field of **human geography** focuses on how humans create places in the natural or physical world, how we interact with each other in and across different places, and how we make sense of others and ourselves. We are all geographers at heart as we navigate through our everyday lives, creating our own private spaces of "home," perhaps travelling to faraway lands, and carefully negotiating the best route to ensure we get our chores done.

While the disciplines of human and **physical geography** are closely related areas of study, physical geographers explore the processes and patterns at work in the physical world, while human geographers examine human activities interacting with that physical world. Human geography is also concerned with the processes of change. We examine past activities to see how they affect contemporary places, and we consider how both past and present activities might shape our world, for better or for worse, in the future.

The quotation from Christopher Hume, a *Toronto Star* architecture and urban affairs columnist, at the beginning of this chapter highlights our dynamic impact on the world around us. But in writing about the winners of the Seven Wonders of Canada contest, Hume's focus was the nation-building activities of Canada's colonizing peoples. He did not mention the presence and activities of First Nations peoples in North America. Also, his quote suggests that human-environment interaction operates in one direction: humans, through their ingenuity, alter their environment for their own benefit. This is an **anthropocentric view**—one in which human interests and perspectives alone are highlighted. Most human geographers take a broader view, arguing that just as human activities constantly change our physical and built environment, so do our physical and built environments have a profound effect on us as individuals and as a society. The places we grow up, and the places we experience, in positive or negative ways, influence our sense of self and our norms,

Anthropocentric view A view in which human interests and perspectives are highlighted.

values, and beliefs. Our sense of self and our norms and values, in turn, affect how we see others and how we understand the world.

Human geographers use the term **sense of place** to highlight our relationships to the places we build and inhabit. This term suggests that we not only think about a location's physical or material characteristics, but we also consider the sentiments we feel and meanings we hold for particular places. This sense of place underpins our everyday decisions, including where we want to live and work and, perhaps, have a family. Our sense of place is also pivotal when we make our most important decisions, such as whether we consider a place worth dying for if we face the choice of defending that place in a war.

Sense of place State of mind derived through the infusion of a place with meaning and emotion by remembering important events that occurred in that place or by labelling a place with a certain character.

One deceptively simple concept in human geography is the idea that "place matters." Where we are literally affects our life chances—the possibilities for success or failure, health and happiness, life or death. Place has an impact on our ability to access public services, such as health care, or to find employment, afford a house, or breathe less polluted air. Whether we live in Newfoundland or Alberta affects whether we can find a job, what kind of job we will work at every day for many years, and our resulting quality of life. Place determines whom we meet and get to know and whom we do not. The familiar phrase "a place for everything and everything in its place" tells us something about our expectations—about who we should expect to find in certain places and when people might be seen as "out of place"—which in turn have serious implications for individuals and groups that might be regarded as being in places where they do not belong (Figure 1.3). Often, whom we expect to see and where we expect to see them depends on our ideas about age, race, ethnicity, gender, and other markers of the self. The geography of our everyday lives is pivotal in influencing who we are and what we might become.

No place on Earth is untouched by people. As people explore, travel, migrate, interact, play, live, and work, they make places. They organize themselves into communities, nations, and broader societal networks, establishing political, economic, religious, linguistic, and cultural systems that enable them to function in space. People adapt to, alter, manipulate, and cope with their physical geographic environment and are, in turn, influenced by their experiences in that environment. No place stands apart from human action, nor is human action undertaken apart from place.

Clearly, places do not exist in splendid isolation, and human geographers are interested in the interconnections between different places. Throughout human history, advances in communication and transportation technologies have made places and people more interconnected. Only 100 years ago, the fastest modes of transportation were the steamship, the railroad, and the horse and buggy. Today we can cross the globe in record time, with easy access to automobiles, airplanes, and ships.

(a)

(b)

FIGURE 1.3 (a) A Segregated Beach in South Africa, 1982. (b) Breast Feeding in Public, Toronto, Ontario. (UN Photo; Mark Blinch/Reuters/Landov)

The interconnections between places are not only about how humans move from one place to another. Aspects of popular culture, such as fashion and architecture, are in some ways making many people and places seem more alike. Despite all these changes, our world still encompasses a multitude of ways in which people identify themselves and others. Nearly 200 countries, a diversity of religions, thousands of languages, and any number of settlement types, from small villages to enormous cities, come together in different ways around the globe to create a world of endlessly diverse places and people. Understanding and explaining this diversity is the mission of human geography.

One term used frequently to describe the contemporary interconnections between places is *globalization*, a concept discussed in detail in Chapter 2. For now, the term can be understood as referring to a set of processes that reflect increasing interactions and heightening interdependence among and between places,

with diminishing regard for national borders. Globalization also refers to a set of outcomes that result from these processes. These outcomes are unevenly distributed—that is, the processes of globalization are experienced differently in different locations, with different results across the world. For example, the fashion industry encompasses a far-reaching set of global processes that include consumerism, advertising, manufacturing, and shipping. However, the fashion industry experienced by a garment worker in Cambodia (Figure 1.4) is significantly different from that experienced by a teenager in Winnipeg, Manitoba.

Discussions about the processes of globalization often focus on the pull between the global—seen as a blanket covering the world—and the local—seen as a continuation of the traditional despite the blanket of globalization. Geographers are well positioned to understand globalization as much more than this. When they describe the outcomes of globalization as unevenly distributed, they are not only talking about effects and changes at the local level. Geographers use the concept of **scale** to understand the networked interrelationships among individual, local, region-

> **Scale** Representation of a real-world phenomenon at a certain level of reduction or generalization. In cartography, the ratio of map distance to ground distance; indicated on a map as a bar graph, representative fraction, and/or verbal statement.

al, national, and global. Globalizing processes occur at the world scale and are visible in such things as the global financial markets or even global environmental change. However, the processes of globalization do not magically appear at the global scale: *what happens at other scales (individual, local, regional, national) helps create the processes of globalization and shape the outcomes of globalization.* To reduce our understanding of the world to a consideration of only the local and the global is to miss all the complex interactions across, and cutting through, a multiplicity of scales. In this book, we study these processes and outcomes of globalization, and we use scale to assess the dynamic effects and impacts on place.

FIGURE 1.4 Garment Workers in Cambodia. (Tang Chhin Sothy/ AFP/Getty Images)

- Human geographers study human-environment relations—both the impact we have on the physical and built environment, and the interrelated impact the physical and material world has on us, individually and collectively.

- Human geographers are concerned with our sense of place—that is, how we make sense of place and our emotions, sentiments, and attachments to place.

- Human geographers argue that "place matters." Where we are affects our sense of self (individually and also collectively, as a society), determines our ability to access services such as education and health care, and influences who we expect to see in which places.

- Places are interconnected in complex ways. Globalization is a set of processes that reflect increasing interactions, deepening relationships, and heightening interdependence among and between places without regard to national borders. It also refers to a set of outcomes that are felt from these global processes—outcomes that are unevenly distributed and differently manifested across the world.

1.2 What Are Geographic Questions?

Geographer Marvin Mikesell defines geography succinctly as the "why of where." Why and how do things come together in certain places to produce particular outcomes? Why are some things found in certain places but not in others? To what extent do things in one place influence those in other places? To these questions, we add "so what?" Why does it matter that things are different across space? What role does a place play in its region and in the world, and what does that mean for people there and elsewhere? Questions such as these are at the core of geographic inquiry—whether human or physical—and they are of critical importance in any effort to make sense of our world.

If the field of geography deals with so many aspects of our world, ranging from people and places to coastlines and climates, what do the various facets of this wide-ranging discipline have in common? The answer lies in a perspective that both human and physical geographers use: the **spatial**. Virtually all geographers are interested in the spatial arrangement of places and phenomena: how they are laid out, organized, and arranged on the Earth, and how they appear in the landscape.

> **Spatial** Pertaining to space on the Earth's surface; sometimes used as a synonym for *geographic*.

THE SPATIAL PERSPECTIVE

Geography, and being geographically literate, involves much more than memorizing places on a map. In this sense, the disciplines of geography and history have much in common. History is not merely memorizing dates. To understand history is to appreciate how events, circumstances, and ideas came together at particular times to produce certain outcomes. Knowledge of how events have developed over time is critical to understanding who we are and where we are going.

Understanding change over time is critically important, and understanding change across space is equally important. The great German philosopher Immanuel Kant argued that we need to pay scholarly attention not only to particular phenomena (such as economics and sociology), but also to the perspectives of time (history) and space (geography). The disciplines of history and geography have intellectual cores defined by perspective rather than by subject matter.

Human geographers use a **spatial perspective** as they study a multitude of phenomena ranging from political elections and shantytowns to gay urban neighbourhoods and folk music. The goal here is for you to develop a spatial perspective on the world around you and the everyday spaces you experience. While there are many possible ways to conceptualize the spatial, we have selected **five themes** derived from the spatial perspective in geography to organize this book.

> **Spatial perspective** Observing variations in geographic phenomena across space.
>
> **Five themes (of geography)** The five themes derived from the spatial perspective of geography are location, region, place, landscape, and movement.

THE FIVE THEMES

Throughout this book, we draw in five major themes or concepts: location, region, place, landscape, and movement. This means that in every discussion about human-environment relations, we will use one or more of these themes. Many of these themes overlap or have similarities in meaning, and human geographers use the concepts in different combinations as they think about the geographical.

Location. To have a spatial perspective is to be thoughtful about or aware of **location**. Thinking about location highlights how the geographical position of people and things on the Earth's surface matters in terms of what happens where, how, and why. A concern with location underlies almost

> **Location** The first theme of geography; the geographical situation of people and things.

all geographical work, as location helps to establish the context within which events and processes are situated.

Some geographers develop elaborate (often quantitative) models describing the locational properties of particular phenomena—even predicting where things are likely to occur.

> **Location theory** A logical attempt to explain the locational pattern of an economic activity and the manner in which its producing areas are interrelated. The agricultural location theory contained in the von Thünen model in Chapter 9 is a leading example.

Such undertakings have fostered an interest in **location theory**, an element of contemporary human geography that seeks answers to a wide range of questions—some of them theoretical, others highly practical—such as, Why are villages, towns, and cities spaced the way they are? A geographer versed in location theory might make a decision about where a Canadian Tire store or Tim Hortons should be built, based on an assessment of the demographics and median income of the surrounding neighbourhoods, the locations of other shopping areas, and the existing and future road system. Similarly, a geographer could determine the best location for a wildlife refuge, given existing wildlife habitats and migration patterns, human settlement patterns, and road networks.

Region.

From our spatial perspective, we can determine that phenomena are not evenly distributed on the surface of the Earth. Instead, features tend to be concentrated in particu-

> **Region** The second theme of geography; an area on the Earth's surface marked by a degree of formal, functional, or perceptual homogeneity of some phenomenon.

lar areas, which we call **regions**, the second concept we will draw on. Novelist James Michener once wrote that whenever he started writing a new book, he first prepared himself by turning to books written by regional geographers about the setting for his story. Understanding the regional geography of a place allows us to make sense of much of the information we have about that place and to digest new information as well.

In geography, an area characterized by shared physical or cultural attributes constitutes a region. To identify and delimit a region, geographers must establish the criteria that will define it. Those criteria can be physical, cultural, functional, or perceptual. A physical region, such as the Canadian Shield, is defined by a shared physical geographic criterion. When geographers choose

> **Formal region** A type of region marked by a certain degree of homogeneity in one or more phenomena; also called uniform region or homogeneous region.

one or more physical or cultural criteria to define a region, they are looking for a **formal region**. A formal region has a shared trait—it can be a shared cultural trait or a physical trait. In a formal cultural region, people share one or more cultural traits. For example, the region of Europe where a majority of the people speak French can be thought of as a French-speaking region. When the scale of analysis shifts, the formal region changes. If we shift scales to the world,

the French-speaking formal region expands beyond France into former French colonies of Africa and into the overseas departments that are still associated politically with France.

A **functional region** is defined by a particular set of activities or interactions that occur within it. Places that are part of the same function-

> **Functional region** A region defined by the particular set of activities or interactions that occur within it.

al region interact to create connections. They also share a political, social, or economic purpose. Functional regions are not necessarily culturally homogeneous. Instead, the people within the region function together politically, socially, or economically. The city of Toronto is a functional region, and the city itself has internal functional regions, such the central business district. Alternatively, the city of Mississauga is nested within the Golden Horseshoe, a larger functional region linked politically, economically, and socially. The name reflects a geographical shape and a consolidated economic region.

Regions may be primarily in the minds of people—a product of our imagination (think, for example, about our perceptions of Newfoundland, the North, or the Maritimes). This does not mean the region is not "real." Rather, such a region has less to do with material locations and more to do with how we understand a place.

Perceptual regions are intellectual constructs designed to help us understand the nature and distribution of phenomena in human geography. As Figure 1.5 demonstrates, per-

> **Perceptual region** A region that exists only as a conceptualization or an idea and not as a physically demarcated entity. For example, the North or the Maritimes.

ceptual regions can sometimes take on a comedic character. Geographers do not agree entirely on their properties, but we do concur that we all have impressions and images of various regions and cultures. How people think about regions has influenced everything from daily activity patterns to large-scale international conflict. A perceptual region can include people, their cultural traits (such as dress, food, and religion), places and their physical traits (such as mountains, plains, or coasts),

FIGURE 1.5 Perceptual Regions of Canada. (Brian Gable, *The Globe and Mail*)

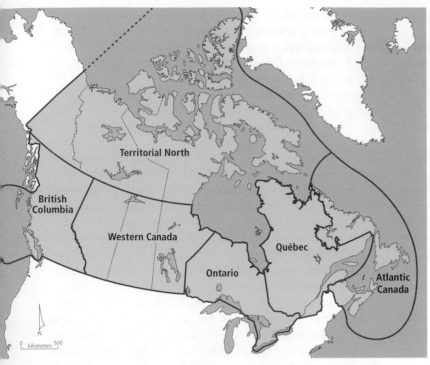

FIGURE 1.6 Regional Distinctions within Canada. From Robert M. Bone, *The Regional Geography of Canada* (3rd ed.), Figure 1.2, p. 11. © Oxford University Press Canada 2005. Reprinted by permission of the publisher.

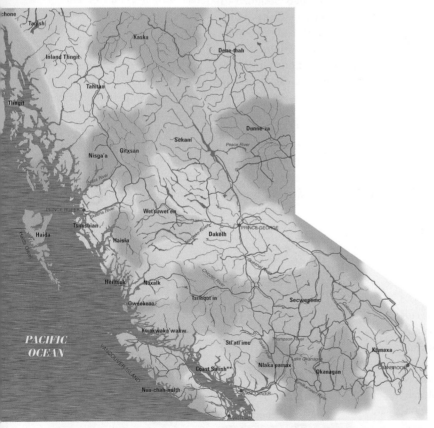

FIGURE 1.7 Boundaries between Territories for First Nations People in British Columbia. In this presentation, the boundaries are deliberately blended to demonstrate the complex territorial relations being negotiated. Accessed October 28, 2011 at the Government of British Columbia website, http://www.bced.gov.bc.ca/abed/map.htm. First Nations Peoples of BC, 7530879086, copyright © 2011, Province of British Columbia.

and built environments (such as windmills, barns, skyscrapers, or beach houses).

Regions, whether formal, functional, or perceptual, are a form of spatial classification. They provide a means by which we can organize humans geographically or handle large amounts of information so we can make sense of it.

In her classic study of the forces of regionalism in Canada, Mildred Schwartz argues that regionalism in the Canadian context is shaped by shared past economic experiences, which have led to unequal development and political and social relationships. Regions in Canada have developed as a result of distinctive settlement patterns, distinctive cultural groups, and the ensuing economic and political regionalization. As Figure 1.6 illustrates, many of us have a collective sense of Canadian regions that are a blend of these various factors. In thinking about Canada and its regions, we can consider the physical characteristics of regions, such as the Rockies or the Canadian Shield, or the cultural and social history of a place, such as the unique history of the peoples of Quebec or the North. We can also consider economic structures and political identities as well as transportation systems and urban development.

It is important to remember, however, that these political, cultural, physical, and perceptual regions are largely based on British and French colonial settlement patterns and not on an understanding of underlying indigenous populations. Ongoing land claims disputes remind us that First Nations' histories and understandings of the Canadian landscapes may be different from those reflected in our standard textbooks (Figure 1.7).

Place. The third theme arising from our spatial perspective is the seemingly simple idea of **place**, which is a key concept in geography. All places on the surface of the Earth have unique human

> **Place** The third theme of geography; uniqueness of a location.

and/or physical characteristics, and one of the purposes of geography is to study the special character and meaning of places. While place may be thought of as a bounded area or territory, it may also be a location with no clear boundaries that is part of our collective or imagined memory. We can, therefore, be interested in place as a point on a map, or we can study individual experiences of place in terms of emotions and attachments. People individually and collectively develop a sense of place based on the ways in which places take on meaning and emotion in various ways—we can remember important events that occurred in a place, or we can imbue a place with a certain character. Canadian geographer Edward Relph has argued that our sense of place is "an innate faculty, possessed in some degree by everyone, that connects us to the world" (1997, p. 208).

Some geographers note that we may also be developing a sense of "placelessness" because of the way so many landscapes seem similar or indistinguishable. For example, the layouts of airports, strip malls, food chains, and shopping centres have become largely interchangeable so that no matter where we are in the world, these spaces may seem exactly the same. Geographer Yi-Fu Tuan coined the term "topophilia" to describe the emotional bond people have to place and to highlight his argument that the loss of the diversity and authenticity of place may lead to forms of alienation. We will explore the intricate relationships between people, place, identity, and social relations more deeply in chapters 7 and 8, on social geography and cultural geography, respectively.

Landscape.

Landscape is the fourth core theme related to a spatial perspective. Human geographers generally understand landscapes to be the visible imprint of human activity on the physical environment.

> **Landscape** The fourth theme of geography; the overall appearance of an area. Most landscapes comprise a combination of natural and human-induced influences.

Carl Sauer, formerly a professor at the University of California at Berkeley, is the geographer whose name is most closely identified with this concept (we consider Sauer's work in more detail in Chapter 8). In 1927, Sauer wrote an article, "Recent Developments in Cultural Geography," in which he argued that cultural landscapes comprise the "forms superimposed on the physical landscape" by human activity.

The Tanzanian city of Dar-es-Salaam provides an interesting urban example of a landscape possessing visible imprints of changing occupancy. Arabs from Zanzibar first chose the African site in 1866 as a summer retreat. Next, German colonizers imprinted a new layout and architectural style (wood-beamed Teutonic) when they chose the city as the centre of their East African colonies in 1891. After World War I, when the Germans were ousted, a British administration took over the city and began yet another period of transformation. The British encouraged immigration from their colony in India to Tanzania. The new Asian migrant population created a zone of three- and four-storey apartment houses, which look as if they were transplanted from Mumbai, India (Figure 1.8). Then, in the early 1960s, Dar-es-Salaam became the capital of newly independent Tanzania. Thus, the city experienced four stages of cultural dominance in less than one century, and each stage of the sequence remains imprinted in the cultural landscape.

The cultural landscape can be seen as a kind of book offering clues into each chapter of the cultural practices, values, and priorities of its various occupiers. As geographer Peirce Lewis explained in *Axioms for Reading the Landscape* (1979), "Our human landscape is our unwitting autobiography, reflecting our tastes, our values, our aspirations, and even our fears, in tangible, visible form." Lewis recommends looking for layers of history in cultural landscapes, adding that most major changes in the cultural landscape occur after a major event, such as a war, an invention, or an economic depression.

Movement.

The fifth theme drawing on a spatial perspective is **movement**, which refers to the mobility of people, goods, and

> **Movement** The fifth theme of geography; the mobility of people, goods, and ideas across the surface of the planet.

(a)

(b)

FIGURE 1.8 (a) Mumbai, India. Apartment buildings throughout Mumbai (formerly Bombay), India, are typically four storeys with balconies. **(b) Dar-es-Salaam, Tanzania.** This four-storey walk-up stands where single-family African dwellings once stood, reflecting the sequential occupancy of the city. (© Alexander B. Murphy)

Spatial interaction The nature and extent of interconnections and linkages. This depends on the distance between places, the accessibility of places, and the transportation and communication connectivity among places.

Distance Measurement of the physical space between two places.

Accessibility The degree of ease with which it is possible to reach a certain location from other locations. Accessibility varies from place to place and can be measured.

Connectivity The degree of direct linkage between one particular location and other locations in a transport network.

ideas across the surface of the planet. Movement is an expression of the interconnectedness of places. **Spatial interaction** between places depends on the **distance** (the measured physical space between two places) between places, the **accessibility** (the ease of reaching one location from another) of places, and the transportation and communication **connectivity** (the degree of linkage between locations in a network) among places. Interactions of many kinds shape the human geography of the world, and understanding these interactions is an important aspect of comprehending the global spatial order.

MAIN POINTS 1.2 What Are Geographic Questions?

- Human geographers are concerned with questions arising from a spatial perspective. The discipline of geography has an intellectual core defined by perspective rather than by subject matter.

- A spatial perspective can be developed through attention to five basic themes: location, region, place, landscape, and movement.

- Using these themes, human geographers work to make sense of the complexities of human-environment relations. Many of these themes overlap or have similarities in meaning, and human geographers use the concepts in different combinations as they think about the geographical.

FIGURE 1.9 Average Annual Precipitation of the World. A generalized map of the mean annual precipitation received around the world. (© H.J. de Blij, P.O. Muller, and John Wiley & Sons, Inc.)

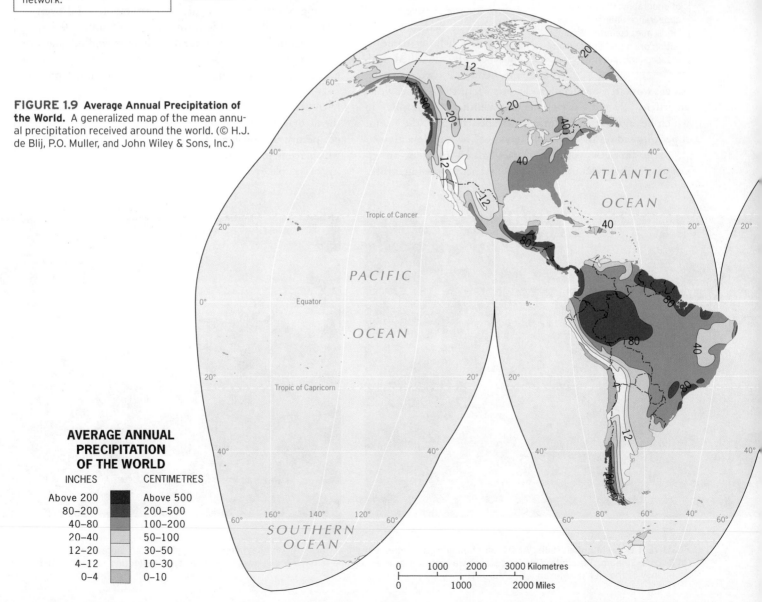

1.3 Why Do Geographers Use Maps and What Do Maps Tell Us?

Maps are an incredibly powerful geographic tool, and **cartography**, the art and science of making maps, is as old as geography itself. (For details on the cartographic arts, see Appendix A). Maps have countless purposes—they can be used to wage war, promote political propaganda, solve medical problems, locate shopping centres, guide refugees, and warn of natural hazards. There are many distinctive kinds of mapping that convey incredible amounts of information. In our daily lives, most of us make use of several relatively common types of maps: reference maps, thematic maps, and mental maps help us make sense of the world. New technologies such as remote sensing and

> **Cartography** The art and science of making maps, including data compilation, layout, and design. Also concerned with the interpretation of mapped patterns.

Global Positioning Systems (GPS) add to our arsenal of technical tools for navigating our physical world.

It is important to bear in mind that all maps simplify the world. A reference map of the world cannot show every place there is. Likewise, a thematic map of hurricane tracks in the Atlantic Ocean cannot pinpoint every hurricane and its precise path for the last 50 years. The very act of mapping—that is, putting pen to paper—erases some places from human memory and brings others into being. This is also illustrated in Figure 1.7, which details indigenous territorial understandings in British Columbia. When they map data, geographers make decisions about what information to include and generalize the information they present on maps. Many of the maps in this book are thematic maps of the world in which shadings show how much or how little of some phenomenon can be found on a part of the Earth's surface. While these generalized maps help us see broad trends, we cannot see all cases of a given phenomenon. For example, the map of world precipitation (Figure 1.9) is a generalized map of mean annual precipitation received around the world. The areas shaded burgundy, dark blue, and vibrant green indicate places that receive the most rain, and

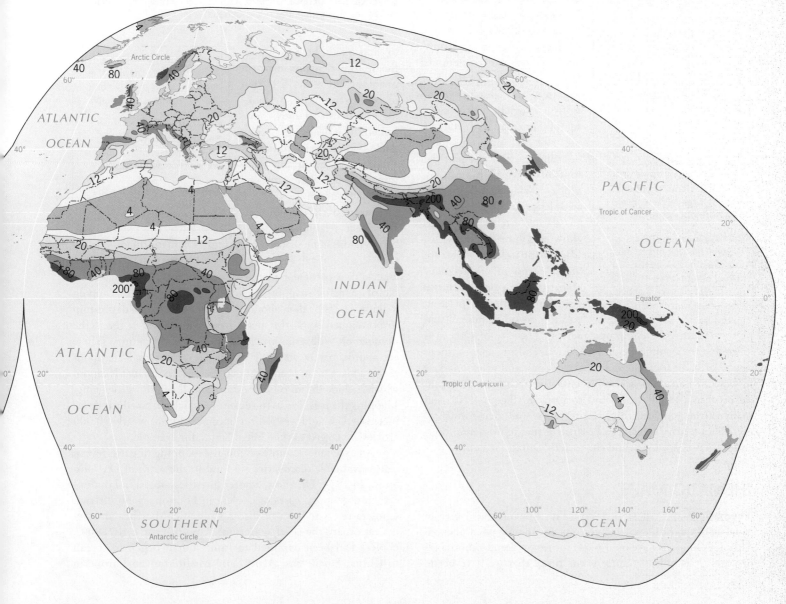

those shaded orange receive the least rain on average. Take a pen and trace along the equator on the map. Notice how many of the high-precipitation areas on the map are along the equator. The consistent heating of the equator over the course of the year brings consistent precipitation to the equatorial region. At the scale of the world, we can see general trends in precipitation like this, but it is difficult to see the micro-scale areas of intense precipitation everywhere in the world.

REFERENCE MAPS

Reference maps show locations of places and geographic features, focusing on accuracy in showing the **absolute locations** of places. These maps use a coordinate system that allows you to plot precisely where something is on Earth. Imagine taking an orange, drawing a dot on it with a marker, and then trying to describe the exact location of that dot to someone who is holding another orange so she can mark the same spot on her orange. If you draw and number the same coordinate system on both oranges, the task of drawing the absolute location on each orange is not only doable but is also simple. The most frequently used coordinate system is latitude and longitude. For example, the absolute location of Mogadishu, the capital of Somalia, is 2° 04' N and 45° 22' E. Using these coordinates, you can plot the location of Mogadishu on any globe or map that is marked with latitude and longitude.

> **Reference maps** Maps that show the absolute location of places and geographic features determined by a frame of reference, typically latitude and longitude.
>
> **Absolute location** The position or place of a certain item on the surface of the Earth as expressed in degrees, minutes, and seconds of latitude, 0° to 90° north or south of the equator, and longitude, 0° to 180° east or west of the Prime Meridian passing through Greenwich, England (a suburb of London).
>
> **Relative location** The regional position or situation of a place relative to the position of other places. Distance, accessibility, and connectivity affect relative location.

While reference maps show absolute locations, we often want to know where we are in terms of our relationship to other places. **Relative location** describes a place in relation to other human and physical features. Descriptors such as "The city of Ottawa is located at the confluence of the Ottawa, Rideau, and Gatineau rivers" or "Calgary is the hub of the oil, gas, and wheat markets in western Canada" locate a place relative to other features. In eastern Ontario, all roads lead to Ottawa (Figure 1.10), and many of the people within that region would define much of their lives relative to Ottawa because of the tight interconnectedness between Ottawa and the eastern Ontario region.

THEMATIC MAPS

Thematic maps tell stories, typically showing the degree of some attribute or the movement of a geographic phenomenon. Although humans have used maps for navigation for thousands of years, it is only in more recent times that we have begun

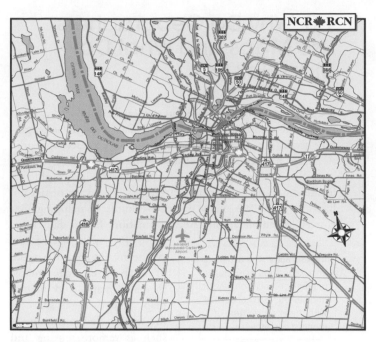

FIGURE 1.10 Ottawa, Ontario. Capital and central hub. (Public Works and Government Services Canada)

to appreciate how mapping the **spatial distribution** of a phenomenon is the first step to understanding it. By looking at a map that shows how something is distributed across space, we can raise questions about how the arrangement came about, what processes create and sustain the particular **pattern** of the distribution, and what relationships exist between different places and things. Thematic maps portray the social, political, economic, physical, agricultural, and other aspects of a particular place, region, or area. A unique example of thematic mapping is shown in Figure 1.11, Mapping Wikipedia. Using data obtained from the Wikipedia data dump in November 2009, this map has been created to reveal the number of Wikipedia articles tagged to each country. There are approximately 500,000 Wikipedia articles that are about either a place or an event that occurred in a particular location, which include the absolute location coordinates for geotagging. Mapping the tags reveals the extent to which Wikipedia is dominated by U.S. and western European countries. Nearly 90,000 articles are tagged to the United States, for example.

> **Thematic maps** Maps that tell stories, typically showing the degree of some attribute or the movement of a geographic phenomenon.
>
> **Spatial distribution** Physical location of geographic phenomena across space.
>
> **Pattern** The design of a spatial distribution (e.g., scattered or concentrated).

An excellent example of how the mapping of patterns can lead to valuable discoveries is found in the work of Dr. John Snow. In 1854, Dr. Snow, a noted anesthesiologist in London, England, mapped cases of cholera in London's Soho district. Cholera refers to a set of diseases in which diarrhea and dehydration are the chief symptoms. Up until the early 1800s, cholera had been confined to India, but it began to spread to China, Japan, East Africa, and Mediterranean Europe in

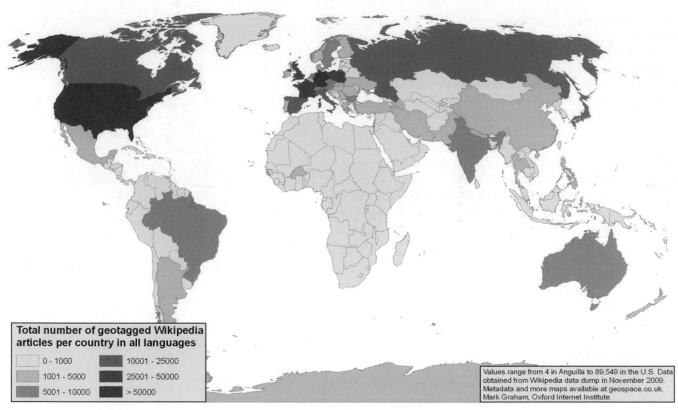

FIGURE 1.11 Mapping Wikipedia. (Courtesy of Mark Graham Ph.D., Oxford Internet Institute)

Total number of geotagged Wikipedia articles per country in all languages	
0 - 1000	10001 - 25000
1001 - 5000	25001 - 50000
5001 - 10000	> 50000

Values range from 4 in Anguilla to 89,549 in the U.S. Data obtained from Wikipedia data dump in November 2009. Metadata and more maps available at geospace.co.uk. Mark Graham, Oxford Internet Institute.

Pandemic An outbreak of a disease that spreads worldwide.

the first of several **pandemics**, a worldwide outbreak of the disease. This initial wave abated by 1823, but by then the very name cholera was feared throughout the world, for it had killed people everywhere by the thousands. A second cholera pandemic struck North America from 1826 to 1837, and during a third pandemic, England was severely hit, and cholera again spread into North America.

When the pandemic that began in 1842 reached England in the 1850s, cholera swept through Soho. In an effort to understand the disease, Dr. Snow mapped London's Soho district, marking all the area's water pumps, where residents obtained their water supply for home use. Dr. Snow marked these pumps with the letter P and also marked with a dot the residence of each person who died from cholera (Figure 1.12). Approximately 500 deaths occurred in Soho, and as the map took shape, Snow noticed that an especially large number of those deaths clustered around the water pump on Broad Street. Plotting the spatial distribution of the phenomenon made visible certain patterns that had previously been undetected. At Snow's request, city authorities removed the handle from the Broad Street pump, making it impossible to get water from that pump. The result was dramatic: almost immediately the number of reported new cases fell to nearly zero. Snow's theory about the role of water in the spread of cholera was confirmed, partly through the use of a thematic map.

Cholera has not been defeated completely, however, and in some ways risks have risen in recent years. In the teeming shanty-towns of the growing cities of the developing world, and in the refugee camps of Africa and Asia, cholera remains a

threat. For example, in the aftermath of the Haitian earthquake in January 2010, damage to water supply systems and deteriorating sanitary conditions led to an outbreak of cholera in that

FIGURE 1.12 Cases of Cholera in the Soho District of London, England, 1854. Adapted with permission from L.D. Stamp, *The Geography of Life and Death*, Cornell University Press, 1964. Reprinted by permission of HarperCollins Publishers Ltd. © 1964, L.D. Stamp.

country for the first time in 100 years. Until the 1990s, major outbreaks remained few and limited (after remaining cholera-free for a half century, Europe had its first reappearance of cholera in Naples in 1972), and most cases were reported in Africa. But an outbreak in the slums of Lima, Peru, in December 1990 became a fast-spreading **epidemic** (regional outbreak of a disease) that, although confined

> **Epidemic** Regional outbreak of a disease.

to the Americas, touched every country in the hemisphere, infected more than one million people, and killed over 10,000. In 2006, a cholera outbreak in Angola spread quickly, abruptly ending Angola's civil war. This allowed people to move around the country more easily, which inadvertently helped spread the disease. Proper hygiene prevents cholera, but contaminated water abounds in many of the tropical world's cities. A cholera vaccine exists, but it is costly and remains effective for only six months. Dr. Snow achieved a victory through the application of geographical reasoning, but the war against cholera is not yet won.

MENTAL MAPS

While we often think about maps as something we can hold and touch, it is also important to think about how we all carry maps in our minds of places we have been and places we

> **Mental map** Image or picture of the way space is organized as determined by an individual's perception, impression, and knowledge of that space.

have merely heard of—our internal **mental maps**. Even if you have never been to the Maritimes, for example, you may have studied wall maps and atlases or come across descriptions of the region in books, magazines, newspapers, websites, or television advertisements frequently enough to envision the provinces of the region (Nova Scotia, Prince Edward Island, and New Brunswick) in your mind. If you hear on the news that a hurricane caused damage in Halifax, you use your mental map of the region to make sense of where the hurricane occurred and its impact.

Our mental maps of the places within our **activity spaces** (those places we travel to routinely in our rounds of daily activity)

> **Activity space** The space within which daily activity occurs.

are more accurate and detailed than our maps of places we have never been (Figure 1.13). If your friend calls and asks you to meet her at the movie theatre you go to all the time, your mental map will engage automatically. You will envision the hallway, the front door, the walk to your car, the lane to choose in order to be prepared for the left turn you must make, the spot where you will park your car, and your path into the theatre and up to the popcorn stand.

Geographers who study human-environment behaviour have made extensive studies on how people develop their mental maps. The earliest humans, who were nomadic, had incredibly accurate mental maps of where to find food and shelter. Today, people use mental maps to find their way through the intricacies of cities and suburbs. Geographers have also studied how

FIGURE 1.13 An Example of Mental Mapping. (Courtesy of Hilary Nixon, Department of Urban and Regional Planning, San Jose State University)

children, the blind, new residents to cities, men, and women form mental maps. Each group uses slightly different processes. To learn new places, for example, women tend to use landmarks, whereas men tend to use paths. Activity spaces vary by age, and the extent of people's mental maps depends in part on their ages. Mental maps include *terra incognita*, unknown lands that are off-limits. If your path to the movie theatre includes driving past a school that you do not go to, your map on paper will likely label the school but will not show any details about the place. However, if you have access to the school and you are drawing a mental map of how to get to the school's cafeteria, your mental map of the school might be quite detailed.

GEOMATICS TECHNOLOGIES

Geomatics technologies have had a profound impact on how geographers map the earth. These new technologies include remote sensing (RS), geographic information systems (GIS), and Global Positioning System (GPS).

Geographers use **remote sensing** (RS) to monitor the Earth from a distance. Their data are collected by satellites, aircraft, or other technology located some distance away from the place being studied, and the resulting information is available almost instantaneously. After a major

> **Geomatics technologies** Those processes and tool used in the collection and analysis of spatial data, including remote sensing (RS), geographic information systems (GIS), Global Positioning System (GPS), and related forms of earth mapping.
>
> **Remote sensing** A method of collecting data or information through the use of instruments (e.g., satellites) that are physically distant from the area or object of study.

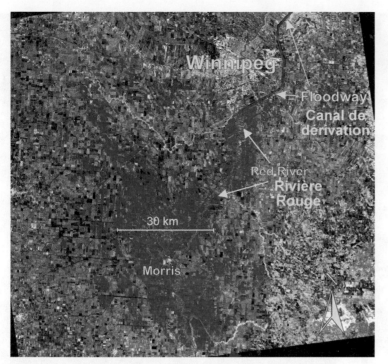

FIGURE 1.14 Remotely Sensed Image of the Red River Flood in Manitoba in 1997. This image was acquired by RADARSAT-1, an earth observation satellite developed in Canada. Since water bodies and wet surfaces produce lower levels of radar backscatter, flooded areas appear in darker tones on this radar image, while dry or upland areas appear in lighter tones. On this image, the extent of flooding is also highlighted in blue. (Canadian Space Agency)

FIGURE 1.15 Airborne Remote-Sensing Image of Flood Waters Surrounding the Town of Morris, Manitoba, during the 1997 Red River Flood. (Greg Brooks/Natural Resources Canada)

weather event, such as the Red River flood in 1997 (figures 1.14 and 1.15) or the unprecedented hurricane season in the Gulf of Mexico in 2008 (Figure 1.16), remotely sensed data show us the major areas of impact.

Remote sensing helps geographers understand the physical and human geography of a place, and the Internet ensures such information is widely available. Google Earth, for example, is an on-line set of remotely sensed images from around the world that are freely accessible to anyone with Internet access. You can think of Google Earth as a quilt of remotely sensed images, taken all over the world. The images come from several sources and are sewn together like a patchwork quilt. As a result, the resolution (the measure of the smallest object or the degree of detail that can be resolved by the sensor) of the images differs.

Geographers can incorporate remotely sensed images in a map and study absolute locations over time by plotting the changes depicted in remotely sensed images. Advances in computer technology and data storage, increasing accessibility to locationally based data and GPS technology, and creation of software products tailored to specific geographic uses have all driven incredible advances in **geographic information systems** (GIS) over the last two decades. Geographers use GIS to compare a variety of spatial data by creating digitized representations of the environment (figures 1.14, 1.16), combining layers of spatial data, and creating maps on which patterns and processes are superimposed. Geographers also use GIS to analyze data, which can give us new insight into geographic patterns and relationships.

> **Geographic information system (GIS)** A collection of computer hardware and software that permits spatial data to be collected, recorded, stored, retrieved, manipulated, analyzed, and displayed to the user.

Geographers trained in GIS apply the software technologies in countless fields today. Students who earn undergraduate degrees in geography are employed by software companies, government agencies, and businesses to use GIS to survey wildlife, map soils, analyze natural disasters, follow diseases, assist first responders, plan cities, plot transportation improvements, and track weather systems. For example, a group of geographers working for one GIS company tailors its software to serve branches of the military and the defence intelligence community. The vast amounts of data gathered by the various intelligence agencies can be integrated into a GIS and then analyzed spatially. Geographers working in the defence intelligence community can use GIS to query a vast amount of intelligence, interpret spatial data, and make recommendations on issues of security and defence.

The establishment of satellite-based **Global Positioning System** (GPS) allows us to locate things on the surface of the Earth with extraordinary accuracy. Researchers collect data quickly and easily in the field, and low-priced GPS units are encouraging fishers, hunters, and hikers to use GPS in their hobbies. Many new cars are equipped with GPS units, and dashboard map displays help commuters navigate traffic and travellers find their way. These new

> **Global Positioning System (GPS)** Satellite-based system for determining the absolute location of places or geographic features.

(a)

(b)

FIGURE 1.16 Quickbird Satellite Images of a Causeway in Galveston, Texas, (a) Before Hurricane Ike and (b) After. Image was collected on September 22, 2005, while (b), acquired on September 15, 2008, shows the impact of Hurricane Ike. Note the extensive damage to the marina directly south of the causeway. (Copyright © 2011 GeoEye)

geomatics technologies are being used in new and unexpected ways. As Vickie Tasker and Dr. Marilyne Jollineau discuss in their *Guest Field Note*, geomatics technologies can offer new information and data useful for cultivating grapes and making wine. As well as improving wine production and taste, these techniques also help improve soil and water quality, reduce pesticide and herbicide use, and improve land management practices.

Geographic information science (GISc) is an emerging research field concerned with studying the development and use of geospatial concepts and techniques to examine geographic patterns and processes. Your school may have a program in GISc that draws across disciplines, bringing together the computer scientists who write the programs, the engineers who create sensors that gather data about the Earth, and the geographers who combine layers of data and interpret them to make sense of our world. One more intriguing use of new technologies is the hobby of **geocaching**. Geocachers use their GPS units to play a treasure hunt game all over the world. People find a location for the treasures ("caches"), mark the coordinates on their GPS, and post clues on the Internet. If you find the cache, you sign either an electronic or physical logbook, indicating your success. If you choose to take the

> **Geocaching** A hunt for a cache, the global positioning system (GPS) coordinates of which are placed on the Internet by other geocachers.

treasure, you must leave something of equal or greater value for the next geocacher to find. According to www.geocaching.com, there are now over 1.2 million active geocaches located around the globe. What makes geocaching so much fun is that caches are hidden in such a way that most people would walk right past them. Geocachers are highly creative in hiding their caches, which makes the seeking, aided with GPS technologies, more challenging (Figure 1.17).

FIGURE 1.17 Hidden Geocache. A geocache is carefully hidden. (© Taplight/Alamy)

GUEST FIELD NOTE   A Geomatics Perpective to Wine Production in the Niagara Region

Have you ever noticed that some wines are remarkably delicious while others are not so tasty? Or that some wines cost under $10 per bottle while others are worth hundreds of dollars? The methods of wine production permit significant variation in quality and cost. There are multiple explanations for this variation, but it all starts with simple geography—the location of the vineyard. The effect of location on grape production is known as the *terroir*: the interaction of soil, geology, microclimate, and choice of grape variety. The wine industry in Canada is small because it has limited *terroir* suitable for grape production, but it is gaining a reputation as a producer of premium wines. However, quality must go beyond *terroir*.

Many Old World wine regions have had thousands of years to develop the best management practices and now produce high-quality grapes due to the experienced viticulture techniques passed down generation after generation. Conversely, Canadian wine makers have not had generations to develop vineyard management techniques best suited for the production of premium grapes, but they are now turning to geomatics technologies—including geographic information systems (GIS), global positioning systems (GPS), and remote sensing—to improve methods of assessing, monitoring, and managing vineyards. The Niagara region of Ontario, in particular, contains some of the most fertile agricultural lands in the world and is an ideal location to integrate geomatics technologies to improve wines.

Situated at 43° north latitude, the Niagara region is bounded by the shores of Lake Erie and Lake Ontario and is characterized by a unique microclimate and a rich diversity of glacial soils (see Figure 1.18 for the location of the region). These characteristics provide ideal conditions for growing grapes with complex and intense flavours for wine production. Historically, Niagara grapes were of the native *Vitis labrusca* variety, which produced poor-quality wines with maximum alcohol content. These were affectionately called "block and tackle wines"—after consuming a bottle, you could walk a block and tackle anyone. In the early 1980s, experienced viticulturalists introduced French *Vitis vinifera* and hybrid varieties associated with premium wines (e.g., chardonnay, riesling, pinot noir, and cabernet franc) to Niagara, despite warnings that they would not survive the harsh winter. The French varieties did unexpectedly well in Niagara's *terroir*, and by 1988, Labrusca grape varieties were banned from Ontario wines, forever improving their quality. Since these varieties are at the northern

fringe of adaptability, proper management techniques are essential to successful production.

As geographers, we have the opportunity to use various tools to contribute to the improvement of wine production and quality in the Niagara region. One of our studies sought to understand the spatial variability in vine quality and yield in order to produce higher-quality, higher-value wines. Vineyard managers rely on the availability of detailed, accurate, and reliable datasets that describe spatial variation in the fields. Many vineyard management practices treat fields as though they are of uniform quality when, in actuality, they are varied and complex. Figure 1.19 illustrates the spatial variation in vine vigour on a standard false-colour satellite image, where red represents areas of high vine vigour and healthy vegetation, and blue-green (known as cyan) represents areas of low vine vigour and possibly unhealthy vegetation. Managers can make better decisions if they understand and manipulate these underlying spatial variations to the advantage of the grape grower.

Stratus Wines, a 22-hectare vineyard and winery in Niagara-on-the-Lake, Ontario, is a specific area of study. Stratus is a reputable winery committed to responsible stewardship of the land while producing superior wines. Successfully integrating geomatics technologies into Stratus's existing vineyard system requires multiple steps. It begins by quantifying the vineyard's spatial variability on the ground through on-site data collection. Then the vineyard is divided into blocks, the sample vines are geolocated using a GPS device, and pertinent information is collected at these points. The data collected provide important information such as leaf water potential, soil moisture, soil composition, and temperature throughout the growing season. Finally, at harvest, grapes are collected from the sample vines and analyzed according to five indicators of grape quality: size (by weight),

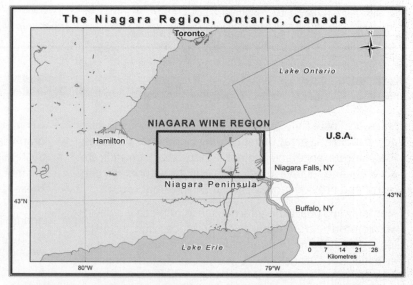

FIGURE 1.18 Location of the Niagara Wine Region. (© Victoria Tasker)

brix (sugar content), pH, total acidity, and colour. We can then quantify the spatial variability of grape quality throughout the vineyard.

The field data are subsequently correlated with air- and space-borne remotely sensed data to determine spatial trends that are visible from above. Over time, the need for detailed field-based data should decrease as our understanding of the spectral reflectance characteristics of vines, and their condition, improves. Recent advances in remote sensing provide opportunities to acquire much of the detailed information needed to assess plant condition in a timely manner.

Since 2008, Brock University and University of Guelph have assembled a multi-disciplinary research team to explore the spatial variation and apply geomatics techniques to vineyard management (Figure 1.20). Geographer Dr. Marilyne Jollineau and I are focused on Stratus Wines in particular. We

FIGURE 1.20 Collecting Field Data. (© Victoria Tasker)

are fortunate to be funded by the Ontario Centres of Excellence (Centre for Earth and Environmental Technologies), which are concerned that improper management practices within vineyards (e.g., the widespread or excessive application of fertilizer or pesticides) can have a negative impact on the natural environment (especially surrounding local water bodies, including Lake Ontario). Integrating geomatics technologies into existing vineyard management practices has the potential to significantly increase vineyard productivity, production efficiency, and profitability over the long term while minimizing the impact of farm operations on the natural environment. Geomatics technologies are an important tool in promoting environmental sustainability while ensuring profitability of the grape and wine industry in the Niagara region of Canada.

Victoria Tasker and Dr. Marilyne Jollineau, Department of Geography, Brock University, St. Catharines, Ontario

FIGURE 1.19 Vineyard Spatial Variability. (SPOT satellite image over Niagara, July 22, 2007. Image from Brock University Map Library Controlled Access G [accessed September 2010]. © 2007 CNES, licensed by the Alberta Terrestrial Imaging Center, www.imagingcenter.ca)

MAIN POINTS   **1.3 Why Do Geographers Use Maps and What Do Maps Tell Us?**

- Maps are incredibly powerful tools that allow us to plot and visualize an array of data for any number of purposes. We use reference and thematic maps that can indicate absolute and relative locations, highlight unforeseen patterns, and provide more generalized information.

- Mental maps chart the internal sense of place we develop from our actual experiences in places and from the information we hear about places we perhaps have never been. Not surprisingly, researchers find differences in how we draw our mental maps depending on age, race, gender, and class.

- Geomatics technologies, including remote sensing, geographical information systems, and Global Positioning System, are another set of powerful mapping tools with a range of economic, social, and political uses. Use of these technologies can capture the processes of change in places over time, track the movement of people and goods, and aid in providing assistance and information to those in need. They have also proven to be powerful weapons in waging war.

1.4 Why Are Geographers Concerned with Scale and Connectedness?

Geographers study places and patterns at a variety of scales, including local, regional, national, and global. Scale has two meanings in geography: it refers to the distance on a map compared to the distance on the Earth; it can also refer to the territorial extent of something. When we refer to scale throughout this book, we are generally using the second of these definitions. As geographers, the scale of our research or analysis matters because we can make different observations at different scales. We can study a single phenomenon across different scales in order to see how what is happening at the global scale affects localities and how what is happening at a local scale affects the globe. Geographers recognize that phenomena, whether human or physical, happen in a context, and that context looks different at different scales.

The scale at which we study a geographic phenomenon tells us what level of detail we can expect to see. We also see different patterns at different scales. For example, when we study the distribution of wealth on a global scale, we see the countries in western Europe, Canada, the United States, Japan, and Australia are the wealthiest, and the countries of sub-Saharan Africa and Southeast Asia are the poorest (Figure 1.21). Does that mean everyone in the United States is wealthy and everyone in Indonesia is poor? Certainly not, but on a global-scale map of states, that is how the data appear.

When you shift scales to North America and examine the data for U.S. states and Canadian provinces, you see that the wealthiest areas are on the coasts and the poorest are in the interior and the extreme northeast and south. The State of Alaska

and Canada's Northwest Territories have high gross per capita incomes stemming largely from oil revenues that are shared among the residents (Figure 1.22).

Shifting scales to just one city—for example, the Census Metropolitan Area (CMA) of Montreal, Quebec (see Figure 1.23 on page 21)—we can see how less than 13 percent of the population in surrounding areas, such as Dorval, are considered low income, whereas there is greater diversity of income within the more central parts of the city, such as near the region of Westmount. Shifting scales again, to the individual, if we conducted fieldwork in Saskatoon, Saskatchewan, and interviewed people who live below the poverty line, we would quickly find that each person's experience of poverty and reasons for being in poverty vary—making it difficult to generalize. We might find some trends—such as how women who have children cope with poverty differently than single men, or how illegal immigrants cope differently from legal immigrants—but the details would still vary from person to person.

Because the level of detail and the patterns observed change as the scale changes, geographers must be sensitive to their scale of analysis and must also be wary of researchers who make generalizations about a people or a place at a particular scale without considering other scales of analysis.

Geographers are also interested in how people use scale politically. Local political movements, such as the Zapatistas in southern Mexico, have learned to **rescale** their actions—to involve players at other scales and create a global outcry of support for their position. By taking their political campaign from the individual and local

> **Rescale** Involvement of players at other scales to generate support for a position or an initiative (e.g., use of the Internet to generate interest on a national or global scale for a local position or initiative).

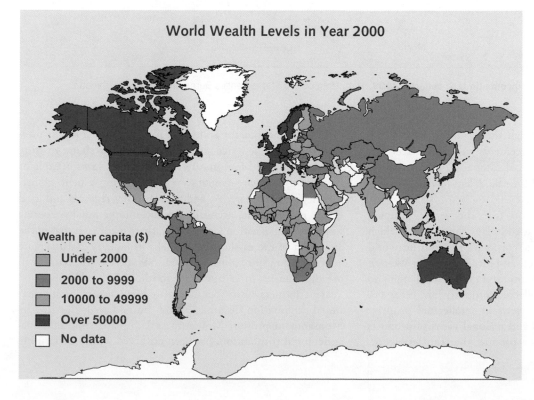

World Wealth Levels in Year 2000

Wealth per capita ($)
- Under 2000
- 2000 to 9999
- 10000 to 49999
- Over 50000
- No data

FIGURE 1.21 Global Distribution of Wealth by Country, 2000. This map, in U.S. dollars, depicts global wealth per capita, wherein wealth is understood not as income, but rather as the value of physical and financial assets less debts. United Nations University, World Institute for Development Economics Research. (UNU-WIDER Study © United Nations University)

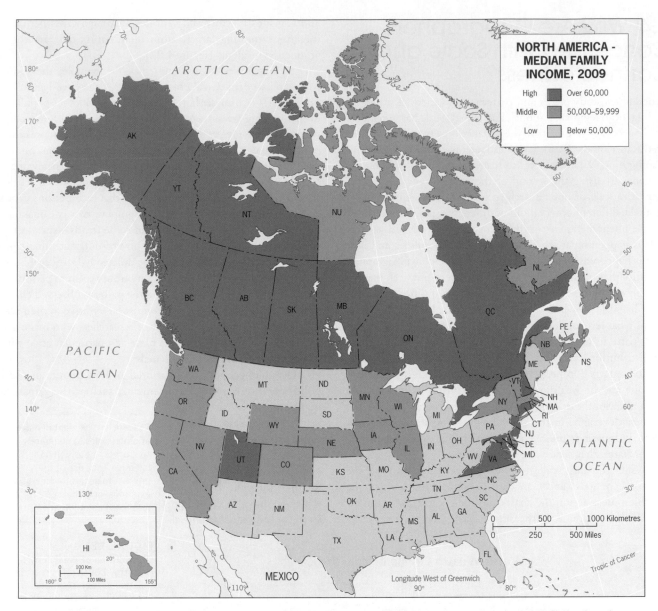

FIGURE 1.22 Median Family Income (in U.S. dollars), 2009. Data from United States Census Bureau and Statistics Canada.

scale to the national scale through their protests against the North American Free Trade Agreement, and then effectively using the Internet to wage a global campaign, the Zapatistas gained attention from the world media, a feat few local political movements achieve.

Geographer Victoria Lawson uses the term "jumping scale" to describe rescaling. She compares the ways in which Western countries, multinational corporations, and the World Trade Organization take products and ideas created in Western places and by Western corporations and globalize all rights to profits from them through intellectual property law. Efforts to push European and American views of intellectual property on the globe negate other local and regional views of products and ideas. To the West, rice is a product that can be owned,

privatized, and bought and sold. To East Asians, rice is integral to culture; new rice strains and new ideas about growing rice can help build community, not just profit. Lawson explains that taking a single regional view and jumping scale to globalize it legitimates that view and negates other regional and local views. For example, according to the international corporate watchdog organization CorpWatch, there is concern that in the aftermath of the earthquake in Haiti in January 2010 (Figure 1.24), large multinational corporations such as Monsanto will use this disaster to gain a larger foothold in local economies. Peasant farmers, wary because of a long history of international exploitation disguised as aid, burned seeds donated by Monsanto in protest. Monsanto, a U.S.-based multinational agricultural corporation, has been criticized widely by farming

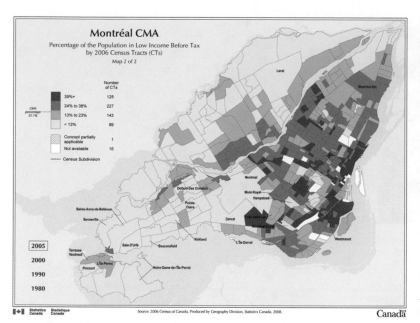

FIGURE 1.23 Montreal Percentage of Population in Low-Income, 2006. Statistics Canada, Thematic Maps 2006 Census, 92-173-XIE 2006001, July 2008; http://www.statcan.gc.ca/bsolc/olc-cel/olc-cel?lang=eng&catno=92-173-X

groups for its practice of copyrighting genetically modified seeds; copyrighting seeds reduces or eliminates farmers' ability to harvest seeds and replant the following year, a critical aspect of sustainable farming.

CONNECTEDNESS THROUGH DIFFUSION

Geographers focus on the "connectedness" of places. By this we mean the ways in which sometimes distant and apparently unrelated places exhibit unexpected linkages. We find these connections through the various processes of **diffusion**. Diffusion occurs when people, goods, or ideas move across space and across a number of different scales. (Remember that movement is one of the five themes organizing this book.) The process by which an idea or innovation spreads from its hearth (source area) to other places is known as **cultural diffusion**. Carl Sauer focused attention on this process in his book *Agricultural Origins and Dispersals*, in which he defined the ancient hearths of agriculture and traced the diffusion of agricultural practices from the hearths. In 1970, Swedish geographer Torsten Hägerstrand published pioneering research on the role of time in the diffusion process. Hägerstrand's research revealed how time, as well as distance, affects individual human behaviour and the diffusion of people and ideas. Sauer and Hägerstrand's fascinating research attracted many geographers to the study of diffusion processes. For example, cultural diffusion has been used to study the historic spread of hearth cultures globally, such as the spread of Roman Catholicism in the Americas during the 16th and 17th centuries. More recent research considers the interrelationship between culture and corporations, studying such phenomena as the "McDonaldization" of the world, in which American culture is diffused internationally through the franchising of McDonald's restaurants on a global scale. Geographers are still using principles of diffusion to model movement and dissemination through GIS and other geographic techniques.

> **Diffusion** The spatial spreading or dissemination of a culture element (such as a technological innovation) or some other phenomenon (e.g., a disease outbreak).
>
> **Cultural diffusion** The expansion and adoption of a cultural element, from its place of origin to a wider area.

Not all spaces and places view the diffusion of new ideas, concepts, or goods as a positive outcome, and **cultural barriers** can work against diffusion. Certain innovations, ideas, or practices may not be acceptable or adoptable in particular cultures because of prevailing attitudes or even taboos. For example, cultural barriers against practices such as the use of contraceptives influences diffusion processes and are highly politicized in some places where the transmission of HIV/AIDS is being fought. Other places may seek to preserve their language, history, and geography from the diffusion of ideas and such cultural artefacts as music, writing, and technology. In Canada, the Province of Quebec considers that legislative and policy initiatives to protect Québécois culture and language are crucial to the province's survival. As

> **Cultural barrier** Prevailing cultural attitude rendering certain innovations, ideas, or practices unacceptable or unadoptable in that particular culture.

FIGURE 1.24 Earthquake in Haiti, January 12, 2010. (Ryan Remiorz/The Canadian Press)

FIGURE 1.25 Altered Street Sign in Quebec. The English word "street" has been changed to "Rue," the French word for street. (Copyright © Francis Mariani)

Figure 1.25 illustrates, changing signs to enforce these requirements can be awkward. At the national level, the Canadian Radio-television and Telecommunications Commission has the task of protecting Canadian culture (the television, radio, and telecommunications industries) from foreign (mainly U.S.) domination.

EXPANSION DIFFUSION

Geographers divide diffusion processes into two broad categories: expansion diffusion and relocation diffusion. In the case of **expansion diffusion**, an innovation or idea develops in a hearth, which is an area where cultural traits develop and from which the cultural traits diffuse, and remains strong there while also spreading outward (Figure 1.26). For example, we can study the spread of Islam from its hearth on the Arabian Peninsula to Egypt and North Africa, through Southwest Asia, and into West Africa. If we were to draw a series of maps of followers of Islam (Muslims) at 50-year intervals beginning in 620 CE, the area of adoption of Islam would be larger in each successive period.

Expansion diffusion takes several forms. **Contagious diffusion** is diffusion in which nearly all adjacent individuals and places are affected. A disease can spread in this way, infecting almost everyone in a population (although not everyone may show symptoms of the disease). However, an idea such as a new fashion or new genre of music may not always spread throughout a contiguous population. For example, the spread of Crocs footwear is a case of **hierarchical diffusion**, in which the main channel of diffusion is some segment of those who are susceptible to (or adopting) what is being diffused. In the case of Crocs, founder Scott Seamans found a clog manufactured by a Canadian company that was created out of the unique croc resin material. Seamans, an avid sailor, put a strap on the back of the clog and added a few holes to allow for drainage. He and two co-founders set up their company in Boulder, Colorado, had the shoes manufactured, and sold them at boat shows in 2002 and 2003. Crocs footwear diffused from boating enthusiasts to gardeners to the American and Canadian public—becoming especially popular among children who adorned their Crocs with Jibbitz, or charms designed for Crocs. The hierarchy of boaters, gardeners, and then the contagious diffusion that followed helps explain the rapid growth of the Crocs brand, whose revenues peaked in 2007 at $800 million, having sold over 30 million pairs of shoes worldwide in that year alone.

A third form of expansion diffusion is **stimulus diffusion.** Not all ideas can be readily and directly adopted by a receiving population; some are simply too vague, too unattainable, too different, or too impractical for

> **Expansion diffusion** The spread of an innovation or an idea through a population in an area in such a way that the number of those influenced grows continuously larger, resulting in an expanding area of dissemination.

> **Contagious diffusion** The distance-controlled spreading of an idea, innovation, or some other item through a local population by contact from person to person—analogous to the communication of a contagious illness.

> **Hierarchical diffusion** A form of diffusion in which an idea or innovation spreads by passing first among the most connected places or peoples. An urban hierarchy is usually involved, encouraging the leapfrogging of innovations over wide areas, with geographic distance a less important influence.

> **Stimulus diffusion** A form of diffusion in which a cultural adaptation is created as a result of the introduction of a cultural trait from another place.

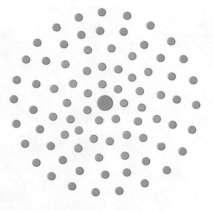

A. Contagious Diffusion

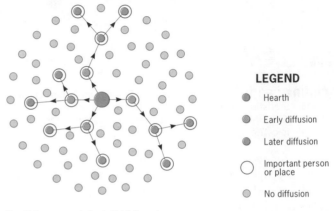

B. Hierarchial Diffusion

LEGEND

- ● Hearth
- ● Early diffusion
- ● Later diffusion
- ○ Important person or place
- ● No diffusion

FIGURE 1.26 Contagious and Hierarchical Diffusion. (© E.H. Fouberg, A.B. Murphy, H.J. de Blij, and John Wiley & Sons, Inc.)

(a)   (b)

FIGURE 1.27 (a) New Delhi, India and (b) Vrindavan, India. Hindus believe cows are holy, and evidence of that belief can be seen everywhere in India, from cows roaming the streets to the menu at McDonald's. In 1996, the first McDonald's restaurant opened in New Delhi, India, serving Maharaja Macs and vegetable burgers with cheese. In Indian towns, such as Vrindavan, cows are protected and share the streets with pedestrians, bicyclists, and motorists. (© Douglas E. Gurran/AFP/Getty Images; John Moore/Associated Press)

immediate adoption. Yet these ideals can still have an impact. They may indirectly promote local experimentation and eventual changes in the ways people do things. For example, the diffusion of mass-produced food items in the late 20th century—pushed by multinational retailers—led to the introduction of the hamburger in India. The Hindu religion in India prohibits consumption of beef, which was a major cultural obstacle to the adoption of the hamburger (Figure 1.27). However, retailers experimented and began selling burgers made of vegetable products, an adaptation stimulated by the diffusion of the hamburger, which took on a new form in the cultural context of India.

RELOCATION DIFFUSION

Expansion diffusion spreads across space without requiring people to physically move to become "knowers" of the trait or innovation. Instead, the people stay put and the innovation, idea, trait, or disease does the moving. **Relocation diffusion**, in contrast, involves the actual movement of individuals who have already adopted the idea or innovation, and who carry it to a new, perhaps distant, locale, where they proceed to disseminate it.

Relocation diffusion occurs most frequently through migration. When migrants move from their homeland, they take their cultural traits with them. Developing an ethnic neighbourhood in a new country helps immigrants maintain their culture in the midst of an unfamiliar one. If the homeland of the immigrants loses enough of its population, the cultural customs may fade in the hearth while gaining strength in the ethnic neighbourhoods abroad.

> **Relocation diffusion**
> Sequential diffusion process in which the items being diffused are transmitted by their carrier agents as they evacuate the old areas and relocate to new ones. The most common form of relocation diffusion involves the spreading of innovations by a migrating population.

MAIN POINTS **1.4** **Why Are Geographers Concerned with Scale and Connectedness?**

- The scale of geographical research or analysis matters because we can make different observations at different scales. Geographers can study a single phenomenon across different scales or any number of phenomena at a single scale. Often what is happening at the global scale affects localities, and what is happening at a local scale may have global implications.

- Geographers study places and patterns at a variety of scales, usually focusing on the territorial extent of a phenomenon. The scale determines the level of detail we can expect to see. By "jumping scales" or rescaling, we can see how political and social ideas are mobilized at different scales.

- Using scales, we can see how people, goods, or ideas move across space (movement being one of the five themes in this text). A good example of this is the cultural diffusion of cultural artefacts such as music or fashion. Sometimes places try to set up cultural barriers to prevent ideas or goods from coming to a place or as an attempt to preserve local language and culture. Geographers divide diffusion into two broad categories: expansion diffusion (which can take the form of contagious, hierarchical, or stiumulus diffusion) and relocation diffusion.

1.5 What Does It Mean to "Think Geographically" and How Do We Do It?

Today's research, thought, and writing in human geography are grounded in a variety of theories and philosophies that can be traced back thousands of years. You might be surprised by the depth and range of research topics explored by geographers. Human beings are decidedly geographical because where we are matters to us very much. As nomads, early humans covered vast distances in search of shelter and sustenance, and our earliest written records are often pictograms or drawings of where we have come from and, perhaps, where we would like to go.

Geography as a distinct subject taught in what we now consider to be the formal education system evolved in western Europe from the 17th century onward as part of the formation of higher institutions of learning called universities or colleges. By tracing the numerous ways scholars approached their task, we can see how their ideas about what is "geographical" and how we should "do" geography changed over time. New geographical work (and academic work as a whole) often comes about because of critiques of older or established approaches. These critiques create a divergence in perspectives, foci, and methods as scholars shift their thinking about the nature of the geographical. A history of geographical thought demonstrates how diverse theoretical and philosophical ideas produce different ideas about what we consider geographical knowledge. It is important to remember that changes in perspective are influenced by the historical context of the era.

The main focus in this text is on contemporary human geography as it developed in the Western world after World War II, although there is some reference to pre-war scholarship. In this section, we get a taste of how geographical scholarship evolved from the age of exploration and "discovery" in western Europe to the present day. We will then consider 20th-century perspectives on the geographical—perspectives such as environmental determinism and possibilism, regional geography, geography as a spatial science, humanistic and behavioural geography, radical and Marxist geographies, and feminist geographies. While adherents of environmental determinism and possibilism have largely fallen by the wayside, geographers today continue to approach geographical questions using any number and combination of these approaches. This generates a diverse and intriguing body of geographical knowledges for study.

THEORIZING THE GEOGRAPHICAL

Most scholars agree that the formal discipline of geography emerged as a result of the participation of adventurer/scholars in the European age of exploration and "discovery" during the 13th and 14th centuries. Western Europeans travelled the globe, mapping and documenting a seemingly limitless array of new discoveries—new peoples and places, new species of plants and animals, new technologies, architecture, and cultures. (It is worth pointing out that these were discoveries for European explorers only, as the indigenous peoples already knew about the places, plants, animals, and cultures around them!) Considerable labour was required to catalogue, classify, and categorize this endless stream of new and often perplexing information. Scholars such as Alexander von Humboldt (1769–1859) and the German Carl Ritter (1779–1859) are recognized as among the first to look for underlying universal patterns and structures organizing all earthly phenomenon into some coherent whole. Carl Ritter produced a 19-volume work, entitled *Erdkunde*, in which he struggled to organize geographical data into a coherent whole to provide a sense of unity and purpose.

ENVIRONMENTAL DETERMINISM

Drawing on this vast array of new data, 20th-century geographers turned their attention to theorizing about why certain peoples and phenomena appeared in certain places and not in others and displayed particular and collective characteristics and traits. The notion of **environmental determinism**, which argues that human behaviour, individually and collectively, is strongly affected by—even controlled or determined by—the physical environment, became popular. This philosophy has its roots in the biological and sociological thinking of such scholars as Charles Darwin and Herbert Spencer. Environmental determinists conceptualize human society as a social organism displaying traits similar to those of a biological organism that responds to its need to expand, develop, and interact with its surrounding environment.

> **Environmental determinism** The view that the natural environment has a controlling influence over various aspects of human life, including cultural development.

The idea that there is a strong interconnection between peoples, their social organization, and their territories or environment has a long history. The ancient Greeks, finding that some of the peoples subjugated by their expanding empire were relatively docile while others were rebellious, attributed such differences to variations in climate. Over 2,000 years ago, Aristotle described northern Europeans as "full of spirit ... but incapable of ruling others" and characterized Asian people (by which he meant inhabitants of modern-day Turkey) as "intelligent and inventive ... [but] always in a state of subjection and slavery." Aristotle attributed these traits to the respective climates of the regions—the cold north versus the more tropical Mediterranean.

These views resurfaced as recently as the first half of the 20th century in the work of such geographers as the German Friedrich Ratzel and the American Ellen Churchill Semple. As Ron Johnston argues, some geographers went to great lengths to suggest that human behaviours and patterns can be directly linked to an environmental cause. An example is found in the *Principles of Human Geography* (1940), by Ellsworth Huntington and S.W. Cushing:

The well-known contrast between the energetic people of the most progressive parts of the temperate zone and the inert inhabitants of the tropics and even of intermediate regions, such as Persia, is largely due to climate ... the people of the cyclonic regions rank so far above those of the other parts of the world that they are the natural leaders.

Cushing and Huntington suggested that climate is the critical factor in how humans behave. Yet what constitutes an "ideal" climate lies in the eyes of the beholder. For Aristotle, it was the climate of Greece. More recent commentators from western Europe and North America see the climates most suited to progress and productiveness in culture, politics, and technology as (you guessed it) those of western Europe and the northeastern United States. Such perspectives arguably served to legitimize the colonial and imperial aspirations of European rulers in the new lands they came to govern.

Despite the appeal of explanations provided by environmental determinism, many geographers doubted whether such sweeping generalizations about human-environment connections were valid. They recognized exceptions to the environmental determinists' theories (for example, the Maya civilization in the Americas arose in a tropical climate that most assumed was incapable of complex cultures; see Figure 1.28) and argued that humanity was capable of much more than merely adapting to and being constructed by the natural environment. Environmental determinist theories that suggest Europe is superior to the rest of the world because of the climate and location of the region ignore the fact that for thousands of years the most technologically advanced civilizations were found outside Europe in North Africa, Southwest Asia, Southeast Asia, and East Asia.

Geographers grew increasingly cautious about such speculative notions and began asking new questions about human-environment relationships. They believed that if generalizations were to be made, they ought to arise from detailed, carefully designed research. Everyone agrees that the natural environment affects human activity in some ways, but people are the decision makers and the modifiers—not just the slaves of environmental forces. People and their cultures shape environments, constantly altering the landscape and affecting environmental systems. For those who think less carefully about the human-environment dynamic, environmental determinism continues to hold an allure, leading to some highly questionable generalizations about the impact of the environment on humans and a multitude of popular books that use environment as the dominant force in explaining complex histories.

POSSIBILISM

Reactions to environmental determinism produced critique and counterargument. An approach known as **possibilism** emerged, espoused by geographers who argued that the natural environment merely serves to limit the range of choices available to a culture. The choices that a society makes depend on what its members need and on what technology is available to them. Geographers increasingly accepted the doctrine of possibilism, and increasingly discredited environmental determinism.

> **Possibilism** Geographic viewpoint—a response to determinism—that holds that human decision making, not the environment, is the crucial factor in cultural development. Nonetheless, possibilists view the environment as providing a set of broad constraints that limits the possibilities of human choice.

Even possibilism has its limitations, however, because it encourages a line of inquiry that starts with the physical environment and asks what it allows. Human cultures frequently push the boundaries of what is "environmentally possible" through advances in technology, which are the result of their own ideas and ingenuity. In the interconnected, technologically dependent world we live in today, it is possible to do many things that are at odds with the local environment.

REGIONAL GEOGRAPHY

Dissatisfaction with environmental determinism in Europe and North America took some geographers in a new direction, and **regional geography** vied for a central place as the framework for undertaking geographical work. Proponents such as Richard Hartshorne (1899–1992) and Alfred Hettner (1859–1941) argued for a descriptive geography that di-

> **Regional geography** The study of a region's unique characteristics, including its natural and human characteristics, in order to understand how areas differ from each other.

vided the world into natural regions by identifying phenomena that grouped themselves in distinctive ways in particular areas. Regional geographers argued that places are unique, disputing the idea that universal and generalizable statements could be

FIGURE 1.28 Mayan Ruins in Guatemala. The Maya civilization caused many geographers to question environmental determinists' belief about human-environment connections. The civilization flourished in a tropical climate, which environmental determinists assumed was incapable of complex cultures. (Wilbur E. Garrett/ National Geographic/Getty Images)

made. This notion of "areal differentiation," or the distinctiveness of places, narrowed the geographer's task to a systematic but largely descriptive undertaking. Geography, according to Hartshorne in his *The Nature of Geography: A Critical Survey of Current Thought in the Light of the Past* (1939), was

> *a science that interprets the realities of areal differentiation as they are found, not only in terms of the differences in certain things from place to place, but also in terms of the total combination of phenomenon in each place, different from those of every other place.* (p. 462)

While Hartshorne's approach was dominant in this period, the work of Carl Sauer and the Berkley school marked a distinct specialization in the study of cultural landscapes (see Chapter 8 as well as the discussion of landscape in section 1.2 earlier in this chapter). Sauer made important contributions through his focus on both the cultural and natural processes at work in human interactions with the environment.

GEOGRAPHY AS A SPATIAL SCIENCE

In the post-war period, many geographers found the regional focus too narrow and descriptive. While it is important to understand a place in detail, description is only the first step in asking questions about why things are they way they are. Regional geography as it was then practised lacked scientific rigour and had little to say about contemporary political, social, and economic issues. In 1953, geographer Frederick Schaefer authored a paper strongly critical of Hartshorne's regional geography. In "Exceptionalism in Geography: A Methodological Examination," Schaefer argued that geography needed to integrate methods from the positivist sciences and concern itself not only with description but also with explanation. Geography, he argued, should be approached as "a science concerned with the formulation of laws concerning the spatial distribution of certain features on the surface of the earth" (p. 227). In other words, geography should concern itself with the search for the laws of location and spatial organization. This was a marked departure from the work of regional geographers, who regarded regions as unique in all respects. This perceived uniqueness made it impossible to develop general, universal, quantitative laws governing spatial organization.

Schaefer's paper marked the beginning of a new approach to geography called **spatial analysis**. By spatial analysis, we

Spatial analysis Quantitative procedures used to understand the spatial arrangement of phenomena and the related patterns of connections and flows.

mean those quantitative procedures used to understand the spatial arrangement of phenomena and the related patterns of connections and flows. His appeal for systematic analysis and scientific methods sparked what some call a "quantitative revolution" in geography as practitioners began testing hypotheses and identifying repeatable and recognizable causal factors governing spatial relations. Scholars both within and outside geography, such as J.H. von Thünen and Walter

Christaller, developed models predicting certain spatial patterns and regularities—approaches we will consider in Chapter 10. This approach remains popular in a number of subdisciplinary areas today, including urban planning, transportation, and economic geographies.

HUMANISTIC AND BEHAVIOURAL GEOGRAPHY

While "quantitative" approaches yielded models and laws of spatial organization, a growing critique in the 1960s argued that these models and laws provided poor descriptions of reality. Some geographers suggested that spatial analysis, with its scientific focus, could not take the unpredictability of human actions into account. These behavioural geographers sought to understand and model human behaviour and the decision-making processes implicated in human relationships with place. This involved thinking about the cultural and social norms and values guiding human decision-making processes. **Behavioural geography** covered a wide range of topics, from human-natural environment interactions to conceptual or mental mapping

Behavioural geography An approach that seeks to understand and model human behaviour and the decision-making processes implicated in human relationships with place.

and time-geography. Much of this work drew on other social sciences, such as sociology and psychology, but many practitioners continued to use the statistical processes developed by spatial analysts for analyzing behavioural data, which made them the target of a wider critique of positivistic approaches.

While behavioural geographers were attempting to predict human behaviour using a spatial science approach, another group of geographers developed yet another form of geographical inquiry: humanistic geography. As geographer Nicholas Entrikin notes, this approach rejected what adherents regarded as the "overly objective, narrow, mechanistic and deterministic view" of human beings found in behavioural geography (1976, p. 16). Humanistic geographers argued that geography's main interest should be the human aspects of place, including human emotions, values, and desires. Yi-Fu Tuan defined **humanistic geography** as the study of "people's relations to nature, their geographical behaviour as well as their feelings and ideas in regard to space and place" (1976, p. 266). Geographers turned to phenomenology, existentialism, and hermeneutics as they attempted to understand humans' every-

Humanistic geography An approach that focuses on the human aspects of place, including human emotions, values, and desires.

day interactions in place. Canadian geographer Edward Relph (1970) asserted that our ability to know and learn about place is fundamental to human existence and those geographers should investigate how our direct experience of the material world is foundational to all geographical knowledge. Much of the research carried out from this perspective underpins more recent work in cultural and social geography that addresses how people's sense of identity and collective community is bound up with place. We will explore this approach further in Chapter 7.

RADICAL AND MARXIST GEOGRAPHY

Both behavioural and humanistic geographers focused on human choices and experiences in place, albeit from different perspectives. During the social and political upheavals of the 1960s and early 1970s, other geographers looked for more direct ways to engage with the ideological and activist debates beyond the academy. As Richard Peet (1998) argues, the revolutionary and often violent social movement activism in Western countries "made the concerns of the traditional discipline of geography, for all its quantitative update and even humanistic concerns, seem socially and politically irrelevant" (p. 67). Radical and Marxist geographers sought to make the study of geography more useful and relevant, and they pressed the discipline to produce research that contributed to furthering social justice. David Harvey urged geographers to enter the fray, arguing that, as Peet says, "geography can no longer be simply an academic discipline, isolated in its ivory towers." Geographers interested in these pursuits turned to social theory and methodologies based on the work of Karl Marx (1818–1883), Henri Lefebvre (1901–1991), and Raymond Williams (1921–1988), which positioned spatial production and organization at the heart of social justice issues and gave geography a role in working for and reshaping society.

GEOGRAPHY AND IDENTITY

In the 1970s, and in conjunction with the feminist social movements beyond the academy, women in geography increasingly asserted that gender and gender relations had serious but largely overlooked geographical implications (Figure 1.29). What it means to be a "woman" or a "man" varies geographically as well as historically. Spaces and places themselves can also be gendered in that some places are seen as more appropriately feminine, such as the home or domestic spaces, and other spaces more properly masculine, such as the public space of work and

FIGURE 1.29 Feminist Protest, 1970. (York University Libraries, Clara Thomas Archives & Special Collections, Toronto Telegram fonds, ASCO4612)

political engagement. A number of different perspectives have emerged—liberal feminism, socialist feminism, Marxist feminism, lesbian feminism, postmodern/poststructuralist feminism—and a substantial body of research attests to the spatial implications of gender and gender relations. As we shall see in chapters 7 and 8, geographers have also examined how sexualities are constituted and regulated in and through the spatial. Much of this work also emphasizes the importance of race, ethnicity, age, able-bodiedness, and other social and cultural markers of identity in how we experience spaces and understand ourselves in space.

POSTMODERNISM AND THE CULTURAL TURN

By the 1980s, broad philosophical shifts were challenging the very foundations of modern thought, including assumptions about the nature of truth and knowledge, the objectivity of the scientific method, and the possibilities of finding universal laws and an underlying coherence at the heart of much of the work in geography. Termed "postmodernism," this complex and highly contested world view has informed contemporary geographical research across many subdisciplines, from economic and political geographies to social and cultural geographies. It is beyond the scope of this text to explore postmodernist ideas in any great detail, but it is enough to say that geographers have taken up the challenges of postmodern thought in myriad ways, and students of geography will come across this thinking in many subdisciplines, particularly in social and cultural geographies, feminist and queer geographies, and geographies of sexuality.

CONTEMPORARY HUMAN GEOGRAPHY

As this overview suggests, human geographers undertake their studies from a variety of theoretical and conceptual perspectives, producing a wide array of geographical knowledges that are often contradictory and contested. Human geographers focus on an impressive range of topics, which are reflected in the variety of subdisciplines, including population geography and demographics, political geography, social and cultural geography, economic geography, transportation geography, and urban geography. We touch on many of these areas in this text. To appreciate more fully the vast topics researched by human geographers, examine the multitude of occupations filled by human geographers, including location analyst, urban planner, diplomat, remote sensing analyst, geographic information scientist, area specialist, travel consultant, political analyst, intelligence officer, cartographer, educator, soil scientist, transportation planner, park ranger, or environmental consultant. All of these careers and more are open to geographers because each of these fields is grounded in place and is advanced through spatial analysis.

MAIN POINTS **1.5   What Does It Mean to "Think Geographically" and How Do We Do It?**

- What we might consider modern geographical research and knowledge began in the 1500s and is largely associated with the age of exploration, when European nations travelled the globe discovering (for themselves) new lands and peoples, animals, plants, rocks, and minerals.

- From its earliest beginnings, geography has used a number of different philosophical and theoretical approaches to study human-environment relations.

These include environmental determinism, possibilism, regional geography, spatial science, humanistic and behavioural geography, radical and Marxist geography, and feminist, queer, and postmodern/poststructuralist geographies.

- Geographical scholarship today employs a range of philosophical and theoretical perspectives that make the discipline a rich and intriguing area of study.

SUMMARY

Geography matters. It affects our life changes, structures our understandings of ourselves and others, and organizes our daily experiences. Geographers are interested in myriad questions related to human-environment interactions from a number of perspectives. In particular, geographers use a spatial perspective to understand events, activities, and human behaviours, focusing expressly on the themes of location, place, region, landscape, and movement. While these themes clearly overlap, they also provide a distinct conceptualization of human-spatial interactions. Geographers have also used a variety of philosophical, theoretical, and conceptual frameworks for thinking through geographical questions. These include regional perspectives and spatial analysis, Marxist and feminist perspectives, as well as more contemporary postmodern viewpoints. All of these contribute to the existence of

a rich and complex body of geographical thought and knowledge, much of which we highlight in the chapters that follow.

Our study of human geography will analyze people and places and explain how they interact across space and time to create our world. Chapters 2 and 3 lay the basis for our study of human geography by looking at the changing political territorial organization through colonialism, imperialism, and globalization. Chapters 4 and 5 focus on populations and immigration while chapters 7 and 8 focus on aspects of social organization and how people use culture and identity to make sense of themselves in their world. The remaining chapters examine how people have created a world in which they function economically and how they organize themselves across both rural and urban spaces as well as how their activities in those realms re-create themselves and their world.

DISCUSSION AND REVIEW QUESTIONS

1. What was the *Seven Wonders of Canada* competition and what does it reveal about the nature of human geography as a field of inquiry? Further, what would you have chosen for the competition and why?

2. While maps are the most familiar and recognizable tool of geography, the concept of "place" is what arguably unifies the field. Discuss this concept of place, paying particular attention to notions of "sense of place," "place matters," and "the globalization of place."

3. "Landscape" is another important theme related to a spatial perspective. What is landscape and with whom is the concept most associated? How does the Tanzanian

city of Dar-es-Salaam illustrate the variety of forces involved in landscape practices?

4. Compare and contrast reference maps with thematic maps. Who was Dr. John Snow and how was he able to use mapping in the field of medicine?

5. Human geographers approach their studies from a variety of theoretical and conceptual perspectives, which in turn lead to the production and dissemination of a wide array of geographical knowledge. Compare and contrast two such theoretical and conceptual perspectives focusing on key individuals, concepts, and outcomes.

GEOGRAPHIC CONCEPTS

ADDITIONAL RESOURCES ONLINE

Association of American Geographers: www.aag.org

Canadian Association of Geographers: www.cag-acg.ca

Canadian Geographic Magazine: www.cangeo.ca

Canadian Canoe Museum: www.canoemuseum.net

Royal Canadian Geographical Society: www.rcgs.org

Geocaching: www.geocaching.org

Globalization: www.learner.org/resources/series180. html#program_descriptions. Click on Video On Demand for "One Earth, Many Scales".

Globalization and Geography: www.lut.ac.uk/gawc/rb/rb40.html

John Snow and His Work on Cholera: www.ph.ucla.edu/epi/ snow.html

The State of Food Insecurity in the World: www.fao.org

World Hunger: www.wfp.org

Google Earth: www.googleearth.com

Indigenous knowledges: www.nativemaps.org

Yi-Fu Tuan: www.yifutuan.org

Zapatista Revolution: www.zapatistarevolution.com

chapter 2

GLOBALIZATION AND GEOGRAPHIES

Global Consumption

WALKING into a Gap store, one's eyes are immediately drawn to a display of T-shirts on a circular table at the store's entrance. Each T-shirt has a special tag identifying it as Gap (PRODUCT)RED. This means that a portion of the shirt's sale price goes directly to the Global Fund, which finances projects to combat AIDS in sub-Saharan Africa. (RED) is a business model that creates partnerships with corporations, such as The Gap and Hallmark (Figure 2.1), to establish a network of private sector funding for designated AIDS projects in Africa.

Economic geographers study the geographies of consumption, which includes retail centres such as the Mall of America, as well as consumer choices—how consumers make choices and whether social or political concerns, such as AIDS in sub-Saharan Africa, play a role in their purchasing decisions. According to geographer Jon Goss, economic geographers observe an "attitude-behavior gap": they have found that "consumers are not willing to pay higher prices for 'cause-related products,' lack adequate information to make effective choices, suffer from 'care fatigue,' respond more to short-term negative campaigns," and at the same time are concerned about "exploitation of labor and environment."

(RED) works to overcome the attitude-behaviour gap by keeping the prices of its products the same as non-(RED) products, by sustaining a dynamic marketing campaign, and by advocating transparency and disseminating information about the projects supported through funds raised. The success of (RED) and other goods with connections to social concerns is one of many processes creating and recreating globalization.

FIGURE 2.1 (Red). Products offered include items from The Gap, Converse, and Motorola. (© Tony Cenicola/*The New York Times*/Redux)

KEY QUESTIONS FOR CHAPTER 2

1. What is globalization, and what are the major debates about globalization?

2. What are the connections between globalization and the geographical?

3. Why do some people or groups oppose or resist globalization?

2.1 What Is Globalization, and What Are the Major Debates about Globalization?

As you read this paragraph, take a quick inventory of your possessions and surroundings. Who made your shoes? What about your pants? Does your shirt or blouse have a "Made in Canada" label? Where was your purse or knapsack made? Are you drinking a Tim Horton's coffee or one from Starbucks? Is it organic or fair trade coffee? Do you care? When we stop to think about our daily routines, we realize how tightly our consumption choices connect us to people and their labour in places all over the globe. If

> **Commodity chain** Series of links connecting the many places of production and distribution and resulting in a commodity that is then exchanged on the world market.

you own a laptop, you could probably map the process of its manufacture down a global **commodity chain**—a complex network of people, labour, and production processes starting with the extraction of raw materials from the earth itself and ending with your purchase of the final product. The fruit you eat, the fish you consume, the music you play, your knapsack, your hat, your pens and paper, cell phone, and iPod all circulated through these global commodity chains until you "consumed" them (see Figure 2.14). While these interconnected production circuits provide a wealth of material goods at inexpensive prices, as a knowledgeable "player" in this global "game," you are implicated at a very personal level in its success and failures, its exploitative and oppressive regimes, and its possibilities for positive change and progress.

Our role as consumers is just one of many ways we may find ourselves drawn into social and political debates that are taking place far beyond our local neighbourhoods or even our own country. In this chapter, we consider the definition of the term "globalization" and introduce the main issues related to globalization processes and outcomes. In particular, we consider the debates about what globalization means, when it began, and whether it is a positive or negative process, or both. Finally, we consider why there is resistance or opposition to globalization. As noted in Chapter 1, questions about globalization, its processes, and outcomes are fundamental to human geographers' consideration of the current organization of place at a variety of scales and to our understanding of location, region, place, landscape, and movement—our spatial perspective.

WHAT IS GLOBALIZATION?

The meaning of the term "globalization" is a hotly contested topic, and any position we take has serious political, social, and economic implications. Scholars disagree about how to define globalization; they argue over when these globalizing processes began and they debate vigorously whether globalization has positive or negative consequences (or both). Some scholars go so far as to argue that there is no such thing as globalization and that, economically at least, the world is no more interconnected now than in previous eras. Steven Firth and Peter McMichael suggest that globalization is more properly understood as an "agenda" or a "project" in which dominant Western countries work to actively create opportunities for themselves to accumulate capital and profit. Others argue that the processes, activities, and outcomes of globalization are so fundamentally different from previous global interactions that we are experiencing radical and decisive economic, social, and political shifts in relations at many scales, including the global.

Among those who do agree that the world is experiencing something understood as globalization, it remains difficult to reach a consensus on what the term actually means. George Ritzer suggests that various definitions have a number of common elements. Based on those shared attributes, he defines **globalization** as "an accelerating set of processes involving flows that encompass ever-greater numbers of the world spaces and that lead

> **Globalization** The expansion of economic, political, and cultural processes to the point that they become global in scale and impact. The processes of globalization transcend state boundaries and have outcomes that vary across places and scales.

to increasing integration and interconnectivity among those spaces" (2007, p. 1). This text uses Ritzer's definition as the starting point from which to argue that we are experiencing something unique called "globalization," and that its processes and outcomes have spatial consequences.

Two important points spring to mind from Ritzer's definition. First, it refers to "processes" without specifying what those processes might be. While the processes of globalization are often understood as largely economic (that is, the activities of capitalist enterprise), the term "processes" also refers to cultural, political, social, and technological activities and practices. For example, technological processes can accelerate the flow of cultural traits (such as music or fashion) and political ideas into new and increasingly interconnected places (see Chapter 8 for details). Globalization comes about through improved technologies, new and emerging international financial and labour markets, and the growth of global consumer markets with an appetite for an ever-increasing array of goods.

Second, the definition highlights the geographical implications of globalization by focusing on how processes involve flows that, for better or worse, increase interactions, deepen relationships, and heighten interdependence between peoples and places. A geographer's spatial perspective helps in understanding the geographical implications of globalization. We need to

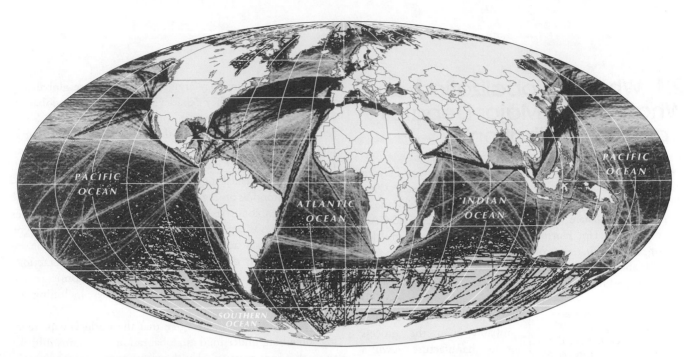

FIGURE 2.2 Global Shipping Lanes. This map traces over 3,000 shipping routes used by commercial and government vessels during 2006. The red lines mark the most frequently used shipping lanes. Courtesy of National Center for Ecological Analysis and Synthesis. Accessed October 28, 2011 at http://ebm.nceas.ucsb.edu/GlobalMarine/impacts/transformed/jpg/shipping.jpg.

consider spatial processes at a variety of intertwined scales, from the local to the global, and to think about how global processes and activities are continually forging links and connections. Canadian geographer Glen Norcliffe emphasizes that the processes and outcomes of globalization are not predictable or orderly and are best understood as chaotic and unruly, with places and people experiencing its effects in highly variable ways. The global shipping lanes illustrated in Figure 2.2 help us visualize how trade in various goods creates linkages and connections among and between numerous places—but not everywhere with everyone. Globalization processes and outcomes are not evenly distributed through time and space. Global interactions pass by some places and include others only tangentially, resulting in both positive and negative implications for those places. A geographical eye helps us consider these different experiences of globalization.

THE BEGINNINGS OF GLOBALIZATION

Scholars disagree about when globalizing processes began. We might argue that we have been living in a globalizing world since the early 14th century, when newly emerging nation states in western Europe, including Spain, Portugal, France, and Great Britain, began exploring and colonizing on a global scale. In the early 1400s, the first wave of sailing adventurers and explorers, including Christopher Columbus (Spain) and Vasco da Gama (Portugal), led expeditions to the shores of the Americas and around Africa's Cape of Good Hope to India and beyond—the outer reaches of the known world. In a second wave of exploration in the early 1800s, Spain and Portugal, the Netherlands, Great Britain, and France established colonies

around the world, consolidating a global system of trade and commerce (Figure 2.3). The colonizing countries' relations with the colonized were largely exploitative. Colonizers organized the administration of their colonies to ensure the most efficient processes for moving raw materials from the interior of the country to the coast for export. By the end of the 1800s, most of the world's territories had been drawn into the capitalist economy.

The *world systems approach* or theory, developed by Immanuel Maurice Wallerstein in the early 1970s, provides one way to understand the organizational structure of these colonial and imperial enterprises. According to this approach, discussed in more detail in Chapter 11, the interaction and exchange resulting from these successive waves of exploration, colonization, and imperialism resulted in the current organization of nation states. In Wallerstein's system, states are classified as *core*, *periphery*, and *semi-periphery* (Figure 2.4). Natural resources, foodstuffs, and labour are redistributed from the periphery to the core through the operation of the world market.

Colonizing countries, mainly in the Western industrialized regions, constitute the core of the world economy because of their ability to dominate commercial, financial, and production activities. Core regions control the major production facilities and technologies, lead in trade and investment, and can maintain and protect their interests through political and military strength. Periphery regions, drawn into the global capitalist economy to varying degrees through colonization and engagement in trade, remain underdeveloped, supplying the core with raw materials, labour, and foodstuffs. Semi-periphery regions are able to make use of the resources of peripheral regions but also

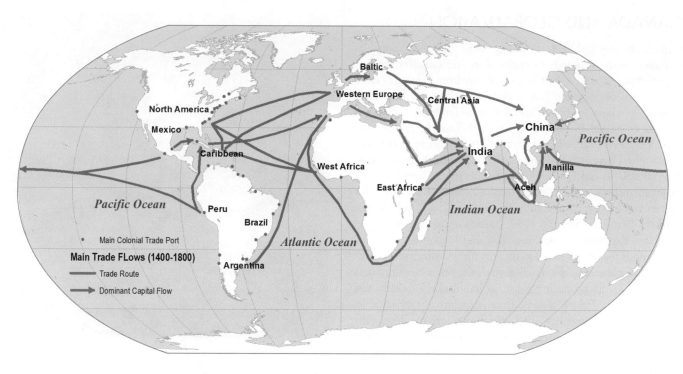

FIGURE 2.3 Major Global Trade Routes, 1400-1800. (Copyright © Dr. Jean-Paul Rodrigue, Department of Global Studies & Geography, Hofstra University.)

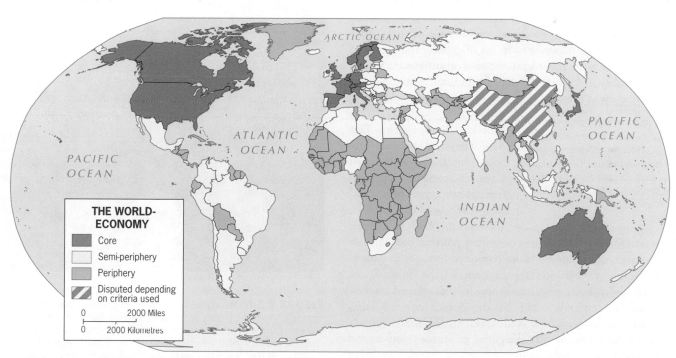

FIGURE 2.4 The Three-Tier Structure of the World Economy. One representation of core, peri phery, and semi-periphery based on a calculation called World-Economy Centrality, derived by sociologist Paul Prew. The authors took into consideration factors not quantified in Prew's data, including membership in the European Union, in moving some countries from the categories Prew's data recommended to other categories. Data from: *Paul Prew, World-Economy Centrality and Carbon Dioxide Emissions: A New Look at the Position in the Capitalist World-System and Environmental Pollution, American Sociological Association, 12, 2 (2010) 162 -191.*

find themselves exploited by core regions. Many semi-peripheral countries were once members of the periphery, but through various circumstances they shifted their positioning within the world system. Obviously, the world system has organized itself differently depending on the historical era. Varying perspectives regarding the prospects for countries to move along the peripheral—semi-peripheral—core trajectory are discussed at length in Chapter 11.

CANADA AND GLOBALIZATION

Canada's history highlights the nature of the shifting relationships initiated by the processes of exploration and colonization that began in the 1400s. As the *Guest Field Note* from Sarah de Leeuw argues, this colonization had a profound effect on the North American indigenous population that is still felt today. The country was colonized by successive waves of Spanish, French, and British explorers, settlers, and adventurers, beginning in the mid-1550s when Basque fishers and whalers explored the sea coasts of Newfoundland and Labrador. The St. Lawrence River became a major inland waterway, opening up the interior of Canada to fur traders and lumber barons shipping raw goods back to European markets. Between 1550 and 1750, Canada developed as a staples economy, exporting its rich resources and importing manufactured goods that were needed to support the growing export trade. Local manufacturing, always modest, developed as an adjunct to the export trade, producing ships, agricultural equipment, and steel machinery for the railway. Because it initially served as an exporter of raw materials, Canada was drawn into the developing world system as a peripheral region. The country's long association with the sea (Figure 2.5) as the primary means of moving our exports is reflected in our art and music.

With successive waves of industrialization, Canada was increasingly incorporated into the world economy but with continued dependence on the global core—at that time, the colonial core countries of Europe. As the west was settled, Canada added wheat and mineral resources to its list of exports and by World War II was one of the leading producers of oil and gas. As Harold Innis describes it, Canada developed a distinctive staples-based economy even as it emerged as part of one of the world's three

> **Staples thesis** The theory that Canada's economy developed through the export of raw resources to Europe and that, as a result, Canada did not develop a strong manufacturing base, preferring to import finished goods.

major core regions—North America, Europe, and East Asia. The **staples thesis**, proposed by Innis, argues that Canada's economy developed through the export of "staples" such as fish, lumber, fur, wheat, and minerals back to Europe.

However, Canada holds a less dominant position today due to its geographical location and its economic linkages to what is currently one of the world's largest economies, the United States. As Glen Norcliffe argues, Canada may have developed a manufacturing and service base but "the staples economy still looms larger in Canada's hinterland" (2001, p. 18). This makes Canada vulnerable to fluctuations in the global prices for resources and hinders economic development in manufacturing. In its reliance on resource export, Canada has been slower to develop the technologies and processes to refine and manufacture raw materials from those resources, preferring to import finished goods. While a contested perspective, the staples thesis does help explain Canada's seemingly contradictory position as both a member of the global core and a secondary economic player.

The world system is constantly reorganizing, and the growing global importance of China, South Korea, Taiwan, and Japan as emergent economic and political centres refocused the global economy on the Pacific Rim in the 1990s. By the end

(a)

(b)

FIGURE 2.5 (a) Whaling. The dangers of traditional whaling are shown in this 19th-century lithograph. **(b) Ship Building.** Shipyard workmen and women gathered to witness the launching of a ship from the Burrard yard, Vancouver circa 1944. (Library and Archives, Canada C-32706; National Film Board of Canada. Still Photography Division/Library and Archives Canada, R1196-14-7-E)

of that decade, Japan had become an economic powerhouse, with major investments in North America and Europe and a host of multinational corporations engaged in automobile manufacturing (Honda, Toyota, Nissan, and Mitsubishi) and electronics production (Fujitsu, Sharpe, Sony, and Panasonic) exporting goods around the world. However, the instability of the world's markets in the fall of 2008 and the subsequent recession had a serious impact on the world's major economies.

GUEST FIELD NOTE Geographies of a Neocolonial British Columbia

At the age of 12, I stood beside Bill Reid on a long rocky beach stretching the length of the Skidigate Indian Reserve on Haida Gwaii. Bill Reid was an old man on that sunny afternoon in 1986. I was participating in the launch of *Loo Taas*, or *Wave Eater* in English, a 15-metre war canoe Reid carved from a single red cedar tree (Figure 2.6b). At the time, I did not understand Reid was one of Canada's most talented artists, dedicated to the revitalization of the Haida Nation and culture (Figure 2.6a). Instead, I stood beside a man I knew was about the same age as my Opa, had a grandfatherly-like presence, and was draped in a beautiful button blanket. I remember he had a gentle handshake and a shock of white hair.

Like many British Columbians, or arguably like many Canadians, I knew nothing about the long geographic history of that relatively small space where, for a relatively short moment in the closing years of the 20th century, I stood watching *Loo Taas* break, and then for the first time hungrily eat, waves crashing on the shore of the Pacific Ocean. In 1986 I did not know that the islands where I lived were once called something other than The Queen Charlotte Islands, a name that referenced both an English monarch and the ship of Captain George Dixon, the man who surveyed the islands in 1787. I did not know that an Indian reserve was a specific jurisdiction, governed under different policies than the town of Queen Charlotte City where my family and I lived, about 9 km up the highway. And, as I stood and listened to speeches made in a language I did not comprehend, made by men and women I simply thought of as the grandparents of children I went to school with, I had no idea that, not so long ago, many of those elderly people would have been placed in schools where they likely suffered beatings for speaking in their Haida language.

Given the plethora of my other naiveties, I certainly had no idea that linkages existed between those historic violences and the tragedies like suicide and drug addiction that claimed too many of my young classmates from the Indian reserves on the islands I knew only by an English name. I also had no idea that the ravens and killer whales and beavers and bears that stretched out across the button blankets and headdresses that the speakers wore, or that reached skywards in the totem poles dotting the beach behind us, were testaments to a strong, complex, self-determining, and sovereign people. Because I was young, and a product of a school system that taught me Christopher Columbus "discovered" the Americas in 1492, I had no idea what self-determining or sovereign meant. And I certainly had never heard words like postcolonial, or neocolonial, and a concept like "edge of empire" would have just made me giggle.

Over the years, I have become fascinated with that moment on a beach in 1986. In a way, what I research today is always in reference to Skidegate Village, Bill Reid, and *Loo Taas*. The work I do involves producing a deeper understanding

about how that moment, the small space in which it unfolded and the people of which it was composed, embodied a history of missionary activity, a production of reserves, the renaming of lands, efforts to transform indigenous peoples, and the sustained work of Haida people to maintain social, cultural, and even geographic sovereignty.

Broadly speaking, I am interested in the relationships between indigenous peoples and people who might best be described as settlers in the province. More specifically, I am interested in the ways that British Columbia's colonial history manifests in certain kinds of geographies, in particular types of power dynamics, and in a variety of social naiveties, tensions, and injustices in the province. To this end, I undertake cultural, social, and historic geographic research. This includes, for in-

(a)

(b)

FIGURE 2.6 *The Spirit of Haida Gwaii–The Jade Canoe.*
(a) The six-ton sculpture by Bill Reid is on display at Vancouver International Airport. (b) The launch of Bill Reid's *Loo Tass (Wave Eater)* in 1986. (Photo by Media2oProductions. "The Spirit of Haida Gwa: The Jade Canoe" by Haida artist Bill Reid, 1993. The second and final bronze casting in the collection of the Vancouver International Airport Authority;© Sarah de Leeuw)

stance, searching archives in order to find records and documents of indigenous peoples' responses to colonial projects like residential schooling. I also analyze historic and contemporary government policies and laws so as to demonstrate linkages between 19th and 20th century ideas about "savage Indians" and 21st century realities, including unprecedented high rates of child apprehensions from indigenous families. I also write creatively, but always with an emphasis on geographic themes. I think of all these efforts as part of my broader research agenda.

In efforts to demonstrate that British Columbia is not a post-colonial geography–a space, in other words, no longer shaped and reshaped in the present day by settler colonial peoples and our polices–I write and produce research that links the past to the present. To this end, some of my work has argued that when Aboriginal patients visit a doctor they are met with a medical system that does not fully account for a history of residential schooling, living on an Indian reserve, or being governed under the *Indian Act*, each of which have particular impacts on

people's health. At other times, and usually in partnership with Aboriginal organizations, my work has focused on feelings of trust–or mistrust–that indigenous peoples may have toward various spaces and peoples with which they interact.

All of these different research projects are connected because, at base, I am concerned with ameliorating the significant disparities that exist between indigenous and settler colonial peoples in British Columbia and, arguably, around the world. Ultimately, I hope for a future in British Columbia and elsewhere wherein grave naiveties, like mine in 1986, do not dominate understandings about relationships between indigenous and settler peoples in the province. Geographic research can assist in building this future, and undertaking this research from a variety of angles will lead to a richer, more nuanced and complex, array of understandings.

Sarah de Leeuw, Northern Medical Program, UNBC, Faculty of Medicine, UBC

The gross domestic product (GDP) of several of the world's major economies declined significantly in the fourth quarter of 2008 and the first quarter of 2009. Several economies, including those of Japan and the United States, began to rebound in 2009, but by early 2010, declines were again apparent in the economies of Japan, the United States, and Greece. Canada weathered the economic storm reasonably well but did experience a modest economic downturn.

China, the world's most populous county (an estimated 1.3 billion in 2008), continues to gain strength in the global economy. Since the death in 1976 of Mao Zedong, leader of the governing Communist Party from 1949, China's government has increasingly drawn the country into the global economic system and

encouraged rapid economic growth, particularly in the last 30 years. China joined the World Trade Organization in 2001 and has experienced a marked increase in exports and foreign investment. According to the World Bank, Japan's economy grew by some 5 percent while China's experienced a staggering 261 percent growth between 2000 and 2008. Much of China's industrial and manufacturing development takes place along the eastern shore, in Beijing and port cities such as Shanghai and the former British Territory of Hong Kong, which are the contact points for international trade. China has experienced rapid urbanization (for example, the population of Beijing was estimated at 20 million in 2010), and cities such as Shanghai and Tianjin are centres of economic, social, and cultural development (Figure 2.7).

(a)

(b)

FIGURE 2.7 Urbanization and development in China. (a) A Starbucks Coffee shop inside the Forbidden City, Beijing. (b) The Lujiazui Financial District in Pudong, Shanghai. (© Macduff Everton/Corbis; © Qilai Shen/In Pictures/Corbis)

FIGURE 2.8 *ATB Victorious/John J. Carrick.* (Courtesy of McAsphalt Industries Ltd.)

Canada has worked hard to develop an economic relationship with China. In June 2010, China's president Hu Jintao visited Canada as part of efforts on behalf of both countries to establish stronger economic, political, and social ties. As of 2010, China ranks among Canada's largest trading partners, with over $40 billion in trade annually. Of the many industries caught up in Canadian-Chinese relations, shipbuilding has become increasingly significant.

Shipbuilding is not only an important aspect of Canada-China economic relations but also exemplifies the processes of globalization generally when we consider the complicated history of its construction and deployment. For example, *Victorious/John J. Carrick* is a Canadian articulated tug-barge (ATB) unit built at the Penglai Bohai Shipyard in Penglai City, China, in 2009. ATB *Victorious/John J. Carrick* is owned and operated by Toronto-based McAsphalt Marine Transportation Ltd. The Articouple system that connects the tug and barge is Japanese; the NORIS system that provides engine-room monitoring and controls is German; most of the navigational equipment is provided by British-based Sperry Marine; the main engines are from MaK, another German company; the thermal oil heaters on the barge are Swedish; the Collomatic winches are made in Canada; and the main switchboards and motor control centres use Telemecanique components, relays, overloads, and programmable logic circuits—all made in France. There are at least 10 countries involved in making this Canadian vessel (Figure 2.8). Once complete, the ATB was sailed from China to Canada via the Pacific Ocean, through the Panama Canal, before picking up its first load of asphalt in Louisiana. It now regularly sails the Great Lakes–St. Lawrence Seaway system to the east coast of North America, moving asphalt between the United States and Canada.

WORLD CITIES

Globalization is having a profound effect on urban areas as cities take up new positions that were not anticipated. Many of the most important processes in global relations occur among and between cities. In fact, what we now call **world cities** function as the service centres of the world economy, often superceding state borders. These world cities are connected to other cities at the global level, and the forces shaping the world economy pulse across these connections and through the cities.

> **World city** Dominant city in terms of its role in the global political economy. Not the world's biggest city in terms of population or industrial output, but rather centers of strategic control of the world economy.

World cities currently operate within a hierarchy (which we will discuss in detail in Chapter 10). Many geographers agree that that New York, London, and Tokyo are the most important world cities, but after those three, the list and the definition of what makes a world city changes depending on the perspective of the person defining the term. Two Canadian cities, Toronto and Vancouver, are often on the list of world cities, but they usually appear far down that list. Various ranking systems are used to identify world cities, with each system emphasizing different characteristics and giving cities a higher or lower rank based on, for example, their livability and sustainability, their economic or technological functions, and/or their position in relation to other cities. Researchers adopt the system that reflects what they consider the most important criteria for evaluating urban areas.

World cities do not exist merely as players in the global economy; they often continue their role as the capital cities of states. For example, even though London and Paris are only a short distance apart, both function as world cities, in part because of the role they play within their respective states. Each became a magnet for economic and political activity within Great Britain and France, respectively, and then the globe. In each case, the national government concentrated on developing the country's capital city, thereby bolstering that city above other cities in the state, and also encouraged interconnectedness between that city and the rest of the world. World cities, such as London, serve as major financial capitals, transportation links, and centres of tourism and service industries partly because of their geographical location. Such cities usually go to great lengths to ensure they have impressive landscapes with distinctive architecture and historic sites (Figure 2.9).

FREE TRADE ZONES

In addition to the emergence of world cities, **free trade zones (FTZs)** have also become increasingly important for the movement of goods and capital on a global scale. FTZs are areas set aside

> **Free trade zones** Areas set aside within countries to make foreign investment and trade easier by reducing or eliminating trade barriers, and providing inexpensive labour and raw materials.

within countries to make foreign investment and trade easier by reducing or eliminating trade barriers, including tariffs and bureaucratic requirements. The zones, which usually emerge in

(a)

(b)

FIGURE 2.9 World Cities. (a) The London Eye, the world's largest cantilevered observation wheel, was completed in 2000. Standing next to it is the London Sea Life Aquarium, formerly the headquarters of the London County Council, opened in 1922. (b) Toronto's distinctive skyline boasts the iconic CN Tower and the dome of the Rogers Centre, home of the Toronto Blue Jays baseball team. (© Richard Nowitz/National Geographic Society/Corbis; © Robert Glusic/Getty Images)

peripheral nations, are labour-intensive manufacturing centres where inexpensive labour and raw materials are brought together to produce clothing, electronics, and other mass-produced consumer goods for transnational corporations. The earliest FTZs were established in the 1920s in Argentina and Uruguay, but the idea spread quickly; as of 1999, over 40 million people were employed in more than 3,000 FTZs in 116 countries. In developing or peripheral nations, the establishment of FTZs is considered central to economic growth because the zones provide an important opportunity for the periphery to connect economically with core countries. For example, 14 FTZs have been set up in Sri Lanka since the 1970s. They employ over 250,000 people, 80 percent of whom are women drawn to these locations by the promise of steady employment (Figure 2.10). The garment and textile industries make up the vast majority of manufacturing

FIGURE 2.10 Female Workers at a Factory in One of Sri Lanka's Free Trade Zones. (Anuruddha Lokuhapuarachchi/Reuters/Landov)

in Sri Lankan FTZs. Criticism of FTZs comes from a variety of sources, including labour unions that are concerned for the rights and safety of workers who toil in poor conditions for low wages and often lack job security and basic labour rights.

DEBATING GLOBALIZATION

The world systems approach provided a valuable conceptualization of world economic organization up to World War II. However, most scholars agree that this system began to undergo fundamental changes in the 1950s. One of the most influential writers describing these changes was Canadian literary critic Marshall McLuhan, whose description of the new world order is captured in the term "global village." McLuhan was reflecting on the rapid and profound impacts new technologies and communications were having on social and cultural life. Human geographers might agree, somewhat tentatively, that global processes, activities, and outcomes are continuing to foster substantial economic, political, and social transformation at myriad scales—a process described by the term "globalization." However, vitriolic disagreement persists over whom these alterations benefit and whether they are generally for better or for worse.

Thomas Friedman, in his book *The World Is Flat,* presents globalization in a positive light, arguing that we are seeing a "flattening" of the world as nations drop barriers to trade and migration. Friedman suggests that the **friction of distance**—the increase in time and cost that usually comes with increasing distance—has been overcome by technological improvements as well as free trade agreements.

> **Friction of distance**
> The increase in time and cost that usually comes with increasing distance.

This neoliberal political perspective understands globalization as a mainly progressive economic process that, with a few bumps along the way, promotes democracy, prosperity, and peace. Geographer David Harvey defines **neo-liberalism** as a political-economic theory that suggests that human well-being will come about by "liberating individual entrepreneurial freedoms and skills" through state protection of "private property rights, free markets and free trade." (2005, p. 2). In this framework, the role of the state is not only to maintain these protections but also to see they become as much a part of the global condition as possible. Proponents of neoliberalism argue that greater participation in the world economy and in democratic politics by individuals, corporations, and states will ensure improved conditions for all. Economist Keith Maskus asserts, "Free trade raises the well-being of all countries by inducing them to specialize their resources in those goods they produce relatively most efficiently" (2004, p. 98–116), resulting in lower production costs. By engaging in global competition through trade, a country can expect to increase its long-term growth rate by gaining access to global technologies and becoming more innovative.

> **Neo-liberalism** An ideologically driven set of practices that seek to open and expand capitalist markets, reduce or eliminate government regulation and constraint of the free market, and the development of frameworks that enhance global market processes.

Other observers argue that the neoliberalism currently underpinning the economic and political policies of core countries has resulted in unchecked free market capitalism, which benefits some individuals, corporations, nation-states, and regions over others. This has led to new or continued economic, social, and cultural domination by some of the beneficiary countries, which exploit and marginalize other countries. From this perspective, globalization processes are understood as operating unevenly or generating uneven or inequitable outcomes, creating an ever-widening gap between the "haves" and the "have-nots" in terms of income, access to education and health care, and global environmental justice issues. Scholars largely agree that inequities between people have increased dramatically, although they disagree about whether these inequalities will diminish (as we will see in Chapter 11).

Despite the concerns of critics, globalization is not likely to stop. Even if there were a desire to reverse the processes, there are powerful forces opposed to such a move. Many scholars and grassroots organizations suggest that globalization itself is not the problem but, rather, the way it operates. If globalization in its current form leads to economic exploitation and domination for the benefit of some over others, then perhaps there is a way to redirect or transform global processes so they lead to less inequality and exploitation and greater democratic reform (which is not always viewed positively by all), economic and social development, and prosperity. Numerous grassroots organizations and international governmental and non-governmental organizations (IGOs and INGOs) have proposed reforms to address the inequities stemming from globalizing forces while taking advantage of the benefits of participation and engagement; we will discuss some of these proposals in the final section of this chapter.

Whether in favour of or opposed to globalization, most people would agree that the process is not a natural evolution in humanity. We need to question whether the overwhelming dominance of capitalism as an economic system makes globalization necessary and unstoppable. According to geographers John O'Loughlin and his colleagues, globalization is "neither an inevitable nor an irreversible set of processes" (2004), while Andrew Kirby states that it is "not proceeding according to any particular playbook" (2004, p. 133–158). Globalization is perhaps better understood as an unpredictable and highly selective set of processes and outcomes created by people, be they corporate CEOs, university administrators, readers of blogs, or protesters at a trade meeting. The processes of globalization and the connectedness created through globalization are not limited to state-to-state interaction. Rather, the connection occurs across scales and across networks, regardless of state borders. The focus on human agency, participation, and choice highlights how both scholarship and grassroots protest might be harnessed to work with the possibilities and potentials of globalizing processes to foster more beneficial, universal outcomes.

MAIN POINTS   2.1   What Is Globalization, and What Are the Major Debates about Globalization?

- Globalization, according to George Ritzer, is an accelerating set of processes involving flows that encompass ever-greater numbers of the world spaces and that lead to increasing integration and interconnectivity among those spaces.

- The processes involved are often seen as economic but are also political, cultural, social, and technological. Although globalization is often seen as a global process, it has profound local implications.

- The current world system, in which globalization is a contemporary process, is rooted in some 500 years of colonial and imperial exploration by European countries. In this world system, countries are viewed as constituting part of the core, periphery, or semi-periphery.

- Globalization processes have changed the nature and organization of cities, creating what we now call world cities, such as London, New York, and Tokyo. These cities are often centres of finance, information, and administration and are interconnected at the global scale.

- There is considerable debate about the form, definition, characteristics, and outcomes of globalization as well as contestations over how its positive and negative outcomes should be addressed.

2.2 What Are the Connections between Globalization and the Geographical?

The world seems smaller as a result of the explosion in information and communication technologies since World War II. We can send information great distances in the blink of an eye, travel anywhere on the globe relatively quickly, and pluck vast amounts of information out of the cyberspace ether with the click of a mouse. We make intellectual and emotional connections with people and places whether we have actually met them or been there, creating a complex network of relationships, linkages, and interdependencies. These rapid and unprecedented transformations have provoked some scholars, including Richard O'Brien, to herald "the end of geography," declaring that in economic matters, at least, "geographic location no longer matters" (1992, p. 1). Needless to say, geographers and other social scientists have resisted this somewhat cavalier dismissal of the importance of the geographical. In this section, we consider how geographers, using their spatial perspective, have attempted to conceptualize the geographical operations of globalizing processes and outcomes. Here we consider several different approaches: David Harvey's notion of "time-space compression," the idea of networks, the concept of "placelessness," and the new relations of the global-local captured in the term "glocalization."

TIME-SPACE COMPRESSION

Globalization arguably transforms time and space in novel and unexpected ways. We know that social life is experienced in material places, so changes in how we comprehend time and space must have an effect on social relations. Sociologist Anthony Giddens argues that globalization brings about time-space distanciation, which means we experience "the intensification of worldwide social relations" such that local experiences are being shaped by events occurring at great distances and vice versa. Geographer David Harvey links globalization directly to the dynamics of the capitalist market system, suggesting it is responsible for a surge in

> **Time-space compression**
> The social and psychological effects of living in a world in which time-space convergence has rapidly reached a high level of intensity; associated with the work of David Harvey.

time-space compression: the process by which global markets seem to reorganize the perception of time so as to reduce the constraints of space on their activities. In other words, as new technologies such as telephones, telegraph, radio, automobiles, and now the Internet appear to be speeding time up, the barriers of space seem to be removed. Take, for example, Harvey's depiction of the Shrinking Map of the World (Figure 2.11). Here, Harvey shows us that in 1500, the average speed of horse-drawn carriages and ships was 10 miles per hour. In 1960, the average speed of a jet was 700 miles per hour. Thus, according to Harvey's time-space compression, the world feels 70 times smaller in 1960 than it did in 1500.

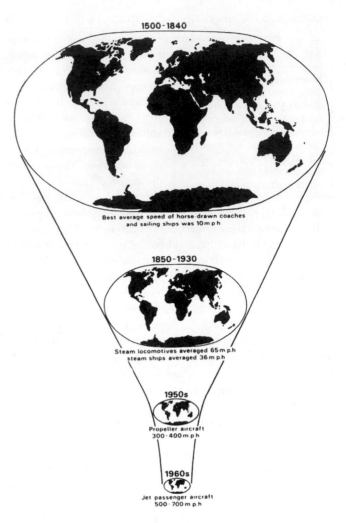

FIGURE 2.11 The Shrinking Map of the World. David Harvey, *The Condition of Postmodernity.* Oxford and Cambridge, MA: Basil Blackwell, 1989, p. 241, plate 3.1.

These changes have a profound effect on how human beings understand and operate in their world. Artist Julie Mehretu graphically captures how we, as individuals, might be experiencing these changes (Figure 2.12). According to the Williams College Museum of Art, her work "combines maps, urban grids, and architectural renderings to articulate complex social and geopolitical structures," and to "[query] what impact an individual can have, and what one person contributes to the construction of a larger narrative."

Time-space compression means that certain places, such as world cities, are more interconnected than ever as a result of their access to communication and transportation networks, while other places are farther removed than ever. A major divide in access to information technology networks is a hallmark of the current world and an example of the uneven outcomes of globalization among peripheral, semi-peripheral, and core regions. In 2004, the United Nations Development Programme's Human Development Report divided the world's states into high income, middle income, and low income (according to gross domestic product) and reported on accessibility to technology according to these classes. At the same time, high-income states had, on average, 507 telephone mainlines,

the globalized world and magnifies the global technological divide. We may be shocked to see how quickly technology has changed and diffused. In 1992, the highest-income states had, on average, only 10 cellular subscribers and 2.5 Internet users per 1,000 people (contrasted with 582 and 382.6, respectively, in 2002). In Canada, governments at the local, provincial, and national levels are concerned with the uneven availability of high-speed Internet access, which has become increasingly important in our ability to access government services and information. As Figure 2.13 illustrates, there is a vast divide between rural and urban access. As part of its economic action plan, the federal government implemented *Broadband Canada: Connecting Rural Canadians*, a $225 million investment in providing broadband Internet access to unserved and underserved Canadian areas.

FIGURE 2.12 *Stadia II.* This work by artist Julie Mehretu captures how individuals might experience globalization's transformation of time and space. (Carnegie Museum of Art, Pittsburgh; Gift of Jeanne Greenberg Rohatyn and Nicolas Rohatyn and A. W. Mellon Acquisition Endowment Fund; © 2004 Julie Mehretu. By permission. Photo by Richard Stoner.)

582 cellular subscribers, and 382.6 Internet users per 1,000 people. Middle-income states had, on average, 111 telephone mainlines, 104 cellular subscribers, and 37.2 Internet users per 1,000 people, while states in the low-income class had an average of 11 telephone mainlines, 15 cellular subscriptions, and 5.9 Internet users per 1,000 people. The uneven access to, and use of, these technologies suggests that those excluded from the technology networks will experience increasing disadvantage and marginalization. The quickening pace of change in technology is another hallmark of

NETWORKS

As our definition of globalization suggests, places are interconnected now in such complex ways that we need to think conceptually across bounded and defined spaces and envision the connections, or networks, between places. Scholar Manuel Castells defines a **network** as "a set of interconnected nodes," and an increasing multitude of net-

> **Networks** A set of interconnected nodes without a centre, as defined by Manuel Castells.

works—financial, transportation, communication, kinship, corporate, nongovernmental, trade, government, media, education, and dozens of others—exist in the world, enabling globalization to occur and creating a higher degree of interaction and interdependence among people than ever before in human history.

As we noted earlier, commodity chains—those networks of labour and production processes that begin with the extraction or production of raw materials and end with the delivery of the finished product—are just such a network. Figure 2.14 takes us through the production of an iPod. Central to the iPod is the microchip that runs the iPod's wheel, stores your favourite songs and movies, and provides high-quality sound. The iPod's microchip is produced by PortalPlayer, a California company with offices in India. In "The World in an iPod," his article on PortalPlayer, journalist Andrew Leonard explains that the company has a 24-hour development cycle because engineers in California and in India can work around the clock (with time zones 12 hours apart) to design and redesign the microchip. The actual microchips are created in Taiwan, and the commodity chain for PortalPlayer reveals how people and places around the world interconnect to design and create the company's microchip.

The act of consumption is the end of a commodity chain; it is also the beginning of the product's afterlife. What happens when you discard or donate the item, and what are the costs or benefits created by the funds (whether revenue for a charity or profits for a corporation) generated by your purchase? Corporations such as Apple, which sells the

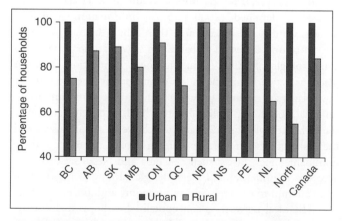

FIGURE 2.13 Broadband Availability in Canada: Urban versus Rural, 2009. From Figure 1 Broadband Availability in Canada: Urban Versus Rural, 2009, Publication No. 2011-57-E. Data from Communications Monitoring Report, July 2010. Courtesy of Information Service, Parliament of Canada/Bibliothèque du parlement.

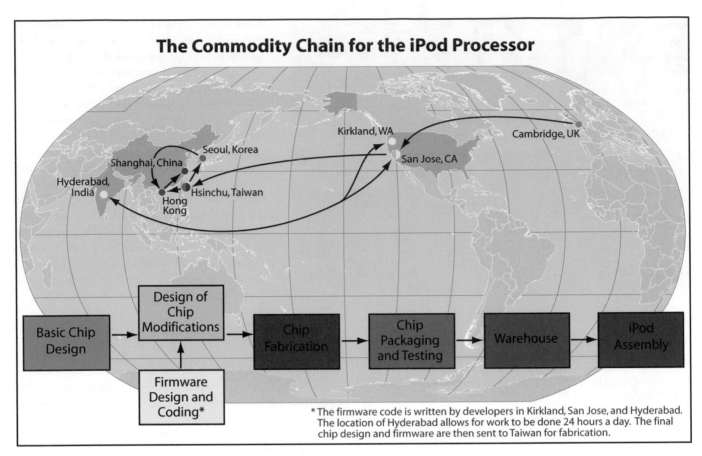

The Commodity Chain for the iPod Processor

Kirkland, WA

Cambridge, UK

Seoul, Korea

San Jose, CA

Shanghai, China

Hyderabad,
India

Hsinchu, Taiwan

Hong
Kong

| Basic Chip Design | → | Design of Chip Modifications | → | Chip Fabrication | → | Chip Packaging and Testing | → | Warehouse | → | iPod Assembly |

Firmware Design and Coding*

*The firmware code is written by developers in Kirkland, San Jose, and Hyderabad. The location of Hyderabad allows for work to be done 24 hours a day. The final chip design and firmware are then sent to Taiwan for fabrication.

FIGURE 2.14 Inside an iPod: The PortalPlayer World. Map designed by Stephen P. Hanna, based on information from Andrew Leonard, "The World in the iPod," *Spiegel Online*, August 8, 2005.

generated by your purchase? Corporations such as Apple, which sells the iPod, might attempt to reduce consumer waste by recycling iPods and computers, and by offering discounts to consumers who recycle their old iPods. Nonetheless, in many world cities in poorer parts of the globe, adults and children work in garbage dumps to recover valuable copper wire and other components of

FIGURE 2.15 China Recycling. Circuit boards in Guiyu, Guangdong Province, 2004. (© Photos 12/Alamy)

computers and electronics made by Apple and its competitors (Figure 2.15).

While networks have always existed, Castells argues that they have fundamentally changed over the last 20 years. He suggests that globalization has proceeded via information technology networks, albeit unevenly, by "linking up all that, according to dominant interests, has value anywhere in the planet, and discarding anything (people, firms, territories, resources) which has no value or becomes devalued" (2000, p. 5–24). Information technology networks link some places more than others, helping to create the spatial unevenness of globalization as well as the uneven outcomes of globalization. Thinking about connections between places as networks and flows lets us imaginatively conceptualize how places are situated (or excluded) in these communication, financial, social, and political networks. It also helps us understand the struggle of some places to achieve greater inclusion and the desire of others to perhaps remain beyond the reach of these dominant forces. Places such as China and Nepal seek to limit access to the Internet and the wider global flow of information in an attempt to preserve culture autonomy and distinctiveness.

The ideal network is conceptualized as horizontally structured, with no centre of power. While we know this type of structure encourages frequent interaction among nodes, we also know that power relations within networks mean that flows are uneven and inequitable, with some places experiencing greater access to and advantage within these global networks than others. In this section, we examine two major networks in the world today—media and retail corporations—and the scales at which they operate in the globalized world. Within each type of network, nodes interact on a global scale, but individuals have also created their own local or regional networks, often in response to network operations at the global scale. We will consider both the global and local or regional scales of activity for each type of network.

NETWORKS IN MEDIA

Global diffusion of products and ideas in popular culture depends largely on global media and retail store networks as well as the advertising in which both engage. Today's global media encompass much more than print, radio, and television. They also include spaces of entertainment, such as the New Amsterdam Theatre in Times Square in New York (owned by Disney); songs produced for record labels like RCA, Jive, and BMG (all owned by Bertelsmann); games played on PlayStation (owned by Sony); information about movies from MovieFone and directions to movie theatres from MapQuest (both owned by Time-Warner, as is the New Line Cinema movie you chose to see).

Through a series of mergers and consolidations occurring mostly in the post-Cold War era, global media are now largely controlled by six global corporations: Time-Warner, Disney, Bertelsmann, Viacom, News Corporation, and Vivendi Universal. These six media corporations (along with other smaller media corporations) are masters of **vertical integration**. A vertically integrated corporation owns companies and, in this case, media, at a variety of points along the production and consumption nodes of a commodity chain.

> **Vertical integration**
> Ownership by the same firm of a number of companies that exist along a variety of points on a commodity chain.

In a 2003 report, Miguel Mendes Pereira stated that media companies compete for three things: content, delivery, and consumers. Through consolidation and mergers, global media companies such as the Walt Disney Corporation (Figure 2.16) become vertically integrated in order to gain content (e.g., production companies, radio shows, television programming, films, books) and delivery (e.g., radio and television stations, magazines, movie theatres). Delivery of content also refers to the infrastructure of technology—the proprietary technologies used for creating and sharing digital media. Vertical integration helps media giants attract and maintain customers through **synergy**, or the cross-promotion of vertically integrated goods. For example, within the vertical integration of Disney, you can visit Disney's Hollywood Studios at Walt Disney World, go to a *High School Musical* pep rally, and meet Muppet characters at Muppet*Vision 3D. Then, you can hop over to Disney's Animal Kingdom to catch the *Festival of the Lion King*, based on the Disney theatrical production that was based on the Disney movie *The Lion King*.

> **Synergy** The cross-promotion of vertically integrated goods.

Vertical integration of media changes the geography of the flow of ideas globally by limiting the ultimate number of gatekeepers—that is, the people or corporations who control access to information. A gatekeeper can choose not to tell a story and

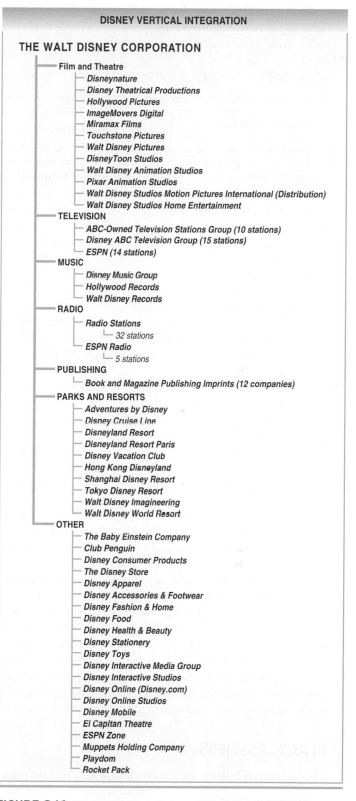

DISNEY VERTICAL INTEGRATION

THE WALT DISNEY CORPORATION

- Film and Theatre
  - Disneynature
  - Disney Theatrical Productions
  - Hollywood Pictures
  - ImageMovers Digital
  - Miramax Films
  - Touchstone Pictures
  - Walt Disney Pictures
  - DisneyToon Studios
  - Walt Disney Animation Studios
  - Pixar Animation Studios
  - Walt Disney Studios Motion Pictures International (Distribution)
  - Walt Disney Studios Home Entertainment
- TELEVISION
  - ABC-Owned Television Stations Group (10 stations)
  - Disney ABC Television Group (15 stations)
  - ESPN (14 stations)
- MUSIC
  - Disney Music Group
  - Hollywood Records
  - Walt Disney Records
- RADIO
  - Radio Stations
    - 32 stations
  - ESPN Radio
    - 5 stations
- PUBLISHING
  - Book and Magazine Publishing Imprints (12 companies)
- PARKS AND RESORTS
  - Adventures by Disney
  - Disney Cruise Line
  - Disneyland Resort
  - Disneyland Resort Paris
  - Disney Vacation Club
  - Hong Kong Disneyland
  - Shanghai Disney Resort
  - Tokyo Disney Resort
  - Walt Disney Imagineering
  - Walt Disney World Resort
- OTHER
  - The Baby Einstein Company
  - Club Penguin
  - Disney Consumer Products
  - The Disney Store
  - Disney Apparel
  - Disney Accessories & Footwear
  - Disney Fashion & Home
  - Disney Food
  - Disney Health & Beauty
  - Disney Stationery
  - Disney Toys
  - Disney Interactive Media Group
  - Disney Interactive Studios
  - Disney Online (Disney.com)
  - Disney Online Studios
  - Disney Mobile
  - El Capitan Theatre
  - ESPN Zone
  - Muppets Holding Company
  - Playdom
  - Rocket Pack

FIGURE 2.16 The Walt Disney Corporation. Data from "Who Owns What," *Columbia Journalism Review.* Accessed October 28, 2011 at http://www.cjr.org/resources/index.php?c=disney.

the story will not be heard. We can interpret the consolidation of media as an attempt to limit the number of gatekeepers to the big media conglomerates. Or we can focus on the competition media (e.g., the vast number of cable television channels, radio stations, Internet sources, and magazines) and argue that there are more gatekeepers in the world.

NETWORKS OF RETAIL CORPORATIONS

While major media corporations are vertically integrated, major retail corporations are typically **horizontally integrated**. In a horizontally integrated retail corporation, stores that at first glance appear to be owned by different retail companies in pursuit of different market shares turn out to be owned by the same parent corporation. For example, if you go to the mall to buy a pair of jeans, you can choose to shop at Banana Republic, The Gap, or Old Navy, but your money will go to one parent company, Gap Inc. If you take a break at the food court to drink Gatorade, eat a bag of Doritos, and buy a Quaker granola bar for later, all your dollars go to PepsiCo. You may look up and wonder when Taco Bell started selling Kentucky Fried Chicken and Pizza. Hut pizza. (All three are part of Yum! Brands Inc., which also owns A&W and Long John Silvers. YUM! is a spinoff of PepsiCo.)

> **Horizontal integration**
> Ownership by the same firm of a number of companies that exist at the same point on a commodity chain.

Neil Wrigley, Neil Coe, and Andrew Currah have studied the globalization of retail corporations such as Walmart (U.S.), Costco (U.S.), IKEA (Sweden), Metro (Germany), and Carrefour (France). In their comparison of manufacturing and retail corporations, they found that global retailers are more spatially disaggregated, with stores in hundreds or thousands of locations, whereas global manufacturers are more spatially concentrated, especially at production sites. In addition, global retailers engage directly with consumers and have a local presence that manufacturing corporations do not. Consumers who enter local stores interact directly with the global retailer at the local scale. While some individuals view global retail as a positive presence in their area and organize networks to invite stores to their community, others create networks of protest against the building of a global retail store.

By analyzing the global networks of development, global consolidation of media, and the global presence of retail corporations, we see the diversity in global networks, with some increasingly centralized and others increasingly disaggregated. In each case, the global network does not change local places in the same way. People interact with the global network, shaping it, resisting it, embracing it, and responding to globalization in unique ways.

PLACELESSNESS

Many observers believe globalization is creating a sense of **placelessness**, or a loss of heterogeneity between places. In their view, every place is becoming the same, with the same restaurant franchises, retail stores, books, movies, fashion, automobiles, and architecture. This idea is aptly captured in George Ritzer's term "McDonaldization," which encapsulates

> **Placelessness** The loss of uniqueness of place in the cultural landscape so that one place looks like the next, as defined by geographer Edward Relph.

what some see as a trend to reduce diversity across cultural boundaries. Ritzer coined the term to describe how notions of efficiency, predictability, and control are embedded in global consumerism. We might be seeing a worrying diminishment in the variety and uniqueness of places and, perhaps, in the "authenticity" (a highly contested notion) of local experience. The images of Vancouver International Airport and the Tokyo International Airport in Figure 2.17 illustrate this idea of placelessness. In many ways it is impossible to tell where the airports are from the architecture. While this similarity provides comfort for some of us, travelling to unfamiliar places, we might also experience a generic blandness obliterating the distinctive nature of places. Globalization is seen as creating a universal placelessness, to the detriment of the local and the specific.

If we accept that globalization is experienced unevenly and differentially, we must acknowledge that the impacts and reactions at the local level vary as well. In some places, a defensive response to the perceived ills of global capital has resulted in a

(a)

(b)

FIGURE 2.17 (a) Vancouver International Airport. (b) Tokyo International Airport, Japan. (Vancouver International Airport Authority; © DAJ/Getty Images)

response to the perceived ills of global capital has resulted in a resurgence of claims to local community ties and territories. This suggests that peoples' sense of place is distinctly individual and experiential and that total homogenization of the meaning and sense of place is impossible. It also reasserts the heterogeneity of people in place—an individual's gender, race, class, age, sexuality, and religion, for example, profoundly affect how that individual understands place and his or her position in that place—which in turn highlights how globalizing processes and outcomes are experienced differently by individuals who live and work in the same place.

These varied responses raise a key point about human agency. Just as globalization is not inevitable, neither are the people caught up in these processes powerless or passive. The differences among and between places exist because of local reactions to and engagement with globalization, as well as the complicated intersections of social relations across places and space.

GLOBAL-LOCAL

> **Glocalization** The process by which people in a local place mediate and alter regional, national, and global processes.

The term **glocalization** was coined by geographer Eric Swyngedouw in an attempt to counter the concept of "deterritorialization" behind geographical notions of placelessness. Swyngedouw argues that places are both heterogeneous and homogeneous simultaneously, and that despite our sense of people, goods, and money moving rapidly and nimbly from place to place, these activities are in fact deeply materialistic, embedded in place, and grounded, if only for a moment. As Peter Dicken argues, cultural, political, and economic processes have a "spatial fixedness" that must be taken into account. The reinsertion of the local and the material is a necessary corrective to the tendency of thinking about globalization as only a set of macro-processes.

Places themselves have a history and a spatial fixity that they bring to bear on globalizing processes of flows, networks, and time-space compression. The history of how a place or region came into the current world system; its relations with other places; its internal infrastructure and location in circulating networks of goods, foodstuffs, and resources; and the resources it has to inject into the system are all significant in glocal relations. We must look to the socio-spatial, historical, cultural, and political specificity as part of the larger tale. This perspective helps us focus on the fact that we are experiencing forms of homogeneity and homogenization that, according to Douglas Goodman's examination of consumer culture, "make people more different but in a similar way."

Globalization networks interlink us. The flow of information technology is one way we are interlinked with the globe every day. A person may be overwhelmed by the flow of information and choose to ignore it, but even this person has a global identity. As the flow of information continues, many people feel a need to make sense of the world by identifying with or against other people and places at the local, regional, and global scale. People personalize the flow of information and in so doing feel more or less connected to the globe, altering their local cultural landscapes to reflect their feeling of connectedness.

For example, news of the death of Michael Jackson in June 2009 travelled quickly from global media sources, through social networking sites, and among friends, family, and even strangers. Many felt the need to mourn Jackson's death with others they had never met in a place they had never been. Some wanted to leave a token offering—a note, a candle, CDs, songs, photographs. Memorials to Jackson sprang up in many cities and towns, marking the personal connection many felt because of his music (Figure 2.18).

In an incredibly divided world in which the rift between rich and poor is growing at the global scale, what made people feel connected to a person who was a distant image and a member of an elite group of people of wealth and privilege? The idea that people around the world are linked and share experiences, such as death, tragedy, and sorrow, draws from Benedict Anderson's concept of the nation as an "imagined community." Anderson argues that a nation "is imagined because the members of even the smallest nation will never know most of their fellow-members, meet them,

(a)

(b)

FIGURE 2.18 Michael Jackson Memorials. (a) A Michael Jackson memorial at an HMV store in London, England, in 2009. (b) Basra Arte, from Canada, stands outside Staples Center, in Los Angeles, before a memorial service for Michael Jackson on Tuesday, July 7, 2009. (© Rune Hellestad/Corbis; ©Jae C. Hong/Associated Press)

or even hear of them, yet in the minds of each lives the image of their communion" (1991, p. 224). The desire to personalize or localize a tragedy springs from the hope that all people in the imagined global community feel or experience the loss tangentially.

When a death or a tragedy does happen, how do people choose a local space in which to express a personal and/or global sorrow? Although many academics argue that place and territory are unimportant because things like global superhighways of information transcend place, people continue to recognize territories and create places. In the case of Michael Jackson's death, people created hundreds of spaces of sorrow to mourn the loss of a larger-than-life person whose life was cut short. In the case of the destruction of the World Trade Center on September 11, 2001, people transformed homes, schools, public spaces, and houses of worship into places of reflection by creating human chains, participating in moments of silence, or holding prayer vigils for the victims.

MAIN POINTS   2.2   What Are the Connections between Globalization and the Geographical?

- Global processes and outcomes are geographical in nature. They operate unevenly across a variety of scales and are experienced differently in different places with different results.

- Globalization is constantly reordering relations between places on a variety of scales, creating interdependencies, linkages, and interconnections, although it does not do so the same way each time or for all places.

- Geographers conceptualize the geographical operations of globalizing processes and outcomes using a number of overlapping approaches, including time-space compression, networks, placelessness, and glocalization.

2.3 Why Do Some People or Groups Oppose or Resist Globalization?

Globalization processes and outcomes have not been greeted favourably in all places or by all peoples because of the uneven and inequitable outcomes. The term "anti-globalization" is perhaps a misnomer, as most organizations believe it is unrealistic to seek an end to globalization processes; for groups seeking social justice, the term "alter-globalization" may be more accurate. However, resistance or opposition movements run the gamut from the progressive to the most right-wing and conservative. All take a critical view of globalization, albeit for different reasons, which is not surprising given that globalization itself is seen as complex and contradictory, operating unevenly across time and space.

Those opposing the processes and forces of globalization are often conceptualized as constituting some form of global civil society, itself a globalizing process that struggles to create new political and social forums as it agitates for participatory democracy and social justice on a global scale (Figure 2.19). This exemplifies how globalization may take positive as well as negative forms.

Opponents of neoliberal economic policies argue that international organizations such as the World Bank, International Monetary Fund, and World Trade Organization are set up to benefit the countries of the global economic core. Proponents of the dependency theory, outlined in Chapter 11, contend that the countries of the core continue to protect their own economies while forcing the countries of the semi-periphery and periphery to open their economies to foreign direct investment and remove protections on their domestic production. As Keith Maskus suggests, the rules negotiated for the World Trade Organization "inevitably reflect the economic interest of powerful lobbyists" in states such as the United States and the European Union. From this perspective, free trade is not "free" nor is it fair. Rather, it builds up a global economic network that sends most benefits to the core.

In response to the uneven and inequitable distribution of globalization's disadvantages and possibilities, a number of non-governmental organizations (NGOs) have sprung up in the last two decades. These groups, which often originate at the local or regional level, have fostered a web of global development networks in response to what they see as top-down decision making by hegemonic global organizations dominated by Western interests (e.g., the World Bank and the International Monetary Fund). The development networks serve a counter-hegemonic or resistive function, opposing or challenging the major global decision makers. The aim of these NGOs is to advocate for the poor, the marginalized, and those directly affected by global development processes, permitting these groups to engage with and oppose the processes they see as unfavourable or negatively affecting their lives. Within these development networks, northern and southern NGOs strive to work together to reach a consensus on how to achieve favourable and ameliorative economic development in a particular place.

Visible opposition in the form of public protests has been a part of every major economic and political meeting since the

FIGURE 2.19 Opponents of Neoliberal Economic Policies at the World Social Forum in Porto Alegre, Brazil. (© Agliberto Lima/Gamma-Presse, Inc.)

(a)

(b)

FIGURE 2.20 (a) Summit of the Americas Conference in Quebec City, 2001. Thousands of protesters from Canada, the United States, and abroad arrived in Quebec City to speak out against globalization. **(b) Protesters in Downtown Toronto during the G20 Summit, June 26, 2010.** (© Tom Hanson/The Canadian Press; © Carolyn Kaster/Associated Press)

World Trade Organization ministerial conference in Seattle during 1999. In Canada, protestors picketed the Summit of the Americas conference in Quebec City in April 2001—an event marred by what many regard as excessive security and police action (Figure 2.20a). The G20 meeting of world leaders in Toronto in 2010 precipitated a repeat of that violence (Figure 2.20b), although the global movement has been refining its style and message, using communications technology such as the Internet and cell phones to draw together disparate and loosely associated political and social organizations at the global scale.

This change in approach speaks to a growing global solidarity and is reflected in the formation of the World Social Forum, which since 2001 has been holding counter-summits to the World Economic Forum. These new movements have made certain issues a focus of global concern, especially questions of environmental degradation, justice (specifically human rights), health and security, and the development of a global normative culture.

Resistance to globalization at the extreme right of the political spectrum is driven by concern about the perceived threat to local, traditional cultures and values. The possibility of global governance has given rise to strong nationalist movements and religious fundamentalism.

Global social movements of all political stripes, networked on a local, regional, national, or international scale, have developed practical local approaches for dealing with globalizing processes. We will examine two of these local solutions to development: participatory development and local currencies.

PARTICIPATORY DEVELOPMENT

Participatory development The notion that locals should be engaged in deciding what development means for them and how it should be achieved.

Participatory development—the idea that locals should be engaged in deciding what development means for them and how to achieve it—is one response to top-down decision making. Stuart Corbridge has studied how the global push for participatory development encouraged the government of India to enact participatory development programs. Corbridge and his colleague Sanjay Kumar describe the goal of participatory development as giving the people who are directly affected by policies and programs a voice in making the policies and programs—that is, to use local networks to shape development for local goals.

Kumar and Corbridge studied a program in India that was meant to get seeds to farmers and create irrigation schemes. The program was successful for many farmers, though not for the poorest farmers because, the geographers discovered, local politics factored into the distribution of poverty-alleviation schemes, and richer farmers and elites in rural areas tended to be most involved with the program. However, Kumar and Corbridge claimed that the poorer farmers' lack of participation was not a reason to abandon the participatory program. They concluded that all participatory development programs have to "operate in an environment that is dominated by better off farmers and particular community groups"; therefore, the definition of success must change because development organizations cannot expect the poorest to "participate in groups that have little meaning for them." Nevertheless, awareness of the local factors that cause inequalities in the benefits of a program means those delivering such programs should work to minimize these problems.

The World Bank, the International Monetary Fund, and even state governments are increasingly embracing the ideal of participatory development and reducing demands for trade liberalization in the periphery and semi-periphery. As Kumar and Corbridge explain, politics will enter participatory development, just as they enter the development networks and the global development organizations. The goal of participatory development is worthwhile, even if the short-term results do not mesh with Western concepts of success.

LOCAL CURRENCIES

Uneven development affects not just the periphery but also the core and semi-periphery. Economic downturns are a common occurrence in local places of all regions, and unemployment is frequently the result. As Michael Pacione explains, finding families and neighbours who can help in times of economic hardship may be difficult because globalization results in less connectedness:

> Social trends inherent in global capitalism, including decreasing household size, increasing distance between relatives, and attenuation of neighbouring relations within cities, have served to inhibit the operation of informal relations in which disadvantaged households could exchange goods and services for partial or no payment within the "moral" economy of their own family or neighbourhood. (1997, p. 1179–1199)

One way people can cope with such downturns, whether in the core, semi-periphery, or periphery, is by establishing a local currency. During the 1980s, the people of the Comox Valley in British Columbia established the first **local exchange trading system (LETS)**. When the two major employers in the area closed, many of the area's 50,000 residents faced severe

> **Local exchange trading system (LETS)** A barter system whereby a local currency is created through which members trade services or goods in a local network separated from the formal economy.

economic hardship. The community began a local exchange system, LETS, through which members traded services or goods in a local network separated from the formal economy. People who needed services (such as plumbing) would pay others with their own services or goods (such as providing accounting services in exchange for the plumbing call).

LETS systems and other local currency systems are alternatives to global norms of development, serving as a local response to global or regional economic change affecting a community or region (Figure 2.21). Because the currency is local and can

only be traded locally, it fuels the local economy. The person who spends LETS credits for shoes, for example, can only spend them at the local shoe store, and not at an online store or in a catalogue.

The number of local currencies in use in the world today totals well over 1,000. Many are used in rural areas, but local currency systems have also been successful in cities as diverse as Glasgow, Scotland, and Berkeley, California. In Berkeley, the local currency did not develop as a response to economic hardship but rather as a desire to avoid supporting the global currency system.

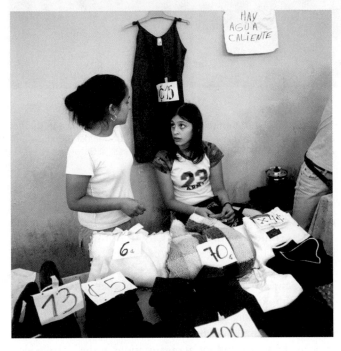

FIGURE 2.21 Bernal, Buenos Aires, Argentina. When the Argentinian economy collapsed in 1999, the number of local currencies in the country proliferated, eventually hovering around 5,000 different currencies and barter clubs. In this suburb of Buenos Aires, girls sold clothing that was priced with "credits" based on values established in their local currency system. (© Network Photographers/Alamy)

MAIN POINTS   2.3 Why Do Some People or Groups Oppose or Resist Globalization?

- There are different perspectives on whether globalization produces positive or negative results. Many argue that globalization benefits the core regions to the detriment of the periphery and the semi-periphery.

- Resistance or oppositional movements develop their own views on what is wrong with globalization and how these difficulties might be fixed.

- Participatory development and local currencies are two examples of distinctive approaches to dealing with the perceived ills of globalization.

SUMMARY

Globalization is a complicated and contested concept. As a starting point, globalization can be understood generally "as an accelerating set of processes involving flows that encompass ever-greater numbers of the world spaces and that lead to increasing integration and interconnectivity among those spaces." Space and places are increasingly connected by improved technologies as more and more locations are drawn into the global capitalist markets. The current world system is the result of some 500 years of exploration and colonialism that unevenly positioned places within that system for different purposes. Canada, as a colonized country, developed a staples economy, supplying resources to an almost insatiable European market. Canada's colonial past established some of the historical factors that partially explain the country's current role as part of a global core region.

Globalization processes operate in chaotic and unruly ways, with uneven and varying impacts. Human geographers have been compelled to imagine new ways of thinking about the

geographical in response to these processes and outcomes, and concepts such as "time-space compression," networks, "placelessness," and "glocalization" have emerged as a result.

Those who oppose globalization processes for different reasons have formed a global counter-movement, comprising a loose collection of different groups, that has successfully pushed a number of items onto the global agenda—including environmental justice, human rights, and health and security.

The spatial perspective of human geographers is particularly useful for coming to grips with the possibilities, limitations, and uncertainties of these globalizing processes.

DISCUSSION AND REVIEW QUESTIONS

1. What is globalization? Think about the place where you live: how has it been affected by and/or how does it affect modern globalization?

2. What is the "staples thesis," and what does it reveal about how Canada has historically been integrated into the processes of globalization?

3. To succeed in the globalized economy requires a variety of corporate strategies. Two such strategies are "vertical" and "horizontal" integration. Explain these strategies and discuss the specific industries where they have proven most successful.

4. Many observers believe globalization is creating a sense of "placelessness." What do they mean by this and based on your experience and where you live, do you agree or disagree?

5. Globalization processes and outcomes have not been favourably viewed in all places or by all peoples. The movement that has arisen to challenge the logic of globalization has been dubbed, "alternative globalization." Identify who are the proponents of this movement and discuss their arguments against globalization. What are their ideas for improving globalization?

GEOGRAPHIC CONCEPTS

commodity chain   31
free trade zones   37
friction of distance   38
globalization   31
glocalization   45
horizontal integration   44
local exchange trading system (LETS)   48
neo-liberalism   39

networks   41
participatory development   47
placelessness   44
staples thesis   34
synergy   43
time-space compression   40
vertical integration   43
world cities   37

ADDITIONAL RESOURCES ONLINE

About media ownership in Canada: www.crtc.gc.ca/ownership/eng/title_org.htm

About media ownership in the U.S., *Columbia Journalism Review's* Who Owns What website: www.cjr.org/tools/owners

About PRODUCT (RED): www.joinred.com

About the GlobalFund: www.theglobalfund.org/EN

About Global Cities Index 2010: www.foreignpolicy.com/node/373401

About the Network of World Cities: www.brook.edu/metro/pubs/20050222_worldcities.pdf

About the World Social Forum: www.forumsocialmundial.org.br

About the World Trade Organization: www.wto.org

About Unionizing Workers in Sri Lankan free trade zones: www.ftzunionlanka.org

Canadian Naomi Klein takes aim at transnational corporations: thefilmarchived.blogspot.com/2010/10/naomi-klein-on-no-logo-taking-aim-at.html

No Logo, on-line documentary: topdocumentaryfilms.com/no-logo-brands-globalization-resistance

Meltdown: A Global Tsunami: www.cbc.ca/video/#/Shows/Doc_Zone/1242299559/ID=1593906827

chapter 3

POLITICAL GEOGRAPHY

FIGURE 3.1 **Statue of Kwame Nkrumah, the First President of Ghana, Dressed in Hospital Gown and Bandage.** (© H.J. de Blij)

Independence Is Better Than Servitude

I ARRIVED IN Ghana in 1962 just after an assassination attempt on the country's first president, Kwame Nkrumah. As I drove through the capital city of Accra, I saw a statue of President Nkrumah. Ghanians had dressed the statue in a hospital gown and bandaged its head (Figure 3.1). The proclamations on Nkrumah's statue read: "To me the liberation of Ghana will be meaningless unless it is linked up with the liberation of Africa" and "We prefer self-government with danger to servitude in tranquility."

Ghana, the first black African colony to become independent, gained its independence in 1960. A wave of decolonization swept through the continent in the 1960s (see Figure 3.2)—fuelled by the hope that decolonization would bring political and economic independence. But independence did not eliminate political and economic problems. As former colonies became states, achieving political independence under international law and having the ultimate say over what happened within their borders, new political problems arose within the sovereign countries. Each had to deal with a mixture of peoples, cultures, languages, and religions amalgamated during colonialism. Economically, the new countries found themselves fully intertwined in the world economy, unable to control fundamental elements of their own economies.

For many of the new African states, Nkrumah's words rang true—independence was better than servitude, even if it meant danger instead of tranquility. Nkrumah was overthrown by the military in 1966 and died in exile in 1972.

The story of Ghana and President Nkrumah is a familiar one. After decades of European colonial rule, peoples around the world sought independence; they wanted to have their own country, and they wanted to have a voice in what happened in their country. European colonialism had set the world up as a huge functional region for Europe—one where Europe benefited the most economically. Colonialism also brought the European way of politically organizing space to the rest of the world. This system and its lack of fit for most of the world has caused political strife. Yet peoples still seek to become independent countries because, in Nkrumah's words, they know independence is better than servitude.

KEY QUESTIONS FOR CHAPTER 3

1. How is space organized into states and nations?

2. How did the modern nation-state come into being?

3. How is the governance of states spatially organized?

4. How do geopolitics and critical geopolitics help us understand the world?

5. What are supranational organizations, and what is the future of the state?

3.1 How Is Space Organized into States and Nations?

Politics and place are intertwined. Our lives—where we live, the taxes we pay, the schools we attend, and the places we travel or work—are regulated by various levels of government and state institutions. We come to understand ourselves as people living in bounded places, either imagined or otherwise. We have mental maps of our neighbourhoods, our school districts, and the "city limits." We identify as being from a particular province, and we see ourselves as Canadians living in an identifiable and bounded territory. Political geographers are interested in nations and states, their territories and boundaries, and the ideologies of nationalism and sovereignty that constitute the geographies of everyday lives. As Canadians, we should be deeply concerned about the politics of geography and the geography of politics—about Arctic sovereignty (Figure 3.3), Afghanistan, offshore drilling in the Beaufort Sea, or the security or permeability of our borders.

> **Political geography** A subdivision of human geography focused on the nature and implications of the evolving spatial organization of political governance and formal political practice on the Earth's surface. It is concerned with why political spaces emerge in the places that they do and with how the character of those spaces affects social, political, economic, and environmental understandings and practices.

In Chapter 1, we noted that human geographers are interested in the geography of human-environmental interrelations. In this chapter, we focus on the political aspects of these relationships in terms of the themes of location, region, place, landscape, and movement as they relate to the subdiscipline of **political geography**. When we speak about the "political," we generally mean the organization, structure, and administration of a country and its relationships with other countries. When a country acts in particular ways, there are distinctive spatial effects. For example, when one country invades another country, boundaries change, people are displaced, and new relationships are formed between people and place: people may be forced to flee their homeland and become "refugees"—a new political and social entity grounded in a different location through forced movement or migration.

THE MODERN STATE

At the global scale, we have a world divided into individual countries or, more properly, states. A **state** is a politically organized entity with a permanent population, a defined territory, and a government. To achieve statehood, an entity must be recognized as such by other states. Article 2 of the United Nations Charter enshrines the principle that all member states must uphold the territorial integrity of other member states and not interfere in their internal domestic affairs. While states and international relations are an important focus for political geographers, many work at the microscale, studying smaller administrative units such as regions, urban areas, provinces, or electoral districts.

> **State** A politically organized entity that is administered by a sovereign government and is recognized by a significant portion of the international community. A state has a defined territory, a permanent population, a government, and is recognized by other states.

The present-day division of the world into states is the result of endless contests and accommodations within and between human societies. On the conventional political map, a mosaic of colours represents more than 200 countries and territories, a visualization that accentuates the separation of these countries by boundaries (see Figure 3.4 on page 54). The political map is the world map most of us learn first. We look at it, memorize it, and name the countries and perhaps each country's capital. It hangs in the front of our classrooms, is used to organize maps in our textbooks, and becomes so familiar to us that *we begin to think it is natural*.

Yet we must think carefully about how "natural" these divisions are and consider the implications flowing from such assumptions. As geographer Richard Jackson argues:

> *When school children are repeatedly shown a political map of the world...they can easily end up regarding [states] in the same light as the physical features such as rivers, or mountain ranges which sometimes delimit their natural boundaries...Far from being natural entities, modern sovereign states are entirely historical artefacts the oldest of which have been in existence in their present shape and alignment only for the past three or four centuries. (1990, p. 7)*

FIGURE 3.2 Dates of Independence for States throughout the World. The first major wave of independence movements between 1750 and 1939 occurred mainly in the Americas. The second major wave of independence movements after 1940 occurred mainly in Africa and Asia. South Sudan became the most recently recognized independent state in July 2011, bringing the total number of member states in the United Nations to 193. *Data from: United Nations, 2011.*

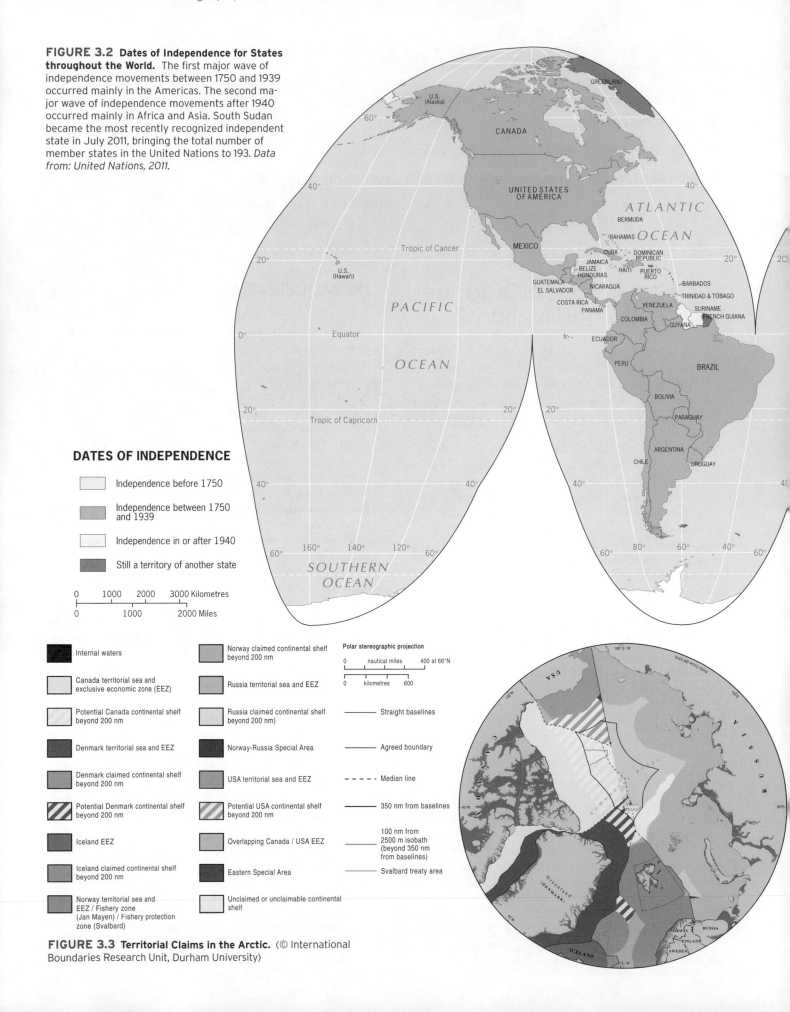

DATES OF INDEPENDENCE

- Independence before 1750
- Independence between 1750 and 1939
- Independence in or after 1940
- Still a territory of another state

| 0 | 1000 | 2000 | 3000 Kilometres |
| 0 | 1000 | | 2000 Miles |

- Internal waters
- Canada territorial sea and exclusive economic zone (EEZ)
- Potential Canada continental shelf beyond 200 nm
- Denmark territorial sea and EEZ
- Denmark claimed continental shelf beyond 200 nm
- Potential Denmark continental shelf beyond 200 nm
- Iceland EEZ
- Iceland claimed continental shelf beyond 200 nm
- Norway territorial sea and EEZ / Fishery zone (Jan Mayen) / Fishery protection zone (Svalbard)

- Norway claimed continental shelf beyond 200 nm
- Russia territorial sea and EEZ
- Russia claimed continental shelf beyond 200 nm)
- Norway-Russia Special Area
- USA territorial sea and EEZ
- Potential USA continental shelf beyond 200 nm
- Overlapping Canada / USA EEZ
- Eastern Special Area
- Unclaimed or unclaimable continental shelf

Polar stereographic projection

| 0 | nautical miles | 400 at 66°N |
| 0 | kilometres | 600 |

——— Straight baselines
——— Agreed boundary
- - - - Median line
——— 350 nm from baselines
——— 100 nm from 2500 m isobath (beyond 350 nm from baselines)
——— Svalbard treaty area

FIGURE 3.3 Territorial Claims in the Arctic. (© International Boundaries Research Unit, Durham University)

The world map of states is anything but natural. Just as people create places, imparting character to space and shaping culture, people, their actions, and their history make, shape, and refine states and state boundaries.

> **Territoriality** In political geography, a country's or more local community's sense of property and attachment toward its territory, as expressed by its determination to keep it inviolable and strongly defended.

Central to the idea of the state is the concept of **territoriality**, which geographer Robert Sack (1986) defines as "the attempt by an individual or group to affect, influence, or control people, phenomena, and relationships, by delimiting and asserting control over a geographic area." Sack sees human territoriality as a key ingredient in the construction of social and political spaces. He argues that human territoriality takes many different forms, depending on the historical, social, and geographical context. He calls for a better understanding of the human organization of the planet through a consideration of how and why different territorial strategies are pursued at different times and in different places.

Political geographers study territoriality across scales, cultures, and time. They examine how people have changed the way territoriality is expressed and how ideas about territoriality vary over space and time. Today, territoriality is tied closely to the concept of **sovereignty**, which refers to a state's right to exercise power and control over people in a particular territory, a right that is recognized in international law. The UN principle that requires the

> **Sovereignty** A principle of international relations that holds that final authority over social, economic, and political matters should rest with the legitimate rulers of independent states.

international community of states to recognize an entity as a legitimate state and as being sovereign within its borders stems from the concept of territoriality.

Sometimes states will refuse to recognize other places that claim to be states in their own right. For example, territoriality has

FIGURE 3.4 States of the World, 2011.
(© H.J. de Blij, P.O. Muller, and John Wiley & Sons, Inc.)

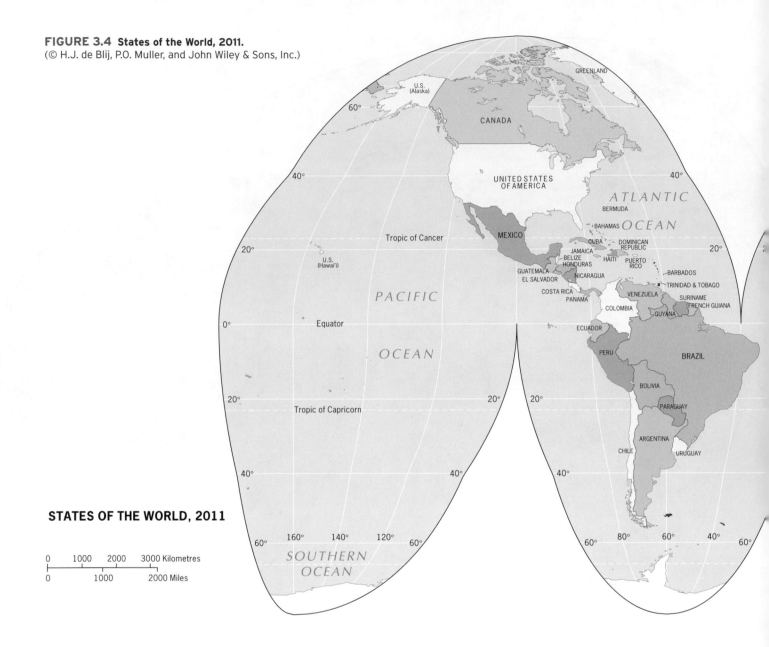

STATES OF THE WORLD, 2011

```
0    1000    2000    3000 Kilometres

0           1000          2000 Miles
```

led to the heavy contestation of space in the former Yugoslavia. The Republic of Kosovo declared independence on February 17, 2008. By April 2009, some 52 of the 198 member states in the United Nations (including Canada, the United States, Australia, and most of the European Union) recognized Kosovo as a sovereign state. However, many states did not, including Serbia and Russia (Figure 3.5). The notion of recognition is a complicated one. A state may be recognized as having a particular territory by its government but may not be recognized if the government is perceived as invalid such as the result of internal military action. A state government may not be recognized formally but may maintain informal relations with a large number of other states. Under international law, states have the right to defend what they perceive as

their **territorial integrity** against incursion from other states, which means they could go to war if invaded by another state. These modern ideas of how state, sovereignty, and territory are intertwined began in mid-17th-century Europe and diffused to the rest of the world.

BOUNDARIES

International boundaries or borders separate individual states. Boundaries may appear on maps as straight lines or may twist and turn to conform to the bends of rivers and the curves of hills and valleys. But a boundary is more than a line and is far more than a fence or wall on the ground. A **boundary**

> **Territorial integrity** The right of a state to defend sovereign territory against incursion from other states.

> **Boundary** Vertical plane between states that cuts through the rocks below (called the subsoil), and the airspace above the surface, dividing one state territory from another.

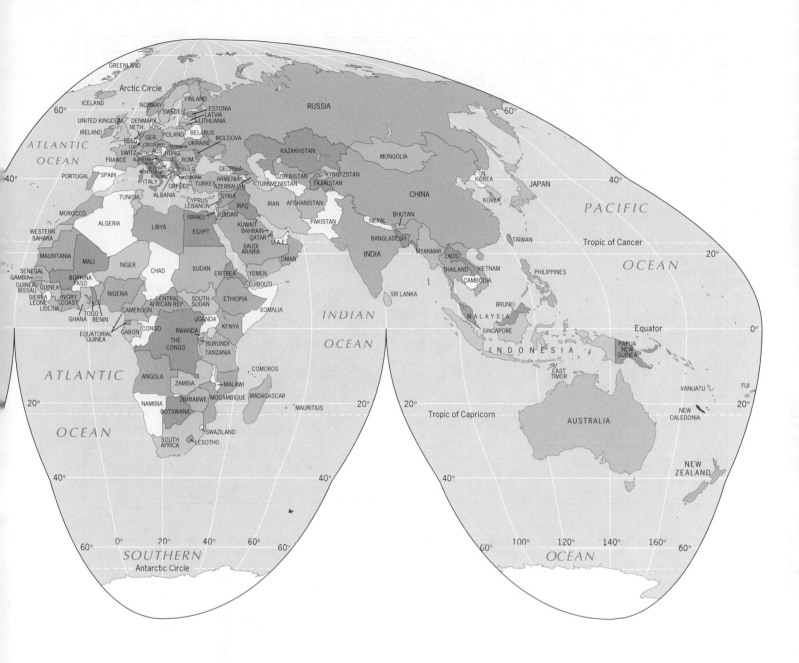

between states is actually a vertical plane that cuts through the rocks below (called the subsoil) and the airspace above, dividing one state territory from another (Figure 3.6). Only where the vertical plane intersects the Earth's surface (on land or at sea) does it form the line we see on a map.

Many boundaries on the contemporary world map were established before the extent or significance of subsoil resources was known. A major issue between Iraq and Kuwait, which in part led to Iraq's invasion of Kuwait in 1990, was the oil in the Rumaylah reserve that lies underneath the desert and crosses the boundary between the two states. The Iraqis asserted that the Kuwaitis were drilling too many wells and draining the reserve too quickly; they also alleged that the Kuwaitis were drilling oblique boreholes to penetrate the vertical plane extending downward along the boundary. At the time the Iraq-Kuwait boundary was established, however, no one knew this giant oil reserve lay in the subsoil or that it would help create an international crisis (Figure 3.7).

Above the ground, too, the interpretation of boundaries as vertical planes has serious implications. A state's "airspace" is defined by the atmosphere above its land area as marked by its boundaries, as well as by what lies beyond, at higher altitudes. But how high does the airspace extend? Most states insist on controlling the airline traffic over their territories, but states do not yet control the paths of satellite orbits.

ESTABLISHING BOUNDARIES

Demarcating and controlling territory is a central function of the state. Clearly, the ability to control the border is a primary concern. A boundary helps define who belongs and who does not, who must stay and who can go. Boundaries affect

FIGURE 3.5 The Former Yugoslavia. The contested geography of the former Yugoslavia, and in particular Kosovo, as discussed, provides a good example of territoriality. Map from the United Nations Department of Peacekeeping Operations Cartographic Section, June 2007. The Former Yugoslavia, Map No. 3689 Rev. 12 UNITED NATIONS.

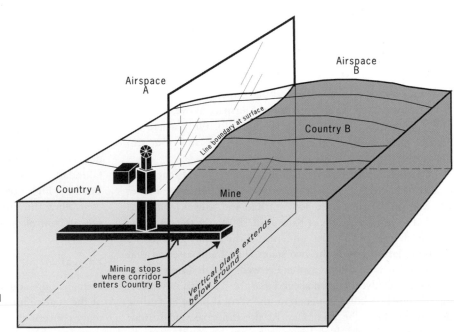

FIGURE 3.6 The Vertical Plane of a Political Boundary. (© E.H. Fouberg, A.B. Murphy, H.J. de Blij, and John Wiley & Sons, Inc.)

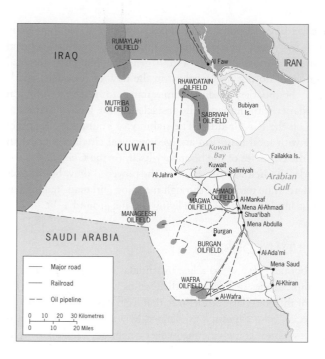

FIGURE 3.7 **The International Boundary between Iraq and Kuwait.** Kuwait's northern boundary was redefined and delimited by a United Nations boundary commission; it was demarcated by a series of concrete pillars 2 kilometres apart. (© E.H. Fouberg, A.B. Murphy, H.J. de Blij, and John Wiley & Sons, Inc.)

FIGURE 3.8 The Mexico-United States Barrier. The border wall goes up near the Rio Grande in southern Texas in January 2009. (Copyright Wendy Shattil and Bob Rozinski)

the movement of people from different places, locations, and regions; by allowing or inhibiting movement they affect life changes, influence the possibilities for work or travel, and, in some cases, determine whether or not one will survive.

Practically speaking, establishing a boundary between two states typically involves four steps. First, states *define* the boundary through a treaty-like legal document in which actual points in the landscape or points of latitude and longitude are described. Next, cartographers *delimit* the boundary by drawing it on a map. Third, if either or both of the states on each side of the border so desire, they can *demarcate* the boundary by using steel posts, concrete pillars, fences, walls, or some other visible means to mark the boundary on the ground. A good example of unilateral fence building is illustrated in Figure 3.8. The border between the United States and Mexico spans over 3,100 kilometres, crossing a vast array of terrain from urban centres to deserts. The barrier comprises a variety of technologies, including steel and wire fencing, floodlighting, surveillance cameras and equipment, and tightly controlled border crossings. By no means are all boundaries on the world map demarcated. Demarcating a lengthy boundary is expensive, and it is hardly worth the effort in high mountains, vast deserts, frigid polar lands, or other places with few permanent settlements. The final step is to *administrate* the boundary—to determine how the boundary will be maintained and how goods and people will cross the boundary.

TYPES OF BOUNDARIES

When boundaries are drawn using grid systems such as latitude and longitude or township and range, political geographers refer to them as **geometric boundaries**. In North America, the United States and Canada used a single line of latitude west of the Great Lakes to define their boundary (Figure 3.9).

At different times, political geographers and other academics have advocated "natural" boundaries over geometric

> **Geometric boundary** Political boundary defined and delimited (and occasionally demarcated) as a straight line or an arc.

FIGURE 3.9 The 49th Parallel, Facing West with the U.S. (Montana) on the Left and Canada (Alberta) on the Right. The border between the United States and Canada follows the 49th parallel for 2,043 kilometres, from Lake of the Woods (Minnesota/Manitoba) to the Pacific Ocean. A six-metre-wide path is clearcut along this stretch of the border, marked by over 900 survey markers. (Copyright © Carolyn Cuskey)

Physical political (natural-political) boundary Political boundary defined and delimited (and occasionally demarcated) by a prominent physical feature in the natural landscape—such as a river or the crest ridges of a mountain range.

boundaries because they are visible on the landscape as physical geographic features. **Physical-political boundaries** (also called natural-political boundaries) follow an agreed-upon feature in the physical geographic landscape, such as the centre point of a river or the crest of a mountain range. The Rio Grande is an important physical-political boundary between the United States and Mexico; an older boundary follows crest lines of the Pyrenees between Spain and France. Lakes sometimes serve as boundaries as well; for example, four of the five Great Lakes of North America (between the United States and Canada) and several of the Great Lakes of East Africa (between Congo and its eastern neighbours) serve as boundaries.

Physical features sometimes make convenient political boundaries, but topographic features are not static. Rivers change course, volcanoes erupt, and, slowly, mountains erode. People perceive physical-political boundaries as more stable, but many states have entered territorial conflicts over physical-political boundaries (notably Chile and Argentina). Similarly, physical boundaries do not necessarily stop the flow of people or goods across boundaries, leading some states to reinforce physical boundaries with human-built obstacles (as the United States has done on the Rio Grande). The stability of boundaries has more to do with local historical and geographical circumstances than with the character of the boundary itself. As the *Guest Field Note* from Jason Grek Martin suggests, the power to draw boundaries and determine territories through mapping and map-making has serious implications for those living "on the ground".

BOUNDARY DISPUTES

The boundary we see as a line on an atlas map is the product of a complex series of legal steps that begins with a written description of the boundary. Sometimes that legal description is old and imprecise. Sometimes it was dictated by a stronger power that is now less dominant, giving the weaker neighbour a reason to argue

GUEST FIELD NOTE
Maps and Power in a Canadian Colonial Context

"As much as guns and warships, maps have been the weapons of imperialism." With these words, map historian J. B. Harley (2001, p. 57) seeks to debunk the notion that cartography offers a neutral and objective depiction of the world. Rather than showing the terrain "as it is," maps make arguments about the geographies they represent. They naturalize particular and often quite contested spatial understandings at the expense of competing perspectives. To paraphrase another map historian, maps work by serving interests—by "showing this but not that" (Wood, 1992, pp. 4 and 48).

I have been a cartophile my whole life and spent hours as a child pouring over atlases and drawing elaborate maps of my own. This fascination intensified as an undergraduate student after the insights of Harley and Wood showed me that maps were powerful geopolitical statements, worthy of careful intellectual scrutiny. As Harley suggests, this is especially apparent with maps made in the context of colonialism and imperialism.

George Dawson's geological map of Haida Gwaii (formerly the Queen Charlotte Islands), published in 1880, is a good example. As a field scientist for the Geological Survey of Canada, Dawson was responsible for exploring vast portions of the western territories acquired by Canada from Great Britain in 1870-71. The Survey aimed to provide the scientific knowledge to help Canada effectively colonize its new acquisi-

tions in the West. Dawson surveyed Haida Gwaii and several other portions of British Columbia's coastline in 1878. His task was to locate, examine, and document the natural amenities of the islands to assist future settlement and resource extraction. Dawson also studied the Haida, the archipelago's native population, to advance an anthropological understanding of their fascinating society. His season's work produced the first detailed report describing the indigenous Haida inhabitants and the abundant resource wealth of the islands. The report was accompanied by an impressive geological map of the islands that significantly improved upon previous maps.

Dawson's map of the archipelago largely erased the Haida from the landscape despite their extensive presence. Their most significant villages were marked and labelled but the vast majority of the mapped terrain bore no trace of human presence. The extensive, intimate and often quite formalized proprietary relations the Haida had with their homeland were not inscribed on Dawson's map, even though he had taken care to document this complex cultural geography in the accompanying report. In place of a cultural landscape, the map presented the islands as an uninhabited geological landscape of colour-coded rock formations and topographic relief. By focusing on underlying geology, Dawson's cartography stripped away the human landscape of the islands, rendering the Haida invisible.

Dawson took the cartographic erasure of the Haida a step further through the renaming of topographical features on the archipelago. In the colonial context, assigning names to places imposed order and signified authority over territory. Published maps formally codified new place names and erased the old. This quest for order and authority was particularly important on Haida Gwaii, which had never been thoroughly surveyed and mapped prior to Dawson's work in 1878. According to the colonial conventions of the day, Dawson had the right to name any previously "unmarked" topographical features that he should happen to "discover" in the course of his surveys. But, this notion of discovery was Eurocentric, given the indigenous Haida population had long since applied their own names to the unmarked landscapes Dawson (re)-named in 1878. While Dawson adopted a few of these existing indigenous names, he assigned a significant number of new names to the islands, headlands, and waterways found along the eastern coastline of the archipelago. Dawson entrenched a colonial tradition begun over a century earlier, when English explorer George Dixon—oblivious to the fact that these islands had already been named *Haida Gwaii* by their indigenous inhabitants–christened them the *Queen Charlotte Islands*.

In place of Haida toponyms, Dawson imposed new place names paying tribute to early European explorers to the region as well as to some of the leading figures in 19th-century science. Figure 3.10 shows Dawson's cartographic depiction of Juan Perez Sound, a place name created to commemorate the first European explorer to set eyes on the islands in 1774. On the map, the inlets and headlands of Juan Perez Sound are sprinkled with the names of prominent geologists and naturalists: Charles Darwin, Charles Lyell, Roderick Murchison, Thomas Huxley, Abraham Werner, James Hutton, and many others. The symbolism of this naming practice is profound: Dawson inscribed the leading figures of science into the topography of Haida Gwaii, symbolically asserting scientific authority over landscapes that his surveying had just begun to make legible. Dawson's commemoration of Perez made reference to the early exploration of the islands and connected his 1878 survey to a long history of celebrated Pacific exploration. Through his place naming, Dawson was able to symbolically position himself at the intersection of two great imperial traditions—exploration and natural science. Dawson's surveying merged both traditions into an enterprise enhancing his own reputation and symbolizing the power of the Canadian State to assert its authority over even its most remote territorial outposts.

In the process, the Haida presence on these islands was overwritten on Dawson's geological map. A people that had occupied this archipelago since time immemorial were callously mapped out of the landscapes they considered their exclusive home. In their place, an enticing picture of resource abundance and available real estate was inserted, beckoning settlers westward. In the colonial context of late 19-century Western Canada, Dawson's geological map of Haida Gwaii was not the neutral territorial depiction it purported to be. Rather, it was precisely the kind of weapon of imperialism that Harley describes.

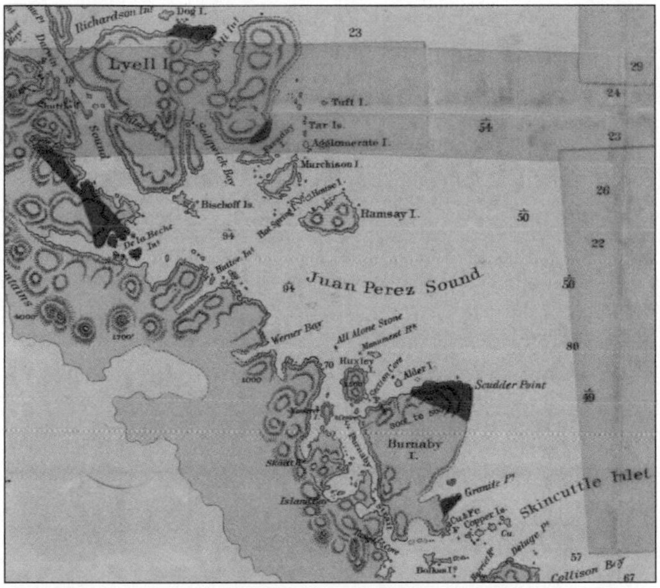

FIGURE 3.10 George Dawson's Map Showing Juan Perez Sound, Haida Gwaii (known then as the Queen Charlotte Islands). Source: George Dawson, "Report on the Queen Charlotte Islands, 1878." In *Report of Progress for 1878-1879*, Geological Survey of Canada, Montreal: Dawson Brothers, 1880, 1B-239B. © Department of Natural Resources Canada. All rights reserved.

Jason Grek-Martin, Assistant Professor, St. Mary's University, Halifax, Nova Scotia

---

for change. At other times, the geography of the borderland has actually changed; the river that marked the boundary may have changed course, or a portion of it could be cut off. Resources lying across a boundary can lead to conflict. In short, states often argue about their boundaries. These boundary disputes take four principal forms: definitional, locational, operational, and allocational.

Definitional boundary disputes focus on the legal language of the boundary agreement. For example, a boundary definition may stipulate that the median line of a river will mark the boundary. That would seem clear enough, but the water levels of rivers vary. If the river valley is asymmetrical, the median line will move back and forth between low-water and high-water stages of the stream. This may involve hundreds of metres of movement—not very much, it would seem, but enough to cause serious argument, especially if there are resources in the river. The solution is to refine the definition to suit both parties.

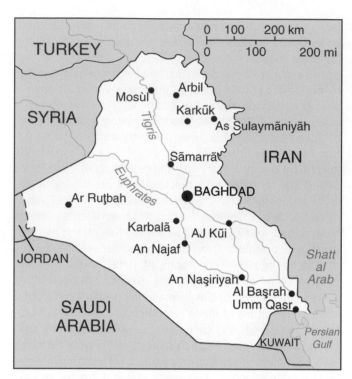

FIGURE 3.11 Euphrates–Tigris River Basin. (The World Factbook 2009. Washington, DC: Central Intelligence Agency, 2009.)

Locational boundary disputes centre on the delimitation and possibly the demarcation of the boundary. The definition is not in dispute, but its interpretation is. Sometimes the language of boundary treaties is vague enough to allow mapmakers to delimit the line in various ways. For example, when the colonial powers defined their empires in Africa and Asia, they specified their international boundaries rather carefully. But internal administrative boundaries often were not strictly defined. When those internal boundaries became the boundaries of independent states, there was plenty of room for argument. In a few instances, locational disputes arise because no definition of the boundary exists at all. An important case involves Saudi Arabia and Yemen, whose potentially oil-rich boundary area is not covered by a treaty.

Operational boundary disputes involve neighbours who differ over the way their border should function. When two adjoining countries agree on how cross-border migration should be controlled, the border functions satisfactorily. However, if one state wants to limit migration while the other does not, a dispute may arise. The United States now requires Canadian citizens to have passports when crossing into the United States. Canada has not imposed a similar requirement on Americans entering Canada. Similarly, efforts to prevent smuggling across borders sometimes lead to operational disputes when one state's efforts are not matched (or are possibly even sabotaged) by its neighbour's. And in areas where nomadic lifeways still prevail, the movement of people and their livestock across international borders can lead to conflict.

Allocational boundary disputes, of the kind described earlier involving Iraq and Kuwait over oil, are becoming more common

as the search for resources intensifies. Today, many such disputes involve international boundaries at sea. Oil reserves under the sea floor below coastal waters sometimes lie in areas where exact boundary delimitation may be difficult or subject to debate; the contested terrain in the Arctic described earlier is such an example. Another growing area of allocational dispute has to do with water supplies: the Tigris, Nile, Colorado, and other rivers are subject to such disputes. When a river crosses an international boundary, the rights of the upstream and downstream users of the river often come into conflict. The Euphrates–Tigris River Basin (Figure 3.11) is a contested region in the Middle East. Turkey, Iraq, and Syria all rely upon the water supply in the basin, and the site has become known as a potential "water wars" region. Issues such as dam building water navigation, and access to fresh water are central to this allocation boundary dispute.

NATIONS

The popular media and press often use the words "nation," "state," and "country" interchangeably. Political geographers use "state" and "country" interchangeably (often preferring "state"), but the word "nation" is distinct. "State" is a legal term in international law, and the international political community has some agreement about what this term means. "Nation," on the other hand, is a culturally defined term, and few people agree on exactly what it means. Definitions are important as few words are as politically charged as the concept of nation.

The *Dictionary of Human Geography* (4th edition) defines a **nation** as

> *a community of people whose members are bound together by a sense of solidarity rooted in an historic attachment to a homeland and a common culture, and by a sense of consciousness of being different from other nations.* (p. 532)

A nation, then, is a group of people who think of themselves as collectively bound together based on a sense of shared culture and history, and who have some identification with a territory or place—a homeland. This idea encompasses different kinds of culturally and historically defined nations. Nations variously see themselves as sharing a religion, a language, an ethnicity, or a history. The French are often considered to be the classic example of a nation, but the most French-feeling person in France today is the product of a melding of a wide variety of cultural groups over time, including Celts, ancient Romans, Franks, and Goths. If the majority of inhabitants of modern France belong to the French nation, it is because they claim the French nation as an identity—not because the French nation exists as an always existing primordial group. Historically, nations were treated as something we are born into, something

> **Nation** A tightly knit group of people possessing bonds of language, ethnicity, religion, and other shared cultural attributes. Such homogeneity actually prevails within very few states.

natural that changes over time. The widely held view was that all people belong to a nation and always have. Recently, scholars have argued that nations are constructed, that people create nations to give themselves an identity at that scale. Benedict Anderson, one of the most widely read scholars on nationalism today, defines the nation as an "imagined community"—imagined because, even though you will never meet all of the people in your nation and community, you still see yourself as part of a collective.

Because a nation is identified by those who are able to define and control membership, we cannot simply define a nation as the people within a territory. Indeed, rarely does a nation's extent correspond precisely with a state's borders. For example, in the country of Belgium, two nations—the Flemish and the Walloons—exist within the state borders. While some groups who envision themselves as nations do not seek territorial control and autonomy, there are numerous examples of groups seeking independence and the creation of their own territorially defined nation-state—for example, the Kurds of Iraq, Turkey, Syria, and Iran; Tamils in northern Sri Lanka; and the Québécois in the province of Quebec here in Canada.

While we may think that everyone is a citizen or member of a nation-state, some people can be rendered "citizenshipless"

or "stateless" and government policies that determine the rights to citizenship may affect people's ability to claim rights to territory and nationality or citizenship. For example, on October 7, 2010, CBC Radio's *The Current* told the story of Chloe Goldring, who is officially stateless. Her father is a Canadian citizen, born in Bermuda to a Canadian father and Bermudan mother, and her mother is Algerian. Chloe is 15 months old and lives with her parents in Brussels, Belgium, where her father runs a consulting company. Her father grew up in Canada, went to the University of Guelph and York University, and currently resides in Belgium for his work. Due to a change in the *Canadian Citizenship Act* in 2009, Chloe's parents are unable to get a Canadian passport for her because although her father is a Canadian citizen, he was not born in Canada, and neither was Chloe. They are unable to get an Algerian passport, because in Algeria a woman does not possess the same automatic rights to citizenship for her children if she marries a foreigner. The end result is that Chloe is caught up in a maelstrom of political decisions from no fewer than three states. Her case illustrates the complexities of state policies around citizenship, immigration, and territory within the context of globalization. Political geographers study these spatial manifestations of political processes at various scales from the global to the local.

MAIN POINTS   **3.1**   How Is Space Organized into States and Nations?

- Political geographers are interested in nations and states, their territorial organization and boundaries, and nationalist ideologies. Political geographers are also interested in the political organization of space from the global to the local.

- A state is not a "natural" organizational structure. It is a particular form of political and social order created by humans. The state is a politically organized territory with a permanent population, a defined territory, and a government. It must be recognized as such by the international community in accordance with international law.

- States need to establish boundaries and do so in a number of different ways. Disputes between countries about boundaries take a number of different forms including definitional, locational, operational, and allocational.

- A nation is a group of people who collectively understand themselves as having a shared history and a common culture attached to a particular homeland. Some states are made up of many nations, and many nations do not have their own state.

3.2 How Did the Modern Nation-State Come into Being?

Human beings have organized themselves into groups claiming control over territories for most of known human history. The great kingdoms of China and Japan, the earliest beginnings of human settlement in Mesopotamia some 7,000 years ago, and the long-lost civilizations of the Aztecs and the Incas speak to the territorial complexity of human social and political organization. The dominant modern European idea of the "state" is a relatively recent invention, emerging some 500 years ago out of the peculiar histories and geographies of exploration, and

colonialism, imperialism, and revolution. Prior to that time, medieval Europe was a hodgepodge of city-states, small kingdoms, duchies, and principalities engaged in seemingly endless petty feuds, minor skirmishes, and multiple wars over boundaries and territorial control. Figure 3.12 illustrates the organization of Europe in 1190, which looks considerably different than it does today.

By the early 17th century, such European locales as the Republic of Venice, Brandenburg, the Papal States of central Italy, the Kingdom of Hungary, and several minor German states were part of a complicated patchwork of political entities, many with poorly defined borders. The emergence of the contemporary European state as we know it is intertwined with

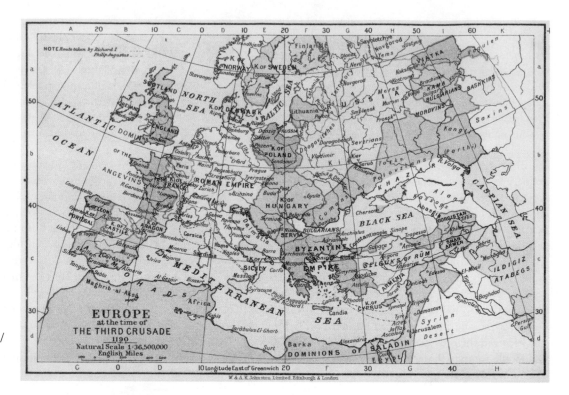

FIGURE 3.12 Medieval Europe, c. 1190. From *Historical Atlas*, published by W. & A.K. Johnston Limited, 1911 (colour litho) by English School (20th century) Private Collection/ Ken Welsh/The Bridgeman Art Library. Reprinted by permission.

changing economic relations from the Dark Ages onward. A growing land and sea trade beginning in the 1150s gave rise in many European urban centres to the merchant class—a new grouping distinguishable from the aristocracy on the one hand and landless, labouring classes on the other. As a group, the merchants increasingly used forms of money as a means of exchange as they developed long-distance trade in spices, woods, fabric, and slaves. Trade routes sprang up across the globe, drawing more of the world's territory into these global circuits.

By the early 1300s, competitive rivalries sprang up between the great trading nations of Spain, Portugal, Holland, Britain, and France. These rivalries escalated with the increasing belief in **mercantilism**, which began to take hold in the 1500s. Adherents to this belief argued that it was the state's responsibility to directly finance foreign trade by hiring merchants, explorers, and adventurers in order to promote the state's economic interests abroad. Each state sought to accumulate wealth through plunder, colonization, and the protection of home industries and foreign markets. Rivalry and competition intensified in Europe as well as abroad. Powerful royal families struggled for dominance in eastern and southern Europe. Instability was the rule, strife occurred frequently, and repressive governments prevailed. Some states were able to expand and consolidate their control and to raise revenues through increasingly

> **Mercantilism** In a general sense, associated with the promotion of commercialism and trade. More specifically, a protectionist policy of European states during the 16th to the 18th centuries that promoted a state's economic position in the contest with other countries. The acquisition of gold and silver and the maintenance of a favourable trade balance (more exports than imports) were central to the policy.

sophisticated means of government control and bureaucratic regulation. In his work on the emergence of the English and Welsh states during the 17th century, Miles Ogborn (1998) argues that these states' ability to efficiently institute taxation and collect revenue was central to their consolidation as a form of modern state. The ability to raise funds to support state activities remains crucial today to the stability and effectiveness of the modern state.

In 1648, relative peace and stability was achieved in Europe when the **Peace of Westphalia** was negotiated among the princes of the states making up the Holy Roman Empire, as well as the rulers of a few neighbouring states (Figure 3.13). The treaties that constituted this peace concluded the Thirty Years' War, Europe's most destructive internal struggle over religion. These treaties contained new language recognizing the rights of rulers within defined, demarcated territories. The language of the treaties laid the foundations for a Europe made up of territorially defined states. They originally applied only to the states that were party to the treaty, but they gave rise to a political-territorial order that spread throughout western and central Europe.

> **Peace of Westphalia** Peace negotiated in 1648 to end the Thirty Years' War, Europe's most destructive internal struggle over religion. The treaties contained new language recognizing statehood and nationhood, clearly defined borders, and guarantees of security.

The Westphalian treaties set the stage for the emergence of a state system that marked a fundamental change in the relationship between people and territory. In previous eras, societies had largely defined their territories. In the Westphalian system, territories defined societies (for example, the French are the people who live in France). Territory is treated as a fixed element of political identification, and states define exclusive,

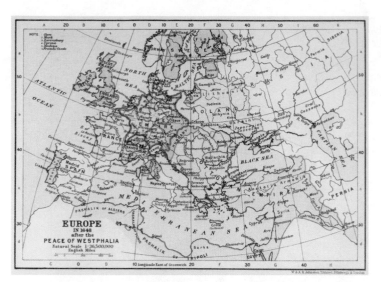

Figure 3.13 Peace of Westphalia. The treaties that became known as the Peace of Westphalia ended the Thirty Years' War in Europe in 1648. The result was the drawing of new boundaries around European states, including an independent Portugal and Netherlands, and the growth of the Ottoman Empire. From 'Historical Atlas', published by W. & A.K. Johnston Limited, 1911 (colour litho), English School, (20th century)/Private Collection/Ken Welsh/The Bridgeman Art Library International. Reprinted by permission.

non-overlapping territories. State rulers are sovereign over their territories and the people who inhabit them.

Well after the Peace of Westphalia, absolutist rulers continued to control most European states. During the later 17th and 18th centuries, however, the development of an increasingly wealthy middle class proved to be the undoing of absolutism in parts of Western Europe. City-based merchants gained wealth and prestige, while the nobility declined. Money and influence were increasingly concentrated in urban areas, and the traditional measure of affluence—land—became less important. Merchants and businessmen demanded political recognition. In the 1780s, a series of upheavals began that would change the sociopolitical face of the continent—most notably the French Revolution of 1789. That revolution, conducted in the name of the French people, ushered in an era in which the foundations for political authority came to be seen as resting with a state's citizenry, not with a hereditary monarch.

THE NATION-STATE

Nation-state Theoretically, a recognized member of the modern state system possessing formal sovereignty and occupied by a people who see themselves as a single, united nation. Most nations and states aspire to this form, but it is realized almost nowhere. Nonetheless, in common parlance, nation-state is used as a synonym for country or state.

A **nation-state** is a politically organized area in which nation and state occupy the same space. That is, people who collectively understand themselves as a nation, bound together by history, identity, and/or culture, occupy a bounded territory governed by a state. Few (if any) states are nation-states. Many states, such as Canada, are made up of groups who consider themselves

a different nation—Quebec nationalists and First Nations peoples, for example. Given this reality, the importance of the nation-state concept lies primarily in the idea behind it. States, and the governments that run states, desire a unified nation within their borders to create stability and to replace other politically charged identities that may challenge the state and the government's control of the state.

People began to see the idea of the nation-state as the ultimate form of political-territorial organization, the right expression of sovereignty, and the best route to stability. The key problem associated with the idea of the nation-state is that it assumes the presence of reasonably well-defined, stable nations living contiguously within discrete territories. Very few places in the world come close to satisfying this requirement. Nonetheless, in Europe during the 18th and 19th centuries, many believed the condition could be achieved.

The quest to form nation-states in the Europe of the 1800s was associated with a rise in **nationalism**. Flint and Taylor (2007) define nationalism as an ideology and a political practice that assumes all nations should have their own state—a nation-state—in their own territory—the national homeland. In this sense, nationalism is a relatively recent phenomenon and constitutes a powerful link between politics, place, and culture. It requires that a group of people feel they belong to a nation (a collective imagined community) that corresponds to a particular bounded territory. In Canada, this feeling of collective imagined community is evident every year as thousands of flag-waving Canadians gather on Parliament Hill for Canada Day celebrations.

Nationalism Both an ideology and a political practice that all nations need their own sovereign government and territory.

We can view nationalism from two vantage points: that of the people and that of the state. When *people* in a nation feel a strong sense of nationalism, they have a loyalty to the nation and a belief in the nation. This loyalty to a nation does not necessarily coincide with the borders of the state. A *state* does not have a strong sense of nationalism; rather, the government of a state is nationalistic. In this sense, the government promotes the nation, and because the government is the representative of the state, it seeks to promote a nation that coincides with the borders of the state. In the name of nationalism, a state that contains more than one nation can attempt to build a single national identity out of the divergent people within its borders. In the name of nationalism, a state can also promote a war against another state that threatens its territorial integrity.

In 19th-century Europe, states used nationalism to achieve a variety of goals. In some cases they integrated their population into an ever-more-cohesive national whole (e.g., France, Spain), and in other cases they brought together people with shared cultural characteristics within a single state (e.g., Germany and Italy). Similarly, people who saw themselves as a separate nation within another state or empire launched successful separatist movements and achieved independence (e.g., the Republic of Ireland, Norway, and Poland).

European state leaders used the tool of nationalism to strengthen the state. The modern map of Europe is still

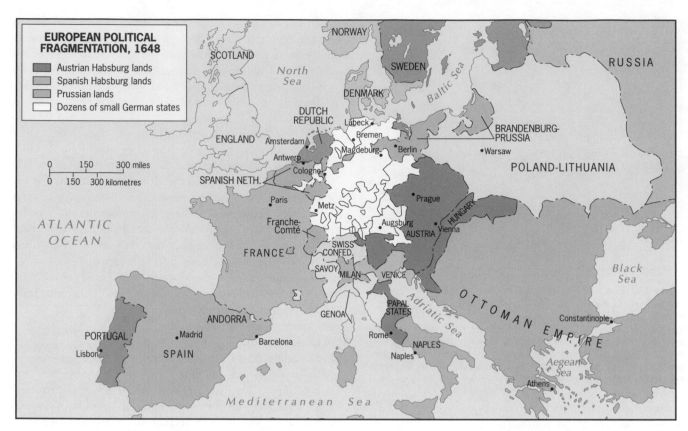

FIGURE 3.14 European Political Fragmentation in 1648. A generalized map of the fragmentation of Western Europe in the 1600s. Adapted with permission from Geoffrey Barraclough, ed., *The Times Concise Atlas of World History*, 5th edition Hammond Incorporated, 1998.

fragmented, but much less so than it was in the 1600s (Figure 3.14). In the process of creating nation-states in Europe, states absorbed smaller entities into their borders, resolved conflicts by force as well as by negotiation, and defined borders.

To help people within the borders relate to the dominant national ideal, states provide security, goods, and services to the citizens. They support education, infrastructure, health care, and a military to preserve the state and to create a connection between the people and the state—to build a nation-state. European states even used the colonization of Africa and Asia in the late 1800s and early 1900s to promote nationalism. People could take pride in their state, in their nation, and in its vast colonial empire. People could identify themselves with their French, Dutch, or British nation by contrasting themselves with the people in the colonies—people whom they defined as mystical or savage. By identifying against an "other," the state and the people helped identify the traits of their nation—and in so doing, they worked to build a nation-state.

An important aspect of the building of a nationalist ideology is the development of a discourse of militarism; the role of the military and of civilians who support the military is central to the imagery of the nation-state. The British recruitment posters in Figure 3.15 exemplify the ways in which governments encourage their citizens to enlist in armies. In Figure 3.15a the poster not only employs a sense of difference in terms of "us versus them," but it also uses gendered representations of the ways in which men (as protectors) and women (as victims in

need of protecting) are understood within the nation-state to encourage enlistment. In Figure 3.15b the poster demonstrates the other side of this gendered narrative as it encourages women to "come into the factories" to do their part in the war effort.

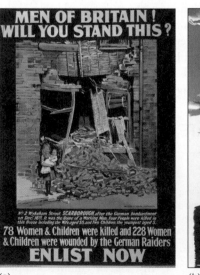

(a)   (b)

FIGURE 3.15 (a) British World War I Pre-Conscription Recruitment Poster. (b) Specialist War Recruitment Poster Urging Women to Go to Work in Factories. (Courtesy of Library of Congress; Mary Evans Picture Library/Onslow Auctions Limited)

MULTISTATE NATIONS, MULTINATIONAL STATES, AND STATELESS NATIONS

The sense of belonging to a nation rarely meshes perfectly with state borders. The lack of fit between nation and state creates complications, such as states with more than one nation, nations with more than one state, and nations without a state. Nearly every state in the world is a **multinational state**, a state with more than one nation inside its borders. Millions of people who were citizens of the former state of Yugoslavia never had a strong sense of Yugoslav nationality—instead they identified

> **Multinational state** A state with more than one nation within its borders.
>
> **Multistate nation** A nation that stretches across borders and across states.

themselves as Slovenes, Croats, Serbs, Armenians, or members of other nations or ethnic groups within the state or region. Yugoslavia was a state that always had more than one nation, and eventually the state collapsed (see Figure 3.5).

When a nation stretches across borders and across states, it is called a **multistate nation**. Political geographer George White studied the states of Romania and Hungary and their overlapping nations. The territory of Transylvania is currently in the middle of the state of Romania, but for two centuries, Hungary's borders stretched far enough east to incorporate Transylvania into the state of Hungary. The Transylvania region today is populated by Romanians and by Hungarians, and both states claim a desire and a right to control the territory. Both states identify places within Transylvania that they see as pivotal to the histories of their nations. The desire to control the territory and to stretch the Hungarian state in order to mesh with what Hungarians see as their nation requires the movement of state borders. In the case of Romania and Hungary, and in similar states where the identity of the nation is tied to a particular territory, White explains that nations will defend their territories as strongly as they defend their "language, religion, or way of life."

Another complication that arises from the lack of fit between nations and states is that some nations do not have

> **Stateless nation** A nation that does not have a state.

a state; they are **stateless nations**. The Palestinians are an example of a stateless nation. Palestinian Arabs have gained control of the Gaza Strip and fragments of the Occupied Territories, which may form the foundations of a future state. Well over half of the approximately 8 million Palestinians continue to live in Israel, Jordan, Lebanon, Syria, and other Arab states. The international community does not yet recognize the Palestinian lands as a state.

A much larger stateless nation is that of the over 27 million Kurds who live in an area called Kurdistan that covers parts of six states (Figure 3.16). In the aftermath of the 1991 Gulf War, the United Nations established a Kurdish Security Zone north of the 36th parallel in Iraq, but subsequent events have dashed any Kurdish hopes that this might one day become a state. The Kurds form the largest minority in

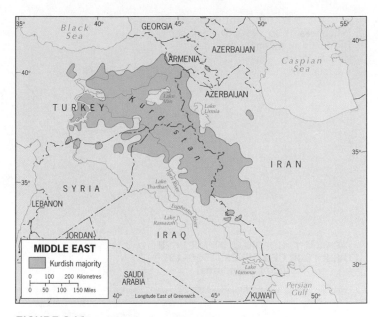

FIGURE 3.16 Kurdish Region of the Middle East. (© H.J. de Blij, P.O. Kuller, and John Wiley & Sons, Inc.)

Turkey, and the city of Diyarbakir is the unofficial Kurdish capital; however, relations between the 10 million Kurds in Turkey and the Turkish government in Ankara have been volatile. Without the consent of Turkey, establishing a truly independent Kurdish state will be difficult.

EUROPEAN COLONIALISM AND THE DIFFUSION OF THE NATION-STATE MODEL

Europe exported its concepts of state and sovereignty, and the desire for nation-states, to much of the rest of the world through two waves of colonialism. In the 16th century, Spain and Portugal took advantage of their increasingly well-consolidated internal political order and new-found wealth to expand their influence to increasingly far-flung realms during the first wave of colonialism. Later joined by Britain, France, the Netherlands, and Belgium, the first wave of colonialism established a far-reaching capitalist system. After independence movements in the Americas during the late 1700s and 1800s, a second wave of colonialism began in the late 1800s. This time the major colonizers were Britain, France, the Netherlands, Belgium, Germany, and Italy. Driven by motives ranging from economic profit to the desire to bring Christianity to the rest of the world, colonialism projected European power and a European approach to organizing political space into the non-European world (Figure 3.17).

With Europe in control of so much of the world, Europeans laid the ground rules for the emerging international state system, and the modern European concept of the nation-state became the model exported and imposed around the world. European colonial states also established and defined the ground rules of the capitalist world economy, creating a system of economic interdependence that persists today.

FIGURE 3.17 Dominant Colonial Influences, 1550-1950. The map shows the dominant European or Japanese colonial influence in each country over the four centuries. (© H.J. de Blij, John Wiley & Sons, Inc.)

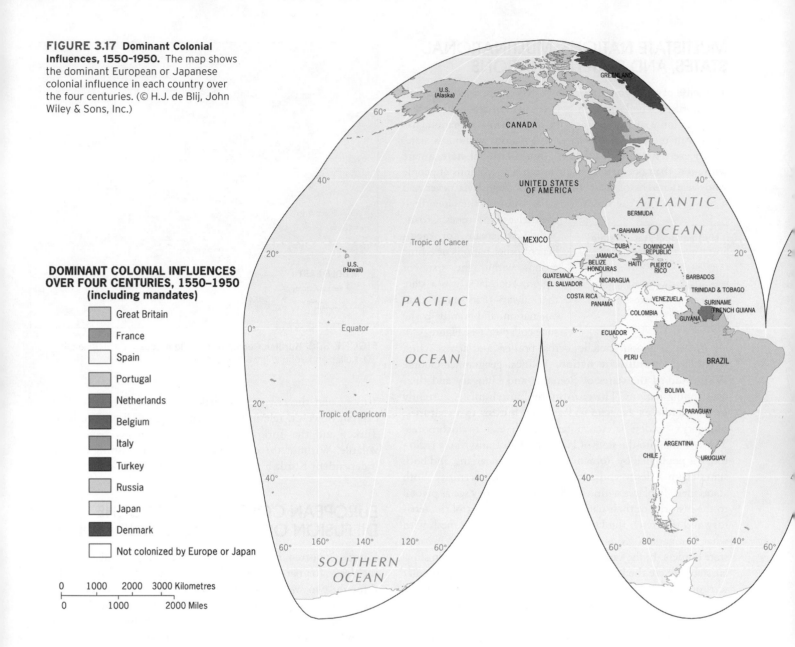

DOMINANT COLONIAL INFLUENCES OVER FOUR CENTURIES, 1550–1950 (including mandates)

- Great Britain
- France
- Spain
- Portugal
- Netherlands
- Belgium
- Italy
- Turkey
- Russia
- Japan
- Denmark
- Not colonized by Europe or Japan

0   1000   2000   3000 Kilometres

0   1000   2000 Miles

Colonialism Rule by an autonomous power over a subordinate and alien people and place. Although often established and maintained through political structures, colonialism also creates unequal cultural and economic relations. Because of the magnitude and impact of the European colonial project of the last few centuries, the term is generally understood to refer to that particular colonial endeavour.

During the heyday of **colonialism**, the imperial powers exercised ruthless control over their domains and organized them for maximum economic exploitation. The capacity to install the infrastructure necessary for such efficient profiteering is itself evidence of the power relationships involved: entire populations were regimented in the service of the colonial ruler. Colonizers organized the flows of raw materials for their

own benefit, and we can still see the tangible evidence of that organization (i.e., plantations, ports, mines, and railroads) on the cultural landscape.

Although many formerly colonized countries have gained their independence, the political organization of space and the global world economy that arose from colonialism remain. As a result, the economies of these now independent countries are anything but independent. In many cases, raw material flows are as great as they ever were during the colonial era. For example, today in Gabon, Africa, the railroad goes from the interior forest (which is logged for plywood) to the major port and capital city, Libreville. The second largest city, Port Gentil, is located to the south of Libreville, but the two cities are not connected by road or railroad. Like Libreville, Port Gentile is

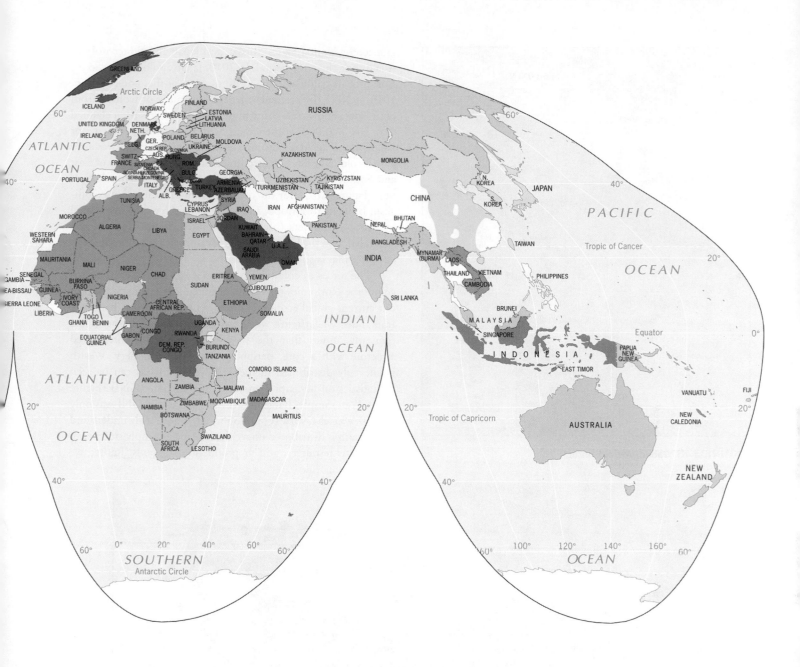

CONSTRUCTION OF THE CAPITALIST WORLD ECONOMY

As we discussed in Chapter 2, the long-term impacts of colonialism are many and varied and are important to our understanding of the current processes of globalization. One of the most powerful impacts of colonialism was the construction of a global order characterized by great differences in economic and political power. The European colonial enterprise gave birth to a globalized economic order in which the European states, and areas dominated by European migrants, emerged as the major centres of economic and political activity. Through colonialism, Europeans extracted wealth from colonies and established the colonized as subservient in the relationship.

Of course, not all Europeans profited equally from colonialism. Enormous poverty persisted within the most powerful European states. Similarly, not all colonizers profited to the same degree. Spain had a large colonial empire in the late 17th century, but by then the empire was economically draining Spain. Moreover, Europeans were not the only people to profit from colonialism. During the period of European colonialism (1500–1950), Russia and the United States expanded over land instead of overseas, profiting from the taking of territory and the subjugation of indigenous peoples. Great Britain, the Netherlands,

export-focused, with global oil corporations responsible for building much of the city and its housing, and employing most of its people (Figure 3.18).

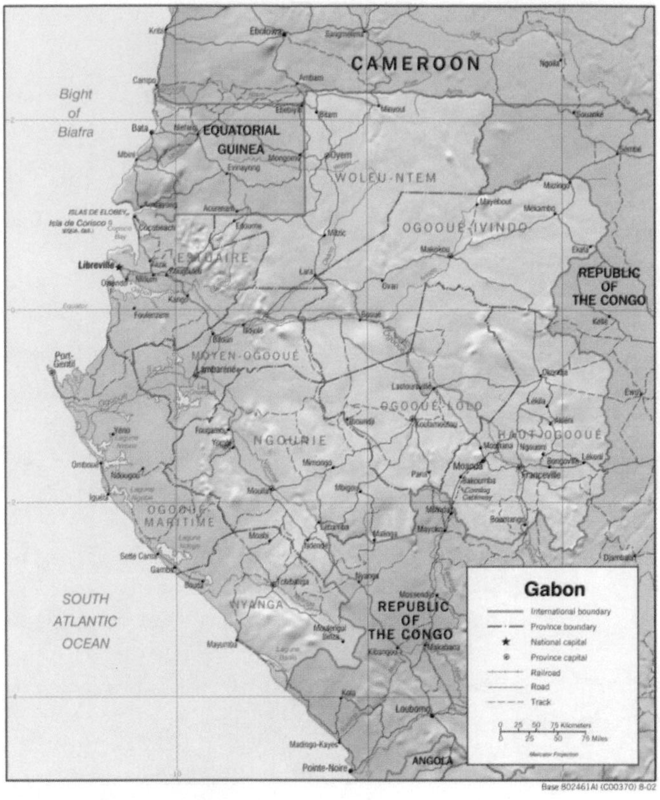

FIGURE 3.18 Gabon, Africa. (Intute)

France, the United States, Russia, and Japan all held territory in Asia during this time period. In 2010, Japan apologized to South Korea for its colonization and occupation of that country from 1910 to 1945. In particular, Japan's treatment of women from both Korea and China came under scrutiny; it has been claimed that over 200,000 women were used as "comfort women" for Japan's Imperial Army during this time period. Japan was a regional colonial power, controlling Korea and other parts of East and Southeast Asia as well as Pacific Islands through colonization (Figure 3.19). But the concentration of wealth that colonialism brought to Europe, and to parts of the world dominated by European settlers (such as the United States, Canada, and Australia), is at the heart of the highly uneven global distribution of power that is still with us today.

The forces of colonialism played a key role in knitting together the economies of widely separated areas—giving birth to our current global economic order. As we noted in Chapter 2, Immanuel Wallerstein's world systems approach to the global economy argues that the world economy is a three-tiered structure with a core, periphery, and semi-periphery. Wealth is unevenly distributed in the world economy, as can be seen in statistics on per capita gross national income (GNI) (Figure 3.20). For example, Bangladesh's 2009 per capita GNI was only $1,550, whereas Norway's was $55,420. But to truly understand why wealth is distributed unevenly, we cannot simply study each country, its resources, and its production of goods. Rather, we

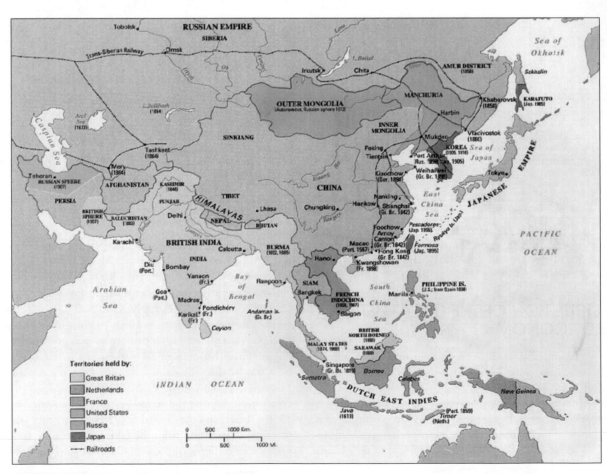

FIGURE 3.19 Colonized Asia, Circa Early 1900s.

need to understand where countries fit in the world economy. That is, we need to see the big picture. To study a single country or even each country individually, we miss the whole. We need to step back and see the whole, as well as the individual elements, studying how one affects the other. This should sound familiar—it is one of the ways geographers think about **scale**.

> **Scale** Representation of a real-world phenomenon at a certain level of reduction or generalization. In cartography, the ratio of map distance to ground distance; indicated on a map as a bar graph, representative fraction, and/or verbal statement.

Not all core countries in the world today were colonial powers. Countries such as Switzerland, Singapore, and Australia have significant global clout even though they were never classic colonial powers, and that clout is tied in significant part to their positions in the global economy. They gained these positions as a result of their access to the networks of production, consumption, and exchange in the wealthiest parts of the world and their ability to take advantage of that access. Canada was once a peripheral country providing raw materials, goods, and resources to markets around the world. Now Canada is considered part of the core, although not as a major economic power. Conversely, China, formerly a peripheral player, is now a major player on the global stage and actively engaged in re-working global political and economic power relations.

But, are economic power and political power one and the same? No, but economic power can certainly bring political power. In the current system, economic power means wealth, and political power refers to the ability to influence others to achieve your goals. Political power is not defined by sovereignty. Each state is sovereign, but not all states have the same ability to influence others or achieve their political goals. Having wealth helps leaders amass political power. For instance, a wealthy country can establish a mighty military. But political influence is not simply a function of hard power; it is also diplomatic. Switzerland's declared neutrality, combined with its economic might, aids the country's diplomatic efforts.

Finally, the idea of meshing the nation and state into a nation-state was not confined to 19th-century Europe or 20th-century Africa. Major players in international relations still see the validity of dividing nations with state borders—of creating nation-states. This remains the case, even in the face of the globalizing processes discussed in Chapter 2 that seem to ignore national boundaries as they weave locations, places, and regions into an ever-more-complex network of economic, political, and social relations. Nevertheless, as we seek solutions to complex political conflicts, we continue to work with the nation-state idea as the social and institutional framework capable of bringing long-term peace. People trying to find solutions to the conflicts in the former Yugoslavia and in Israel/Palestine have tried to draw state boundaries around nations—to make nation and state fit. In all of these ways, the European state became the world model and is still shaping the political organization of space in the world.

MAIN POINTS   3.2   How Did the Modern Nation-State Come into Being?

- The nation-state, a politically organized area in which the nation and the state occupy the same territory, is a modern institution.

- The modern nation-state is a product of the historical, cultural, and geographical processes at work in Europe between the 1100s and the present day. The imperial and colonial activities of European states ensured that some form of nation-state government was transported around the world.

- Multistate nations, multinational states, and stateless nations focus our attention on the complicated relationship between the collective sense of being a nation, the territorial affiliations of nations, and the state institutions that govern those territories. We have many examples of multiple nations within the borders of one state or single nations that straddle several states. Finally, we have nations that have no state at all.

- The export of the nation-state model around the globe by colonial and imperial states is the foundation for the current world order. This occurred in part because of the dominance of the capitalist economic system and the legacies of colonial conquest.

- In the world systems approach, developed by Wallerstein, states find themselves organized in a hierarchical relationship as core, peripheral, or semi-peripheral participants in the global economy. This means that some states gain greater benefits than others as a result of their position in the global economy.

- A state's position in the world system can change. Canada was once a peripheral country but is now considered part of the economic core.

FIGURE 3.20 Per Capita Gross National Income (GNI), 2009. Data from the World Bank.

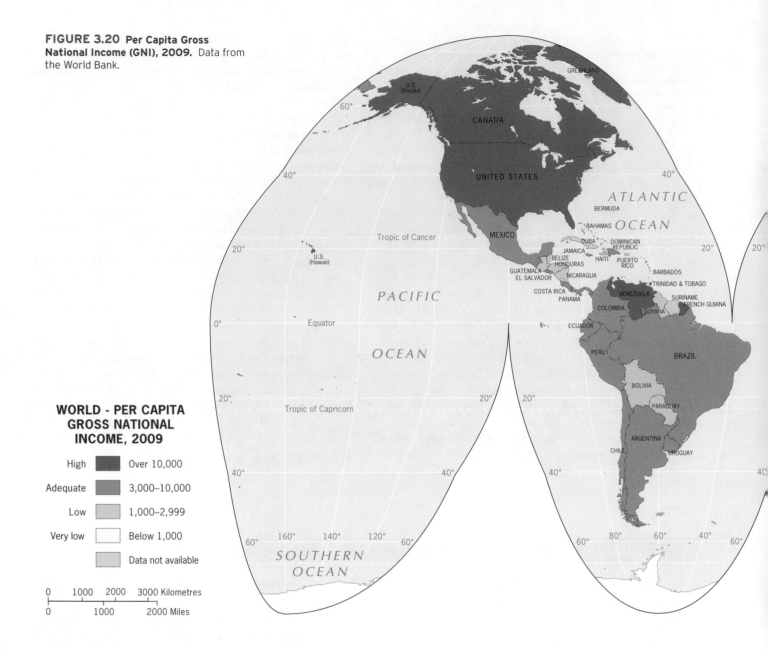

WORLD - PER CAPITA GROSS NATIONAL INCOME, 2009

High		Over 10,000
Adequate		3,000–10,000
Low		1,000–2,999
Very low		Below 1,000
		Data not available

0   1000   2000   3000 Kilometres

0   1000   2000 Miles

3.3 How Is the Governance of States Spatially Organized?

In the 1950s, political geographer Richard Hartshorne described the forces that unify people within a state as **centripetal** and the forces that divide them as **centrifugal**. According to Hartshorne, a nation's (or a state's) continued existence depends on the balance between centripetal and centrifugal forces. Many political geographers have thought about Hartshorne's theory, and most have concluded that

> **Centripetal** Forces that tend to unify a country—such as widespread commitment to a national culture, shared ideological objectives, and a common faith.
>
> **Centrifugal** Forces that tend to divide a country—such as internal religious, linguistic, ethnic, or ideological differences.

we cannot take a given event or process and declare it to be centrifugal or centripetal in isolation from the context in which it is situated. An event, such as a war, can pull the state together for a short time and then divide the state over the long term. Timing, scale, interaction, and perspective factor into unification and division in a state at any given point.

Instead of creating a balance sheet of centripetal and centrifugal forces, governments attempt to unify a state by nation-building, by structuring the government in a way that melds the nations within, by defining and defending boundaries, and by expressing control over all of the territory within those boundaries. When we look at how different governments have attempted to unify their states, we are reminded how important geography is. Governance does not take place in a vacuum. The uniqueness of place helps determine whether any possible governmental "solution" solves or exacerbates matters.

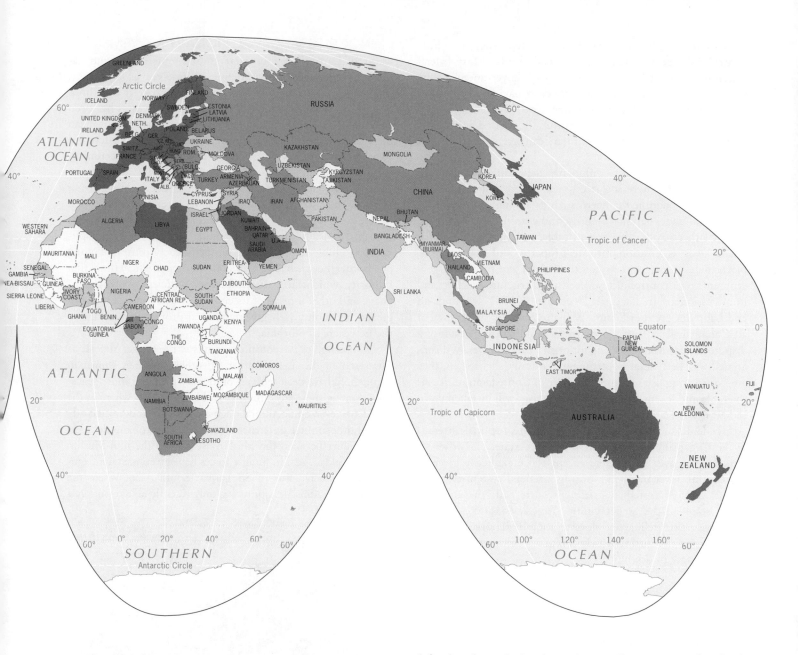

THE STRUCTURE OF GOVERNMENT

One way states promote unification is by choosing a governmental structure that promotes nation-building and quells division within. Two common governmental structures are unitary and federal.

To address multination states, governments, even democratic governments, can and have suppressed dissent by forceful means. Until the end of World War II, most European governments were **unitary** governments: they were highly centralized, with the capital city serving as the focus of power. States made no clear efforts to accommodate minorities or outlying regions where identification with the state was weaker. Europe's nation-states were unitary states, with the culture of the capital city

> **Unitary** (state) A nation-state that has a centralized government and administration that exercises power equally over all parts of the state.

defined as the nation's culture. Any smaller nations within (such as Bretons in France or Basques in Spain) were repressed and suppressed. A unitary government's administrative framework ensures the central government's authority and control over all parts of the state. The French government divided the state into more than 90 *départements,* whose representatives came to Paris not to express regional concerns but to implement governmental decisions back home.

Another way to govern a multinational state is to construct a **federal** system, organizing state territory into regions, substates, provinces, or cantons. In a strong federal system, the regions have a lot of control over government

> **Federal** (state) A political-territorial system wherein a central government represents the various entities within a nation-state where they have common interests—defence, foreign affairs, and the like—yet allows these various entities to retain their own identities and to have their own laws, policies, and customs in certain spheres.

policies and funds; in a weak federal system, they have little control over government policies and funds. Most federal systems are somewhere in between, with governments at the state scale and at the substate scale each having control over certain revenues and certain policy areas. By giving control over certain policies (especially culturally relative policies) to smaller-scale entities, a government can keep the state as a whole together.

Federalism functions differently depending on the context. In Canada, there is a strong central government dealing with issues of national concern such as air transportation, international trade, national security, and criminal law. Provinces, on the other hand, have considerable authority over internal affairs such as taxation, private property, and civil matters. Nevertheless, disputes between the federal and provincial governments over control of resources, infrastructure funding, and immigration are frequent. In December 2004, Newfoundland and Labrador premier Danny Williams ordered the removal of all Canadian flags from government buildings as a result of a dispute about revenue sharing for offshore oil reserves. Williams argued, "[The federal government] basically slighted us, they are not treating us as a proper partner in Confederation. It's intolerable and it's insufferable and these flags will be taken down indefinitely."

Federalism attempts to accommodate regional interests by vesting primary power in provinces, states, or other regional units over all matters except those explicitly given to the central government. Choosing a federal system does not always quell nationalist sentiment. After all, the multinational states of the Soviet Union, Yugoslavia, and Czechoslovakia fell apart despite their federalist systems, and the future of Belgium as a single state is increasingly in doubt.

DEVOLUTION

Devolution is the movement of power from the central government to regional governments within the state.

> **Devolution** The process whereby regions within a state demand and gain political strength and growing autonomy at the expense of the central government.

Sometimes devolution is achieved by reworking a constitution to establish a federal system that recognizes the permanency of the regional governments, as Spain has done. In other places, governments devolve power without altering constitutions, almost as an experiment. In the United Kingdom, the Northern Ireland Assembly (a parliamentary body) resulted from devolution; the British government suspended its activities in 2002 but then reinstated it in 2007. Devolutionary forces can surface in all kinds of states, old and young, mature and emergent. These forces arise from several sources: ethnocultural, economic, and spatial.

ETHNOCULTURAL DEVOLUTIONARY MOVEMENTS

Many of Europe's devolutionary movements came from nations within a state that define themselves as ethnically, linguistically, or religiously distinct. The capacity of ethnocultural forces to stimulate devolutionary processes has been evident in Eastern Europe. Parts of the Eastern European map have changed drastically over the past two decades, and two countries—Czechoslovakia and Yugoslavia—succumbed to often violent devolutionary pressures. In the case of Czechoslovakia, the process was peaceful: Czechs and Slovaks divided their country along a new international border. As Figure 3.21 shows however, one of the two new states, Slovakia, is not homogeneous: about 11 percent of the population is Hungarian, and that minority is concentrated along the border between Slovakia and Hungary. The Hungarian minority, which faces discriminatory policies involving language and other aspects of its culture, has at times demanded greater autonomy (self-governance) to protect its heritage in the new state of Slovakia.

Compared to the constituent units of the former Yugoslavia (discussed in detail in Chapter 7), other countries shown in Figure 3.22 have dealt with devolutionary pressures more peacefully. Among these are Lithuania and Ukraine. Elsewhere in the world, however, ethnocultural fragmentation has produced costly wars. Ethnocultural differences lie at the heart of the decades-long conflict between the Muslim North and the non-Muslim South in Sudan, Africa. Similar forces have given rise to a seemingly endless civil war in Sri Lanka (South Asia), where the Sinhalese (Buddhist) majority was only recently able to suppress

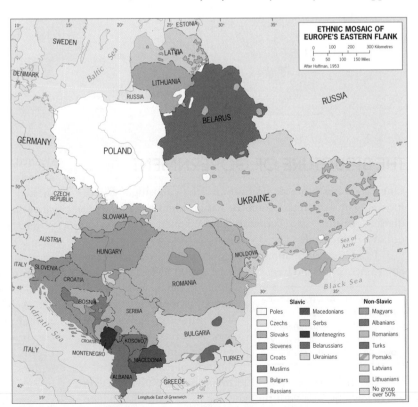

FIGURE 3.21 Ethnic Mosaic of Eastern Europe. Adapted (in part) with permission from George Huffman, ed., *Europe in the 1990s: A Geographical Analysis,* 6th rev. ed. (New York: Wiley), p. 551.

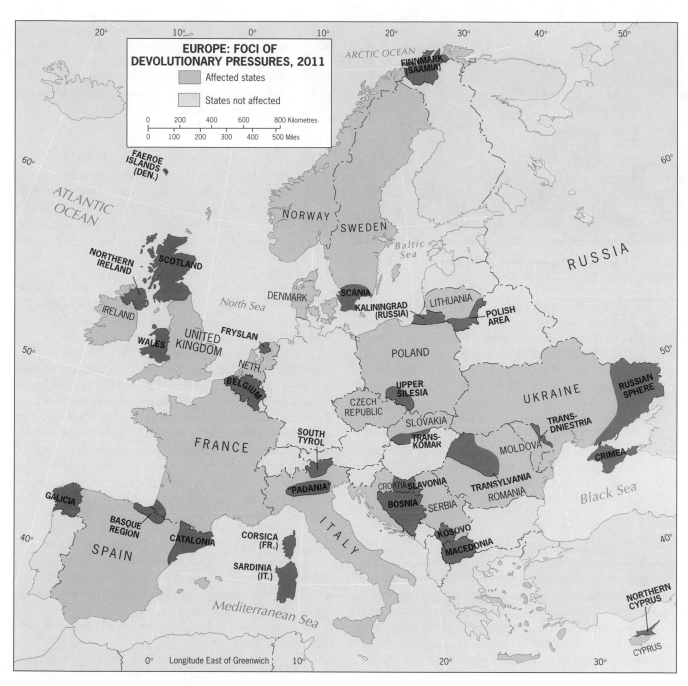

FIGURE 3.22 Europe: Foci of Devolutionary Pressures, 2011. (© H.J. de Blij, P.O. Muller, and John Wiley & Sons, Inc.)

revolutionary activities of the Tamil (Hindu) minority. Moreover, devolutionary forces are gaining momentum in places that have long looked stable from the outside. China's far west is a case in point, where Tibetan and Uyghur separatist movements are gaining momentum. The point is that ethnocultural differences are weakening the fabric of many states in today's global political framework. The trend appears to be in the direction of more, rather than fewer, calls for autonomy, or even independence.

In Canada, these ethnocultural devolutionary processes have been seen at critical junctures in Canadian history, particularly in relation to the province of Quebec. Nationalistic sentiments sent Quebec voters to the polls in two referendums,

in 1980 and 1995, seeking to gain enough support to secede from Canada. In each case, the "no" side, voting against secession, won the vote (by 59.56 percent in 1980, and by a very narrow margin of 50.58 percent in 1995).

The drive for Quebec's independence takes many forms, with some proposing a form of sovereignty association with Canada and others suggesting full independence as a separate nation-state. Beginning in the 1960s with the so-called Quiet Revolution, more radical and violent calls for Quebec independence emerged in the form of the Front de Libération du Québec (FLQ), an organization responsible for some 200 bombings and the deaths of five people (Figure 3.23). On October 5,

FIGURE 3.23 Quebec Student Rally in Support of the FLQ (undated). (Montreal Gazette/The Canadian Press)

1970, the FLQ kidnapped British trade commissioner James R. Cross; five days later they kidnapped, and later murdered, Quebec labour minister Pierre Laporte. The "October Crisis" continued, as Prime Minister Pierre Trudeau invoked the *War Measures Act* and sent the Canadian Army into Quebec to maintain order and protect public figures. The army withdrew on December 28, 1970. Since then, negotiations between the federal government and the province have sought some form of reconciliation. The Meech Lake and Charlottetown accords failed, but on November 27, 2006, the House of Commons passed a motion recognizing that "Québécois form a nation within a united Canada." Still, devolutionary forces grounded in ethnocultural sentiments are alive and well in Quebec.

ECONOMIC DEVOLUTIONARY FORCES

Devolutionary pressures often arise from a combination of sources. In Catalonia, Spain, ethnocultural differences play a significant role, but Catalonians also cite economics; with about 6 percent of Spain's territory and just 17 percent of its population, Catalonia produces some 25 percent of all Spanish exports by value and 40 percent of its industrial exports. Such economic strength lends weight to devolutionary demands based on Catalonian nationalism.

Economic forces play an even more prominent role in Italy and France. In Italy, Sardinia's demands for autonomy are deeply rooted in that island's economic circumstances, with accusations of neglect by the government in Rome high on the list of grievances. Italy also faces serious devolutionary forces on its mainland peninsula. One stems from regional disparities between the wealthy north and the poorer Mezzogiorno region to the south, below the Ancona Line (an imaginary border extending from Rome to the Adriatic coast at Ancona). Despite the large subsidies granted to the Mezzogiorno, the development gap between the north, very much a part of the European core, and the south, part of the European periphery, has been widening. Some Italian politicians have exploited widespread impatience with the situation by forming organizations to promote northern interests, including devolution. The most recent of these organizations was the Northern League, which raised

the prospect of an independent state called Padania in the part of Italy lying north of the Po River. After a surge of enthusiasm, the Padania campaign faltered. But it did push the Italian government to give more rights to the country's regions, moving it toward a more federal system.

SPATIAL INFLUENCES ON DEVOLUTION

We have seen how political decisions and cultural and economic forces can generate devolutionary processes in states. Devolutionary events have at least one feature in common: they most often occur on the margins of states. Note that every one of the devolution-affected areas shown in Figure 3.22 lies on a coast or on a border. Distance, remoteness, and marginal location are allies of devolution. The regions most likely to seek devolution are those far from the national capital. Many are separated by water, desert, or mountains from the centre of power and adjoin neighbours that may support separatist objectives.

Note also that many islands are subject to devolutionary processes: Corsica (France), Sardinia (Italy), Taiwan (China), Singapore (Malaysia), Zanzibar (Tanzania), Jolo (Philippines), Puerto Rico (United States), Mayotte (Comoros), and East Timor (Indonesia) are notable examples. Some of these islands became independent states, while others were divided during devolution. Insularity clearly has advantages for separatist movements.

Not surprisingly, the United States faces its most serious devolutionary pressures from the islands of Hawai'i. The year 1993 marked the hundred-year anniversary of the U.S. annexation of Hawai'i; in that year, a vocal minority of native Hawai'ians and their sympathizers demanded the return of rights lost during the "occupation." These demands included the right to reestablish an independent state called Hawai'i (before its annexation Hawai'i was a Polynesian kingdom) on several of the smaller islands. Their hope is that ultimately the island of Kauai, or at least a significant part of that island, which is considered ancestral land, will become a component of the independent Hawai'ian state.

At present, the native Hawai'ians do not have the numbers, resources, or influence to achieve their separatist aims. The potential for some form of separation between Hawai'i and the mainland United States does exist, however. The political geographer Saul Cohen theorized in 1991 that political entities situated in border zones between geopolitical powers may become gateway states, absorbing and assimilating diverse cultures and traditions and emerging as new entities, no longer dominated by one or the other. Hawai'i, he suggests, is a candidate for this status.

Spatial influences can play a significant role in starting and sustaining devolutionary processes. Distance can be compounded by differences in physical geography—a feeling of remoteness can be fuelled when people are isolated in a valley or separated by mountains or a river. Basic physical-geographic and locational factors can thus be key ingredients in the devolutionary process.

FIELD NOTE   Honolulu, Hawai'i

As I drove along a main road through a Honolulu suburb I noticed that numerous houses had the Hawai'i state flag flying upside down (Figure 3.24). I knocked on the door of this one house and asked the homeowner why he was treating the state flag this way. He invited me in and we talked for more than an hour. "This is 1993," he said, "and we native Hawai'ians are letting the state government and the country know that we haven't forgotten the annexation by the United States of our kingdom. I don't accept it, and we want our territory to plant our flag and keep the traditions alive. Why don't you drive past the royal palace, and you'll see that we mean it." He was right. The Iolani Palace, where the Hawai'ians' last monarch, Queen Liliuokalani, reigned until she was deposed by a group of American businessmen in 1893, was draped in black for all of Honolulu to see. Here was devolutionary stress on American soil.

FIGURE 3.24 Honolulu, Hawai'i. (© H.J. de Blij)

MAIN POINTS   3.3   How Is the Governance of States Spatially Organized?

- There are centrifugal and centripetal forces at play in any state. States seek to encourage a sense of unity through nation-building, territorial control, and strong state institutions and governance.

- Multination states can be classified as unitary or federal governments that are distinctive ways of organizing relationships between a central government and its constituent parts.

- While states attempt to create unity and stability, there are often internal pressures calling for the devolution of state power from central governments to a state's regions, provinces, or states. We have many examples of ethnocultural, economic, and spatial devolutionary movements.

3.4 How Do Geopolitics and Critical Geopolitics Help Us Understand the World?

Geopolitics is an area of study that considers the interplay between space, power, and international relations. In political science, for example, scholars tend to focus on governmental institutions, systems, and interactions in international relations. Geopolitics brings the importance of geography to the enquiry with a focus on locational considerations, environmental contexts, territorial perspectives, and spatial assumptions. Geopolitics helps us understand the arrangements and forces that are transforming the map of the world.

CLASSICAL GEOPOLITICS

Geopolitical study has a long history. Classical geopolitics of the late 19th and early 20th centuries generally fit into one of two camps: the German school, which sought to explain why certain states are powerful and how to become powerful; and the British school, which sought to offer strategic advice for states and explain why states interact the way they do. A few scholars tried to bridge the gap, blending the two schools, but for the most part the British school offers classic geostrategic perspectives on the world.

THE GERMAN SCHOOL

Why are certain states powerful, and how do states become powerful? The first political geographer who studied these issues was the German professor Friedrich Ratzel (1844–1904). Influenced by the writings of Charles Darwin, Ratzel postulated that the state resembles a biological organism whose life cycle extends from birth through maturity and, ultimately, decline and death. To prolong its existence, the state requires nourishment, just as an organism needs food. Such nourishment is provided by the acquisition of territories (what Ratzel deemed *lebensraum*) belonging to less-powerful competitors and by the people who live there. If a state is confined within permanent and static boundaries and deprived of overseas domains, Ratzel argued, it will atrophy. Territory is the state's essential, life-giving force. Unfortunately, some of Ratzel's German followers in the 1930s translated his abstract writings into policy recommendations that ultimately led to Nazi expansionism.

THE BRITISH SCHOOL

Not long after the publication of Ratzel's initial ideas, other geographers began studying the physical geographic map of the world with a view to determining where the most strategic places on Earth were located. Prominent among these geographers was Sir Halford J. Mackinder (1861–1947) of Oxford University whose ideas formed the foundation for the British school of classical geopolitics. In 1904, he published an article, "The Geographical Pivot of History," in the Royal Geographical Society's *Geographical Journal*. That article became one of the most intensely debated geographic publications of all time.

Mackinder was concerned with power relationships at a time when Britain had acquired a global empire through its strong navy. To many of his contemporaries, the oceans—the paths to colonies and trade—were the key to world domination, but Mackinder disagreed. He concluded that a land-based power, not a sea power, would ultimately rule the world. His famous article contained a lengthy appraisal of the largest and most populous land mass on Earth—Eurasia (Europe and Asia together). At the heart of Eurasia, he argued, lay an impregnable, resource-rich "pivot area" extending from eastern Europe to eastern Siberia (Figure 3.25). Mackinder issued a warning: if this pivot area became influential in Europe, a great empire could be formed.

Mackinder later renamed his pivot area the heartland, and his warning became known as the **heartland theory**. In his book *Democratic Ideals and Reality* (1919), Mackinder (calling

> **Heartland theory** A geopolitical hypothesis, proposed by British geographer Halford Mackinder during the first two decades of the twentieth century, that any political power based in the heart of Eurasia could gain sufficient strength to eventually dominate the world. Mackinder further proposed that since Eastern Europe controlled access to the Eurasian interior, its ruler would command the vast "heartland" to the east.

Eurasia "the World Island") issued a stronger warning to the winners of World War I, stating:

> *Who rules East Europe commands the Heartland*
> *Who rules the Heartland commands the World Island*
> *Who rules the World Island commands the World*

When Mackinder proposed his heartland theory, there was little to foretell the rise of a superpower in the heartland. Russia was in disarray, having recently lost a war against Japan (1905), and was facing revolution. Eastern Europe was fractured. Germany, not Russia, was gaining power. But when the Soviet Union emerged and World War II gave Moscow control over much of eastern Europe, the heartland theory attracted renewed attention.

In 1943, Mackinder wrote a final paper. He was concerned about the power wielded by Joseph Stalin in the Soviet Union and was worried the Soviet Union could exert control over the states of eastern Europe. He offered strategies for keeping the Soviets in check, including preventing the expansion of the Heartland into the Inner Crescent (Figure 3.25) and creating an alliance around the North Atlantic to join the forces of land and sea powers against the Heartland. Within the next 10 years, the United States began its containment policy (to stop the expansion of the Soviet Union), and the United States, Canada, and Western Europe formed an alliance called the North Atlantic Treaty Organization (NATO).

INFLUENCE OF GEOPOLITICS ON POLITICS

Ratzel and Mackinder are only two of many geographers who influenced international relations. Their writings, grounded in history, current events, and physical geography, sounded logical and influenced many politicians. In some ways, they still do. NATO still exists, and although it has not invited Russia to join the military alliance, it has extended membership to Eastern European states and is working in partnership with former republics of the Soviet Union.

Because of the influence of Ratzel's geopolitical theory on Adolf Hitler and his aspirations for a German homeland, the term "geopolitics" acquired a negative connotation. For some decades after World War II, the term was in such disrepute that few political geographers, even those studying the spatial implications of international power relationships, would identify themselves as students of geopolitics. Time, along with more balanced perspectives, has reinstated geopolitics as an appropriate name for the study of the spatial and territorial dimensions of power relationships past, present, and future.

CRITICAL GEOPOLITICS

Contemporary geographers engaged in geopolitical analysis do much less predicting and prescribing the spatial implications of state actions; instead they focus on revealing and explaining

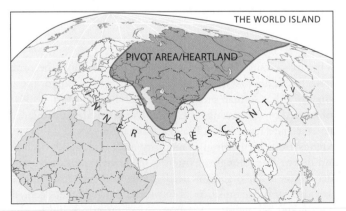

FIGURE 3.25 The Heartland Theory. The Pivot Area/Heartland, the Inner Crescent/Rimland, and the World Island described by Halford Mackinder.

the underlying spatial assumptions and territorial perspectives of politicians guiding state policy. Political geographers Gearoid O'Tuathail and John Agnew refer to the politicians in the most powerful states, the core states, as "intellectuals of statecraft." The basic concept behind today's **critical geopolitics** is that intellectuals of statecraft construct ideas about places, and these ideas, in turn, influence and reinforce their political behaviours and policy choices. The ideas also affect how we, the people, process our own notions of places and politics. In other words, critical geopolitics suggests that we need to be conscious of the political power relations driving our understanding of people, ideas, and places. If, for example, we conceptualize a place as "backward" or "primitive," we may then treat that place (and its peoples) in less than respectful ways.

> **Critical geopolitics** Process by which geopoliticians deconstruct and focus on explaining the underlying spatial assumptions and territorial perspectives of politicians.

In a number of publications, O'Tuathail has studied American geopolitical reasoning by examining the speeches and statements of U.S. intellectuals of statecraft regarding certain wars, certain places, and certain times. He has highlighted how American intellectuals of statecraft spatialize politics into a world of "us vs. them." By drawing on American cultural logic and certain representations of America, presidents have repeatedly defined an "us"

that is pro-democracy, independent, self-sufficient, and free, and a "them" that is in some way against all of these things.

During the Cold War (1945–1991), the United States and its allies were involved in a series of military, political, social, and economic clashes with the Soviet Union and its allies. In 1983, when the Cold War was escalating, then U.S. president Ronald Reagan coined the term "Evil Empire" for the Soviet Union and represented the United States as "the shining city on a hill," an example of the "us versus them" spatialization (Figure 3.26).

Over the last three presidencies, terrorism has replaced the Soviet Union as the "they." Sounding remarkably similar, Democratic president William J. Clinton and Republican president George W. Bush justified military actions against terrorists. In 1998, President Clinton explained American military action in Sudan and Afghanistan as a response to the terrorist plans, stating that the terrorists "come from diverse places but share a hatred for democracy, a fanatical glorification of violence, and a horrible distortion of their religion, to justify the murder of innocents. They have made the United States their adversary precisely because of what we stand for and what we stand against." Immediately after September 11, 2001, President George W. Bush exclaimed to the world, "They [the terrorists] stand against us because we stand in their way." Statements such as these are rooted in a particular geopolitical perspective on the world—one that divides the globe into opposing political

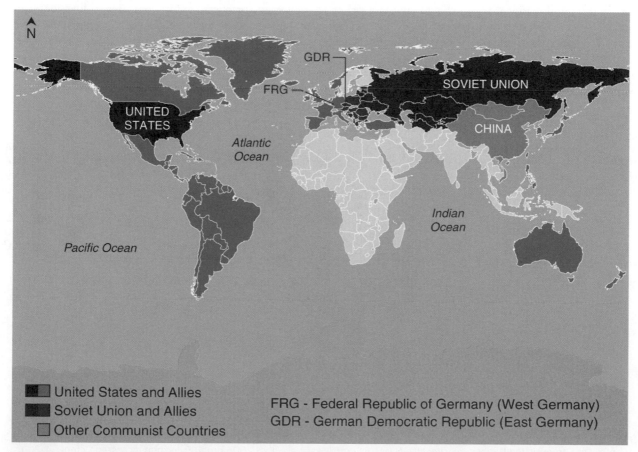

FIGURE 3.26 Map of the Cold War Countries. This map shows the various actors in the Cold War, and illustrates the clash in ideologies of the capitalist West and communist East. (Encarta)

camps. But critical geopolitics seeks to move beyond such differences to explore the spatial ideas and understandings that undergird particular political perspectives and shape policy approaches. The goal of critical geopolitics is to understand the ideological roots and implications of geopolitical reasoning by intellectuals of statecraft as they shape the policies that are pursued and affect what happens on the ground.

GEOPOLITICAL WORLD ORDER

Political geographers study the geopolitical world order—the temporary periods of stability in the way international politics are conducted. For example, during the Cold War, the geopolitical world order was bipolar—the Soviet Union versus the United States and its close allies, including Canada (see Figure 3.26). After a stable geopolitical world order breaks down, the world goes through a transition, eventually settling into a new geopolitical world order.

After the Soviet Union collapsed in 1991, the world entered a transitional period, where a range of world orders was possible. Politicians spoke optimistically about a new world order—one where a standoff of nuclear terror between two superpowers would no longer determine the destinies of states. Supposedly this new geopolitical order would be shaped by forces that connect nations and states—by supranational unions like the European Union (discussed in the next section of this chapter), and by multinational action should any state violate international rules of conduct. The risks of nuclear war would recede, and negotiation would replace confrontation. When Iraq was driven out of Kuwait by a United Nations coalition of states led by the United States in 1991, the framework of a new world order seemed to be taking shape. Russia, which a

few years earlier might have led the Soviet Union in support of Iraq, endorsed the United Nations operation. Arab as well as non-Arab forces helped repel the invaders.

Soon, however, doubts and uncertainties began to cloud hopes for a mutually co-operative geopolitical world order. Although states were more closely linked to each other than ever before, national self-interest still acted as a powerful force. For all its faults and changed circumstances, the state continued to function as a central building block in the new global framework. Nations wanted to become states, and many did—the number of United Nations members increased from 159 in 1990 to 184 by 1993 and 192 as of 2006 (Figure 3.27). The number and power of economic and social networks that extend across state borders increased. The new world order includes nonstate organizations, such as the World Trade Organization, with political and economic agendas that are not channelled through states—and are often spread across the world.

Some see the new geopolitical world order as one of **unilateralism**, with the United States in a position of hard-power dominance and with U.S. allies following rather than taking part in the political decision-making process. However, in the early 2000s the United States' unabashed unilateralism, its abandonment of traditional diplomatic practices, and its controversial invasion of Iraq significantly undermined its influence in many parts of the globe. Southeast Asian states that had long been oriented toward the United States began to turn away. A significant rift developed between the United States and some European countries, and anti-Americanism surged around the world. Challenges to

> **Unilateralism** World order in which one state is in a position of dominance with allies following rather than joining the political decision-making process.

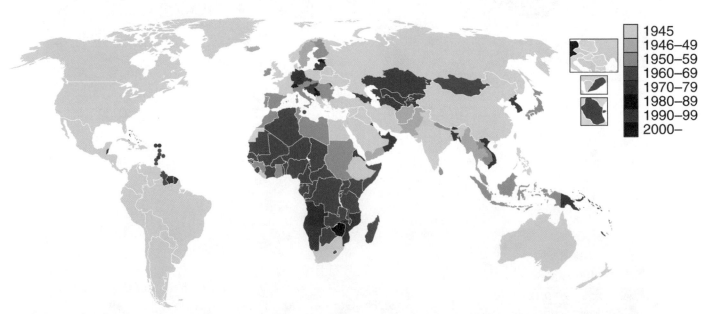

1945
1946–49
1950–59
1960–69
1970–79
1980–89
1990–99
2000–

FIGURE 3.27 United Nations Member Countries. This map illustrates the countries represented at the United Nations, colour-coded by year of entry. Data from United Nations website, http://www.un.org/News/Press/docs/2006/org1469.doc.htm. Accessed October 4, 2011.

American unilateralism also came from the processes of globalization, the diffusion of nuclear weapons, the emergence of China and India as global powers, the growth of terrorist groups, and the economic strength of the European Union.

Canada, despite its close economic and political ties to the United States, has strongly asserted its independence in international relations. For example, Canada did not join the United States in the Iraq War and continues to maintain open relations with Cuba. Canada is a strong proponent of multilateralism—it attempts to foster co-operation and alliance building when seeking solutions to international conflict. Canada is also known as a peacekeeping nation, heavily involved in sending troops to support United Nations efforts in troubled areas around the globe—though some would argue that Canada's peacekeeping role has been called into question in recent years, given its

combative activities in Afghanistan. Canada is often considered a "middle power" in international relations—a country that is not among the superpowers but that has sufficient international presence to be an important contributor in world issues.

When geopolitical strategists and intellectuals of statecraft predict future geopolitical orders, they often assume that individual states will continue to be the dominant actors in the international arena. Yet with the traditional powers of the state under increasing strain, other geopolitical arrangements may emerge. A new multi-polar order may arise, with states clustering together as regional forces; or, as we will discuss in Chapter 10, global cities may gain increasing power over issues typically addressed by states. In the final section of this chapter, we consider several other challenges to the state that may influence the next geopolitical order.

MAIN POINTS **3.4** How Do Geopolitics and Critical Geopolitics Help Us Understand the World?

- Classical geopolitics originated in Britain and Germany in the late 1800s. Practitioners were primarily interested in how states came into being and how they expanded and prospered. Halford Mackinder took a global view of the organization and relationships of states based on the idea that control of the Eurasian "pivot area" might lead to global domination.

- Classical geopolitics was very influential. Unfortunately, Hitler used Ratzel's ideas about state expansionism and territorial growth to justify attacking surrounding countries. Mackinder's ideas about a geographical heartland governed Western foreign policy well into the 1970s.

- Contemporary critical geopolitics focuses on the "intellectuals of statecraft" and considers how these individuals create various ideas or conceptualizations

- about relationships between states. These ideas then influence how we see, understand, and react to other peoples and states.

- The current geopolitical world order can be understood by examining the historical changes in power relations between states. During the Cold War years (1945–91), the geopolitical world order was bipolar, with the Soviet Union and the United States and its allies developing global spheres of influence.

- Today, the United States is the dominant world power with the ability to act unilaterally. Many argue this has been detrimental to global stability and contributed to a surge of anti-Western sentiment worldwide.

- Canada, as a middle power, is part of the global core.

3.5 What Are Supranational Organizations, and What Is the Future of the State?

Ours is a world of contradictions. Globalization, as George Ritzer defines it, is "an accelerating set of processes involving flows that encompass ever-greater numbers of the world spaces," which suggests we are seeing increasing integration and interconnectivity among different locations. Technological processes accelerate the flow of cultural traits (e.g., music or fashion) and political ideas into new and increasingly interconnected places. We seem to know more about each other and our feelings, desires, and ambitions, which should lead to

greater understanding, appreciation, and integration. Yet in many places, the opposite appears to be happening. Over the past couple of decades, some Québécois have demanded independence from Canada even as Canada joined the United States and Mexico in the North American Free Trade Agreement (NAFTA). At soccer games in Scotland, fans drown out "God Save the Queen" with a thunderous rendition of "Flower of Scotland," while in London, Parliament debates Britain's position on the European Monetary Union. At every turn we are reminded of the interconnectedness of nations, states, and regions, yet separatism and calls for autonomy are rampant. In the early years of the 21st century, we appear to be caught between the forces of division and those of unification.

Despite the conflicts arising from these contradictory forces, hardly a country exists today that is not involved in some

> **Supranational organization**
> A venture involving three or more nation-states involving formal political, economic, and/or cultural co-operation to promote shared objectives. The European Union is one such organization.

supranational organization. A **supranational organization** is an entity composed of three or more states that forge an association and form an administrative structure for mutual benefit and in pursuit of shared goals. The 20th century witnessed the establishment of numerous supranational associations in political, economic, cultural, and military spheres. States have now formed over 60 major supranational organizations (such as NATO and NAFTA), many of which have subsidiaries that bring the total to more than 100. The more states participate in such multilateral associations, the less likely they are to act alone in pursuit of a self-interest that might put them at odds with neighbours. Ample research has established that participation in a supranational entity is advantageous to the partners and that being left out can have serious negative effects on states and nations.

FROM LEAGUE OF NATIONS TO UNITED NATIONS

The modern beginnings of the supranational movement can be traced to conferences following World War I. Woodrow Wilson, president of the United States, proposed an international organization that would include all the states of the world (fewer than 75 states existed at that point). This led to the creation of the League of Nations in 1919 (Figure 3.28). In all, 63 states participated in the League, although the total membership at any single time never reached that number. Costa Rica

and Brazil left the League before 1930; Germany departed in 1933, shortly before the Soviet Union joined in 1934. In the mid-1930s, the League had a major opportunity when Ethiopia's Haile Selassie made a dramatic appeal for help in the face of an invasion by Italy, a member state until 1937. However, the League failed to take action, and in the chaos of the beginning of World War II, the organization collapsed.

Despite its demise, the League of Nations laid the groundwork for the formation of other international organizations. Between World War I and World War II, states created the Permanent Court of International Justice to adjudicate legal issues between states, such as boundary disputes and fishing rights. The League of Nations also initiated international negotiations on maritime boundaries and related aspects of the law of the sea. The conferences organized by the League laid the groundwork for the final resolution on the size of nations' territorial seas decades later.

After World War II, states formed a new organization to foster international security and co-operation: the United Nations (UN). Membership in the UN has grown significantly since its 1945 inception (see Figure 3.27). A handful of states still do not belong to the United Nations, but with the most recent additions in 2006, it now has 192 member states and manages a budget of about U.S. $4 billion, excluding peacekeeping efforts. The United Nations Security Council, the United Nations General Assembly, and their work are frequently in the news. The United Nations includes numerous other subsidiaries—some more visible than others—such as the Food and Agriculture Organization (FAO), United Nations Educational, Scientific and Cultural Organization (UNESCO), United Nations Children's Fund (UNICEF), and World Health Organization (WHO). Not all UN members participate in every subsidiary, but their work has benefited all humanity.

We can find evidence of the important work of the United Nations in the "world" section of any major newspaper. UN peacekeeping troops have helped maintain stability in some of the most contentious regions of the world (Figure 3.29). The UN High Commissioner on Refugees is called upon to aid refugees in crises throughout the world. UN documents on human rights standards, such as the Universal Declaration on Human Rights, the Covenant on Civil and Political Rights, and the Covenant on Economic and Social Rights, set precedents and laid the groundwork for countless human rights groups working in the world today.

By participating in the United Nations, states commit to upholding internationally approved standards of behaviour. Many states still violate the standards set out in the United Nations Charter, but such violations can lead to collective action (e.g., economic sanctions or Security Council-supported military action). Scholars of international relations and political geography point to UN actions in South Africa (against apartheid), Iraq (the Gulf War), and North Korea (preventing nuclear proliferation) as examples of the organization's success.

FIGURE 3.28 League of Nations. The first assembly of the League of Nations in Geneva, Switzerland, 1920. (UNOG Library, League of Nations Archives)

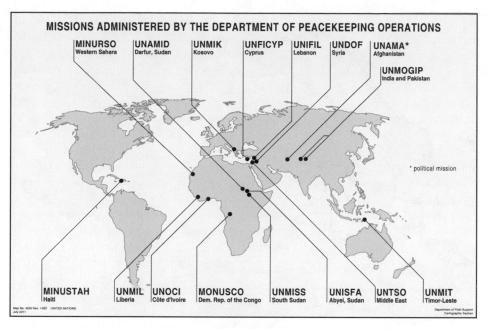

FIGURE 3.29 United Nations Peacekeeping Operations, 2011. This map depicts United Nations peacekeeping operations as at July 2011. There is no clear definition of "peacekeeping" in the UN Charter, leaving it a somewhat ambiguous, flexible term that can be interpreted differently over time and space. From missions administered by the Department of Peacekeeping Operations, Map No. 4259 Rev.14 (E), July 2011.

REGIONAL SUPRANATIONAL ORGANIZATIONS

The League of Nations and the United Nations are global manifestations of a phenomenon expressed even more strongly at the regional level. States organize supranational organizations at the regional scale to position themselves more strongly economically, politically, and even militaristically.

Belgium, the Netherlands, and Luxembourg undertook the first major modern experiment in regional economic co-operation. The three countries have much in common culturally and economically. Dutch farm products are sold on Belgian markets, and Belgian industrial goods go to the Netherlands and Luxembourg. During World War II, representatives of the three countries decided to create common tariffs and eliminate import licences and quotas. In 1944, even before the end of the war, the governments of the three states met in London to sign an agreement of co-operation, creating the Benelux (Belgium, the Netherlands, and Luxembourg) region.

Following World War II, U.S. secretary of state George Marshall proposed that the United States finance a European recovery program. A committee representing 16 Western European states, including what was then known as West Germany, presented the United States Congress with a joint program for economic rehabilitation, and Congress approved it. From 1948 to 1952, the United States gave Europe about $12 billion under the Marshall Plan. This investment revived European national economies and also spurred a movement toward co-operation among European states.

THE EUROPEAN UNION

From the European states' involvement in the Marshall Plan came the Organization for European Economic Co-operation (OEEC), which in turn gave rise to other co-operative organizations. Soon after Europe established the OEEC, France proposed the creation of a European Coal and Steel Community (ECSC), with the goal of lifting the restrictions and obstacles that impeded the flow of coal, iron ore, and steel among the mainland's six primary producers: France, West Germany, Italy, and the three Benelux countries. The six states entered the ECSC, and gradually, through negotiations and agreement, enlarged their sphere of co-operation to include reductions and even eliminations of certain tariffs and a freer flow of labour, capital, and non-steel commodities. This led, in 1958, to the creation of the European Economic Community (EEC).

The success of the EEC induced other countries to apply for membership. Denmark, Ireland, and the United Kingdom joined in 1973; Greece in 1981; and Spain and Portugal in 1986. The organization became known as the European Community (EC) because it began to address issues beyond economics. By the late 1980s, the EC had 12 members: the three giants (Germany, France, and the United Kingdom), the four southern countries (Italy, Spain, Portugal, and Greece), and the five small states (the Netherlands, Belgium, Luxembourg, Denmark, and Ireland). These 12 members initiated a program of co-operation and unification that led to the formal establishment of a European Union (EU) in 1992. In the mid-1990s, Austria, Sweden, and Finland joined the EU, bringing the total number of members to 15. Today there are 27 member countries in the European Union, with 4 "candidate" countries and 5 "potential candidate" countries (Figure 3.30).

In the late 1990s, the EU began preparing for the establishment of a single currency—the euro. First, all electronic financial transactions were denominated in euros, and on January 1, 2002, the EU introduced euro coins and notes. Not all EU member states are currently part of the euro-zone, but they may join soon as the euro begins to creep into their economies and as the euro gains strength against other global currencies.

The integration of 10 eastern European and Mediterranean island states into the European Union in 2004, and the addition of two more in 2007, are significant developments. Integration is a difficult process and often requires painful adjustments because of the diversity of the European states. For example,

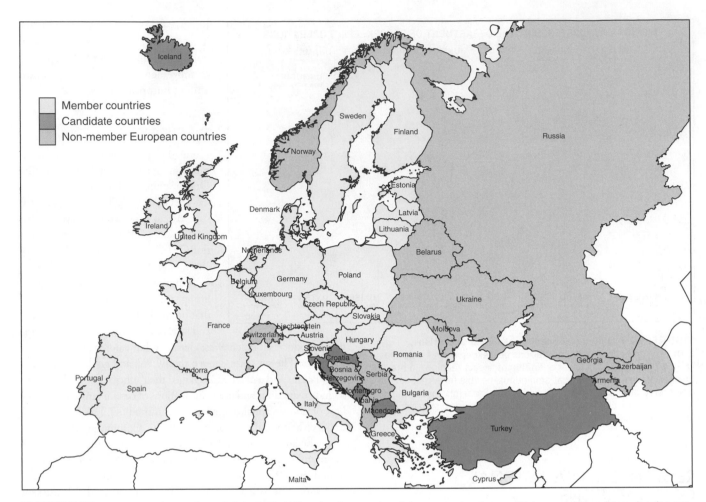

FIGURE 3.30 European Union (EU) as at July 2011. Yellow denotes member states, green denotes candidate countries, and grey denotes non-member European countries. Data from European Union website, http://europa.eu/about-eu/countries/index_en.htm. Accessed October 4, 2011.

agricultural practices and policies have always varied widely. Yet some general policy must govern agriculture throughout the European Union. Individual states have found these adjustments difficult at times, and the EU has had to devise policies to accommodate regional contrasts and delays in implementation. In addition, integration requires significant expenditures. Under the rules of the EU, the richer countries must subsidize (provide financial support to) the poorer ones; therefore, the entry of eastern European states adds to the financial burden on the wealthier western and northern European members.

Another concern is the loss of traditional state powers. The EU is a patchwork of states with many different ethnic traditions and histories of conflict and competition. Economic success and general well-being tend to submerge such differences, but in the face of difficult economic or social times, divisive forces can, and have, reasserted themselves. Moreover, as the EU grows, it becomes increasingly difficult for individual states to exert significant influence.

A current problem involves Turkey, which is a "candidate" state. Some western Europeans would like to see Turkey join the EU, thereby widening the organization's reach into the Muslim world. The government of Turkey has a strong interest

in joining, but many Greeks are hesitant to support Turkish integration for several reasons, though the main one is the long-standing dispute between Greece and Turkey over the island of Cyprus. Other EU members have expressed concerns about Turkey's human rights record, specifically its treatment of the Kurdish minority, which would not meet the standards set by the European Union. Behind these claims lies an unspoken sense among many that Turkey is not "European" enough to warrant membership. Moreover, the debate within the EU about Turkey has alienated many Turkish people, causing them to question their support for EU membership.

EU member states will determine future policies of the European Union. Since 2000, member states have rejected a constitution for the organization, while at the same time the European Union has become more activist in international affairs.

HOW DOES SUPRANATIONALISM AFFECT THE STATE?

Supranationalism is a worldwide phenomenon. Other economic associations, such as the North American Free Trade Agreement (NAFTA), the Association of Caribbean States (ACS), the

Central American Common Market, the Andean Group, the Southern Common Market (MERCOSUR), the Economic Community of West African States (ECOWAS), the Asia-Pacific Economic Cooperation (APEC), and the Commonwealth of Independent States (CIS), have drawn up treaties to reduce tariffs and import restrictions in order to ease the flow of commerce in their regions. Not all of these alliances are successful, but economic supranationalism is a sign of the times, a grand experiment still in progress.

Yet when we turn back to the European Union, we are looking at a supranational organization that is unlike any other. It is not a state, nor is it simply an organization of states. The European Union is remarkable in that it has taken on a life of its own—with a multi-faceted government structure, three capital cities, and billions of euros flowing through its coffers. The EU is extending its reach into foreign relations, domestic policies, and military policies, with sovereignty over certain issues moving from the states to the organization. In fact, citizens in the Benelux countries (the first members) and in regions where people have been disempowered by their state governments often identify more strongly with the European Union than with their state. With the EU, we may be witnessing a transformation in the political organization of space similar to the development of the modern state system in Europe in the 17th century.

Other major challenges to the state as we know it include the demands for independence from nations within states (discussed earlier), the proliferation of nuclear weapons, economic globalization, and increasing connectedness among people and cultures. These and similar developments raise questions about the logic, effectiveness, and even the necessity of the spatial organization of the world into states. Sociologist and urban geographer Manuel Castells became an important figure in articulating the shifting notions of geopolitical space and power in the age of digitization and the rise of the "network society." Castells sees the global shift that privileges information and communication technologies as a challenge to traditional hierarchies of nation-states. He believes power now resides in the "logic of the network" in and around emerging world cities such as New York, London, and Tokyo. According to Castells, it is in the "space of flows" of these global financial centres that the world economic order is structured, controlled, and maintained.

Nuclear weapons give even small states the ability to inflict massive damage on larger and distant adversaries. Combined with missile technology, this may be the most serious danger the world faces. This explains, in part, United Nations efforts to force the dismantling of Iraq's nuclear capacity after the 1991 Gulf War and international concerns about Iran's and North Korea's progress in the nuclear arms arena (Figure 3.31). Some states publicize their nuclear weapons programs, and others keep their nuclear abilities a carefully guarded secret. Reports of an enemy's nuclear proliferation have led to military actions

FIGURE 3.31 Anti-Nuclear Protest. Protestors in Seoul, South Korea, demonstrate against North Korea's nuclear test and missile launch in May 2009. North Korea announced that it had conducted a "successful" nuclear test, raising concerns and prompting calls for sanctions against the country and the impeachment of its leader, Kim Jong Il. (© Bloomberg/Getty Images)

in the last 30 years. For example, in 1981, when reports of Iraq's nuclear program reached Israel, the Israelis attacked Iraq. During the apartheid period, South Africa built nuclear weapons; adversaries India and Pakistan both possess nuclear weapons, and Iran may be building itself up as a nuclear power. As nuclear weapons have become smaller, and as "tactical" nuclear arms have been developed, the threat of nuclear weapons sales has to be taken seriously. It is now possible for a hostile state or group to purchase the power with which to threaten the world.

The state still provides the territorial foundations from which producers and consumers operate, and it continues to exert considerable regulatory powers. However, economic globalization (discussed in Chapter 2) makes it more difficult for states to control economic relations. States are responding to this situation in a variety of ways, with some giving up traditional regulatory powers and others seeking to insulate themselves from the international economy. Still others are working to build supranational economic blocs that they hope will help them cope with an increasingly globalized world. The impacts of many of these developments are as yet uncertain, but it is increasingly clear that states now compete with a variety of other forces in the international arena.

Some scholars argue that the state's traditional position is being further eroded by the globalization of social and cultural relations. Networks of interaction are being constructed in ways that do not correspond to the map of states. When unrest breaks out in southern Mexico, for example, activists use the Internet to contact interested people throughout the world. Increased mobility brings individuals from far-flung places into much closer contact than before. Paralleling all this change is the spread of popular culture in ways that make national borders virtually meaningless. Fans from Iceland to Australia listen to Céline Dion; fashions developed in northern Italy are hot items among Japanese tourists visiting Hawai'i; Thai restaurants are found in towns and cities across the United States; Russians hurry home to watch the next episode of soap operas made in Mexico; and movies produced in Hollywood are seen on screens from Mumbai to Santiago.

Another global phenomenon with major implications for a future world order is the role of religion as a force in global affairs. In Chapter 6 we note that extremist religious movements commit violent acts in the name of their faith. Whether at the local scale, with an individual acting alone, or at the global scale, with an entire network operating, violence by extremists challenges the state. The state's mission to defeat extremism often produces support for the state government in the short term, but the state's inability to defeat extremist attacks may weaken the state in the

long term. A wave of international terrorism toward western states began in the 1980s, with events such as the bombing of an airplane in Lockerbie, Scotland, in 1988. Terrorism came to dominate the international scene on September 11, 2001, with the attacks on the World Trade Center and the Pentagon and the downing of Flight 93 in Pennsylvania.

Globalization has produced economic, social, and cultural geographies that look less and less like the map of states. At the same time, nationalism continues to be a fundamental social force in the world today. The state system is unlikely to disappear anytime soon, but we are headed for a world in which the spatial distribution of power is more complex than the traditional map of states would suggest. Describing that spatial distribution will be a challenge for geographers for generations to come.

MAIN POINTS   3.5   What Are Supranational Organizations, and What Is the Future of the State?

- The nation-state remains a primary political and social institution for human organization despite globalizing processes and the emergence of supranational organizations.

- Since World War II, numerous supranational organizations have come into being. Some are economic, such as the World Trade Organization, while others have a broader mandate, such as the United Nations.

- Regional supranational organization between states are often designed to promote the economic interests of member states (e.g., European Economic Community) or

- to ensure they will come to each other's aid in the event of aggression by non-members (e.g., North Atlantic Treaty Organization [NATO]).

- Scholarship is divided on the state's traditional position given the emergence of supranational organizations. Some argue the state's traditional ability to control its own economic and political direction is being eroded. Others argue that the mutual aid, co-operation, and increased stability offered by such alliances will ensure a more peaceful globe. Whether this will be the result remains to be seen.

SUMMARY

Political geographers are interested in the political aspects of human-environment relations and how politics at a variety of scales have spatial implications. The primary unit of interest is the state, an entity exercising control over people occupying a bounded territory and recognized by other states. While we might take the idea of the state for granted, the modern concept of the state is less than 400 years old and, as an idea and ideology, was transported around the globe, primarily through colonialism, imperialism, and globalizing processes. The state may seem natural and permanent, but it is not. New states are still being recognized, and existing states are vulnerable to destructive forces.

We can only understand the current world order—the economic, social, and political relationships—by understanding the history of the modern nation-state and colonialism and imperialism. European explorers and adventurers travelled the globe, conquering various locales and divvying up

the spoils for the benefit of their home country. A world systems approach argues that, in a global economy, there is one global market and a global division of labour. Further, states in that world economy are currently organized in a three-tiered structure with a core, periphery, and semi-periphery. This results in uneven participation in the global economy for the benefit of some over others. Political geographers have a great deal to contribute to both understanding and finding solutions for those inequalities. Canada, despite its colonial beginnings and its continued reliance on resources, is part of the core.

Since World War II, a number of supranational organizations have emerged and changed the nature of the political and socio-economic relationships among states at local, regional, and national levels. While some approve of these changes, others do not. It remains to be seen how future geographies will evolve.

DISCUSSION AND REVIEW QUESTIONS

1. J.B. Harley (2001) observed that "As much as guns and warships, maps have been the weapons of imperialism." What does he mean by this and how does this relate to the specific example of George Dawson's mapping of the Queen Charlotte Islands.

2. "Nation" and "state" are concepts that often used interchangeably; however, to a political geographer they are not the same. Discuss how these concepts differ. Discuss the concept of a "nation-state"?

3. One of the strategies by which states promote unification is by choosing a governmental structure that promotes nation-building and mitigates internal divisions. Two such

structures are "unitary" and "federal." Explain these structures and identify which one most fits Canada. Has Canada's structure been successful?

4. Geopolitics is the branch of political geography that considers the interplay between space, power, and international relations. How has the study of geopolitics changed since its beginnings in late 19th-century Germany and Britain?

5. What is "supranationalism" and why has it become an important political-territorial strategy? Discuss the specific case of the European Union and how it is a historically unique form of supranationalism.

GEOGRAPHIC CONCEPTS

boundary   54
centrifugal   70
centripetal   70
colonialism   66
critical geopolitics   77
devolution   72
federal   71
geometric boundary   57
heartland theory   76
mercantilism   62
multinational state   65
multistate nation   65
nation   60
nation-state   63

nationalism   63
Peace of Westphalia   62
physical-political boundary   58
political geography   51
scale   69
sovereignty   53
state   51
stateless nation   65
supranational organization   80
territorial integrity   54
territoriality   53
unilateralism   78
unitary   71

ADDITIONAL RESOURCES ONLINE

About Canada's peacekeeping operations: www.international.gc.ca/peace-paix/index.aspx

About the case of the stateless citizen: www.cbc.ca/thecurrent/2010/10/oct-710---pt-3-citizens-of-nowhere.html

About the countries of the world: lcweb2.loc.gov/frd/cs/cshome.html

About the European Union: europa.eu/index_en.htm

About international refugees: www.refugeesinternational.org

About nationalism: www.nationalismproject.org

About political geography: www.politicalgeography.org

Colonialism, *The Story of India*, PBS: www.pbs.org/thestoryofindia

Cuban Missile Crisis: The Other Side of Armageddon: www.bbc.co.uk/bbcfour/documentaries/features/cuban-missile-crisis.shtml

Devolution: Slovakia: New Sovereignty. Click on "Video

on Demand": www.learner.org/resources/series180.html#program_descriptions

International Boundaries: Boundaries and Borderlands. Click on "Video on Demand": www.learner.org/resources/series180.html#program_descriptions

October Crisis: Action: The October Crisis of 1970: www.onf-nfb.gc.ca/eng/collection/film/?id=10471

Refugees and territorial disputes: CBC Doczone: Darfur: On Our Watch: www.cbc.ca/doczone/darfur/

Supranationalism and the European Union: Strasbourg: Symbol of a United Europe. Click on "Video on Demand": www.learner.org/resources/series180.html#program_descriptions

The United Nations in Rwanda: *Shake Hands with the Devil: The Journey of Roméo Dallaire*: www.whitepinepictures.com/dallairesite/

The U.S.-Mexico Barrier: Border Stories: A Mosaic Documentary: http://borderstories.org

chapter 4

POPULATION

Where Are the Children?

MY MIND WAS on wine. I was in Bordeaux, France, walking down the street to the Bordeaux Wines Museum (Musée des Vins de Bordeaux) with a friend from the city. Having just flown from Dakar, Senegal, after spending several weeks in sub-Saharan Africa, I found my current surroundings strikingly different. Observing the buildings and the people around me, I noticed that after having been among so many young children in sub-Saharan Africa, the majority of the inhabitants I encountered in Bordeaux represented an aging population.

I turned to my friend and asked, "Where are all the children?"

He looked around, pointed, and replied, "There goes one now!"

In Bordeaux, in Paris, in all of France and the rest of Europe, there are fewer children and populations are aging (Figure 4.1). To reach replacement levels—to keep a population stable over time without immigration—the women of childbearing age in a country need a total fertility rate (TFR) of 2.1. The TFR reports the average number of children born to a woman of childbearing age. At the beginning of this century, more than 60 countries, containing 45 percent of the world's population, had fallen below this replacement level (Figure 4.2).

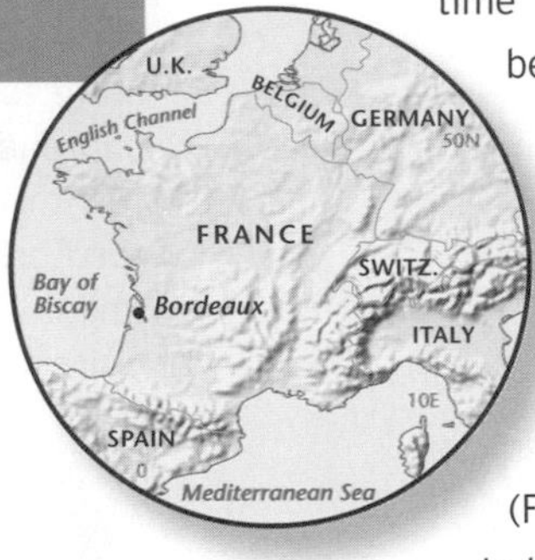

In the 1980s, in the midst of a population explosion, Kenya recorded one of the highest TFRs ever, 8.1. Today, parts of Italy are recording the lowest TFRs ever, as low as 0.8 in Bologna. Not a single country in Europe is above replacement levels at present. By 2030, people over 65 may well account for nearly half the adult population in Germany, as compared with one-fifth now. Many other European countries are on a similar trajectory, and even countries with large populations, such as Brazil and China, will likely experience substantial aging of the population as their growth rates decline.

Why are women having fewer children? In wealthier countries, more women are choosing to stay in school, work on careers, and marry later, delaying childbirth. Couples worry about the higher cost of raising children and delay starting a family in order to be better prepared financially. In some countries, such as China, governments are administrating lower birth rates. In other countries, such as India, the cultural costs associated with having children, such as providing

FIGURE 4.1 Bordeaux. People stroll through the historic streets of Bordeaux, France. (© H.J. de Blij)

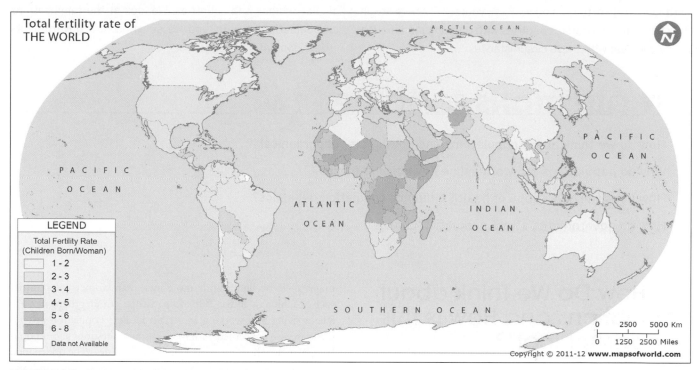

FIGURE 4.2 Total Fertility Rate of the World, 2009. This map indicates the expected number of births per woman in her childbearing years for the year 2009. (Copyright © 2009 www.mapsoftheworld.com)

dowries for girls, are resulting in higher abortion rates, particularly if the woman is pregnant with a girl.

An aging population requires substantial social adjustments. Older people retire and eventually suffer health problems, so they need pensions and medical care. The younger people in the population must work in order to provide the tax revenues to enable the state to pay for these services. As the proportion of older people in a country increases, it means there are fewer young workers providing tax revenues to support programs that offer services for the growing number of retired people. To change the age distribution of an aging country and provide more taxpayers, the only answer is immigration: influxes of younger foreign workers to do the work locals are unable (or unwilling) to do. Yet immigration can create its own set of social issues, as has already happened in Germany with its large increase in Turkish and Kurdish immigration, in France with its Algerian-Muslim influx, and in the United States with the arrival of immigrants from Latin America.

What will happen when a country resists immigration despite an aging population? Over the next half century, Japan will be an interesting case study. Japan's population is no longer growing, and projections indicate the population will decline as it ages, falling from just over 128 million in 2008

to around 100 million in 2050 (some predictions are lower). Japan was a closed society for hundreds of years, and even today the Japanese government discourages immigration and encourages homogeneity of the population. More than 98 percent of the country's population is Japanese, according to government statistics. The British newspaper *The Guardian* reported that the Japanese government's efforts to maintain the homogeneity of the population are often "lauded domestically as a reason for the country's low crime rate" and strong industrial economy.

Today, TFRs are falling almost everywhere on Earth, in large part because of access to birth control. In some countries, fertility rates are declining dramatically. Kenya's TFR is now down to 4.8; China's fell from 6.1 to 1.75 in just 35 years. Once the government of Iran began to allow the use of birth control, the TFR fell from 6.8 in 1980 to 1.7 in 2008.

Having a low TFR was once a status symbol—a goal few governments were able to reach. Realizing now that a young, working population is a necessity for providing tax revenues to support the aging population, governments are getting creative. Countries that desire a larger, younger population, such as Sweden, are providing major financial incentives, like year-long paid maternity leaves and state-funded daycare, to encourage women to have children. These programs have had limited success in encouraging sustained population growth. When you walk down the streets of Stockholm, Sweden, or Bordeaux, France, today, you may ask yourself, "Where are all the children?" Of course, countries with a strong immigration policy can deal with these circumstances.

In this chapter, we discuss where people live and why they live where they do. We also examine the rising world population and contrast it with the aging population in particular regions and countries. We look at the ramifications of population change, and we question how governments affect population change.

KEY QUESTIONS FOR CHAPTER 4

1. How do we think about populations and how is this "geographical"?
2. Why do populations grow or decline in particular places?
3. How does the geography of health influence population dynamics?
4. How do governments affect population change?

4.1 How Do We Think about Populations and How Is This "Geographical"?

Wilbur Zelinsky, a prominent cultural geographer, argues that, as geographers, we need to ask questions about where people live and why they live where they do. We need to think about how many and what sorts of people inhabit different parts of the world. If patterns emerge (or if they do not), we need to understand what meanings lie behind these areal patterns. We must also ask much more troubling questions: Where do people die, when do they die, how, and why? Clearly embedded in these questions are our spatial perspectives—location, region, landscape, place, and movement. Populations have distinctive locations and regions, they create distinctive landscapes and places, and, as we discuss in Chapter 5, populations migrate, relocate, and alter locations as they move from place to place.

Population geographers, working with demographic information, are concerned with spatial variations in distinctive populations. **Demography** is the study of the characteristics of a population, such as race, age, sex, and ethnicity. Geographers ask questions about the number of men and women in a particular population, or the number of elderly people compared with the number of young. **Population geography** focuses on why populations have certain characteristics and why they distribute themselves across space in particular ways. Once we understand the characteristics of populations and their locations, other questions arise. Why are some populations aging more quickly than others (as is the case in France, discussed in the opening field note)? Why

> **Demography** The study of the characteristics of a population, such as race, age, sex, and ethnicity.
>
> **Population geography** The study of why populations have certain characteristics and why they distribute themselves across space in particular ways.

might there be significantly more men than women in countries such as China or India? Why do particular ethnic groups seem to favour living and working in certain locales? Population geographers are also concerned with more abstract questions about populations, such as how the term "population" comes to be understood as an object or a "thing," who becomes part of a "population," and how these "populations" are regulated and controlled through state policy and governance.

Before we can begin to work through some of these more detailed questions, we need to compile and understand a few basic facts about the populations we are interested in studying. Population geographers undertake basic calculations about a particular population, such as population density, population distribution, and population composition. This information provides the starting point for considering the complex spatial organization and movement of populations.

POPULATION DENSITY

Demographers report the **population density** of a country as a measure of total population in relation to total land area. They usually calculate density as the number of people located in a particular territorial unit—usually a square kilometre. Population density assumes an even distribution of the population over the total land or territory in question. Clearly, populations are rarely evenly distributed as people tend to congregate within favourable environments, such as near water or on major transportation routes. In 2005, Canada had a population density of 3.5 people per square kilometre, one of the lowest densities in the world. In the United States, the population density is 31 people per square kilometre (9 times higher); France has 109 people per square kilometre (31 times higher), and the United Kingdom has 246 people per square kilometre

> **Population density** A measurement of the number of people per given unit of land.

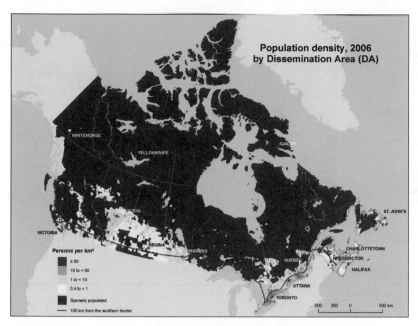

FIGURE 4.3 **Population Density Map of Canada, 2006.** The most populated areas are within 210 kilometres of the Canada–U.S. border. (Statistics Canada Population and Dwelling Counts, 2006 Census, Catalogue 97-550-XWE2006001, http://www12. statcan.ca/census-recensement/2006/as-sa/97-550/vignettes/m1-eng.htm)

Arithmetic population density The population of a country or region expressed as an average per unit area. The figure is derived by dividing the population of the areal unit by the number of square kilometres or miles that make up the unit.

(70 times higher). This density figure is also known as the country's **arithmetic population density**—a simple calculation that divides the total land area by the number of people in that area. For example, a region that is 100 square kilometres with 10 people has 1 person for every 10 square kilometres.

No country has an evenly distributed population, and arithmetic population figures do not reflect the sparse population in northern Canada or the fact that two out of three Canadians live within 210 kilometres of the Canada–U.S. border (Figure 4.3). Prince Edward Island has the highest population density with 23.9 people per square kilometre; Yukon has the lowest at 0.01 people per square kilometre. In other cases, an arithmetic calculation is actually quite misleading. Egypt, with a population of 78.6 million in 2008, has a seemingly moderate arithmetic population density of 78 people per square kilometre. However, Egypt's territory of just over 1 million square kilometres is mostly desert, and the vast majority of the population is crowded into the valley and delta of the Nile River. An estimated 98 percent of all Egyptians live on just 3 percent of the country's land, so the arithmetic population density figure is meaningless (Figure 4.4).

PHYSIOLOGIC POPULATION DENSITY

Given that populations are unevenly dispersed within a territory, with most people residing in places that are more hospitable to human life, a superior index of population density relates the total population of a country or region to the area of arable (farmable) land it contains. The **physiologic population density**, defined as the number of people per unit area of agriculturally productive land, gives us a much better sense of how people are distributed. When we measure the entire population of Egypt relative to the arable land in the country, the resulting physiologic density figure for Egypt in the year 2008 is 2,616 people per square kilometre—a density illustrated so well by Figure 4.4. This number is far more reflective of Egypt's population pressure, and it continues to rise rapidly despite Egypt's efforts to expand its irrigated farmlands.

Physiologic population density The number of people per unit area of arable land.

Appendix B, at the end of this book, provides complete data on both arithmetic and physiologic population densities, calculated using a land area measure in square kilometres. Some of the data stand out markedly. Mountainous Switzerland's high physiologic density should be expected: it is 10 times as high as its arithmetic density. But note Ukraine, with its vast farmlands: its physiologic density is only 1.7 times as high as its arithmetic density. Also compare the high physiologic densities in Central America (see Puerto Rico) to the moderate data for South America, where Argentina has one of the lowest indices in the world. Furthermore, note that India's physiologic density is the lowest in South Asia despite its huge population (and is less

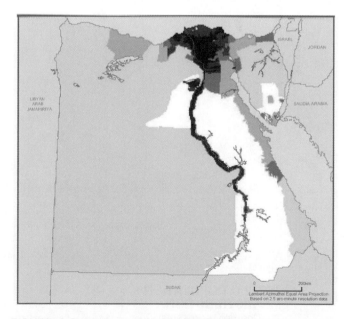

FIGURE 4.4 **Population Density of Egypt, 2000.** The population is situated mainly along the valley and delta of the River Nile. (Center for International Earth Science Information Network (CIESIN), Columbia University and Centro Internacional de Agricultura Tropical (CIAT), 2005. Gridded Population of the World Version 3 (GPWv3). Palisades, NY: NASA Socioeconomic Data and Applications Center (SEDAC), CIESIN, Columbia University, http://sedac.ciesin.columbia.edu/gpw.)

FIELD NOTE
Yangon, Myanmar (Burma)

An overpass across one of Yangon's busy streets provides a good perspective on the press of humanity in lowland Southeast Asia (Figure 4.5). Whether in urban areas or on small back roads in the countryside, people are everywhere—young and old, fit and infirm. When population densities are high in areas of poverty and unsophisticated infrastructure, vulnerability to natural hazards can be particularly great. This became stunningly evident in 2008 when a tropical cyclone devastated a significant swath of the Irrawaddy Delta south of Yangon, killing some 100,000 people and leaving millions homeless.

FIGURE 4.5 Yangon, Myanmar (Burma). (© Alexander B. Murphy)

FIGURE 4.6 World Population Distribution. (© H.J. de Blij, P.O. Muller, and John Wiley & Sons, Inc.)

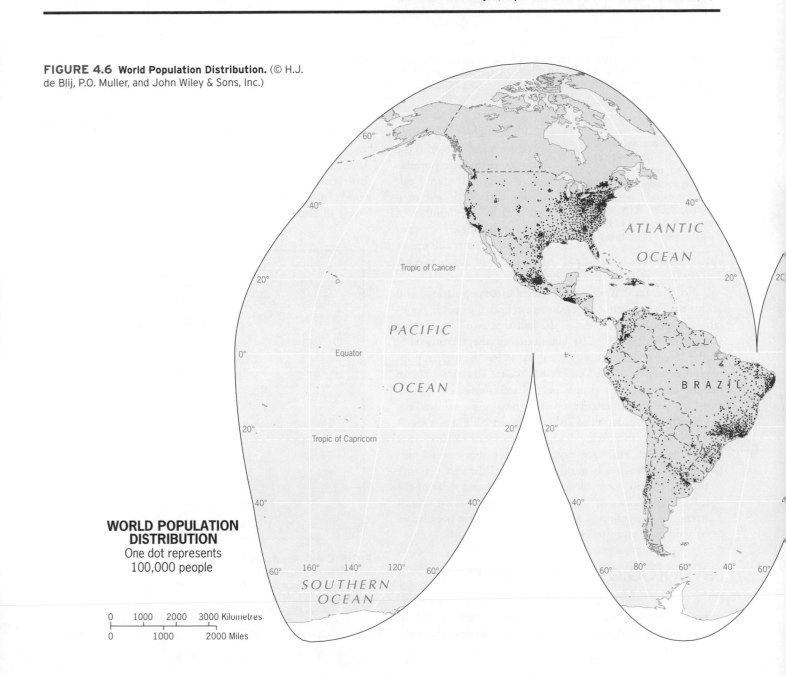

WORLD POPULATION DISTRIBUTION
One dot represents 100,000 people

than twice as high as its arithmetic density), whereas China's physiologic density in 2008 was some 40 percent higher than India's. Both China and India have populations well over 1 billion, but according to the physiologic density, India has much more arable land per person than China. Canada has an arithmetic population density of 3 and a physiologic density of 66. Contrast this to Russia with 8 and 137 respectively, the United States with 31 and 157, Europe with 32 and 157, and Haiti with 321 and 971.

POPULATION DISTRIBUTION

People are not distributed evenly across the world or within a country. One-third of the world's population lives in China and India. Yet each country has large expanses of land where people are absent or sparsely distributed (the Himalayas in

India and a vast interior desert in China). In addition to studying population densities, geographers study **population distributions**, which describe where on the Earth's surface individuals or groups (depending on the scale) live. Canada's population distribution shows Canadians live close to the Canada–U.S. border and are clustered around major urban areas. Geographers often represent population distributions on **dot maps**, in which one dot represents a certain number of people or objects. At the local scale, for example, a dot map of population can show each individual farm in a sparsely populated rural area. At the global scale, the data are much more generalized (see Figure 4.6).

Population distribution Description of locations on the Earth's surface where populations live.

Dot maps Maps where one dot represents a certain number of a phenomenon, such as a population.

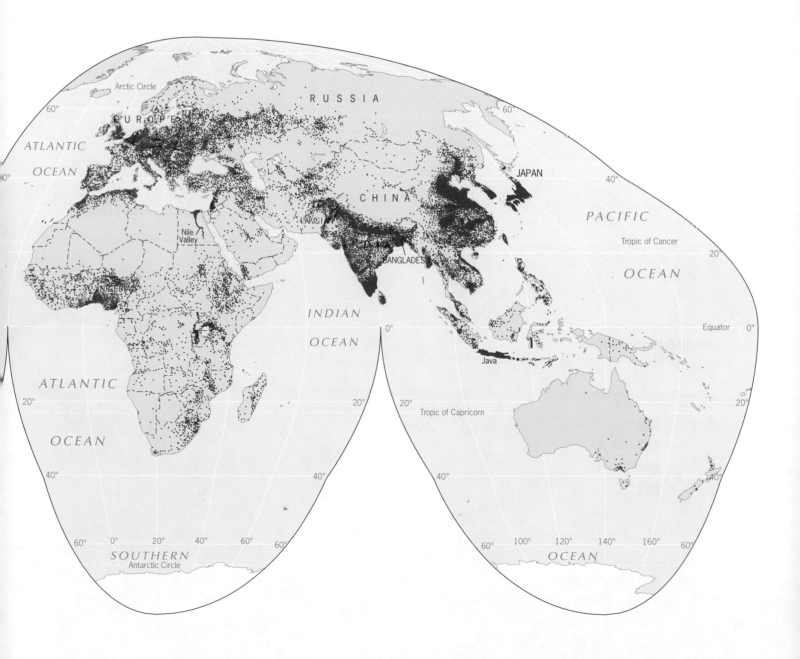

WORLD POPULATION DISTRIBUTION AND DENSITY

From the beginning, people have been unevenly distributed across the globe. Today, contrasts between crowded countrysides and bustling cities on the one hand and empty reaches on the other hand have only intensified. Historically, people tended to congregate in those parts of the world where they could grow food. This meant there was a high correlation between arable land and population density. Cities began in agricultural areas, and for most of our existence, people lived closest to the most agriculturally productive areas. Recent advances in agricultural technology and in transportation of agricultural goods have begun to change this pattern.

In Figure 4.6, where each dot on the map represents 100,000 people, three major clusters of population jump out:

East Asia, South Asia, and Europe. Each of the three largest population clusters is on the Eurasian (Europe and Asia combined) landmass. The fourth largest is in North America.

EAST ASIA

Although the distribution map (Figure 4.6) requires no colour contrasts, Figure 4.7 depicts population density through shading: the darker the colour, the larger the number of people per unit area. The most extensive area of dark shading lies in East Asia, primarily in China but also in Korea and Japan. Almost one-quarter of the world's population is concentrated here—over 1.3 billion people in China alone. In addition to high population density in China's large cities, ribbons of high population density extend into the interior along the Yangtze and Yellow River valleys (Figure 4.8). Farmers along China's major river valleys produce

FIGURE 4.7 **World Population Density.** (© E.H. Fouberg, A.B. Murphy, H.J. de Blij, and John Wiley & Sons, Inc.)

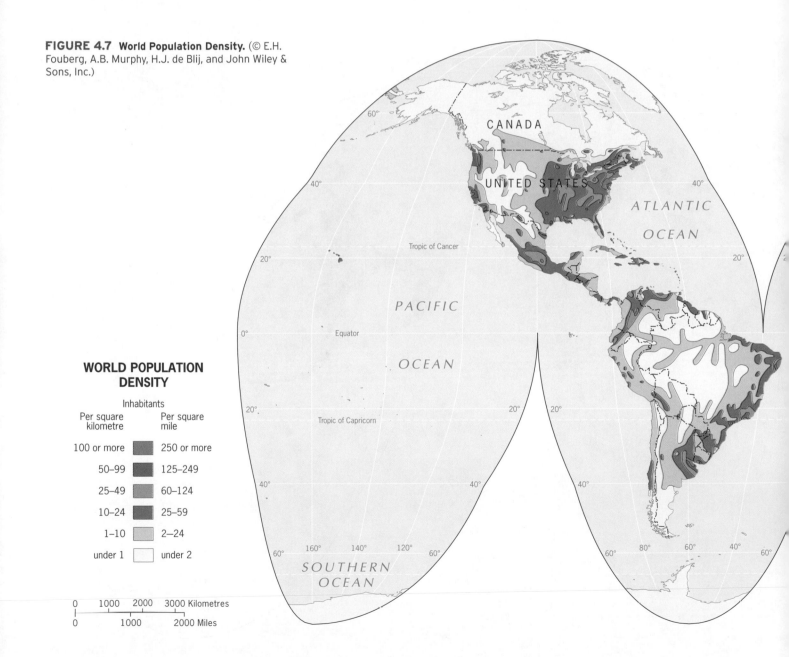

WORLD POPULATION DENSITY

Inhabitants

Per square kilometre		Per square mile
100 or more		250 or more
50–99		125–249
25–49		60–124
10–24		25–59
1–10		2–24
under 1		under 2

0   1000   2000   3000 Kilometres
0   1000   2000 Miles

crops of wheat and rice to feed not only themselves but also the population of major Chinese cities such as Shanghai and Beijing.

SOUTH ASIA

The second major population concentration also lies in Asia and is similar in many ways to that of East Asia. At the heart of this cluster of more than 1.5 billion people lies India. The concentration extends into Pakistan and Bangladesh and onto the island of Sri Lanka. Here, people again cluster in major cities, on the coasts, and along rivers, such as the Ganges and Indus.

Two physical barriers create the boundaries of the South Asia population cluster: the Himalayan Mountains to the north, and the desert west of the Indus River Valley in Pakistan. This is a confined region with a rapidly growing population. As in East Asia, the overwhelming majority of the people are farmers, but in South Asia the

pressure on the land is even greater. Over large parts of Bangladesh, the rural population density is between 1,153 and 1,922 people per square kilometre. By comparison, in 2006, the population of Alberta was just under 3 million people, and the rural population density was well under 12 people per square kilometre.

EUROPE

A band of dense population extends from Ireland and Great Britain into Russia, encompassing large parts of Germany, Poland, Ukraine, and Belarus and including the Netherlands and Belgium, parts of France, and northern Italy. This European cluster contains over 715 million inhabitants, less than half the population of the South Asia cluster. A comparison of the population density and physical maps indicates that in Europe, terrain and environment are not as closely related to population

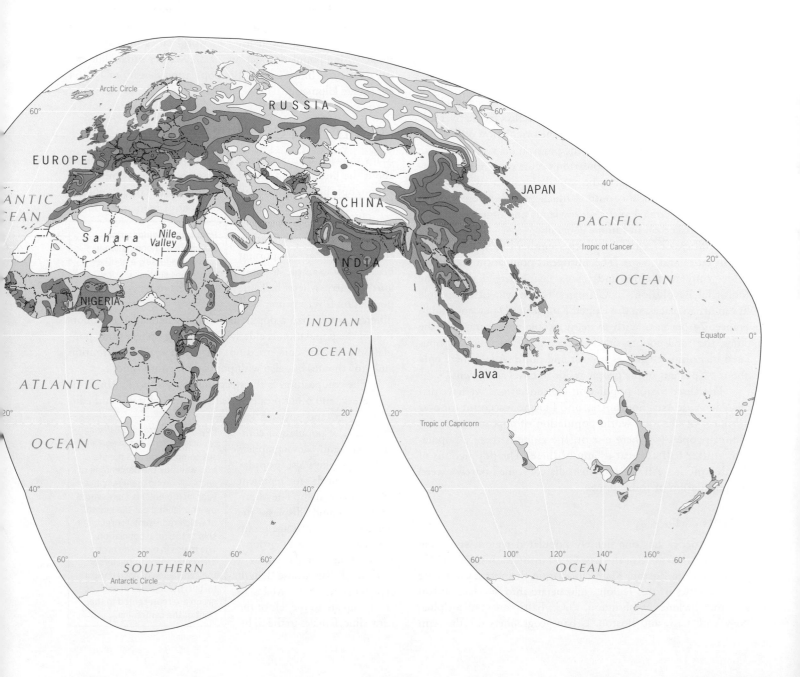

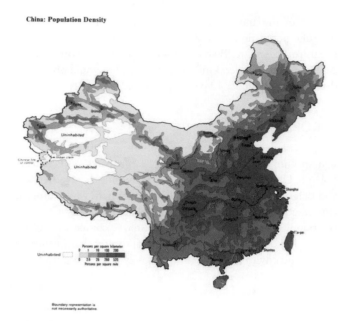

China: Population Density

Persons per square kilometer
0   10   100   200

Persons per square mile
0   2.6   26   260   520

Boundary representation is
not necessarily authoritative.

FIGURE 4.8 China, Population Density. (Courtesy of the University of Texas Libraries, The University of Texas at Austin)

distribution as they are in East and South Asia. For example, note the population density "protrusion" into Russia in Figure 4.7. Unlike the Asian protrusions, which reflect fertile river valleys, the European extension reflects the orientation of Europe's coalfields. If you look closely at the physical map, you will note that comparatively dense population occurs even in mountainous, rugged country, such as the boundary zone between Poland and its neighbours to the south. A much greater correspondence exists between coastal and river lowlands and high population density in Asia than in Europe generally.

Another contrast is seen in the number of Europeans who live in cities and towns. The European population cluster includes numerous cities and towns that emerged during the Industrial Revolution. In Germany, 88 percent of the people live in urban places, in the United Kingdom, 89 percent, and in France, 74 percent. With so many people concentrated in the cities, the rural countryside is more open and sparsely populated in Europe than it is in East and South Asia (where only about 30 percent of the people reside in cities and towns).

The three major population concentrations we have discussed—East Asia, South Asia, and Europe—account for over 4 billion of the total world population of approximately 6.7 billion people. Nowhere else on the globe is there a population cluster half as great as any of these. The populations of South America, Africa, and Australia combined barely exceed the population of India alone.

NORTH AMERICA

North America has one densely populated region, stretching along the urban areas of the East Coast from Washington, D.C., in the south to Boston, Massachusetts, in the north. On Figure 4.7, the cities in this region agglomerate into one large urban area that includes Washington, D.C., Baltimore, Philadelphia, New York City, and Boston. Urban geographers use the term **megalopolis** to refer to such huge urban agglomerations. The cities of this megalopolis account for more than 20 percent of the U.S. population. In Canada, as of 2006, roughly 80 percent of Canadians live in urban areas.

If you examine the global scale map in Figure 4.7, you will notice the dense population concentration of a megalopolis that includes the Canadian cities of Toronto, Ottawa, Montreal, and Quebec City. Adding these Canadian cities to the population of the megalopolis creates a population cluster that is about one quarter the size of Europe's population cluster. If you have lived or travelled in a megalopolis, you can think about traffic and comprehend what dense population means. However, the total population of the megalopolis is 2.8 percent of the East Asian population cluster, and the 10,194 people per square kilometre density of New York City does not rival the density in world cities like Mumbai, India, with a population density of 22,922 per square kilometre, or Jakarta, Indonesia, with a population density of 14,464 per square kilometre.

> **Megalopolis** Large coalescing supercities that are forming in diverse parts of the world; formerly used specifically with an uppercase "M" to refer to locations such as the Boston–Washington multimetropolitan corridor on the northeastern seaboard of the United States.

POPULATION COMPOSITION

Maps showing distribution and density of populations tell us about the number and organization of people in a country or region, but they do not reveal the characteristics of those populations, such as, for example, the number of men and women, or their ages. These aspects of population, the **population composition**, are important because, for example, a populous country where half the population is very young faces different issues than a populous country where a large proportion of the population is elderly. When geographers study populations, they are concerned not only with spatial distribution and growth rates but also with population composition.

The composition is the structure of a population in terms of age, sex, and other properties such as marital status and education. Age and sex are key indicators of population composition, and demographers and geographers use **population pyramids** to represent these traits visually. The population pyramid displays the percentages of each age group (normally five-year groups) in the total population by a horizontal bar whose length represents its share. Males in the group are to the left of the centreline, females to the right.

> **Population composition** Structure of a population in terms of age, sex, and other properties such as marital status and education.

> **Population pyramids** Visual representations of the age and sex composition of a population whereby the percentage of each age group (generally five-year increments) is represented by a horizontal bar the length of which represents its relationship to the total population. The males in each age group are represented to the left of the centre line of each horizontal bar; the females in each age group are represented to the right of the centre line.

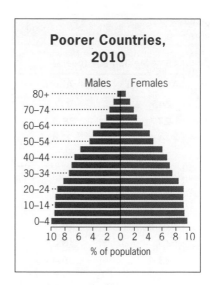
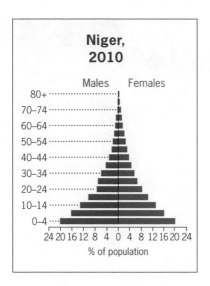
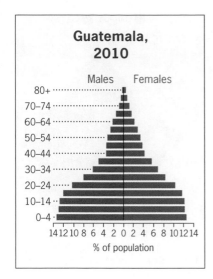

FIGURE 4.9 Age-Sex Population Pyramids for Countries with High Population Growth Rates. Countries with high total fertility rates, high infant mortality rates and low life expectancies will have population pyramids with wide bases and narrow tops. Data from United Nations Population Division, *World Population Prospects: The 2010 Revision*.

A population pyramid can instantly convey the demographic situation in a country. In the poorer countries, where birth and death rates generally remain high, the pyramid looks like an evergreen tree, with wide branches at the base and short ones near the top (Figure 4.9). The youngest age groups have the largest share of the population; in the composite pyramids in Figure 4.9, the three groups up to age 14 account for more than 30 percent. Older people, in the three highest age groups, represent only about 4 percent of the total. Slight variations of this pyramidal shape mark the population structure of such countries as Niger and Guatemala. From the 15-to-19 age group upward, each group is smaller than the one below it.

In countries with economic wealth, the pyramid shapes change. Families become smaller, children fewer. A composite population pyramid for wealthier countries looks like a slightly lopsided vase, with the largest components of the population in the middle. The middle-age bulge is moving upward, reflecting the aging of the population (Figure 4.10) and the declining total fertility rate (TFR). Overall, wealthier countries fit into this pyramid mode, including Italy, France, and the United States.

The Canadian population pyramid (Figure 4.11) demonstrates that the Canadian population is aging, given that the base of the pyramid is smaller than the middle. In 2006, the median age in Canada reached 38.8, the highest it has ever been. Statistics Canada projects that by the year 2056, this median age will reach 46.9 years. The largest population group is between 35 and 54 years of age. Figure 4.12 illustrates Canada's aging population in more detail over time, showing how, since 1921, the median age has gone up and the number of babies born has gone down. While net international migration has been the

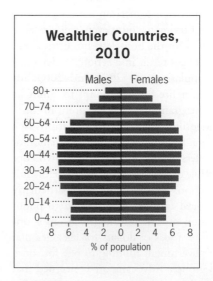
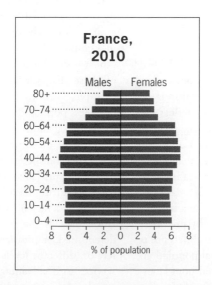
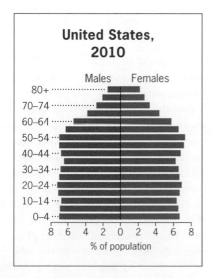

FIGURE 4.10 Age-Sex Population Pyramids for Countries with Low Population Growth Rates. Countries with lower total fertility rates and longer life expectancies have population pyramids shaped more uniformly throughout. Data from United Nations Population Division, *World Population Prospects: The 2010 Revision*.

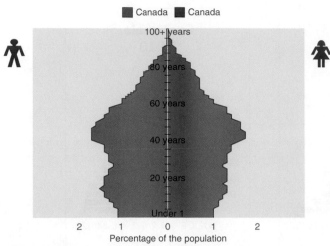

FIGURE 4.11 Age-Sex Population Pyramid for Canada, 2006.
Data from Statistics Canada.

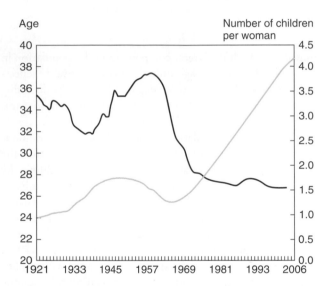

**FIGURE 4.12 Median Age and Number of Children in Canada,
1921-2006.** The light blue line indicates the median age, which has
gone up; the dark blue line indicates the average number of children
per woman, which has declined. Data from Statistics Canada.

TABLE 4.1	Median Age for Population Reporting Aboriginal Identity and Non-Aboriginal Population, Canada, 2001	
	Median age (years)	
	Aboriginal	Non-Aboriginal
Canada	24.7	37.7
Newfoundland and Labrador	27.7	38.5
Prince Edward Island	24.6	37.4
Nova Scotia	25.3	38.7
New Brunswick	28.2	38.5
Quebec	27.9	38.5
Ontario	27.9	37.1
Manitoba	22.8	38.5
Saskatchewan	20.1	38.8
Alberta	23.4	35.4
British Columbia	26.8	38.7
Yukon Territory	28.6	37.7
Northwest Territories	24.0	34.5
Nunavut	19.1	35.2

Median age is the point at which exactly half of the population is older,
and the other half is younger. Data from Statistics Canada.

RELIABILITY OF POPULATION DATA

A **census** is an official enumeration of a population, completed periodically, that usually provides demographic information about a population. In Canada, a census is taken every five years, and Canadian citizens, landed immigrants, refugee claimants, and those holding a work or student permit are legally bound to complete the census questionnaire. The reliability of population data varies from country to country depending on the technologies available, the skill of the data collector, and the mobility and visibility of the population. In the North American context, various groups protest the practice of trying to count every single person in a country. Many advocates for the homeless, minorities, and others insist the census practices result in a serious undercount of these disadvantaged populations. In 2006 and 2009, for example, Toronto came under fire for its attempt to count its homeless population. The program, which used "point in time" methodology and visual identification, was criticized for its lack of verifiable or accurate data, leading to the underestimation of the actual number of homeless. Many homeless people who opt to "couch-surf" are not visible on the street and are therefore not counted during data collection. This is important, particularly because federal and provincial funding is often tied to population data. If the population of a disadvantaged group is undercounted, it translates into a loss of dollars for agencies that rely on different levels of government funding to pay for social services to disadvantaged groups. Advocates are concerned that people who are already members of a disadvantaged group suffer further as a result of census undercounts.

> **Census** A periodic and official count of a country's population.

main driver of population growth in Canada since the 1990s, it has not affected the overall structure of our aging population.

It is important to remember that Canada's population is diverse and that these overall trends do not necessarily reflect the population composition of various groups within Canada. For example, as Table 4.1 reveals, the median age of those Canadians who claim Aboriginal identity is significantly lower than those of non-Aboriginal identity. Data from Statistics Canada in 2001 reveal a median age for the Aboriginal population, Canada-wide, of 24.7, approximately 13 years younger than the Canadian average. Table 4.1 also breaks down the median age by province, which shows distinct variation based on place. This difference is due, in part, to a higher birth rate in the Aboriginal population. According to Statistics Canada, Canada's Aboriginal population is nevertheless aging, albeit more slowly than the rest of Canada, in part due to increased life expectancy and declining birth rates.

Being undercounted also translates into less government representation when the number of seats for an electoral district is allocated based on census data. Prosperous countries such as Canada and the United States often experience problems conducting an accurate census. For example, as outlined in more detail in Chapter 7, there has been a great deal of controversy over issues such as "race" and "ethnic origin" in terms of collecting census data. Greater difficulties must be overcome in less well-off countries, where the cost, organization, and reporting of a census exceed what many countries can afford or handle.

In the summer of 2010, a massive controversy erupted in Canada over the Conservative government's decision to scrap the long-form census questionnaire for the 2011 Census, replacing it with a voluntary national household survey. The mandatory long-form questionnaire has been used by governments, businesses, educators, and social service agencies to provide services and funding to a vast array of Canadians. As well, academics, including geographers, rely upon this data to analyze population

trends and movements over time (see Chapter 7). Critics of the government's decision to replace the mandatory questionnaire with a voluntary one argue that voluntary surveys are not as statistically rigorous as mandatory ones, and that many groups will be underrepresented in the new voluntary program. The head of Statistics Canada, Munir Sheikh, tendered his resignation over the issue, claiming that the voluntary survey is no replacement for the mandatory long-form questionnaire.

Several agencies collect data on world population. The United Nations records official statistics that national governments assemble and report. The World Bank and the Population Reference Bureau also gather and generate data and report on the population of the world and of individual countries. If you compare the population data reported by each of these sources, you will find inconsistencies. Data on population, growth rates, food availability, health conditions, and incomes are often informed estimates rather than actual counts. It is important to always think carefully about the source and veracity of the statistics you are using.

MAIN POINTS **4.1** **How Do We Think about Populations and How Is This "Geographical"?**

- Population geographers, working with demographic information, are concerned with spatial variations in distinctive populations. Population geography focuses on why populations have certain characteristics and are distributed across space in particular ways.

- While it is important to understand a population's density and distribution, the next stage is to understand a population's composition or characteristics—the number of men and women, their age, income, health, education, and other attributes.

- Population density, distribution, and composition provide the basic data for asking broader geographical

questions, including those related to our spatial perspectives: Where are populations located? Who lives in what places and why? Why is the world's population distributed in four main regions? How does a particular population order its landscape and why? How do people and groups move from place to place and why?

- Population data is often difficult to gather, and different sources may have different data. How data is collected, what is included, and what is overlooked can have a serious effect on the quality of life of particular populations in certain places.

4.2 Why Do Populations Grow or Decline in Particular Places?

THE POPULATION GROWTH DEBATE

The concern over the burgeoning world population can be traced back to 1798, when British economist Thomas Malthus published *An Essay on the Principles of Population*. Malthus reasoned that food supplies grew *linearly*, adding acreage and crops incrementally by year, whereas population grew *exponentially*, compounding on the year before. This suggested that the world's population was increasing faster than the food supplies needed to sustain it. Malthus's work has resonated with other writers, including Paul Ehrlich, whose book *The Population Bomb* was published in 1968. Ehrlich and others warned that the world's population was increasing too quickly and outpacing our food production.

On the other side of the debate, scholars including Danish economist Ester Boserup, who published *The Conditions of Agricultural Growth: The Economics of Agrarian Change under Population Pressure* in 1965, argue that it is not food supply that determines population, but, rather, society's capacity to develop new technologies and farming techniques that ensures the production of enough food supplies to meet the needs of growing populations.

Moreover, Malthus assumed food production is confined spatially—what people can eat within a country depends on what is grown in that country. We now know this assumption does not hold true; countries are not closed systems. Malthus did not foresee how globalization would aid the exchange of agricultural goods across the world. As discussed in Chapter 3, mercantilism, colonialism, and capitalism brought interaction among the Americas, Europe, Africa, Asia, and the Pacific. Through global interaction, new agricultural methods developed, and commodities and livestock diffused across oceans.

In the 1700s, farmers in Ireland grew dependent on a South American crop that was well suited for their country's rocky soils, the potato. Today, wealthier countries that lack arable land, such as Norway, can import the majority of their food-stuffs, circumventing the limitations of their lands.

Modern food production has grown exponentially as the acreage under cultivation expands, mechanization of agricultural production diffuses, improved strains of seed are developed, and more fertilizers are used. In the 21st century, bioengineering continues to bring new hybrids, genetically modified organisms (GMOs), and countless herbicides and pesticides that enable exponential growth in food production. Conversely, these changes also raise concerns about food safety, the possible risks of GMOs, and the potential dangers of pesticide use to humans and the environment.

Debates about food and our ability to feed ourselves continue and are intimately bound up in our relationship with the environment (see Chapter 6 for more on human-environment relations). In November 2010 *The Globe and Mail* ran a series of articles examining food production in Canada, contextualizing the subject in terms of globalization, food safety, and environmental and climate concerns, among other issues. With headlines proclaiming Canada's reputation as a world agricultural "superpower" was slipping, the newspaper reported that while we export over $30 billion in agricultural products annually, we are losing our position on the world's markets due to increased competition globally. Canada's share of the global wheat market has shrunk from 23 percent to 19 percent, and its overall export position has dropped from third to ninth. While Canada's economic investment in agriculture has increased to $8 billion annually, we continue to struggle in a competitive global environment. The Canadian Federation of Agriculture is attempting to address these issues by developing a national food strategy driven by consumer groups, producers, and government representatives.

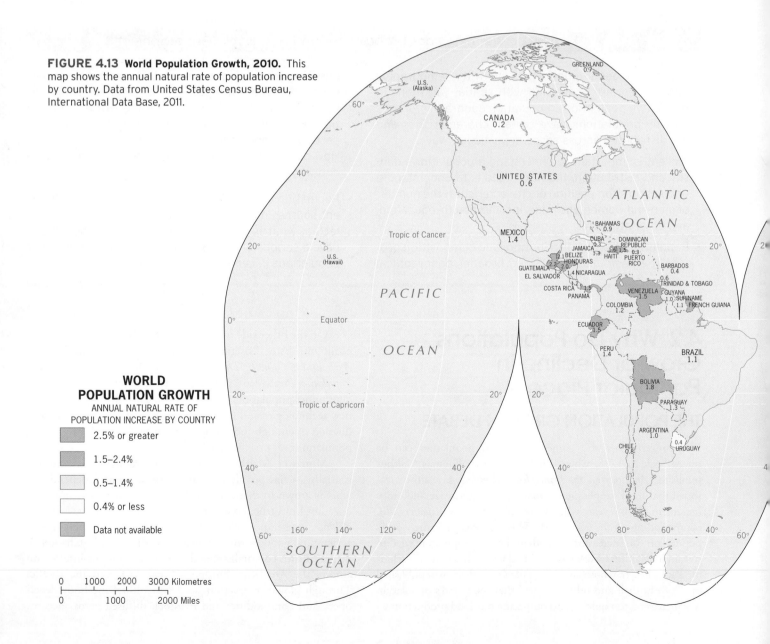

FIGURE 4.13 World Population Growth, 2010. This map shows the annual natural rate of population increase by country. Data from United States Census Bureau, International Data Base, 2011.

POPULATION CHANGE AT WORLD, REGIONAL, NATIONAL, AND LOCAL SCALES

Analysis of population change requires attention to scale. While we can consider population growth and decline at different scales, we must be mindful that what happens at one scale can be affected by what is happening at other scales and in other places at the same time. Therefore, we usually begin by considering population change within a defined territory or unit of a country (or other administrative unit, such as a province or city). One basic indicator of population change is the **rate of natural increase (RNI)** in a country's population. The RNI is calculated by subtracting the deaths from births for the total population over a particular period of time, usually one year. For example, Canada's RNI in 2010 was 2.99 per thousand.

> **Rate of natural increase (RNI)** An indicator of population change, calculated by subtracting the crude death rate from the crude birth rate.

This is a relatively simple statistic to calculate and comprehend; however, calculating the natural increase misses two other key components in a country's population: immigration, which along with births adds to the total population; and emigration (outmigration), which along with deaths subtracts from the total population. Using these four components, we can calculate demographic change within a territory.

POPULATION CHANGE AT THE WORLD SCALE

World population growth is mapped in Figure 4.13. Most of the world's population growth is expected to be in Africa, Asia, and Central and South America. This measure of population growth does not, however, take into account emigration and immigration, which we will discuss in Chapter 5. Other maps and tables

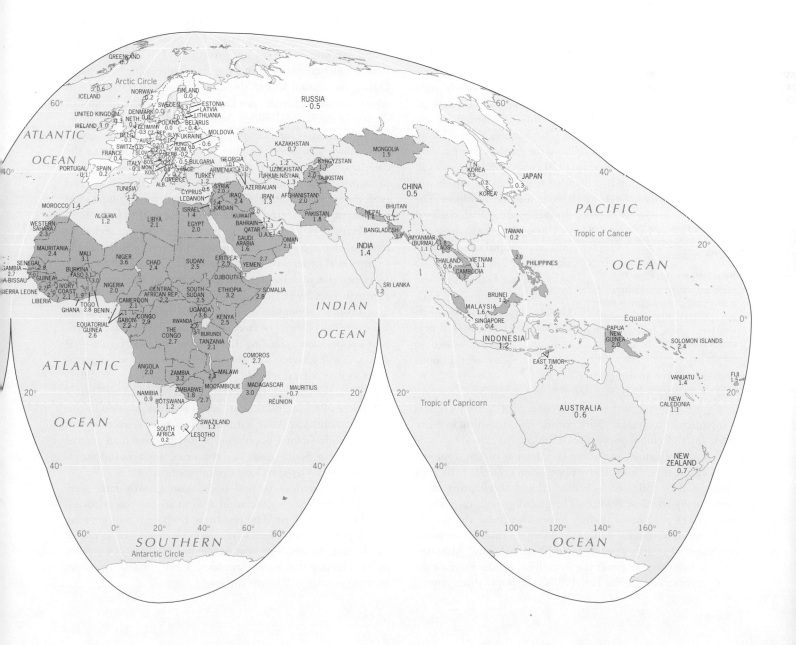

of population growth may take into account emigration and immigration. Statistics for each population trait can be calculated globally, by region, by country, or even for smaller locales. When studying population data across scales, we must constantly remind ourselves of exactly what is being calculated and for where. Otherwise, many of the statistics we read will seem contradictory.

> **Total fertility rate (TFR)** The average number of births per woman of childbearing years, usually considered between 15 and 49 years of age.

For example, we began this chapter with a Field Note discussing the low and declining **total fertility rates (TFRs)** in a number of countries around the world. How can the worldwide population continue to increase when so many countries are experiencing low TFRs and population decline? Despite declining population growth rates and even negative growth rates (growth rates below 0.0) in a number of the world's countries, the global population continues to rise. The worldwide TFR was 2.6 in 2007, above the replacement level of 2.1. (The replacement level is the TFR needed to maintain a population.) The Population Reference Bureau estimates global population will rise to over 9.3 billion by 2050. This is because the low TFRs and low population growth rates enumerated in this chapter are dwarfed by continued additions to the population in countries where growth rates are still relatively high, such as India, Indonesia, Bangladesh, Pakistan, and Nigeria.

Two thousand years ago, the world's population was an estimated 250 million. More than 16 centuries passed before this total had doubled to 500 million, the estimated population in 1650. Just 170 years later, in 1820 (when Malthus was still writing), the population had doubled again, to 1 billion. Barely more than a century later, in 1930, it reached 2 billion. The

> **Doubling time** The time required for a population to double in size.
>
> **Population explosion** The rapid growth of the world's human population during the past century, attended by ever-shorter doubling times and accelerating rates of increase.

doubling time had declined to 100 years and was dropping fast; the **population explosion** was in full gear. Only 45 years elapsed before the next doubling, to 4 billion (1975). During the mid-1980s, when the rate declined to 1.8 percent, the doubling slowed to 39 years. Today, world population is expected to double in 54 years.

For demographers and population geographers studying global population growth today, the concept of doubling time is losing much of its punch. With populations declining in many places, fears of global population doubling quickly are subsiding. Many indicators, including the slowing of the doubling time, suggest that the explosive population growth of the 20th century will be followed by a marked and accelerating slowdown during the 21st century. The global growth rate is now down to 1.4 percent or slightly lower. But today the world's population is about 6.7 billion, yielding an increase in world population that still exceeds 80 million annually. Although this is an improvement over the 90 million annual increase the world experienced in the late 1980s, the population growth

rate of the globe will have to come down well below 1.0 percent to significantly slow global population growth.

POPULATION CHANGE AT THE REGIONAL AND NATIONAL SCALES

The world map of population growth rates by country (Figure 4.13) confirms the wide range of RNIs in different geographic regions. These variations have existed as long as records have been kept and are the result of countries and regions going through stages of expansion and decline at different times. In the mid-20th century, the population of the former Soviet Union was growing vigorously. Thirty years ago, India's population was growing at nearly 3 percent, more than most African countries; then India's growth rate fell below that of sub-Saharan Africa. Today, Africa's RNI remains higher than India's (2.4 percent to 1.7 percent), but now sub-Saharan Africa faces the impact of the AIDS epidemic, which is killing millions and orphaning children, reducing life expectancies, and curtailing growth rates.

The map also reveals continuing high growth rates in Muslim countries of north Africa and Southwest Asia. Saudi Arabia has one of the highest growth rates in the world, but some smaller countries in this region are increasing even faster. During the second half of the 20th century, countries in this region saw their growth rates increase even as those in most of the rest of the world declined. More recently, several fast-growing populations—for example, those of Iran and Morocco—have shown significant declines. Demographers point to the correlation between high growth rates and the low standing of women: where cultural traditions restrict educational and professional opportunities for women, and men dominate as a matter of custom, rates of natural increase tend to be high.

South Asia is the most important geographic region in terms of the population growth rate. The region includes the country that appears destined to overtake China as the world's most populous: India. Only one country in this region has a growth rate lower than the world average: Sri Lanka. But Sri Lanka's total population is only 20.4 million, whereas the fast-growing countries of Pakistan and Bangladesh have a combined population exceeding 326 million. India, as Figure 4.13 shows, is still growing well above the world average. The situation in East Asia, the world's most populous region, is different. China's official rate of natural growth has fallen well below 1.0 percent (0.6 in 2008), and Japan's population is no longer growing. Southeast Asia's natural growth rates remain higher, but this region's total population is much lower than that of either East or South Asia; key countries, such as Indonesia, Thailand, and Vietnam, have declining growth rates.

South America's natural population growth rates were alarmingly high just a generation ago but are now experiencing significant reductions. The region as a whole is still growing at 1.5 percent, but Brazil's population growth, for example, has declined from 2.9 percent in the mid-1960s to 1.4 percent today. The populations of Argentina, Chile, and Uruguay are growing at rates well below the world average.

As Figure 4.13 shows, the slowest-growing countries—including those with declining rates of natural population increase—lie in the economically wealthier areas of the world extending from the United States and Canada across Europe, and Japan. In the Southern Hemisphere, Australia, New Zealand, and Uruguay are in this category as well. Wealth is not the only reason for negative population growth rates. Russia's population is declining because of social dislocation in the wake of the collapse of the Soviet Union; deteriorating health conditions, high rates of alcoholism and drug use, and economic problems combine to shorten life expectancies (especially among males) and to lower birth rates (in recent years, Russia's economy has improved, but its birth rate remains low). Similar problems afflict Ukraine and Kazakhstan, two of Russia's neighbours, which also show slow or negative growth.

No single factor can explain these variations. Economic prosperity and social dislocation reduce natural population growth rates. Economic well-being, associated with urbanization, higher levels of education, later marriage, family planning, and other factors, lowers population growth. Using Appendix B, compare the indices for natural population increase and the percentage of the population that is urbanized; in general, the higher the population's level of urbanization, the lower its natural increase. Cultural traditions also influence rates of population growth. Religion, for example, has a powerful impact on family planning and thus on growth rates, not only in Islamic countries but also in traditional Christian societies (note the growth rate in the Roman Catholic Philippines) and in Hindu-dominated communities (such as India).

POPULATION CHANGE AT THE LOCAL SCALE

The information provided in Figure 4.13 is based on countrywide statistics. Significant demographic variations also occur *within* countries. In India, for example, some states record population growth rates far above the national average; these states lie mostly in the east of the country (Figure 4.14). Other states, in the west and southwest region, are growing much more slowly. India is a federation of 28 states and 7 union territories, and the individual states differ greatly both culturally and politically.

After becoming independent in 1947, India began a population planning program in the 1950s, long before the modern era's fear of worldwide overpopulation and a global population bomb spread. In the 1960s, when census numbers revealed extreme growth rates in parts of the country,

the Indian government instituted a national population planning program, encouraging states to join. As in any federation, the will of the federal government cannot be forcibly imposed upon the states; however, when it became evident that early population planning that was not national in scope was not working, a federal effort was implemented.

Despite the federal effort, rapid population growth continued, especially in the eastern states. Social problems arose in some of the states where governments pursued the campaign vigorously. During the 1970s, the Indian government began a policy of forced sterilization of any man with three or more children. The State of Maharashtra sterilized 3.7 million people before public opposition led to rioting, and the government abandoned the program. Other states also engaged in compulsory sterilization programs, with heavy social and political costs—eventually, 22.5 million people were sterilized.

The horrors of the forced sterilization program of the 1970s are haunting India again. In 2004, three districts in the State of Uttar Pradesh (India's most populous state, with over 170 million people) instituted a policy of exchanging gun licences for sterilization. The policy granted a shotgun licence in exchange for the sterilization of two people, and a revolver licence in exchange for the sterilization of five people. Abuse began almost

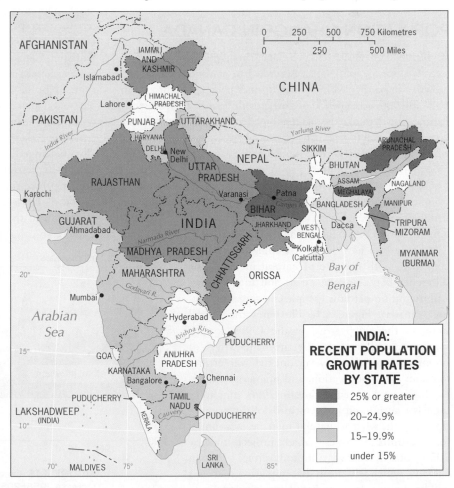

FIGURE 4.14 Population Growth Rates in India. Data from India Census Bureau, 2011.

immediately, with wealthy landowners sterilizing their labourers in exchange for gun licences. Before the "guns for sterilization" policy, districts in Uttar Pradesh encouraged sterilization by providing access to housing and extra food for people who agreed to be sterilized.

Today, most Indian state governments are using advertising and persuasion—not guns for sterilization—to encourage families to have fewer children. Posters urging people to have small families are everywhere, and the government supports a network of family-planning clinics even in the remotest villages. The southern states continue to report the lowest growth rates, correlating with higher wealth and education levels in these states. The eastern and northern states, the poorer regions of India, continue to report the highest growth rates. In countries such as China and India, where there is a preference for male children, there has been a startling increase in the infanticide and abortion of female children. The result is populations with a far greater number of men than women.

POPULATION CHANGE IN CANADA

As Figure 4.15 illustrates, the Canadian population has grown steadily since the mid-1850s. According to Statistics Canada, this growth can be divided into three distinct phases. The first, from 1851 to 1900, was a period of slow growth because there was little natural growth due to the fact that high fertility rates were offset by very high mortality rates. The second phase, from 1901 to 1945, which included World War I and II, was defined by accelerated growth, due mostly to immigration and the settlement of western Canada. The third phase, from 1946 to the present, is characterized by an even faster pace of growth due to both the baby boom and strong immigration. Canada's population increased from 12.3 million in 1946 to approximately 34 million in 2010.

Yet, as we have learned, population growth comprises both the rate of natural increase (the difference between total births and total deaths) and migration patterns (people entering and leaving Canada). Figure 4.16 illustrates the overall trend in these two areas. In the 1990s, for instance, natural increase was the main driver of population growth. However, due to lower fertility rates, an aging population, and migratory changes, this is no longer the case. In 2006, migratory increases accounted for two-thirds of the population growth, whereas natural increases accounted for one-third. Statistics Canada projects that by 2030, total deaths will outnumber total births in Canada, which will mean that migration increases will be the sole driver of population growth.

Furthermore, these statistics speak to population at the national scale, but we are also interested in population growth and changes at

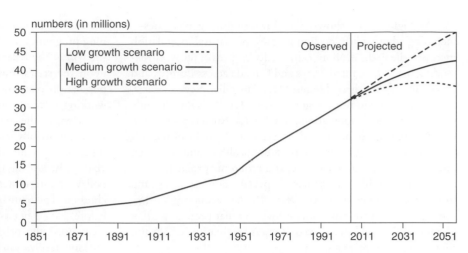

FIGURE 4.15 Canadian Population Growth, 1851 to 2051. From Statistics Canada, Figure 1: "Population of Canada, 1851 to 2056," *Canadian Demographics at a Glance, 2007*, Catalogue 91-003-XWE2007001, http://www.statcan.gc.ca/pub/91-003-x/2007001/figures/4129857-eng.htm. Accessed November 23, 2011.

the local scale. Figure 4.17 breaks down population growth by province and territory. (Note that this includes population growth from both migratory and natural increases.) Since 2001, population growth has increased in every province and territory except Prince Edward Island (where it remains unchanged), Newfoundland and Labrador, and Saskatchewan. Statistics Canada attributes growth rates in most regions to international immigration patterns, inter-province migration, or both. Two-thirds of the overall growth since 2001 has taken place in Alberta and Ontario. The territories all report significant population growth since 2001. For the most part, the Atlantic region's population remains steady, virtually unchanged between 2001 and 2006. Quebec reported its second-highest growth rate since the end of the baby boom, growing three times faster than it did in the previous reporting period of 1996–2001. This is due to increased international migration to the province, along with less movement out of Quebec to other provinces and territories. The territories all

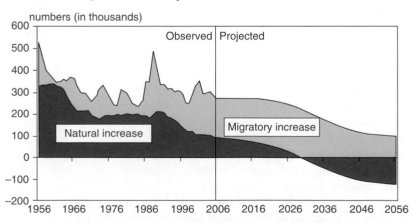

FIGURE 4.16 Canadian Population: Migratory and Natural Increase, 1956–2056. From Statistics Canada, Figure 3: "Migratory and natural increase of the Canadian population, 1956 to 2056," Canadian Demographics at a Glance, Catalogue 91-003-XWE2007001, http://www.statcan.gc.ca/pub/91-003-x/2007001/figures/4129879-eng.htm. Accessed November 23, 2011.

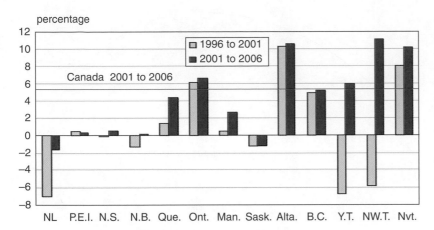

FIGURE 4.17 Population Growth of Provinces and Territories, 1996–2001 and 2001–2006. From Statistics Canada, Figure 4: "Population growth of provinces and territories, 1996 to 2001 and 2001 to 2006," *Population and Dwelling Counts, 2006 Census*, Catalogue 97-550-XWE2006001, http://www12.statcan.ca/census-recensement/2006/as-sa/97-550/figures/c4-eng.cfm. Accessed November 23, 2011.

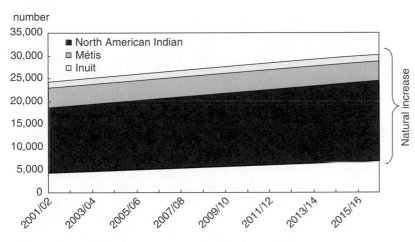

FIGURE 4.18 Natural Increase in the Aboriginal Populations of Canada, 2001–2002 to 2016–2017. From Statistics Canada, Figure 4: "Population growth of provinces and territories, 1996 to 2001 and 2001 to 2006," *Population and Dwelling Counts, 2006 Census*, Catalogue 97-550-XWE2006001, http://www12.statcan.ca/census-recensement/2006/as-sa/97-550/figures/c4-eng.cfm. Accessed November 23, 2011.

reported growth in the 2001–2006 cycle, which can be attributed to improvement in migration exchanges with other provinces, as well as the region's higher Aboriginal populations, which tend to have a higher fertility rate (Figure 4.18).

THE DEMOGRAPHIC TRANSITION

The high population growth rates now occurring in many poorer countries are not necessarily permanent. In Europe, the rate of population growth changed several times in the last three centuries. Demographers used data on baptisms and funerals from churches in Great Britain to study changes in birth and death rates of the population. They expected the RNI of the population—the

Crude birth rate (CBR) The number of live births yearly per thousand people in a population.

Crude death rate (CDR) The number of deaths yearly per thousand people in a population.

difference between the number of births and the number of deaths—to vary over different time periods. Demographers calculated the **crude birth rate (CBR)**, the number of live births per year per thousand people in the population (Figure 4.19), and the **crude death rate (CDR)**, the number of deaths per year per thousand people (see Figure 4.20 on page 106).

The church data gathered in Great Britain reveals that before the Industrial Revolution began in the 1750s, the country experienced high birth rates and high death rates, with small differences between the two. The result was low population growth. After industrialization began, the death rates in Great Britain began to fall because of better and more stable access to food and improved access to increasingly effective medicines. With a rapidly falling death rate and a birth rate that remained high, Britain's population exploded. From the late 1800s through the two world wars, death rates continued to fall. Birth rates also began to decline but stayed higher than the death rates, resulting in continued, but slower, population growth. Finally, in recent history, both the birth rate and death rate in Great Britain declined to low levels, resulting in slow or stable population growth.

Demographers call the shift in population growth experienced in Great Britain and elsewhere the **demographic transition**. They have developed a five-stage model, shown in Figure 4.21 (see page 106) to illustrate the process. The model is based on the kind of shift that Britain experienced and

Demographic transition Multistage model, based on Western Europe's experience, of changes in population growth exhibited by countries undergoing industrialization. High birth rates and death rates are followed by plunging death rates, producing a huge net population gain; this is followed by the convergence of birth rates and death rates at a low overall level.

can be used to compare the transition in other places. Some locations underwent a similar shift in their population growth while others are in the process of doing so.

The initial low-growth phase (Stage 1), which in all places endured for most of human history, is marked by high birth rates and equally high death rates. In this phase, epidemics and plagues keep the death rates high among all sectors of the population—in some cases so high that they exceed birth rates. For Great Britain and the rest of Europe, death rates exceeded birth rates during the bubonic plague (the Black Death) of the 1300s, which hit in waves beginning in Crimea on the Black Sea. The plague was diffused through trade to Sicily and other Mediterranean islands, largely because of the travel of rats (which hosted the vector—the flea—that spread the plague) north from the Mediterranean.

Once the plague hit a region, it was likely to return within a few years, bringing another wave of human suffering. Estimates

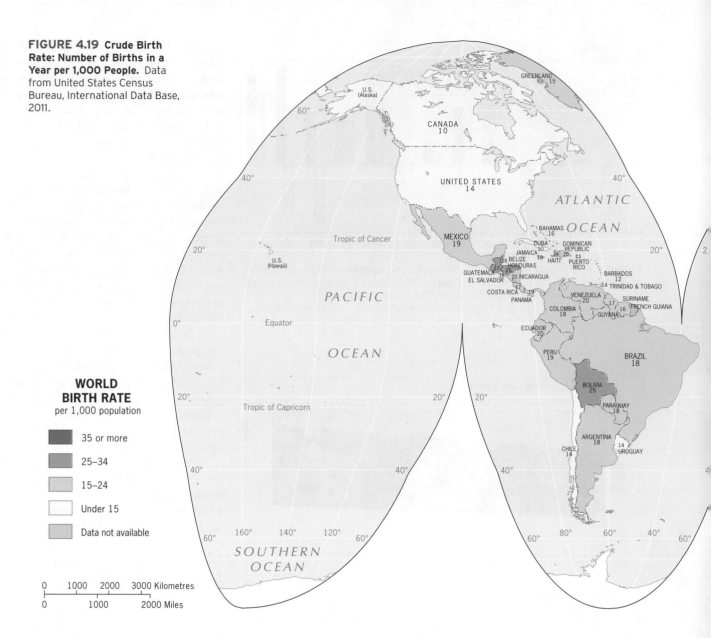

FIGURE 4.19 Crude Birth Rate: Number of Births in a Year per 1,000 People. Data from United States Census Bureau, International Data Base, 2011.

WORLD BIRTH RATE
per 1,000 population

- 35 or more
- 25–34
- 15–24
- Under 15
- Data not available

0   1000   2000   3000 Kilometres
0   1000   2000 Miles

of plague deaths vary between one-quarter and one-half of the population, with the highest death rates recorded in the west (where trade among regions was the greatest) and the lowest in the east (where cooler climates and less-connected populations delayed diffusion). Across Europe, many cities and towns were decimated. Historians estimate the population of Great Britain fell from nearly 4 million when the plague began to just over 2 million when it ended.

Famines also limited population growth. A famine in Europe just prior to the plague likely facilitated the diffusion of the disease by weakening the people. Records of famines in India and China during the 18th and 19th centuries document millions of people perishing. At other times, destructive wars wiped out population gains. As mentioned previously, the world's population did grow from 250 million people 2,000 years ago to 1 billion people in 1820. However, the lines in

Stage 1 of Figure 4.21 show there was not a steady upward trend. Rather, they turn up and down frequently, reflecting the impacts of disease, crop failures, and wars, as well as changing farming practices and technologies.

The beginning of the Industrial Revolution ushered in a period of accelerating population growth in Europe (Stage 2). Before workers could move from farms to factories, a revolution in agriculture had to occur, and during the 18th century the Second Agricultural Revolution did take place (the first, which occurred thousands of years earlier, is described in Chapter 9). During the Second Agricultural Revolution, farmers improved seed selection, practised new methods of crop rotation, selectively bred livestock to increase production and quality, employed new technology such as the seed drill, expanded storage capacities, and consolidated landholdings for greater efficiencies. With more efficient farming methods,

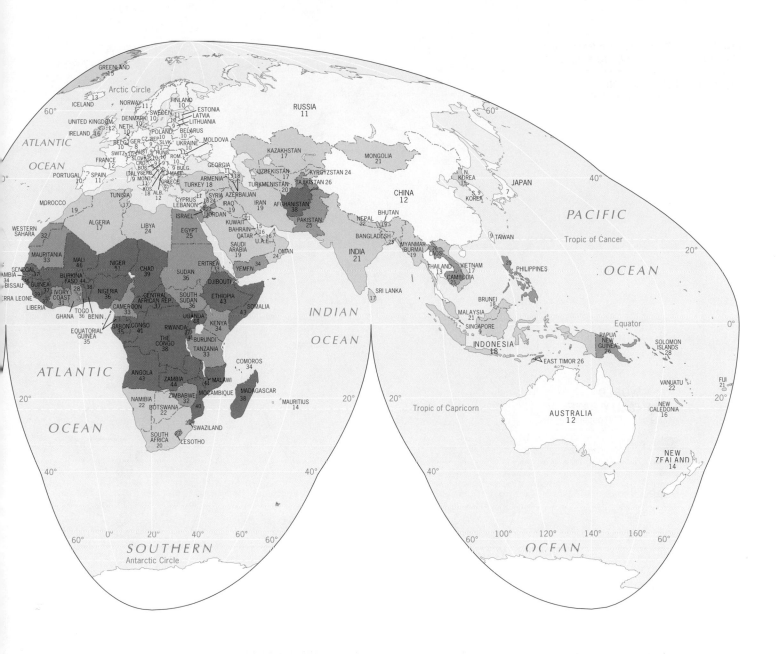

the number of people needed in farming decreased and the food supply increased, thereby supporting a higher population overall.

In the 1800s, as the Industrial Revolution diffused through continental Europe, other advances also helped lower the death rates. Sanitation facilities made the towns and cities safer from epidemics, and medical practices improved. Disease prevention through vaccination introduced a new era in public health. The combined improvements in food supply and medical practice resulted in a drastic reduction in death rates. Before 1750, death rates in Europe probably averaged 35 per 1,000 (birth rates averaged under 40 per 1,000), but by 1850 the death rate was down to about 16 per 1,000.

Birth rates fell at a slower rate, leading to a population explosion (Stage 3). The increase in the rate of population growth in Europe spurred waves of migration. Millions of people left

the squalid, crowded, industrial cities and poor rural regions to emigrate to other parts of the world. They were not the first to make this journey. Adventurers, explorers, merchants, and colonists had gone before them. In a major wave of colonization from 1500 through the 1700s, European migrants decimated native populations through conquest, slavery, and the introduction of diseases against which the local people had no natural immunity.

When a second wave of European colonization began in Africa and Asia during the late 1800s, the Europeans brought with them their newfound methods of sanitation and medical techniques, and these had the opposite effect. By the mid-1900s, declining death rates in Africa, India, and South America brought rapid population increases to these regions. At this point, new alarms and cautions of worldwide overpopulation rang out.

FIGURE 4.20 Crude Death Rate: Number of Deaths in a Year per 1,000 People. Data from United States Census Bureau, International Data Base, 2011.

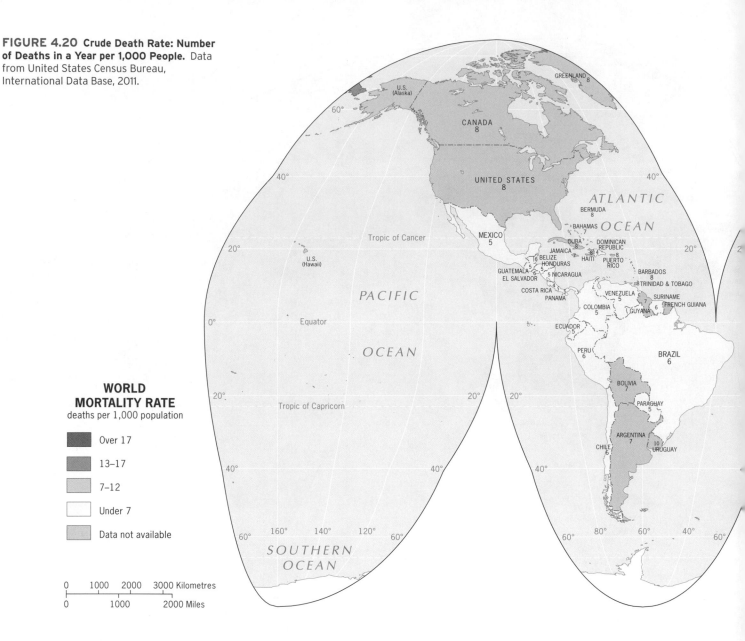

WORLD MORTALITY RATE
deaths per 1,000 population

- Over 17
- 13–17
- 7–12
- Under 7
- Data not available

FIGURE 4.21 Model of the Demographic Cycle. This model shows the five stages of the demographic transition. (© H.J. de Blij, P.O. Muller, and John Wiley & Sons, Inc.)

MODEL OF THE DEMOGRAPHIC CYCLE

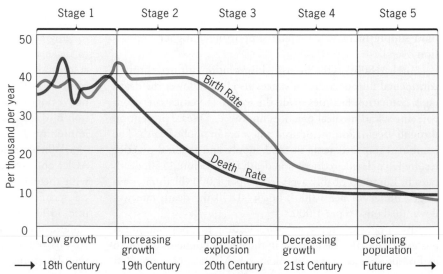

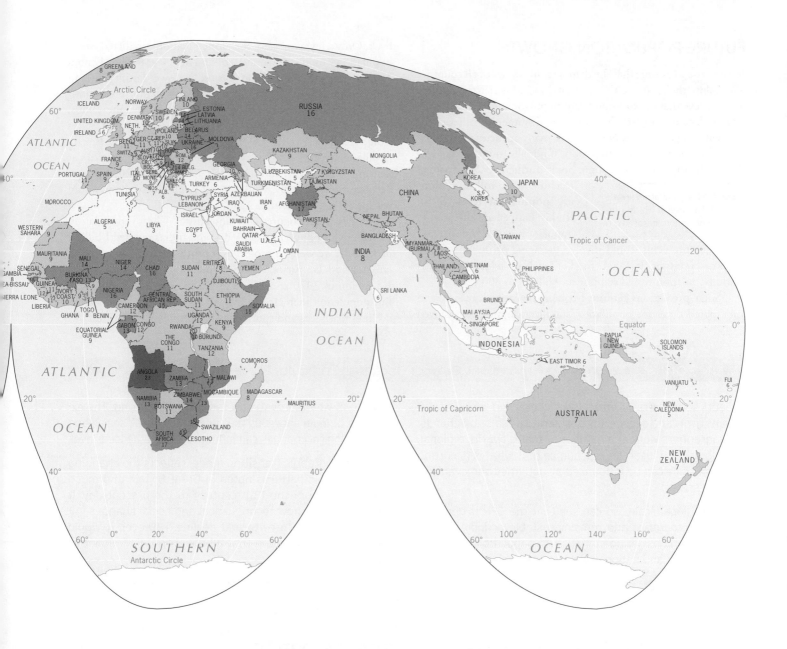

These alarms subsided for populations in Europe and North America when population growth rates began to decline in the first half of the 1900s (Stage 3) as a result of a significant decline in birth rates. Populations continued to grow, but at a much slower rate. Many countries in Latin America and Asia experienced falling birth rates later in the 20th century, which helped slow the global population growth rate.

Why have birth rates declined? Throughout the 1900s, lower birth rates appeared first in countries with greater urbanization, wealth, and medical advances. As more and more people moved to cities, both the economics and the culture of large families changed. Children who were valued as workers on the family farm became a drain on the family finances in urban areas. At the same time, new employment opportunities—especially for women—were often not compatible with the level of care women were expected to provide to large families. Hence,

women often delayed marriage and childbearing. Medical advances lowered infant and child mortality rates, lessening the sense that multiple children were necessary to sustain a family. In recent history, the diffusion of contraceptives, the accessibility to abortions, and conscious decisions by many women to have fewer children or to start having children at a later age have all lowered birth rates within a country.

In some parts of the world, countries are now experiencing exceptionally low total fertility rates (Stages 4 and 5). Low birth rates along with low death rates put these countries in a position of negligible, or even negative, population growth. Birth rates are lowest in countries where women are the most educated and most involved in the labour force. For example, in Canada, half of the women between the ages of 25 and 44 have a post-secondary degree, compared to only 40 percent of men in the same age range. In 2008, Canada's TFR was 1.57, one of the lowest in the world.

FUTURE POPULATION GROWTH

It is unwise to assume that the demographic cycles of all countries will follow the sequence that occurred in industrializing Europe or to believe that the still-significant population growth currently taking place in Bangladesh, Mexico, and numerous other countries will simply subside. Nonetheless, many agencies monitoring global population suggest that most, if not all, countries' populations will stop growing at some point during the 21st century,

> **Stationary population level (SPL)** The level at which a national population ceases to grow.

reaching a so-called **stationary population level (SPL)**. If this happened, the world's population would stabilize and the major problems would involve the aging of the population in some countries. In 2004, the United Nations predicted that world population would stabilize at 9 billion in 300 years.

Such predictions require frequent revision, however, and anticipated dates for population stabilization are often moved back. Only a few years ago, the United Nations predicted world population would stabilize at 10 billion in 200 years. The United Nations changed its predictions based on lower fertility rates in many countries. All agencies reporting population predictions have to revise their predictions periodically. In the late 1980s, for example, the World Bank predicted that the United States would reach SPL in 2035 with 276 million inhabitants. Brazil's population would stabilize at 353 million in 2070, Mexico's at 254 million in 2075, and China's at 1.4 billion in 2090. India, destined to become the world's most populous country, would reach SPL at 1.6 billion in 2150.

Today these figures are unrealistic. China's population passed the 1.2 billion mark in 1994, and India's reached 1 billion in 1998. If we were to project an optimistic decline in growth rates for both countries, China's population would "stabilize" at 1.5 billion in 2070 and India's at 1.8 billion in the same year. But population increase is a cyclical phenomenon, and overall declines mask lags and spurts as well as regional disparities.

MAIN POINTS   4.2   Why Do Populations Grow or Decline in Particular Places?

- Geographers are interested in where and why populations grow and decline. In considering population change, geographers work at a number of scales (world, regional, national, and local) and recognize that what is occurring at one scale can be influenced by activities and events at other scales.

- At the global scale, we can see that the TFR is declining in some countries and remaining stable or increasing in others. By considering statistics on population change at the regional and national scale, we can get a much better

sense of where growth and decline are occurring. The example of India shows us that internal political, social, and technological changes can influence TFR at the local level.

- The demographic transition model reflects the changing demographic patterns noted in Great Britain and much of Europe from the 18th century to the present day. It demonstrates how technological and social changes impact population growth and decline. However, it would be unwise to presume that all countries will follow this model.

4.3 How Does the Geography of Health Influence Population Dynamics?

Understanding the nature of a country's population requires much more than simply knowing the total population or the growth rate, densities, distribution, and composition. Also of significance is the welfare of the country's people across regions, ethnicities, or social classes. Among the most important influences on population dynamics are geographical factors. Location influences access to health care, availability of clean water and good sanitation, prevalence of diseases, and quality of housing, nutrition, and education. It is important to consider how different groups, from the elderly to the disabled, experience their everyday geographies. For example, the *Guest Field Note* by Nicole Yantzi illustrates how geography affects and is experienced by those with chronic illnesses and disabilities.

INFANT MORTALITY

One of the leading measures of the condition of a country's population is the **infant mortality rate (IMR)**. Infant mortality records the death of babies during the first year of life. Child mortality records death between ages 1 and 5. Infant mortality is usually given as the number of deaths per thousand for every thousand live births.

> **Infant mortality rate (IMR)** A figure that describes the number of babies that die within the first year of their lives in a given population.

Infant and child mortality reflect the overall health of a society. High infant mortality has a variety of causes, the physical health of the mother being a key factor. In societies where most women bear a large number of babies, women also tend to be inadequately nourished, exhausted from overwork, suffering from disease, and poorly educated. Demographers report that many children die because their parents do not know how to cope with the routine childhood problem of diarrhea. This

GUEST FIELD NOTE
Measuring Accessibility

Geographer David Sibley (1995) states that the role of human geography is to interrogate "the assumptions of inclusion and exclusion which are implicit in the design of places and spaces." As a person who uses a walker, I have experienced the daily challenges of negotiating inaccessible spaces and how this makes me feel. My overall research goal is to take this personal experience and Sibley's challenge and go beyond examining, questioning, and critiquing, and work toward improving the accessibility and inclusiveness of the spaces that children with disabilities must negotiate.

This work involves developing tools to measure the accessibility and inclusiveness of indoor and outdoor school environments for children who use mobility aids such as crutches, walkers, and wheelchairs. These tools are based on my research training in the areas of the geographies of health and health care, the geographies of children and youth, and the geographies of disabilities. My research is based on the premise that the organization and design of spaces conveys messages of belonging or not belonging to people with disabilities. This is clearly shown by research findings based on a tool that I developed to measure the accessibility and suitability of school playgrounds. Although important physical, intellectual, and emotional skills are learned on the playground, data collection and analysis provides evidence that many children cannot get into, move around, or play in these spaces. Figure 4.22 provides examples of typical elementary school playgrounds in which there are often large plastic or perimeter boarders with no breaks, soft surfaces such as sand, and very few, if any, play opportunities. In one Ontario school board I found that almost 60 percent of the playgrounds had this type of large perimeter border that would prevent a child with a mobility aid from entering the playground. This definitely conveys a message to a child, even if unintentional, that they do not belong in this space.

Another researcher and I are developing a tool to examine the accessibility of the interior spaces of schools. Development of this tool required careful consideration of how children are expected to move around their classroom and school on a daily basis. Therefore, our tool examines children's movement both between and within a diversity of school spaces such as classrooms, washrooms, and libraries, and helps identify barriers that a child might experience.

The effectiveness of these two tools was dependent on two key aspects of the research process. First, it was important to go beyond the walls of the university, and seek out feedback from health and educational professionals, and parents and children in the community. The tool to measure interior school spaces was revised several times based on discussions with school therapists, school board staff, and most importantly students who use mobility aids. This feedback has helped to ensure that the tool covers all aspects of school accessibility, and that it is relatively easy to use.

After examining the accessibility of 18 schools we conducted a focus group with students to ensure that the tool was picking up on their key areas of concern. When we asked the students what school space was the most difficult to manage the unanimous decision was the stage. From this discussion we found that several of the students had not been able to participate in plays, ceremonies, and ultimately graduation because most of the stages had stair access (Figure 4.23). They said that the stage is where students' accomplishments and contributions are recognized. Existing school accessibility tools do not collect data for the stage. Our study found that less than 20 percent of stages were deemed accessible in one school board. Our discussion with the students resulted in revising the tool to ensure that it reflects the importance of the stage.

Second, after completing key parts of the research it is important to report the findings to those who may benefit. In academic circles this is referred to as knowledge translation. Part of developing and testing the accessibility tools is sharing the research with health and educational professionals, accessibility advisory groups, and most importantly children with disabilities and their families. In order to improve the accessibility of schools and work toward creating school spaces that promote the belonging and participation of all students, the research must end up in the hands of those responsible

(a)

(b)

FIGURE 4.22 Typical Organization and Design of School Playgrounds. (S. Wendorf and L. Stevens)

for funding and developing policies to promote accessibility, and also individuals who have daily interactions with students with disabilities. While this step can be very time consuming it is an important part of the research process. Upon completion of each school assessment we sent the principal a report that provided an in-depth analysis of the advantages and challenges for accessibility. That means that we wrote 18 separate reports. We also wrote a very detailed report for the local school board that carefully documented the key challenges for accessibility. We met with board representatives and went over our findings in terms of particularly problematic spaces and also provided some suggestions. Effective knowledge translation involves putting the research in a format and language that will resonate with the intended audience.

In research, when students hear the word *field* it often conjures up images of a researcher trekking through the bush, or travelling to another country to collect data. This field note shows that the field can be a school or playground in your local community. More and more research is a collaborative process, which recognizes the value of different types of expertise. The tools discussed above would not be as effective if I relied only on my own personal knowledge and experience. The professional and experiential knowledge and contributions of all those involved were essential. Finally,

FIGURE 4.23 Typical Organization and Design of a Stage.
(A. Rose)

reporting back to your target audience is essential if one of your goals is to unveil, challenge, and rectify the assumptions of inclusion and exclusion found in society.

Dr. Nicole Yantzi, Department of Environmental Studies, Laurentian University. Photos were taken by research assistants S. Wendorf, L. Stevens, and A. Rose as part of various research projects led by Dr. Yantzi.

condition, together with malnutrition, is the leading killer of children throughout the world. Poor sanitation is also a threat to infants and children. Estimates are that more than one-fifth of the world's population lacks ready access to clean drinking water or hygienic human waste disposal facilities.

The map plotting infant mortality rates at the global scale (see Figure 4.24 on page 112) reveals high rates in many poorer countries. Infant mortality patterns are mapped at five levels, ranging from 100 or more per thousand (one death for every eight live births) to fewer than 15. Compare this map to that of overall crude death rate (CDR) in Figure 4.20, and the role of infant mortality in societies with high death rates is evident.

The lowest infant mortality rate among larger populations has long been reported by Japan, with 3.0 deaths per thousand live births in a country of over 128 million people. Some less-populated countries show even lower IMRs. Singapore has over 4.5 million people and an incredibly low IMR of just under 3.0, and Sweden's nearly 9 million people record an IMR of 2.8. Note how much lower these are than the rates in some of the countries in Africa and East Asia.

Canada's IMR has remained relatively constant in recent years (Table 4.2). In 2009, the infant mortality rate was 5.0 deaths per thousand live births. However, in 2010 the CBC reported that in Manitoba, which already has a high IMR, the Aboriginal IMR is more than twice the Canadian average. Researchers suggest that this is due to several factors including

location in rural areas, inadequate access to health care services, and lack of effective use of these facilities due to language and cultural barriers. Overall, however, infant mortality rates are declining in Canada.

In 2008, 22 countries reported an IMR of 100 or more, and several had rates of 125 or higher—that is, one or more deaths among every eight newborns. Sierra Leone and Afghanistan had the highest IMR: 165. Dreadful as these figures are, they are a substantial improvement over the situation 20 years ago (although they are not much improved since 1997). Globally, infant mortality has been declining, even in the poverty-stricken regions of the world.

Each of these observations about infant mortality rates considers what is happening within an entire country. The IMR varies within countries and provides a lens through which we can see variations in access to health care and health education within a country. The statistic typically varies by region, ethnicity, social class, or other criteria. South Africa's IMR is 48 per thousand, an average of all the people within the country's borders. Using the demographic terminology employed by South Africa, the IMR for South African whites is near the European average; for black Africans it is nearer the African average; and for the Coloured and Asian populations it lies between these two figures. The reported average for South Africa does not tell us about ethnic and class differences within the country.

TABLE 4.2	Canadian Infant Mortality Rates (both Sexes), by Province and Territory, 2003-2007				
	2003	2004	2005	2006	2007
Canada	5.3	5.3	5.4	5.0	5.1
Newfoundland and Labrador	5.0	5.1	6.2	5.3	7.5
Prince Edward Island	4.9	4.3	2.2	2.1	5.0
Nova Scotia	5.7	4.6	4.0	4.0	3.3
New Brunswick	4.1	4.3	4.1	4.0	4.3
Quebec	4.4	4.6	4.6	5.1	4.5
Ontario	5.3	5.5	5.6	5.0	5.2
Manitoba	8.0	7.0	6.6	6.0	7.3
Saskatchewan	6.3	6.2	8.3	6.1	5.8
Alberta	6.6	5.8	6.8	5.3	6.0
British Columbia	4.2	4.3	4.5	4.1	4.0
Yukon	6.0	11.0	0.0	8.2	8.5
Northwest Territories	5.7	0.0	4.2	10.2	4.1
Nunavut	19.8	16.1	10.0	13.4	15.1

This infant mortality rate is calculated as the number of deaths of children less than one year of age per 1,000 live births in the same year. Data from Statistics Canada.

CHILD MORTALITY

Child mortality rate (CMR) A figure that describes the number of children who die between the first and fifth years of their lives in a given population.

Infants who survive their first year of life still do not have a long life expectancy in poorer areas of the world. The **child mortality rate (CMR)**, recording the deaths of children between the ages of 1 and 5, remains staggeringly high in much of Africa and Asia, notably in the protein-deficient tropical and subtropical zones. *Kwashiorkor* (also known as protein malnutrition), a malady resulting from a lack of protein early in life, afflicts millions of children; *marasmus*, a condition that results from inadequate protein and insufficient calories, causes the deaths of millions more. In some countries, more than one in five children still die between their first and fifth birthdays, a terrible record in the 21st century. In Canada, the most recent statistics available indicate a CMR that is dropping over time. In 1990, the CMR was 8 per thousand live births. In 2007, it was 6 per thousand live births. The leading cause of child mortality in Canada is accidents.

The Canadian International Development Agency (CIDA) argues that, at the global scale, child mortality rates can be lowered through better access to health care, nutrition, and basic medical treatment. As a result, CIDA plays a leadership role internationally through its Children and Youth Strategy, working to promote immunization, micronutrient supplementation, HIV/AIDS prevention and treatment, and malaria control around the world.

LIFE EXPECTANCY

Another indicator of a society's well-being is provided by calculating the **life expectancy** of its members at birth—the number of years, on average, someone may

Life expectancy A figure indicating how long, on average, a person may be expected to live. Normally expressed in the context of a particular state.

expect to remain alive. Figure 4.25 (on page 114) shows the average life expectancies of populations by country and thus does not take into account gender differences. Women outlive men by about four years in Europe and East Asia, three years in sub-Saharan Africa, six years in North America, and seven years in South America. In Russia today, the difference is approximately 14 years.

The map does reveal huge regional contrasts. At the start of the century, world average life expectancy was 68 for women and 64 for men. Not only are these levels now exceeded in the wealthy countries of the Western world, but great progress has also been made in East Asia, where Japan's life expectancies are the highest in the world. With its low infant and child mortality rates and low fertility rates, Japan's life expectancy is predicted to rise to 106 by the year 2300. By contrast, the spread of AIDS in sub-Saharan Africa over the past two decades has lowered life expectancies in some countries below 40, a level not seen for centuries. As a result, these countries have the world's lowest life expectancies.

Life expectancies can change in relatively short order. In the former Soviet Union, and especially in Russia, the life expectancies of males dropped quite precipitously following the collapse of communism, from 68 to 62 years. Today, Russia's life expectancy is only 58 for males; female life expectancy also declined, but only slightly, from 74 to 72.

In Canada, life expectancies have risen steadily over the past 100 years. As Table 4.3 shows, men born in 1920 had a life expectancy of 59, while for females the figure was 61. For those born in 2007, this changed to 78 and 83, respectively. It is noteworthy that the gap between men's and women's life expectancy in Canada seems to be closing; from 7 years in the 1970s and 1980s to 4.7 years in 2007. Researchers attribute this to men's focus on health, nutrition, and avoiding smoking, coupled with less stress as men are less likely to be the sole breadwinner in a family unit. Table 4.3 also shows that location matters in terms of life expectancy. The lowest life expectancy rates are in Newfoundland and Labrador, and the highest are in British Columbia.

Life expectancy figures do not mean everyone lives to a certain age. The figure is an average that takes into account the children who die young and the people who survive well beyond the average. The dramatically lower life expectancy figures for the world's poorer countries primarily reflect high infant mortality. A person who has survived childhood may live long past the recorded life expectancy. The low life expectancy figures for the malnourished countries remind us again how difficult life is for children in poorer parts of the world.

FIGURE 4.24 Infant Mortality Rate, 2008. Data from *CIA World Factbook*, 2011 estimate.

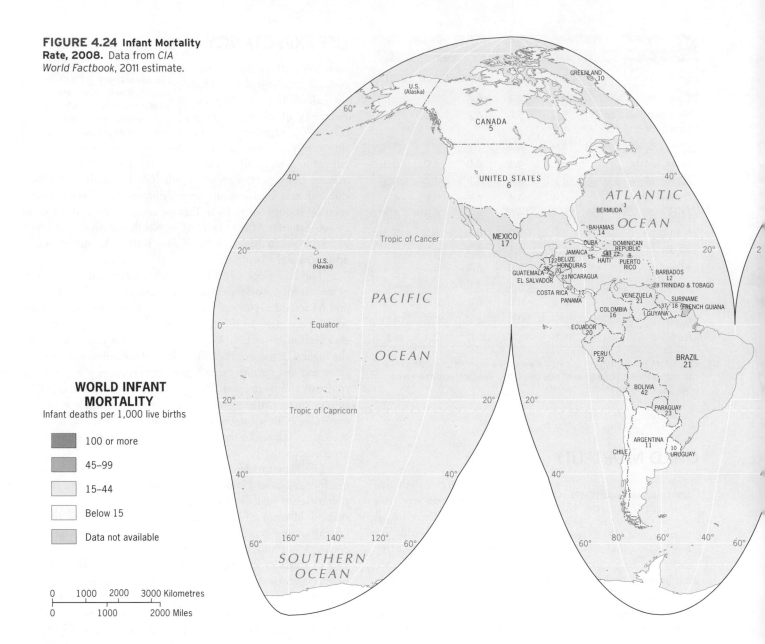

WORLD INFANT MORTALITY
Infant deaths per 1,000 live births

- 100 or more
- 45–99
- 15–44
- Below 15
- Data not available

TABLE 4.3	Life Expectancy at Birth, by Sex and Province					
	Number of Years				**Number of Years**	
Canada (Year of Birth)	**Males**	**Females**		**2005 to 2007 (Year of Birth)**	**Males**	**Females**
1920 to 1922	59	61		**Canada**	**78**	**83**
1930 to 1932	60	62		Newfoundland and Labrador	76	81
1940 to 1942	63	66		Prince Edward Island	78	83
1950 to 1952	66	71		Nova Scotia	77	82
1960 to 1962	68	74		New Brunswick	77	83
1970 to 1972	69	76		Quebec	78	83
1980 to 1982	72	79		Ontario	79	83
1990 to 1992	75	81		Manitoba	77	82
2000 to 2002	77	82		Saskatchewan	77	82
				Alberta	78	83
				British Columbia	79	84

Data from Statistics Canada.

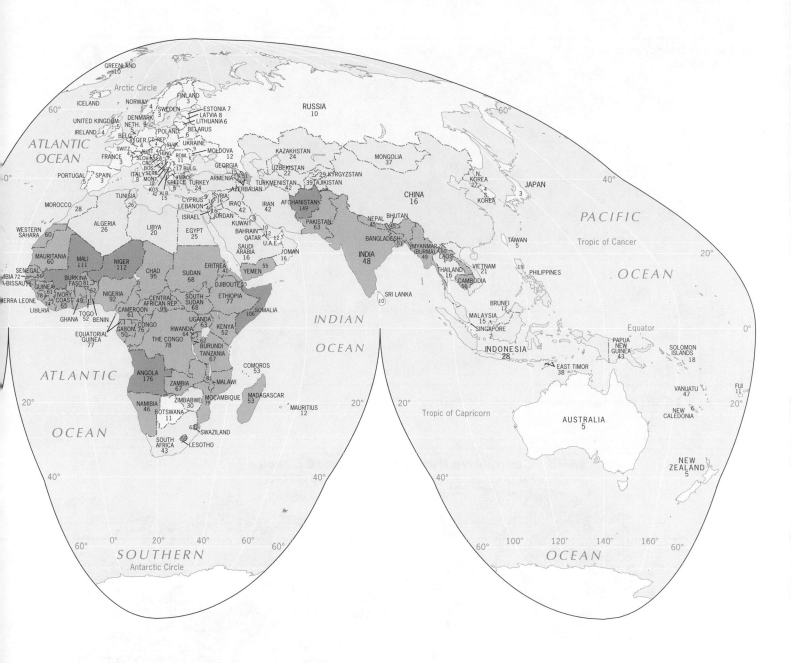

GEOGRAPHY'S INFLUENCE ON HEALTH AND WELL-BEING

Health and well-being are closely related to location and environment. People who live in Iceland, where mosquitoes are rare, do not need to worry about contracting malaria unless they travel to parts of the tropics where malaria is prevalent. People who live in close proximity to animals, including livestock, run a greater risk of catching certain diseases than do people who live in cities. When an outbreak of disease occurs—for example, H5N1 avian influenza in East Asia, or severe acute respiratory syndrome (SARS) on a global scale—its source and diffusion are studied by specialists in medical geography. Medical geographers can reveal the complexity of such outbreaks. For example, Canadian researchers Roger Keil and S. Harris Ali studied the outbreak of SARS and point to its spread through globalized metropolitan areas, including Toronto (Figure 4.26). The lessons, they contend,

are geographical. Infectious diseases spread rapidly at a global scale because there is unprecedented connectivity between communities and bioregions that were previously separated by oceans and land masses. Importantly, Keil and Ali argue that "the geography of globalization is a geography of disease" (2006, p. 108).

Medical geographers study diseases; they also use locational analysis to predict diffusion and prescribe prevention strategies. A medical geographer can answer questions such as: Where is avian flu most likely to diffuse, and according to what timeline, if an outbreak occurs in New York City? If a country receives enough funding to build 25 clinics for people in rural areas, where should these clinics be located to enable the maximum number of patients to reach them? These questions become critical during moments of international crisis. For instance, in the aftermath of the earthquake in Haiti in 2010, the international community paid a great deal of attention to the possibility of disease outbreaks, which could be devastating in

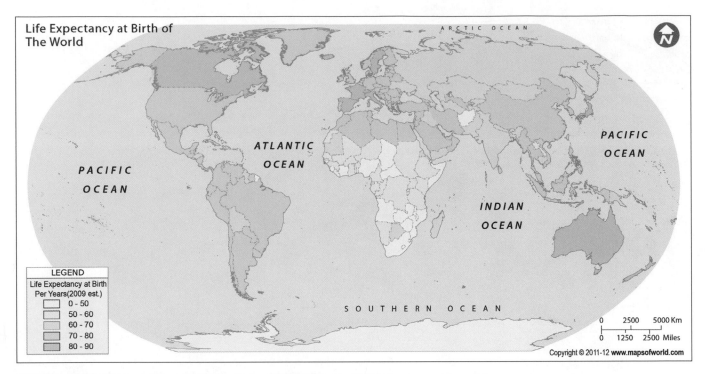

FIGURE 4.25 Life Expectancy at Birth in Years, 2009 estimate. (© 2009 www.georules.com)

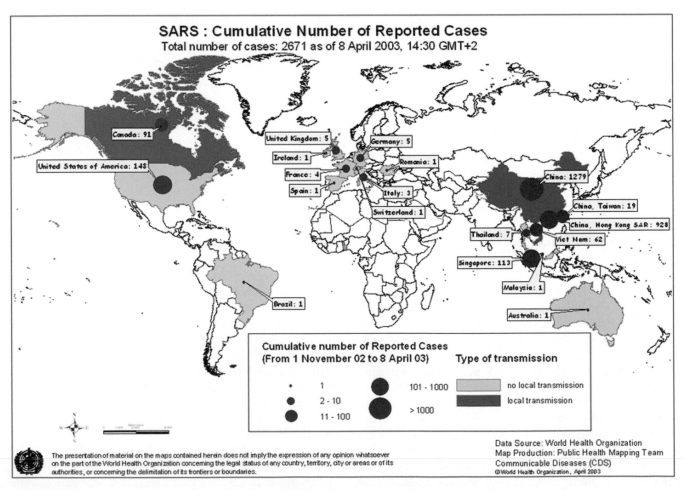

FIGURE 4.26 SARS: Cumulative Number of Reported Cases, 2003. (World Health Organization, 2003)

the already-precarious circumstances in the aftermath of the earthquake. In late October 2010, approximately 10 months after the earthquake struck, media began to report on an outbreak of cholera in Haiti. How quickly the disease could spread was an immediate concern, particularly in the densely populated camps erected in the capital city of Port-au-Prince. Poor sanitation, the build-up of garbage, lack of fresh water, and widespread poverty are all contributing factors that raise the alarm for aid workers, medical staff, officials, and international agencies working in the region.

Diseases can be grouped into categories to make it easier to understand the risks they pose. About 65 percent of all diseases are known as **infectious diseases**, resulting from an invasion of parasites and their multiplication in the body. Malaria is an infectious disease. The remainder can be divided into **chronic or degenerative** diseases, the maladies of longevity and old age such as heart disease, and **genetic or inherited diseases** we can trace to the chromosomes and genes that define our makeup. Sickle-cell anemia, hemophilia, and lactose intolerance are genetic diseases. These can be of special geographic interest because they tend to appear in certain areas and in particular populations, suggesting the need for special, local treatment.

Infectious diseases Diseases that are spread by bacteria, viruses, or parasites. Infectious diseases diffuse directly or indirectly from human to human.

Chronic or degenerative diseases Generally, long-lasting afflictions now more common because of higher life expectancies.

Genetic or inherited diseases Diseases caused by variation or mutation of a gene or group of genes in a human.

Endemic When a disease prevails over a particular locality or region.

Epidemic Regional outbreak of a disease.

Pandemic An outbreak of a disease that spreads worldwide.

Three geographic terms are used to describe the spatial extent of a disease. A disease is **endemic** when it prevails over a small area. A disease is **epidemic** when it spreads over a large region. A **pandemic** disease is global in scope.

INFECTIOUS DISEASES

Infectious diseases continue to sicken and kill millions of people annually. Malaria, an old tropical disease, alone still takes more than a million lives annually and infects about 300 million people. HIV/AIDS, an affliction that erupted in Africa only about 30 years ago, has killed about 25 million people since that time. These two maladies illustrate two kinds of infectious disease: vectored and non-vectored.

A vectored infectious disease, such as malaria, is transmitted by an intermediary vector—in the case of malaria, a mosquito. A mosquito stings an already-infected person or animal, called a host, and sucks up some blood carrying the parasites. These then reproduce and multiply in the mosquito's body and reach its saliva. The next time that mosquito stings someone, some of the parasites are injected into that person's bloodstream. Now that person develops malaria as the parasites multiply in his or her body, and he or she becomes a host.

Mosquitoes are especially effective vectors of infectious diseases ranging from yellow fever (another historic illness) to dengue fever (a newer disease that is spreading quickly). But mosquitoes are only one kind of vector. Fleas, flies, worms, snails, and other vectors transmit such terrible diseases as sleeping sickness, river blindness, guinea worm, elephantiasis, and numerous others. Tropical climates, where biological activity is most intense, are the worst-afflicted areas of the world, but infectious diseases are a global phenomenon.

No disease in human history has taken more lives than malaria, and the battle against this scourge still is not won. On the day you read this, about 3,000 people will die from malaria, the great majority of them in Africa and most of them children. What these numbers do not tell you is that an estimated 3 to 5 million people live lives that are shortened and weakened by malaria infection. If you do not die from malaria as a youngster, you are likely to be incapacitated by it or will struggle in exhaustion with chronically severe anemia throughout your life.

Non-vectored infectious diseases, such as influenza, are transmitted by direct contact between host and victim. A kiss, a handshake, or even the slightest brush can transmit influenza, a cold, or some other familiar malady. Standing close to another person means that tiny moisture particles in exhaled air can transmit the disease to you. HIV/AIDS is a non-vectored infectious disease that is transmitted primarily through sexual contact and secondarily through sharing needles in intravenous drug use.

As mentioned earlier in this section, the world is experiencing new waves of influenza: H1N1 or "swine flu" in 2009, H5N1 or "avian flu" in 2006 and 2007, SARS in 2003. Geographers have discussed these diseases in terms of their global scale, noting the incidence of pandemics, which spread quickly around the world. They are diseases of global cities.

CHRONIC AND GENETIC DISEASES

Chronic diseases (also called degenerative diseases) are the afflictions of middle and old age, reflecting higher life expectancies. Among the chronic diseases, heart disease, cancers, and strokes rank as the leading diseases in this category, but pneumonia, diabetes, and liver diseases also take their toll. In Canada 100 years ago, tuberculosis, pneumonia, diarrheal diseases, and heart diseases (in that order) were the chief killers. Today, cancer and heart disease head the list, with cerebrovascular diseases (including strokes) next, and accidents also high on the list (Table 4.4). In the early 1900s, tuberculosis and pneumonia caused 20 percent of all deaths; today they cause fewer than 5 percent.

The battles against cancer and heart disease, however, are far from won. Recent decades have brought new lifestyles, new pressures, new consumption patterns, and exposure to new chemicals, and we do not know how these will affect our health. In order to distribute adequate food supplies to populations in huge urban areas, we add various kinds of preservatives to foods without knowing exactly how they will affect our health in the long run. We substitute artificial flavouring for sugar and other calorie-rich substances, but some of those substitutes have been proven to be dangerous. Despite all the sugar substitutes,

TABLE 4.4 Leading Causes of Death in Canada, 2006			
	Rank	Number	Percent
Total, all causes of death	...	228,079	100.0
Malignant neoplasms [cancers]	1	67,807	29.7
Diseases of the heart	2	49,893	21.9
Cerebrovascular diseases	3	13,805	6.1
Chronic lower respiratory diseases	4	9,786	4.3
Accidents (unintentional injuries)	5	9,640	4.2
Diabetes mellitus	6	7,261	3.2
Alzheimer's disease	7	5,675	2.5
Influenza and pneumonia	8	5,152	2.3
Nephritis, nephrotic syndrome, and nephrosis	9	3,686	1.6
Intentional self-harm (suicide)	10	3,512	1.5

Data from Statistics Canada.

obesity plagues a significant percentage of the western population, bringing with it heart disease and diabetes. Even treating drinking water with chemicals is a recent development in the scheme of global population change, and we do not know its long-term effects. Future chronic diseases may come from practices we take for granted as normal now.

Genetic diseases are of particular interest to medical geographers because they tend to be transferred from one generation to the next and display clustering that raises questions about environment and long-term adaptation. Prominent among these are metabolic diseases, in which the body is unable to process all elements of the diet. Enzymes play a key role in these diseases. If the body fails to produce enough (or any) of a particular enzyme used in digestion, the result can be serious metabolic malfunction. For example, some people suffer from a malady called primary lactose intolerance: they do not have an adequate supply of one (or a set) of enzymes needed to break down lactose, a sugar in milk.

AIDS

Low life expectancies in some parts of the world are caused by the ravages of diseases such as **AIDS** (acquired immune deficiency syndrome), which was identified in Africa in the early 1980s. AIDS took hold in Africa years, perhaps decades, earlier, but its rapid diffusion worldwide began in the 1980s, becoming one of the greatest health catastrophes of the past century. Nowhere has its impact been greater than in Africa itself.

Medical geographers estimate that in 1980, about 200,000 people were infected with HIV (the human immunodeficiency virus, which causes AIDS), all of them Africans. By 2007, according to the United

AIDS (acquired immune deficiency syndrome) Immune system disease caused by the human immunodeficiency virus (HIV) which over a period of years weakens the capacity of the immune system to fight off infection so that weight loss and weakness set in and other afflictions such as cancer or pneumonia may hasten an infected person's demise.

Nations AIDS Program, the number worldwide exceeded 33.2 million, with 68 percent (22.5 million) of all cases in sub-Saharan Africa. The infection rate has slowed, and some regions are experiencing a downturn, but eastern Europe and central Asia have recently seen a surge in HIV infection.

AIDS is a debilitating disease that weakens the body and reduces its capacity to combat other infections. It is spread through bodily contact that involves the exchange of bodily fluids such as blood or semen. Sexual activity and needles shared among drug users can transmit the virus, but so can blood transfusions. Over a period of years, a person's immune system is impaired, weight loss and weakness set in, and other afflictions, such as cancer or pneumonia, may hasten an infected person's death.

Over the past two decades, the AIDS pandemic has reached virtually all parts of the world, but its full dimensions are unknown. People carrying the HIV virus do not immediately display visible symptoms of the disease; they may carry it for years without being aware of it, and during that period they can unwittingly transmit it to others. In its earliest stages, a blood test is needed to confirm the presence of HIV, but millions go untested. Add to this the social stigma many people attach to this malady, and it is evident that official statistics on AIDS lag far behind the real numbers.

That is true not only in Africa but in other parts of the world as well; both India and China, for example, long denied that AIDS was a serious health threat to their populations. Now China is reporting at least 650,000 cases, and the number in India may well exceed 5 million. Canada reported its first known case of AIDS in 1982, and the Public Health Agency of Canada estimates that 65,000 Canadians are now infected with HIV, an increase of 14 percent since 2005. In Central and South America there are some 2 million cases, but after Africa, the worst-afflicted geographic realm is Southeast Asia, with as many as 6 million people affected.

Nowhere is AIDS having the impact it has had on sub-Saharan Africa. In 2006, some 24 percent of people in Botswana aged 15 to 49 were infected, 20 percent in Zimbabwe, almost 19 percent in South Africa, and 17 percent in Zambia. These are the official data; medical geographers estimate that 20 to 25 percent of the entire population of several tropical African countries is infected. The United Nations AIDS program reports that more than 1.6 million people died of AIDS in sub-Saharan Africa in 2007 alone. Geographer Peter Gould, in his book *The Slow Plague* (1993), calls Africa a "continent in catastrophe," and the demographic statistics support his viewpoint. Life expectancy in Botswana and Swaziland has declined to 34 (and is projected to fall farther), and in Zimbabwe it is 36. In a continent already ravaged by other diseases, AIDS is the leading cause of death.

AIDS is reshaping the population structure of the countries hardest hit by the disease. Demographers look at the projected population pyramids for countries with high rates of infection and see population chimneys, reflecting the major impact AIDS plays on the younger population in the country and its future generations (Figure 4.27).

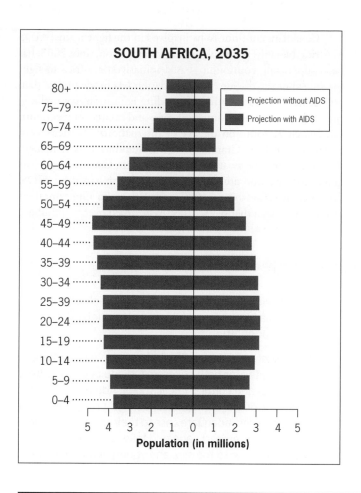

SOUTH AFRICA, 2035

Population (in millions)

Projection without AIDS

Projection with AIDS

FIGURE 4.27 Effect of AIDS on the Population Pyramid for South Africa, Predicted 2035. The estimated population of South Africa, male and female, with AIDS and without AIDS. Data from United States Census Bureau, 2005.

Geographers are engaging in fieldwork to understand the human toll of AIDS locally and within families. Geographer Elsbeth Robson, who has studied the impact of AIDS in hard-hit Zimbabwe, found that global processes, such as the diffusion of AIDS and reductions in spending on health care (often mandated by structural adjustment programs), "shape young people's home lives and structure their wider experiences." In sub-Saharan Africa, the number of children orphaned when parents die from AIDS is growing rapidly. In 2004, UNICEF reported that between 2001 and 2003, the number of global AIDS orphans (children who have lost a parent to AIDS) rose from 11.5 million to 15 million. The United States Agency for International Development estimates that this number will rise to 25 million by 2010. As Robson notes in her *Guest Field Note,* in addition to the rising number of AIDS orphans, many young children, especially girls, are taken out of school to serve as caregivers for their relatives with AIDS. In her interviews with young caregivers, she discovered that "more children are becoming young carers as households struggle to cope with income and labour losses through illness and mortality." There are few positives to report. Uganda, once Africa's most afflicted country, has slowed the spread of AIDS through an

GUEST FIELD NOTE
Marich Village, Kenya

This drawing (Figure 4.28) was done by a Pokot boy in a remote primary school in northwestern Kenya. He agreed to take part in my fieldwork some years after I had started researching young carers in sub-Saharan Africa. Since those early interviews in Zimbabwe I have been acutely aware of

young carers' invisibility—you can't tell who is a young carer just by looking at them. Indeed, invisibility is a characteristic of many aspects of the social impacts of HIV/AIDS. This young person drew himself working in the fields and taking care of cattle. The reasons why African young people help with farming and herding are many, but for young caregivers, assisting their sick family members in this way is especially important.

Elsbeth Robson, Keele University

FIGURE 4.28 Young Carers. A young boy depicts himself working in the fields and taking care of cattle. (Elsbeth Robson)

intensive, government-sponsored campaign of public education and action—notably the distribution of condoms in even the remotest part of the country. In the world's wealthier countries, remedies have been developed that can stave off the effects of AIDS for many years. But African countries cannot afford such luxuries. United Nations calculations suggest that more than $50 billion needs to be spent globally by 2015 to slow AIDS and treat the infected; in 2007, only about $10 billion was available. The impact of AIDS will be felt in African economies and in African demographics for generations to come. HIV/AIDS will constrain African economic development (see Chapter 11) and require world intervention to overcome.

Canadians continue to be involved in the fight against AIDS in Africa. Notably, the Stephen Lewis Foundation, since 2003, has been supporting community-based initiatives in Africa to fight the spread of the disease. The foundation has funded more than 300 projects in 15 countries, providing education, counselling, prevention information, medical care, and community support. On March 7, 2006, on the eve of International Women's Day, Lewis launched the Grandmothers to Grandmothers campaign, which seeks to raise awareness and support in Canada for Africa's grandmothers, who are caring for children orphaned by AIDS. To date, there are over 240 Grandmothers to Grandmothers groups in Canada that have, collectively, raised over $10 million.

MAIN POINTS **4.3** **How Does the Geography of Health Influence Population Dynamics?**

- Populations are influenced by their geography. Where we live, the climate, the government, access to health care, the availability of clean water and good sanitation, the prevalence of disease, and the quality of housing, nutrition, and education affect population composition and dynamics.

- Measures of infant mortality rates, child mortality rates, and life expectancy for particular populations tell us a great deal about the overall health and strength of that population. Clearly, location matters in that poorer countries with fewer health services, a lack of good nutrition, and a high rate of disease suffer high death rates across the population.

- Diseases such as AIDS and malaria not only contribute to high death rates for both children and adults but also have serious social and cultural implications. Adults may be less able to work due to ill health, unable to provide for their families, or to give adequate care to their children. Children are orphaned at an early age and take up the role of caregiver and provider to the sick and young in their families.

4.4 How Do Governments Affect Population Change?

Over the past century, many of the world's governments have instituted policies designed to influence the overall growth rate or ethnic ratios within their country's population. Certain policies directly affect the birth rate by implementing laws and policies ranging from subsidized abortions to forced sterilization. Others influence family size through taxation or subvention. These policies fall into three groups: expansive, eugenic, and restrictive.

The former Soviet Union, and China under Mao Zedong, led other communist societies in **expansive population policies**, which encourage large families and raise the RNI. Ideological, anti-capitalist motives drove those policies, which have now been abandoned. Today, some countries are again pursuing expansive population policies, largely because their populations are aging and population growth is declining. The aging population in Europe has moved some countries to institute policies (such as tax incentives and other fiscal measures) that encourage families to have more children.

Birth rates in Russia plummeted after the 1991 collapse of the Soviet Union. The total fertility rate (TFR) in Russia in 1980 was 2.04; in 2008 it was 1.4, according to the World Bank. Prime Minister Vladimir Putin calls the demographic crisis Russia's greatest

> **Expansive population policies**
> Government policies that encourage large families and raise the rate of population growth.

current problem. The Russian government offers cash subsidies of $10,000 to women who give birth to a second or third child.

In response to concerns over Russia's aging population, the government of Ulyanovsk province has held a National Day of Conception each September 12 since 2005. In 2007, government and businesses in Ulyanovsk offered people the afternoon off so they could participate in the National Day of Conception. The government planned to award a free car to the proud parents of one of the children born nine months later, on June 12—the Russian National Day. On June 12, 2008, 87 children were born in Ulyanovsk, about four times the average daily birth rate in the province. Russia experienced an increase in TFR in the first half of 2008, but the ability to sustain a high TFR will depend on many factors, including alleviating social problems, stabilizing incomes, and continued government support.

In the past, some governments engaged in **eugenic population policies**, which were designed to favour one racial or cultural sector of the population over others. Nazi Germany was a drastic example of eugenics, but other countries also have pursued eugenic strategies, though in more subtle ways. Until the time of the civil rights movement in the 1960s, some observers accused the United States of pursuing social policies tinged with eugenics that worked against the interests of African Americans. Some argue that Japan's nearly homogeneous culture is the result of

> **Eugenic population policies**
> Government policies designed to favour one racial sector over others.

deliberately eugenic social policies. Eugenic population policies can be practised covertly through discriminatory taxation, biased allocation of resources, and other forms of favouritism.

Today, the majority of the world's governments seek to reduce the rate of natural increase through various forms of **restrictive population policies**, ranging from toleration of officially unapproved means of birth control to outright prohibition of large families. China's **one-child policy**, instituted after the end of the Maoist period in the 1970s, drastically reduced China's growth rate from one of the world's fastest to one of the developing world's slowest. Under the one-child policy, families having more than one child were penalized financially and denied educational opportunities and housing privileges.

> **Restrictive population policies** Government policies designed to reduce the rate of natural increase.
>
> **One-child policy** A program established by the Chinese government in 1979 to slow population growth in China. Under the policy, families having more than one child were penalized financially and denied educational opportunities and housing privileges.

Population growth rates in China fell quickly under the one-child policy. In the 1970s, China's growth rate was 3 percent; in the mid-1980s it was 1.2 percent; today, China's growth rate is 0.7 percent. The main goal of the one-child policy was achieved, but the policy also had several unintended consequences, including an increased abortion rate, an increase in female infanticide, and a high rate of orphaned girls (many of whom were adopted in the United States and Canada).

During the 1990s, under pressure to improve its human rights records, and also realizing its population was quickly becoming gender- (Figure 4.29) and age-imbalanced, China relaxed its one-child policy. Several caveats allow families to have more than one child. For example, if you live in a rural area and your first child is a girl, you can have a second child, and if both parents of the child are only children, they can have a second child. With these changes, the National Bureau of Statistics of China estimates that the population growth rate in China will climb again over the next 10 years.

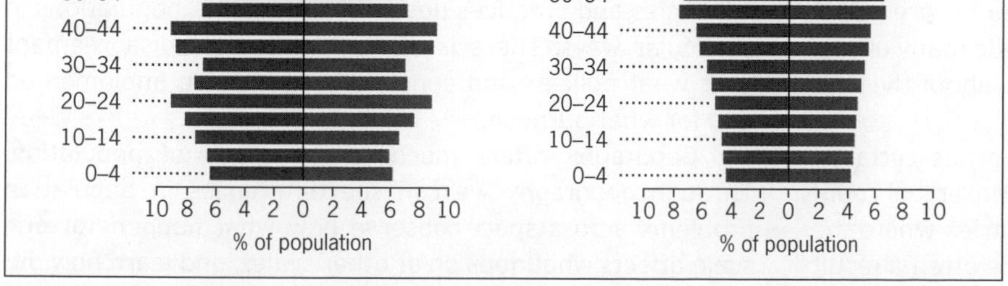

The Canadian government attempted to encourage population growth by introducing a "baby bonus" following World War II. Since that time, various provincial initiatives, most recently in Newfoundland and Labrador, have sought to increase birth rates through various incentives. Debates about the effectiveness of such policies are ongoing. Quebec has been deeply embroiled in these debates. Quebecers historically had large families, thanks to the province's large Roman Catholic population, but Quebec has struggled in the latter half of the 1900s and early 2000s with declining birth rates. In response, the province has taken several pro-natal policy measures. For example, in 1988 Quebec introduced the Allowance for Newborn Children, which paid families up to $8,000 for the birth of a child. Another policy is the $5-a-day childcare program, which encourages young working couples to have children without having to incur the high costs of daycare. The result of such policies has been positive; birth rates continue to rise annually, and in 2007 the provincial birth rate of 1.65 children per woman outranked the national average of 1.59. However, these policies are not without criticism. As Queen's University professor Catherine Krull outlines, some feminists see these policies as marginalizing women by objectifying them as simple demographics. Moreover, the $5-a-day daycare policies cannot meet the growing demand, so Quebec's public daycares have some of the longest waiting lists in the country.

LIMITATIONS

Population policies do not operate independently of circumstances that can influence population growth and decline. In the 1980s, for example, the government of Sweden adopted family-friendly policies designed to promote gender equality and boost fertility rates. The programs focused on alleviating much of the cost of having and raising children. In Sweden, couples who work and have small children receive cash payments, tax incentives, job leaves, and work flexibility that last up to eight years after the birth of a child. The policies led to a mini–baby boom by the early 1990s. When the Swedish economy slowed shortly thereafter, however, so did the birth rate. The children born in 1991 made up a class of 130,000 students in the Swedish education system. But the children born three years later, in 1994, made up a class of only 75,000 students. The government had to build new classrooms for the temporary population boom but then had excess capacity when the boom subsided. Sweden's population policies have helped to produce an RNI that is a little higher than that in many other European countries, but these policies can achieve only so much. With a TFR still well below 2, the Swedish government continues to consider new ways to support families and promote birth rates. One

FIGURE 4.29 Population Pyramids, China: 2010 and 2050. Data from Population Reference Bureau, 2010.

imaginative, but not evidently successful, approach was suggested by a spokeswoman for the Christian Democrat Party, who urged Swedish television to show racier programming at night in hopes of returning the population to a higher birth rate!

CONTRADICTIONS

Some areas of the world with low population growth rates (Figure 4.13) are in the very heart of the Roman Catholic world. Roman Catholic doctrine opposes birth control and abortion. Adherence to this doctrine appears to be stronger in areas remote from the Vatican (the headquarters of the Catholic Church). For example, in the Philippines, thousands of miles from the Vatican, in Asia's only Roman Catholic country, the still-powerful Catholic Church opposes the use of artificial

contraceptives, which the Philippine government supports as a method of controlling population growth. The Catholic Church and the Philippine state agree on abortion, however, as the Philippine constitution prohibits abortion.

Among Islamic countries, the geographic pattern is the opposite. Saudi Arabia, home to Mecca—the heart of Islam—has a population growth rate of 2.7 percent, one of the world's highest. But in Indonesia, thousands of miles from Mecca and near the Philippines, the government began a nationwide family-planning program in 1970. When fundamentalist Muslim leaders objected, the government used a combination of coercion and inducement to negate their influence. By 2000, Indonesia's family-planning program had lowered the growth rate to 1.6 percent, and today it stands at 1.4 percent.

MAIN POINTS   4.4   How Do Governments Affect Population Change?

- Governments are often heavily involved in implementing population laws and policies designed to influence population change and composition. These can take the form of either incentives or prohibitions to dictate the number of children permitted in a family.

- Approaches to the regulation of population composition include tax incentives, the "baby bonus," state-operated daycare, family planning clinics, and parental leave.

- Governments may also impose limits on the number of children permitted through sterilization programs, family planning, and restrictions on access to education.

- Population regulation is also socially and culturally influenced. In particular, religious beliefs about family, the role of women, and the nature of procreation play a substantial role in government and community decision making.

SUMMARY

Population geographers are keenly interested in the demographic and locational aspects of populations. They examine population density, distribution, and composition at a variety of scales from the local to the national, regional, and global. Global population density, distribution, and composition tell us a great deal about the health and stability of particular places. The location of a population or group clearly has an impact on that population's health, survival rate, life expectancy, and quality of life.

In the late 1700s, Thomas Malthus sounded the alarm about the rapidly growing population in Great Britain. He feared a massive famine would soon "check" the growing population, bringing widespread suffering. Although the famine in Great Britain did not take place as he predicted, the rapidly growing worldwide population made many others follow Malthus's lead, issuing similar warnings about the population explosion over the last two centuries.

The growth rate of the world population has certainly slowed, but human suffering is not over yet. Dozens of countries still face high death rates. Even in countries where the death rate is low, slowed population growth is often a result of deplorable sanitary and medical conditions, which cause

high infant and child mortality; diseases such as AIDS, which ravage the population and orphan the young; or famines, which governments deny and global organizations cannot ameliorate.

Population pyramids illustrate that as wealthier countries worry about supporting their aging populations, poorer countries have problems of their own. A high birth rate in a poor country does not necessarily mean overpopulation. Some of the highest population densities in the world are found in wealthy countries. Even poor countries that have lowered their birth rates and their death rates are constantly negotiating what is morally acceptable to their people and their cultures. Governments worldwide are actively engaged in policies and practices designed to regulate populations in particular ways. There is often considerable disagreement over what policies and approaches should be implemented and for what purpose.

Geography offers much to the study of population. Through geography we can see differences in population problems across space, observe how what happens at one scale affects what goes on at other scales, and learn how different cultures and countries approach population questions.

DISCUSSION AND REVIEW QUESTIONS

1. In an historical context, Europe was known as a region of high population that resulted in mass emigration to the New World. However, the situation today is vastly different. Describe this situation today, its causes, and the impacts it will have on European society. What are specific European countries doing to address the challenges they face?

2. Since the first settlements of the Neolithic, people have been unevenly distributed across the globe. Referring to figures 4.6 and 4.7 discuss the where and why of this distribution. For instance, why is the world's population distributed in four main regions?

3. How has population historically changed in Canada? Referencing any of the demographer's tools (fertility,

mortality rates, population pyramid, demographic transition) discuss the current population situation in Canada.

4. Since the first official cases and recognition of HIV/AIDS in the early 1980s, medical geographers have been involved in fighting the disease. Explain the social and demographic affects of this disease and discuss the contributions of medical geographers.

5. Governments have instituted a variety of policies to directly influence their country's demographics. These policies have varied from the controversial to the benign and invariably have been influenced by social ideology. Discuss some of these policies and, by focusing on specific examples, assess their demographic and social impacts.

GEOGRAPHIC CONCEPTS

AIDS   116
arithmetic population density   89
census   96
child mortality rate (CMR)   111
chronic or degenerative diseases   115
crude birth rate (CBR)   103
crude death rate (CDR)   103
demographic transition   103
demography   88
dot maps   91
doubling time   100
endemic   115
epidemic   115
eugenic population policies   118
expansive population policies   118
genetic or inherited diseases   115
infant mortality rate (IMR)   108

infectious diseases   115
life expectancy   111
megalopolis   94
one-child policy   119
pandemic   115
physiologic population density   89
population composition   94
population density   88
population distribution   91
population explosion   100
population geography   88
population pyramids   94
rate of natural increase (RNI)   99
restrictive population policies   119
stationary population level (SPL)   108
total fertility rate (TFR)   100

ADDITIONAL RESOURCES ONLINE

About Population Growth in the World: www.prb.org

About the Composition of the Population of the United States: www.census.gov

About the Global AIDS Crisis: www.unaids.org/en/ www.npr.org/healthscience/aids2004

About International Population Programs: www.unfpa.org

About Stephen Lewis Foundation: www.stephenlewisfoundation.org

About Spread the Net: www.spreadthenet.org

About Grandmothers to Grandmothers Campaign: www.grandmotherscampaign.org

About 2010 World Population and Housing Census Program (United Nations):

unstats.un.org/unsd/demographic/sources/census/ 2010_PHC/default.htm

About the Population Transition in Italy: www.learner.org/ resources/series85.html#program_descriptions

chapter 5

MIGRATION

Mobility for a Reason

IN EARLY AUGUST 2010, Canadian newspapers began reporting that the *MV Sun Sea*, a ship carrying up to 500 Sri Lankan refugees, was expected to arrive on the shores of British Columbia within a few days. The ensuing press coverage was conflicting; editorials in Canada's national newspapers, *The Globe and Mail* and *The National Post*, expressed varying positions on who these refugees were and what Canada's response should be. As I read through the barrage of press coverage, I was struck by the loaded language used in these articles. The men, women, and children aboard *MV Sun Sea* were sometimes "migrants," sometimes "refugees," sometimes "terrorists," amongst other descriptors. What this news coverage revealed is that the arrival of nearly 500 migrants on Canadian shores calls into question how we understand citizenship, belonging, immigration, the role of the nation-state, border security, and refugees, to name but a few. Moreover, it also illustrates what geographer Tim Cresswell calls the "brute materialities" of mobility. Mobility and its regulation have very real effects on the racialized, classed, and gendered bodies of those who often risk their lives to immigrate to countries such as Canada.

(a)   (b)

FIGURE 5.1 "Boat Migrants" from Fujian, China. (a) Migrants arrive by boat in Nootka Sound, B.C., August 3, 1999. (b) Chinese migrants attend an immigration hearing on August 20, 1999. (*Vancouver Sun*)

Across the world, hundreds of thousands of migrants and refugees have left their homelands by boat, plane, train, car, or foot for opportunities in Europe or such countries as Canada, the United States, Australia, and Brazil. Immigrants are sometimes welcomed and sometimes turned away. The Sri Lankans on the *MV Sun Sea* are only the most recent example of the controversies surrounding migrants in Canada. In another instance, during the summer of 1999, some 600 men, women, and children from Fujian, China, arrived off the coast of British Columbia in four dilapidated boats (Figure 5.1). Newspaper and press reports made much of their desperate plight, noting the "boat migrants" had paid human smugglers their life savings for the chance at a new life in Canada. As geographer Alison Mountz notes, their arrival sparked intense debate in Canada about the sovereignty of Canada as a "nation state, manifest in the perception of its ability to police its borders." After spending several years in detention, only 24 individuals received refugee status. Most were deported back to China. While it is difficult to calculate the number of illegal migrants in Canada, estimates place that number between 35,000 and 120,000 in 2007. It is important to remember, though, that these numbers are relative. The estimated number of illegal immigrants in the United States is 11 million.

When we think about mobility—the socially produced movements that make up our everyday lives—we often assume it is universal and always positive. In other words, we assume mobility is inherently good and is something to which we all have equal access. As geographers who are concerned with the world around us, we must engage with and ask questions about the increased movement of goods, people, information, and capital at the global, national, regional, and local scales. Who gets to move and who doesn't? How and why do people move? To where are they moving? How are people's movements blocked or impeded? What does it mean to be forced to move? When we begin to ask these questions, it be-comes apparent that mobility is a complex issue. Sometimes people have to migrate to avoid persecution or to find work. Sometimes people are not allowed to move and are forced underground.

Mobility is tightly regulated and controlled. Think of the Mexico–United States Barrier (see Chapter 3), or of the vast security measures that you have to pass through to enter the United States for a holiday or a shopping trip. We carefully construct "secure" borders through the use of surveillance technologies, walls, fences, border patrols, customs procedures, and so forth. We must also consider the plethora of statutes and legal regulations enacted to manage the movement of immigrants and refugees. In Canada, the primary statute is the *Immigration and Refugee Protection Act* S.C. 2001, c. 27. In the aftermath of the arrival of the Sri Lankan migrants in August 2010, the minority Conservative government introduced a controversial new bill entitled *Preventing Human Smugglers from Abusing Canada's Immigration System Act*, aimed at deterring the practices of human smuggling and illegal immigration into Canada. The proposed act includes stiffer jail times and fines for those found guilty of human smuggling. However, the proposed act has come under attack by the opposition parties, with critics claiming that it criminalizes the victims of smugglers. The Liberals have dubbed it an "anti-immigrant" policy because, they argue, it penalizes migrants seeking refugee status, allowing them to be detained for a year without review, and barring them from becoming permanent residents for five years if their refugee claim is accepted. The new act seems to contradict recent strategies aimed at welcoming immigrants to bolster declining birth rates and to contribute to the nation's pool of skilled labour for economic growth and investment (see Chapter 4). The act is also seen as a departure from Canada's long history as a welcoming destination for many of the world's peoples and a model of a successful multicultural state.

KEY QUESTIONS FOR CHAPTER 5

1. What is migration?
2. Why do people migrate?
3. Where do people migrate?
4. How do governments affect migration?

5.1 What Is Migration?

Migration is about human movement, and movement is one of the five themes this book uses to illustrate how we might employ a spatial or geographical perspective in considering issues and problems. Movement changes people. It changes how they see themselves and their place in the world. Movement changes places—both the places that people leave and the places they settle. Humans bring new ideas and feelings to their new homes, altering the landscape and building a new sense of place and community. Human movement speeds the diffusion of ideas and innovations, intensifies spatial interaction, and transforms regions.

In this chapter, we consider what we mean by "immigration" and we examine various types of migration. We also need to understand why migrants choose to leave a particular place and go to another—the "push" and "pull" aspects of immigration. Some immigration is "voluntary"—that is, people migrate to new employment or to be with family. Others are forced to migrate due to war or political or social persecution. We also examine how government policies shape human migration and consider why government immigration policies might change. By employing some of our five geographic themes, including movement, region, and scale, in our analysis of human migration, we hope to shed light on the nature and meaning of migration flows and to gain an appreciation for why people migrate, where they migrate, and how people, places, and landscapes change as a result.

The events of September 11, 2001, remind us that, within the framework of globalization, a singular event can fundamentally alter our perception of the movement of people. These processes of globalization, discussed in Chapter 2, are now at play in unprecedented ways. We are experiencing increasing integration and interconnectivity among people and places, brought about, in part, by the greater mobility of individuals and groups across state borders, continents, and hemispheres. Globalizing processes seem to be breaking down state borders and challenging the ability of the nation-state to regulate the flows of people and materials, as so clearly illustrated in the opening field note. As we discussed in Chapter 3, nation-states are concerned with borders and boundaries and with preserving sovereignty (or control) over what happens within their borders, including who enters into and leaves their territory. Despite the increasing mobility some people might experience through the processes of globalization, states continue to enforce laws that determine who may enter and who may remain within a country's borders. As noted in Chapter 4, in places such as Canada, where the total fertility rate is falling below replacement levels, setting appropriate immigration targets and ensuring we have people with the skills needed in the Canadian workplace is of paramount importance. A properly functioning immigration policy and practice is central to the economic and social well-being of all Canadians.

Migration is about movement, and the movement of humans takes several forms. Mobility ranges from local to global, from the daily to the once in a lifetime. Mobility has increased markedly for some people in some places over the past decades. Those experiencing greater mobility are able to broaden their perspectives, which perhaps encourages further mobility. People are on the move for numerous reasons—fleeing famine and war, seeking greater economic opportunities, moving closer to relatives, or obtaining a better education.

FORMS OF MOVEMENT AND MIGRATION

There are a variety of ways in which people move from place to place. For example, the traditional nomadic practices of the world's indigenous peoples are dwindling, but they have been a matter of survival, culture, and tradition—and remain so for nomadic peoples who can still be found in parts of Asia, South and Central America, and Africa. Westerners often envision **nomadism** as an aimless wandering across steppe and desert by small groups of rootless roamers—people who

> **Nomadism** Movement among a definite set of places—often cyclic movement.

claim no territory and do not behave territorially. In reality, nomads need to know their territory well in order to find water, food, and shelter in their cyclic movements. Nomadic movement takes place along long-familiar routes followed time and again. The nomads and their animals visit water sources and pastures that have served their ancestors for centuries. Weather conditions may affect the timing of their travel, but barring obstacles such as fenced international borders or the privatization of long-used open country, nomads engage in cyclic movement. Nomadic people can pose a series of problems in terms of government regulation because they do not fit into the categories of migration outlined below. For example, Roma people, sometimes called gypsies, are a heterogeneous ethnic group that travels through Europe, western Asia, and Latin America. In August 2010, France expelled over 700 Roma people who had set up camps in the country, invoking a policy that required them to have a work permit to prove that they could support themselves (Figure 5.2). Most were sent to Romania and Bulgaria. France has faced international scrutiny for its dealings with the Roma people; its policies have been called both xenophobic and racist.

When movement results in permanent relocation across significant distances, we call it **migration**. The process of migration involves the long-term relocation of an individual, household, or larger group to a new locale outside the community of origin—movement that is about leaving home for

> **Migration** A change in residence intended to be permanent.
>
> **International migration** Human movement involving movement across international boundaries.

a significant duration, if not permanently. Clearly, this can occur at a variety of scales. We can migrate to a new neighbourhood in the same town in which we grew up or we can relocate to another country in pursuit of a career or new opportunities.

International migration, or transnational migration, is movement across a country's borders. When people leave their

FIGURE 5.2 France Expels Roma People. Romani gypsies are escorted by French police officers to the check-in desk for their departure flights at Roissy Charles de Gaulle airport, near Paris, August 20, 2010. The French government has come under heavy criticism from human rights groups who have referred to the expulsions as "disgraceful." (© Michel Euler/The Canadian Press)

home country, they are classified as emigrants (those who migrate out) of the home country. When the same migrants enter a new country, they are classified as immigrants (those who migrate in) of the new country—how we are defined depends on where we are. As we discussed in Chapter 4, **emigration** subtracts from the total population of a country, and **immigration** adds to the total

Emigration The act of leaving one location or place for another, from the perspective of the beginning location.

Immigration The act of migrating into a new country or area.

population of a country. The United Nations defines international migrants as "persons born in a country other than that in which they live." According to the International Organization for Migration, there were approximately 214 million international migrants in the world by mid-2010—a number that has increased significantly since 2000, when there were 150 million international migrants. That being said, the share of the world's population who are international migrants has remained stable (3.1 percent of the world's population); in other words, the increase in numbers reflects the growth in world population. As Figure 5.3 illustrates, some regions have a much greater migrant population than others. As a percentage of total population, Qatar has the highest percentage of international migrants, at 87 percent, followed by United Arab Emirates (70 percent) and Kuwait (69 percent). In Canada, 21.3 percent of the total population is composed of international migrants—approximately 7.2 million people.

It is important to remember that international migration is nothing new. As early as the 1600s, some cities had substantial immigrant populations. For example, 25 percent of Amsterdam's population in 1620 was foreign-born. As well, during the last major phase of globalization in the late 1800s, the percentage of the world's population that migrated was slightly higher than it is today. There are some important differences, however. Historically, it was very difficult to migrate from one country to another logistically, but once you arrived at your destination, there were relatively few regulatory and/or legal barriers. Today, the opposite is true. While it may be easier to move around the globe with improved transportation and communication technologies, the legal and regulatory frameworks make it much more difficult to settle in a new country than it has been in the past.

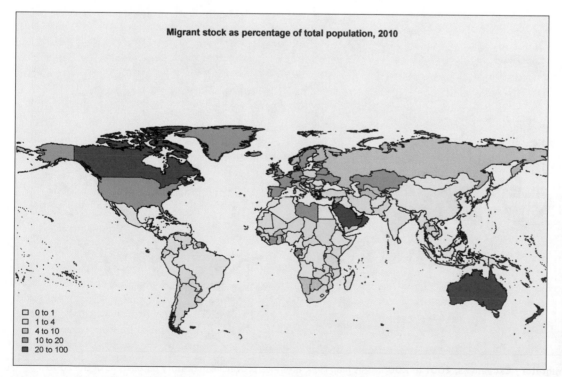

Migrant stock as percentage of total population, 2010

- 0 to 1
- 1 to 4
- 4 to 10
- 10 to 20
- 20 to 100

FIGURE 5.3 Migrant Stock as a Percentage of Total Population, 2010. This map shows international migrants as a percentage of total population. Countries represented as dark green have the highest concentration of international migrants, at 20 percent or greater. From United Nations, Department of Economic and Social Affairs, Population Division, 2009.

Internal migration Human movement within a nation-state, such as ongoing westward and southward movements in Canada.

Countries also experience **internal migration**—migration that occurs within a single country's borders. Mapping internal migration routes reveals well-defined patterns that change over time. Internal migration varies according to the mobility of the population, which can fluctuate over a country's territory. In mobile societies, internal migration over long distances is common. In Peru, which has a less mobile society than Canada, the pattern of internal migration is generally from rural to urban. Migrants leave rural areas and move to Lima, the capital. Global and national investment capital is concentrated in Lima, which represents the major focus of economic opportunity for the rural population. Lima receives the vast majority of Peru's migrants, regardless of age, gender, or marital status.

In Canada, the flow of internal migration is not as simple as rural to urban, although rural to urban migration has been a characteristic of Canada's internal migration for some time (Figure 5.4). During difficult economic times, different regions in Canada experience declining economic conditions, and individuals migrate internally to other parts of the country, often seeking work. For example, after the 1992 cod moratorium, Newfoundland and Labrador experienced 10 years of population decline. While urban centres maintained relatively stable populations, smaller towns and villages—especially those developed around the fishery—experienced losses of up to 18 percent of the total population. Because the population loss was significant and sustained over a long period of time, the province has faced considerable social and economic challenges. Census information from 2006 shows dense out-migration from the Maritime provinces, Saskatchewan, and Manitoba. Ontario, particularly the Golden Horseshoe (Oshawa-Toronto-Hamilton-Niagara), and Alberta show the most significant increases in migratory exchanges, illustrating migration to places that offer greater economic opportunity.

WHO ARE MIGRANTS?

For human geographers, a key part of understanding migration is considering who migrants are. As the opening field note indicates, there is much confusion in the public realm about who migrants are; they are often described as "refugees," "migrants," or "guest workers." In the most general sense, those who move from one region or country to another are called migrants, which includes international and internal migrants discussed above. In this section we take a closer look at guest workers and refugees.

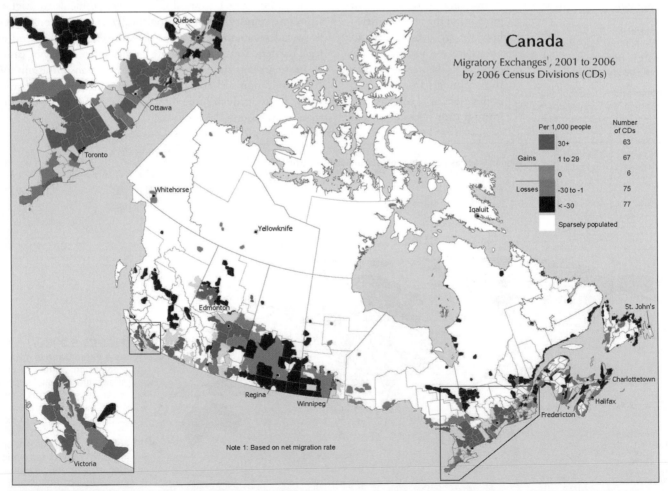

FIGURE 5.4 Canada: Migratory Exchanges, 2001 to 2006. This map illustrates interprovincial migratory patterns as of the 2006 census. Places shaded in green have experienced the greatest increase in population, whereas those shaded in dark purple have experienced the most significant losses. Data from 2006 Census. Map produced by Statistics Canada, Geography Division, 2008.

GUEST WORKERS

After World War II, European countries needed to rebuild their economies and found themselves in need of labourers. Two flows of migration into Western European countries began. The first flow of migrants comprised labourers from poorer European countries, who migrated to European countries that were experiencing solid economic growth. The second flow of **migrant labour** came from outside Europe, as millions of foreign workers emigrated from such North African countries as Algeria, Egypt, Libya, and Sudan. In addition, a large number of migrants came to Germany from Turkey, and many migrants from the Caribbean region, India, and Africa came to the United Kingdom.

> **Migrant labour** A common type of periodic movement involving tens of millions of workers worldwide who cross international borders in search of employment and become immigrants, in many instances.

Western European governments called the labour migrants **guest workers**. Guest workers are legal (documented) migrants who have work visas, usually short term, although destination governments will often extend the visas if certain sectors of the economy still need labourers. The international flow of guest workers changes the ethnic, linguistic, and religious mosaic of the places where they go regardless of whether their stay is short or long term. The laws allowing guest workers into Europe assumed the workers were temporary and would fill the void left by those who died during World War II before returning to their home countries. Instead, the guest workers often stayed—both because they wanted to and because they were needed. Two to three generations of Turks have now been born in Germany, making them far more than "guests." The German government, which for decades defined German citizens as those of German descent, only recently allowed Turks to become German citizens.

> **Guest worker** Legal immigrant who has a work visa, usually short term.

In many countries around the world, millions of guest workers live and work far from their home country and send **remittances** back to their families. Guest workers are often employed as agricultural labourers or in service industries (e.g., hotels, restaurants, tourist attractions). The home states of these workers are fully aware that their citizens have visas and are working abroad; in fact, the economies of many poorer countries in the Caribbean, Africa, Central and South America, and Eurasia depend in part on remittances sent to their citizens. Haitian immigrants living in the United States, Canada, and the Caribbean, for example, sent home over $1 billion in remittances in 2007, a figure equivalent to 30 percent of Haiti's gross domestic product and far outpacing the value of Haitian exports. The 2001 census in Haiti estimates that one in five households in Haiti receives remittances from abroad. In 2007, Mexican immigrants sent $23.98 billion in remittances home, up from $23.05 billion the year before. In total, at the global scale, 2009 estimates indicate that approximately $414 billion in remittances are sent round the world.

> **Remittances** Money migrants send back to family and friends in their home countries, often in cash, forming an important part of the economy in many poorer countries.

Home governments work with destination countries and with international labour organizations to protect the rights of the guest workers, but despite the legal status of guest workers, and despite the efforts of governments and international organizations to protect them, many employers abuse them with impunity because guest workers are often unaware of their rights. Long hours and low pay are common, but guest workers continue to work because the money is better than they would ordinarily receive and because they are supporting families at home.

In Canada, seasonal agricultural workers are granted admission to enter Canada to fill labour shortages in the agricultural sector during peak periods, mainly in southern Ontario and central British Columbia (Figure 5.5). The Canadian Seasonal Agricultural Worker Program (CSAWP) is run jointly by the Canadian government, under the *Immigration and Refugee Protection Act*, with the governments of Mexico and participating Caribbean states. According to the North-South Institute, in 2004, there were 10,777 seasonal workers from Mexico and 8,110 from various Caribbean states working in Canada's agricultural industries. CSAWP is not without controversy and critique, mostly focused on the working conditions for seasonal agricultural workers, who work 60 to 70 hours a week for minimum wage—conditions that most Canadians will not accept. It is also precarious work, with workers reliant on their employers for transportation, housing, and regular payment of wages. In November 2010, the CBC reported on a small group of Mexican agricultural workers in Simcoe, Ontario, who were stranded when their employer left the country without paying their wages. Owed thousands of dollars, the Mexicans were awaiting support from the Mexican consulate to fly them home. This case makes evident the extent to which guest workers rely on their employers for fair and equitable employment standards. It also shows how easily their situations can become dire when employers do not live up to their agreements.

FIGURE 5.5 Migrant Farm Workers, Leamington, Ontario. These workers toil for long hours for minimum wage. Under the CSAWP, a worker's flight to and from their home country is paid for, as is their accommodation. All other expenses, including food, must be paid for by the workers. Still, their remittances go a long way toward supporting their families. (© 2011 UFCW Canada/www.ufcw.ca)

REFUGEES

You may have seen a story on television news showing thousands upon thousands of people fleeing a crisis in their home region or country by walking. They put their few earthly possessions and their babies on their backs and walk. They walk to another town. They walk beyond their country's border. They walk to a refugee camp without adequate food, water, or amenities. International agencies attempt desperate relief efforts while disease spreads, dooming infants and children and emaciating adults. For example, when the former Yugoslavia, composed of a federation of six republics, began to disintegrate in 1991, more than 2.3 million people fled their homelands for other nations such as Germany, Hungary, Austria, and Sweden, leading to the largest refugee crisis in Europe since World War II (Figure 5.6).

The world's refugee population has grown steadily since the 1951 establishment of the United Nations' Convention Relating to the Status of Refugees, an international law specifying who is a refugee and what legal rights they have. The convention defines a

> **Refugees** People who have fled their country because of political persecution and seek asylum in another country.

refugee as "a person who has a well-founded fear of being persecuted for reasons of race, religion, nationality, membership of a particular social group, or political opinion." Countries interpret this definition in different ways, especially since the phrase "well-founded" leaves much room for judgement. The main goal of the 1951 Refugee Convention was to help European refugees following the end of World War II. The United Nations High Commissioner for Refugees (UNHCR) helped to repatriate (return to their homeland) most of the refugees from World War II.

In 1970, the United Nations reported 2.9 million persons were refugees; the majority were Palestinian Arabs dislocated by the creation of the state of Israel and the armed conflicts that followed. In 1980, the refugee total had nearly tripled, to over 8 million. In 2007, the UNHCR reported 11.4 million refugees

(not counting Palestinian refugees in Jordan and Syria) forced from their homes and across country borders. While there are approximately 15.2 million refugees worldwide in 2010, this is lower than it has been historically. Refugee numbers peaked in the early 1990s, with people trying to escape wars in the former Yugoslavia and Afghanistan. At that time, there were 20 million refugees worldwide.

The UNHCR is the agency that monitors the refugee problem and is the key organization supporting refugees. It organizes and funds international relief efforts and negotiates with governments and regimes on behalf of refugees. But UNHCR is not alone in tracking this global problem; other agencies often contradict UNHCR data, arguing that the situation, especially for **internally displaced persons** (called IDPs or internal refugees) is even worse than the United Nations suggests. The United Nations and international law

> **Internally displaced persons (IDPs)** People who have been displaced within their own countries and do not cross international borders as they flee.

distinguish between refugees, who have crossed one or more international borders during their move and encamped in a country other than their own, and IDPs, who abandon their homes but remain in their own countries (such as the victims of Hurricane Katrina). IDPs tend to remain undercounted, if not almost invisible. In 2007, UNHCR estimated that 26 million people (in addition to the 11.4 million official refugees) were IDPs.

Because the status of a refugee is internationally defined and recognized and comes with legal rights, the UNHCR and nation-states distinguish between people who are refugees and those migrants who may be just as poor or desperate but who do not qualify for refugee status. When a refugee meets the official criteria, he or she becomes eligible for assistance, including possible **asylum** (the right to protection in the first country in which the refugee arrives),

> **Asylum** Shelter and protection in one state for refugees from another state.

to which other migrants are not entitled. Such assistance can extend over decades and become the very basis for a way of life, as has happened in the Middle East. In Jordan, Palestinian refugees have become so integrated into the host country's national life that they are regarded as permanent refugees; in Lebanon, however, Palestinians wait in refugee camps for resettlement and still qualify as temporary refugees.

In another example, *The Globe and Mail* reported that in early February 2011, in the wake of the overthrowing of Tunisia's dictator Zine El Abidine Ben Ali, thousands of Tunisians fled the country, seeking asylum on the tiny Italian island of Lampedusa. Lampedusa, an isolated island in the southern Mediterranean, is close to both Libya and Tunisia, and due to this proximity many have chosen to take the risky boat voyage across the Mediterranean Sea. By early February, over 6,000 refugees had arrived, which is greater than the entire island population. In what became known as "a Libyan solution" the Berlusconi government paid dictator Moammar Gadhafi a large sum of money to round up those attempting to flee Libya, and to police its beaches. In response to the Tunisian situation, United Nations Secretary-General Ban

FIGURE 5.6 Yugoslav Refugees. This photograph, taken in 1999, shows Kosovar refugees fleeing their homeland in the former Yugoslav Republic of Macedonia. (© UN Photo/R. LeMoyne)

Ki-moon reminded Italy of its responsibilities to the refugees, in ensuring that their basic human rights are protected.

The United Nations helps ensure that refugees and IDPs are not forcibly returned to a homeland where persecution continues. Once the violence subsides and the conditions improve, the UNHCR helps return refugees to their homelands, a process called **repatriation**. In the 1990s, hostilities broke out between the Hutu and Tutsi ethnic groups in Rwanda that led to the **genocide** of hundreds of thousands of people and a disastrous exodus of more than one million refugees, who fled to neighbouring Democratic Republic of Congo (then called Zaire), Tanzania, and Uganda. The Tutsi-Hutu strife in Rwanda spread to neighbouring Burundi and dislocated tens of thousands there. After the civil war in Rwanda in 1996, the UNHCR and the World Health Organization watched and helped as 500,000 Rwandans returned from nearby nations, including the Democratic Republic of Congo and Uganda (Figure 5.7).

> **Repatriation** A refugee or group of refugees returning to their home country, usually with the assistance of government or a non-governmental organization.
>
> **Genocide** The deliberate and systematic destruction, in whole or in part, of an ethnic, racial, religious, or national group.

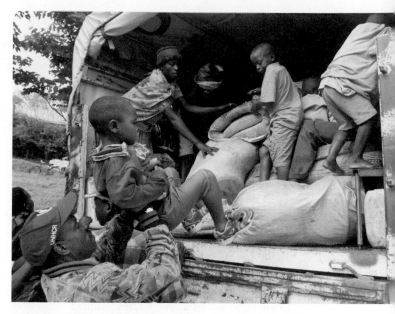

FIGURE 5.7 Rwandans Return Home. A UNHCR official helps a Rwandan child to board a truck at Nakivavele refugee camp in western Uganda, January 19, 2004, as a first group 242 Rwandan refugees, mostly children born after the 1994 genocide, began returning home. (© Patrick Olum/Stringer/Reuters/Corbis)

MAIN POINTS 5.1 What Is Migration?

- Migration is a form of human movement, which can take many forms depending on the nature and permanence of that movement.

- Migration can be international or transnational, meaning the individual crosses state borders.

- An emigrant is defined as a person who leaves a place to settle elsewhere, while an immigrant is someone who comes from elsewhere to settle in a place.

- Migration can also be examined on a more local scale. Geographers study population movement within a country's boundaries, such as movement between provinces. They study the movement of people from rural to urban areas or from urban to suburban areas. Finally, they consider movement between neighbourhoods in the same region, city, or town.

- Migrants can be guest workers, refugees, or internally displaced persons.

5.2 Why Do People Migrate?

Migration can be the result of a voluntary action, a conscious decision to move from one place to the next. It can also be the result of involuntary action, a forced movement imposed by one group of people on another group of people. **Voluntary migration** occurs after a migrant weighs options and choices (even if desperately or not so rationally), and can be analyzed and understood as a series of options or choices that result in movement. **Forced migration** involves the imposition of authority or power, producing involuntary movement that cannot be understood based on theories of choice.

> **Voluntary migration** Movement in which people relocate in response to perceived opportunity, not because they are forced to move.
>
> **Forced migration** Human migration flows in which the movers have no choice but to relocate.

The distinction between voluntary and forced migration is not always clear-cut. The enormous European migration to North America during the 19th and early 20th centuries is often cited as a prime example of voluntary migration. However, some European migration can be construed as forced. The British treatment of the Irish during their colonial rule over Ireland can be seen as political persecution—a cause for forced migration. During British colonialism in Ireland, the British took control of nearly all the Irish Catholic lands and discouraged the operation of the Catholic Church in Ireland. Until 1829, the British enforced penal laws preventing Irish Catholics from buying land, voting, or carrying weapons. The mass exodus of migrants from Ireland to North America in the mid-1800s can be seen as forced, both because of the British treatment of the Irish and because of the potato famine, but it can also be seen as voluntary in that the Irish chose to go to North America. What is clear is that the notion of "choice" in examples such as this is subject to much debate and controversy.

At the scale of an individual region or country, we can question whether a decision to migrate is forced or voluntary. At the scale of the household, the decision to migrate is all the more complex. For certain members of a migrating household, the move may be under duress, while for others, the move may be a preferred choice. The neutral title "migrant" veils the complexities of decision making at the household scale including distinctions based on such things as gender or age. At the household scale, geographers consider power relationships, divisions of labour, and gender identities as they attempt to understand migration flows. Here, decisions are made, in geographer Victoria Lawson's terms, in a "cooperative conflict bargaining process." Who has a say in this process and how much of a say each individual has depends on gendered power relationships and responsibilities in the household.

Studies of gender and migration find that, in many regions, men are more mobile than women, and men migrate farther than women. Generally, men have more choices of employment than women, and women earn less than men in the jobs they find at the destination. One study of migration in Mexican households

found that strongly patriarchal households shield young women from migration, sending young men out to work. Mexican households without a strong patriarchy send young, unmarried women to the city or another country to gain employment. Geographer Gerry Pratt, in her study of Filipina domestic workers in Vancouver, found that despite their educational credentials, a segregated labour market ensured narrowed occupational possibilities based on assumptions about women's "natural" abilities as caregivers regardless of their level of education.

Geographers cannot easily describe migration flows in terms of men and women or forced and voluntary. Ultimately, the decision or directive to migrate happens to an individual migrant within a household, place, country, region, and world, each of which has its own dynamics. The key difference between voluntary and forced migration, however, is that voluntary migrants have an option (at the very least—where to go or what to do once there); forced migrants do not.

FORCED MIGRATION

The largest and most devastating forced migration in the history of humanity was the Atlantic slave trade, which carried tens of millions of Africans from their homes to South America, the Caribbean, and North America, with huge loss of life. The number of Africans sold into slavery will never be known (estimates range from 12 million to 30 million). However, as Figure 5.8 shows, a considerable majority of Africans forced

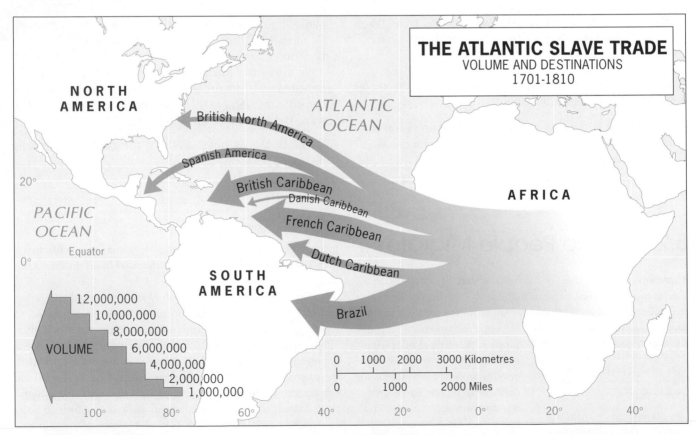

FIGURE 5.8 The Atlantic Slave Trade. Adapted with permission from Philip D. Curtin, *The Atlantic Slave Trade* (University of Wisconsin Press, 1969), p. 57; and Donald K. Fellows, *Geography* (John Wiley & Sons, Inc., 1967, p. 121.)

across the Atlantic went to the Caribbean, Spanish Central America, and Brazil, a Portuguese colony until 1822. In North America the destination was more often coastal Middle America (especially Maryland and Virginia) rather than the Deep South.

The Atlantic slave trade began during the 16th century, when Africans were first brought to the Caribbean. In the early decades of the 17th century, they were brought in small numbers to plantations developing in coastal eastern North America. Plantation economies from the southeastern United States to Brazil helped drive the slave trade. Plantation work, both planting and harvesting, was labour-intensive, and plantation owners realized their wealth through the exploitation of slave labour. Of all crops produced on plantations in the Americas and Caribbean during the 1700s, sugar was the most important economically, followed by coffee and fruit. The wealth promised by plantation agriculture created a demand for slaves by plantation owners, who paid European shippers for slaves. The shippers, in turn, paid African raiders.

The terror and destruction of slave raiding afflicted large areas of Africa. Much of West Africa, from Liberia to Nigeria and inland to the margins of the Sahara, was exploited. So many Africans were taken to Bahia, in Brazil, from the area that is now Benin that significant elements of the local culture remained intact in the transition. Today there are strong ties between Bahia and Benin, and cultural exchanges are growing stronger. The entire Equatorial African coastal region was victimized as well, and Portuguese slave traders raided freely in the Portuguese domains of Angola and Mozambique. Arab slave raiders were active in East Africa and the Horn, penetrating Equatorial Africa and often cooperating with the Europeans. Zanzibar, off the coast of mainland Tanzania, was long a major slave market.

We know proportionately where slaves were ultimately relocated, but we can never gauge the full impact of this horrific period. In *A Colonizer's Model of the World*, geographer James Blaut discusses the loss to African civilizations that occurred when significant populations were enslaved. The Atlantic slave trade also changed the Caribbean, where on many islands the vast majority of people are of African-Caribbean descent, and few, if any, indigenous peoples remain. In combination, the slave trade inflicted incalculable damage on African societies and communities, and changed the cultural and ethnic geography of Brazil, Central America, and the United States.

Canada's role in the history of slavery is most often connected to the Underground Railroad, which in the mid-1800s was a series of secret routes and safe houses used to help black slaves escape to Canada, where slavery had been abolished. Estimates indicate that between 30,000 and 100,000 American slaves came secretly to Canada from 1840 to 1860, settling mostly in a triangle between Toronto, Niagara Falls, and Windsor, Ontario. However, Canada played an important role in the Atlantic slave trade as a colony of both France and Britain, two of the world's largest traffickers of slaves. Research has shown that at least 60 of the ships used by the British to transport slaves were built in Canada. Moreover, from 1628 to 1834, slavery was institutionalized in Canada. Canada's dubious history of involvement in slavery has become evident in at least two historical accounts

published in 2007 and 2005, respectively. Canadian novelist Lawrence Hill's *The Book of Negroes* was based on a handwritten ledger of the same name that kept account of over 3,000 blacks who left New York for Nova Scotia in search of freedom, only to find poverty, disease, and further servitude. Another book, *Rough Crossings* by Simon Schama, recounts the ill treatment of Black Loyalists sent from London to Nova Scotia after the American War of Independence. In the world's first back-to-Africa voyage, 1,000 of these individuals, angry at Britain's betrayal of them, sailed to Sierra Leone within 10 years of arriving in Nova Scotia.

These two historical accounts both centre on the town of Birchtown, Nova Scotia (Figure 5.9). Birchtown was home to the largest population of free Blacks outside Africa in the late 1700s. The term used to describe the migration away from their ancestral homeland by a group of people sharing an ethnic background is **diaspora**. Indeed, the Black community that emerged in Birchtown would be considered a diaspora in that they were displaced forcibly from their ancestral homeland in Africa and felt a common desire to return. During the American War of Independence from British colonial rule in the 1770s, Black Loyalists (those remaining loyal to the king of Britain) agreed to take arms against the Americans, with the promise of free land in Nova Scotia. Many found their way to Shelburne, Nova Scotia, and settled in nearby Birchtown, only to discover that the British promises would not be kept.

Diaspora From the Greek "to disperse," a term describing forceful or voluntary dispersal of a people from their homeland to a new place. Originally denoting the dispersal of Jews, it is increasingly applied to other population dispersals, such as the involuntary relocation of Black peoples during the slave trade or Chinese peoples outside of Mainland China, Taiwan, and Hong Kong.

FIGURE 5.9 The Birchtown Plaque. This Historic Sites and Monuments Board plaque, located in Birchtown, Nova Scotia, and erected in 1996, commemorates more than 3,500 black Loyalists who once resided there. (© United Empire Loyalists' Association of Canada)

Forced to work at rates below those of white workers in order to survive, racial tensions grew, and in 1784, Birchtown became the site of the first race riot in North America. In 1791, nearly half the population of Birchtown decided to depart on ships bound for Sierra Leone. Other diasporas include the Irish exiled by the British from their homelands and, perhaps the most well-known example, the Jewish diaspora, when the Israelites were expelled from Israel, Jordan, and parts of Lebanon, beginning in the eighth century BC.

Although no forced migration in human history compares in magnitude to the Atlantic slave trade, there have been other forced migrations that have changed the world's demographic map. For 50 years, beginning in 1788, tens of thousands of convicts were shipped from Britain to Australia, where they had a lasting impact on the continent's population geography. In the 1800s, the Canadian government took lands from thousands of First Nations peoples and forcibly moved them to other areas of the country—sometimes far from their traditional homelands. In the Soviet Union during Stalin's ruthless rule between the late 1920s and 1953, the government forcibly moved millions of non-Russians from their homes to remote parts of Central Asia and Siberia for political reasons. During the 1930s in Germany, the Nazis were responsible for a significant forced migration of Jews from portions of western Europe that fell under their control. Forced migration still happens today, often in the form of counter-migration, where governments return migrants caught entering their countries illegally. As noted in the opening field note, Canada deported most of the 600 Chinese "boat immigrants" who landed illegally on the west coast in the summer of 1999.

VOLUNTARY MIGRATION

Why do people choose to migrate? Researchers have been intrigued by this question for more than a century. Studies of voluntary migration flows indicate that the intensity of a migration flow varies with such factors as similarities between the source (place of origin) and the destination, the effectiveness of the flow of information from the destination back to the source, and the physical distance between the source and the destination.

Over a century ago, British demographer Ernst Ravenstein sought an answer to the question of why people voluntarily migrate. He studied internal migration in England, and on the basis of his data he proposed several **laws of migration**, many of which are still relevant today, including the following five:

> **Laws of migration** Developed by British demographer Ernst Ravenstein, five laws that predict the flow of migrants.

1. Every migration flow generates a return or counter-migration.
2. The majority of migrants move a short distance.
3. Migrants who move longer distances tend to choose big-city destinations.
4. Urban residents are less migratory than inhabitants of rural areas.
5. Families are less likely to make international moves than young adults.

Ravenstein also posited an inverse relationship between the volume of migration and the distance between source and destination; that is, the number of migrants to a destination declines as the distance they must travel increases.

Ravenstein's ideas were an early articulation of the **gravity model**, which predicts interaction between places based on their population size and the distance between them. The gravity model assumes any form of spatial interaction (such as migration) is directly related to the populations and inversely related to the distance between them—an assumption that had more meaning in an age before airplane travel and the Internet. In mathematical terms, the equation for the gravity model is the multiplication of the two populations divided by the square of the distance between them.

> **Gravity model** A mathematical prediction of the interaction of places, the interaction being a function of population size of the respective places and the distance between them.

PUSH AND PULL FACTORS INFLUENCING MIGRATION

Although the gravity model gives us a guide to expected migration, migration is not as simple as a mathematical equation. When a person, family, or group of people makes a voluntary decision to migrate, push and pull factors come into play. **Push factors** are the conditions and perceptions that help the migrant decide to leave a place. **Pull factors** are the circumstances that effectively attract the migrant to certain locales from other places—the decision about where to go. Migrants' decisions to emigrate from their home country and migrate to a new country are the result of a combination of push and pull factors—and these factors play out differently depending on the circumstance and scale of the migration. Because migrants are likely to be more familiar with their place of residence (source) than with the locale to which they are moving (destination), they will likely perceive push factors more accurately than pull factors. Push factors include individual considerations such as work or retirement conditions, cost of living, personal safety and security, and, for many, environmental catastrophes or even issues such as weather and climate. Pull factors tend to be vaguer and may depend solely on perceptions based on things heard and read rather than on personal experiences in the destination place. Often migrants move on the basis of excessively positive images and expectations regarding their destinations.

> **Push factor** Negative conditions and perceptions that induce people to leave their abode and migrate to a new locale.
>
> **Pull factor** Positive conditions and perceptions that effectively attract people to new locales from other areas.

Many migration streams that appear on maps as long, unbroken routes in fact consist of a series of stages, a phenomenon known as **step migration**. A peasant family in rural Brazil, for example, is likely to move first to a village, then to a nearby town, later to a city, and finally to a metropolis such as Sao Paulo or Rio de Janeiro. At each stage, a new set of pull factors comes into play.

> **Step migration** Migration to a distant destination that occurs in stages; for example, from farm to nearby village and later to town and city.

Not all migrants from one place follow the same steps. For example, when 1,000 people leave a village and migrate to a town in a given year, most, if not all, of them may dream of making it to—and in—the "big city." But perhaps only 500 people actually move from town to city, and of these, only, say, 200 eventually reach the metropolis that impelled them to move in the first place. Along the way, the majority are captured by **intervening opportunity**. In Canada, for example, many migrants from Atlantic Canada make their way westward by way of Montreal and Toronto. While many continue their journey, others find opportunities in these cities and do not carry on to their original destination.

> **Intervening opportunity** The presence of a nearer opportunity that greatly diminishes the attractiveness of sites farther away.

Whether people are forced to migrate or choose to move, there are various factors that shape their mobility. What specific factors impel people to pull up stakes and leave the familiar for the uncertain? What specific factors help migrants choose a destination? Research has shown that typically a combination of factors, not just one, leads to a decision that it is time to move and a particular decision about where to go. Any single factor can be either a push for the migrant to leave the home country or a pull to the new country, and which factor matters most depends on the migrant and the circumstances surrounding the decision to migrate.

LEGAL STATUS

Migrants can arrive in a country with the consent of the host country (i.e., legally) or without that consent (illegally). All countries establish rules to determine who is allowed to migrate to their country and under what circumstances. If you apply for and receive a work visa from another country, you are legally allowed to live in the country and work there for the time allotted on the visa (usually a period of months or years). Having a visa makes you a legal migrant because you have your documents, your visa, to show your legal right to be in the place. If you do not have a visa, you are an illegal, or undocumented, migrant in the country. Undocumented or illegal migrants choose very different options for finding their way into the country than legal migrants do, simply because they do not want to be caught for fear of **deportation** (being sent back home).

> **Deportation** The act of a government sending a migrant out of its country and back to the migrant's home country.

ECONOMIC CONDITIONS

Poverty has driven countless millions from their homelands and continues to do so. Perceived opportunities in places such as western Europe and North America impel numerous migrants, both legal and illegal, to cross the Atlantic, the Mediterranean, the Caribbean, and the Rio Grande in search of a better life. The lower economic position of migrants in their host countries can lead to exploitation by employers and others. The United Nations Convention on the Protection of the Rights of All Migrant Workers and Members of Their Families recognizes the precarious position of migrant workers—their need for work and their desire to not be deported. The convention establishes standards of treatment for migrant workers. Although only 22 states have signed on to the convention, its statements on human trafficking and the right of migrant workers to equal wages have some influence on non-signatory's migration policies. Although migrant workers are essential to the economies of southern Ontario and central British Columbia, Canada is not a signatory.

POWER RELATIONSHIPS

Gender, ethnicity, race, and money are all factors in the decision to migrate. The power relationships already embedded in society enable the flow of migrants around the world for the benefit of some and to the detriment of others. Employers who hire migrant workers often have perceptions of what kinds of migrants would best work for them.

Women in the Middle East hire Southeast Asian women to work as domestic servants, housekeepers, and nannies. Geographer Paul Boyle points out that by hiring women from abroad, the female head of household establishes a relationship in which the employee's "ethnicity and citizenship status differentiates them from their female employer and this influences the power relationships that underpin the working arrangements." In their study of placement agencies that help people hire domestic workers, Stiell and England found that certain ethnicities were portrayed according to a scripted stereotype. For instance, workers from the Caribbean went from being portrayed as "docile, jolly and good with children" to being depicted as "difficult, aggressive and selfish"; women from the Philippines are in demand now as they are being portrayed as "'naturally' docile, subservient, hard-working, good natured, domesticated, and willing to endure long hours of housework and child-care with little complaint."

Race is also a factor in the hiring of migrant workers. For example, carpet companies in Dalton, Georgia (the carpet capital of the world), began hiring Mexican workers after the 1986 passage of the *Immigration Reform and Control Act* (IRCA) because they saw them as hard workers who were loyal to one company. In the same period, North and South Carolina have also experienced surges in the Mexican migrant population. Geographer Jamie Winders cites the work of several researchers in the South whose research "raises the issue of displacement of black workers by Mexican migration—a topic hinted at by many studies but addressed by few." Issues of race and migrant status in hiring can spill over into neighbourhoods, as they have recently in Raleigh, North

Carolina, where in the last 10 years conflicts over the available affordable housing have arisen between the African Americans who have lived in the neighbourhoods for years and Mexican migrants who have recently moved into the neighbourhoods.

Paul Boyle also cites the power relationships based on money in the growing migration industry, whereby migration flows are contractually arranged in order to fill labour needs for particular economic sectors throughout the world. Contractors give migrants advances on their income, help them migrate to the new country or region within a country, and then take wages in order to pay for advances and other needs the contractor supplies to the migrants.

POLITICAL CIRCUMSTANCES

Throughout history, oppressive regimes have engendered migration streams. Desperate migrants fled Vietnam by the hundreds of thousands after the communists took control of the country in 1975. In 1972, Uganda's dictator, Idi Amin, expelled 50,000 Asians and Ugandans of Asian descent from his country. The Cuban communist dictatorship expelled more than 125,000 Cubans in 1980 in the "Mariel Boatlift." Politically driven migration flows are marked by both escape and expulsion.

ARMED CONFLICT AND CIVIL WAR

The dreadful conflict engulfing the former Yugoslavia during the 1990s drove as many as 3 million people from their homes, mostly into western Europe. Many people became permanent emigrants, unable to return home. During the mid-1990s, a civil war engulfed Rwanda in Equatorial Africa, a conflict that pitted militant Hutus against the minority Tutsis and "moderate" Hutus. The carnage claimed an estimated 800,000 to 1 million lives and produced huge migration flows into neighbouring Democratic Republic of Congo (then called Zaire), Uganda, and Tanzania. More than 2 million Rwandans fled their homeland. Canadian Roméo Dallaire, who was commander of the United Nations Assistance Mission for Rwanda in 1994, has become well known for speaking out against the atrocities that took place in Rwanda. His book *Shake Hands With the Devil: The Failure of Humanity in Rwanda* won the Governor General's Literary Award for Non-Fiction in 2004 and was turned into a feature film in 2007.

ENVIRONMENTAL CONDITIONS

A major example of migration induced by environmental conditions is the movement of hundreds of thousands of Irish citizens from Ireland to North America during the 1840s. The potato blight destroyed the potato crop, creating famine. The famine was exacerbated by a set of political conditions for which the British government has recently apologized—a reminder that environmental conditions rarely operate in a social vacuum. This migration with an environmental component permanently altered the demographics of both Ireland (the source) and the northeastern region of the United States (the chief destination).

Some environmental crises, such as volcanic eruptions, bring long-term environmental changes to the landscape, making

FIGURE 5.10 Montserrat. This photo shows the damage caused by the 1995 eruption of the Soufrière Hills volcano on the Caribbean island of Montserrat. Many Montserratians fled to the United States when the capital city, Plymouth, was destroyed and they were given "temporary protected" immigration status. In 2005, the U.S. government told Montserratian refugees to leave—not because the volcanic crisis was over but rather, the U.S. government expected the volcanic crisis to last at least 10 more years, and so the Montserratians no longer qualified as "temporary" refugees. (Jason Dittmer)

return migration difficult, if not impossible. For example, the Caribbean island of Montserrat had a small population of about 10,000 prior to a volcanic eruption that began in 1995. The volcano has been active since then, prompting a migration flow. Geographer Jason Dittmer has studied how drastically the physical and cultural landscapes of Montserrat have changed since the onset of volcanic activity. According to Dittmer, roughly half the island is designated an "exclusion zone"—a region that includes the capital city of Plymouth—and people are banned from this zone of active volcanic activity (Figure 5.10). Over 7,000 people have migrated off the island. The remaining 3,000 migrated to the northern coast of the island where the effects of the volcano are less serious; however, the soils are thin, the land is rocky, and making a living is difficult.

CULTURE AND TRADITIONS

People who fear that their culture and traditions will not survive a major political transition, and who are able to migrate to places they perceive as safer, will often do so. When British India was partitioned into a mainly Hindu India and an almost exclusively Muslim Pakistan, millions of Muslim residents of India migrated across the border to the new Islamic state. As well, millions of Hindus migrated from what became Muslim Pakistan to secular India, as illustrated so clearly in the movie *Gandhi*. Similarly, in the 1990s, after decades of Soviet obstruction, more than 2 million Jews left the former Soviet Union for Israel and other destinations. And turbulent political conditions in South Africa during the mid-1990s impelled many whites to emigrate to Australia, Europe, and North America.

TECHNOLOGICAL ADVANCES

For some migrants, emigration is no longer the difficult and hazardous journey it used to be. Although most migrants still move by simple and even difficult means, some use modern forms of transportation and communication, the availability of which can itself encourage migration.

Gone is the time when would-be emigrants waited months, even years, for information about distant places. News today travels faster than ever, including news of job opportunities and ways to reach desired destinations. Television, radio, and telephone stimulate millions of people to migrate by relaying information about relatives, opportunities, and already established communities in destination lands. Advances in communication technology strengthen the role of **kinship links** as push or pull factors. When deciding where to go, a migrant is often pulled to places where family and friends have already found success.

> **Kinship links** Types of push factors or pull factors that influence a migrant's decision to go where family or friends have already found success.

Thus, Turks quickly heard about Germany's need for immigrant labour. Algerians knew where the most favourable destinations were in France. Haitians knew that a "Little Haiti" had sprung up in the Miami area.

When migrants move along and through kinship links, they create what geographers call chain migration. **Chain migration** occurs when the migrant chooses a destination and writes, calls, or communicates through others to tell family and friends at home about the new place. The migrant may help create a positive perception of the destination for family and friends, and may promise help with migration by providing housing and assistance obtaining a job. Reassuring family and friends that a new community has been formed, a place where they can feel at home, encourages further migration along the same chain. Chains of migration built upon each other create **immigration waves**—swells in migration from one source to the same destination.

> **Chain migration** Pattern of migration that develops when migrants move along and through kinship links (i.e., one migrant settles in a place and then writes, calls, or communicates through others to describe this place to family and friends who in turn then migrate there).
>
> **Immigration wave** Phenomenon whereby different patterns of chain migration build upon one another to create a swell in migration from one origin to the same destination.

MAIN POINTS   5.2 Why Do People Migrate?

- Migration may be *voluntary* or *forced*. Sometimes people choose to leave their home for economic or social reasons, including better employment opportunities or reunion with family members. In other circumstances, individuals are forced to leave due to war, intimidation, or brute force, as in the case of slavery.

- In the case of voluntary migration, Ernst Ravenstein developed laws of migration some 100 years ago that are still relevant today. His work marks an early formulation of the gravity model, which predicts interactions between places based on population size and distance.

- Push and pull factors, including legal status, economic conditions, power relationships, political circumstances, armed conflict and civil war, environmental conditions, culture and traditions, and technological advances, are useful to consider when analyzing the migration choices made by different groups.

- Migrants tend to move along migration chains that are linked to kinship and that may build to create immigration waves from one place to another. The location and composition (age, gender, and ethnicity) of these waves change over time and have an impact not only on the point of departure but on the place of relocation as well.

5.3 Where Do People Migrate?

It is tempting to reduce the flow of migration to simple economics—a chance for a job in another place trumps the lack of a job at home. However, migration is much more complicated. As we have discussed, migration depends on various push and pull factors, ranging from persecution in civil war to environmental disaster, from disempowerment in the home to discrimination in the country. Each migration flow is helped or hampered by existing networks and governmental actions.

In this section, we examine where people migrate—that is, what destinations they choose. At the global, regional, and national scales, we can see several major migration flows over the past 500 years, flows where hundreds of thousands of people migrated along the same general path. We will focus on the "where," on the destinations in these major migration flows. A large movement of migrants changes places—both the place the migrants left and the destination. As we discuss migration flows at the global, regional, and national scales in this chapter, remember that these flows give only an overview of migration. At the local and household scales, each individual or family migration required life-altering decisions, and those decisions fostered global change.

GLOBAL MIGRATION FLOWS

In 2010, the United Nations Population Division estimated there were some 214 million international migrants, about 3.1 percent of the world's total population. Between 1846 and 1939, some 59 million people travelled from Europe to North America, Australia, South Africa, and New Zealand. Before 1500, long-distance global-scale migration occurred haphazardly, typically in pursuit of spices, fame, or exploration. To put exploration in perspective, we need to remember that a complete map of the world's continents did not exist until the early 1800s. European **explorers**, who included surveyors and cartographers, played a major role in finally mapping the world. On the heels of exploration came European **colonization**—a physical process whereby the colonizing country takes over another place, putting its own government in charge and either moving its

> **Explorer** A person examining a region that is unknown to them.

> **Colonization** Physical process whereby the colonizer takes over another place, putting its own government in charge and either moving its own people into the place or bringing in indentured outsiders to gain control of the people and the land.

own people into the place or bringing in indentured outsiders to gain control of the people and the land. From the 1500s to the 1800s, Europeans colonized the Americas and the coasts of Africa and parts of Asia. Then they colonized interior Africa and Asia, starting in the late 1800s and continuing into the 1900s.

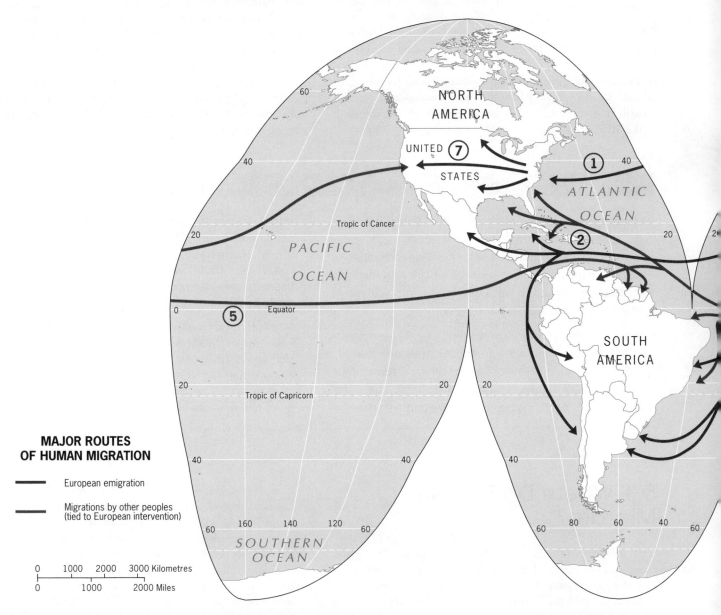

MAJOR ROUTES OF HUMAN MIGRATION

—— European emigration

—— Migrations by other peoples (tied to European intervention)

0   1000   2000   3000 Kilometres
0   1000   2000 Miles

FIGURE 5.11 Major Routes of Human Migration between 1500 and 1950. The major flows of global migration include movements from Europe to North America (marked 1 on the map), from southern Europe to South and Central America (2), from Britain and Ireland to Africa and Australia (3), from Africa to the Americas during the period of slavery (4), and from India to eastern Africa, Southeast Asia, and Caribbean America (5). (© H.J. de Blij, P.O. Muller, and John Wiley & Sons, Inc.)

The past five centuries have witnessed human migration on an unprecedented scale, much of it generated by European colonization. Among the greatest human migrations in recent centuries was the flow from Europe to the Americas. Emigration from Europe (1 and 2 in Figure 5.11) began slowly. Before the 1830s, perhaps 2.75 million Europeans left to settle overseas. The British went to North America, Australia, New Zealand, and South Africa (3). From Spain and Portugal, many hundreds of thousands of Europeans emigrated to Central and South America. Early European colonial settlements grew, even in coastal areas of present-day Angola, Kenya, and Indonesia. The rate of European emigration increased sharply between 1835 and 1935, with perhaps as many as 75 million departing for colonies in Africa and Asia and for economic opportunities in the Americas. Although millions of Europeans eventually returned to their homelands, the net outflow from Europe was enormous, as evidenced by the sheer number of Canadians and Americans who identify themselves as being of European ancestry. As already discussed, the Americas were the destination of another mass of immigrants: African slaves (4). Although this migration is mapped as just one of the eight major migrations, its immense and lasting impact on both sides of the Atlantic sets it apart from all the others.

Even as the Atlantic slave trade was in progress, the European impact was generating other major migrations as well. The British, who took control of South Asia, transported tens of thousands of "indentured" workers from present-day India, Pakistan, and Sri Lanka to East and South Africa (see route 5 on Figure 5.11).

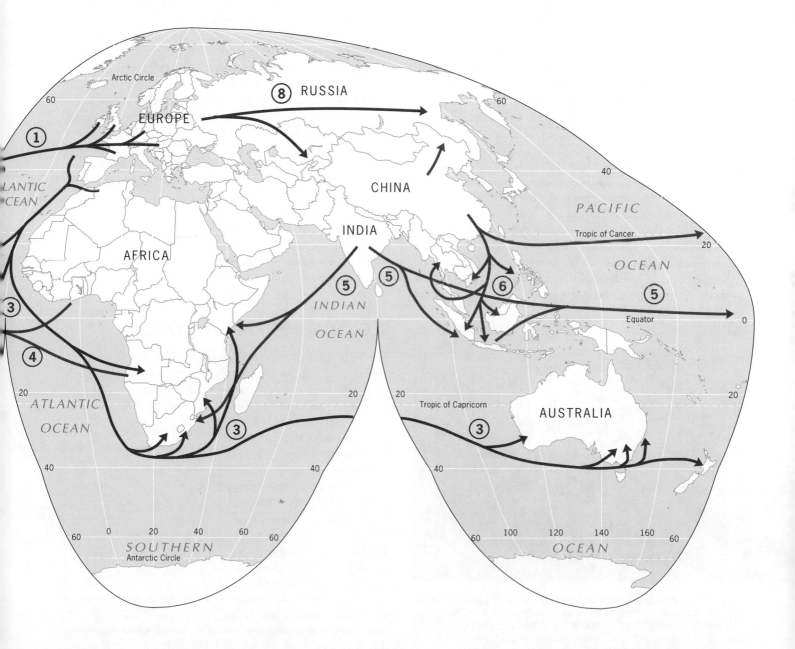

Today, people of Indian ancestry form substantial minorities in South Africa, Kenya, and Tanzania and, until their forced migration from Uganda, in that country as well. Their disproportionate share of commerce and wealth is now a major source of ethnic friction. Long before the British arrived in India, Hindu influences radiated into Southeast Asia, reaching the Indonesian islands of Java and Bali. Later, the British renewed the Indian migration stream, bringing South Asians to the Malay Peninsula (including Singapore) and to their Pacific holdings, including Fiji. The British were also instrumental in relocating Asians, mainly from India, to such Caribbean countries as Trinidad and Tobago and Guyana (shown by the trans-Pacific stream on Figure 5.11). The Dutch brought many Javanese from what is today Indonesia to their former dependency of Suriname along the same route.

An example of global migration flows involving Canada can be seen with the British Home Children program. Between 1869 and 1930, an estimated 150,000 British children between the ages of 4 and 18 were sent to Canada and other British colonies during the child emigration movement in Britain. Of this amount, an estimated 100,000 was sent to Canada (Figure 5.12). Called British Home Children, these impoverished children were sent abroad to work as indentured labourers on Canadian farms or as domestic servants until they reached the age of 18. The practice of sending poor, orphaned children to the colonies dates back to the 1600s, when homeless children, mostly from Scotland, were rounded up in a forced emigration scheme and sent overseas. In the mid-1800s, British philanthropist Annie McPherson saw opportunity for impoverished British children who were being exploited in urban industrial factories to find a better life overseas. She began setting up distribution homes in Canada where these children could be fed and educated in exchange for work. However, critics of the program reported child abuse, exploitation, and displacement

as a result of the program. As well, because it was a forced emigration program, children were often told, falsely, that their parents were dead, or that great prosperity awaited them in Canada, in order to gain their compliance. Once in Canada, they were frequently mistreated, ill cared for, not educated, and forced to stay in their placement homes.

The program shrank in the 1930s due to the economic hardships brought about by the Great Depression, and was officially ended in the 1960s. During an official inquiry in the 1990s, the scope of the tragedy was revealed. British Prime Minister Gordon Brown issued an official apology in 2010 and set up a compensation fund for families torn apart by the program. Likewise, Australian Prime Minister Kevin Rudd issued a formal apology in 2009 to the children subjected to the forced migration scheme to that country; his government set up a travel fund to help surviving participants locate their families. Canadian immigration minister Jason Kenney, in response to these apologies, stated that there was "no need for Canada to apologize for abuse and exploitation" of British Home Children in Canada (*Toronto Star*, 2009).

Many of these migration patterns persist even as new forms emerge. According to Castles and Miller (2003), we are seeing several generalizable trends in global migration. A larger number of countries are affected by the acceleration of migration. Countries accepting migrants do so from a much larger number of places. Countries such as Canada are becoming more diverse, particularly in urban areas. As well, countries accept diverse types of migrants—labourers, refugees, family sponsorship—and have seen a substantial increase in the number of women migrants. Immigration is also becoming an increasingly politicized process, with states experiencing serious internal division over the role of immigrants in the nation's future.

REGIONAL MIGRATION FLOWS

The huge flows of migrants mapped in Figure 5.11 were unprecedented and have few rivals in terms of sheer numbers today. Although some global migration flows already discussed were forced and some were voluntary, each occurred across an ocean. Migration also occurs at a **regional scale**, with migrants going to a neighbouring country to take advantage

Regional scale Interactions occurring within a region, in a regional setting

of short-term economic opportunities, to reconnect with their cultural group across borders, or to flee political conflict or war.

European colonialism helped establish **islands of development** throughout the world. Islands of development are places within a region or country where most foreign investment goes, where the

Island of development Place built up by a government or corporation to attract foreign investment and that has relatively high concentrations of paying jobs and infrastructure.

vast majority of paying jobs are located, and where infrastructure is concentrated. Islands of development are often coastal cities because their establishment was based on access to trade.

FIGURE 5.12 British Home Children. British immigrant children from Dr. Barnardo's Homes at the landing stage, Saint John, New Brunswick. In this undated photograph, children who were sent to Canada as part of the British Home Children program await placement in Canadian homes as indentured labourers and domestic servants. (© Isaac Erb/Library and Archives Canada/PA-041785)

An example of such a phenomenon is found in Figure 5.13, which shows the islands of development in sub-Saharan Africa.

To understand migration flows from one poor country to another, it is not sufficient to analyze the flow at the global scale. We need to understand where the region fits into the picture of global interaction, and to see how different locations within the region fit into interaction patterns at both the global and regional scales. For example, within the region of West Africa, the oil-producing areas of Nigeria are islands of development. In the mid-1970s, poor people in Togo, Benin, Ghana, and the northern regions of Nigeria, perceiving that economic life was better in coastal Nigeria, migrated to the coast for short-term jobs while the oil economy was good. The migrants, usually young men, worked as much as they could and sent almost all of the money they earned home as remittances to support their families. They worked until the oil economy took a fall in the early 1980s. At that point the Nigerian government decided the foreign workers were no longer needed and forcibly pushed out 2 million of them.

Global economic processes and the lasting effects of European colonialism certainly played a role in this West African migration flow. If we study such a flow only at the global scale, we see migrants moving from one poor country to another poor country. But if we use both the global and regional scales to study this flow, we understand regional economic influences and the pull of islands of development in Nigeria.

European colonialism also had an impact on regional migration flows in Southeast Asia. Europe's colonial occupation of Southeast Asia presented economic opportunities for the Chinese. During the late 1800s and early 1900s, many Chinese immigrated to cities in the region to work in trade, commerce, and finance (Figure 5.14). Many remained, and today Chinese minorities in Southeast Asian countries account for substantial portions of national populations: 14 percent in Thailand, 32 percent in Malaysia, and 76 percent in Singapore. The Chinese minority in Indonesia accounts for only about 3 percent of the total population, but Indonesia has more than 200 million people, so its Chinese minority is one of Southeast Asia's largest clusters.

RECONNECTION OF CULTURAL GROUPS WITHIN REGIONS

Regional migration flows also centre on reconnecting cultural groups across borders. A migration stream with enormous consequences is the flow of Jewish immigrants to Israel. At the turn of the 20th century, fewer than 50,000 Jewish residents lived in what was then Palestine. From 1919 to 1948, Great Britain held control over Palestine, and Britain encouraged Jews (whose ancestors had fled more than a thousand years earlier from the Middle East to Europe) to return to the region. As

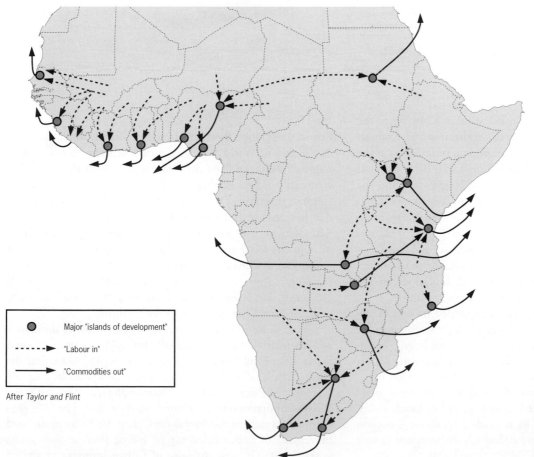

●	Major "islands of development"
----▶	"Labour in"
⟶	"Commodities out"

After *Taylor and Flint*

FIGURE 5.13 Islands of Development in Sub-Saharan Africa. Adapted with permission from Peter J. Taylor and Colin Flint, *Political Geography: World-Economy, Nation-State and Locality,* 5th Edition, © 2007, p. 96. Reprinted by permission of Pearson Education, Inc. Upper Saddle River, NJ.

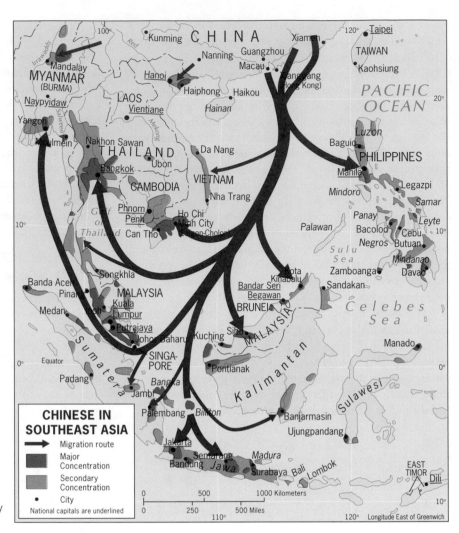

FIGURE 5.14 Chinese in Southeast Asia.
The great majority of Chinese who live in
Southeast Asia migrated from southeastern
China. (© H.J. de Blij, P.O. Muller, and John Wiley
& Sons, Inc.)

CHINESE IN SOUTHEAST ASIA
→ Migration route
■ Major Concentration
■ Secondary Concentration
• City
National capitals are underlined

many as 750,000 Jews resided in Palestine in 1948, when the
United Nations intervened to partition the area and establish
the independent state of Israel (the original boundaries of the
new state are shown in orange in Figure 5.15). After the land
was divided between the newly created Israeli state and the
state of Palestine, another migration stream began—600,000
Palestinian Arabs fled or were pushed out of Israeli territories.
Many sought refuge in neighbouring Jordan, Egypt, Syria, and
elsewhere. Israel's Law of Return gives residence and Israeli citizenship to Jews from anywhere in the world. This has resulted
in significant numbers of Ethiopian Jews (Falashas) residing in
Israel, as well as an obscure tribe from northeast India.

Through a series of wars, Israel expanded its area of territorial control (Figure 5.15) and actively built settlements for
new Jewish immigrants in Palestinian territories (Figure 5.16).
Jewish immigrants from the Eurasian region continue to migrate to Israel. Following the collapse of the Soviet Union in the
early 1990s, thousands of Jews who had been unable to practise their religion in the Soviet Union migrated to Israel. Today,
Israel's population of 7.4 million (including about 1 million
Arab citizens) continues to grow through immigration as well
as substantial natural increase.

CONFLICT AND WAR

Regional migration flows are often the result of conflict and war.
At the end of World War II, as many as 15 million Germans
migrated westward from their homes in Eastern Europe, either
voluntarily or because they were forced to leave. Before the East
German government built the Berlin Wall and the Iron Curtain
was lowered, several million Germans fled Soviet-controlled
East Germany into what was then West Germany. And millions
of migrants left Europe altogether to go to the United States
(1.8 million), Canada (1.1 million), Australia (1 million), Israel
(750,000), Argentina (750,000), Brazil (500,000), Venezuela
(500,000), and other countries. As many as 8 million Europeans
emigrated from Europe in this postwar stream.

Even before Cuba became a communist state, thousands
of Cuban citizens applied annually for residency in the United
States after Fidel Castro came to power in 1959. During the
1960s, while the Cuban government was establishing the
Communist Party of Cuba and formalizing a communist state,
Cuban immigration to the United States swelled. The U.S. government formalized the flow as the Cuban Airlift, an authorized
movement of persons desiring to escape from a communist
government. The vast majority of Cuban immigrants arrived

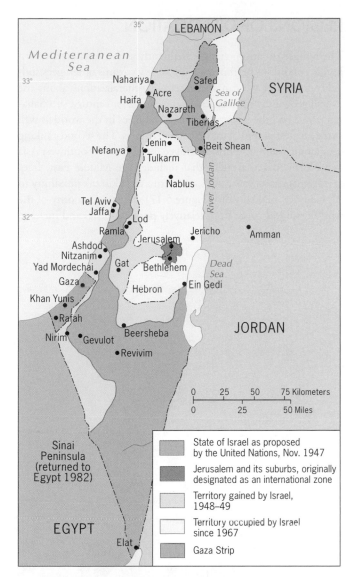

FIGURE 5.15 **Changing Boundaries of Israel.** Adapted with permission from M. Gilbert, *Atlas of the Arab-Israeli Conflict* New York: Macmillan, 1974, p. 38.

and remained in the greater Miami area. They developed a core of Hispanic culture in southern Florida, and in 1973, Dade County, Florida, declared itself bicultural and bilingual. In 1980, another massive, organized exodus of Cubans occurred, the Mariel Boatlift, bringing more than 125,000 Cubans to U.S. shores; the migrants qualified for refugee status under U.S. regulations. The Cuban influx persisted throughout the 1980s, and in 1994, over 30,000 Cubans fled for the United States. By that point, the Soviet Union had collapsed, and the Soviet Union's financial support for the Cuban government had dwindled. The 1994 exodus pushed diplomats in both the United States and Cuba to come to an agreement on Cuban migration, called the "wet foot, dry foot policy." The Cuban government agreed to patrol its seas more closely for boats attempting to leave, and to impose no reprisals on those caught and returned by patrolling U.S. Coast Guard fleets. However, the general rule is that once Cubans reach American soil and are out of American waters, they are allowed to remain in the United States.

NATIONAL MIGRATION FLOWS

National migration flows can also be thought of as internal migration flows. Different countries, with distinctive social, historical, and cultural traditions, have very different internal migration patterns. We outlined the recent internal migration patterns in Canada earlier in this chapter. Another example comes from Russia, which experienced a major internal migration from the heartland of the Russian state (near Moscow and St. Petersburg) east as far as the shores of the Pacific. This eastward migration significantly altered the cultural mosaic of Eurasia, and understanding this migration flow helps us understand the modern map of Eurasia. During the czarist (1800s–1910s) and communist periods (1920s–1980s), Russian and Soviet rulers tried to occupy and consolidate the country's far eastern frontier, moving industries eastward, building railroads and feeder lines, and establishing Vladivostok

FIELD NOTE
Jerusalem, Israel

Just a few miles into the West Bank, not far from Jerusalem, the expanding Israeli presence could not be missed. New settlements dot the landscape—often occupying strategic sites that are also easily defensible (Figure 5.16). These "facts on the ground" will certainly complicate the effort to carve out a stable territorial order in this much-contested region. That, of course, is the goal of the settlers and their supporters, but it is salt on the wound for those who contest the Israeli right to be there in the first place.

FIGURE 5.16 **Jerusalem, Israel.** (Alexander B. Murphy)

on the Pacific coast as one of the world's best-equipped naval bases. As Russia and then the Soviet Union expanded outward and to the east, the country incorporated numerous ethnic minorities into its population. During the communist period, the Soviet government also employed a policy of Russification, which sought to assimilate all the people in the Soviet territory into the Russian culture. One way the Soviets pushed this policy was by encouraging people of Russian heritage to move out of Moscow and St. Petersburg and fill in the country. By 1980, as many as 30 million Russians had moved out toward the borders. After the collapse of the Soviet Union in 1991, some people moved back to their original homelands, but the map will long carry the impact of Russia's eastward expansion.

REGIONS OF DISLOCATION

The refugee situation changes frequently as some refugees return home, conditions permitting, and as new streams of refugees suddenly form. Yet we can make certain generalizations about the overall geography of refugees. In the early 21st century, sub-Saharan Africa had the largest number of refugees in the world as well as the greatest potential for new refugee flows. The second-ranking geographic realm in terms of refugee numbers was Southwest Asia and North Africa, a realm that includes the Middle East, Iraq, and Afghanistan. South Asia, as a result of Pakistan's proximity to Afghanistan, ranked third (Figure 5.17). The vast majority of the world's refugees come from relatively poor countries and travel to

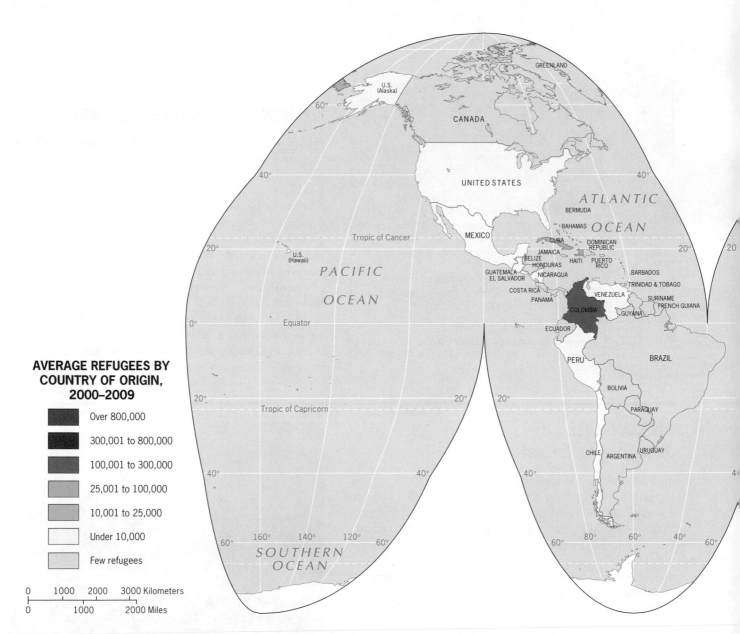

FIGURE 5.17 Average Refugee Populations between 2000 and 2009 by Country of Origin. Data from World Health Organization, Global Health Atlas, 2009.

neighbouring countries that are equally poor. The impact of refugee flows is certainly felt most in the poorest countries of the world. In 2009, according to the United Nations High Commissioner for Refugees (UNHCR), there were 43.3 million forcibly displaced people worldwide, the highest since the mid-1990s.

AFRICA

Africa's people are severely afflicted by dislocation—and not just in terms of the 8 million "official" refugees accounted for by international relief agencies. Many millions more are internally displaced persons. Of all regions in the world, sub-Saharan Africa experiences the greatest impact from migration because

the majority of the world's migration flows involve refugees, and the majority of refugees are in sub-Saharan Africa. Add to that the extreme poverty and devastation of disease in many parts of the region, and each day is a humanitarian crisis somewhere in sub-Saharan Africa.

At the beginning of the 21st century, several of the world's largest refugee crises occurred in sub-Saharan Africa. In West Africa, civil wars in Liberia and Sierra Leone sent columns of hundreds of thousands of refugees streaming into Guinea and Ivory Coast; in 1997, the UNHCR reported more than 1.5 million refugees in this small corner of Africa. And Angola, strife-torn ever since the days of the Cold War, still has well over 1 million IDPs (some estimates put the total nearer 2 million).

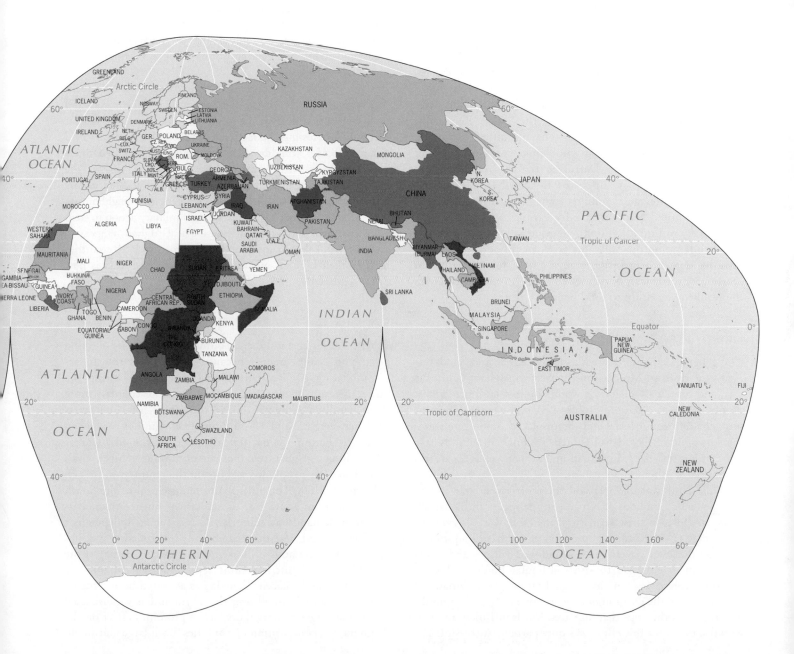

Sudan, which has been in a civil war for two decades, is the site of one of the worst refugee crises in Africa today. The country's borders, drawn by European colonialism, forced together a largely Arab and Muslim population in the north, and a mostly black African and Christian or animist (a follower of a traditional religion) population in the south. (Christianity was brought by Western missionaries, while Islam was introduced by North African traders.) The war between north and south has caused immense damage—over 2.2 million people have died in the fighting or have starved as a result of the war. More than 5 million people have been displaced, with over 1.6 million in neighbouring Uganda alone. Both sides in the Sudanese civil war have interfered with the efforts of international agencies to help the refugees.

This long-lasting refugee crisis in Sudan helps us understand the complexity of political conflict and migration flows in sub-Saharan Africa. The multi-ethnic and religious conflicts occurring, most recently, in and around Darfur demonstrate that conflict can be generated for numerous reasons, including ethnic tension, religious division, and political manoeuvring. Actors at the regional and global scale strive to deal with the human suffering in the Sudan. Regionally, the African Union, an organization committed to finding African solutions to African problems, has sent Nigerian and Rwandan troops to Darfur to try to solve the crisis. The African Union is supported by North American and European monies and military strategizing. On the global scale, the United Nations Security Council met in Kenya in 2004 to try to find a solution and eventually passed a resolution condemning the Sudanese government and threatening punitive damages against the government for its actions in Darfur. Nevertheless, hostilities continue in the region, with the resulting hardship to local peoples.

NORTH AFRICA AND SOUTHWEST ASIA

The geographic region known as North Africa and Southwest Asia extends from Morocco in the west to Afghanistan in the east, and contains some of the world's longest-lasting and most deeply entrenched refugee problems. A particularly significant problem centres on Israel and the displaced Arab populations that surround it. Decades of United Nations' subventions have more or less stabilized this situation, but many refugees are still in motion or in temporary camps.

The Gulf War of 1991 and the more recent war in Iraq have generated millions of refugees in the region in the last 20 years. In 1991, in the aftermath of the Gulf War, a significant percentage of the Kurdish population of northern Iraq, threatened by the Iraqi government, abandoned villages and towns and streamed across the Turkish and Iranian borders. This migration involved as many as 2.5 million people. International pressure led to the creation of a secure zone for Kurds in northern Iraq, with the hope that displaced Kurds in Turkey and Iran would return, but this effort was only partially successful. The Kurdish people of Iraq were severely dislocated by events surrounding the Gulf War; many remain refugees in Turkey as well as Iran. The war in Iraq has generated upwards of 2 million refugees, most of whom are living in neighbouring Syria and Jordan.

The Soviet invasion of Afghanistan at the end of 1979 generated a double migration stream that carried millions westward into Iran and eastward into Pakistan. At the height of the exodus, it was estimated that some 2.5 million Afghans were living in camps in Iran, and an additional 3.7 million were gathered in tent camps in Pakistan's northwestern province and in southern Baluchistan. The Soviet invasion seemed destined to succeed quickly, but the Russian generals underestimated the strength of Afghan opposition, and the Soviets eventually withdrew. A power struggle among Afghan factions ensued and generated substantial internal instability and turmoil. As a result, most of the more than 6 million Afghani refugees in Iran and Pakistan—about one-quarter of the country's population—stayed where they were.

In 1996, the Taliban, an Islamic fundamentalist movement that began in northwest Pakistan, emerged in Afghanistan and took control of most of the country, imposing strict Islamic rule and suppressing the factional conflicts that had prevailed since the Soviet withdrawal. Although several hundred thousand refugees moved back to Afghanistan from Pakistan, the harsh Taliban rule created a counter-migration and led to further movement of some 2.5 million refugees into neighbouring Iran. After September 11, 2001, Western military action to stem global violence drove tens of thousands of Afghan refugees to seek safety in Pakistan and Iran despite efforts by both countries to close their borders, intensifying a refugee crisis that is now nearly a quarter-century old.

SOUTH ASIA

In terms of refugee numbers, South Asia is the third-ranking geographic realm, mainly because of Pakistan's role in accommodating Afghanistan's forced emigrants. During the Soviet invasion in the 1980s, the UNHCR counted more than 3 million refugees; during the 1990s, the total averaged between 1.2 and 1.5 million. That number rose when Allied retaliation against terrorist bases began in October 2001. Today, Afghanistan has an enormous refugee crisis with 3 million people living outside the country, mostly in Pakistan and Iran. The other major refugee problem in South Asia stems from a civil war in Sri Lanka. This conflict, arising from demands by minority Tamils for an independent state on the Sinhalese-dominated and -controlled island, has cost tens of thousands of lives and has severely damaged the economy. The United Nations reports about 200,000 are now internally displaced. Canada has accepted both refugees and immigrants from all over the world and as we discussed in Chapter 4, new immigrants have a profound effect on the demographic composition of our cities, both large and small.

GUEST FIELD NOTE Living in Toronto, Studying Immigrant Lives

With the exception of the First Nations, Canada is a country of immigrants with thousands of people arriving in search of a new life and a better future. According to the 2006 Census, about 20 percent of the population was born outside the country.

Often, until one actually lives in Canada for a while, however, one does not realize that all of Canada is not the same. In the urban context, some cities are "richer" than others, socio-culturally, economically, and politically. Toronto, Montreal, and Vancouver, for instance, are more diverse than many other Canadian cities. One reason for this is that, traditionally, these cities have served as immigrant gateways. Almost 70 percent of immigrants who arrived between 2001 and 2006 settled in Toronto (40 percent), Montreal (15 percent), and Vancouver (14 percent). As a result, whereas in a large city like Toronto it is difficult to find someone who is *not* from one's own ethnic background, in a smaller town like Elora (in Southern Ontario), you may find your family to be the only one who looks different or has a lifestyle that is distinct from the general population.

Socio-cultural, economic, and political differences are common within Canadian cities as well. For example, whereas some neighbourhoods of Toronto have more Caucasian immigrants (e.g., British, French, Greeks, Italians, Russians, and Portuguese), in other areas most residents may belong to a visible minority group (e.g., Chinese, Indian, Filipino, Caribbean, Pakistani, and Sri Lankan). Beyond being predominantly a Caucasian or visible minority area, Toronto's neighbourhoods are further segregated along the axes of economic class (income and employment) and culture (language and religion). Some areas of Toronto, however, are also mixed; that is, there is no one dominant racial, economic, or cultural group living in that area.

Why are all neighbourhoods not mixed? Why don't visible minority immigrants live in all neighbourhoods? A variety of exogenous and endogenous factors influence immigrant households to gravitate toward their own ethnic neighbourhoods. Sometimes it is only in areas where most people belong to their own socio-cultural groups that newcomer households are received without prejudice. They may also get a cushion of economic and socio-psychological support from these people until they begin to grasp the "Canadian system" and find a job or a home.

As a new Canadian, when I first landed at Toronto's Pearson airport, I thought to myself, "Where am I"? Contrary to my expectations, I saw a multitude of people who looked like me! In the next few months, as I began to settle down in this new country, I found distinct ways of life in every nook and corner of Toronto—new languages, ways of dressing, religions, dietary habits, festivals, histories, and struggles. It is the vibrancy, dynamicity, and chaos of Toronto that inspired me to ask: How do a multitude of diverse people (whom we loosely call "immigrants") make Toronto their "home"—a home that is not just of bricks and mortar, but rather a space that they can call their own?

To find answers to my questions, I began to study immigrant settlement experiences. How do immigrants survive in a country that is so different from their own in terms of climate, society, and culture? In which specific ways do they transform the city into their own spaces? I found that it is essential to explore the everyday lives of households. Understanding the atomic, everyday life situations is important because everyday lives of immigrant families are laden with complex webs of challenges and triumphs, be it while searching for suitable shelter and employment, or attempting to express and retain specific elements of their culture. Moreover, this understanding leads the researcher toward questioning and evaluating some of the larger societal forces. What factors cause immigrants to earn less than the Canadian born? Is it the lack of Canadian experience? How can an immigrant acquire Canadian experience when they have just landed in Canada? What are the specific reasons that make it harder for a visible minority household to find a residence of their choice? Are there any discrete discriminatory practices that restrict their access to specific parts of the city?

My research corroborated previous findings that not all immigrants have similar settlement experiences. Settlement experiences differ between and within immigrant groups in multifaceted ways. In my research I found that although the two South Asian subgroups studied—Indian Bengalis and Bangladeshis—speak the same language (Bangla), migrated to Canada from the same region (South Asia) at the same time (mid to late 1990s), mostly as independent class immigrants (young, with high levels of education and employment experience), their housing experiences have been very different. Also, whereas Indian Bengalis disperse, Bangladeshis cluster in specific neighbourhoods in the inner suburbs and the city core. While many Indian Bengalis moved into ownership housing within the first five years of their arrival in Canada, most Bangladeshis live in private rental housing that is unaffordable, inadequate, and unsuitable. Some were already in social housing and many were on the waiting list.

Despite these problems, however, within a decade of their arrival in Canada, Bangladeshis have successfully transformed three areas of Toronto into their own spaces: the Victoria Park area—also known as "Little Bangladesh"; Regent Park, a social-housing complex immediately east of downtown Toronto, built in the 1940s and 1950s (Figure 5.18); and the Markham Road and Eglinton Avenue area in Scarborough. All three areas contain several Bangladeshi retail stores and services, including grocery and clothing stores, beauty parlours, photographic studios, entertainment stores, remittance centres, and immigration consultants. In addition, the main offices of two Bengali newspapers and community agencies serving Bangladeshi-Canadians are also located here. Several mosques are also located in the immediate vicinity. This relatively high level of institutional completeness has also played an important role in attracting more Bangladeshi newcomers to these neighbourhoods, thus increasing their residential concentration in these areas.

What my research broadly reflects is that immigrants are not just "economic bodies" (earning wages and paying taxes). They are in fact, the "life of the party"—filling our cities with vibrant colours and cultures. What should we do today to make their lives easier, particularly when they first arrive?

Sutama Ghosh, Department of Geography, Ryerson University

FIGURE 5.18 Regent Park, Toronto. Just east of downtown Toronto, Regent Park, one of Canada's oldest social housing projects, has been home to many immigrant groups. Seen here in 2005, a 12-year, $1 billion redevelopment project is underway. (© Simon Hayter/*Toronto Star*)

As the *Guest Field Note* by Sutama Ghosh suggests, immigration patterns in cities such as Toronto contribute to the emergence of new and distinctive neighbourhoods.

SOUTHEAST ASIA

Southeast Asia is a reminder that refugee problems can change quickly. Indochina was the scene of one of the 20th century's most desperate refugee crises—the stream of between 1 and 2 million people who fled Vietnam in the aftermath of the long war that ended in 1975. In the early 1990s, Cambodia produced an exodus of 300,000 refugees escaping from their country's seemingly endless cycle of violence, and ending up in refugee camps on the Thailand side of the border. Today, the largest refugee camps in this realm are internal refugees in Myanmar (formerly Burma), victims of the 2004 tsunami, the 2008 cyclone, and the repressive rule of the generals who are seeking to subjugate the country's minorities.

EUROPE

In the 1990s, the collapse of Yugoslavia and its associated conflicts created the largest refugee crisis in Europe since the end of World War II. In 1995, the UNHCR reported the staggering total of 6,056,600 refugees, a number that some observers felt was inflated by the Europeans' unusually liberal interpretations of the United Nations' rules for refugee recognition. Nevertheless, even after the cessation of armed conflict and the implementation of a peace agreement known as the Dayton Accords, the UNHCR still reports as many as 1.6 million internal refugees in the area—people dislocated and unable to return to their homes.

OTHER REGIONS

The number of refugees and IDPs in other geographic realms is much smaller. In the Western Hemisphere, only Colombia has a serious IDP problem, numbering between 2 and 3 million people, caused by the country's chronic instability associated with its struggle against narcotics. Large areas of Colombia's countryside are vulnerable to armed attack by "narcoterrorists" and paramilitary units; these rural areas are essentially beyond government control, and thousands of villagers have died in the crossfire. Hundreds of thousands more have left their homes to seek protection.

This section has focused on the "where" of migration, on where refugees, IDPs, and others move on a global, regional, and national scale. It is important to remember that where people move is partly contingent upon countries' immigration policies. As a result of these global, regional, and national trends, scholars argue there are three main issues shaping immigration policy for countries such as Canada. The first is what Janice Stein calls the "global economic divide." The current division in the world is based on age. Core countries such as Canada and European states have an aging population, while peripheral countries have youthful populations. Core countries are increasingly looking to immigration to supply young, skilled workers to the labour market. Second, there is a growing demographic inequality in terms of wealth, quality of life, and access to technologies. This has the potential to increase tensions between the more well-off core and the increasingly poor periphery. Finally, we are seeing more barriers to immigration based on security concerns. With the tightening of borders, immigration policy is seen as a security issue that will severely restrict, perhaps unfairly, who gains admission to core countries such as Canada.

MAIN POINTS   **5.3**   **Where Do People Migrate?**

- The world has experienced major immigration flows over the last century. Prior to 1500, migration was haphazard, and preliminary population movement was based on colonial settlement patterns.

- In the last five centuries, major immigration flows occurred from southern Europe to North America; from Britain and Ireland to North America; from Africa to the Americas due to slavery; and from India to eastern Africa, Southeast Asia, and Caribbean America.

- We can consider immigration on global, regional, and national scales as well as on more local scales. Many people immigrate for employment opportunities, to reconnect with cultural groups, and because of conflict and war. Many countries have witnessed internal migration for distinctive historical, social, and cultural reasons.

- Refugees are found in every corner of the globe and represent a serious humanitarian issue for all countries.

5.4 How Do Governments Affect Migration?

The control of immigration, legal and illegal, the granting of asylum to refugees, and the fate of cross-border refugees, permanent and temporary, are sensitive issues in countries around the world. Efforts to regulate, organize, and sometimes limit immigration have been a concern of states for millennia. In the 14th century, China built the Great Wall (Figure 5.19a) in part as a defensive measure but also as a barrier to emigration (by Chinese trying to escape the control of the Chinese authorities) and immigration (mainly by Mongol "barbarians" from the northern plains). The Berlin Wall (Figure 5.19b), the Korean DMZ (demilitarized zone), the fences along the Rio Grande, and the new wall being constructed by Israel are all evidence of the desire of governments to control the movement of people across their borders.

POST–SEPTEMBER 11

Since September 11, 2001, government immigration policies in the United States and Canada, and around the world, have incorporated new security concerns. The U.S. response to the September 11 attacks is a good example of how international immigration policy can be transformed. Prior to that date, the U.S. border patrol was concerned primarily with drug trafficking and human smuggling. Immediately after September 11, the George W. Bush administration cracked down on asylum seekers. The U.S. government marked 33 countries as places where al-Qaeda or other terrorist groups operate, and the government automatically detained anyone from one of these 33 countries who entered the United States seeking asylum.

New U.S. government policies also affect illegal immigrants. The U.S. Justice Department currently has a policy that allows it to detain any illegal immigrant, even if the person has no known ties to terrorist organizations. This policy stems from the department's concern that terrorists may use Haiti as a "staging point." The idea

(a)

(b)

FIGURE 5.19 Barriers to Immigration. (a) The Great Wall of China, undated, and (b) the Berlin Wall. (© Eddie Granlund/Naturbild/Corbis; © Owen Franken/Corbis)

behind this law is that terrorists could travel to Haiti temporarily and then illegally migrate from Haiti to the United States to commit terrorist attacks. Similarly, the government fence-building along the United States–Mexico border is a response in part to the concern that terrorists will use Mexico as a staging ground to enter the United States illegally and commit terrorist attacks.

In addition to focusing on asylum seekers and illegal immigration, the post–September 11 world is concerned with legal immigration. *The 9/11 Commission Report*, released in 2004, discusses the issue of terrorists using fabricated or altered papers to migrate to the United States. The 9/11 terrorists entered the United States using visas. The commission reported that the Federal Aviation Administration flagged more than half of the 9/11 hijackers with the profiling system they had in place. However, the policy at the time was to check the bags of those flagged, not the people themselves. The commission explains, "For terrorists, travel documents are as important as weapons"; it recommends stepping up inspections and questioning at travel checkpoints, and to view these checkpoints as "a chance to establish that people are who they say they are and are seeking access for their stated purpose, to intercept identifiable suspects, and to take effective action."

People and organizations opposed to the post–September 11 policies counter that raising fences and detaining people will not combat terrorism; rather, it will intensify hatred of the U.S. government, thus promoting terrorism. Organizations such as Human Rights First, Amnesty International, and the Migration Policy Institute claim that the new government crackdowns have violated civil liberties and have done nothing to make Americans safer. Others opposed to the new border regulations argue the crackdown has only slowed traffic and the flow of business and tourism, and has utterly failed to slow illegal immigration, which along the United States–Mexico border is increasing.

Regardless of which side of this debate you are on, we can all agree that concern about migration will continue to shape security policy in North America, Europe, and beyond in the decades to come.

MANAGING AND CONTROLLING BORDERS

According to Eric Weiner at NPR, "In years past, it was difficult to travel from one country to another, yet relatively easy to clear any regulatory hurdles once you arrived. The reverse is true today. Modern technology makes it easy to travel, but migration is now highly regulated in most parts of the world." This high regulation of migration is due in large part to the roles of governments, and their legal and regulatory frameworks, that seek to control who enters and leaves nation-states. The attacks on September 11, 2001, have brought to light issues around global security, in particular the protection of borders, and have led to increased control of immigration. Indeed, the United States has tightened immigration policy at its southern borders with Mexico, as well as along its Canadian borders, in the wake of the terrorist attacks. For example, Canadians were previously able to fly or drive to the United States without a passport. Now, all Canadians over the age of 16 must have a passport to enter the United States.

There are various tools that governments use to control and affect migration. While some of these are more visible—such as the building of walls, the patrolling of borders, and the use of a variety of surveillance technologies—others are built into the legislative and judicial systems of governance. In the opening field note, for example, we discussed Canada's *Immigration and Refugee Protection Act* and the proposed bill to prosecute human smugglers. Along with legal statutes, procedures such as visa applications, or the U.S. "green card" process, control who can work in a particular country, and for how long.

Most of the laws and regulations that come to mind, however, seem to focus on controlling those who are permitted to enter a given country—the concern is with who we allow in. Yet there are many countries where the exit process is tightly controlled as well. In recent history, we have heard stories of people "defecting" from Eastern European countries, such as East Germany prior to the collapse of the Berlin wall, and of Cubans escaping to the Miami area of Florida by boat. In 2009, the London *Telegraph* published an article about migrant workers in the Kingdom of Saudi Arabia. According to Saudi law, migrant workers must surrender their travel papers, passports, and exit documents to their employer upon arrival in the country. This means that, while it is possible to enter the Kingdom for work, it can be very difficult to leave without their employer's permission. With over 7 million migrant workers, accounting for nearly 28 percent of the Kingdom's population, Saudi Arabia's treatment of its migrant workers has come under international scrutiny.

The Canadian government manages its temporary migrant workforce through the Temporary Foreign Worker Program (TFWP), which is facilitated by Human Resources and Skills Development Canada and by Citizenship and Immigration Canada. In recent years the TFWP has expanded significantly, making it easier for Canadian employers to hire foreign workers to fill labour shortages. While the expansion of this program has allowed migrant worker populations in Canada to increase, the program has also come under a great deal of scrutiny from labour and human rights groups. For example, the Alberta Federation of Labour has called for the provision of better working conditions and has even called for an end to the program in its current form, to be replaced by a program that enables foreign migrant workers to apply for permanent residency. The federation states this would better protect foreign workers' rights.

THE BRAIN DRAIN

One of the impacts of migration that governments have wrestled with since the end of World War II is the "brain drain." Originally coined by the Royal Society of London for Improving Natural Knowledge (now known as "The Royal Society") to describe the outflow of scientists from Britain to the United States and Canada in the 1950s and 1960s, the term refers to the emigration of doctors, scientists, engineers, and other trained professionals once their training is complete. The concern arises when publicly funded institutions invest in and train a particular skilled labour pool, only to watch this skilled labour force emigrate to countries offering greater opportunity. As we have discussed in this chapter, there are a variety of push and pull factors that lead skilled people to emigrate, including economic opportunity, political unrest and conflict, health concerns, and so forth. Many countries struggle to devise methods to "keep" their skilled labour force. In Canada, a recent study of Canadian doctoral graduates revealed that 12 percent of doctoral graduates from 2005 were living in the United States in 2007. Of these, the majority specialized in life sciences, or in computer, mathematics, and physical sciences.

In the remainder of this section, we focus on some of the specific issues related to the ways in which government affects migration patterns in Canada.

WAVES OF IMMIGRATION IN CANADA

Governments have a tremendous impact on immigration through the passage of laws and policies setting out who may immigrate to Canada and for what reasons. Canada is a nation of immigrants, from the arrival of Aboriginal populations some 30,000 years ago to the current influx of immigrants from around the world. In 2008, some 300,000 immigrants came to Canada. Who we are and what we might become depends on the composition of the Canadian population, which is increasingly made up of immigrants from diverse places. Understanding the history of Canadian immigration policy will put us in a better position to direct our future.

While certainly not a result of immigration policy, most historians, archaeologists, and anthropologists argue that the first human groups in North America were Aboriginal groups who arrived in Canada via a land bridge from Siberia to Alaska between 10,000 and 30,000 years ago. The first Europeans thought to set foot in Canada were Norse seafarers. L'Anse aux Meadows, located on the northernmost tip of Newfoundland, is recognized as the earliest known European settlement in North America and has been designated a UNESCO World Heritage site (Figure 5.20). Portuguese and Basque fishermen and sailors explored the coast of Newfoundland and Labrador throughout the late 1400s and early 1500s. The Italian explorer John Cabot, funded by the British monarch Henry VII, made several voyages to North America in the late 1490s, claiming much of the eastern seaboard of Canada and the northern United States for the British.

The French began to explore inland along the St. Lawrence River in the early 1500s, with Jacques Cartier documenting Aboriginal settlements along the St. Lawrence at what is now Quebec City (founded in 1608) and Montreal. While countries such as France, Portugal, and Britain made annual trips to the area for fish and furs throughout the 1500s, it was not until 1604 that a permanent settlement was established at Port Royal in the Annapolis Valley on the Bay of Fundy. This colony grew slowly

FIGURE 5.20 Replica Norse Sod Houses at L'Anse aux Meadows National Historic Site, Newfoundland. Dating back to the 11th century, L'Anse aux Meadows is recognized as the earliest known European settlement in North America. (© Wolfgang Kaehler/Corbis)

but reached a population of 500 by the early 1700s. Samuel de Champlain, a French navigator and mapmaker, also settled a permanent site at Quebec City, which became the capital of the new colony, New France (Figure 5.21). Immigration to New France was slow, and by 1759, New France had a modest population of about 65,000 French men and women.

FIGURE 5.21 Map of New France by Samuel de Champlain, 1613. Champlain's 1613 map shows Newfoundland ("terreneuve"), Acadia ("Acadye"), and Labrador, among other locations. Notice the label "Canadas" on the north shore of the Gulf of Saint Lawrence. (Centre d'études acadiennes Anselme-Chiasson, Université de Moncton (image no: Cb-4-1613))

Over this same period, the British were busy establishing colonies along the eastern seaboard of what is now the United States. The British also laid claim to parts of Newfoundland and Labrador as well as Hudson's Bay and its drainage basin, based on the trading and exploration activities of the Hudson's Bay Company. French exploration to the west of the British settlements in the United States all the way to the Gulf of Mexico seemed to pin the British to their coastal lands, foreclosing further expansion westward. France and Britain fought a series of wars over the 17th and 18th centuries that ultimately resulted in France losing control of its North American colonies to the British under the Treaty of Paris.

In 1710, the British conquered Acadia, an area we now know as the Maritime provinces of Canada, which had been under French rule. However, the French-speaking Acadian people refused to sign an oath of allegiance to Britain. Despite the Acadians' status as politically and commercially neutral people, the British came to believe they posed a threat to British control of the region, so 45 years later, between 1755 and 1763, the British expelled all Acadians from the area, deporting them to American colonies, Britain, and France. The "Expulsion of the Acadians" resulted in the deaths of thousands of people and is known as an early example of "ethnic cleansing" in Canada.

British control of the colonies ensured a steady influx of British settlers, supplemented by British Loyalists fleeing the American Revolution. Throughout the 1800s, a steady stream of British and Irish settlers came to Canada, partly to bolster the army ranks in anticipation of a feared American invasion and partly in flight from the Irish potato famine of the 1840s. Some 100 years of immigration substantially changed the demographic base from French-speaking to English-speaking peoples with a mixture of English, Irish, Scottish, and Welsh.

The British Isles' domination as a source of immigrants began to wane after Confederation in 1867, and the newly formed Canadian government looked farther afield in search of immigrants to populate the Prairies and British Columbia, partly to shore up Canadian claims to these territories against U.S. interest (Figure 5.22). At first the Canadian government worked to attract mainly American and British immigrants, but when they failed to draw enough to populate the west, they began to focus on Central European immigrants instead. From the late 1870s to the early 1950s, Central Europeans immigrated to western Canada, causing a demographic shift and new regional differentiation. While Quebec and Ontario were dominated by the French and British, respectively, the Prairies and British Columbia were settled by Ukrainians, Hungarians, Doukhobors, and peoples from Scandinavia and Tsarist Russia—giving western Canada its distinctive cultural roots. Nevertheless, despite language and religious differences, immigrants to Canada remained largely European. The port city of Halifax became an important location through which many immigrants entered Canada. Between 1928 and 1971, 1.5 million passed through the doors of Pier 21 in Halifax (Figure 5.23).

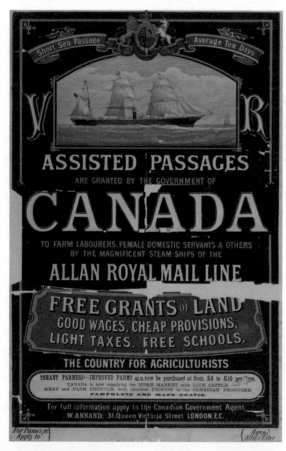

FIGURE 5.22 **Passage to Canada, 1870s to 1880s.** Posters in Britain and Europe promoting immigration to Canada offered assisted passages and promised free land, good wages, and free schools. (Library and Archives Canada/C-063484)

FIGURE 5.23 **New Arrivals Being Examined and Documented at Pier 21, Halifax, 1952.** Millions of immigrants passed through Pier 21 between 1928 and 1971, and in June 2009, the federal government declared its intention to create a National Museum of Immigration on the site. (Chris Lund/National Film Board of Canada. Photothèque collection/Library and Archives Canada/PA-111579)

FIGURE 5.24 Chinese Railway Workers, 1884. (Ernest Brown/Boorne & May/Library and Archives Canada/C-006686B)

Europeans remained the "preferred nationality" in government policy on immigration until the passage of the *Immigration Act* in 1967. The act refined Canada's system for processing those considered to be refugees and developed two distinct streams of immigrants: family members, who could be sponsored; and those assessed on a point system that analyzed skills and education. This new process was designed, in part, to ensure Canada could attract certain types of skilled workers during labour shortages.

This policy change ushered in a new era that encouraged immigration from all countries, substantially changing Canada's demographic composition over the next 40 years. Prior to 1961, 90 percent of Canadian immigrants came from Europe. By 2001, that figure had declined to less than 20 percent. Over that same period, immigration from Asia increased from just 3 percent before 1961 to over 58 percent in 2001. Between 1991 and 2001, most Asian immigrants came from China, India, Hong Kong, and Sri Lanka. As a result, Canada now has a much more diverse society that includes non-European languages and non-Christian religions. Today, Canadian immigration policy assesses immigrants in three broad classes: family class immigrants, who enter to reunite with family members already here; economic class, made up of individuals assessed on a point system considering occupational skills, experience, and adaptability; and refugees.

One measure of the importance of immigration to Canada is the proportion of immigrants in the total population. In 1996, immigrants made up 17.4 percent of Canada's population. By 2001, that figure had risen to nearly 20 percent. As Canada's rate of natural increase has declined, the government's **quota** for landed immigrants has increased in order to stabilize Canada's population. This demographic shift means Canada is an increasingly diverse country, which has led to growing debate and conflict over

> **Quotas** Established limits by governments on the number of immigrants who can enter a country each year.

what it means to be "Canadian." As we saw in Chapter 2, states strive to foster an internal sense of unity around a shared sense of history and culture underlying nationalist sentiments. This has become increasingly difficult in Canada given the country's shifting demographic composition.

One group meriting particular attention is the Chinese, who have a long history of immigration to Canada, first appearing in substantial numbers in the 1850s as part of the Fraser River gold rush. However, it was the building of the Canadian Pacific Railway, linking British Columbia and eastern Canada in the 1870s, that spurred Chinese immigration (Figure 5.24). With the completion of the railway, the Canadian government sought to stifle Chinese immigration, and from 1885 to the 1920s it imposed an increasingly harsh levy or "head tax" on Chinese immigrants. In 1923, the Canadian government passed the *Chinese Exclusion Act,* banning all Chinese immigration except for special circumstances. The act remained in place until 1947 (when it was repealed) and caused significant hardship for the mainly male immigrants who were already here, as they were unable to marry or raise a family. With the change in immigration policy in 1967, Chinese immigration has increased considerably. In June 2006, Prime Minister Stephen Harper made a formal apology for the injustices of the "head tax" and offered compensation to the families of those affected.

As we will discuss in more detail in Chapter 10, most immigrants to Canada gravitate to large cities. Between 1991 and 1995, 93.5 percent of all immigrants located in an urban area; of those, 77 percent located in one of four major metropolitan areas—Toronto, Vancouver, Montreal, and Calgary. Immigrants can have a profound impact on the social, political, and cultural aspects of place at a variety of scales. For example, as geographer Margaret Walton-Roberts has shown, by becoming active participants in the political process, immigrant women in Canada saw some of their concerns about gender equity in immigration addressed through policy changes. The social and ethno-cultural organization of these cities' neighbourhoods has changed substantially. On the one hand, this increased diversity has contributed to the vibrancy and economic health of these cities. On the other hand, some scholars argue we are seeing increasing social polarization, segregation, and not necessarily positive shifts in patterns of suburbanization. City administrators, planners, and social service providers are facing new and distinctive challenges in the development of Canada's largest cities.

MULTICULTURALISM AS GOVERNMENT POLICY—THE CASE OF CANADA

As a matter of government policy and cultural tradition, Canada has always been a multicultural nation given its settler history. *The Dictionary of Human Geography* defines "multiculturalism" as "the belief that different ethnic or cultural groups have the right to remain distinct rather than assimilating into 'mainstream' norms" (p. 528). The fact that Canada has adopted multiculturalism as government policy and in legislation impacts immigration flows; in this section, we consider some of the ways in which multiculturalism policy is intertwined with immigration. Geographer Audrey Kobayashi suggests that the multicultural nature of Canada occurred in three broadly defined stages.

In the first demographic stage, Canada became increasingly ethno-culturally diverse, although there was no official policy in place encouraging that diversity. While the French and then the English initially settled Canada, the drive to settle the Prairies broke the English/French domination with an influx of Ukrainians, Poles, Germans, Slavs, and Russians in the late 1800s and early 1900s (Figure 5.25). After World War II, Canada experienced increases in immigration from Eastern and Central Europe. Throughout this time period, immigration policy was committed to notions of assimilation, which ensured the continuing predominance of white, European, and Christian peoples. The *Immigration Act* in 1967 paved the way, yet again, for an increase in numbers of other ethnic groups beyond Europe and increasingly from Africa, China, India, and South America.

The second, or "symbolic," stage occurs when the Canadian government put in place policies that recognized and promoted multiculturalism without a firm commitment to legislate it as an official government objective. It is largely acknowledged that this shift in policy came out of the report from the Royal Commission on Bilingualism and Biculturalism (1963), which acknowledged the bicultural character of the country but argued Canada also needed to take into account other ethnic groups' contributions to Canadian society and to undertake measures to safeguard their contributions. By 1971, largely due to the Royal Commission recommendations, the Canadian government announced a new official policy of multiculturalism within a bilingual framework. Multiculturalism granted official recognition of the diverse cultures of a plural society and encouraged immigrants to retain their linguistic and ethnic cultures rather than assimilating into the dominant culture. In order to protect the right to retain distinctive cultural traits, the Canadian Human Rights Commission was created in 1978. These rights were further protected with the passage of section 15 of the Charter of Rights and Freedoms in 1982.

The third and final stage is "structural multiculturalism," in which formal government legislation is passed to address core issues such as equality of opportunity, cultural diversity, and protection from discrimination. The *Multiculturalism Act* of 1988 provided a strong legal base by consolidating existing policies and practices and providing a more detailed statement on multiculturalism. Many argue that there are a number of benefits to Canada from promoting multiculturalism. Not only does it make Canada a more interesting place; it also enhances Canada's international image and influence by ensuring demographic links to almost every other country in the world.

FIGURE 5.25 Immigrant Settlement Farm.
A Polish immigrant breaks new land on his farm in Saskatchewan, ca. 1920-1930. (Library and Archives Canada, C-052313)

However, not everyone is convinced that multiculturalism is a useful or successful policy. For example, Neil Bissoondath, in his book *Selling Illusions: The Cult of Multiculturalism in Canada*, argues that multiculturalism promotes ghettoization by encouraging immigrants to remain separate and apart from the dominant culture, and it discourages newcomers from thinking of themselves as Canadians. This arguably detracts from national unity and tends to emphasize people's differences rather than their similarities. All this is to say that ensuring immigrants are welcome and contributing members of Canadian society is a complicated business. While "multiculturalism" as formal government policy has been successful in terms of ensuring reasonably harmonious relations between "old-timers" and "newcomers," whether it remains the best approach is under reassessment. Nevertheless, Canada will continue to become increasingly diverse given current immigration policy.

MAIN POINTS   **5.4**   **How Do Governments Affect Migration?**

- The events of September 11, 2001, have singularly shaped immigration policy around the world.

- Governments influence immigration patterns in both informal and formal ways. In Canada, informal government policies in the late 1800s encouraged immigration from a wide range of European countries through advertisements and incentives. More formally, new Canadian legislation in 1967 opened the door to immigration from all countries in the world and substantially changed Canada's demographic composition.

- Multiculturalism, the official policy of the Canadian government, promotes cultural diversity, distinctiveness, and accommodation of difference. Not everyone agrees that multiculturalism is a successful approach to immigration.

- Historical events may force countries to re-evaluate government policies. The attacks of September 11, 2001, meant that many countries, including Canada, tightened their immigration requirements in ways that limited or excluded certain groups. In other cases, countries seek to exclude migrants by building physical barriers.

SUMMARY

In the last 500 years, humans have travelled the globe, mapped it, connected it through colonization and imperialism, and migrated from one part of the globe to another. Migration can occur as a result of a conscious decision, resulting in a voluntary migration flow, or it can occur under duress, resulting in forced migration. Both kinds of migration have left an indelible mark on the world and on its cultural landscapes. When we consider migration, we can do so at a number of scales, from the national to the regional and the global. Governments attempt to strike a balance among the need for migrant labour, the desire to help people in desperate circumstances, and the desire to stem the tide of migration. Immigration policy, in whatever form it takes, can have a profound effect on the internal composition of a country's population.

Canada is, of course, a country of immigrants. Recent immigration and multiculturalism policy means Canada accepts immigrants from all over the globe, substantially enriching its human resources. Yet increasing diversity has the potential to be problematic as people seek some common ground in their understanding of what it means to be a "Canadian." Canada relies on immigrants to ensure stable population growth given our declining rate of natural increase and our aging population.

As the world's population mushrooms, the volume of migrants will expand. In an increasingly open and interconnected world, neither physical barriers nor politically motivated legislation will stem tides that are as old as human history. Migrations will also further complicate an already complex global cultural pattern—raising questions about identity, race, ethnicity, language, and religion, topics we turn to in upcoming chapters.

DISCUSSION AND REVIEW QUESTIONS

1. What does the case of the *MV Sun Sea* reveal about the issue of migration both for Canada and the world? What do you feel is an appropriate response to the issue posed by this event?

2. As a key part of studying and understanding migration, human geographers focus on determining who migrants are. Discuss and assess the typology constructed to understand the migrant experience. What, if any, is your personal experience with migration?

3. The Atlantic slave trade is arguably one of the most devastating and pernicious cases of forced migration in human history. It profoundly altered the human geographies of Africa, the Caribbean, North America, and South America. Discuss its history and the geographic impacts. What was Canada's role in the history of slavery?

4. Canada has often been described as a "multicultural" nation. What does this mean and how is it related to the history of the country? What, if any, criticisms are there of Canada's multicultural policy?

5. Re-read the guest field note *Living in Toronto*. Have you ever thought about your own or your family's migratory experience? When did your ancestors move to Canada? What were the "push" or "pull" factors that brought them to the country? Where did they first arrive and how have they moved since? Has it been mainly a positive or a negative experience?

GEOGRAPHIC CONCEPTS

asylum   128
chain migration   135
colonization   136
deportation   133
diaspora   131
emigration   125
explorers   136
forced migration   129
genocide   129
gravity model   132
guest workers   127
immigration   125
immigration wave   135
internal migration   126
internally displaced persons (IDPs)   128
international migration   124

intervening opportunity   133
islands of development   138
kinship links   135
laws of migration   132
migrant labour   127
migration   124
nomadism   124
pull factors   132
push factors   132
quota   151
refugees   128
regional scale   138
remittances   127
repatriation   129
step migration   133
voluntary migration   129

ADDITIONAL RESOURCES ONLINE

About foreign policy and international development issues (North-South Institute): www.nsi-ins.ca

About refugees: www.unhcr.org

About internally displaced persons: www.internal-displacement.org

About migration (International Organization for Migration): www.iom.int/jahia/Jahia/lang/en/pid/1

About geographic mobility and movement in the United States: www.census.gov/population/www/socdemo/migrate.html

About *Rough Crossings*: www.youtube.com/watch?v=2nnAB3xOMW4

About Canada's Temporary Foreign Worker Program: www.hrsdc.gc.ca/eng/workplaceskills/foreign_workers/index.shtml

About migration and identity: www.learner.org/resources/series85.html#program_descriptions (Click on Video On Demand for "A Migrant's Heart")

About the United States-Mexico border region: www.learner.org/resources/series180.html#program_descriptions (Click on Video On Demand for "Boundaries and Borderlands")

About Latin American migrant workers in the United States: www.cbc.ca/documentaries/passionateeyeshowcase/2010/whichwayhome

About Mexican migrant workers on an Ontario farm: www.nfb.ca/film/el_contrato

About The Royal Society: http//royalsociety.org

chapter 6

HUMAN-ENVIRONMENT RELATIONS

Disaster Along Indian Ocean Shores

WATCHING THE HORRORS of the tsunami of December 26, 2004, unfold on my television screen (Figure 6.1), I found it eerie to see such devastation in places where earlier I walked and drove and rode. I took a group of students, including my own children, on this Sri Lankan train in 1978; now it was smashed by the waves, the carriages toppled, killing more than a thousand passengers, both locals and tourists. And the beaches near Phuket, Thailand, so serene and beautiful in memory, now proved a fatal attraction leading to disaster for thousands more, tourists and workers alike.

I went on-line to follow the events of that day and those that followed, horrified by the rising death toll and by the images of destruction and devastation. My e-mail in-box began to include messages from former students who remembered my in-field assessment of the tsunami risks in Southeast Asia. But I had not been especially prescient. Like those people who choose to farm the fertile soils on the slopes of an active volcano, anyone living at or near sea level near an earthquake zone lives with risk.

A few weeks later, I began to hear stories about an English girl named Tilly Smith, who was vacationing with her parents at a hotel on Maikhao Beach at Phuket when she saw the water suddenly recede into the distance. Tilly had just completed a geography class in her school near London. Her teacher, Andrew Kearney, had told the class what happens when a tsunami strikes: the huge approaching wave first sucks the water off the beaches; then the sea foams, rises, and returns as a massive, breaking wall that crashes over and inundates the whole shoreline. Tilly saw this happening on Maikhao Beach that day and alerted her parents; her father told hotel security; and they ran back and forth, screaming at beachgoers to seek shelter on higher ground in the hotel behind them. About a hundred people followed the Smith family into the building. They all survived. Many others did not. Being aware of some of the basics of physical geography has its advantages.

FIGURE 6.1 Galle, Sri Lanka. The December 26, 2004, Indian Ocean tsunami destroyed this passenger train in Sri Lanka, ripping apart tracks and killing more than a thousand people. (AP/Wide World Photos)

Newspaper editors could use some of this awareness. Many headlines referred to the tsunami as a tidal wave, but a tsunami has nothing to do with the tides that affect all oceans and seas. A tsunami results from an undersea earthquake involving a large displacement of the Earth's crust. Most submarine earthquakes do not generate tsunamis, but in some cases, fortunately relatively rarely, a large piece of crust is pushed up or pulled under (or both), and this causes the water overhead to pile up and start rolling away in all directions. If you were on a cruise ship somewhere in the middle of the ocean, nothing catastrophic would mark the passing of this tsunami wave; your ship would be lifted up and then lowered, but it would not overturn. But when such a huge wave reaches a beach, it does what all waves do: it breaks. Most of us have seen this happen with waves several metres (or even tens of metres) high. But imagine a wave over 60 metres high approaching a beach. As it begins to break, it pulls the water away, exposing wide swaths of muddy bottom. Then it comes crashing into the shore, pushing deep inland.

Tsunamis of the magnitude of the 2004 wave are rare, but the hazard is continuous. As the Earth's human population has grown, so have the numbers of people vulnerable to such a calamity. As we learn more about the submarine zones where earthquakes are most likely to occur, we can begin to determine where the hazards are greatest. Here we combine two major fields of study in geography, physical geography and human geography. Both fields are clearly very dynamic. The environment is not static, and environmental change affects human societies. At the same time, humans have an impact on their natural environments. The study of hazards, not just from tsunamis but also from volcanic eruptions, terrestrial earthquakes, landslides, floods, avalanches, and other threats, is a key part of this research. Geography is a discipline in which the relationship between humans and the environment is a primary concern.

KEY QUESTIONS FOR CHAPTER 6

1. How do geographers think about the concept of "nature"?

2. What impact do humans have on the environment?

3. How are humans responding to environmental change?

6.1 How Do Geographers Think about the Concept of "Nature"?

In Chapter 1, we defined the discipline of geography as the study of human-environmental relations. In this definition, the term "environment" included both the natural world and the built environment. In this chapter, we will consider the concept of "nature" as it has been taken up by geographers and as something we consider separately from the built environment. Although the centrality of our environment to our very existence may fade into the background as we go about our daily business, as the opening field note suggests, we may be sharply reminded of its significance when we suffer through hurricanes, experience smog or high ultraviolet exposure, or pay higher prices for food or fuel. Conversely, we are becoming increasingly aware that our individual daily activities, from driving our cars to recycling to the temperature we set in our homes, have an impact on our environment.

As geographers, we are interested in how human-nature relations can be considered in light of our five major themes—location, region, place, landscape, and movement. In this chapter, we begin by examining geographical approaches to thinking about or conceptualizing human-environment interrelationships. Although these are often framed as "binary" relationships—that is, as an interconnection between two things (humans and nature)—we will soon see that the complexity of the human-nature relationship evades straightforward binary descriptions. We then consider the impacts human beings are having on the natural world. In the third and final section, we explore the approaches humans are employing to address such challenges as climate change, species extinction, diminishing air quality, and resource depletion.

Cultural and literary critic Raymond Williams argues that "[the word] nature is perhaps the most complex word in the [English] language" (1988, p. 221). We may use the term "nature" in a number of different ways. For example, we may mean the nature of an object, its inherent and unchanging characteristics—as in the phrase "it is just the nature of things." We may be talking about a physical world untouched by humankind, such as the "wilderness," or we may be thinking about a natural world that may or may not include human beings. Clearly, these are overlapping ideas, and we cannot usually think of one conceptualization without thinking of the others. Our conceptualization of nature determines our relationship to nature, how we see our place in nature, and how we think we should interact with the natural world.

Many human populations regard human beings and our society or culture as separate from the natural world—they believe we are somehow standing outside or beyond nature. In this conceptualization, nature tends to be a place we look out at or step into, a place we go to for recreation and leisure, relaxation and rest. Nature is portrayed as an undisturbed landscape waiting to be discovered (and possibly developed) by humans. We often see nature as something to be conquered and overcome, brought under the control of humans for their own purposes. Television reality shows such as *Survivorman* and *Mantracker* portray humans battling the forces of nature (Figure 6.2). A common element of these ways of thinking is their organization of ideas about nature and humanity as a set of binaries or a set of opposing concepts: nature-culture, nature-society, nature-human. In each of these, we see reflected the idea that humans and human social relations (society and culture) are outside nature.

We might question whether understanding nature as something separate from humankind fairly represents our relationship. Some argue that the current conceptualization of nature as distinct from society emerged during the Western Age of Enlightenment

(17th and 18th centuries). In the late 18th and early 19th centuries, rapid urbanization and industrialization in Western societies radically altered human landscapes, making the distinction between human society (urban) and undeveloped "nature" (the rural) quite stark. As we examined in the chapters on globalization and political geography (chapters 2 and 3 respectively), this was also the age of imperial and colonial exploration by countries such as France, Spain, Britain, Belgium, and Portugal. Colonial enterprises sought to map a vastly expanding world teeming with an unimaginable array of plants, animals, and sea creatures that had previously been unknown to Europeans. It is not surprising that Western nations saw themselves as discoverers of vast new natural resources for human use. Geographers and scientists "discovered" and studied a "nature" that was seen as remote and removed from human society and culture. This perception is distinct from views of nature held by many of the world's Aboriginal populations or by such religions as Buddhism and Taoism, which regard human existence as fully enmeshed in and inseparable from the natural world (see Chapter 8).

How we view our relationship with nature affects how we use or treat the natural world. If the dominant view is that nature is a resource for human use, we will think about nature only in the context of its usefulness for humans—an **anthropocentric** perspective. On the other hand, if we see ourselves as intrinsically bound up with nature or if we believe that nature is valuable in its own right and not merely as determined by its usefulness to humans, we may see our interaction with the natural world in a different light.

> **Anthropocentric view** A view in which human interests and perspectives are highlighted.

Recent geographical scholarship questions whether the nature-human binary is the best or most accurate way to understand our relationship with nature. Perhaps there are other, more useful, ways to think about these connections given our current concerns about climate change and resource depletion. In this section, we first consider three different ways geographers have thought about our relationship with nature—Marxist-based scholarship, research in cultural geography, and the political ecology approach. Then we consider the history of environmentalism and environmental movements and their ideas about the human-nature relationship.

MARXIST GEOGRAPHY AND THE PRODUCTION OF NATURE

Geographer Neil Smith, in his book, *Uneven Development* (1984), draws on the work of Karl Marx to think about how changes in the world economy brought about by the advent of a new economic system, capitalism, fundamentally altered how we conceive of nature. Capitalism is a relatively new system for organizing the exchange of goods and services that developed during the age of Western exploration, imperialism, and colonialism in the 17th and 18th centuries (see Chapter 3). During that period, urbanization, rapid population growth, and new technologies transformed the organization of human societies around the globe. In core countries, dominant social, economic,

FIGURE 6.2 Survivorman. Canadian Les Stroud, a filmmaker and survival expert, uses his skills and knowledge to survive in the wilderness, battling nature for days at a time with little food or water. (Laura Bombier/© Discovery Channel/Courtesy: Everett Collection/ The Canadian Press)

FIGURE 6.3 *Food, Inc.* In his documentary *Food, Inc.*, filmmaker Robert Kenner examines corporations' control of the food industry. This control illustrates one way in which we manipulate and commodify nature. (Joe Kohen/Wire Image/Getty Images)

and political relations shifted from small rural and agricultural communities to rapidly expanding cities operating within an increasingly global trading system. A new form of government also developed—the democratically constituted nation-state.

Karl Marx (1818–1883) lived during the height of the Industrial Revolution in Europe, a time of dramatic political and economic upheaval and unprecedented social change. He eyed these massive changes with some anxiety and spent his life writing about their implications for humankind. One concept central to his thinking is the idea that human beings increasingly used new technologies to transform nature into something else—mills transformed wood into lumber and furniture, or water into power; plants were modified to produce larger and better crops; and raw materials were extracted to make various metals. Marx argued that through this human manipulation of nature, humans were not only producing something new but were "producing nature" as well. By this he means that humans, in their interactions with nature, produce a new kind of nature. For example, human use of plants and animals led to their domestication in fields and in fenced yards. We began planting crops in tidy rows for human harvest, differentiating miscellaneous plants from "crops" that could be eaten or used for other human needs. We began evaluating forests and rocks with an eye to their resource value, changing our view of them as an object in their own right to a commodity whose value is measured in its worth for human consumption. Setting aside land as a hunting reserve transformed animals into "game"—a truly human-centred way of understanding living creatures.

As geographer Noel Castree argues, there are three important reasons to think about how humans "produce nature" through their technological and intellectual efforts. First, if we understand that we produce nature, we force ourselves to think about how humans interact and change nature—that is, we can examine how our production of nature changes historically and geographically. For example, hunter-gatherer societies clearly used nature in a different manner than industrial societies did. Second, recognizing that humans produce nature ensures we realize that nature is not unchanging and static but constantly

interwoven into human activity. We can consider how, in the process of transforming nature for our own use, we alter the very foundation of the natural world and our relationship to it. Finally, thinking about the production of nature requires that we focus on how we manipulate nature into something to be sold—a commodity—for profit (Figure 6.3).

CULTURAL GEOGRAPHY AND THE CONCEPT OF NATURE

In contrast to Marxist thinkers, cultural geographers argue that what we understand as nature comes as much from the human imagination as it does from technological intervention. How we envision nature, and the meanings we give it, affect how we come to use nature and regard our place in it. The subdiscipline of landscape studies has directed considerable attention to the implications of how humans "see" landscapes. As geographers point out, the term "landscape" can mean both the actual world we inhabit and a representational quality we might find in landscape paintings or other art forms. When we look at paintings of landscapes, we see the world through an artist's eye and get a sense of how nature is represented or understood by that artist. How the artist represents nature—the colours used, the items included or excluded, the positioning and organizing of trees, people, and buildings—can tell us a great deal about "ways of seeing" nature-human relationships in different cultures and in different historical periods.

In their book *Iconography of Landscape* (1988), geographers Stephen Daniels and Denis Cosgrove argue that we all have our own way of seeing landscape, both individually and collectively as a society. We can argue that the representation of nature in paintings, art, or writing is not a neutral process, as it is influenced by the social norms of the time. One example that cultural geographers have used to illustrate how landscapes draw together nature and culture is a painting, *Mr. and Mrs. Andrews*, by 18th-century artist Thomas Gainsborough (Figure 6.4). In this painting, the landowners are seated on the left, and nature appears on

FIGURE 6.4 Mr. and Mrs. Andrews, 1748. Cultural geographers often use Thomas Gainsborough's painting as an example of how landscapes provide a way of seeing the relationship between nature and culture. (National Gallery, London)

the right as a wide-open vista, ready for exploitation. Nature, at the time this painting was produced, was seen as proprietary, and the fact that those who worked the land were not depicted is a commentary of the class relations of the time. When European explorers saw landscapes as literally "empty" (with no indigenous peoples) or as "undeveloped" or "vacant," they could only understand what they saw through the particular cultural lens of that historical era. It follows that whatever the "real" world of nature is, it is also something mediated through human expectations, experiences, and representations. This has serious implications for how we view or think about the world around us. How we understand landscapes influences, for example, which places we assume are important enough to be protected in national parks or designated World Heritage sites, and which are the proper locations for ATV (all-terrain vehicle) trails or human development. All of this suggests that there might be no common or typical way of understanding landscapes and nature. It also suggests, perhaps to our benefit, that how we see nature might change and, in turn, prompt a reassessment of humankind's place in it. The approaches of both Marxist and cultural geographers challenge us to reconsider how we think about human-environment relations.

POLITICAL ECOLOGY AND ENVIRONMENTAL CHANGE

The third method geographers have used to think about our relationship with nature, the political ecology approach, emerged in geographical scholarship in the 1970s and 1980s. This approach suggests the connection between nature and society is better understood if we focus on political and social relations under capitalism. The perspective has been particularly useful in development studies, which examine the positioning of peripheral and semi-peripheral countries within the processes of globalization (see Chapter 11) and the various forms of environmental degradation that seem to occur as these countries are increasingly caught up in the global capitalist economy.

Economic development is clearly linked to environmental change, and as we will see in Chapter 11, many argue that the benefits of development are captured by core countries while developing countries inequitably bear the costs in the form of environmental degradation and deteriorating social and cultural relations. For example, in the late 1980s, geographers Harold Brookfield and Piers Blaikie argued that ecological problems, such as environmental degradation, actually reflect social and political problems rather than lack of technical or managerial expertise. Brookfield and Blaikie suggested that problems such as soil erosion in Nepal could be explained as environmental mismanagement or overpopulation. Subsequent scholarship developed a more formal political ecology approach, arguing we might need to take a broader view and look at how globalization has changed social relations at the local level in ways that alter how a community farms or accesses resources. We might also consider how new government regulations, such as taxes or levies, could influence how local communities operate. This approach asserts that to properly understand environmental problems, one needs to take a multiscalar approach that is sensitive to broader historical, political, and social circumstances.

A political ecology approach helps us focus on human-nature relations and on the transformation in social relations among and between social groups based on class, race, gender, or ethnicity within a wider capitalist economic system. Political ecologists focus on questions of property rights, resource control, traditional land management techniques, and labour and production, all central concerns when considering the changing human-nature relationship in peripheral and semi-peripheral countries.

ENVIRONMENTALISM

How we think about or understand our relationship with nature is reflected in the history of the environmental movement in both Canada and the United States. Environmentalism is both an ideology and an activity; that is, it is a particular perspective or set of beliefs about human-environment relations that promote a set of actions designed to effect change. Put simply, how we understand our relationship with nature has influenced the distinctive perspectives of environmental activism over the last 200 years.

During the age of imperialism, colonialism, and global exploration, the dominant world view was that of manifest destiny—that man is destined to expand over territory. Sociologist Charles Harper argues that the idea of manifest destiny provided the moral and economic rationale for human exploitation of nature. Such a position, Harper notes, assumes that "nature has no intrinsic value, that human welfare depends on the exploitation and development of nature and that human inventiveness and technology can transcend any resource problem." Such a perspective clearly provided support for the European conquest and exploitation of the resources and peoples of its colonies and continues to provide a rationale for those who support the continued free-market commodification and use of the natural world.

Despite the prominence of this widely held view, concern about environmental degradation and the abuse of nature began to surface in the early 1800s. In Europe, the rapid urbanization occurring as a result of the Industrial Revolution alarmed civic leaders, women's organizations, religious groups, and social planners who believed the overcrowded, dirty, tenement housing and slums of the working poor were unhealthy for children and adults alike. Humans' need for access to the countryside, sunshine, and fresh air became an increasing preoccupation for many.

NORTH AMERICAN ENVIRONMENTALISM

In North America, deforestation, desertification, soil erosion, and the extermination of creatures such as carrier pigeons and the buffalo increased worries about human impacts on nature and paved the way for the first wave of environmentalists. Writers such as Henry David Thoreau, Ralph Waldo Emerson, and James Fenimore Cooper, and politicians including Theodore Roosevelt, argued for the "scientific management" of natural resources and their conservation. Clear divisions emerged between such individuals as John Muir, who founded the Sierra Club in 1892 and who favoured wilderness preservation, and Gifford Pinchot, a member of the American forestry service who argued that natural resources should be used for human benefits but in a responsible way.

Conservationism, the view that humans are part of nature and in destroying our resources are undermining our own ability to survive, advocates the conservation of resources for future use. This is in contrast to **preservationism**, which argues for the preservation of wildlife for its own sake and allows only minimal human use. Tensions between the two views are clearly seen in today's environmental debates.

> **Conservationism** A human-centred view of nature that advocates for conservation of resources for future human use.
>
> **Preservationism** A view asserting that nature should be preserved for its own sake, rather than for human use.

In this early movement, Canadian responses were legislative and reflected the view that the natural world was there to provide respite and relief to humans wishing to escape their urban environments. For example, the *Dominion Forest Reserves and Parks Act* of 1913 stated that forests "shall be maintained and made use of as public parks and pleasure grounds for the benefit, advantage, and enjoyment of the people of Canada," clearly a conservationist view of nature.

The first national park in Canada was established when Sir John A. Macdonald's government passed the *Rocky Mountains Park Act* in 1887, designating some 674 square kilometres as a protected area that came to be known as Banff National Park. Increasing concern in both the United States and Canada over the hunting of migratory birds led to the passage of the *Migratory Birds Act* in 1911. This law sought to protect migratory birds and their habitats from hunting and trafficking. It is important to note that while the act protects the birds themselves, it does not protect the land or water resources they use. Canada's Dominion Parks Branch, the world's first national park service, was also established in 1911. (Now known as Parks Canada Agency, it is under the purview of Environment Canada.) The Dominion Parks Branch saw to the creation and management of national parks and wildlife areas. The *National Parks Act* was passed in 1930 and includes a clause that "dedicates" the parks to the people of Canada. These early legislative interventions demonstrate the desire to preserve certain natural areas largely for the benefit of human beings and, potentially, for the future use of those resources. Today, Canada has 36 national parks and 6 national park reserves—areas designated to be national parks once Aboriginal land claims have been settled. The goal is to have a system of national parks that represents Canada's 39 national regions (Figure 6.5).

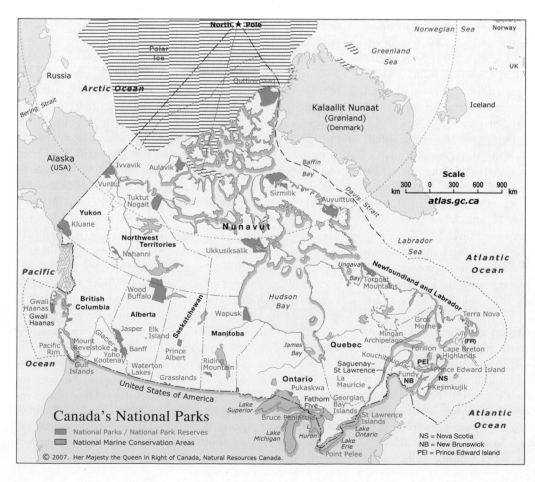

FIGURE 6.5 Canada's National Parks and Marine Conservation Areas, 2007. Canada has 36 national parks and 6 national park reserves (areas set aside to become national parks once Aboriginal land claims have been settled), as well as 4 national marine conservation areas (which take in the seabed, the water, and any species it contains), spread across the 10 provinces and 3 territories. (© 2007, Her Majesty the Queen in Right of Canada, Natural Resources Canada)

Canada's provincial governments also have a long history of creating and maintaining park lands for public use. One of the earliest and largest provincial parks is Ontario's Algonquin Park, created in 1893 as a wildlife and timber preserve, which covers some 7,630 square kilometres. As of 2007, Ontario had 329 parks and 292 conservation reserves. Other provinces have followed suit, although each province has developed its own distinctive classification system. For example, British Columbia has 14 designations that include marine parks, provincial heritage sites, and ecological reserves. Saskatchewan has created 34 provincial parks, 130 recreational areas, 8 historic sites, and 24 protected areas—each designation reflecting a specific natural or historic feature with a range of recreational and educational purposes. The distinctive modes of designation, protection, preservation, and use of various types of landscapes reflect the range of philosophies behind such designations, from the aspiration to preserve untouched wilderness areas to the wish to generate income from recreational uses that will support the costs of the parks system.

The second phase of the North American environmental movement began in the 1950s and 1960s, and focused on air and water quality and human health issues arising from pollution and from chemical and toxic waste. In the previous phase, environmental activism took the form of government policies and direct intervention. New forms of environmental activism were largely directed by grassroots organizations struggling to address local environmental problems. A series of influential books, including Rachel Carson's *Silent Spring*, Paul Ehrlich's *The Population Bomb*, and Garrett Hardin's *Tragedy of the Commons*, drew public attention to environmental problems. Several high-profile environmental disasters, such as toxic waste in the Love Canal (Niagara Falls, New York), environmental degradation in Burlington Bay (Hamilton, Ontario), and the Sydney Tar Ponds (Sydney, Nova Scotia), as well as oil spills off the coast of California in the late 1960s, spurred growing concern for the well-being of both humans and nature. The first Earth Day was celebrated in 1970, organized by American senator Gaylord Nelson. It was attended by 20 million people, and organizers were shocked by the event's success. Greenpeace, now a well-known international environmental organization, was established in Vancouver, B.C., in 1971 to protest American underground nuclear testing at Amchitka Island, off the Alaskan coast, which is home to endangered wildlife (Figure 6.6).

The new environmental activists and their organizations took many different approaches to highlight environmental concerns and crises. Some were conservationist, seeking to ensure resources were maintained for future generations; others were strictly preservationist in their attempts to preserve nature for nature's sake; still others walked a fine line between these two perspectives. Collectively, the organizations were referred to as the "environmental lobby." Some groups acted locally, protesting local actions by companies causing pollution or

FIGURE 6.6 Greenpeace MV *Arctic Sunrise* in Leith, Edinburgh, **2007.** Established in Vancouver, B.C., in 1971, Greenpeace is now a well-known international environmental organization. (© Choice/ Alamy)

demanding the cleanup of toxic sites. Others lobbied for legislative and policy changes, demanded funding for scientific research, and worked to raise environmental awareness. Over the last several decades, environmental activism has expanded to include broader concerns such as global ecological issues, biodiversity, and climate change.

Grassroots activism on environmental issues experienced a resurgence in the late 1980s and early 1990s, particularly in relation to environmental justice, with activists arguing that environmental issues could not be considered separately from questions of race, class, and gender. For example, Blue Planet Project, an organization founded by Canadian Maude Barlow, explicitly considers access to fresh water a woman's issue given that women around the world, particularly in the peripheral and semi-peripheral countries, struggle to provide fresh water to their families for washing clothes, bathing, domestic cleaning, and human consumption (Figure 6.7). Scholars and activists also claim that environmentally undesirable projects, such as garbage dumps, toxic waste sites, nuclear waste facilities, or oil exploration or drilling sites, are often unfairly located near poor or disadvantaged groups with little ability to protest or engage in community activism. Environmentalism tied to global climate change has increased in visibility with projects such as Al Gore's 2006 film *An Inconvenient Truth* capturing international interest. In Canada, David Suzuki continues to raise environmental issues on *The Nature of Things*, and projects like the Canadian government's One-Tonne Challenge encourage Canadians to act in environmentally responsible ways. Today's environmental movement is complicated, made up of local grassroots organizations, national non-governmental and governmental organizations, and global movements focused on global issues.

FIGURE 6.7 Maude Barlow. Maude Barlow, founder of Blue Planet Project, attends the People's World Water Forum in New Delhi, January 12-14, 2004. (Photo courtesy of The Council of Canadians.)

FIGURE 6.8 D5 Demonstrations, 2009. On December 5, 2009, protestors in Portland, Oregon, participated in the global days of action against the World Trade Organization, which became known as the "D5 Demonstrations." (Bette Lee)

GLOBAL ENVIRONMENTALISM

Environmental activism has also gone global, with alliances of nation-states, United Nations organizations, non-governmental organizations (NGOs), and international non-governmental organizations (INGOs). Global organizations with distinctive but interrelated concerns are forming alliances too, including groups working for women's rights or workers' rights, environmentalists, and student groups. These alliances link concerns about globalization with environmental degradation and the exploitation of workers, particularly women and the poor. The World Trade Organization protests in Seattle, Washington, in 1999 brought together diverse groups for a common goal. In more recent WTO protests, such as the D5 demonstrations in 2009 in Portland, Oregon, placards read "teamsters and turtles, together at last" and "... together still" (Figure 6.8).

There is no doubt that global environmental issues are a growing concern. Disappearing tropical rainforests, loss of soil, desertification, access to clean water, air pollution, and renewable/non-renewable energy sources have become central issues. The United Nations has sponsored a series of environmental conferences—first the United Nations Conference on the Human Environment in Stockholm, Sweden, in 1972, followed by the United Nations Conference on Environment and Development (UNCED) in Rio de Janeiro in 1992. While no treaties emerged from these conferences, delegates did attain a broad consensus about pollution, biodiversity, and global warming. Progress is slow and often sidelined by acts of global terror. However, the World Summit on Sustainable Development (WSSD) in Johannesburg in 2002 did make some progress. Overall, and despite considerable disagreement, there seems to be a consensus emerging on the need for sustainable development and environmental protection at the global

level. We will revisit this discussion in more detail in the final section of the chapter.

ANTI-ENVIRONMENTALISM

In the 1980s and 1990s, corporations and businesses began organizing against the environmental lobby, usually presenting arguments that supported free market activity and the right to use private property as the owner wishes. When protestors attempted to sabotage the Trans-Alaska Pipeline, the corporation spent thousands of dollars to locate the protestors, even using eavesdropping technologies and surveillance to track them down. Interestingly, while corporations fought government regulation of environmental issues in their industries, they also began public relations campaigns and "green" advertising campaigns to capture the new green consumer.

More recently, scholars have pointed to the formation of a so-called wise use movement, made up predominantly of lumber and mining industries, that works to counter initiatives of the environmental movement. Wise use groups resemble grassroots organizations but are financed by industry and argue against claims that climate change is a problem and that fish stocks are declining. These groups also argue against environmental regulation because it infringes on private property rights and free enterprise; they claim that tough environmental regulations threaten jobs and makes it more expensive to do business; and they insist that by making certain resources, such as oil and natural gas, off-limits by designating parks or wildlife preserves, countries like Canada and the United States will be unable to develop their resources to their own advantage. Regardless of one's position, the process of thinking through environmental issues and finding information and perspectives that might responsibly guide future decision making has become increasingly complicated.

MAIN POINTS   6.1   How Do Geographers Think about the Concept of "Nature"?

- Geographers study human-environmental relations. The term "environment" encompasses both the natural world (or "nature") and the built environment. "Nature" is a complicated concept, and how we understand the term influences our relationship to it.

- Human societies have conceptualized "nature" and their relationship with it differently in different historical periods and geographical locations. In core countries, views of human-environment relations are generally structured around a set of binaries or opposing concepts: nature-culture, nature-society, nature-human.

- Geographers use three main conceptual approaches (although there are others) to think about the

human-environment relationship—Marxism, the notion of cultural landscapes, and political ecology.

- The history of the environmental movement in North America demonstrates that activists and grassroots movements as well as governments and their agencies take different approaches to the environment, falling along a continuum between preservationism and conservationism.

- The global environmental movement demonstrates the interconnectedness of the environment at the global level while maintaining a focus on specific local concerns.

6.2 What Impact Do Humans Have on the Environment?

While we tend to think of serious human impacts on the environment as a modern event, humans have had an effect on their environment for all of their history. In search of food, they set fires to kill herds of reindeer and bison. They hunted entire species of large mammals to extinction. The Maori, who arrived in New Zealand not much more than 1,000 years ago, greatly altered native species of animals and plants long before the advent of modern technology. Elsewhere in the Pacific region, Polynesians reduced the forest cover to brush and, as a result of their penchant for wearing bird-feather robes, exterminated more than 80 percent of the regional bird species by the time the first Europeans arrived. European fashions over the last 800 years had a disastrous impact on African species ranging from snakes, crocodiles, and birds to leopards and elephants.

In this section, we consider the impact humans have on their environment by considering such human activities as consumption and energy use, and the effects these have on ecosystems—the biological community of plants and animals that live in a particular region and interact with each other and their environment, including water, atmosphere, and land. We begin, however, with a discussion of the Columbian Exchange—a process arising from exploration and colonization (discussed in Chapter 3) that continues today.

THE COLUMBIAN EXCHANGE

The age of exploration, which began in the 1400s, had profound environmental impacts. European explorers travelled the world, bringing their technologies, cultures, norms, and beliefs to previously unknown peoples and places. These travellers also carried home a staggering array of seemingly exotic and

unknown plants, animals, and peoples. The historian Alfred Crosby, in his book *The Columbian Exchange*, argues that the voyage of Christopher Columbus to the Americas in 1492 launched a large-scale exchange of plants, animals, cultures, ideas, and diseases that had a profound effect on agriculture, the environment, and culture in both the Old World of Europe and the New World of the Americas. As Figure 6.9 indicates, the global circulation and exchange of plants, animals, and illnesses was incredible.

In the Americas, indigenous people were deeply affected by European contact, particularly by European diseases for which they had no immunity. It is estimated that the indigenous populations experienced losses between 50 and 90 percent due to disease. Some groups, including the Incas and the Aztec, disappeared altogether. Conversely, new varieties of crops and domesticated animals moved between the Old and the New Worlds. In Europe, crops such as maize, potatoes, and tomatoes became important by the early 18th century. The dandelion, previously unknown in North America, arrived with colonial settlers as an herb for cooking and is now considered a noxious weed to be eradicated by herbicides. Europeans introduced the horse to North America, and indigenous populations took advantage of the possibilities for migration, resettlement, and new, more efficient hunting strategies. Latin American plantations were established to grow coffee from Africa and sugar cane from Asia for export to both Europe and North America.

Even today we confront the unintended consequences of species introduction into new habitats. In Canada, for example, the zebra mussel and purple loosestrife threaten various habitats. Asian carp, originally introduced as pond fish in the southern United States, escaped into local waterways and have been making their way north through the river system (Figure 6.10). Recreational and commercial fishers fear that these carp will reach the Great Lakes and decimate the native fish, forever altering the ecosystem.

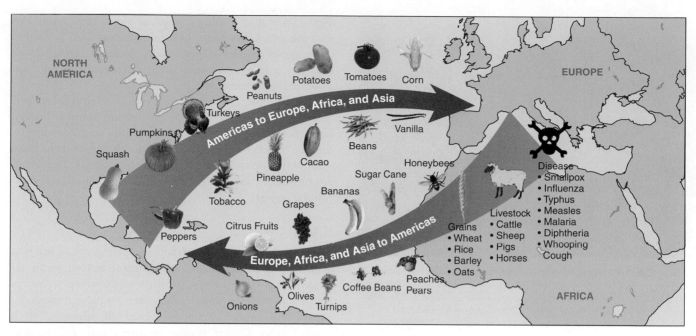

FIGURE 6.9 The Columbian Exchange. A partial list of the plants, animals, and diseases travelling between the Old World and the New World.

FIGURE 6.10 Asian Carp Threaten the Great Lakes. Asian carp leap from the water of a U.S. river, demonstrating their size and numbers. An electronic barrier has been erected in an attempt to prevent Asian carp from reaching the Great Lakes. (Nerissa Michaels, Illinois River Biological Station via the *Detroit Free Press*/AP/The Canadian Press)

HUMAN FACTORS

Several interrelated factors are responsible for humans' expanding impact on the environment over the past two centuries. One factor is the dramatic growth of the human population, discussed in Chapter 4. In addition, our consumption of natural resources has intensified, while technological change has increased both our capacity to alter the environment and our demand for energy. All these factors have significant environmental impacts, although the nature of that impact varies depending on the local and regional context.

PATTERNS OF CONSUMPTION

Humans rely on the Earth's resources for our very survival. We consume water, oxygen, and organic and mineral materials, and we have developed increasingly complex technologies, including intensive agricultural processes and industrial production, to collect them. Consequently, many societies now consume resources at a level and rate that far exceed basic subsistence needs. In a 1996 article on "Humanity's Resources" in *The Companion Encyclopaedia of Geography: The Environment and Humankind*, I.G. Simmons notes that a hunter-gatherer could subsist on the resources found within an area of about 26 square kilometres. Today, many people living in urban centres in the global economic core have access to resources from all over the planet.

Generally, the smaller numbers of people in the world's core countries make far greater demands on the Earth's resources than do the much larger numbers in the periphery and semi-periphery. A baby born in the United States during the first decade of the 21st century is estimated to consume about 250 times as much energy over a lifetime as a baby born in Bangladesh. In terms of food, housing, metals, paper (and thus trees), and many other materials, individuals in affluent countries consume far more than people in poorer countries. Rapid population growth in the periphery tends to have local or regional environmental impacts as the growing number of people put pressure on soil, natural vegetation, and water supplies, and pollute the local air with the smoke from their fires. The reach of affluent societies is much more extensive, so population growth in the core is a matter of local, regional, and global concern. For example, North American demand for low-cost meat for hamburgers has led to deforestation in Central and South America as ranchers

FIGURE 6.11 Deforestation in the Amazon, Mato Grosso, Brazil.
Fuelled by the increasing demand for meat around the world, farmers burn swaths of land in the Amazon to make way for more land to raise cattle and to grow more food grain. (John Stanmeyer/VII/Corbis)

clear land for pastures and cattle herds (Figure 6.11). This, in turn, has increased water demand in such areas (Table 6.1) and demonstrates how North American, European, Japanese, and Australian consumers have a detrimental impact on distant environments. All this underscores the importance of thinking geographically about human impacts on the natural world.

Technological advances have increased rapidly since the Industrial Revolution and today affect all aspects of our lives. We continually develop technologies we hope will improve our standard of living, protect us against disease, and allow us to work more efficiently. These technologies do not come without a cost, however. Resource extraction practices, such as mining and logging, provide the materials to produce new technologies but also create severe environmental problems. Energy from fossil fuels (coal, oil, and natural gas) is required to develop new technologies and to use them, but fossil fuel consumption contributes to many types of pollution and is a factor in climate change. Technological innovations produce hazardous and toxic by-products, creating pollution and health problems that we are only now beginning to recognize. The United Nations Environment Programme, Division of Technology, Industry and Economics works to characterize and assess the environmental impacts of new technologies, organizing these impacts into human health impacts, local natural environment

TABLE 6.1	Estimated Litres of Water Required to Produce One Kilogram of Food	
Crop	Litres/Kg
Potatoes	500
Wheat	900
Corn	1,400
Rice	1,912
Chicken	3,500
Beef	100,000

Data from D. Pimentel et al., *Bioscience*, 47, no. 2 (February 1997): p. 98.

impacts, social and cultural impacts, global impacts, and resource sustainability. In its most recent report (2007), the division suggests steps to address climate change, increase resource efficiency, reduce harmful substances and hazardous wastes, and mobilize the private sector.

The industrialized core has access to a vast array of transportation and communication technologies that stimulate demand for particular goods from around the world. Understanding the complex ties between technology and environmental change requires that we consider several different facets of the technology picture, including organizational, technological, and sociocultural aspects.

TRANSPORTATION

Different modes of transportation represent some of the most important technological advances in human history. Each innovation makes greater demands on resources, which are needed not only to make the vehicles that move people and goods, but also to build and maintain the related infrastructure—roads, railroad tracks, airports, parking structures, and facilities. With each innovation, there is a larger impact on the environment, not least because humans achieve access to more remote areas of the planet. Technology now allows people to travel through extreme climates, to the bottom of the ocean, and across the polar ice caps. These places, in turn, have been altered by human activity.

Transportation is also implicated in global environmental change—albeit sometimes indirectly. Advances in transportation have produced significant pollution, as seen, for example, in the extent of oil spills along major shipping lanes (Figure 6.12). Transportation facilitates the types of global networks necessary to sustain the patterns of consumption, as many of the products available in stores come from distant places. Resources are required to produce and ship these products, and, except for those that meet basic subsistence needs, they all contribute to the strains placed on the environment by those living, for the most part, in wealthier regions of the world. This realization has led some individuals to reduce their levels of consumption or to consume more environmentally friendly, locally produced products. In 2005, two Canadians, Alisa Smith and J.B. MacKinnon, began the 100-Mile Diet, pledging to eat only foods grown within a 100-mile radius of their residence for one year. Their local food activism, described in a series of magazine articles, a how-to book, and a Food Network challenge, inspired thousands of individuals. The 100-Mile Diet, which is tied in to a growing "locavore" movement that espouses the environmental, ecological, and health benefits of eating locally, provides a good example of the vital relationship between transportation and environmental change. While the locavore movement has had some effect, so far its impact on the geography of global consumption has been marginal.

Not everyone is convinced that the local food movement is the right way to go environmentally. University of Toronto geography professor Pierre Desrochers disagrees with the claim that transportation of products from around the globe is the problem. He argues that transportation accounts for only 10 percent of the energy needed to produce food and that large industrial farms are still the best and most efficient way to produce food. Nevertheless,

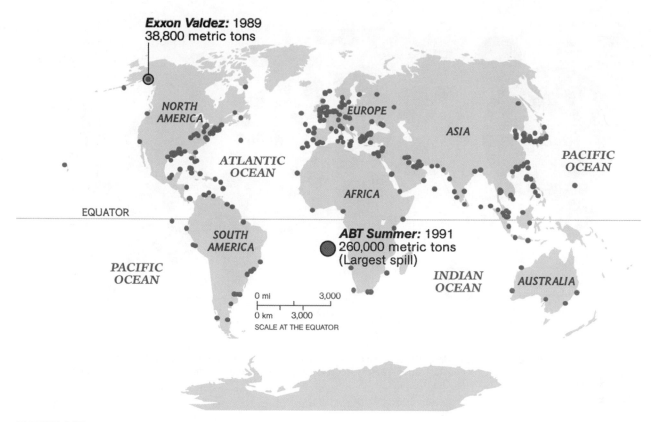

Exxon Valdez: 1989
38,800 metric tons

NORTH
AMERICA

EUROPE

ASIA

ATLANTIC
OCEAN

PACIFIC
OCEAN

AFRICA

EQUATOR

SOUTH
AMERICA

ABT Summer: 1991
260,000 metric tons
(Largest spill)

PACIFIC
OCEAN

INDIAN
OCEAN

AUSTRALIA

0 mi   3,000

0 km   3,000
SCALE AT THE EQUATOR

FIGURE 6.12 Oil Spills from 1989 to 2007. Between 1989 and 2007 there were a reported 439 oil spills of 10 or more metric tonnes from tankers and barges. (National Geographic Maps; data from International Tanker Owners Pollution Federation, Exxon Valdez Oil Spill Trustee Council)

this perspective does not address concerns about pesticide use, mono-cropping, the ethical treatment of animals, and the damage caused by thousands of kilometres of infrastructure (roads, rail, and sea or air corridors) needed to transport goods.

ENERGY

Consumption of material goods is closely linked to the consumption of energy. It takes energy to produce material goods, energy to deliver them to markets, and, for many products (such as appliances and automobiles), energy to keep them running. The resulting demand for energy is a factor in environmental change. Resources that are replenished even as they are being used are **renewable resources**; resources that are present in finite quantities are **non-renewable resources**. Much of

> **Renewable resources**
> Resources that can regenerate as they are exploited.
>
> **Non-renewable resources**
> Resources that cannot regenerate as they are exploited.

our energy supply comes from non-renewable fossil fuels, such as coal, oil, and natural gas. As populations grow, so does their demand for energy, and we can expect that energy production will increase over the coming decades to meet the growing demand. In developing countries in particular, the need for more energy leads to the development of new sources of fossil fuel. This may help explain why, according to the United States Energy Information Administration, global oil production increased from 45.89

million barrels per day in 1970 to 73.27 million barrels per day in 2007. Canada ranks seventh in the world in oil production, at 3.35 million barrels per day in 2008. In terms of global oil consumption in 2008, the United States ranked first, with 21.5 percent share of the world's total oil consumption, followed by China with 10.4 percent and Japan with 5.1 percent. Canada used 2.5 percent (Figure 6.13).

Oil is a finite resource. That means there is no question that the world's oil supply will run out someday. The question is *when* it will run out. Because geologists continue to discover new reserves, and because the extraction of fossil fuels is becoming ever more efficient, it is difficult to predict exactly how much longer oil will remain a viable energy source. Many scientists suggest that the current level of oil consumption can be sustained for up to 100 years, although some argue for much shorter or much longer time frames. Despite the range of opinion, the majority of scientists believe that we will have to be developing alternative energy sources by the middle of this century. When we consider that oil could become an increasingly scarce commodity, the importance of finding alternative energy sources is apparent. Adding further urgency are the pollution problems associated with the burning of fossil fuels and the geopolitical tensions that arise from global dependence on a resource concentrated in one part of the world. Moreover, the risk of environmental damage from oil drilling and shipping highlights the need for alternate energy sources that would have less of an environmental impact. The oil spill caused when the

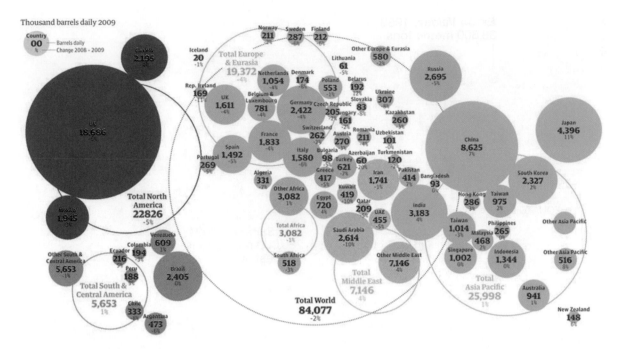

FIGURE 6.13 World Oil Consumption, 2009. Each circle on the map indicates how many thousands of barrels of oil each country used per day in 2009. (Illustration by Mark McCormick for *The Guardian*. Copyright Guardian News & Media Ltd 2010.)

Exxon Valdez ran aground off the coast of Alaska in 1989, and the explosion and subsequent leaking of the BP-owned MC252 oil well in the Gulf of Mexico in 2010, graphically illustrate the environmental dangers of reliance upon oil (Figure 6.14). Moving away from a dependence on oil carries with it some clear positives, but it could lead to wrenching socio-economic adjustments as well. Nuclear power is a possible alternative non-renewable energy source, but the long-term radioactivity associated with this form of energy production, and the potential for accidents, have limited the expansion of nuclear energy.

The effects of a shift away from oil will certainly be felt to some degree in the industrial and post-industrial countries, where considerable retooling of the economic infrastructure will be necessary. Oil-producing countries will face the greatest adjustments, however. More than half of the world's oil supply is found in the Middle Eastern countries of Saudi Arabia, Iraq, Kuwait, the United Arab Emirates (UAE), and Iran. In each of these countries, the extraction and export of oil accounts for at least 75 percent of total revenue and 90 percent of export-generated income.

ALTERATION OF ECOSYSTEMS

Human alteration of the environment continues in many forms today. For the first time in history, however, the combined impact of humanity's destructive and exploitative actions is capable of producing environmental changes on a global scale. While we have always had an impact on our environment, over the last 500 years both the rate and scale at which humans modify the Earth have increased dramatically. During the last half century, humans transformed every place on Earth, either

FIGURE 6.14 BP's Transocean Deepwater Horizon Rig Burns in the Gulf of Mexico, April 20, 2010. The explosion of the Transocean Deepwater Horizon rig resulted in the deaths of 11 people and the largest oil spill in U.S. history. Scientists are still assessing the environmental impact of the disaster. (Gerald Herbert/AP/The Canadian Press)

directly or indirectly. Our patterns of consumption, technological and transportation advances, and energy consumption have generated environmental stress on our water supply, social and atmospheric quality, and biodiversity.

The natural environment is modified by human activity in many obvious and some less obvious ways. Among the more obvious actions causing **environmental stress** (obvious because they take place around human habitats) are clear-cutting forests and emitting pollutants into the atmosphere. Less obvious actions include burying toxic wastes that foul groundwater supplies, dumping vast amounts of garbage into the oceans, and using pesticides in farming. All these activities have an impact on the environment and raise a number of concerns about the future of water supplies, the state of the atmosphere, and our impact on the terrain.

> **Environmental stress** The threat to environmental security by human activity such as atmospheric and groundwater pollution, deforestation, oil spills, and ocean dumping.

WATER

Water, the essence of life, is a renewable resource. But the available supply of fresh water is not distributed evenly across the globe. The world distribution of precipitation reveals the largest totals recorded in equatorial and tropical areas of Southeast Asia, South Asia, central and coastal West Africa, and Central and South America. That distribution is sustained through the hydrologic cycle, which brings rain and snow from the oceans to the landmasses (Figure 6.15). The volume of precipitation in the world as a whole is enormous; spread out evenly, it would cover the land area of the planet with about 83 centimetres of water each year. Much of that water is lost through runoff and evaporation, but enough of it seeps downward into porous, water-holding rocks called **aquifers** to provide millions of wells with steady flows.

> **Aquifers** Subterranean, porous, water-holding rocks that provide millions of wells with steady flows of water.

Despite such favourable data, the supply of water is anything but plentiful, and access to fresh water has become a global concern. Chronic water shortages afflict tens of millions of farmers in Africa and hundreds of thousands of city dwellers in southern California. Water rationing has been imposed in rainy south Florida and in Spain, which borders the Mediterranean Sea. In Canada, a severe drought in the 1930s had devastating effects on the Prairies for nearly a decade, turning once fertile land into a "dust bowl." At the same time as the Great Depression, when poverty and unemployment ravaged much of the world, precipitation on the Canadian prairies

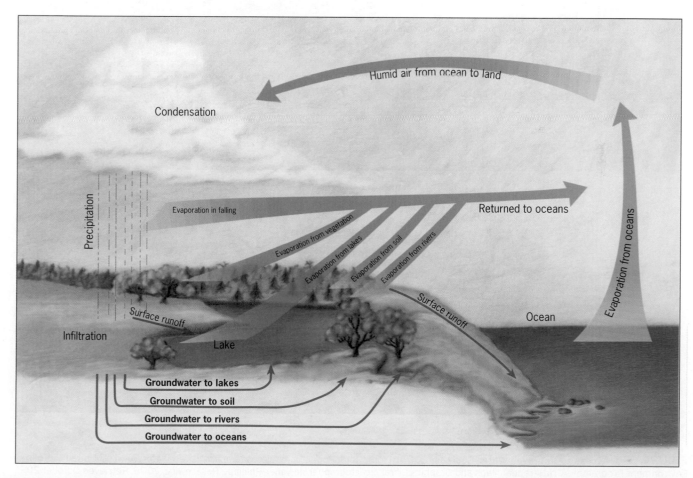

FIGURE 6.15 The Hydrologic Cycle. The hydrologic cycle carries moisture from the oceans and from other water bodies over the land, where precipitation, runoff, and evapotranspiration sustain the system. (© E. H. Fouberg, A. B. Murphy, H. J. de Blij, and John Wiley & Sons, Inc.)

averaged 40 percent below normal amounts, leading to massive crop failures, grasshopper swarms, dust storms, and the wholesale destruction of livestock herds due to starvation.

H.E. Miguel D'Escorto Brockmann, president of the United Nations General Assembly, has declared access to fresh water a basic human right, and efforts are underway to revise the UN Declaration of Human Rights to reflect this change. Using "rights" language to claim humans have a "right" to water requires us to think about how we conceptualize nature. As we discussed in the introduction to this chapter, humans often understand themselves as separate from nature and therefore see themselves having dominion over it. From a Marxist perspective, nature is often "produced" or commodified within a capitalist system. For example, when companies such as Nestlé's bottles water for sale, they are privatizing nature for profit. Canadian Maude Barlow, founder of the Blue Planet Project, works with international activist organizations to protect water from becoming a traded

commodity and from the threat of privatization. Blue Planet Project's research shows that over 1 billion people worldwide do not have access to clean water, and 1 million children die each year from diseases attributed to lack of fresh water. These statistics are supported by the World Health Organization and UNICEF (Figure 6.16). As she fights the increasing commodification of water, occurring through the privatization of water utilities and the bottled water industry, Barlow argues that water should be considered a "commons," a shared natural resource.

As human populations have expanded, people have increasingly settled in arid regions. One of the great ecological disasters of the 20th century occurred in Kazakhstan and Uzbekistan, whose common boundary runs through the Aral Sea. Streams that fed this large body of water were diverted to irrigate the surrounding desert (mainly for commercial cotton production). Heavy use of chemical pesticides ruined the groundwater, causing a health crisis that some observers describe as an "ecological Chernobyl,"

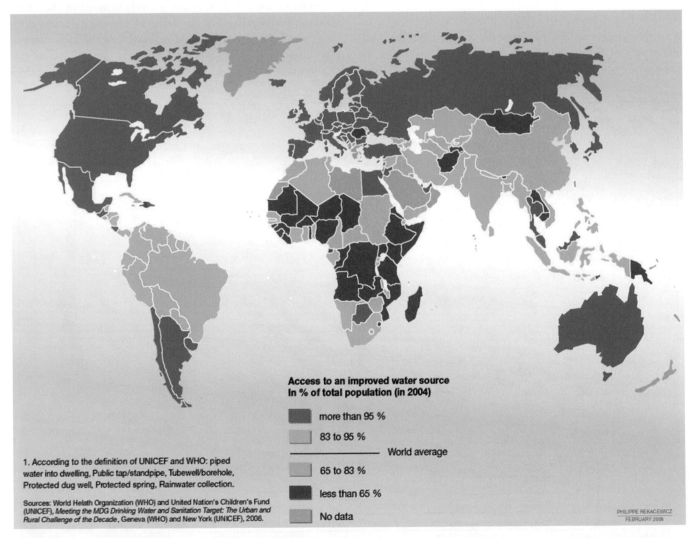

FIGURE 6.16 Access to Improved Water Sources, 2004. From "Total Population: Access to an Improved Water Source." United Nations Environment Programme/Grid-Arendal Maps and Graphics Library, cartographer/designer Phillippe Rekacewicz, 2006. Retrieved October 20, 2011 from http://maps.grida.no/go/graphic/total-population-access-to-an-improved-water-source.

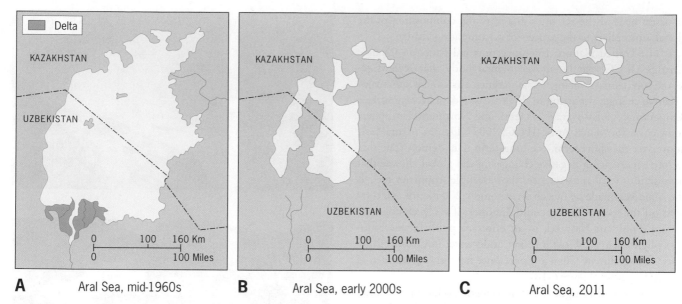

A   Aral Sea, mid-1960s   **B**   Aral Sea, early 2000s   **C**   Aral Sea, 2011

FIGURE 6.17 The Dying Aral Sea. Affected by climatic cycles and afflicted by human interference, the Aral Sea, on the border of Kazakhstan and Uzbekistan, is dying. In over a quarter of a century, it lost three-quarters of its surface area. (© E. H. Fouberg, A. B. Murphy, H. J. De Blij, and John Wiley & Sons, Inc.)

a reference to the 1986 nuclear reactor meltdown in the Ukraine. Then the Aral Sea began to dry up. In 1960, the Aral Sea was the world's fourth-largest lake (Figure 6.17a). However, by 2011 it was one-tenth of its original size (Figure 6.17b). Philip Micklin and Nikolay Aladin, in a 2008 *Scientific American* article, describe a process of what they call "reckless starvation," which siphoned off the Aral's water supply for crop irrigation. The environmental and economic ramifications are vast: fish species declined from 32 varieties to 6, and 60,000 commercial fishermen lost their jobs when the fisheries closed. Inland waterways have shut down, and toxins, both airborne and ground-based, have become a serious problem for humans and nature alike. The average lifespan for a local resident has dropped from 65 to 61 years of age.

THE ATMOSPHERE

> **Atmosphere** Blanket of gases surrounding the Earth and located some 600 kilometres above the Earth's surface.

The Earth's **atmosphere** is a thin layer of air lying directly above the lands and oceans. We depend on the atmosphere for our survival: we breathe its oxygen; it shields us from the destructive rays of the sun; it moderates temperatures; and it carries moisture from the oceans over the land, sustaining crops and forests and replenishing soils and wells. The atmosphere has a truly amazing capacity to cleanse itself. In 1883, the Indonesian volcano Krakatau erupted catastrophically, throwing 10 cubic kilometres of rock and ash into the atmosphere. Total darkness prevailed in the area for nearly three days; dust from the explosion encircled the Earth and created vividly coloured sunsets for years afterward. However, the atmosphere eventually cleared and all traces of the eruption disappeared. In 1980, the eruption of Mount St. Helens in the northwestern United States caused a similar, though much

smaller, globe-encircling cloud of volcanic dust in the upper atmosphere. Again, the atmosphere soon cleansed itself.

Human pollution of the atmosphere will likely result in longer-lasting and possibly permanent damage. While the atmosphere can disperse even the densest smoke and most acrid chemical gases, some waste may be producing irreversible change. The nature of the change is still being debated, but two centuries of industrial expansion have caused an enormous increase in global atmospheric pollution, and the rapid industrialization of countries like China, India, and Brazil is compounding the problem. Although global concern and action to limit atmospheric pollution are much in evidence, the problem remains.

Climate Change. Climate change and its effects are an increasing concern around the globe. The United Nations Framework Convention on Climate Change is an international treaty developed during the UN's Conference on Environment and Development in Rio de Janeiro in June 1992. That document defined climate change as:

> *a change of climate which is attributed directly or indirectly to human activity that alters the composition of the global atmosphere and which is in addition to natural climate variability observed over comparable time periods.*
> (1994 Article 1).

This definition acknowledges that climate change may occur naturally but that the changes we are interested in are those attributable to human activity. More recent definitions take a more scientific perspective, suggesting that climate change is "a statistically significant variation in either the mean state of the climate or in its variability, persisting for an extended period (typically decades or longer)" (Houghton, 2001). This shifts the focus from an assessment of the activities that alter the composition of the global atmosphere to the process of documenting change.

The United Nations Intergovernmental Panel on Climate Change (IPCC), an intergovernmental body that reviews research on climate change data, argues that there are major negative changes occurring in three areas: global average surface temperature, global average sea level, and Northern Hemisphere snow cover for March-April (IPCC, 2007). Despite natural variation over the short term, the long-term data demonstrate that we are experiencing negative changes in the global climate that have serious local consequences. For example, countries such as the Maldives, made up of a chain of some 1,200 islands and coral reefs off the coast of India, could disappear if sea levels continue to rise. President Nasheed, in an effort to publicize his country's plight, held a cabinet meeting underwater in October 2009 prior to the Climate Change Conference held in Copenhagen in December 2009 (Figure 6.18).

Most scientists argue that tropospheric pollution (pollution in the lowest layer of the atmosphere), particularly the release of "greenhouse" gases, causes the Earth to retain more heat (hence the term "greenhouse"). Greenhouse gases include methane, ozone, nitrous oxide, and carbon dioxide. The full effect of this heating will not be felt until well into the 21st century. Estimates of **global warming** differ: in the early 2000s, computer models still predicted a warming of 2.7°C to 3.7°C over the next 50 years. This might be enough to melt some glacial ice and raise sea levels as much as 15 centimetres. Indeed, this is already happening, as evidenced by the disappearance of two uninhabited islands in the Pacific atoll state of Kiribati. Changes in climate involve changes in the hydrologic cycle, which affect patterns of precipitation. These changes can, in turn, affect where certain types of vegetation grow, which can alter

> **Global warming** Theory that the Earth is gradually warming as a result of an enhanced greenhouse effect in the Earth's atmosphere caused by ever-increasing amounts of carbon dioxide produced by various human activities.

(a)

(b)

FIGURE 6.19 Grinnell Glacier, Glacier National Park, Montana. Grinnell Glacier retreated substantially between (a) 1940 and (b) 2006. (U.S. Geological Survey Department of the Interior/USGS: (a) Unknown photographer, courtesy of GNP Archives; (b) photo by Karen Holzer)

everything from agricultural patterns to the location of animal habitats. One of the most obvious impacts of climate change is the melting of glaciers and ice packs (Figure 6.19).

Although there is some debate about how much the Earth will warm, there is no question that growing populations and increased human activity, ranging from the burning of tropical forests to pollution of the atmosphere by industry and automobiles, are having an unprecedented impact on the atmosphere. The amounts of key "greenhouse" gases in the atmosphere have been increasing at a rate of about 2 percent per decade. Automobiles, steel mills, refineries, and chemical plants account for a large part of this increase. Figure 6.20 shows that core countries are the largest producers of carbon dioxide (CO_2) emissions, with the United States, China, Russia, India, and Japan leading the way. We can also see the difference in carbon dioxide production between high-income and low-income nations.

The United Nations Environment Programme (UNEP) argues that in order to understand climate change, we need an emissions inventory that identifies and quantifies a country's sources of greenhouse gas. Questions of accuracy are a concern, although we can have some confidence about emissions calculations from energy and industrial processes (bearing in mind problems with self-reporting). However, agricultural emissions, such as methane and nitrous oxide, are difficult to calculate because they arise from biological processes that are quite variable. Feed lots—large penned areas where beef cattle

FIGURE 6.18 Underwater Cabinet Meetings. To draw attention to rising sea levels, which they fear will ultimately cover their island nation, the cabinet of the Maldives government held a meeting underwater in 2009. (Mohammed Seeneen/AP/The Canadian Press)

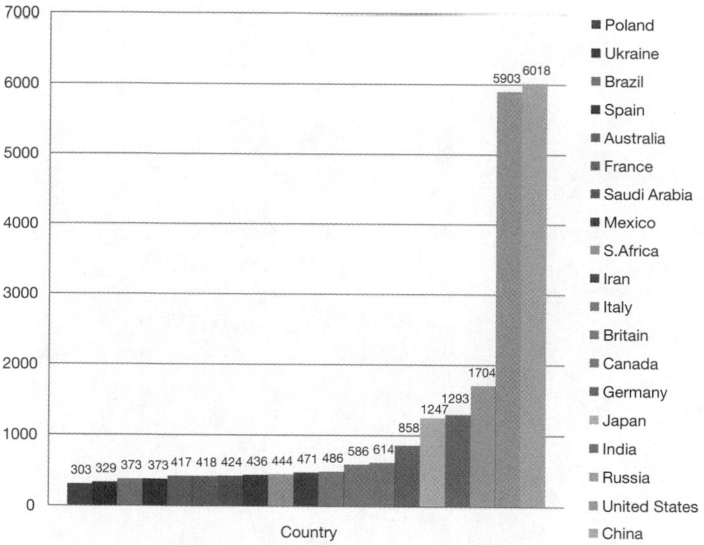
7000
6000
5000
4000
3000
2000
1000
0
303 329 373 373 417 418 424 436 444 471 486 586 614 858 1247 1293 1704 5903 6018
Country
Poland
Ukraine
Brazil
Spain
Australia
France
Saudi Arabia
Mexico
S.Africa
Iran
Italy
Britain
Canada
Germany
Japan
India
Russia
United States
China

FIGURE 6.20 Carbon Dioxide Emissions by Country (Million Metric Tonnes), 2009. In 2009, China and the United States had significantly more carbon dioxide emissions, in million metric tonnes, than the next highest emitters. Data from Ecosystem Marketplace.

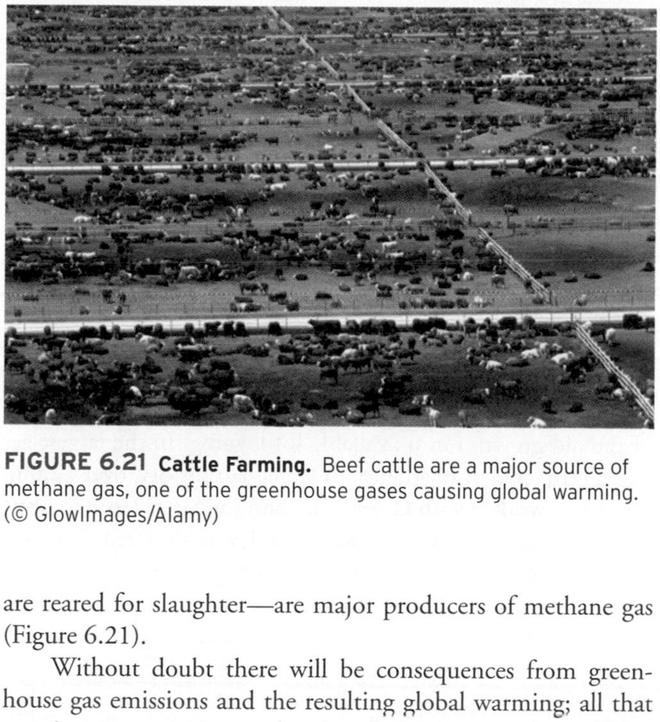

FIGURE 6.21 Cattle Farming. Beef cattle are a major source of methane gas, one of the greenhouse gases causing global warming. (© GlowImages/Alamy)

are reared for slaughter—are major producers of methane gas (Figure 6.21).

Without doubt there will be consequences from greenhouse gas emissions and the resulting global warming; all that remains uncertain is exactly what those consequences will be. In the face of these concerns, international action around climate change is gaining momentum.

Acid rain A growing environmental peril whereby acidified rainwater severely damages plant and animal life; caused by the oxides of sulphur and nitrogen that are released into the atmosphere when coal, oil, and natural gas are burned, especially in major manufacturing zones.

Acid Rain.

A by-product of the enormous volume of pollutants spewed into the atmosphere is **acid rain**. Acid rain forms when sulphur dioxide and nitrogen oxides are released into the atmosphere by the burning of fossil fuels. These pollutants combine with water vapour in the air to form dilute solutions of sulphuric and nitric acids, which are washed out of the atmosphere by rain or other types of precipitation, such as fog and snow. Although acid rain usually consists of relatively mild acids, they can be caustic enough to harm certain natural ecosystems. Acid rain is causing acidification of lakes and streams (which, in turn, kills fish that are unable to adapt to the change in acidity of the water), stunted growth of forests, and loss of crops in affected areas.

In cities, acid rain accelerates the corrosion of buildings and monuments. Sudbury, Ontario, has become a case study for the effects of acid rain. Sudbury boasts large deposits of ore, most prominently nickel and copper. The smelting process, which turns the ore into metal, releases high levels of sulphur into the atmosphere, which combines with water vapour to make acid rain. As a result, Sudbury became infamous for its destroyed vegetation and wildlife, and more than 7,000 lakes in the area were deemed contaminated due to acid rain. However, scientific and activist engagement, demanding that emissions be cleaned up and controlled, played a key role in the revitalization of the Sudbury region. Since 1980, emissions from smelters have been drastically reduced. Two of the main smelting companies, Inco and Falconbridge, reduced their emissions 75 percent and 56 percent respectively between 1980 and 1997. The ecosystem is slowly responding to the environmental changes, and the area's flora and fauna are showing signs of recovery. In addition to smelters, emissions from cars, trucks, airplanes, and ships also contribute to the production of acid rain (see Chapter 12).

The geography of acid rain is most closely associated with patterns of industrial concentration and middle- to long-distance wind flows. The highest emissions from coal and oil burning are associated with large concentrations of heavy manufacturing, such as are found in western and eastern Europe, the United States, and eastern China. As these industrial areas began to experience increasingly severe air pollution in the second half of the 20th century, many countries (including the United States in 1970) enacted legislation establishing minimal clean-air standards. The United States and western Europe saw positive results as industry complied with legislated emission reductions. In Canada, acid rain from U.S. industrial regions near the border damaged forests and acidified lakes, although some recovery came faster than scientists had predicted. This evidence encourages other countries to impose stricter controls on factory emissions.

THE LAND

Over the centuries, human population growth has increased pressure on the land surface. More land is cleared and placed under cultivation, rivers are dammed, and cities expand. The effects are seen almost everywhere and are so extensive that it is often difficult to picture what an area might be like in the absence of humans. Yet when we try to imagine a world without human intervention, the results can be startling (Figure 6.22). Human impact on the Earth's land surface has several key aspects; the most significant are deforestation, soil erosion, waste disposal, and loss of biodiversity.

FIGURE 6.22 The Mannahatta Project. The Mannahatta Project at the Wildlife Conservation Society provides a fascinating exploration of what Manhattan Island would have looked like, circa 1609. The project traces 55 different ecological communities, including a deciduous forest, bears, wolves, fish, and birds. (left, Stephen Amiaga (www.amiaga.com); right, Markley Boyer/The Mannahatta Project/Wildlife Conservation Society)

Deforestation.   From the tropical Amazon Basin to high-latitude North America and Eurasia, humans have cut down forests and whittled away woodlands. The world's forests, especially those of lower and middle latitudes, play a critical role in the **oxygen cycle**. In that cycle, atmospheric oxygen is consumed by natural processes as well as by human activities. Forests counteract this loss through photosynthesis and related processes, which release oxygen into the atmosphere. The destruction of vast tracts of forest—known as **deforestation**—alarms ecologists and others, who warn of unforeseeable and incalculable effects for the affected areas but also for the planet as a whole. As the *Guest Field Note* by Valerie Thomas indicates, geographers are also engaged in research focusing on deforestation and climate change, particularly as it applies to Canadian forests.

> **Oxygen cycle** Cycle whereby natural processes and human activity consume atmospheric oxygen and produce carbon dioxide and the Earth's forests and other flora, through photosynthesis, consume carbon dioxide and produce oxygen.
>
> **Deforestation** The clearing and destruction of forests to harvest wood for consumption, clear land for agricultural uses, and make way for expanding settlement frontiers.

In the early 1980s, the Food and Agriculture Organization (FAO) of the United Nations undertook a study of the rate at which forests were being depleted. This analysis showed that 44 percent of the tropical rainforest had already been affected by cutting and that more than 1 percent was being logged every year. In 1990, the FAO predicted that if this rate of cutting were to continue, the entire equatorial rainforest would be gone in less than 90 years. In 2005, the FAO released a comprehensive 10-year study of the world's forests. It found that the annual net loss of forests globally was 7.3 million hectares per year between 2000 and 2005—a rate that was lower than the 8.9 million hectares per year lost between 1990 and 2000.

While there has been much international focus on clear-cutting of rainforests in Central and South America, Canada has experienced its share of conflict over clear-cutting rights and practices. In 1993, the B.C. government revisited a previous decision on logging in Clayoquot Sound and deemed two-thirds of the old-growth forest available for logging. In the largest act of peaceful civil disobedience in Canadian history, over 12,000 protestors worked with Greenpeace and the Sierra Club to resist clear-cutting plans. Clayoquot Sound was declared a World Biosphere Reserve by UNESCO in 2000.

GUEST FIELD NOTE   Studying the Changes to Canada's Boreal Forests

My work involves the use of remote sensing to study the boreal forest. I was led to this research through my concerns about deforestation and climate change. The boreal forest, which spans the circumpolar region and covers about half of Canada's landmass, contains more carbon stored in vegetation and soil than any other forest ecosystem, including the tropics (Figure 6.23). This makes it a significant contributor to the global carbon cycle and to global climate. Unfortunately, the vast size and complexity of the boreal forest makes it difficult to study and monitor. My goal is to help improve our ability to predict the impacts of human activities on boreal ecosystem health and function. Remote sensing has facilitated this objective because it allows me to obtain repeated measurements over Canada's boreal landscape, which aids me in characterizing changes over time.

I use two cutting-edge remote sensing technologies for my research. The first, light detection and ranging (lidar), uses laser pulses to penetrate the forest canopy from above.

FIGURE 6.23 Writing Field Notes in a Mixed Wood Forest, Northern Ontario. (Valerie Thomas)

(a)

(b)

FIGURE 6.24 Light Detection and Ranging (LIDAR). (a) Lidar data showing the ground surface (light brown) and vegetation (green). (b) Lidar side profile of a forest canopy. The mature, natural canopy (left) is approximately twice as tall as the young plantation canopy (right). The gap in the middle is a road. (Valerie Thomas)

This gives us very detailed information about the ground surface below the canopy (Figure 6.24a). Using geographic information systems (GIS), we can develop high-resolution digital elevation models that show small stream features, hills, valleys, objects on the surface, and other useful information about the terrain.

Lidar data also give us information about the size, shape, and spatial arrangement of trees (Figure 6.24b). This enables us to quantify and map variables related to forest structure, including tree height, basal area, stem density, biomass, crown closure, and crown shape. Among other things, we use forest structural information for forest inventories and to obtain estimates of the amount of carbon stored in the vegetation.

The second technology I use in my research is hyperspectral remote sensing. These data are a series of images that show how much sunlight is reflected off the top of the forest canopy at different wavelengths (Figure 6.25). We know from previous research that leaves contain different amounts of pigments, chlorophyll, and nutrients under changing environmental conditions. We refer to this as a leaf's biochemistry. Subtle differences in leaf biochemistry will affect the way sunlight reflects off the canopy at different wavelengths and hyperspectral sensors are capable of detecting these variations. Differences in leaf biochemistry, especially chlorophyll and nitrogen, are closely related to vegetation health, and can control a leaf's ability to photosynthesize (or, in other words, a leaf's ability to extract carbon from the atmosphere). This is all part of a tree's function, or physiology.

By combining the structural information (i.e., heights of trees) derived from lidar data with the physiological information (i.e., amount of stored carbon) derived from hyperspectral data, we can construct a more complete model of forest ecosystem structure and function than is possible with either technology alone. This will help us to develop better models of the forest carbon cycle at local, regional, and national scales. Ultimately, the long-term research goal is to use these technologies to monitor global carbon exchange and integrate them into climate models so that we can generate more accurate predictions of future climate conditions.

Valerie Thomas, Department of Forest Resources and Environmental Conservation, Virginia Polytechnic Institute and State University

FIGURE 6.25 Hyperspectral Remote Sensing. Hyperspectral image of a boreal mixed wood forest in northern Ontario, Canada. This is a false colour image, where red/pink indicates healthy closed canopies of trembling aspen, and blue indicates open canopies with low chlorophyll (black spruce). The depth indicates reflectance from blue to near infrared wavelengths along the edge of the image. (Valerie Thomas)

Soil Erosion.   The loss of potentially productive soil to erosion is described as a "quiet crisis" of global proportions. Ecologists Lester Brown and Edward Wolf point out that the increasing rate of soil loss over the past generation is not the result of a decline in the skills of farmers but rather of the pressures on farmers to produce more—an explanation grounded in the political ecology approach. In an integrated world food economy, the pressures on land resources are not confined to particular countries; they permeate the entire world.

Why has **soil erosion** increased so much? Part of the answer lies in population pressure: world population is moving toward 7 billion. Associated with population growth is the cultivation of ever-steeper slopes, with hastily constructed terraces or without any terraces at all (Figure 6.26). As the pressure on land increases, farmers are less able to leave part of their soil fallow (unused) so it can recover its nutrients. Shifting cultivators (see Chapter 9) must shorten their field rotation cycle, which means their soil is less able to recover. Altogether, 99.7 percent of all human food is grown in soil (the rest is grown in water), and annual soil erosion shrinks the cropland available for agriculture. Globally, about 10 million hectares of cropland are lost to soil erosion each year.

> **Soil erosion** The wearing away of the land surface by wind and moving water.

Soil erosion is caused by a variety of factors: livestock grazing in areas where they destroy the natural vegetation; farmers ploughing lands too dry to sustain farming, followed by wind erosion follows. Soil is a renewable resource because with proper care it can recover. International cooperation in food distribution, education of farmers and governments, and worldwide dissemination of soil conservation methods are three interrelated solutions that are urgently needed to solve this "quiet crisis."

FIGURE 6.26 Guangxi-Zhuang, China. Overuse of land in this area of China was leading to the collapse of formerly sound terracing systems. (© H. J. de Blij)

Waste Disposal.   If anything has grown faster than population itself, it is the waste generated by households, communities, and industries—much of it a matter of bulk, some of it a source of danger. The United States, the world's largest consumer of resources, is also the largest producer of **solid waste**, debris, and garbage discarded by urban populations, industries, mines, and farms. According to current estimates, the United States produces about 1.7 kilograms of solid waste per person per day, which adds up to well over 160 million metric tonnes per year. But the United States is not alone. Other high-technology economies with a high ratio of disposable materials (containers, packaging) face the same problems. Canada, for instance, produces 30 million tonnes of solid waste per year, or 1.2 kilograms per person per day.

> **Solid waste** Non-liquid, non-soluble materials ranging from municipal garbage to sewage sludge; agricultural refuse; and mining residues.

When old electronic goods, such as computers, become obsolete, they become "e-waste." Disposal of this e-waste is becoming a global concern. The United Nations Environment Programme estimates that there will be 40 million tonnes of global e-waste per year in 2010. This e-waste is often hazardous: chemicals from discarded electronics leach into the ground or enter the atmosphere. Disposal of this waste has become a global issue, as recycling programs, filled to capacity domestically, turn to international dump sites. Ghana, Nigeria, Pakistan, India, and China are among the nations that have become hazardous e-waste sites for North American and European recycling. These countries, which often have lax worker and environmental protection laws, process tens of thousands of tonnes of e-waste each year, recovering valuable constituent materials of electronic items, including copper, iron, gold and silicon. At the same time, it is significantly cheaper for North American and European countries to ship recycling offshore than to manage it domestically.

Disposal of waste more generally is a major worldwide problem. For example, in Hagersville, Ontario, a huge pile of discarded tires burned for 17 days in 1990. There were an estimated 12 to 14 million tires in the pile, and over 4,000 homes had to be evacuated as such fires produce a huge amount of toxic smoke. The aftermath of the fire was devastating for nature and humans alike, as toxic chemicals leached into the air and groundwater. Millions of dollars were spent on the environmental clean-up. Years later, firefighters reported developing rare, aggressive forms of cancer that the Workers' Safety Insurance Board attributed to the fire. Demands for tougher regulations permeated public discourse, but it was not until September 1, 2009, that Ontario enacted the Used Tires Stewardship Program.

Finding locations for waste disposal is no longer easy. In poorer countries, waste is thrown onto open dumps, where vermin multiply, decomposition sends methane gas into the air, and rain and waste liquids carry contaminants into the groundwater below. In countries that can afford it, such open dumps

Sanitary landfills Disposal sites for non-hazardous solid waste that is spread in layers and compacted to the smallest practical volume. The sites are typically designed with floors made of materials to treat seeping liquids and are covered by soil as the wastes are compacted and deposited into the landfill.

have been replaced by **sanitary landfills**, where waste is placed in a specially prepared excavation that has a floor of materials to treat seeping liquids. Operators cover each load with soil as it is compacted and deposited in the fill.

The United States, the European Union, and Japan export solid (including hazardous) wastes to countries in Africa, Central and South America, and East Asia (Figure 6.27). While these countries are paid for accepting the waste, they do not always have the capacity to treat it properly, so the waste is often dumped in open landfills, where it creates the very hazards that the exporters want to avoid. In the late 1980s, the richer countries' practice of "managing" waste by exporting it became a controversial issue, and in 1989 a treaty was drawn up to control it. The treaty did not prohibit the exporting of hazardous waste, which is what many poorer countries had desired, although it did place some restrictions on trade in hazardous materials.

It is useful to differentiate between two types of hazardous waste: **toxic wastes**, which are dangerous because they may contain chemicals, infectious materials, and the like; and **radioactive wastes**, which are of two types: low-level radioactive wastes, which give off small amounts of radiation and are produced by industry, hospitals, research facilities,

Toxic waste Hazardous waste causing danger from chemicals and infectious organisms.

Radioactive waste Hazardous-waste-emitting radiation from nuclear power plants, nuclear weapons factories, and nuclear equipment in hospitals and industry.

and nuclear power plants; and high-level radioactive wastes, which emit strong radiation and are produced by nuclear power plants and nuclear weapons factories. In the United States, low-level radioactive wastes have for many years been disposed of in steel drums placed in six special government-run landfills, three of which are now closed. High-level radioactive waste is extremely dangerous. No satisfactory means of disposal or place for storage of this waste has been found, although many ideas have been suggested, including deep shafts in the bedrock, chambers dug in salt deposits (salt effectively blocks radiation), ice chambers in Antarctica, sediments beneath the ocean floor, and volcanically active mid-ocean trenches. None of these is a completely safe solution.

BIODIVERSITY. Another significant change due to human impact is the accelerating loss of **biodiversity**. An abbreviation of "biological diversity," biodiversity refers to the diversity of all aspects of life found on the Earth. Although the term is commonly used when referring to the diversity of species, it encompasses the entire range of biological diversity, from the genetic variability within individuals of a species to the diversity of ecosystems on the planet.

Biodiversity The total variety of plant and animal species in a particular place; biological diversity.

How many species are there? Estimates range from 10 million to 100 million, although only 1.75 million species have been identified. New species, particularly new species of insects, are being discovered regularly. Yet species are also becoming extinct at a rapid rate. We can't say exactly how quickly extinctions are occurring, though, because we do not know how many species there are. Although extinction is a natural process, humans have dramatically increased rates of extinction, particularly over the last few hundred years. The United Nations Environment Programme's Global Biodiversity Assessment estimates that 8 percent of plants, 5 percent of fish, 11 percent of birds, and 18 percent of the world's mammal species are currently threatened.

Where is biodiversity most threatened? If a species with a small range, a high degree of scarcity, and a small geographic concentration has its habitat threatened, extinction can follow. Because most species have small ranges, change in a small area can be unexpectedly devastating. A 2005 report in *Scientific American* explained that "clearing a forest, draining a wetland, damming a river or dynamiting a coral reef to kill its fish can more readily eliminate species with small ranges than more widespread species."

Human impacts on biodiversity have increased over time. The domestication of animals, followed by the agricultural domestication of plant life, caused significant changes in our relationship with other species. Large vertebrates have always been particularly hard hit by human activities. Many birds and mammals have been hunted not only for food but also for their skin, feathers, and so forth. During the 18th and 19th centuries, beaver populations in North America were drastically reduced as the beavers were trapped and skinned for their pelts; many

FIGURE 6.27 Shipbreaking in Chittagong, Bangladesh. Bangladeshi workers dismantle old ships, including oil tankers, and salvage everything from the steel sides to the doorknobs and toilets. The workers have no safety protection, no labour regulations, and are paid very little. (© Allan Ivy/Alamy)

MORTALITY RISKS

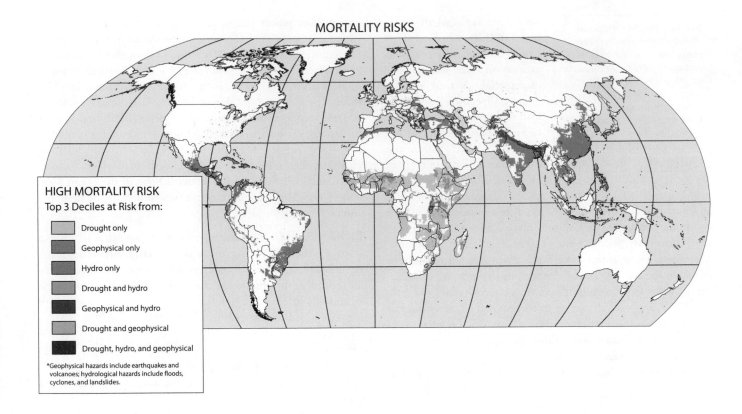

HIGH MORTALITY RISK

Top 3 Deciles at Risk from:

Drought only

Geophysical only

Hydro only

Drought and hydro

Geophysical and hydro

Drought and geophysical

Drought, hydro, and geophysical

*Geophysical hazards include earthquakes and volcanoes; hydrological hazards include floods, cyclones, and landslides.

ECONOMIC LOSS RISKS

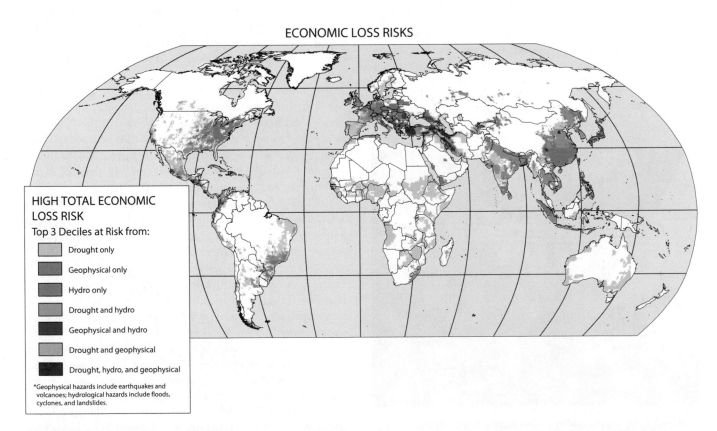

HIGH TOTAL ECONOMIC LOSS RISK

Top 3 Deciles at Risk from:

Drought only

Geophysical only

Hydro only

Drought and hydro

Geophysical and hydro

Drought and geophysical

Drought, hydro, and geophysical

*Geophysical hazards include earthquakes and volcanoes; hydrological hazards include floods, cyclones, and landslides.

FIGURE 6.28 Natural Disaster Hot Spots. The top map shows the potential mortality risks if major natural disasters occur in global natural disaster hot spots; the bottom map shows the potential economic risks if major natural disasters occur in natural disaster hot spots. From Figure 8A and Figure 8B on page 22 in: Dilley, M., Chen, R. S., Deichmann, U., Lerner-Lam, A. L., Arnold, M. Agwe, J., Buys, P., Kjekstad, O., Lyon, B., and Yetman, G. 2005. Natural Disaster Hotspots: A Global Risk Analysis, Synthesis Report. Palisades, NY: Socioeconomic Data and Applications Center (SEDAC), CIESIN, Columbia University. Available at http://sedac.ciesin.columbia.edu/hazards/hotspots/synthesisreport.pdf.

bird species were hunted for their feathers, which were sold to decorate fashionable hats. Elephants and walruses continue to be hunted for their ivory tusks. From historical records we know that over 650 species of plants and over 480 animal species have become extinct in just the last 400 years. These represent only the documented extinctions. The actual number of extinctions that occurred during this period is almost certainly much higher.

A second and more complicated step is to consider the forces driving these changes. Environmental change affects human groups differently depending, in part, on who they are and where they live. To underscore the spatial differences in environmental impact on humans, we can consider two 2005 global maps of natural disaster hot spots published by the Earth Institute at Columbia University and the World Bank. The maps highlight the places most susceptible to natural disasters, whether caused by drought, tectonic activity (earthquakes and volcanoes), or hydrological hazards (floods, cyclones, and landslides) (Figure 6.28). If we compare the map of mortality risk with the map of total economic loss risk, we see that when a natural disaster hits a wealthier area of the world, the result will more likely be financial loss, while disasters in poorer areas will cause both financial loss and loss of life. To understand the differences in mortality and financial risks shown on these maps, we need to focus on the spatial differences in human impacts on environment.

MAIN POINTS   6.2   What Impact Do Humans Have on the Environment?

- Human beings have had an impact on their environment for all of their existence. Humans have brought animals to the brink of extinction in hunter-gatherer societies, and through technologies such as irrigation and genetic engineering they have fundamentally altered both landscapes and life forms.

- Human patterns of consumption vary between the core, periphery, and semi-periphery. The type and severity of environmental impacts vary geographically. Technologies, modes of transportation, and energy use all have a serious impact on ecosystems and the resources we rely on, including water, the atmosphere, and the land. Increasingly, we are seeing tensions between nation-states as they compete for access to the world's resources while at the same time balancing the need to protect shared resources such as the Great Lakes and St. Lawrence Seaway.

- Negative environmental impacts are unevenly distributed around the globe, with peripheral and semi-peripheral countries often bearing the larger human and environmental costs.

6.3 How Are Humans Responding to Environmental Change?

In this final section, we consider the global responses to the environmental problems discussed in this chapter. It is important to note, however, that local and regional initiatives are also significant, from our individual consumer choices and our responsibility to recycle to the actions of all levels of government regarding waste disposal, air pollution, and energy consumption. A major challenge in addressing environmental problems is that they do not occur within a single jurisdiction. Designing policy responses is complicated by the fact that the political map does not reflect the geography of environmental issues. The problem is particularly acute when environmental problems cross international boundaries, for there are few international policy-making bodies with significant authority over multinational environmental spaces. Moreover, those that do exist—the European Union, for example—often have limited authority and must heed the concerns of member states. Those concerns, in turn, may not coincide with the interests of the environment. Within democracies, politicians with an eye to the next election may hesitate to tackle long-term problems that require short-term sacrifices. Most authoritarian regimes have an even worse record, as was seen in the policies of the Soviet-dominated governments of Eastern Europe during the communist era. More recently, in October 2010, chemical waste from an alumina plant in Hungary broke through the retaining wall of a reservoir, flooding into the streets and houses of neighbouring towns and villages (Figure 6.29).

The United Nations Framework Convention on Climate Change currently guides international governmental activity on environmental issues and continues to play a crucial role in international efforts to curb climate change. This treaty was drafted at the United Nations Conference on Environment and Development (UNCED), held in Rio de Janeiro in June 1992. Delegates to UNCED gave the Global Environment Facility (GEF)—a joint project of the United Nations and the World Bank—significant authority over environmental action on a global scale. The GEF funds projects related to six issues: loss of biodiversity, climate change, protection of international waters, depletion of the ozone layer, land degradation, and persistent organic pollutants. Delegates to UNCED believed that significant progress could be made through these funded projects, along with bilateral (that is, government-to-government) aid.

(a)

(b)

FIGURE 6.29 Hungary Toxic Sludge Flood. Over one million cubic metres of poisonous chemical sludge from an alumina factory near Ajka, Hungary, flooded three villages, killing nine people and injuring over a hundred. (a) An aerial view of the broken dike of the reservoir containing the red chemical waste, October 5, 2010. A village in the path of the toxic sludge is visible in the background. (b) Residents attempt to clean up in the aftermath of the toxic sludge flood. (AP Photo/MTI, Gyoergy Varga; © Tamas Kovacs/epa/Corbis)

These actions hold the promise of a more coherent approach to environmental problem solving than is possible when decisions are made on a state-by-state basis. Yet even though the GEF is charged with protecting key elements of the global environment, it still functions in a state-based world, and individual states continue to influence decisions. As Figure 6.30 illustrates, the major forested regions in sub-Saharan Africa straddle a number of nation-states. Clearly, the effectiveness of the GEF in protecting distinct regions is often limited by state boundaries and individual state interests. Nevertheless, the GEF serves an important role in providing financial resources to four major international conventions on the environment: the Convention on Biological Diversity, the UN Framework Convention on Climate Change, the UN Convention to Combat Desertification, and the Stockholm Convention on Persistent Organic Pollutants.

A few global environmental issues are so pressing that efforts have been made to create guidelines for action, which take the form of international conventions or treaties. The most prominent examples are in the areas of global climate change, biological diversity, and protection of the ozone layer.

GLOBAL CLIMATE CHANGE

Beginning in the late 1980s, growing concern about climate change led to a series of intergovernmental conferences on the nature and extent of human impacts on Earth's climate. The second of these conferences, which took place in Geneva in 1990, was sponsored by the World Meteorological Organization, the United Nations Environment Programme, and other international organizations, and brought together representatives from 137 states and the European Community. The delegates concluded that there was enough evidence of human impacts on climate to justify a treaty on climate change. The final declaration, adopted after hard bargaining, did not specify any international targets for reducing emissions. Instead, it proclaimed

climate change as a "common concern of humankind," while noting that "common but differentiated responsibilities" existed between the industrialized core and the less industrialized periphery.

In December 1990, the United Nations General Assembly approved the start of treaty negotiations. A draft convention, prepared and submitted to UNCED delegates for consideration, called on the developed countries to take measures to reduce their emissions to 1990 levels by the year 2000 and to provide technical and financial support for emission-reduction efforts in the developing countries. The convention was signed by 154 states and the European Community at UNCED in Rio de Janeiro.

For several years after UNCED, various committees met to discuss matters relating to the convention. By 1995, mounting concerns about the nature of long-term commitments under the convention led the participants in these discussions to call for a revised treaty that would cover the post-2000 period. They appointed a group to draft an agreement to be considered at a 1997 meeting in Kyoto, Japan. After 10 days of tough negotiations, delegates reached an agreement that required compromises from practically every participating country. The new agreement, known as the Kyoto Protocol, set a target period of 2008–12 by which time the United States, the European Union, and Japan were to cut their greenhouse gas emissions by 7, 8, and 6 percent, respectively, below 1990 levels (see Figure 6.20 for 2009 emissions by country). However, the new agreement did not obligate less-developed countries to adhere to specific reduction goals; instead it called for those countries to implement their own voluntary emission-reduction plans, with financial assistance from industrialized countries.

Neither the United States nor China, the world's two largest emitters of carbon dioxide, signed the Kyoto Protocol, which is slated to expire in 2012. The pressure is high for the United States (which continues to be the largest producer of carbon dioxide emissions, per person, in the world) to play a

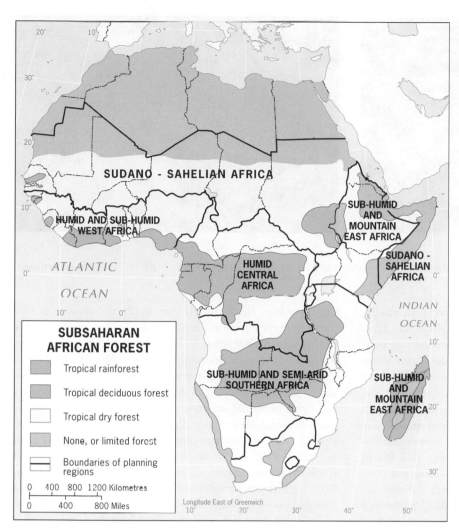

FIGURE 6.30 Major Regions and Forest Zones in Sub-Saharan Africa. Major forest regions in sub-Saharan Africa cross state boundaries, but planning regions are contained within those boundaries. Source: International Bank for Reconstruction and Development/The World Bank: N.P. Sharma, S. Rietbergen, C.R. Heimo, and J. Patel, "A Strategy for the Forest Sector in Sub-Saharan Africa," World Bank Technical Paper No. 251, Africa Technical Department Series, 1994. Adapted with permission.

role in this agreement and in future accords addressing climate change, and ongoing discussions of climate change will inevitably concentrate on China as well. In 2006, China took the lead as the world's largest total emitter of carbon dioxide, pushing the United States out of the top spot. The 2008 Beijing Olympics opened the world's eyes to the incredibly high level of emissions in China.

Canada signed the Kyoto Protocol on April 29, 1998, with formal ratification taking place on December 17, 2002. Under the Liberal government of the day, Canada pledged to reduce greenhouse gas emissions to 6 percent below 1990 levels between 2008 and 2012. The government developed a three-stage strategy of incentives, regulations, and tax measures that would reduce total greenhouse gas emissions by 240 million tonnes by 2012. However, when the Conservative government came into power in 2006, it made no mention of Kyoto and instead proposed a "made-in-Canada" solution. As a result of Canada's poor showing on environmental issues, the country received the Colossal Fossil award at the 2009 Climate Change Conference in Copenhagen, presented to the country making the least-constructive contributions to the process. Canada also received three Fossil of the Day awards at the opening of the

2010 Climate Change Conference in Cancun, Mexico. More than 400 international organizations voted for the winner of this award, which goes to the country regarded as doing the most to undermine UN climate talks. Canada won first, second, and third place for allowing the defeat of a climate change bill, for gutting clean energy programs and reducing funding for Canada's climate science foundation, and for having no plan to meet emissions targets.

One reason for Canada's sullied international reputation is the activity at the Alberta oil sands (Figure 6.31). The oil sands, located in northeastern Alberta, are the second-largest proven reserve of crude oil in the world; only Saudi Arabia has a larger reserve. The bitumen (heavy crude oil) deposits are located across 141,000 kilometres of boreal forest and peat bogs. Economically, the oil sands are crucial to Alberta's economy, providing plentiful job opportunities in the Fort McMurray area. As well, in fiscal year 2009–10 the Alberta government collected over $3 billion in royalties. In 2009, companies working in the oil sands produced approximately 170 billion barrels of oil; 1.4 million barrels per day were exported to the United States, accounting for 15 percent of U.S. crude oil imports.

(a)   (b)

FIGURE 6.31 Alberta Oil Sands (Athabasca Tar Sands). (a) Oil residue landfill. (b) Excavation of tar sands by truck. (© Yann Arthus-Bertrand)

Despite the economic advantages, the Alberta oil sands development has been heavily criticized for the environmental impacts that result from processing practices in the region. Activist groups express concern about clear-cutting of the boreal forest, pollution in the Athabasca river, and toxins in the air and water that threaten birds, fish, and other wildlife. At the same time, according to Greenpeace Canada, human social and health concerns have become an issue: local First Nations groups have reported high incidences of rare cancers and autoimmune diseases; and the high cost of living in the area, along with lack of housing due to the massive influx of workers, have put pressures on long-time residents. After she flew over the area, activist Maude Barlow referred to the tar sands as "Mordor"—a reference to the blackened landscape of Middle-earth in *Lord of the Rings*. Canadian filmmaker James Cameron called the oil sands a "black eye" for Canada's international image.

Canada has a direct and pressing stake in the impacts of climate change, particularly in the Canadian Arctic. In September 2010, the CBC reported that because the waters of the Northwest Passage are free of ice to a greater extent and a longer period than

they have been historically (Figure 6.32), the amount of ship traffic is up considerably. The Canadian Border Services Agency reports that by September 2010, 18 ships had cleared customs in Inuvik, NWT, up from only seven in 2009. The Northwest Passage is a shortcut from northern Europe to Alaska and Asia, and as shipping increases, so do concerns for Arctic sovereignty and rights to natural resources beneath the surface of the Arctic (see Chapter 3 for a map and detailed discussion of interested parties). Moreover, climate change has increased concerns about the future of Arctic wildlife. For instance, polar bears may be at risk because they rely on the sea ice for hunting and breeding. With warmer temperatures, polar bears face shorter hunting seasons and poor den conditions, among other issues.

Despite these and other concerns about the social, environmental, political, and economic impacts of climate change, Canada continues to receive international criticism for its lack of response. In late 2010, Germanwatch and Climate Action Network Europe (CAN Europe) released their annual index rating 57 countries for their efforts to halt climate change. Canada was fourth worst.

BIOLOGICAL DIVERSITY

International concern arising from the loss of plant and animal species led to calls for a global convention (agreement) regarding biodiversity as early as 1981. By the beginning of the 1990s, a group working under the auspices of the UN Environment Programme reached agreement on the wording of the convention, and it was submitted to UNCED for approval. The Convention on Biological Diversity came into effect in late 1993; by 2001, 168 countries had signed it. The convention calls for the establishment of a system of protected areas and for a coordinated set of national and international regulations on activities that can have significant negative impacts on biodiversity. It also provides funding for developing countries that are trying to meet the terms of the convention.

The biodiversity convention is a step forward as it both affirms the vital significance of preserving biological diversity and provides a framework for cooperation to achieve that end.

FIGURE 6.32 Open Waters of the Northwest Passage. For centuries the Northwest Passage was an icebound barrier to ships attempting to travel across the top of Canada, but in recent years the waters have been increasingly free of ice, due to the warmest temperatures in four centuries. (© Ocean/Corbis)

However, the agreement has proved difficult to implement. There is an ongoing struggle to find a balance between the need of poorer countries to promote local economic development and the need to preserve biodiversity. Also, there has been controversy over how countries will share the costs of conservation programs, which has led to heated debates over ratification of the convention in some countries. Nevertheless, this convention, along with a host of voluntary efforts, has helped focus attention on biodiversity and has promoted the expansion of protected areas. Whether those areas will succeed in providing long-term species protection is an open question.

One approach to environmental protection is biodiversity conservation, which usually takes the form of national parks and World Heritage sites. Protecting areas by using these sorts of designations is seen as the best way to ensure environmental preservation and species survival. The number of such designations has increased substantially in recent years, predominantly in tropical peripheral and semi-peripheral countries. The logic is that biodiversity can only be protected by setting aside vast territories beyond the reach of human development or use. Usually the protecting party is the state, which takes ownership of, or establishes regulatory control over, land that may be used or occupied by others. This raises questions about who is responsible for environmental protection, how resources are monitored and controlled, and how environmental benefits and costs are distributed. Indigenous peoples may find their access to and use of traditional grazing and pasture lands curtailed, or certain areas may become open for tourism and recreation in ways that threaten indigenous ways of life. Regulatory schemes also tend to overlook the impact that indigenous communities had on what is portrayed as a pristine wilderness area. Clearly, a more inclusionary and participatory process that recognizes the linkages between local communities and their habitat may be better able to foster conservation and include these communities in ongoing stewardship. As we noted earlier, in the Canadian context, the federal government has designated areas as national park "reserves" until such time as Aboriginal land claims issues can be settled, a process that may prove to be more inclusionary.

PROTECTION OF THE OZONE LAYER

When found in the troposphere (the layer of atmosphere from 0 to 16 kilometres above the Earth's surface), ozone (O_3) gas is a harmful pollutant associated with the creation of smog (Figure

Ozone layer The layer in the upper atmosphere located between 30 and 45 kilometres above the Earth's surface where stratospheric ozone is most densely concentrated. The ozone layer acts as a filter for the sun's harmful ultraviolet rays.

6.33). However, a naturally occurring **ozone layer** in the upper levels of the stratosphere (at an altitude of 30 to 45 kilometres) is of vital importance as it protects the Earth from the sun's harmful ultraviolet rays. In 1985, a group of British scientists working in Antarctica discovered that the thickness of the ozone layer above the South Pole had been dramatically reduced, from 300 Dobson units (DUs) in the 1960s to almost 200 DUs by 1985. (A Dobson unit measures ozone from the Earth's surface.) Studies revealed that the main culprits in ozone depletion were a group of human-made gases collectively known as **chlorofluorocarbons** (CFCs). These gases, which had only been used in industrial applications, mainly as refrigerants, fire extinguishers, and in aerosol cans, since the 1950s, were thought to be completely harmless to humans. However, the strength of the scientific evidence pointing to their contribution to the rapid reduction of the ozone layer led to an unusually swift and united international response.

Chlorofluorocarbons (CFCs) Synthetic organic compounds first created in the 1950s and used primarily as refrigerants and as propellants. The role of CFCs in the destruction of the ozone layer led to the signing of an international agreement (the Montreal Protocol).

(a)

(b)

FIGURE 6.33 Beijing, China. In 2004, the World Bank ranked Beijing the 13th most polluted city in the world. Bobak Ha'Eri's 2005 photographs show Beijing before and during the intense smog that covered the city after two days of rain. In 2007, the World Health Organization deemed smog and air pollution in China to be the world's deadliest, killing approximately 656,000 people each year. It was not until the Beijing Olympics in 2008, however, that the pollution levels became an international issue. (Bobak Ha' Eri/Wikipedia Commons, http://commons.wikimedia.org/wiki/File:Beijing_smog_comparison_August_2005.png (CC-BY-SA-2.5))

In 1985, the **Vienna Convention for the Protection of the Ozone Layer** set out a framework for efforts to protect the ozone layer. Two years later, in September 1987, 105 countries and the European Community defined and agreed on specific targets and timetables for phasing out production and consumption of CFCs when they signed the **Montreal Protocol**. The original agreement called for a 50 percent reduction in the production and consumption of CFCs by 1999. At a meeting in London in 1990, scientific data showing that ozone depletion would continue for many years after CFCs were phased out encouraged the signatories of the Montreal Protocol to agree to halt CFC production entirely by the year 2000. Finally, at a meeting in Copenhagen in 1992, the timetable for CFC phase-out was accelerated; participants agreed to eliminate CFC production by 1996 and speed up plans to phase out other ozone-depleting chemicals, such as halons, hydrochlorofluorocarbons, carbon tetrachloride, methyl chloroform, and methyl bromide. This response is an encouraging example of international cooperation in the face of a significant, albeit clearly defined, problem. Unfortunately, CFCs last for a long time in the atmosphere, which means their effects will be felt for years to come.

> **Vienna Convention for the Protection of the Ozone Layer** The first international convention aimed at addressing the issue of ozone depletion. Held in 1985, the Vienna Convention was the predecessor to the Montreal Protocol.
>
> **Montreal Protocol** An international agreement signed in 1987 by 105 countries and the European Community (now European Union). The protocol called for a reduction in the production and consumption of chlorofluorocarbons (CFCs) of 50 percent by 2000. Subsequent meetings in London (1990) and Copenhagen (1992) accelerated the timing of CFC phaseout, and a worldwide complete ban has been in effect since 1996.

As the study of environmental change moves forward, one of the most important lessons we have learned is that global environmental systems are interconnected at numerous temporal and spatial scales. For example, release of CFCs in Japan contributed to the hole in the Earth's ozone layer centred over Antarctica. Industrial production in the Netherlands and Germany contributes to acid rain in Scandinavia. Water drawn from the Rio Grande for irrigation in northern New Mexico affects the amount and quality of water in the river as it flows along the Texas–Mexico border. Human actions, the activities we undertake individually and collectively, are increasingly important factors in all sorts of global environmental changes. To address these changes, we must consider the complex relationship between humans and the environment.

ALTERNATIVE ENERGY

Since the United Nations-sponsored Framework Convention on Climate Change (FCCC) was developed at UNCED in 1992, a number of countries have established implementation programs that encourage the development of "clean" renewable energy technologies and increased energy efficiency in buildings, transportation, and manufacturing.

The European Union (EU) has mandated that a percentage of the funds it provides for regional development be used for renewable energy projects and increased energy efficiency. In 1994 alone, the EU provided 175 million euros (U.S. $159 million) for the development of renewable energy sources in the member states, and the amount of EU money going toward renewable energy programs has increased since then. In one case, in 1997, the EU provided 43 million euros (U.S. $39.1 million) for the construction of three wind energy parks in Navarra, a state in northern Spain (Figure 6.34). The wind energy parks in Navarra and other regions of Spain generated 9,120 GWh (gigawatt hours) of electricity in 2002, creating 695 million euros in income.

These wind energy parks not only help the EU meet its obligations under the FCCC; they also help Navarra achieve a goal of self-sufficiency in energy. Navarra's wind energy parks now provide over 50 percent of the region's electric energy needs. More has changed in Navarra than its energy situation. The wind energy parks, located in the Guerinda Mountains 30 kilometres southeast of the city of Pamplona, have altered the local landscape and economy in ways that will shape the character of Navarra as a place well into the 21st century.

Renewable energy sources, such as water, sun, and wind, are viable alternatives to fossil fuels, although they are often more expensive to harness and are not without environmental impacts. Wind farms provide a viable, renewable alternative to oil and gas but face resistance from local residents who are concerned about their environmental and aesthetic impact. The adverse effect on birds and waterfowl is well documented. Canada has more than 70 wind farms, producing over 2,550 MW, and there are approximately 50 more contracted or under construction. Ontario has the largest wind energy capacity in the country, with 782 MW. Canada is also working to harness the power of the tides; in January 2008 the Nova Scotia government announced that the Fundy tidal power demonstration project would go ahead, setting up a $10 million research facility that

FIGURE 6.34 Wind Energy Parks, Navarra Spain. Spain is the fourth-largest producer of wind power in the world. Wind energy parks, such as this one in Navarra, have a capacity to produce over 16,400 megawatts of power. (Pedro Salaverría/easyFotostock/age fotostock)

FIGURE 6.35 **Three Gorges Dam, China**. The Three Gorges Dam spans the Yangtze River in the Hubei and Sichuan provinces of China. (Meng Liang/ChinaFotoPress/The Canadian Press)

would test the ability of underwater turbines to convert tidal energy into electricity.

Damming rivers for hydroelectric power alters fresh water systems and the surrounding environment. The Three Gorges Dam (TGD) in China is the largest hydroelectric project in the world, measuring over 2 kilometres long and 185 metres high, and costing upwards of U.S. $30 billion (Figure 6.35). Construction began in 1994 and should be completed by 2011. TGD serves three main purposes—flood control, power generation, and navigation—and is considered to be a great success technologically, economically, and socially. When fully operational, TGD is expected to produce 18,200 MW of power, which is the equivalent of 16 nuclear power stations. However, the project is not without controversy. It has been estimated that 1.13 million people have had to be relocated and fertile agricultural land, cultural landmarks, 13 cities, 140 towns, and 1,300 villages are now underwater. Moreover, while many people have benefited from an improved standard of living, others have struggled with integration strategies that aim to bring farmers into urban environments.

Technology is only one part of the human response to environmental change. The extent and rapidity of that change have led to numerous policies aimed at protecting the environment or reversing the negative impacts of pollution. These policies range from local ordinances that restrict urban development in environmentally sensitive areas to global accords on topics such as biodiversity and climate change. Organizations such as United Nations Environment Programme, the Intergovernmental Panel on Climate Change, and a broad array of NGOs, activist groups, and citizens' organizations are all working to affect change by developing policy, building social awareness, and encouraging culture shifts. The 2010 United Nations Conference on Climate Change, discussed earlier in this section, is just one of the ways in which governments and NGOs work together to respond to concerns about climate change.

MAIN POINTS **6.3** How Are Humans Responding to Environmental Change?

- The framework currently guiding international governmental activity on environmental issues evolved from the United Nations Conference on Environment and Development (UNCED), held in Rio de Janeiro in June 1992. UNCED produced the United Nations Framework Convention on Climate Change.

- The most prominent issues being addressed at the international policy level include global climate change, biological diversity, and protection of the ozone layer.

- A number of countries are establishing implementation programs that encourage the development of "clean" renewable energy technologies and increased energy efficiency in buildings, transportation, and manufacturing.

SUMMARY

Geographers are actively engaged in studying human-environment relations. They point out that how we understand nature influences how we understand our relationship to it. Various approaches to understanding nature, including Marxist and cultural perspectives, have informed environmental movements and government policy over the last 150 years. In the present day, environmental activism takes many forms and operates across a variety of scales from small local-food movements to global activism addressing genetically modified foods and questions of environmental justice.

What will the future be like? Many would agree with geographer Robert Kates, who foresees a "warmer, more crowded, more connected but more diverse world." As we consider this prospect, we must acknowledge that global environmental changes illustrate the limits of our knowledge of the Earth. Many of today's global environmental changes were not anticipated. Moreover, many global changes are nonlinear, and some are "chaotic" in the sense that future conditions cannot be reliably predicted. Nonlinearity means that small actions in certain situations may result in large impacts and may be more important than larger actions

in causing change. Thresholds also exist in many systems, which, once crossed, cannot be re-crossed; in other words, some changes are irreversible. This occurs, for example, when the habitat for a species is diminished to the point where the species quickly dies off. Unfortunately, we may not be able to identify these thresholds until we pass them. This leaves open the possibility of "surprises"—unanticipated responses by physical systems.

The complexity and urgency of the environmental challenge will tax the energies of the scientific and policy communities for some time to come. Geography must be an essential part of any serious effort to grapple with these challenges. The major changes that are taking place have different origins and spatial expressions, and each results from a unique combination of physical and social processes. We cannot simply focus on system dynamics and generalized causal relationships. We must also consider emerging patterns of environmental change and how different actions have different impacts on the operation of general processes from place to place. Geography is not the backdrop to the changes taking place; it is at the very heart of the changes themselves.

DISCUSSION AND REVIEW QUESTIONS

1. According to the cultural critic Raymond: "nature is perhaps the most complex word in the English language." Geographers have approached the meaning of nature and our relationship with it in three different ways. What are these three ways and how does each help our understanding of nature?

2. How we think about or understand our evolving relationship with nature is reflected in the history of the environmental movement in both Canada and the United States. The environmental movement has experienced two waves. Discuss the dominant aspects and concerns of these two waves.

3. How is remote sensing used to study the changes to Canada's boreal forests?

4. It is evident that modern humans and the biosphere face many environmental problems and challenges, such as climate change, loss of biodiversity, water pollution, ozone depletion, soil erosion, deforestation, and the disposal of waste. Which one do you feel is the most pressing and why?

5. Despite the numerous environmental problems and challenges, people across the planet have made serious efforts to act and change the unsustainable path. Discuss these efforts, focusing on the various scales at which action is taking place. Do you think these efforts will succeed or are we doomed to the self-imposed catastrophic alteration of the biosphere?

GEOGRAPHIC CONCEPTS

acid rain   173
anthropocentric view   158
aquifers   169
atmosphere   171
biodiversity   177
chlorofluorocarbons (CFCs)   183
conservationism   161
deforestation   174
environmental stress   169
global warming   172
Montreal Protocol   184

non-renewable resources   167
oxygen cycle   174
ozone layer   183
preservationism   161
radioactive waste   177
renewable resources   167
sanitary landfills   177
soil erosion   176
solid waste   176
toxic waste   177
Vienna Convention for the Protection of the Ozone Layer   184

ADDITIONAL RESOURCES ONLINE

About geography and environmental hazards: www.bbc.co.uk/scotland/education/int/geog/envhaz/index.shtml

About Edward Burtynsky's photographs of the human-environment relationship: www.edwardburtynsky.com

Intergovernmental Panel on Climate Change reports: www.ipcc.ch/publications_and_data/publications_and_data_reports.shtml www.ipcc.ch/ipccreports

United Nations Environment Programme: www.unep.org

Mannahatta Project: themannahattaproject.org

Center for Political Ecology: www.centerforpoliticalecology.org

Manufactured Landscapes: www.onf-nfb.gc.ca/eng/collection/film/?id=53006

The Cove: www.thecovemovie.com

Planet Earth: www.bbc.co.uk/programmes/b006mywy

The Nature of Things: www.cbc.ca/documentaries/natureofthings

chapter 7

SOCIAL GEOGRAPHIES— IDENTITIES AND PLACE

FIGURE 7.1 Bedugul, Indonesia. This woman working at a brick-making facility in the village of Bedugul on the Indonesian island of Bali makes about 45 cents (U.S.) per hour and works 10 hours a day, 6 days a week. (© H. J. de Blij)

Building Walls

TRAVELLING ON THE Indonesian island of Bali, I saw a brick-making facility and stopped to visit. Boys and women were building bricks by hand in the hot sun. I watched young boys scoop wet mud from a quarry by a creek into their wheelbarrows. They poured the mud into wooden forms. Once the bricks began to dry and harden in the sun, someone had to turn the bricks repeatedly to prevent them from cracking.

The woman in Figure 7.1 worked 10 hours a day, 6 days a week, turning, stacking, and restacking bricks to prevent them from cracking. For her work she earned about 45 cents (U.S.) per hour. In Bali, women and boys make bricks. In North America and Europe, the vast majority of brick-makers are men, who are aided by machines (one company estimated that 98 percent of its factory employees are men). What makes brick-making a job for women and boys in Bali and a job for men and robots in other places in the world? Does being a brick-maker mean different things in each of these places?

Throughout the world, different cultures and societies have different ideas about what jobs are appropriate for men and what jobs are appropriate for women. Geographers, especially those who study gender, realize people have created divisions of labour that are "gendered," meaning that some jobs are seen as properly men's jobs and other jobs as properly women's jobs. In many societies in poorer countries, families see young women as financial supporters of their families. Thus, many women migrate from rural areas and travel to cities or central industrial locales (such as export production zones–EPZs) to produce and earn a wage that is then sent home to support the schooling of their brothers and younger sisters (until these girls are also old enough to leave home and work). In Indonesia and in neighbouring Malaysia and the Philippines, many women temporarily migrate to the Middle East to work as domestics (cooking, cleaning, and providing childcare) in order to send money home to support the family. In North America, rarely does an oldest daughter leave her family in a rural region and migrate to the city to labour in a factory so she can pay for her younger brothers' schooling.

KEY QUESTIONS FOR CHAPTER 7

1. What is social geography?
2. What is "identity" and how is identity constructed?
3. What is the connection between identity and place?
4. How does geography reflect and shape power relationships among groups of people?

7.1 What Is Social Geography?

Geographers are interested in how our social lives and the places we live, work, and play—our social geographies—are intertwined. Every day we interact with any number of people across a variety of spaces and places. We talk to the members of our household, we nod to strangers and say "good morning," we exchange pleasantries with co-workers, and we mix with others at baseball games or the opera. These are examples of social "relations"—that is, the interactions and relationships we have with others around us.

While these examples speak to our individual or personal interactions, social geographers consider how social relations vary among and between different groups and across differing spatial contexts. We can think about how individuals come to be grouped collectively as a social category of persons, such as "the elderly," and how they might experience different social spaces, or how certain youth groups, such as "skateboarders," are deliberately excluded from certain spaces, such as parks, through city bylaws and ordinances. We can study how various groups of individuals categorized as "black" or "working class" are expected to be present in particular neighbourhoods or streets and not in others. In other words, we can examine how social processes organize people into social categories that are connected to particular spaces, both literally and in our imaginations. We seek to understand these social geographies.

In this chapter, we focus on the relationship between the spatial and the social with a particular focus on contemporary issues of gender, race, class, ethnicity, and sexuality. We examine how people and society construct social categories of identity and how place factors into the constitution of those social categories. The geographies of our lives and social relations are often caught up in power relationships that circulate among different social groups and social relations. We need to think about how social categories are often positioned in hierarchical arrangements—the wealthy class may have better access to services than others, or different ethnic groups may find themselves excluded from certain jobs or institutions.

Social geography, in the Anglo-American tradition, is defined as "a concern with the ways in which social relations, social identities, and social inequalities are produced in their spatial variation and the role of space in constructing them" (Smith et al., 2009). Social geographers are concerned with the nature of the social relations that tie people together or may tear them apart. What we might study as "social relations" can cut across a variety of scales, from that of the body and the household to the street, neighbourhood, or urban, suburban, and rural landscapes, and across regions, nations, and continents. Relations among and between individuals and groups depend upon the meanings given to social identities or categories such as race, class, gender, age, ethnicity, and sexuality. How these identities are understood depends on society's cultural, historical, and geographical circumstances. For example, women as a social group in Canadian society were not considered mature or intelligent enough to vote in federal elections until 1919, and even then the right to vote was not extended to Aboriginal women or women of Asian descent (Figure 7.2).

Contemporary social geography as a distinct area of study emerged during the tumultuous events of the 1960s and 1970s, when newly formed social groups began to collectively agitate

FIGURE 7.2 Executive of the Political Equality League, 1916. While Canadian women didn't get the vote until 1919, at the provincial level they were able to vote as early as 1914, thanks to the work of activists including Manitoban Nellie McClurg. Organizations such as the Political Equality League, pictured here, were instrumental in gaining the right to vote through efforts that took the form of pamphleteering, petitioning, and holding public events to raise awareness and bring about social change. (Archives of Manitoba, Events 190, N12944)

(a)   (b)

FIGURE 7.3 Campaigns for Social Change. (a) Wages for Housework Campaign grew out of feminist political activism in the 1970s. (b) Canadian musician and activist Buffy Sainte-Marie. Buffy Sainte-Marie sings at a benefit concert on Piapot Reserve north of Regina on September 8, 1975. Sainte-Marie was awarded the lifetime contribution award at the Canadian Aboriginal Music Awards in November 2008 for her 40-year commitment to peace and the North American Aboriginal rights movement. (William F. Campbell/Time & Life Pictures/Getty Images; The Canadian Press)

for social change (Figure 7.3). The civil rights movements, the gay liberation movement, and the women's liberation movement brought together individuals who understood themselves to have common bonds based on particular understandings of the social categories of race, sexual orientation, gender, and ethnicity. These groups held public demonstrations calling for social change and the need for social justice to eradicate perceived injustices based on these social categories (Figure 7.4). Geographical research drew attention to structural inequalities, including unequal access to such resources as affordable housing, health care, and public education. Geographers also began to engage in a more activist and radical agenda to push for social change.

FIGURE 7.4 International Women's Day March, Toronto, 1979. (Denis Robinson/The Canadian Press/The Globe and Mail)

In the 1980s and 1990s, social geographers shifted away from a consideration of structural inequalities, such as access to health care or good schools, and began thinking about how social categories themselves came into being. They began to argue that social categories such as sex or race should not be taken for granted or assumed to be "natural" or biologically unchanging attributes. Contemporary social geography argues that social categories such as age, class, or sex are socially constructed, meaning that such categories are unstable and culturally specific. For example, the concept of "teenager" as an identity and a collective group of individuals in core countries has a fairly recent history, developing in the 1950s. Prior to World War II, no such social category existed, and the line between childhood and adulthood was more crisply drawn. With the development of the idea of the "teenager," we see a host of assumptions about what such as person is like (for example, moody, irresponsible, spontaneous, in transition), which affects how such individuals are perceived and, more importantly, treated. This can affect one's life choices or opportunities, including where one might work or live.

How social categories of identity are constructed and lived depends on a person's location or place; they may vary by regions and be influenced by landscapes and change as we move around. This makes the geographer's spatial perspective uniquely important in understanding people and place. From our discussion above and the opening field note, we can see that social identities affect how we operate in social relations. When people migrate between regions and across continents, they bring with them their understandings of social categories and relations that may be different from those in the place they settle. As we discussed in Chapter 5, migration, tensions, and disagreements may erupt when social groups with differing cultural and social understandings come into contact with each other. The nature of a place may change with the influx or emigration of different social groups. As social geographers, we are concerned with understanding social life, social relationships, and the role of place in these interactions.

MAIN POINTS   **7.1**   What Is Social Geography?

- Social geographers are concerned with social relations and identities—how they are produced and the role of space in constructing those identities and relations.

- Social geographers examine how structural inequality is visible in the built environment. Access to resources such as affordable housing, public education, and health care may differ depending on social categories such as gender, age, race, sexual orientation, ability, and class.

- Social geographers also examine how social categories such as age, race, class, and sexual orientation are socially constructed and vary depending on the historical period and geographic location.

7.2 What Is "Identity" and How Is Identity Constructed?

A man gets off an airplane, walks to the baggage carousel to find his suitcase, and is greeted by dozens of black suitcases. He walks to the parking garage to find his car and sees a sea of black cars that all look the same. The narrator intones, "Maintain your identity. Drive a Saab." Identities are marketed through cars, clothing, memberships, jewellery, and houses. Advertisers tell us we can purchase our identity. Yet identity is much more personal than what we drive or wear, what groups we belong to, or where we live; social categories are a constitutive part of the society in which we live.

> **Identity** Defined by geographer Gillian Rose as "how we make sense of ourselves;" how people see themselves at different scales.

Geographer Gillian Rose defines **identity** as "how we make sense of ourselves." How do each of us define ourselves? We construct our own identities through experiences, emotions, and connections that position us within the various social categories available in certain places. That is, if we come to understand ourselves as a "woman," we also come to understand what is expected of us if we fall into that social category. A social identity is a snapshot—an image of who we are able to be at that moment. However, these social categories of identity are fluid, constantly changing, shifting, and becoming. What it means to be a "man" or a "woman" varies depending on cultural and historical circumstances (Figure 7.5). Place and space are integral to our identities because our experiences happen in places, and perceptions of place help us make sense of who we are.

In addition to defining ourselves, we define others and others define us. One of the most powerful ways to construct an identity is by **identifying against** someone else. To identify against, we first define the "other," and then we define ourselves as "not the other." We understand who we are by understanding who we are not. Edward Said wrote thoughtfully about how Europeans, over time, constructed an identity for the region that is now more commonly called the Middle East and Asia, and how Europeans defined the region as the "Orient"—a place populated with strange peoples who displayed mysterious

> **Identifying against** Constructing an identity by first defining the "other" and then defining ourselves as "not the other."

thinking and astonishing traditions. Geographer James Blaut wrote eloquently about how Europeans, during the time of European exploration and colonialism, defined Africans and the Aboriginal people of the Americas as "savage" and also as "mystical." Through these definitions of the "other," Europeans defined themselves as "not mystical" or "not savages" and therefore as "civilized." These ideas about the identities of others still influence our vernacular speech today, through phrases such as "the civilized world" or "before civilization." Phrases such as these invariably mean someone is defining the "other" and, in the process, is defining themselves as superior.

There are several contemporary social categories that seem central to how we understand others in today's world. These are the social categories of race, gender, ethnicity, and sexuality, and they are the factors we consider when we talk about how identities are "constructed." In thinking about these social categories, we need to work with the idea of **intersectionality**, which refers to the complex connections and relationships that exist between these various social categories and that have a material effect on social relations. How we understand ourselves and others depends on the intersection of race, class, gender, and age, among other factors. For example, an elderly white woman sitting in a public park might be viewed very differently than a group of young men of colour standing around in the same location. In thinking about why this might be, we begin by considering the processes of identity construction and place through a specific analysis of gender and race. Then we examine ethnicity and sexuality as identities that simultaneously shape, and are shaped by, space. Our concluding discussion considers the concept of power relationships through the lenses of gender and ethnicity.

> **Intersectionality** The complex connections and relationships between various social categories such as race, class, gender, and sexuality.

GENDER

Feminist geographers Mona Domosh and Joni Seager define **gender** as "a culture's assumptions about the differences between men and women: their 'characters,' the roles they play in society, what they represent." When we think of men and

> **Gender** Social differences between men and women, rather than the anatomical, biological differences between the sexes. Notions of gender differences–that is, what is considered "feminine" or "masculine"–vary greatly over time and space.

(a)   (b)

FIGURE 7.5 (a) Louis XIV of France, the Sun King and (b) Actor, Brad Pitt. What it meant to be a "man" at the turn of the 18th century is very different from how we understand the role today and must also be understood in the context of race and class. Louis XIV, whose portrait was painted in 1701, wears tights and high heels and has long coiffed hair. Compare this image with a more contemporary example, Brad Pitt. (© Arte & Immagini srl/Corbis; Martin Bureau/AFP/Getty Images)

women, we usually begin by identifying individuals by biological sex—those physical features associated with male or female, such as genitals, genetic characteristics, and hormones. The term "gender" is used to describe those socially constructed characteristics expected of bodies identified by biological features as either male or female. Male bodies are expected to exhibit so-called masculine characteristics, and female bodies are expected to demonstrate feminine characteristics. Further, men and women are expected to be heterosexual. Taken together, this reflects the **sex/gender/sexuality matrix**. That is, we expect biologically male bodies to exhibit properly masculine traits and to be heterosexual. Yet feminist geographers and other scholars argue that gender roles based on biological sexual difference vary historically, geographically, and culturally. In various societies and in different places there are ongoing and shifting notions about what men and women are like, what they are capable of, and the nature of the relations between them. This suggests that what it means to be a man or a woman is not fixed but is unstable and capable of change.

> **Sex/gender/sexuality matrix** The expectation that a person is only one of two biological sexes (male or female); that the proper gender characteristics (masculinity or femininity) will be exhibited by that body and that the normative sexuality is heterosexuality.

For example, the opening field note to this chapter described how brick-making is still done by hand by boys and women in Bali. The industry is not technologically sophisticated, and bricks are made one by one. Even beyond brick-making facilities, most of the factory jobs in Indonesia and in poorer countries in the world go to women instead of men. Factory managers in these areas often hire women over men because they see women as an expendable, docile labour pool. Researcher Peter Hancock (2001, p. 18) studied gender relations and women's work in factories in Indonesia and reported, "Research in different global contexts suggests that factory managers employ young women because they are more easily exploited, less likely to strike or form membership organizations, are comparatively free from family responsibilities, and more adept at doing repetitive and delicate tasks associated with assembly line work."

In Canada, there has been a marked shift in the gendered nature of employment—until recently, women were thought to be incapable of working in a large number of occupations based on gendered assumptions about intellect, aptitude, and physical strength. A 2009 Statistics Canada study illustrates this shift, showing a dramatic increase in the number of women in the paid workforce (Figure 7.6). In 1976, 48 percent of women held paid positions, compared to 91 percent of men. By 2009, the gap had closed significantly, with 76 percent of women and 86 percent of men participating in the paid workforce. Women now comprise the majority of post-secondary graduates. Moreover, women are increasingly working in "non-traditional" sectors such as medicine and law.

Figure 7.7 shows the breakdown by sex across occupational areas. While there has been an increase in the overall number

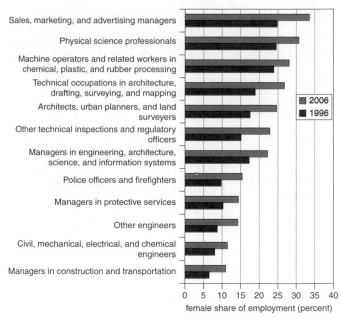

FIGURE 7.8 **Non-Traditional Occupations in Which Women Increased Their Share of Employment between 1996 and 2006.** Source: Statistics Canada, Education Matters: Insights on Education, Learning and Training in Canada, 81-004-XIE2010001, vol. 7 no. 1, April 2010; http://www.statcan.gc.ca/bsolc/olc-cel/olc-cel?catno=81-004-X&lang=eng.

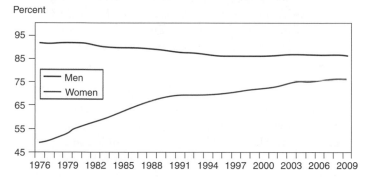

FIGURE 7.6 **Labour Force Participation Rates, Men and Women Aged 25 to 64, 1976 to 2009.** Source: Statistics Canada, Education Matters: Insights on Education, Learning and Training in Canada, 81-004-XIE2010001, vol. 7 no. 1, April 2010; http://www.statcan.gc.ca/bsolc/olc-cel/olc-cel?catno=81-004-X&lang=eng.

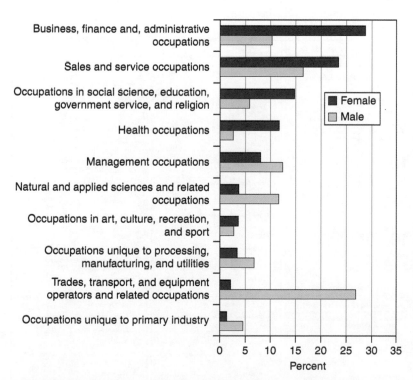

FIGURE 7.7 **Percentage Distribution of Males and Females Aged 25 to 64 across Major Occupational Groups, 2009.** Source: Statistics Canada, Education Matters: Insights on Education, Learning and Training in Canada, 81-004-XIE2010001, vol. 7 no. 1, April 2010; http://www.statcan.gc.ca/bsolc/olc-cel/olc-cel?catno=81-004-X&lang=eng.

of women in the paid workforce, this chart shows the extent to which occupations are still gendered—that is, they are occupations that seem more appropriate for either men or women. For example, over half of all women occupy positions in two categories: business, finance, and administration or sales and service. Men tend to hold positions as trades, transport, and equipment operators or in sales and service or management occupations. Significantly more men than women in Canada today still occupy positions in the natural and applied sciences, trades, management, and manufacturing. Many would argue that this disparity reflects continuing barriers to women being accepted into these occupations rather than any so-called natural difference between men and women.

Statistics Canada data do show an increase in the number of women working in non-traditional jobs, with "non-traditional" defined as sectors previously occupied by a small percentage of women. Figure 7.8 shows the increase in these sectors based upon census data from 1976 and 2006. Professions such as sales, marketing, and advertising; physical sciences; architecture; engineering; and firefighting and policing have all experienced a significant increase in the number of women. All this is to suggest that our assumptions about individual capabilities and proficiencies based on gendered ideas are culturally constructed and that individuals identified as women may do very different things depending on where they live, social expectations, and historical circumstances.

RACE

Most contemporary geographers argue that **race** is also a socially constructed identity and is a perfect example of how identities are built geographically. Biologically, all people are part of the same race—the human race—but find themselves "racialized." That is, they are placed into what amounts to arbitrary social categories based on constructed notions of "race." There is no biological basis for the various "races" to which people refer. Yet countless times we fill out census forms, product warranty information, surveys, medical forms, and application forms that ask us to "check" the box next to our "race" (Figure 7.9). It is important to remember that Caucasian or "white" is also a "race" or a "racialized" identity that is often unremarked.

> **Race** A categorization of humans based on skin colour and other physical characteristics. Racial categories are social and political constructions because they are based on ideas that some biological differences (especially skin colour) are more important than others (e.g., height), even though the latter might have more significance in terms of human activity. With its roots in 16th century England, the term is closely associated with European colonialism because of the impact of that development on global understandings of racial differences.

Where did society get the idea that humans fall into different racialized social categories? Throughout history, societies in different parts of the world have drawn distinctions among peoples based on their physical characteristics, but many modern assumptions about race grew out of the period of European exploration and colonialism discussed in Chapter 3. Benedict Anderson argues that differences in socio-economic classes fuelled the concept of superiority attached to race—what we call **racism**. Anderson notes that even before exploration and colonialism, wealthy Europeans defined themselves as superior to those living elsewhere. During exploration and colonialism, the non-wealthy in colonizing countries defined themselves as superior to the people in the countries they colonized. Anderson (1991, p. 150) explains:

> **Racism** Frequently referred to as a system or attitude toward visible differences in individuals, racism is an ideology of difference that ascribes (predominantly negative) significance and meaning to culturally, socially, and politically constructed ideas based on phenotypical features.

> *Colonial racism was a major element in that conception of "Empire" which attempted to weld dynastic legitimacy and national community. It did so by generalizing a principle of innate, inherited superiority on which its own domestic position was (however shakily) based to the vastness of the overseas possessions, covertly (or not so covertly) conveying the idea that if, say, English lords were naturally superior to other Englishmen, no matter: these other Englishmen were no less superior to the subjected natives.*

The stories the commoners heard about the "barbaric" and "savage" "others" fostered feelings of superiority. One of the easiest ways to define the "other" is through skin colour because it is visible. In building our own identities, an easy way to determine who we are identifying against is by the colour of our skin.

What society typically calls a "race" is in fact a combination of physical attributes in a population. Differences in skin

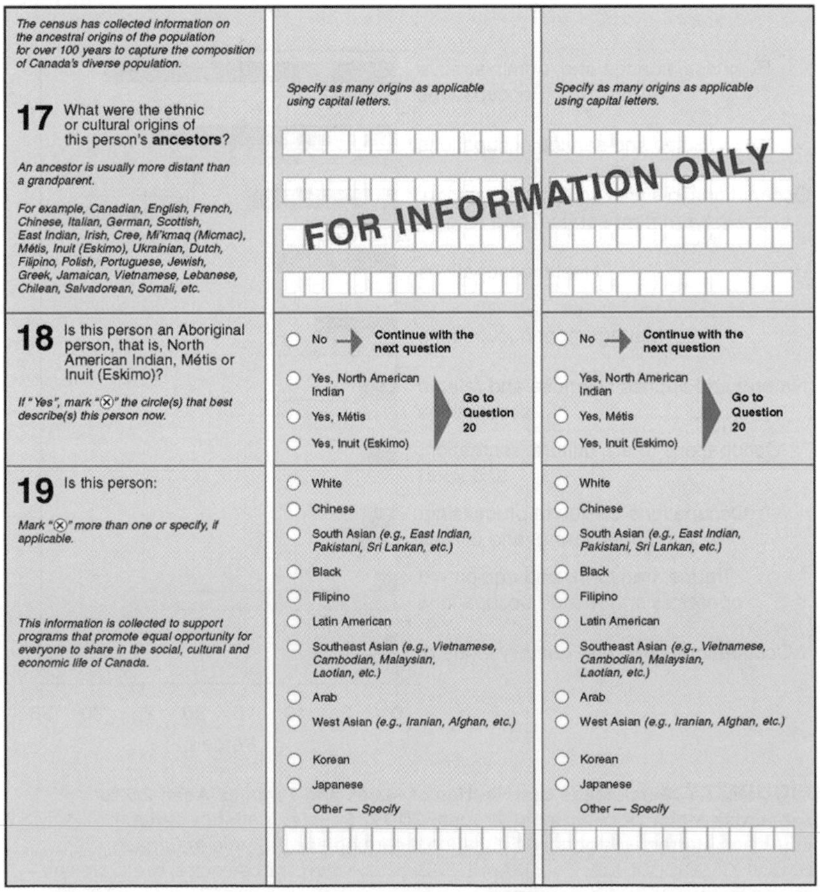
FOR INFORMATION ONLY

The census has collected information on the ancestral origins of the population for over 100 years to capture the composition of Canada's diverse population.

17 What were the ethnic or cultural origins of this person's **ancestors**?

An ancestor is usually more distant than a grandparent.

For example, Canadian, English, French, Chinese, Italian, German, Scottish, East Indian, Irish, Cree, Mi'kmaq (Micmac), Métis, Inuit (Eskimo), Ukrainian, Dutch, Filipino, Polish, Portuguese, Jewish, Greek, Jamaican, Vietnamese, Lebanese, Chilean, Salvadorean, Somali, etc.

Specify as many origins as applicable using capital letters.

18 Is this person an Aboriginal person, that is, North American Indian, Métis or Inuit (Eskimo)?

If "Yes", mark "⊗" the circle(s) that best describe(s) this person now.

○ No → **Continue with the next question**
○ Yes, North American Indian
○ Yes, Métis
○ Yes, Inuit (Eskimo)
Go to Question 20

19 Is this person:

Mark "⊗" more than one or specify, if applicable.

This information is collected to support programs that promote equal opportunity for everyone to share in the social, cultural and economic life of Canada.

○ White
○ Chinese
○ South Asian *(e.g., East Indian, Pakistani, Sri Lankan, etc.)*
○ Black
○ Filipino
○ Latin American
○ Southeast Asian *(e.g., Vietnamese, Cambodian, Malaysian, Laotian, etc.)*
○ Arab
○ West Asian *(e.g., Iranian, Afghan, etc.)*
○ Korean
○ Japanese
Other — *Specify*

FIGURE 7.9 Canadian Census Form, 2006. This figure shows part of the 2006 long-form census, which asked questions about identity and ethnicity. In Canada, explicit references to racial origin were included in census forms from 1901 to 1941. All references to "race" were dropped by 1951, and since that time the focus has been upon "ethnic origin." Scholars Boyd, Goldmann, and White (2000) argue that Canada's erratic enumeration practices around race reflect shifting conceptualizations of "race" and race relations in Canadian society. Source: Statistics Canada, Question #19, 2006 Canadian census long form, http://www.statcan.gc.ca/imdb-bmdi/instrument/3901_Q2_V3-eng.pdf.

colour, eye colour, and hair colour are variations within the human race. The differences likely result from a long history of adaptation to different environments. Sunlight stimulates the production of melanin, which protects skin from damaging ultraviolet rays; the more melanin is present, the darker the skin will be. Many believe that this helps to explain why, over millennia, humans living in lower latitudes—from tropical Africa through southern India to Australia—came to have darker skins. Another (not incompatible) theory holds that the production of vitamin D (a vitamin necessary to live a healthy life) is stimulated by the penetration of ultraviolet rays. Over millennia, natural selection in areas with shorter days in winter and more indirect sun angles (the higher latitudes) favoured those with the least amount of pigmentation, those who most easily absorb ultraviolet rays and in turn produce vitamin D.

Whatever may be said about the link between environment and the development of particular physical characteristics, it is important to recognize that skin colour is *not* a reliable indicator of genetic closeness. The indigenous peoples of southern India, New Guinea, and Australia, for example, are about as dark-skinned as native Africans, but native Africans, southern Indians, and Aboriginal Australians are not closely related genetically. There is no biological basis for dividing the human species into four or five groups based on skin colour. Instead, racial categories are the result of how particular cultures have *viewed* skin colour.

The racial distinctions in place today are drawn from categories of skin colour that are rooted in the cultural history, power relationships, and politics of a place over the past few centuries. Geographer Benjamin Forest (2002) gives us a global overview of racial distinctions:

> In Britain, the term "black" refers not only to Afro-Caribbeans and Africans, but also to individuals from the Indian subcontinent. In Russia, the term "black" is used to describe "Caucasians," that is, people such as Chechens from the Caucasus region. In many parts of Latin America, particularly Brazil, "racial" classification is really a kind of class placement, in which members of the wealthy upper class are generally considered as "white," members of the middle class as mixed race or Mestizo, and members of the lower class as "black." Indeed, because racial classifications are based on class standing and physical appearance rather than ancestry, "the designation of one's racial identity need not be the same as that of the parents, and siblings are often classified differently than one another." (p. 246–247)

In each of these cases, and in countless others, people have constructed racial categories to justify power, economic exploitation, and cultural oppression.

"RACE" IN CANADA

Unlike a local culture or ethnicity to which we may *choose* to belong, race is an identity that is more often *assigned*. Benjamin Forest explains that, "in many respects, racial identity is not a self-consciously constructed collection of

characteristics, but a condition which is imposed by a set of external social and historical constraints." For example, until 1971 the Canadian government hired enumerators to complete census questionnaires. Up to and including 1941, the census included questions that referred specifically to race. Therefore, these enumerators, working within predetermined census guidelines, assigned racial categories to respondents. The next census, in 1951, referred not to race but rather to ethnic origin. Scholars Boyd, Goldmann, and White (2000) marked this watershed moment, noting that the move away from the use of the term "race" was due to a combination of factors, including the sensitization of the Western world after World War II in light of the horrors of Nazi termination policies, and the nation-building project in Canada, which was quickly becoming more diverse due to the massive increase in immigration during the post-war era.

The 2006 long-form census questionnaire (see Figure 7.9) asks respondents to report their ancestral ethnic origin ("ancestral" meaning more distant than a grandparent) as well as their own identity. These statistics reveal a country whose population is increasing in ethnic, cultural, linguistic, and religious diversity (Figure 7.10). The 1901 census revealed 25 ethnic origins, with Aboriginal, French, and English comprising the vast majority. In 2006, census data told a much different story; more than 200 different ethnic origins were reported. As Figure 7.11 shows, predictions for the year 2017 show this diversity to be increasing. As well, the number of people reporting multiple ethnic origins is increasing. The 2006 census data indicated that 41.4 percent of Canadians have more than one ethnic origin.

Additionally, beginning in 1981 and due to increased demand for this information, Statistics Canada began collecting and producing census-based reports addressing another socially constructed category: "visible minorities". While the census questionnaire itself does not ask respondents to identify as a visible minority, Statistics Canada uses the ethnicity identification information (see Figure 7.9) to make determinations

FIGURE 7.10 Visible Minorities in Canada. South Asians celebrate in Mississauga, Ontario, which has the sixth largest visible minority population in Canada. Statistics Canada reported in 2010 that visible minorities in Canada will double by 2031. (Photo courtesy of *The Mississauga News*)

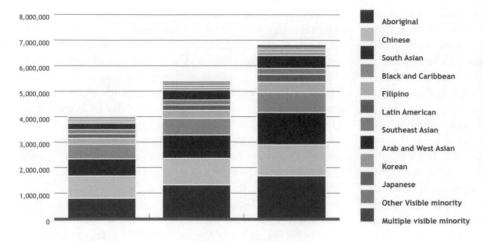

FIGURE 7.11 Diversity in Canada, 1996 to 2006, and 2017 Projections. This bar graph represents the Canadian population, in millions, from 1996 to 2017 (projections). Responses to the "ethnic origin" question on the Canadian census questionnaire reveal an increasingly diverse population, with over 200 different ethnic backgrounds reported. Source: Citizenship and Immigration Canada, Annual Report on the Operation of the Canadian Multiculturalism Act 2007-2008, http://www.cic.gc.ca/english/resources/publications/multi-report2008/part1.asp. Reproduced with the permission of the Minister of Public Works and Government Services Canada, 2011.

about visible minority status. Visible minority status is based on *Employment Equity Act* guidelines that define visible minority persons as "persons, other than Aboriginal peoples, who are non-Caucasian in race or non-white in colour." Since the first year this data was aggregated, there has been a steady increase in the number of persons of visible minority status in Canada. As Figure 7.12 indicates, in 1981 there were 1.1 million visible minority persons in Canada; the number increased to 1.6 million in the next census, 1986. From 1986 to 1991, the number of visible minority persons almost doubled, to 2.5 million. Over these 10 years, the proportion of visible minority persons almost doubled, from 4.7 percent of Canada's population in 1981 to 9.4 percent in 1991. In 1996,

the visible minority population was 3.2 million, constituting 11.2 percent of Canada's population. The growth in the visible minority population continued in 2001, when it was 3.9 million or 13.4 percent of Canada's population. In 2006, it reached over 5 million and constituted 16.2 percent of the total population of Canada.

RESIDENTIAL ORGANIZATION IN CANADIAN CITIES

The statistics in Figure 7.12 reveal a country that is becoming increasingly diverse and multicultural. Canada's visible minority population now accounts for over 16 percent of the total population, and by all accounts this figure will continue to grow. The 2006 census estimated that there were approximately 5.1 million visible minority individuals in Canada (Figure 7.12). This population grew by 27.2 percent between 2001 and 2006, with much of this growth attributed to increased immigration from non-European countries. Consequently, the proportion of new immigrants to Canada who are visible minorities has increased. In the late 1970s, 55.5 percent of new immigrants were members of a visible minority; in 2006, this number had risen to 75 percent.

As we will discuss in Chapter 10, visible minorities have a strong presence in Canadian urban centres. Over 95 percent of visible minorities live in Canadian cities, as compared to just over 68 percent of Canada's population as a whole. Figure 7.13, which depicts the geographic dispersal of visible minorities in Canada during 2006, shows that the major concentrations of this population were in census metropolitan areas (CMA). In fact, 6 in 10 people who were members of visible minorities resided in Toronto or Vancouver. Geographers Harald Bauder and Bob Sharpe (2002) argue that while these statistics reveal an increasingly diverse and multicultural environment, they simultaneously "produce landscapes of fragmentation and ethnic

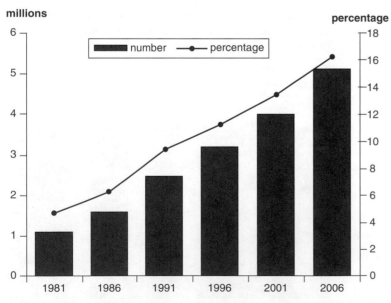

FIGURE 7.12 Number and Percentage of Visible Minority Persons in Canada, 1981 to 2006. The absolute number and the percentage of visible minority people in Canada have been steadily rising over the past 25 years. Source: Statistics Canada, Ethnic Origin and Visible Minorities, 2006 Census, 97-562-XWE2006001, April 2008; http://www.statcan.gc.ca/bsolc/olc-cel/olc-cel?lang=eng&catno=97-562-X2006001.

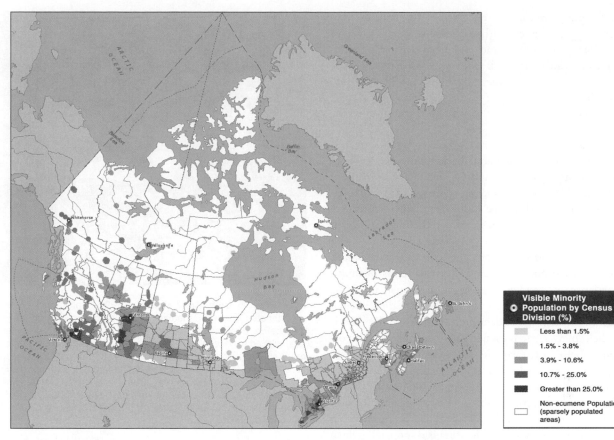

FIGURE 7.13 **Visible Minorities in Canada, 2006.** Data from the 2006 census reveal the geographic organization of visible minority populations in Canada. Source: Visible Minority Population, 2006, http://atlas.nrcan.gc.ca/auth/english/maps/peopleand-society/population/visible_minority/visible_minority_2006. Reproduced with the permission of Natural Resources Canada 2011, courtesy of the Atlas of Canada.

separation." While the spirit of multiculturalism abounds, the geographic reality is potentially one of segmentation and division.

One historic example of the "racial separation" in Canadian cities is Africville, a community that was located in Halifax, Nova Scotia. Africville was settled by Black Loyalists who came to Canada after the War of 1812 in order to escape slavery and accept the promise of free land. In 1849 the first church congregation was established, and in 1883 the first elementary school was built. Although technically part of Halifax, Africville was, by all accounts, a segregated community almost entirely comprised of African Nova Scotians. As a community, Africville struggled to survive, divided by a railway and encroached upon by sewage disposal pits, slaughterhouses, and civic open garbage dumps. The schools were closed in 1953 as children were moved to racially integrated schools. In the early 1960s, through a process of urban renewal, the city of Halifax decided to demolish Africville to make way for a bridge and the industrial development of the Bedford Basin. Figure 7.14 shows Africville prior to the demolition.

The demolition of Africville is an example of what scholars Linda Peake and Brian Ray (2001) call practices of "racialized geography" through the "erasure of people of colour from places, memory and the map." Although Africville was

FIGURE 7.14 **Africville, Nova Scotia, ca. 1965.** Bird's eye view of Africville, showing its location on Bedford Basin, with north end Halifax and the Narrows in the background. Within two years of this photo being taken, the town of Africville, which was part of Halifax, was completely demolished. All its residents were evicted and relocated. (Bob Brooks/Nova Scotia Archives, 1989-468 vol. 16)

a vibrant cultural community, it seemed at the same time to be a "slum" neighbourhood. Urban planners, seeking to solve the urban issues of poverty, crime, and racial tension, opted to flatten the community, erasing it from the Canadian landscape entirely. In February 2010, the government of Nova Scotia issued an official apology to the former residents of Africville and their descendants for the eviction and demolition of the community.

Residential segregation by race/ethnicity has a long history in Canada and can be traced back to the expulsion of Acadians from the Maritimes in 1756 and to the creation of reserves for First Nations peoples, among many other examples. Geographers Bauder and Sharpe (2002), studying census data from 1986, 1991, and 1996, have explored the extent to which residential segregation occurs in Canada's "gateway" cities of Toronto, Montreal, and Vancouver. They conclude that Canada distinguishes itself from the United States in terms of immigrant experiences of residential segregation. Canadian visible minority immigrants are not ghettoized, nor are they isolated in their communities. While data indicate that visible minorities overwhelmingly settle in major urban centres, it is important to remember that the experiences of immigrants are varied and diverse; different levels of racism, historical circumstances, cultural networks, local attitudes, political environments, and economic forces all contribute to unique experiences for new visible minority immigrants. Bauder and Sharpe suggest that Canada's immigration and multiculturalism policies, which stress the importance of adapting to Canadian society while at the same time respecting cultural differences, have resulted in relatively positive immigrant experiences that are neither ghettoizing nor assimilating.

IDENTITIES ACROSS SCALES

The way we make sense of ourselves in this globalized world is complex. We have different identities at different scales: individual, local, regional, national, and global. At the individual scale, we may see ourselves as a son or daughter, a brother or sister, a golfer, or a student. At the local scale, we may see ourselves as members of a community, leaders of a campus organization, or residents of a neighbourhood. At the regional scale, we may see ourselves as Maritmers, Albertans, Torontonians, or newcomers from another region of the world. At the national scale (Figure 7.15), we may see ourselves as Canadian, as college students, or as members of a national political party. At the global scale, we may see ourselves as Western, as educated, as relatively wealthy, or as free. We can understand ourselves as all or some of these social categories at the same time.

One of the most powerful foci of identity in the modern world is the state. State nationalism has been such a powerful force that in many contexts people think of themselves first and foremost as a member of their state, whether that means they

FIGURE 7.15 Unity Rally, Montreal, 1995. On October 27, 1995, an estimated 100,000 Canadians rallied in downtown Montreal just days before a referendum vote that was asking Quebeckers whether they wished to secede from Canada. The referendum was a time of great upheaval across the country and around the world, as people across scales, including sovereigntists, federalists, nationalists, First Nations, and many other identity groups expressed diverse opinions and concerns about the potential of Quebec secession. The "no" campaign won by a narrow margin of 50.58 percent. (Ryan Remiorz/The Canadian Press)

are French, Japanese, or Canadian. Nationalist identities are a product of the modern state system and a form of identity we discussed in Chapter 3. But nationalist identities coexist with all sorts of other identities that divide humanity—identities that can trump state nationalism in certain contexts and certain scales of interaction.

Geographers have frequently conveyed the idea of an individual's various identities by describing the identities as nested, one inside the other; the appropriate identity is revealed at the appropriate scale or in the appropriate situation. In this context, each large geographic territory has its own corresponding set of identities. Today, however, geographers are more likely to visualize identities as fluid and intertwined, rather than neatly nested, using the notion of intersectionality discussed earlier. Identities affect each other in and across scales, and the ways places and peoples interact across scales simultaneously affect identities within and across scales.

THE SCALE OF NEW YORK CITY

One way scale affects identity is by helping shape what is seen—which social category of identity is apparent to others and to us at different scales. To demonstrate this idea, we will focus on one enormous metropolitan area, New York City. New York has a greater number and diversity of immigrants than any other city in the United States. At the scale of New

York, we can see how social categories of identities change so that there is no longer simply Hispanic (as the census enumerates); there is Puerto Rican or Mexican or Dominican from a certain neighbourhood. The people of New York who are defined by the United States census as Hispanic are much more diverse than this one box would indicate. Geographer Inés Miyares has described the importance of Caribbean culture in the Hispanic population of New York. The majority of New York's 2.2 million Hispanics are Puerto Ricans (Figure 7.16) and Dominicans (together accounting for over 65 percent of Hispanics in the city). Historically, the Caribbean culture has made the greatest Hispanic imprint on New York's cultural landscape.

New immigrants to a city often move to areas occupied by older immigrant groups, in a process called **succession**. In

> **Succession** Process by which new immigrants to a city move to and dominate or take over areas or neighbourhoods occupied by older immigrant groups. For example, in the early twentieth century, Puerto Ricans "invaded" the immigrant Jewish neighbourhood of East Harlem and successfully took over the neighbourhood or "succeeded" the immigrant Jewish population as the dominant immigrant group in the neighbourhood.

New York, Puerto Ricans moved into the immigrant Jewish neighbourhood of East Harlem in the early 20th century, successively assuming a dominant presence in the neighbourhood. With the influx of Puerto Ricans, new names for the neighbourhood developed, and today it is frequently called Spanish Harlem or El Barrio (meaning "neighbourhood" in Spanish). As the Puerto Rican population grew, new storefronts catering to the Puerto Rican population appeared, including travel agencies (specializing in flights to Puerto Rico), specialty grocery stores, and dance and music studios.

FIGURE 7.16 Puerto Rican Day Parade, New York City, 2011. On the second Sunday in June since 1968, Americans line the streets of Fifth Avenue in Manhattan to celebrate the Puerto Rican Day Parade. Every year, over 2 million people gather on the streets to watch over 80,000 participants as they celebrate Puerto Rican heritage in the United States. (Gustavo Caballero/Getty Images)

Similar to this immigrant flow from Puerto Rico, the large-scale immigrant flow from the Dominican Republic that began in 1965 resulted in a distinct neighbourhood and cultural landscape. Dominican immigrants landed in Washington Heights or in upper Manhattan, neighbourhoods previously occupied by immigrant Jews, African Americans, Puerto Ricans, and Cubans. Miyares reports that although a Jewish cultural landscape persists, including a Jewish university, synagogues, and Jewish delicatessens, the cultural landscape of Washington Heights is clearly Dominican—from store signs in Spanish to the presence of the colours of the Dominican flag.

New York is unique because of the sheer number and diversity of its immigrant population, and the city's cultural landscape reflects its unique population. Miyares (2004) explains:

> *Since the overwhelming majority of New York City's population lives in apartments as opposed to houses, it is often difficult to discern the presence of an ethnic group by looking at residential housescapes. However every neighborhood has a principal commercial street, and this is often converted into an ethnic main street. It is commonly through business signs that immigrants make their presence known. Names of businesses reflect place names from the home country or key cultural artifacts. Colors of the national flag are common in store awnings, and the flags themselves and national crests abound in store décor. Key religious symbols are also common. Immigrants are so prevalent and diverse that coethnic proprietors use many kinds of visual clues to attract potential customers.* (p. 157)

Throughout the process, new immigrants need not change the facades of apartment buildings to reflect their culture. Instead, they focus their attention on the streetscapes, creating businesses to serve their new community and reflect their culture.

Popular belief in parts of New York holds that the Caribbean presence in the city is so strong that new Hispanic migrants simply acculturate into the Caribbean culture. Miyares cautions, however, that not all Hispanics in the city are categorically assimilated into the Caribbean culture. Rather, the local identities of the Hispanic populations in New York vary by "borough, by neighborhood, by era, and by source country and entry experience" (Miyares, 2004, p. 145). In the last 10 to 15 years, the greatest growth in the Hispanic population of New York has been from Mexico. Mexican migrants have settled in a variety of ethnic neighbourhoods, with new Chinese immigrants in Brooklyn and with Puerto Ricans in East Harlem. The process of succession continues in New York, with Mexican immigrants moving into, and succeeding, other Hispanic neighbourhoods, sometimes creating contention between and among the local cultures.

- Social categories of identity are socially constructed and are differently constructed depending on the place, culture, and historical period. In core countries, the most common social categories of identity are "race," ethnicity, class, gender, sexuality, age, and disability, although many other social categories are also important.

- Gender is defined as a culture's assumptions and expectations about the differences between men and women. This includes expectations about "proper" feminine and masculine characteristics, interests, capabilities, and relations between the sexes. Those expectations and relations can vary over time and geographical location.

- Race is a socially constructed category. People are "racialized"—that is, assigned to a racial category—based on arbitrary physical characteristics. There is no biological basis for the various "races."

- Race has been a category in Canada's national census since its inception. The Canadian population is becoming increasingly diverse, and a growing proportion of the total population is made up of visible minorities. This may lead to certain forms of spatial segregation, but in Canada, immigration and multiculturalism policies tend to reduce this effect.

- How we understand ourselves varies across scales. One aspect of identity may be more relevant in some locations and circumstances than others. For example, nationalistic feelings of pride in being "Canadian" may overshadow gender, race, and age during an event like the Olympics.

7.3 What Is the Connection between Identity and Place?

The processes of constructing identities and identifying ourselves against others, as with any other social or cultural processes, are rooted in places. When we are constituted within particular social categories of identities, we often infuse places with meanings associated with those social categories by attaching memories and experiences to the place. This process of infusing a place with meaning and feeling is what geographer Gillian Rose (1995) and countless other geographers refer to as "developing a sense of place." Our sense of place is fluid; it changes as the place changes and as we change.

What is of particular interest to geographers is how people define themselves through places. Our sense of place be-

> **Sense of place** State of mind derived through the infusion of a place with meaning and emotion by remembering important events that occurred in that place or by labelling a place with a certain character.

comes part of our identity, and our identity affects the ways we define and experience place. Rose explains:

> One way in which identity is connected to a particular place is by a feeling that you belong to that place. It's a place in which you feel comfortable, or at home, because part of how you define yourself is symbolized by certain qualities of that place. The geographer Relph, for example, has even gone so far as to claim that "to be human is to live in a world that is filled with significant places: to be human is to have to know your place."

The uniqueness of a place can become a part of who we are. Certain landscapes can feel like "home"—the smell, sight, and sound of the ocean; the wide-open sky of the prairie; the vastness of a mountainous terrain. Our emotions are deeply attached to and constituted in place, which means we can feel homesick for a place or distinctly out of place in unfamiliar locales. In fact, as the *Guest Field Note* by Sarah Jane Meharg argues, one way enemies attempt to eradicate an ethnic or racial group is to commit "identicide" through the intentional destruction of places that have particular meaning to a people.

GUEST FIELD NOTE
Identicide: The Destruction of Place during Armed Conflict

I embarked upon the study of cultural geography, armed with an educational background in landscape architecture and war studies. Perhaps to the casual observer, these two areas of study seem unrelated, even counterintuitive, yet my aim was to link the two and focus on post-conflict reconstruction—a term that has gained relevance since the U.S. invasion of Iraq in 2003.

Post-conflict reconstruction—the rebuilding of conflict-affected environments—requires research and expertise in designing places for people (landscape architecture) and the study of strategic warfare and its destructive acts (war studies). Through cultural geography, I was able to uniquely bridge theories of the "creation of place" and the "destruction of place" in a doctoral dissertation focused upon post-conflict reconstruction. At the time, there were few research projects that examined the destruction of the relationship between people and their places during war, or the tactical methods used to mete out this type of destruction. It was a worthy area of inquiry to pursue, and I was mentored by scholars in heritage studies, art history, and genocide studies throughout this process. Thankfully, I was surrounded by some multidisciplinary thinkers who were not interested in traditional unidisciplinary projects, rather who encouraged me to connect ideas to inductively develop my theory of warfare: identicide.

Although my entry into the study of cultural geography was from an eclectic perspective, it allowed me to see and understand the phenomenon of war in a way that permitted further insight into the nexus of culture and geography. Since graduating, I have been able to continue researching and publishing on the intentional destruction of symbolic places during armed conflict, and have spoken to NATO, the United Nations, the European Union, and the U.S. Army, among other groups, regarding identicide and why culture matters in war and peace.

We are strongly connected to our places because it is in place that routinized and ritualized daily practices construct our identities. By identity, we mean the characteristics shared by individuals and groups. Identity is space-bound: it refers to the specific places that we create, as well as contributing to the particular experience of our lives in such cultural landscapes. This particularity of place reinforces ethnicities, cultures, and identities. Places, with their defining material elements, become a part of the mythology of cultures and are building blocks of identity. As we act upon our places, they too, act upon us. When they change, we change; when we change, our places seem to shift and alter with our new awareness. We are interconnected and have a relationship with our places that informs who we are, what we do, and what we think.

So what happens when the bond between people and our places is destroyed? I have considered this question for many years, and it is an important one for cultural geographers. Significant places are destroyed in many ways, whether through new land developments in North America,

industrial practices in rural India, or natural disasters such as Hurricane Katrina. Yet none is more potent or traumatic for people than the intentional destruction of their meaningful places during contemporary armed conflict—a phenomenon that I call "identicide."

By identicide, I mean a strategy of warfare that deliberately targets and destroys cultural landscapes through a variety of means in order to contribute to eventual acculturation, removal, and/or total destruction of a particular identity group. Identicide is the killing of identity. Some societies have gone to great lengths to destroy other peoples' cultural places and practices, forcefully dispersing unwelcome groups, and deliberately and systematically destroying an entire people. Identicide is the precursor to genocide, but does not necessarily lead to genocide. Strategies to destroy places and cultural practices are a way to rid an area of a marginalized or openly contested group. Typically, this is achieved through the manipulation and control of symbols and the territorialization of the collective space in which they are embedded.

Identicide kills the relatedness between people and place and attempts to eliminate the bond underpinning individual, community, and national identity. These tactics are some of the most effective war tools and have been used in recent conflicts, such as those in Bosnia-Herzegovina. During the intense armed conflict in Bosnia-Herzegovina in 1993, the famous Bridge of Mostar was intentionally destroyed as a means of severing the two shores of Mostar—one Croat Christian/Catholic and the other Bosnian Muslim (Figure 7.17). Although the ethnic and religious division lines were not so clear cut as the river that divided them, the destruction of the bridge caused local, national, and international outrage, based on the bridge's cultural significance and lack of legitimate military utility. The bridge's destruction is a noteworthy example of identicide because the intention of the perpetrators

(a)   (b)

FIGURE 7.17 The Stari Most, Old Bridge in Mostar, Bosnia-Herzegovina. (a) The destroyed bridge in February 1994. (b) The newly rebuilt bridge in July 2004. The bridge was declared a World Heritage Site in 2005 by the United Nations as "a symbol of reconciliation, international co-operation and of the coexistence of diverse cultural, ethnic and religious communities." (© Nigel Chandler/Sygma/Corbis; © Danilo Krstanovic/Reuters/Corbis)

was to sever the bond between the people of Mostar and their beloved Stari Most, the Old Bridge, hence creating a homogenous culture, rather than allowing the ethnically diverse culture to exist.

Identicide has existed throughout recorded history, including forced Christianization of early pagan symbolic sites in Ireland, and in the changing of Maori place names to the lexicon of the colonists in New Zealand. Identicide takes many forms, but serves a single function: to lead to the decimation of a people, their places, and practices. In my experience, when people learn about identicide, they almost always have had a personal experience related to it. Identicide is a concept for people to better understand their relationships with place, and the bonds that can be affected when places are intentionally destroyed.

Sarah Jane Meharg, Royal Military College of Canada

ETHNICITY AND PLACE

The word "ethnic" comes from the ancient Greek word *ethnos*, meaning "people" or "nation." Cultural theorist Stuart Hall (1995) explains that "where people share not only a culture but an *ethnos*, their belongingness or binding into group and place, and their sense of cultural identity, are very strongly defined." Hall explains that ethnic identity is "historically constructed" and is often considered natural because it implies ancient relations among a people over time. The idea of **ethnicity** as an identity stems from the notion that people are closely bounded, even related, in a certain place over time. Ethnicity offers a good example of how identities affect places and how places affect identities.

> **Ethnicity** Affiliation or identity within a group of people bound by common ancestry and culture.

This definition may sound simple, but the concept of ethnicity is not. In the United States, for example, a group of people may define their ethnicity as Swiss American. Switzerland is a state in Europe. The people in Switzerland speak four major languages and other minor ones. The strongest identities in Switzerland are most often at the level of the canton—a small geographically defined area that distinguishes cultural groups within the state. So which Swiss are Swiss Americans? The way Swiss Americans see Switzerland as part of who they are *may not exist* in Switzerland proper (Figure 7.18). Ethnicity sways and shifts across scales, across places, and across time. A map showing all recognizable ethnic areas would look like a three-dimensional jigsaw puzzle, with thousands of often-overlapping pieces—some no larger than a neighbourhood, others as large as entire countries.

Ethnic identity is greatly affected by scale and place. For example, the Prairie provinces of Alberta, Saskatchewan, and Manitoba are home to a substantial Ukrainian population (Figure 7.19). At the time of the first phase of immigration to Canada in the 1890s, Ukrainian territory was divided into two regions: the vast majority ("Greater Ukraine"), containing some 25 million people, was part of the Russian Empire; Western Ukraine, home to approximately 4 million people, was part of the Austro-Hungarian Empire. Those under the rule of the Russian Empire experienced severe repression of the Ukrainian identity, to the point where even the Ukrainian language was banned. In both regions, oppressive regimes led to a poverty-stricken population whose members were divided among themselves. Between 1891 and 1914, an estimated 170,000 Ukrainians immigrated to Canada's western provinces, drawn by the promise of virtually free land. These immigrants, mostly from the Austro-Hungarian region, were searching for a better life and greater prosperity and settled first in and around Edmonton, with the support of the Canadian government,

FIGURE 7.18 New Glarus, Wisconsin. The town of New Glarus was established by immigrants from Switzerland in 1845. The Swiss American town takes pride in its history and culture, as the artwork on this sign welcoming visitors reveals. (New Glarus Chamber of Commerce, www.swisstown.com)

FIGURE 7.19 Pysanka in Vegreville, Alberta. The Pysanka, or Easter egg, stands as a monument to the diverse ethnicities of Vegreville, Alberta. The dedication message is written in four languages: English, Ukrainian, French, and German. In English it reads: "This Pysanka (Easter Egg) symbolizes the harmony, vitality and culture of the community and is dedicated as a tribute to the One-Hundredth Anniversary of the Royal Canadian Mounted Police who brought peace and security to the largest multi-cultural settlement in all of Canada." (Vegreville & District Chamber of Commerce)

which was seeking to develop the harsh prairie lands. However, concerns about immigrant resistance to Canadian culture led the government, in 1896, to encourage small settlement "pockets" across the Prairie provinces. This first phase of immigration was followed by three more: approximately 68,000 people immigrated between 1922 and 1939; 37,000 arrived between 1946 and 1961; and an ongoing wave began in 1991 with the fall of the former Soviet Union. While there is a complex, rich history behind each wave of immigration, the scale and place of both the Ukrainian territory and the Canadian Prairies shaped the identities of the populations. Historical accounts of Ukrainian immigration to Canada show how different groups redeveloped their identities based upon their experiences in this new land, while at the same time recognizing the regional scales of both their European past and Canadian present.

Cultural groups often invoke ethnicity when race cannot explain differences or antagonisms between groups. Just as "racial conflicts" are rooted in perceptions of distinctiveness based on differences in economics, power, language, religion, lifestyle, or historical experience, so too are "ethnic conflicts." A conflict is often called ethnic when a racial distinction cannot easily be made. For example, an observer may not be able to use physical appearance or skin colour to distinguish between ethnic groups in many of the conflicts around the world. The adversaries in recent conflicts in Northern Ireland, Spain, the former Yugoslavia, Sri Lanka, Ivory Coast, or Rwanda cannot be identified racially, so the parties in the conflicts use "ethnicity" to identify themselves and others.

Ethnicity is also invoked when a distinct cultural group is clustered in one area. Thus, the term "ethnicity" is often used to refer to a small, cohesive, culturally linked group of people

who stand apart from the surrounding culture (often as a result of migration). As with other aspects of culture, ethnicity is a dynamic phenomenon that must be understood in terms of the geographic context and scales in which it is situated.

SEXUALITY AND SPACE

Another way of thinking about place is to consider it as a cross section of space. Doreen Massey and Pat Jess define **space** as "social relations stretched out" and **place** as "particular articulations of those social relations as they have come together, over time, in that particular location." Part of the social relations of a place are the embedded assumptions about ethnicity, gender, and sexuality, assumptions about what certain groups "should" and "should not" do socially, economically, politically, even domestically. Geographers who study social categories of identities, such as gender, ethnicity, race, and sexuality, realize that when people make places, they do so in the context of surrounding social relationships. We can, for example, create places that are **gendered**—places designed for or understood as the appropriate or "normal" location for women or for men. A building can be constructed with the goal of creating gendered spaces within it, or a building can become gendered by the way people use it and interact within it.

Space Defined by Doreen Massey and Pat Jess as "social relations stretched out."

Place The third theme of geography; uniqueness of a location.

Gendered In terms of a place, whether the place is designed for or claimed by men or women.

Sexuality is part of humanity. Just as gender roles are culturally constructed, so too are our ideas of what is "normal" sexual conduct and practice. In their installment on "Sexuality and Space" in *Geography in America at the Dawn of the 21st Century*, geographers Elder, Knopp, and Nast argue that most social science, across disciplines, is written in a **heteronormative** way. This means that, in the minds of the academics who write articles and do research, the default subject is heterosexual, white, middle-class, and male. These geographers and many others are working to find out how the contexts of local cultures and the flow of global culture and politics affect the sexual identities of people.

Heteronormative The assumption in research that the "typical" research subject is heterosexual, white, middle-class, and male.

Geographers' initial forays into the study of sexuality focused largely on the same kinds of questions posed by those who first took up the study of race, gender, and ethnicity: where do people with shared identity cluster? What do they do to create a space for themselves? What kinds of problems do they have? For example, early studies examined gay neighbourhoods in San Francisco, London, and Toronto, focusing on how gay men and lesbians created urban neighbourhoods as their own and what the space meant to their identities and the formation of community. Gay villages now exist in many medium and large cities in North America and Europe. Specific studies have also focused on the role of gay pride parades in creating communities and the political struggle for access to other parades (such as St. Patrick's Day parades in some cities). Other studies in urban geography examine the role gays and lesbians play in the gentrification of neighbourhoods in city centres.

Gay villages played an important role in the political, economic, and social development of gay and lesbian political activism that drove the fight against discrimination on the basis of sexual orientation and the battles for recognition of human rights and for equal access to major social institutions such as marriage, health benefits, the military, and adoption. In the 1970s and 1980s, urban gay spaces provided individuals with a sense of belonging and community. Many gays and lesbians left smaller towns and rural areas for the "big city" in order to find support and acceptance. That is not to say that gays and lesbians are not found in rural areas. Rather, it suggests that at a particular historical and cultural moment, many gays and lesbians found urban life a better location for understanding their identity and social reality.

With the HIV/AIDS pandemic of the 1980s, gay villages became the base from which political activists fought discrimination against those with HIV/AIDS and called for the provision of funding and services that would combat the disease and provide needed community support. Government funding for community and social services helped develop gay and lesbian community centres, hospice facilities, and outreach programs for all those affected by HIV/AIDS. In the last decade, gay villages have been recognized as important indicators of a city's diversity and cosmopolitan nature; they are seen as important assets for attracting well-educated workers to fill jobs in the service sector and tourism.

More recent studies on gay and lesbian neighbourhoods question their purpose and goal in the context of current neoliberal politics. Previous studies assumed that gay and lesbian neighbourhoods were built in opposition to the dominant culture, but according to geographer Natalie Oswin, newer studies see gay and lesbian neighbourhoods as "extending the norm, not transgressing or challenging it" (2008). In other words, residents of gay villages tend to aspire to middle-class, monogamous, and heterosexual norms rather than pressing for more radical challenges to heteronormative gender and sexuality. In a 2006 study, geographer Catherine Jean Nash studied Toronto's gay village, the historical debate over the meaning of homosexual identity, and how that played out in the Toronto neighbourhood. Her research demonstrated that homosexual "identity" and its association with certain urban spaces changed as the gay village developed.

In 2000, the U.S. Census Bureau counted the number of same-sex households in the United States. These data, by census tract (a small area in cities and larger area in rural America), made it possible for Gary Gates and Jason Ost to publish *The Gay and Lesbian Atlas*. Their detailed maps of major cities in the United States show concentrations of same-sex households in certain neighbourhoods of cities, such as Adams-Morgan and DuPont Circle in Washington, D.C. and the West Village and Chelsea in Manhattan (Figure 7.20). Taking the census data by county, we can see a pattern of same-sex households in the United States, with concentrations in cities with well-established gay and lesbian neighbourhoods. We can also see the presence of same-sex households throughout the country, even in states where same-sex unions are illegal.

The 2006 Canadian census provides similar information. However, for the first time, and reflecting the legalization of same-sex marriage in July 2005, Statistics Canada included statistics on same-sex marriages in addition to same-sex households. The 2006 figures show that the number of same-sex partnerships increased by 32.6 percent between 2001 and 2006. A total of 45,345 same-sex couples were reported; of these, 16.5 percent were married. Similar to the findings in the United States, many same-sex couples in Canada reside in urban centres, for the reasons mentioned above. Half of all same-sex couples reside in Toronto (21.2 percent), Montreal (18.4 percent), and Vancouver (10.3 percent). Of those same-sex couples who were married as of 2006, 53.7 percent were men, and 46.3 percent were women. Moreover, 9 percent had children under the age of 24 living in the home.

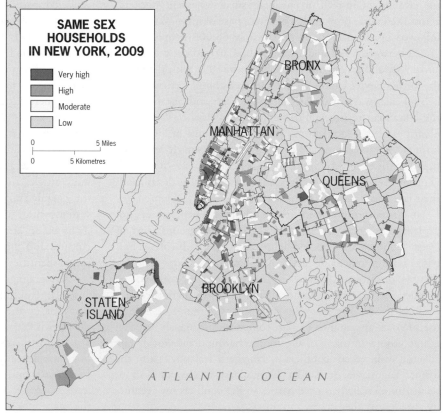

FIGURE 7.20 Same-Sex Households in New York, 2009. Census data were used to show the concentrations of same-sex households in New York, by census tract. Data from U.S. Census Bureau, 2010.

- Social identities are constituted in place. Identities are connected to particular places through the memories and experiences attached to that place. We develop a sense of place through which we inscribe a set of meanings into that place, which can be comfortable or frightening, soothing or worrisome. A sense of place is fluid and changes as places change and as we change.

- Groups of people who share a culture, an *ethnos*, and a sense of cultural identity are said to share an ethnicity that is often tightly bound to place over a certain period of time. Ethnic identities are historically constructed in that understandings of that identity develop over time, making it appear natural and unchanging.

- Sexuality and related practices are socially constructed, which means that what is considered "normal" sexual conduct and practice can vary historically, geographically, and culturally. Geographers are interested in the connections between sexuality and space and have paid particular attention to the formation of gay villages in major cities in North America and Europe.

- With the legalization of same-sex marriage in Canada in 2005, Statistics Canada began to collect information on same-sex couples in the 2006 census. Not surprisingly, given the connections between urban life and gay and lesbian identity, most married same-sex couples live in Canada's three largest cities: Toronto, Montreal, and Vancouver.

7.4 How Does Geography Reflect and Shape Power Relationships among Groups of People?

Social geographers are interested in how different social categories of identity are part of the processes organizing social groups across space, often in uneven and inequitable ways. Certain social groups may have difficulty accessing social services, may be relegated to substandard schools, or may be poorly served by public transit, making it difficult to travel to and from work. The fact that some social groups have better services and nicer accommodation indicates that some people have more "power" than others.

Power relationships (assumptions about, and structures that determine, who is in control and who has power over others) organize the social relations between various social categories of identities in ways that privilege some social groups over others. The nature of those relations depends on the geographical context in which they are situated. Power relationships also affect cultural landscapes, determining what is seen and what is not. Simply put, members of the dominant or hegemonic social group are able to ensure that their idea of what should be visible in the landscape prevails.

Massey and Jess (1995) explain that the cultural landscape is the visible human imprint on the landscape, but only the imprint of the dominant group—so what we see reflects power relationships. They argue:

> The identities of both places and cultures, then, have to be made. And they may be made in different, even conflicting ways. And in all this, power will be central: the power to win the contest over how the place should be

seen, what meaning to give it; the power, in other words, to construct the dominant imaginative geography, the identities of place and culture.

Power relationships do much more than shape the cultural landscape. They can also subjugate entire groups of people, enabling society to enforce ideas about the ways people should behave or where people should be welcomed or turned away. In this way they alter the distribution of peoples. Policies created by governments can limit the access of certain peoples. For example, the Jim Crow laws in the United States separated "black" spaces from "white" spaces, right down to public drinking fountains. Even without government support, people create places where they limit the access of other peoples. In Canada, there is a long history of anti-Semitism dating back to the beginning of the 20th century. By the 1930s, anti-Semitic behaviours were becoming mainstream. In 1937, St. Andrews Golf Club in Toronto posted a notice stating: "After Sunday, June 20, this course will be restricted to Gentiles only. Please do not question this policy." Anti-Jewish immigration policy was enforced, and as a result, boats full of Jewish refugees from Europe were turned away. Even after the *Racial Discrimination Act* was passed in 1944, anti-Semitic practices continued. McGill University restricted Jewish enrolment to 10 percent, for example, and the University of Toronto required higher averages for Jewish students. Toronto's Granite Club and the Royal Canadian Yacht Club restricted access as well.

In another example, Catholics and Protestants in Belfast, Northern Ireland, have defined certain neighbourhoods that exclude the "other" by painting murals, hanging bunting, and painting curbs (Figure 7.21). In major cities in Canada, local governments do not create or enforce laws that define certain spaces as belonging to members of a certain gang, but the people themselves create spaces, much as the people of Belfast do, using graffiti, murals, and building colours.

FIGURE 7.21 Belfast, Northern Ireland. Signs of the conflict in Northern Ireland mark the cultural landscape throughout Belfast. In the Ballymurphy area of Belfast, where Catholics are the majority population, a woman and her children walk past a mural in support of the Irish Republican Army. The mural features images of women who lost their lives in the conflict, including Maureen Meehan, who was shot by the British Army, and Anne Parker, who died when the bomb she planned to detonate exploded prematurely. (© AP/Wide World Photos)

JUST WHO COUNTS?

The statistics governments collect and report reflect the power relationships involved in defining what is valued and what is not. As we mentioned above in the discussion about census information on same-sex relationships, until 2001, no census data was collected on same-sex relationships, thereby erasing the lived realities of same-sex couples from all analyses of "families." Looking further back in history, women in Canada attained the right to vote in 1919. However, they were not considered "persons" under Canadian law, so while they could vote and hold office, they could not be senators. That changed in 1929, when the Justice Committee of the Privy Council (JCPC) in England overturned the decision of the Supreme Court of Canada and declared Canadian women "persons." It was not until 1960 that First Nations peoples were allowed to vote in federal elections without giving up their status under the *Indian Act*. This example shows how voting rights can be tied to assimilation politics; prior to 1960, only those First Nations peoples willing to give up their identity were allowed to vote.

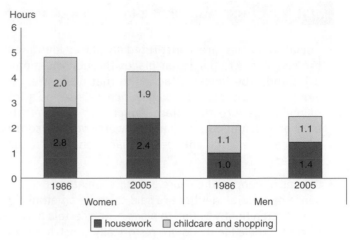

FIGURE 7.22 Average Time Women and Men Spend per Day on Unpaid Domestic Work, 1986 and 2005. In 2005, women were spending slightly less time doing unpaid work (including housework and childcare/shopping) than they were in 1986 (down from 4.8 hours per day to 4.3), while men were doing slightly more (up from 2.1 to 2.5 hours per day). Source: Statistics Canada, Matter of Fact, 89-630-XWE2008001, September 2008; http://www.statcan.gc.ca/bsolc/olc-cel/olc-cel?lang=eng&catno=89-630-X.

When the United States and other state governments began to count the value of goods and services produced within state borders, they did so with the assumption that the work of the household is reserved for women and that this work does not contribute to the productivity of the state's economy. In Canada, as Figure 7.22 shows, household work adds up to a substantial amount of time. In 2005, women were doing an average of 4.3 hours of unpaid domestic work per day, while men were doing approximately 2.5 hours per day. The most commonly used statistic on productivity, the gross national income or GNI (i.e., the monetary worth of what is produced within a country plus income received from investments outside the country), includes neither the unpaid labour of women in the household nor, usually, the work done by rural women in less developed countries.

Scholars estimate that if women's productivity in the household alone were given a dollar value (for example, by calculating what it would cost to hire people to perform these tasks), the world's total annual GNI (that is, the gross national income for all countries combined) would grow by about one-third. In poorer countries, women produce more than half of all the food; they also build homes, dig wells, plant and harvest crops, make clothes, and do many other things that are not recorded in official statistics because they are not seen as being economically productive (Figure 7.23).

Despite these conditions, the number of women in the "official" labour force is rising. In 1990, the United Nations estimated that there were 828 million women in the labour force. All but one geographic region showed increases between 1970 and 1990: in the wealthier countries of the world, from 35 to 39 percent of the labour force; in Middle and South America, from 24 to 29 percent. In East and Southeast Asia the figure rose very slightly, to 40 and 35 percent, respectively. In sub-Saharan Africa, the percentage of women in the labour force actually

FIGURE 7.23 Informal Economy, South Korea. These women sat near one of the ancient temples in southern Korea, selling the modest output from their own market gardens. This activity is one part of the informal economy, the "uncounted" economy in which women play a large role. (© Alexander B. Murphy)

declined from 39 percent in 1970 to 37 percent in the 1990s. These statistics reveal that in stagnating or declining economies, women are often the first to suffer from job contraction.

Even though women are in the official labour force in greater proportions than ever before, they continue to be paid less and have less access to food and education than men in nearly all cultures and places around the world. A 2004 report from the United Nations stated that two-thirds of the 880 million illiterate adults in the world are women, and that women account for 70 percent of the world's poorest citizens.

In most of Asia and virtually all of Africa, the great majority of wage-earning women still work in agriculture. In sub-Saharan Africa, nearly 80 percent of wage-earning women work on plantations and farms; in Asia the figure is over 50 percent. Although the number of women working in industries in these areas is comparatively small, it is rising. The increase has been slowed by the global economic downturn of the early 2000s, as well as by mechanization, which leads to job reductions and hence to layoffs of women workers. In the *maquiladoras* of northern Mexico, for example, many women workers lost their jobs when labour markets contracted between 2001 and 2002.

As the foregoing discussion has highlighted, many women engage in "informal" economic activity—that is, private, often home-based activity such as tailoring, brewing beer, preparing food, and making soap. Women who seek to advance beyond subsistence but cannot enter the formal economic sector often turn to such work. In the migrant slums on the fringes of many cities, informal economic activity is the mainstay of the community. As with subsistence farming, however, it is difficult to assess the number of women involved, their productivity, or their contribution to the overall economy.

Statistics showing how much women produce and how little their work is valued are undoubtedly interesting. Yet the work of geographers who study gender goes far beyond the accumulation of such data. Over the last two decades, geographers have asked why society talks about women and their roles in certain ways

and how these ideas, heard and represented throughout our lives, affect the things we say, the ways we frame questions, and the answers we derive. For example, Ann Oberhauser and her co-authors (2003) explained that people in the West tend to think that women are employed in the textile and jewellery-making fields in poorer countries because the women in these regions are "more docile, submissive, and tradition bound" than women in the core. A geographer studying gender asks where these ideas about women come from and how the ideas themselves bind women to certain jobs and certain positions in society—key elements in making places what they are.

VULNERABLE POPULATIONS

Power relations can have a fundamental impact on which populations or areas are particularly vulnerable to disease, death, injury, or famine. Geographers use mapping and spatial analysis to predict and explain what populations or people will be affected most by natural hazards, such as earthquakes, volcanoes, hurricanes, and tsunamis, or by environmental policies. Vulnerability theory tells us that not all people are affected in the same way by social, political, economic, or environmental change. Rather, the nature and spatial character of existing social structures influence which populations are the most vulnerable.

An example of vulnerable populations and their relationship to their environment is the Hurricane Katrina catastrophe in New Orleans in 2005 (Figure 7.24). Geographers Curtis, Mills and Leitner (2007) studied the events of Katrina, paying close attention to the vulnerability of the urban poor and racial/ethnic minorities. They argue that "vulnerability can be expressed geographically in terms of site (proximity of a neighbourhood to the hazard) and situation (the social context of that neighbourhood). During Katrina, the site of many indigent neighbourhoods made them vulnerable to flooding due to their proximity to a flooding source (such as a levee break), and the elevation of their homes." This study explores how the intersection of class (poverty) and race/ethnicity increased the vulnerability of particular groups to the flooding, which led to greater morbidity. Poor, non-white people, they argue, were less likely to leave, more likely to have existing health conditions, and more likely to lack the economic and social resources to rebound after the disaster.

Geographer Joseph Oppong recognizes that the spatial analysis of a disease can reveal what populations are most vulnerable in a country. In North America and Europe, HIV/AIDS is much more prevalent among homosexual and bisexual men than among heterosexual men and women. In sub-Saharan Africa, however, women have much higher rates of HIV/AIDS than men. Oppong explains that "AIDS as a global problem has unique local expressions that reflect the spatial distribution and social networks of vulnerable social groups."

According to Oppong, in most of sub-Saharan Africa, HIV/AIDS rates are highest for women in urban areas and for women who are sex workers. In Ghana, HIV/AIDS rates were lower for women in the urban area of Accra. Oppong postulates that this is because women in Accra have greater access to health care than women in rural areas. Women in rural areas who were

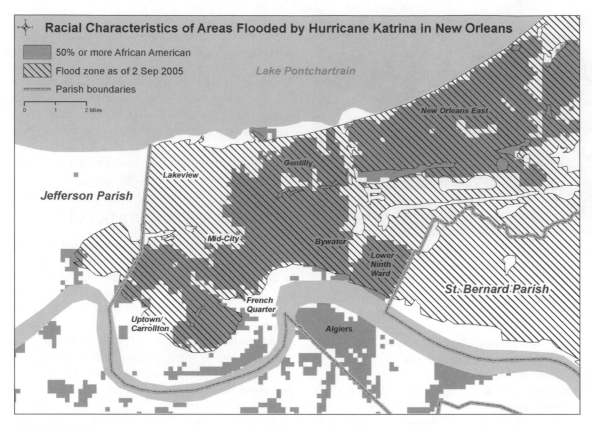

FIGURE 7.24 Racial Characteristics of Areas Flooded by Hurricane Katrina in New Orleans. African Americans were 67 percent of the total population of New Orleans, but 75 percent of the population in the flooded areas. Seirup, L. 2006. Racial Characteristics of Areas Flooded by Hurricane Katrina in New Orleans. Socioeconomic Data and Applications Center (SEDAC), Center for International Earth Science Information Network (CIESIN), Columbia University, http://sedac. ciesin.columbia.edu.

not treated for malaria had higher incidences of HIV/AIDS, according to his research. Oppong also found that women in polygamous relationships in the Muslim part of northern Ghana had lower HIV/AIDS rates. Oppong offers two theories as to why these Muslim women had lower HIV/AIDS rates: first, Muslims have a cultural practice of avoiding sexual promiscuity; second, Muslims in Ghana practise male circumcision, which helps lower the rate of HIV/AIDS transmission.

ABORIGINAL WOMEN IN CANADA

In 2010, the Native Women's Association of Canada issued a report, *Sisters in Spirit Research Report*, to express growing concern about the vulnerability, disappearances, and murders of Aboriginal women and girls in Canada (Figure 7.25). Study results show that there is a disproportionate number of Aboriginal women and girls murdered in Canada. Between 2000 and 2008, 153 murders of Aboriginal women were reported, accounting for 10 percent of the total number of women murdered in Canada during that time period, even though Aboriginal females make up only 3 percent of the population. Well over 100 women and girls are missing. Two-thirds of the cases being tracked in the Sisters in Spirit database are from British Columbia, Alberta, Saskatchewan, and Manitoba. More than half the cases involve women under the age of 31, and the vast majority of disappearances (70 percent) and murders (60 percent) took place in urban centres.

FIGURE 7.25 Candlelight Vigil for Missing or Murdered Aboriginal Women. On October 4, 2009, a candlelight vigil was held on Parliament Hill in Ottawa on behalf of missing Aboriginal women. (Fred Chartrand/The Canadian Press)

The report addresses three interconnected questions: What are the circumstances, root causes, and trends leading to violence against Aboriginal women in Canada? How many Aboriginal women and girls have gone missing or have been found murdered in Canada? And, how has this violence led to such disturbingly high numbers of missing and murdered Aboriginal women and girls in Canada without connection by authorities? Findings reveal that Aboriginals are the group most at risk in Canada for violence against women and that this violence is largely tied to systematic, gendered forms of racism that are the result of colonialism. Thus the violence is both racialized and sexualized. According to Statistics Canada's General Social Survey (2004), Aboriginal women are three and a half times as likely to experience violence as non-Aboriginal women, and Aboriginal women are three times more likely than non-Aboriginal women to experience spousal and sexual assaults. It is important to note that community-based studies reveal statistics much higher than those of government surveys.

The *Sisters in Spirit* report connects these high levels of violence, disappearance, and murder to a combination of social, cultural, geographic, political, and economic factors, including the impacts of assimilation policies, residential schools, lack of education, geographic location, poverty, and the "Sixties Scoop," in which an astonishing number of Aboriginal children were adopted out of their own cultures. Moreover, as discussed above, the power of numbers and the idea of "who counts?" prevails here. The discrepancies between government surveys and community-based research are vast as disappearances go unreported and are not investigated by authorities, or police departments do not ascertain Aboriginal identity.

DOWRY DEATHS IN INDIA

On a 2004 episode of *The Oprah Winfrey Show*, the talk-show host interviewed journalist Lisa Ling about her travels through India and her reports on dowry deaths in India. The Chicago audience looked stunned when it learned that thousands of girls in India are still forced into arranged marriages and that, in extreme cases, disputes over the price (the dowry) to be paid by the bride's family to the groom's father have led to the bride being brutally punished (often burned) or killed for her father's failure to fulfill the marriage agreement. Only a small fraction of India's girls are involved in **dowry deaths**, but the practice is not declining. According to the Indian government, in 1985, the number of dowry deaths was 999; in 1987, 1,786 women died at the hands of vengeful husbands or in-laws; in 1989, 2,436 perished; in 2001, more than 7,000 women died; and in 2006, it was reported that 7,618 women were the victims of dowry deaths. These figures report only confirmed dowry deaths; many more are believed to occur but are reported as kitchen accidents or other fatal domestic incidents.

> **Dowry death** In the context of arranged marriages in India, the death of a bride arising from a dispute over the price (the dowry) to be paid by the family of the bride to the father of the groom.

The power relationships that place women below men in India cannot be legislated away. Government entities in India (federal as well as state) have set up legal aid offices to help women who fear dowry death and seek assistance. In 1984, the national legislature passed the *Family Courts Act*, creating a network of "family courts" to hear domestic cases, including dowry disputes. But the judges tend to be older males, and their chief objective, according to women's support groups, is to hold the family together—that is, to force the threatened or battered woman back into the household. Hindu culture attaches great importance to the family structure, and the family courts tend to adhere to this principle.

Unfortunately, not all women in India (or in many other places around the world) feel empowered enough to stand up to injustices committed against women, nor do they have education, paying jobs, and cell phones that would give them alternatives. Despite the laws against dowry deaths, women remain disempowered in much of Indian society. Some women, when they are pregnant, undergo ultrasound and amniocentesis to determine the gender of their baby and elect to have an abortion when the fetus is a girl. Girls who are born are often victims of infanticide because many parents extend little social value to girls and dread the cost of the dowry they will have to pay when their daughter is married. In all of these cases, moving issues to the global scale has the potential to draw attention to the social ills. Yet for the social ills to be cured, power in social relationships must shift at the family, local, regional, and national scales.

SHIFTING POWER RELATIONSHIPS AMONG ETHNIC GROUPS

The presence of ethnic groups can be seen in the cultural landscapes of places. Many locales are home to more than one ethnic group, and the result is a unique cultural landscape that reveals how power relationships factor into the ways ethnicities are constructed, revised, and solidified; where ethnic groups live; and who is subjugating whom.

In Canada, the visibility of ethnic neighbourhoods is one of the central ways in which we experience urban space. We understand the relation between ethnicity and space through such neighbourhoods as Fisgard Street's Chinatown in Victoria, Toronto's South Asian community on Gerrard Street East and Little Italy on St. Clair West, the Haitian community in Montreal, and African Canadians in Dartmouth, Nova Scotia, just to name a few (Figure 7.26). Research that explores these urban ethnic landscapes in Canada shows the shifting relations in these spaces, often tied to immigration policy and practices, socio-economic factors, and cultural practices. For example, researchers have shown how immigration patterns affect urban spaces and neighbourhoods. Prior to World War II, most of the source countries for immigration into Canada were European; however, this has slowly changed to Asia, Africa, the Caribbean, and South America. As a result, according to Statistics Canada, minority neighbourhoods, defined as census tracts with over 30 percent of their population from a single visible minority group, increased in number from 6 to 254 between 1981 and 2001.

Los Angeles, California, provides a good example of the operation of power relations around notions of ethnicity and race at varying scales. Over the last four decades, the greatest migration flow into California and the southwestern United States has come from Latin America and the Caribbean, especially Mexico. In the 2000 census, the city of Los Angeles had nearly 3.7 million people. Over 46 percent of them were Hispanic,

(a)

(b)

FIGURE 7.26 **Ethnicity and Space.** Our urban landscapes reflect the ethnic composition of neighbourhoods, as illustrated by (a) Chinatown on Fisgard Street in Victoria and (b) Little India on Gerrard Street East in Toronto. (© Gunter Marx Photography/Corbis; Richard Lautens/ Toronto Star)

over 11 percent were black or African American, and 10 percent were Asian (using census categories for race and ethnicity). The Hispanic population in the city grew from 39 percent of the population in 1990 to 46 percent by 2000.

Southeastern Los Angeles County is today "home to one of the largest and highest concentrations of Latinos in Southern California," according to a study by geographer James Curtis (2004). Four decades ago, this area of Los Angeles was populated by working-class whites who were segregated from the African American and Hispanic populations through discriminatory policies and practices. Until the 1960s, southeastern Los Angeles was home to corporations such as General Motors, Bethlehem Steel, and Weiser Lock. During the 1970s and 1980s, the corporations began to close as the process of deindustrialization (see Chapter 11) fundamentally changed where and how goods were produced. As plants closed and white labourers left the neighbourhoods, a Hispanic population migrated into southeastern Los Angeles. A housing crunch followed in the 1980s as more and more Hispanic migrants headed to the area. With a cheap labour supply now readily available in the region again, companies returned to southeastern Los Angeles, this time focusing on smaller-scale production of textiles, pharmaceuticals, furniture, and toys. In addition, the region attracted industrial toxic-waste disposal and petrochemical refining facilities.

In his study of the region, Curtis records the changes to the cultural landscape. He calls the change in neighbourhoods, in which the Hispanic population jumped from 4 percent in 1960 to over 90 percent in 2000, a process of **barrioization** (referring to *barrio*, the Spanish word for "neighbourhood"). With the ethnic succession of the neighbourhood from white to Hispanic, the cultural

> **Barrioization** Defined by geographer James Curtis as the dramatic increase in Hispanic population in a given neighbourhood; referring to *barrio*, the Spanish word for neighbourhood.

landscape changed to reflect the culture of the new population. The structure of the streets and the layout of the housing remained largely the same, giving the Hispanic population access to designated parks, schools, libraries, and community centres built by the previous residents and rarely found in other barrios in southern California. However, the buildings, signage, and landscape changed as "traditional Hispanic housescape elements, including the placement of fences and yard shrines as well as the use of bright house colors," diffused through the neighbourhood. Curtis explains that these elements were added to existing structures, houses, and buildings originally built by the white working class of southeastern Los Angeles.

The influx of new ethnic groups into a region, the replacement of one ethnic group by another within neighbourhoods, changes to the cultural landscape, the persistence of myths such as the belief that Asians are a "model minority," and an economic downturn can create a great deal of volatility in a city. On April 29–30, 1992, the city of Los Angeles became engulfed in one of the worst incidents of civil unrest in United States history. During the two days of rioting, 43 people died, 2,383 people were injured, and 16,291 people were arrested. Property damage was estimated at approximately $1 billion, and over 22,700 law enforcement personnel were deployed to quell the unrest. According to the media, the main catalyst for the mass upheaval was the announcement of a "not guilty" verdict in the trial of four white Los Angeles police officers accused of using excessive force in the videotaped arrest of Rodney King, a black motorist. To the general public, the Los Angeles riots became yet another symbol of the sorry state of race relations between blacks and whites in the United States. Yet a geographic perspective on the Los Angeles riots suggests they were more than a snap response to a single event; they were localized reactions not only to police brutality, but also to sweeping economic, political, and ethnic changes unfolding at regional and even global scales.

The riots took place in South Central Los Angeles. Like southeastern Los Angeles, described above, the South Central area was once a thriving industrial region with dependable, unionized jobs employing the resident population. In the 1960s, however, the population of South Central Los Angeles was working-class African American, and the population of southeastern Los Angeles was working-class white. After 1970, South Central Los Angeles experienced a substantial decrease in the availability of high-paying, unionized manufacturing jobs when plants closed and relocated outside the city and even outside the country. The people of South Central Los Angeles lost over 70,000 manufacturing jobs between 1978 and 1982 alone.

Geographer James Johnson and his colleagues (1992) explored the impact of economic loss on the ethnic and social geography of South Central Los Angeles. They found that the population of the area was over 90 percent African American in 1970, but by 1990 the population was evenly split between African Americans and Hispanics. This change in population composition was accompanied by a steady influx of Korean residents and small-business owners who were trying to find a niche in the rapidly changing urban area (Figure 7.27). Johnson and his colleagues argued that the Los Angeles riots were more than a spontaneous reaction to a verdict. They were rooted in the growing despair and frustration of different

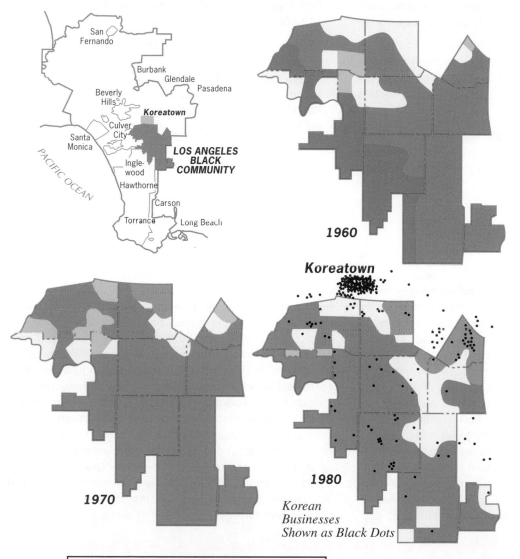

THE CHANGING ETHNIC COMPOSITION
OF SOUTH CENTRAL LOS ANGELES
1960-1980

- ◼ White
- ◼ Black
- ◻ Mixed
- ◻ Asian
- ◼ Hispanic
- ·–·· Community Boundary

FIGURE 7.27 The Changing Ethnic Composition of South Central Los Angeles, 1960-1980. Adapted with permission from J.H. Johnson Jr., C.K. Jones, W.C. Farrell Jr., and M.L. Oliver. "The Los Angeles Rebellion: A Retrospective in View," *Economic Development Quarterly*, 6, no. 4 1992), pp. 356-72.

ethnic groups competing for a decreasing number of jobs in an environment of declining housing conditions and scarce public resources. Their work shows the importance of looking beyond the immediate catalysts of particular news events to the local, national, and global geographical contexts in which they unfold.

MAIN POINTS	7.4 How Does Geography Reflect and Shape Power Relationships among Groups of People?

- Social identities are connected to place, but power relations privilege some groups over others. These power relations affect the built environment, determining what is seen and what is not seen. Dominant social groups are able to ensure their views about what should be visible prevail.

- Power relationships in the built environment can also regulate how people behave in places, who has access to places, and who is included and excluded in certain places.

- How governments gather statistics can ensure that what people do and where they do it is either visible or invisible. By not counting same-sex couples, for example, their presence in certain places can be overlooked. By collecting data on the work that women do in the home, women's unpaid contribution to the productivity of a country can be measured.

- Studies of the locations of vulnerable populations demonstrate that some people are located in better serviced or safer areas than others, as demonstrated by the locational analysis of populations affected by Hurricane Katrina. For other populations, such as Aboriginal women in Canadian cities, many places may be unsafe or dangerous.

SUMMARY

Identity is a powerful concept. The way we make sense of ourselves is a personal journey that is mediated and influenced by the political, social, and cultural contexts in which we live and work. Group identities such as gender, ethnicity, race, and sexuality are constructed by self-realization and by identifying against and across scales. When learning about new places and different people, humans are often tempted to put places and people into boxes, myths, or stereotypes that make them easily digestible. Power relations order social categories and make some categories more powerful than others, and dominant social groups have the ability to ensure that their views of what the built environment should look like prevail. Geographers are interested in how identities are socially constructed and what role place plays in the construction, maintenance, and enforcement of identities.

Geographers, especially those who spend time in the field, recognize that how people shape and create places varies across time and space. Concurrently, time, space, and place shape people, both individually and in groups. James Curtis ably described the work of a geographer who studies places: "But like the popular images and stereotypical portrayals of all places—whether positive or negative, historical or contemporary—these mask a reality on the ground that is decidedly more complex and dynamic, from both the economic and social perspectives." What Curtis says about places is true about people as well. What we may *think* to be positive identities, such as the myths of "Orientalism" or of the "model minority," and what we know are negative social ills, such as racism and dowry deaths, are all decidedly more complex and dynamic than they first seem.

DISCUSSION AND REVIEW QUESTIONS

1. What does the author's experience in the brick-making facility on the island of Bali, Indonesia, reveal about the geography of gender and the division of labour?

2. What is identity and how is our understanding of it enhanced by the incorporation of geographic concepts? What is intersectionality and how does it further our understanding of identity?

3. Discuss the gendered nature of employment in Canada.

4. What was the nature of Sarah Jane Meharg's research, as articulated in the Guest Field Note? What did she discover about the connections between identity and place and "identicide" as a tactic?

5. What does it mean when geographers argue that "places are gendered"? What does the study of Canadian and American gay villages reveal about sexuality and space and the gendering of place?

GEOGRAPHIC CONCEPTS

barrioization   210
dowry deaths   209
ethnicity   202
gender   191
gendered   203
heteronormative   203
identifying against   191
identity   191
intersectionality   191
place   203
race   194
racism   194
sense of place   200
sex/gender/sexuality matrix   192
space   203
succession   199

ADDITIONAL RESOURCES ONLINE

About the Gay and Lesbian Atlas:
   www.urban.org/pubs/gayatlas

About racial and ethnic segregation in the United States, 1980-2000: www.census.gov/hhes/www/housing/resseg/papertoc.html

About ethnicity and the city: www.learner.org/resources/series180.html#program_descriptions. Click on Video On Demand for "Boston: Ethnic Mosaic"

About ethnic fragmentation in Canada: www.learner.org/resources/series180.html#program_descriptions.

Click on Video On Demand for "Vancouver: Hong Kong East" and "Montreal: An Island of French"

About migration and identity:
   www.learner.org/resources/series85.html#program_descriptions. Click on Video on Demand for "A Migrant's Heart"

chapter 8

LOCAL CULTURE, POPULAR CULTURE, AND CULTURAL LANDSCAPES

FIGURE 8.1 Tata sign in Hyderabad. (© Erin H. Fouberg)

Preserving Culture

THE SIGNS WITH the Tata Corporation's logo were everywhere in the landscape of Hyderabad in India (Figure 8.1): a Tata corporate building across the street from our flat; "Tata" emblazoned on the grills of trucks throughout the city; Tata sky satellite dishes bringing television into homes; Tata International consulting buildings in the high-tech district of the city.

I asked my host what the Tata Corporation was and where the name came from. He explained, "Tata is a family name. The Tata family are members of the Parsi religion, and they own many businesses throughout India and the world." I was surprised I had not heard of the Tata family before, but I had heard about the Parsi. The Parsi are an ethnic group and a religion. They are followers of the Zoroastrian religion and came to India from Persia (present-day Iran).

According to Indian folklore, the Parsi were looking for a place of refuge as they fled from Iran. They sent word to a Hindu ruler in western India that they wanted to settle there. The Hindu ruler sent the Parsi a bowl full of milk to symbolize that they should not come to India—that the western states were already full. Legend has it that the Parsi leader placed a gold ring in the bowl of milk and returned it—symbolizing they would bring wealth to the region without displacing the people. Around 1,500 years ago, the Parsi settled in western India, primarily in the city of Mumbai (formerly known as Bombay).

India is overwhelmingly Hindu (85 percent), but the followers of the Parsi religion, who make up 0.0069 percent of the Indian population (fewer than 60,000 Parsi in the Indian population of 1.2 billion people), control a large share of the Indian economy. The Tata Group recorded revenues of $28.8 billion in 2006-7, while the entire gross national income (GNI) of India for the same time frame was around $800 billion. In addition to the Tata family, the Godrej Group, which produces soap, appliances, and office equipment, and the Wadias Company, which produces textiles and owns an airline, are companies established and run by Parsi families in India.

The financial success of the Parsi in India cannot be ascribed to a single cause. Their tight-knit community and maintenance of cultural practices that keep the Parsi together and culturally separate from the dominant Hindu culture were definitely factors in the Parsi success. These same traits now threaten to destroy the Parsi culture, and their numbers are beginning to dwindle.

A local culture such as the Parsi is maintained through the preservation of cultural traits and cultural practices. Today, however, one core cultural practice among the Parsi threatens the existence of the culture itself. According to an edict set down by Parsi religious leaders in 1918, the Parsi religion recognizes only the children who are born of two Parsi parents. Although some Parsi do accept children born to a Parsi father and non-Parsi mother as members of the community, children born of Parsi women married to non-Parsi (called "outsiders" by the Parsi) are not accepted as community members.

This is significant today because the Parsi have a very high literacy rate in India—98 percent—and many Parsi women are highly educated, have good jobs, and choose either not to marry, to have children late (thus reducing fertility rates), or to marry outside the Parsi community. In addition, thousands of Parsi, women and men, have migrated to the United States and Europe over the past few decades. One Parsi high priest sees the historical lack of intermarriage as a major reason the Parsi were able to maintain their culture and religion in a world surrounded by Hindu followers. Parsi in India today question whether to count the women married to "outsiders," and the children born to them, as members of the community. If they do not count these women and children, the Parsi population in India has declined over the last 30 years from 100,000 to 56,000.

As we discussed in Chapter 2, in an era of globalization, popular culture has diffused around the world—embraced by some and rejected by others, yet nonetheless infiltrating every corner of the globe. Local cultures continue to exist, but they face constant pressure from larger cultural groups and from the enveloping popular culture. In the face of these pressures, some members of local cultures have clung more tightly to their customs, some have let go, and others have forged a balance between the two. In this chapter, we explore what we mean by the notion of "culture" and how and why "culture" is geographical.

KEY QUESTIONS FOR CHAPTER 8

1. What do we mean by the term "culture" and how is it geographical?

2. What are local and popular cultures?

3. How are local cultures sustained?

4. How is culture diffused?

5. How is culture reflected in the landscape?

8.1 What Do We Mean by the Term "Culture" and How Is It Geographical?

When we look across our backyards or down our streets, when we glance in the windows of businesses or wander different neighbourhoods, we see the symbols and traditions of different ethnic and racial groups, religions, and cultures. Streetscapes come alive with unexpected architectural features, unfamiliar and intriguing street art, distinctive fashions, unknown languages, and the tantalizing smells of foods yet to be sampled. Distinctive cultural traditions, norms, and values are interwoven into place and have an impact on those of us who live in or experience those places. As geographers, we are interested in how certain values, norms, and ideas become embedded in the landscape. How is it that one group's architecture, lifestyle, or behaviours become what is expected or acceptable in the world around us and others do not? This question asks us to consider notions of power relations and domination, as well as ideas about social justice and our ability to see ourselves reflected in the built environment around us.

Culture A set of shared belief systems, norms, and values practised by a particular group of people. According to cultural theorist Raymond Williams, culture is both "ordinary" and a "whole way of life."

According to cultural theorist Raymond Williams, culture is both "ordinary" and a "whole way of life." A **culture** is a set of shared belief systems, norms, and values practised by a particular group of people. Although this definition of culture sounds simple, the concept is actually quite complex. A group of people who share common beliefs can be recognized as a culture in one of two ways: (1) the people call themselves a culture; or (2) other people (including academics) label them a culture. Some geographers perceive culture as a "way of life" and are intrigued with how certain aspects of that way of life become visible in building styles, music, food, religion, and landscapes. Clearly, not everyone in a particular group may adhere completely to a culture's dominant values, beliefs, and norms. As geographers, we understand that a particular

set of ideas becomes the most prominent within a particular culture. While it is important to understand and study dominant belief systems, we also need to be attentive to those belief systems that are marginal or less visible.

While we can focus on particular forms of literature, dance, or art as being characteristic of a particular group, such as the painting styles of 18th-century Quebec artists or the music of 19th-century Japan, we can also consider the particular shared beliefs, norms, and values of a cross-section or particular grouping of peoples, such as "working class" culture, "skater" culture, or "corporate culture." Shared beliefs, norms, and values also change over time as they are challenged or come into contact with other cultures. Sometimes the cultural changes can seem momentous, as was the case with the radical movements of the 1960s (Figure 8.2), or change can be incremental and subtle, exemplified by the increasing secularization of public life, such as that experienced in Quebec during the Quiet Revolution. Shared beliefs can be based on long-standing traditions, such as religious teachings or community traditions. Shared beliefs can also emerge spontaneously in a particular historical and geographical moment, such as the influential emergence of the grunge music scene in Seattle in the 1980s.

Culture is clearly geographical. Different cultures are present in different places, and culture both shapes and is shaped by the places in which it emerges. As noted in Chapter 1, by taking a spatial perspective, geographers can consider the intimate and important connections between humans and their environment. This can be seen at the global scale when we look at the difference in landscapes between countries such as Australia and the Philippines, for example, or within countries, such as the distinctive landscapes of Newfoundland and Quebec. We can also note distinctive cultural artefacts in rural, suburban, and urban areas and sometimes between inner-city neighbourhoods and outer areas. Using the five geographical themes—location, region, place, landscape, and movement—we can sharpen our spatial perspective to think about how we locate culture, how culture has an impact on place and landscapes, and how cultural traits, values, and characteristics diffuse across space.

Geographers bring particular spatial insights to questions of culture and place, but they have approached the question of connections between culture and landscapes in different ways. Contemporary cultural geography developed in the early 1920s with the work of Carl Sauer and his colleagues and students at the University of California at Berkeley—the so-called Berkeley School of cultural geography. Sauer used the term **cultural landscape** to refer to how a natural landscape, itself always changing (through physical processes such as erosion), is altered by cultural groups in distinctive ways. Sauer's work

Cultural landscape The visible imprint of human activity and culture on the landscape. The layers of buildings, forms, and artefacts sequentially imprinted on the landscape by the activities of various human occupants.

highlights the human–environment relationship at the heart of the geographical endeavour. In his *Morphology of Landscape*, Sauer argued that

FIGURE 8.2 Protesting the Vietnam War: March on the Pentagon, October 21, 1967. Around the globe, the 1960s were known as a time of social upheaval, protest, and the emergence of a "counterculture." The civil rights movement, feminism, gay and lesbian rights movement, anti-war demonstrations, and "flower power," among other movements, came to the forefront during this period. (© Leif Skoogfors/Corbis)

culture was the agent, the natural area the medium, the cultural landscape the result [of cultivation]. Under the influence of a given culture itself changing through time, the landscape undergoes development, passing through phases, and probably reaching ultimately the end of its cycle of development. With the introduction of a different—that is—alien culture [or way of life], a rejuvenation of the cultural landscape sets in, or a new landscape is superimposed on remnants of an older one. (Sauer, 1925, p. 1)

This rather deterministic view of culture was influential in the study of geography, particularly in North America, well into the 1970s. Sauer's model of the relationship between landscape and culture has been critiqued as taking a "super-organic" perspective. In Sauer's work, "culture" is viewed as an overarching or structural agent seemingly creating or determining a cultural landscape that is constantly changing in response to the influence of these cultural forces. Using this approach, geographers studied the historical transformation of place—how rural landscapes were altered by new farming practices and techniques, or how the distribution or organization of villages, towns, and cities changed. This geographical research on cultural landscape was largely descriptive and documented the dominant features that made the landscapes of different groups distinctive. This included the study of specific architectural features in barns and housing or the construction of places of worship and cemeteries of different cultural groups.

The super-organic approach to culture was tested by social upheavals of the 1960s in North America and Europe. Civil unrest and public protest were the hallmarks of the Black civil rights movement, the American Indian movement, the women's movement, the gay and lesbian movement, anti-Vietnam War demonstrations, and the student and worker demonstrations in North America and Europe (most notably France). Any notion of "culture" as an over-arching, unified, and universal or collectively shared set of values and norms seemed unsupportable given the diverse groups arguing for recognition and inclusion in the social fabric. A descriptive geography, interested in documenting the mark of human activities in the landscape, was not at all helpful in explaining or understanding the deeply felt and sometimes violent social and political unrest of the period.

Geographers were intrigued by these rapid and transformative social and political events, and researchers struggled to understand them using a number of different intellectual approaches. In the 1970s and 1980s, geographers such as David Harvey found Marxist notions of class relations and structural inequalities within capitalism useful in understanding the struggles against poverty and exclusion. As the field developed, many began to recognize that class was not the only important social division that distinguished different factions and that, as we discussed in Chapter 7, social divisions along the lines of race, gender, age, and sexual orientation also affected life chances and experiences, often inequitably. This recognition called into question the idea that there was such a thing as a "culture" shared by all individuals in a particular place or region. Geographer Don Mitchell went so far as to argue that "there is no such thing as culture" (1995, p. 102) in terms of an object or area of study distinctive from economics or politics. Political systems and

economic traditions or ways of doing business are clearly influenced by cultural norms and practices, and vice versa—that is, cultural ideas about consumption and the role of government are influenced by political and economic institutions.

Geographers engaged in the so-called cultural turn in geography drew on the postmodernist and poststructuralist frameworks briefly outlined in Chapter 1. These geographers argued that they needed to ask questions about meanings, power relations, and the symbolic in order to make sense of cultural landscapes. Whose meanings and symbols come to dominate the landscape? Who has the power to ensure their beliefs and values are built into the world around them? For some, skyscrapers, highways, and industry represent a landscape that reflects economic development and prosperity. For others, these same landscapes reflect the power of one group (business people or capitalists, for example) to take control of space in particular ways and create landscapes that reflect certain values (Figure 8.3). These ideas recognize that

(a)

(b)

FIGURE 8.3 Pruitt-Igoe Housing Development, St. Louis, Missouri. (a) The Pruitt-Igoe housing development, shown here in 1971, was designed by George Hellmuth and Minoru Yamasaki in 1951 and fully opened in 1956. Considered at the time to be the "epitome of modern architecture," Pruitt-Igoe was upheld as an example of rational, orderly, efficient management of poverty-stricken, mostly Black people. However, within 20 years the development stood in ruins, considered by many to be a disastrous example of attempting to use technological means to solve social and cultural problems. **(b)** In 1972, the first building was demolished, and within four years the entire development was razed. (Bettman/Corbis)

"meanings" are changeable, and that landscapes or the built environment are reflections of power relations.

Some cultural geographers are interested in the subtle and minute ways that oppression, marginalization, and exclusion are built into landscapes in ways that limit or narrow life choices for some and privilege possibilities for others. For example, if the billboards, advertisements, and images in your neighbourhood contain only images of a particular ethnic or racial group of which you are not a member, your sense of belonging in that neighbourhood might be undermined. If people who build streets, walkways, and buildings presume everyone can walk, then individuals with limited mobility or who use a wheelchair are "excluded by design." Geographers use a number of different perspectives to consider questions of social difference and exclusion. For example, feminist geographers, geographers engaged in critical race studies, and geographers of sexualities and queer geographies are all concerned with spatial exclusion and marginalization on the basis of gender, race, and sexuality, respectively. The landscapes we see are the result of contestations and conflict in which the more dominant group is able to successfully mark spaces with its own beliefs and values (Figure 8.4). However, as the *Guest Field Note* by Natalie Oswin suggests, how dominant and marginal groups negotiate or contest controls over space varies from place to place around the globe.

Contemporary cultural geography also considers popular culture as well as what some might see as elite or "high-brow" culture, represented by literature, traditional music, opera, theatre, and high art. Yet all cultural forms, including fashion, mainstream movies, domestic life, and street and folk art, are reasonable objects for geographical enquiry. The everyday lives of individual people and their engagement in the production and consumption of culture, in whatever form, help illuminate broad social, political, and economic processes at work in forging and transforming the built environment and social relations.

FIGURE 8.4 Montreal's Gay Village. Our built environments can also be marked as alternative spaces. Located on Sainte-Catherine Street East, Montreal's Gay Village is one of North America's largest gay villages. (© dbimages/Alamy)

GUEST FIELD NOTE   Excavating Heteronormativity in Singapore

In the Southeast Asian city-state of Singapore, there have been unprecedented debates on the topic of homosexuality in the last several years. Attempting to shed an authoritarian image and foster a "creative economy," the government of this island nation embraced Richard Florida's (2002) contention that gays and lesbians are a crucial part of the creative class (Figure 8.5). As a result, gay and lesbian commercial establishments have been allowed to operate visibly, police raids that were not uncommon in past decades have largely ceased, and gay and lesbian cultural production has flourished. But legislative and policy changes to counter pervasive heterosexual bias have proven stubbornly out of reach. Most significantly, a 2007 lobbying effort to repeal Section 377A of the Penal Code, a colonial era statute that criminalizes "gross indecency" between men, was dismissed. As Singapore's Prime Minister Lee Hsien Loong stated in a speech explaining why the law would stand: "The family is the basic building block of our society...one man one woman, marrying, having children

FIGURE 8.5 Singapore's First Outdoor Gay Event, May 2009. Close to a thousand people dressed in various shades of pink gather to participate in Singapore's first outdoor gay event at Speakers' Corner on May 16, 2009, in Singapore. (Caroline Chia/The Straits Times/Getty Images)

and bringing up children within that framework of a stable family unit." Further, he declared that this family is "part of our landscape."

My current research critically responds to this unjust sexual politics. It asks how and why certain family and sexual norms have been cemented in the urban/national landscape of Singapore. As many critical cultural geographers have argued, landscapes are not *natural*. Rather, they *naturalize*. So I explore how heteronormativity–the societal privileging of heterosexuality that makes heterosexual identification and heterosexual relationships seem normal–is a socially constructed rather than natural fact of Singapore's landscape. It explores the ways that a narrow notion of family (as heterosexual, nuclear, middle- to upper-class, and naturalized) has become a key unit of governance and has led to the advancement of exclusionary discourses and practices of citizenship in the city-state.

Though today the vast majority of households in Singapore are composed of single families, one need not go too far back into the historical record to find a different social formation. Throughout most of its colonial period (1819-1959), Singapore's population was overwhelmingly composed of single male migrant labourers. In the 1920s, however, the colonial administration began to find that its practice of relying on transient labourers was more costly than would be the reproduction of the population in situ. Steps were taken to facilitate this shift including the prioritization of infant and maternal health, the reconfiguration of immigration policies in order to balance the sex ratio and encourage family formation and reunification, the founding of the family planning association, and so on. It is in this period, therefore, in which heteronormativity took root and I focus my study on three case studies from it.

1. *Housing and the modern model family*. Initial public housing efforts by the Singapore Improvement Trust (SIT, formed in 1927) were a central part of a set of initiatives geared toward balancing the sex ratio and accommodating workers' families. While these early initiatives worked with a rather broad notion of family that was open to any "customary" arrangements of the various migrants, by the time the SIT's postcolonial successor the Housing Development Board emerged in 1960, housing was available for those in nuclear family forms only. Since this time, these types of households have become overwhelmingly predominant within Singapore's population. I explore how this change came to be, what kinds of subjects the colonial and postcolonial governments sought to create, and what these shifts in household composition reveal about Singapore's modernization and development processes.

2. *Marriage and (post)colonial authenticity*. Though it valued its own monogamous form of marriage above all others, the British colonial administration left negotiations over marriage customs in the colonized population up to its various communities. This was officially cast as a benevolent act but it served to perpetuate the secondary status of colonized communities by ensuring that they could never be modern subjects. In this aspect of the project, I look at efforts by various colonial elites to lobby for the colonial regulation of marriage and thus gain respectability.

3. *Migrant workers and hetero-nationality*. During the transition to independence of the 1950s and 1960s, a concern with the settlement of the remaining migrant faction of Singapore's population developed in scholarly and government circles alike. Specifically, it was argued that only a settled population would be a "quality" population that could facilitate urban/national development. My research explores the argument that migrants would make improper postcolonial citizens because they did not have "proper" familial home lives.

While contemporary debates in Singapore have pitted homosexuality against a "natural" and "normal" heterosexuality, these three cases suggest that the heterosexual family's privileged place in the city-state is the product of much work. By calling attention to the cultural politics of heteronormativity, perhaps debate that challenges its inevitability might be opened up.

Natalie Oswin, Department of Geography, McGill University

MAIN POINTS 8.1 What Do We Mean by the Term "Culture" and How Is It Geographical?

- A culture is a complex and dynamic set of shared belief systems, norms, and values practised by a particular group of people who define themselves or are defined by others as constituting a cultural group.

- The work of Carl Sauer and geographers of the Berkeley School is one strand of contemporary cultural geography that focuses on how human interaction with natural landscapes created distinctive cultural landscapes.

- Other contemporary strands in cultural geography are concerned with social difference and the built environment and with questions of inequality, social justice, exclusion, and marginalization. Geographers in these areas examine how various markers of difference, including gender, sexual orientation, race, ethnicity, age, and disability, are important in considering how cultural landscapes are created and understood.

- Culture is geographical: dominant cultural beliefs, norms, and values are reflected in cultural landscapes. At the same time, cultural landscapes influence the ideas, beliefs, and values of those who experience them in distinctive and not always predictable ways.

8.2 What Are Local and Popular Cultures?

Academics who accept that there is something called "culture" that can be discerned and studied have traditionally identified cultural groups as either folk cultures or as part of popular culture.

> **Folk culture** Cultural traits such as dress modes, dwellings, traditions, and institutions of usually small, traditional communities.
>
> **Popular culture** Cultural traits such as dress, diet, and music that identify and are part of today's changeable, urban-based, media-influenced western societies.

Folk culture is understood as incorporating a homogeneous population, and as being typically rural with cohesive cultural traits. By contrast, **popular culture** is understood as pervasive, as incorporating heterogeneous populations, and as typically urban with rapidly changing cultural traits. Contemporary academic work tends to reject this polarity of folk and popular cultures in favour of understanding folk and popular cultures as points on a continuum.

Further, folk culture can be a somewhat limiting concept as it requires us to create a list of traits (e.g., religious beliefs, musical styles, fashion) and to look for cultures that meet that list of traits. This methodology of defining folk cultures leaves much to be desired. Once we have our list of traits, we must then find a group that fits our list. Based on these traits, are the Amish a folk culture? Are the Navajo a folk culture? Arguably, it is how the people define themselves that matters more.

> **Local culture** Group of people in a particular place who see themselves as a collective or a community, who share experiences, customs, and traits, and who work to preserve those traits and customs in order to claim uniqueness and to distinguish themselves from others.

A **local culture** is a group of people in a particular place who understand that they share experiences, customs, and traits, and who work to preserve those traits and customs in order to distinguish themselves from others. It is important to bear in mind that just because a certain set of cultural beliefs, values, and norms are dominant in a definable location, it does not mean that everyone in that location is included in these dominant cultural systems. Some may be marginalized based on such things as race, gender, or class. Individuals in a cultural place or region may hold different ideas, may contest certain aspects of local culture, or may adhere to some aspects of the dominant culture while rejecting others. While understanding the dominant culture is important, being attentive to these distinctions is also important.

When we consider local culture instead of folk culture, we are interested in different questions. For example, do the Amish have a group identity? What cultural traits do they share? How do the Amish navigate popular culture and defend their local customs? Why do Canadians in Alberta understand themselves as having a different culture from those individuals from central Canada or the Maritimes? Why do certain North American holidays, such as St. Patrick's Day, transcend ethnicity and are celebrated as a part of popular culture while organizers of a St. Patrick's Day parade prohibit certain groups, such as gays and lesbians, from participating?

Some local cultures rely primarily on religion to maintain their belief systems; others rely on community celebrations or family structures; and still others rely on a lack of interaction with other cultures. Local cultures are constantly redefining or refining themselves based on interactions with other cultures (local and popular) and diffusion of cultural traits (local and popular). Local cultures also affect places by establishing neighbourhoods, by building places of worship or community centres to celebrate important days, and by expressing their material and nonmaterial cultures in certain places. The **material culture** of a group of people includes the things they construct, such as art, houses, clothing, sports, dance, and foods. **Nonmaterial culture** includes the beliefs, practices, aesthetics (what they see as attractive), and values. What

> **Material culture** The art, housing, clothing, sports, dances, foods, and other similar items constructed or created by a group of people.
>
> **Nonmaterial culture** The beliefs, practices, aesthetics, and values of a group of people.

members of a local culture produce in their material culture reflects and reinforces the beliefs and values of their nonmaterial culture. It is vital to note how people in local cultures accept, reject, or alter diffusing cultural traits, depending on what works for them.

In contrast to local cultures, which are found in relatively small areas, popular culture is ubiquitous and is practised by a heterogeneous group of people from any and all local cultures, anywhere in the world. Popular culture encompasses, among other things, architecture, music, dance, clothing, food preference, religious practices, and aesthetic values. The main paths of diffusion of popular culture are the transportation, marketing, and communication networks that interlink vast parts of the

FIGURE 8.6 McDonald's in Hong Kong, 2006. McDonald's operates in more than 119 countries on six continents. Its ubiquity has not come without criticism; sociologist George Ritzer termed the chain's cultural dominance at the global level "McDonaldization." However, while all locations serve menu staples like the Big Mac, they also offer menu items adapted from local cultures to suit local tastes. In this image, McDonald's employees in Hong Kong hold up the toasted shrimp rice burger. (Kin Cheung/AP/The Canadian Press)

FIGURE 8.7 Diffusion of Fashion. Catherine Middleton, Duchess of Cambridge, enters London's Westminster Abbey on her wedding day. Her wedding gown, designed by Sarah Burton of the House of Alexander McQueen, was replicated and on sale by retailers within a few days. (© Samir Hussein/Wire Image/Getty Images)

The hierarchy in this case is the fashion world. Key cities such as Milan, Paris, and New York are the **hearth** (the point

Hearth The area where an idea or cultural trait originates.

of origin) or the cases of first diffusion. The next tier of places includes the major fashion houses in world cities. Finally, the suburban mall receives the innovation. Hierarchical diffusion can also occur through a hierarchy of people. In this case, the designer is the hearth; the models are the next tier; and celebrities, editors and writers of major magazines, and subscribers to fashion magazines follow in close order. Finally, anyone walking through a shopping mall can become a "knower" in the diffusion of this innovation.

Local and popular cultures are not seen as two ends of a continuum; rather, they both operate across multiple scales, affecting people and places in different ways. For example, people from Hutterite or Mennonite communities, dressed in the distinctive clothing of their culture, often visit the ultimate in popular culture: a major international department store such as Walmart. While retaining their local culture, they accept some aspects of the popular culture on sale in the store. Moving the other way, traditions based on centuries-old customs of local cultures, such as painting henna on one's hands or practising Kabbalah beliefs, are carried to the global culture by a popular culture icon or by corporations (such as the media industry) that work to construct popular culture (Figure 8.8).

world (see Chapter 2 for further discussion of these networks). When we study popular culture, we see that some forms of cultural expression appear everywhere, but it is the study of local culture that lets us see how communities, groups, and individuals in particular places take up or reject popular culture. Local culture shows us how those global cultural networks, largely dominated by core countries, touch ground differently in different places and how popular culture is filtered through local traditions and customs (Figure 8.6).

For example, fashions diffuse incredibly quickly today. When Catherine Middleton, Duchess of Cambridge, graced Westminster Abbey in a lace wedding gown designed by Sarah Burton for the House of Alexander McQueen at an estimated cost of $65,000, dress designers around the world interpreted or copied the gown within hours (Figure 8.7). Fewer than ten hours after the wedding aired at 5:30 a.m. Eastern Time, dress designers at Kleinfeld Bridal Salon in New York had replicated Middleton's dress, and started selling it for $3,500 within 48 hours.

In popular culture, fashion trends spread rapidly through the interconnected world in a classic case of **hierarchical diffusion** (discussed in Chapter 1).

Hierarchical diffusion A form of diffusion in which an idea or innovation spreads by passing first among the most connected places or peoples. An urban hierarchy is usually involved, encouraging the leapfrogging of innovations over wide areas, with geographic distance a less important influence.

FIGURE 8.8 Diffusion of Culture. Actor Russell Brand and singer Katy Perry wed in a "traditional" Hindu ceremony at the Sher Bagh Resort near the Ranthambhore tiger sanctuary in India. Perry was adorned with a *nath*, an Indian bridal nose ring, traditionally worn by Indian brides until the wedding night when her husband removes it. (© David Dyson/Retna/Camera Press)

- Local culture involves a group of people in a particular place who understand themselves as a collective or a community; who share experiences, customs, and traits; and who work to preserve those traits and customs in order to claim uniqueness and distinguish themselves from others.

- Popular culture is dominant, ubiquitous, and able to change rapidly, diffusing new ideas across vast distances. It is practised by a heterogeneous group of people from any and all local cultures, anywhere in the world, and encompasses, among other things, music, dance, clothing, food preference, religious practices, and aesthetic values.

- Geographically, we tend to see local cultures as occupying distinctive and discernable places, locations,

and regions. Yet these local cultures are embedded in and influenced by wider popular culture trends that are taken up, rejected, or transformed in local contexts.

- Culture, either local or popular, is not monolithic or universal. Although a certain set of beliefs, norms, and practices may come to dominate, individuals within the cultural group may have their own ideas excluded or rejected. Geographers are interested in the ways in which certain cultural ideas come to dominate and others are actively excluded or simply ignored.

- Cultural geographers are interested in both local and popular cultures that operate within a web of customs and cultures diffused and interlinked across a variety of scales.

Both local and popular cultures operate within a web of innumerable customs and cultures diffused and interlinked at a variety of scales. Distinctive cultural traits and forms circulate through a complex web of political and economic forces that shape and limit their practices. Popular culture is diffused through global communications and transportation networks that intricately link certain parts of the world and distance others. At the same time, local cultures work to preserve their uniqueness even as they are enmeshed in the wider popular culture.

8.3 How Are Local Cultures Sustained?

Local cultures often work hard to preserve and maintain their distinctive features in spite of the pervasive influence of cultural beliefs and norms that may emerge both within and beyond the place or region. A good example is the province of Quebec, which has actively worked for several centuries to preserve its language, music, art, and religious traditions. At the national level, the Canadian Radio-television and Telecommunications Commission (CRTC) works to ensure that Canadian actors, artists, writers, film and television producers, and musicians are given adequate representation within Canadian cultural industries.

> **Assimilation** The process through which people lose originally differentiating traits, such as dress, speech particularities, or mannerisms, when they come into contact with another society or culture. Often used to describe immigrant adaptation to new places of residence.

The drive to preserve certain cultural ideas and eradicate others has a lengthy history in the Canadian context. For example, during the 1800s and into the 1900s, the Canadian government had an official policy of **assimilation**

of indigenous peoples. It wanted to integrate the country's First Nations peoples into the dominant culture, making them "Canadians" rather than "Indians." The United States, Australia, the Soviet Union, and other colonial powers adopted similar policies toward indigenous peoples, using schools, churches, and government agents to discourage native or indigenous practices. In Canada, the federal government forced tribal members to settle in one place, usually on reserves, and to farm rather than hunt or fish on traditional hunting grounds. Residential schools, managed by religions organizations including the Anglican and Roman Catholic churches, were designed to separate First Nations children from their families and to teach them the English language as the first step in assimilating them (Figure 8.9). Missionary school teachers punished tribal members for using their native language. Today, several churches and governments have apologized for assimilationist policies. In 2008, the governments of Australia and Canada each officially apologized to their indigenous populations (Aboriginals in Australia and First Nations and Inuit in Canada). On September 19, 2007, the Indian Residential Schools Settlement Agreement came into effect in Canada; it is the largest class action settlement in the country's history. The measures put in place through this agreement include the Common Experience Payment, a $1.9-billion fund from which compensation will be paid to every eligible former residential school student; the Truth and Reconciliation Commission, which will give former students and their families the opportunity to share their experiences, educate non-natives, and raise awareness of the effects of residential schools; the Independent Assessment Process, established to assist those who suffered sexual and physical abuse and other wrongful acts that led to serious psychological injury; Commemoration, to pay tribute to, honour, and remember students from residential schools and their common experiences; and the Aboriginal Healing Foundation, which will provide healing programs and initiatives.

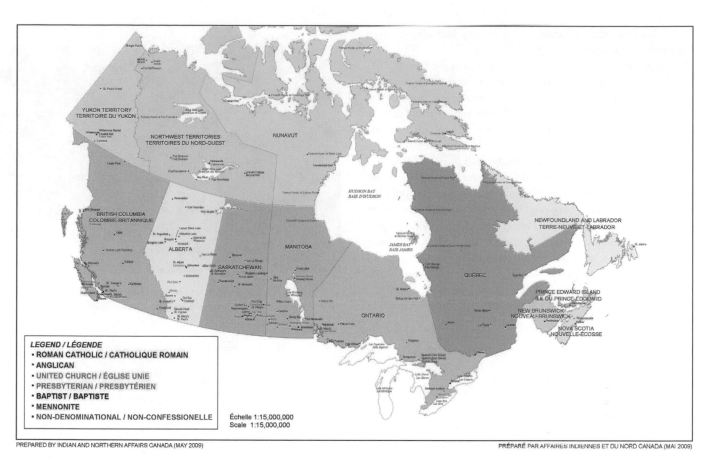

LEGEND / LÉGENDE
- ROMAN CATHOLIC / CATHOLIQUE ROMAIN
- ANGLICAN
- UNITED CHURCH / ÉGLISE UNIE
- PRESBYTERIAN / PRESBYTÉRIEN
- **BAPTIST / BAPTISTE**
- MENNONITE
- NON-DENOMINATIONAL / NON-CONFESSIONELLE

Échelle 1:15,000,000
Scale 1:15,000,000

PREPARED BY INDIAN AND NORTHERN AFFAIRS CANADA (MAY 2009)   PRÉPARÉ PAR AFFAIRES INDIENNES ET DU NORD CANADA (MAI 2009)

FIGURE 8.9 Indian Residential Schools of Canada. The 130 Indian residential schools included in the 2007 Indian Residential Schools Settlement Agreement are indicated on this map, as are the three institutions added since September 19, 2007, through Article 12 of the agreement. From Indian Residential Schools of Canada: List of recognized institutions, map. Ottawa: Indian and Northern Affairs Canada, 2010. Accessed at http://www.aadnc-aandc.gc.ca/eng/1100100015606/1100100015611. Reproduced with the permission of the Minister of Public Works and Government Services Canada, 2011.

As these examples demonstrate, people attempting to maintain a local culture might face tremendous difficulties, including removal from their traditional landscape and a complete dislocation from language and customs particular to a place. Local cultures are sustained through **customs**, which are practices that a group of people routinely follows. People have customs regarding all parts of their lives, from eating and drinking to dancing and sports. These customs may change in small ways over time, but they must be maintained despite the onslaught of popular culture if the local culture is to survive. Members of local cultures, whether rural or urban, often find they are trying to keep their customs for themselves, to prevent others from appropriating their customs for economic benefit. Anthropologists and geographers have studied how others use local cultural knowledge, customs, and even names. For example, a brewery that produced Crazy Horse beer was sued by the estate of Crazy Horse (a Lakota Indian leader).

Researcher Simon Harrison recognizes that local cultural groups purposefully, and often fervently, define themselves as unique, creating boundaries around their culture and distinguishing themselves from other local cultures. In the age of globalization, where popular culture changes quickly and diffuses rapidly, Harrison finds that local cultures typically have two goals: keeping

> **Custom** A practice routinely followed by a group of people.

other cultures out and keeping their own culture in so as to avoid "contamination and extinction." Harrison uses the example of the Notting Hill carnival in London to show how Londoners from the West Indies (the Caribbean) claimed the festival as their own, in conjunction with an increasing sense of collective West Indies culture. The festival did not begin as a Caribbean celebration, but as people from the West Indies shared experiences of "unemployment, police harassment and poor housing conditions" during the 1970s, they began to define themselves as a local culture and redefined the festival as a West Indian celebration.

RURAL LOCAL CULTURES

Members of local cultures in rural areas often have an easier time maintaining their cultures because they are more isolated. By living together in a rural area, members of a local culture can more easily keep external influences on the outside. It is no accident that we find Anabaptist groups, such as the Hutterites, the Amish, and the Mennonites, living in rural areas of South Dakota, Pennsylvania, Virginia, Saskatchewan, and Alberta. During the Protestant Reformation in Europe, Anabaptists broke from both the Catholic Church and the new Protestant churches. Followers of the new religion were called Anabaptists (which means "baptized again") because of their belief in the importance of adult baptism, even if they had already been baptized as infants.

Anabaptists broke from the state as well as the church; they embraced pacifism and soon suffered persecution. In response, Anabaptists migrated east to Moravia and Austria, and then to Russia and the Ukraine, continually moving to rural areas to live apart and avoid persecution. A group of Anabaptists called the Hutterites, named for leader Jacob Hutter, eventually migrated to North America in the second half of the 1800s.

The popular media portrays Old Order Anabaptist groups in stereotypical ways, suggesting all groups are the same, but major differences exist between Old Order Amish, Mennonites, Hutterites, and Brethren. The Hutterites are the only Anabaptist group that lives communally (Figure 8.10). Rather than living with immediate family on a farmstead, Hutterites live in colonies of about 100 people, with individuals ranging in age from infant to elderly. There are 461 colonies in North America, with more than half located in Manitoba and Alberta (Figure 8.11).

FIGURE 8.10 Hutterite Women. A group of Hutterite women near Strathmore, Alberta. (Suzy Thompson/CPI/The Canadian Press)

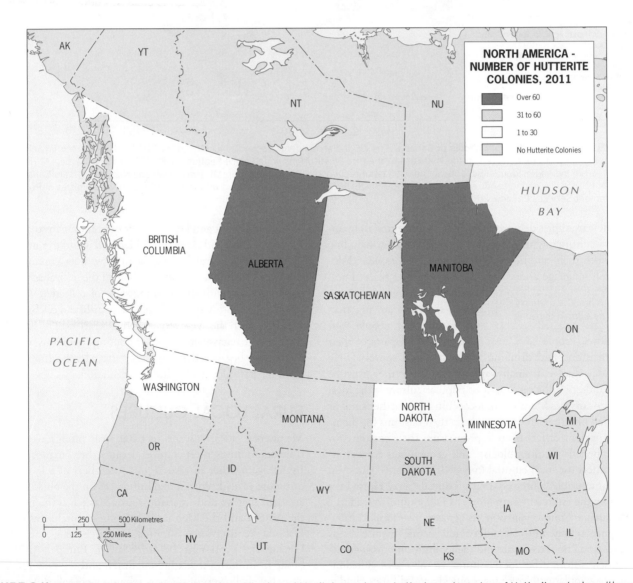

FIGURE 8.11 Hutterite Colonies in North America. Alberta and Manitoba are home to the largest number of Hutterite colonies, although there are groups throughout the four western provinces and five U.S. states. Data from www.hutterites.org/geographicaldistribution.htm. Accessed November 21, 2011.

In their book *On the Backroad to Heaven*, Donald Kraybill and Carl Bowman explain that the linchpin of each colony is the Hutterite religion. Members of the colony join together every night for a 30-minute service as well as on Sundays. The most prominent position in a colony is held by the minister, who speaks in archaic German, reading sermons written in the 16th century.

Unlike the Amish, Hutterites readily accept technologies that help them in their agricultural pursuits. However, they do not accept technologies such as televisions, cameras, and cell phones, which encourage individualistic behaviours or undermine the Hutterite religion. Colonies assign separate jobs and tasks to men and women, which reinforces a patriarchal social structure. Kraybill and Bowman explain that marriages happen across colonies, and women move to their husband's colony after marrying. As a result, a single colony is usually composed of only one or two surnames. Moving to their husband's colony perpetuates women's weak political position in the society. Women are expected to rear many children, averaging five or six currently, but the colony as a whole is responsible for raising and disciplining the children.

Hutterite colonies specialize in diversified agriculture, raising feed, food, and livestock on landholdings as big as 10,000 acres. Hutterite men often barter with neighbouring farmers to fix machinery, trade goods, and lend help. Aside from shopping, it is uncommon for most people in the colony to interact with outsiders. The minister serves as liaison with the outside world, and he works with lawyers and bankers to keep the colony corporation operating smoothly and profitably. The most economically successful colonies have created agricultural products, such as stainless steel animal feeders or animal feed, that they produce in their shops and sell to other farmers. Some colonies have also invested hundreds of thousands of dollars in computerized milking systems for their dairy operations or computerized systems for feeding and raising hogs.

Geographer Dawn Bowen has traced the migration of Mennonites, finding their desire to farm in rural areas led them to the northern reaches of Alberta, where they turned forestlands into farmlands, and as far away as Bolivia to find a place where they could farm, establish their own schools, and practise their religion without pervasive pressures from the popular culture. Rurality can make it much easier for local cultures to keep their culture intact by separating them from other local cultures and from popular culture. Rurality also enables local cultures to define their own space; to create a place, a town, that reflects their values; and to practise their customs unfettered in that place. When a local culture discontinues its major economic activity, it faces the challenge of maintaining the customs that depended on the economic activity and, in turn, sustaining its culture. In the modern world, when a local culture decides to reengage in a traditional economic activity or other cultural custom, it must navigate the limitations and perceptions imposed by different governments and cultures on a variety of scales. In Canada, for example, we often see conflicts between Aboriginal groups, the local community, and the provincial and federal governments over hunting, fishing, and trapping in traditional Aboriginal territories. Conflicts arise where Aboriginals are not required to obtain a licence for these activities, but other groups are required to obtain licences.

URBAN LOCAL CULTURES

Some local cultures have successfully built a world apart, a place to practise their customs, within a major city by constructing tight-knit neighbourhoods. Hasidic Jews in Montreal; the Chinese community in Vancouver; the Afro-Canadian population in Preston, Nova Scotia; and the Sikh community in Richmond, British Columbia, are all able to maintain their distinct local cultures in urban environments. Canada's three "gateway" cities—Toronto, Vancouver, and Montreal—all have vibrant communities. Montreal, with its strong French and English communities, is also home to a variety of ethnic neighbourhoods. Approximately 250,000 Italian Canadians live in Montreal, concentrated in Little Italy and Lasalle, and Italian is the third-most-spoken language in the city. While Montreal's Italian neighbourhoods tend to be family-centred and less apt to establish cultural points of interest outside of the home, the city's Irish community has a more visible presence. Pointe-Saint-Charles and Griffintown are home to a long-standing Irish community that arrived in Montreal after the potato famine in 1847 (Figure 8.12). Upon settling into these two working-class neighbourhoods, the Irish built their own schools, churches, and hospitals.

Several smaller minority neighbourhoods make up the diversity of Montreal. A large Haitian community has emerged since the 1990s; in fact, most Haitians who immigrate to Canada settle in Montreal, and while most are working class, there is a growing number of small businesses, including restaurants, Haitian imports, and travel agencies, to support this community. As well, the Greek community maintains a strong presence, including a large Greek festival organized by the Hellenic Community of Montreal. Finally, Montreal is home

FIGURE 8.12 Ancient Order of Hibernians, Pointe-Saint-Charles, Montreal, 2009. Members of the Ancient Order of Hibernians arrive at St. Gabriel's Church in Pointe-Saint-Charles, which was the starting point of the march to the Black Rock to commemorate the Irish immigrants who died of typhus in Montreal after fleeing the potato famine in 1847. (Graham Hughes/*The Montreal Gazette*)

(a)

(b)

FIGURE 8.13 Gladstone Hotel, Parkdale, (a) circa 1950s and (b) 2011. Built in 1889, the Gladstone Hotel is the oldest continuously operating hotel in Toronto. Located on Queen Street West in the Parkdale neighbourhood, the hotel's rich history—from its heyday in the early 1900s, through its decline in the 1970s, to its current restoration and renaissance as an arts/culture destination and boutique hotel—follows the ebbs and flows of the Parkdale neighbourhood. (Courtesy of the Gladstone Hotel; G. Brown)

to Canada's largest Arab community, according to the 2001 Census, and it too maintains strong social ties, with small businesses emerging to support this demographic group.

Having their own neighbourhood enables members of a local culture in an urban area to set themselves apart and practise their customs. Schools, houses of worship, food stores, and clothing stores all support the aesthetics and desires of members of the local culture. The greatest challenge to local cultures in cities is the migration of members of the popular culture or another local culture group into their neighbourhood. Members of local cultures in Toronto's Parkdale neighbourhood are being challenged by young artists and professionals who are moving into the neighbourhood. Rents and housing costs are rising, and the cultural landscapes are starting to reflect the neighbourhood's new residents, with artistically painted old warehouses converted into residences alongside art galleries and new boutiques and bistros (Figure 8.13).

COMMODIFICATION AND AUTHENTICITY OF PLACES

Local cultures often work to avoid **cultural appropriation**, the process by which other cultures adopt customs and knowledge and use them for their own benefit. In our globalizing world, as Simon Harrison explains, cultural appropriation is a major concern for local cultures because aspects of cultural

> **Cultural appropriation** The process by which cultures adopt customs and knowledge from other cultures and use them for their own benefit.

knowledge, such as natural pharmaceuticals or musical expression, are being privatized by people outside the local culture and used to accumulate wealth or prestige. This is another reason why local cultures might work to keep their customs and knowledge to themselves.

Geographers see both of these processes—cultural preservation and appropriation—happening within local cultures around the world: local cultures desire to keep popular culture out, keep their culture intact, and maintain control over customs and knowledge. Geographers also recognize that through these actions, places become increasingly important. By defining a place (such as a town or neighbourhood) or a space for a short amount of time (such as an annual festival) as quintessentially representing the local culture's values, members of that local culture reinforce their culture and their beliefs. In the process, a local culture can re-establish customs, recreate entire towns, or establish urban neighbourhoods.

The process by which something that was not previously regarded as an object to be bought or sold (e.g., a name, a good, an idea, or even a person) becomes an object that can be bought, sold, and traded in the world market is called **commodification**. One need look no further than eBay

> **Commodification** The process through which something is given monetary value. Commodification occurs when a good or an idea that previously was not regarded as an object to be bought and sold is turned into something that has a particular price and that can be traded in a market economy.

to see commodification. Newspapers frequently report on bizarre objects, such as a cough drop belonging to former California governor Arnold Schwarzenegger or a person's vote for a London mayoral election, being commodified in Internet space.

Commodification affects local cultures in numerous ways. First, material culture such as jewellery, clothing, food, and games, can be commodified by members of the culture or by non-members. Similarly, nonmaterial culture, including religion, language, and beliefs, can be commodified, often by non-members selling local spiritual and herbal cures for ailments. Local cultures may be commodified as a whole, as when tour buses take tourists to "observe" the Amish culture of Lancaster, Pennsylvania, or when hikers trek with "traditional" Nepalese guides on spiritual journeys through the Himalayas. The inukshuk, a traditional Inuit marker of location and direction, has been appropriated by others and can be found in urban gardens and at the side of highways—literally "out of place" in the landscape—and most notably used as the logo for the Vancouver 2010 Winter Olympics (Figure 8.14). Maintaining nonmaterial and material culture while recognizing that culture is not static or fixed is complicated and is a major concern for many groups, from the local neighbourhood to the nation state.

When aspects of a culture are commodified and detached from the culture in which they had significance, the question of **authenticity** follows. Usually one image or experience is typecast as the "authentic" image or experience of that culture (e.g., the igloo for the Inuit, or a horse-drawn buggy for the Mennonites), and it is that image or experience that the tourist or buyer desires. However, local cultures are dynamic, and places and people change over time. An "authentic" local culture cannot be conveyed by a single experience or image, nor can it be represented by an object from a bygone time. Rather, a local culture is complex, multi-dimensional, and constantly changing. To gain a sense of that culture, people need to experience its complexity directly in real time.

> **Authenticity** In the context of local cultures or customs, the accuracy with which a single stereotypical or typecast image or experience conveys an otherwise dynamic and complex local culture or its customs.

The complicated question of authenticity is raised when we examine how certain places are put on display for consumption by others. During the process of colonization, Europeans tagged the cultures they encountered as either savage or mystical. "Authentic" tourist destinations are designed to exploit the mystical or the imagined in local cultures. For example, a South African theme park, the Lost City (built on the site of the Sun City resort), capitalizes on mystical images of Africa described in a legend, thereby "freezing" the continent in a time that never existed (Figure 8.15).

In Canada, similar "living museums" have been created to represent and reflect our early history and provide an "authentic" Canadian historical experience. For example, Sainte-Marie Among the Hurons, near Midland, Ontario, preserves the history of a French Jesuit mission that existed on that site in the 17th century. Tourists can experience Canadian pioneer life (e.g., blacksmithing, cooking, family and community life); learn about the introduction of Christianity to First Nations

FIGURE 8.14 Commodification of Cultural Symbols. The commodification of cultural forms became one of the most blogged about critiques of the 2010 Olympic Games held in Vancouver, specifically the appropriation of the inukshuk for the Games' logo. (© Jennifer Mackenzie/Alamy)

FIGURE 8.15 Sun City, South Africa. The Lost City theme park in Sun City evokes the mystical images of Africa described in a legend. (© Lindsay Hebberd/Corbis Images)

peoples; and walk through a longhouse, among other architectural recreations. Another example is Louisbourg, Nova Scotia (Figure 8.16). Operated as a National Historic Site by Parks Canada, Louisbourg is the largest reconstructed 18th-century fortified French town in North America. The fortress of Louisbourg recreates for its visitors stories of a soldier's life, tales of operating the seaport, building techniques, and religious life, among other things. Both Louisbourg and Sainte-Marie Among the Hurons offer their visitors "authentic"

FIGURE 8.16 Fortress of Louisbourg, Nova Scotia. This national historic site provides visitors with the "authentic" soldier's experience at an 18th-century fortified French town. (Parks Canada/Photographer: Dale Wilson, 2010)

historical experiences, but it is important to remember that a very linear, tidy history is told through these sites.

The commodification of local customs freezes them in place and time for consumption, where claims of "authenticity" abound. The search for "authentic" local cultures implies an effort to identify peoples who are untouched by change or external influence. However, all local cultures (rural and urban) are dynamic, and all have been touched by external influences throughout their existence. The search for an "authentic" local culture merely perpetuates myths about these cultures, whose members are constantly renegotiating their place in this world and making sense of who they are in the midst of the popular culture onslaught.

MAIN POINTS   8.3   How Are Local Cultures Sustained?

- Local cultures often work hard to preserve and maintain their distinctive cultures from the influence of cultural beliefs and norms that may emerge both within and beyond the place or region.

- Local cultures can work for cultural preservation and against cultural appropriation through the practice of local customs, through legislative and policy protection, and through boundary control.

- Local cultures can experience the process of commodification, by which something (e.g., a name, a good, an

idea, a place, or even a person) that was not previously regarded as a sellable item becomes an object that can be bought, sold, and traded in the world market.

- When aspects of a culture are commodified and detached from the culture in which they had significance, the question of authenticity follows. Often a commodity freezes a particular culture in time and does not reflect accurately the complexity of the culture being represented.

8.4 How Is Culture Diffused?

DIFFUSION OF POPULAR CULTURE

Over the past century, the time it takes for people, innovations, and ideas to diffuse around the world has changed dramatically. The early innovations in agriculture that transformed groups of hunter-gatherers into agrarian societies took nearly 10,000 years to diffuse globally. In more recent times, the diffusion of developments such as the printing press or the technologies of the Industrial Revolution was measured in decades or centuries. During the 1900s, the pace of diffusion shrank to months, weeks, days, and in some cases even hours. Simultaneously, the spatial extent of diffusion has expanded, so that more and more parts of the Earth's surface are affected by ideas and innovations from faraway places. For example, as of 2010, the social networking site Facebook had over 400 million subscribers and added many new members each day. In Canada, 16 million people were on Facebook, and in May 2010, 912,000 new

subscribers were added in one month alone. With that many subscribers and various forms of instant communication, news can travel quickly through the Facebook network.

In the past few decades, major world cities have become much closer to each other as a result of modern technologies, including airplanes, high-speed trains, expressways, telephones and fax machines, wireless connections, and e-mail. Conversely, places that lack transportation and communications technologies are now more removed from interconnected places than ever. All of the new technologies create the infrastructure through which innovations diffuse. Because the technologies link some places more closely than others, ideas diffuse through interconnected places rapidly rather than diffusing at constant rates across similar distances.

HEARTHS OF POPULAR CULTURE

As we saw in the section on local culture, even local customs practised for centuries in one place can be swept up into popular culture. How does a custom, idea, song, or object become part of popular culture? It is relatively easy to follow the communications, transportation, and marketing networks that account for the diffusion of popular culture, but how do we find the hearths of popular culture, and how do certain places establish themselves as the hearths of popular culture?

All aspects of popular culture—music, sports, television, and dance—have a hearth, a place of origin. Typically, a hearth begins with contagious diffusion: developers of an idea or innovation may find they have followers who dress as they do or listen to the music they play. A multitude of Canadian musical singers and groups (e.g., Tragically Hip, Bedouin Soundclash, Alexisonfire, Moist) began as college bands or in college towns. They played a few sets in a campus bar or at a campus party and gained followers. The group then started to play at bars and campuses in nearby college towns and soon began selling self-made compact discs at their concerts.

Bands that begin on college campuses or in college towns and build from their base typically follow the path of building a hearth for their sound's diffusion first through contagious diffusion and then through hierarchical diffusion. The Tragically Hip formed in 1983 and created and perfected their sound in Kingston, Ontario, during the mid to late 1980s (Figure 8.17).

The band's members met while still high school students at Kingston Collegiate Vocational Institute, and they attended Queen's University together. Represented early on by Kingston music agent Bernie Dobson, they had limited success playing Rolling Stones and Doors cover music. Their early days were spent playing small venues throughout Ontario, carving out a niche for themselves against the tide of American bands. One of the members, Rob Baker, says, "When we started out, there were a lot of Canadian bands that were trying to look and sound like American bands, and dropping American place names and things as if that would somehow ingratiate themselves into the American market. We found that kind of repulsive." The Tragically Hip's unique sound and contagious diffusion brought them to the attention of

record producers, and they were signed by MCA after playing the Horseshoe Tavern in Toronto in 1987. They didn't gain the attention of critics, however, until 1989 with their album *Up to Here*.

Hierarchical diffusion of the band soon followed. College charts were attracted to the Hip's unique sound, and they began extensive club and concert tours. Their 1992 album *Road Apples* won six Juno awards and two Much Music video awards. They also developed Another Roadside Attraction, a series of tours that raised money for international charities. The Hip has achieved much success in Canada, releasing 12 studio albums, 2 live albums, and 46 singles. Beginning in the late 1990s, the band was heavily promoted internationally but experienced limited success, playing smaller venues in the U.S. and Europe. While the Hip has been heavily promoted in the United States, the group has never really sought "breakthrough" success there. Their distinct Canadian sound and references to Canadian places and stories remain central to their music. For example, they have written songs about Group of Seven affiliate painter Tom Thomson, explorer Jacques Cartier, Toronto Maple Leaf Bill Barilko, and the wrongful conviction of David Milgaard.

The landscape of music production, distribution, and consumption has changed drastically due to processes of digitization and the proliferation of the Internet, particularly social networking platforms like Facebook and Twitter. While contagious and hierarchical diffusion continue to be important aspects of the development of popular culture hearths, digital hearths are becoming increasingly significant. Real-time streaming of live concerts over the Internet is beginning to occur. In 2009, for example, a Phish concert was streamed live from an iPhone, and fans at the show were tweeting updates constantly to those at home. YouTube has been crucial to the diffusion of music, as bands who lack the resources to tour, or who choose not to tour for environmental reasons, are able to promote their music by posting videos on the service. The importance of MySpace and Facebook, where users can be "friends" with bands, or become "fans," cannot be downplayed.

MANUFACTURING A HEARTH

Even in this age of powerful social networking and varied digital possibilities, the question of whether a college band "makes it" depends greatly on the choices and actions of record producers and music media corporate giants. Corporations such as Viacom, the parent company of MTV, generate and produce popular culture, pushing innovations through the communications infrastructure that links it with the rest of the world (Figure 8.18). Geographer Clayton Rosati studied the infrastructure of MTV and its role in the production of popular culture and geographies of popular culture. In his study, he found that MTV produces popular culture by opening globalized spaces to local culture, thereby globalizing the local. Rosati explained that "MTV's incorporation of rap music and Hip Hop expressive forms into its production since 1997" helped produce music celebrities and opened the MTV space to "artists and forms that were often formerly relegated to street corners, block parties and mix tapes—broadening the unification of popular aspirations with the machinery of the industrial production of culture."

FIGURE 8.17 Tragically Hip, Hamilton Place, 2009. A Canadian band, the Hip have much success in Canada but have not actively sought a greater international following, choosing instead to live and work in the Kingston, Ontario, area. (© Igor Vidyashev/Alamy)

FIGURE 8.18 Filming of Total Request Live Show at MTV Studios, New York. MTV's highly visible location in Times Square reflects the network's global reach and influence. (© James Leynse/Corbis)

A 2001 documentary produced by PBS, The Merchants of Cool, looked at the roles corporations and marketing agencies play in creating popular culture. By conducting focus groups with teenagers (the main demographic for innovations in popular culture), by amassing enormous databases of what teenagers do and like, by sending "cool hunters" ("cool" kids themselves) out to talk with other "cool" kids about what is "cool," and by rummaging through teenagers' bedrooms (which, Rosati noted, is what MTV does for casting its reality shows), MTV and marketing companies create what is cool and new in popular culture. The Merchants of Cool producers interviewed Sharon Lee, one of the founding partners of Look-Look, a research company specializing in youth culture, who explained how trends in popular culture are spread from the hearth:

> Actually it's a triangle. At the top of the triangle there's the innovator, which is like 2 to 3 percent of the population. Underneath them is the trend-setter, which we would say is about 17 percent. And what they do is they pick up on ideas that the innovators are doing and they kind of claim them as their own. Underneath them is an early adopter, which is questionable exactly what their percentage is, but they kind of are the layer above mainstream, which is about 80 percent. And what they do is they take what the trendsetter is doing and they make it palatable for mass consumption. They take it, they tweak it, they make it more acceptable, and that's when the mass consumer picks up on it and runs with it and then it actually kills it.

This description is a perfect story of the hierarchical diffusion of traits and trends in popular culture.

With these kinds of infrastructure behind the production of popular culture, we may expect popular culture to act as a blanket, evenly covering the globe. However, even as popular culture has diffused throughout the world, it has not blanketed the world, hiding all existing local cultures underneath it. Rather, one aspect of popular culture (such as music or food) will take on new forms when it encounters a new locality and the people and local culture in that place. Geographers and anthropologists

call this the **reterritorialization** of popular culture: a process by which people start to produce an aspect of popular culture themselves, doing so in the context of their local culture and place, and making it their own.

> **Reterritorialization** With respect to popular culture, a process where people within a place start to produce an aspect of popular culture themselves, doing so in the context of their local culture and making it their own.

STEMMING THE TIDE OF POPULAR CULTURE— LOSING THE LOCAL?

The policies of assimilation practised by colonial powers such as Great Britain, France, and by the Canadian, American, Russian, Australian, and New Zealand governments, were official policies designed for the express purpose of disrupting and changing indigenous, local cultures. Western, democratic governments no longer have official policies of assimilation. Yet for people in many local cultures and in regions that are not hearths of popular culture, popular culture itself can feel like a policy of assimilation.

The influence of western Europe, North America, and Japan in global popular culture makes many people feel threatened by cultural homogenization, especially as popular media such as music, television, and film now diffuse so quickly around the world. If you turn on the television in Harare, Zimbabwe, you can easily find reruns of a 10-year-old American television show or a contemporary CNN broadcast. If you walk down the street in Seoul, South Korea, you might hear a radio broadcasting a song recorded by the Beatles, Madonna, or Justin Timberlake. If you go to a cinema in Santiago, Chile, you can choose among several recently released American films.

The rapid diffusion of popular culture can cause consumers to lose track of the hearth of a good or idea. For example, the Nintendo Wii was, like most video game consoles and games, created in Japan, but the diffusion of the Wii into households and even retirement homes throughout North America was embraced by Americans and Canadians alike, because it has not been seen as a threat to local culture.

However, when the diffusion of popular culture displaces or replaces local culture, it may be met with resistance. In response to the influx of American movies, the Canadian government heavily sponsors its domestic film industry. Ever since the National Film Board was founded in 1939, films have been seen as an important tool for the project of nation-building and cultural coherence in Canada. Both federal and provincial policy has supported not only the production and distribution of Canadian films, but also the making of U.S. films in Canada, thereby providing employment and creative opportunities to "Hollywood North." The largest source of financial support for Canadian film and television production is Telefilm Canada, a federal Crown corporation that oversees the Canadian Feature Film Fund. However, there are also a variety of provincial and private funds available, including the Bell Broadcast and New Media Fund, Bravo!Fact, Cogeco Program Development Fund, and Independent Production Fund, among others. In a market where 90 percent of the feature films shown in Canadian theatres are American, financial support for the production, distribution, and exhibition of Canadian films is critical to the sustainability of the industry. Thanks to this support, Canadian films have received critical acclaim on the international stage, and Canadian filmmakers such as Denys Arcand, Atom Egoyan, David Cronenberg, and Deepa Mehta have become well-known globally (Figure 8.19).

Canada has also developed a series of Canadian content (CanCon) regulations for its music and television industries to ensure that Canadian content receives adequate exposure to the Canadian marketplace. The Canadian Radio-television and Telecommunications Commission (CRTC) oversees the implementation of CanCon regulations, which state, generally, that 35 percent of the music played on English pop music radio stations between 6:00 a.m. and 6:00 p.m. on weekdays must be Canadian. For French language radio, 55 percent must be Canadian within the same parameters. A recording is deemed to be Canadian if it meets two of the following criteria (known as the MAPL system): the music is composed by a Canadian (M), the artist who performs music and/or lyrics is Canadian (A), the recording is produced in Canada (P), and the lyrics are written by a Canadian (L). Scholars such as Scott Henderson (2008) have argued that the presence of the quota system has led to the development of a "Canadian scene" that previously did not exist. It is important to mention, as well, that digitization and the pervasiveness of the Internet have called into question the logic of the policy because it is nearly impossible to regulate music, television, and film downloading and file sharing.

Concern over the loss of local distinctiveness and identity is not limited to particular cultural or socio-economic settings.

FIGURE 8.19 Denys Arcand Wins Academy Award. In 2004, Canadian filmmaker Denys Arcand won the Academy Award for Best Foreign Language Film for his 2003 release, *The Barbarian Invasions*. (Laura Rauch/AP/The Canadian Press)

Such concern is also present among the dominant societies of wealthier countries, where it is reflected in everything from the rise of religious fundamentalism to the establishment of semi-autonomous communes in remote locations; among minorities (and their supporters) in wealthier countries, where it can be seen in efforts to promote local languages, religions, and customs by constructing barriers to the influx of cultural influences from the dominant society; among political elites in poorer countries, who promote a nationalist ideology that is explicitly opposed to cultural globalization; and among social minorities in poorer countries, who seek greater autonomy from regimes promoting acculturation or assimilation to a single national cultural norm.

Geographers realize that local cultures will interpret individual cultural productions in very different ways, depending on the cultural context in which they view them. What people choose to adopt from popular culture, how they reterritorialize it, and what they reject helps shape the character and culture of people, places, and landscapes.

Cultures are made up of a number of characteristics, from music and dress to religion and languages. Geographers can study one particular **cultural trait** or aspect of a complex cultural system of practices to understand how it has diffused geographically or been transformed. Two fundamental cultural traits are language and religion. Throughout the course of human history, both religious belief systems and languages have travelled the globe, creating connections and associations across vast networks of peoples and places. Understanding how language and religion are diffused across a variety of scales helps us to understand the formation and transformation of these networks.

> **Cultural trait** A single element of normal practice in a culture, such as the wearing of a turban.

LANGUAGE AND CULTURAL DIFFUSION

A scene in Quentin Tarantino's cult classic movie *Pulp Fiction* shows Vincent and Jules in the front seat of a car, talking about France. Vincent, trying to demonstrate his knowledge of French culture, turns to Jules and says, "You know what they call a ....a ....a quarter pounder with cheese in Paris?" Jules replies, "They don't call it a quarter pounder with cheese?" Vincent, ever the expert, explains in a few choice words that France uses the metric system and that the French would not know what a quarter pounder is. Then he explains, "They call it a 'royale' with cheese." Jules, surprised, asks, "What do they call a Big Mac?" Vincent explains, "Well a Big Mac is a Big Mac, but they call it 'Le Big Mac.'"

This humorous exchange juxtaposes two opposing forces in our globalized world: globalization of culture and preservation of local and national culture. Are the two contradictory, or can we have globalization of restaurants, food, music, and culture while preserving local languages?

Language is a fundamental element of local and national culture. The French government has worked diligently, even aggressively, to protect the French language, dating back to 1635 and the creation of the Académie française, an institution charged with standardizing and protecting the French language.

INTERNET CONTENT, BY LANGUAGE

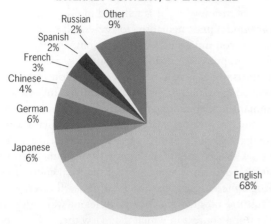

INTERNET USERS, BY LANGUAGE SPOKEN

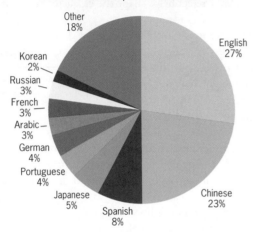

TOP 10 LANGUAGES, BY MILLIONS OF SPEAKERS

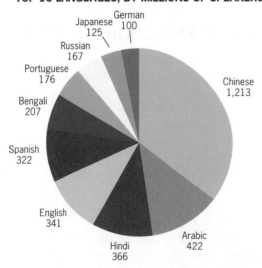

FIGURE 8.20 Languages Used on the Internet. Data from Internet World Stats: Usage and Population Statistics, www.internetworldstats.com/stats7.htm.

In the last few decades, diffusion of globalized terms into France has posed a huge challenge for the Académie française. With the support of many French people, the French government passed

a law in 1975 banning the use of foreign words in advertisements, television and radio broadcasts, and official documents unless no French equivalent could be found. In 1992, France amended its constitution to make French the official language. In 1994, the French government passed another law to stop the use of foreign (mainly English) words in France, with a hefty fine imposed for violations. The law mandates French translations for globalized words and requires that accepted French terms be used in official communications rather than anglicizations like "le meeting," "le weekend," "le drugstore," or "le hamburger." The Internet, where more than 65 percent of all content is in English (Figure 8.20), has posed another set of challenges. Some of the translations the Académie requires are somewhat cumbersome—for example, the official French term for e-mail is "courrier electronique," and the official term for hacker is "pirate informatique." In addition to demonstrating the conflicting forces of globalized language and local or national language, the example of France reveals that language is much more than a set of sounds and symbols used to communicate. It is also an integral part of culture, reflecting and shaping it.

This helps illustrate the claim that language is one of the cornerstones of culture; it shapes our very thoughts. We can use vast vocabularies to describe new experiences, ideas, and feelings, or we can create new words that represent these things. Who we are as a culture, as a people, is reinforced and redefined moment by moment through shared language. Language reflects where a culture has been, what a culture values, even how people in a culture think about, describe, and experience things.

Perhaps the easiest way to understand the role of language in culture is to examine people who have experienced the loss of language under pressure from others. During colonization, both abroad and within countries, colonizers commonly forced the colonized people to speak the language of the colonizer. These language policies continued in many places until recently and were enforced primarily through public (government) and church (mission) schools.

American, Canadian, Australian, Russian, and New Zealand governments each had policies of forced assimilation during the 20th century, including rules that did not allow indigenous peoples to speak their native languages. For example, the United States forced American Indians to learn and speak English. Both mission schools and government schools enforced English-only policies in hopes of assimilating American Indians into the dominant culture. In an interview with the producers of the educational video *Alaska: The Last Frontier*, Clare Swan, an elder in the Kenaitze band of the Dena'ina Indians in Alaska, eloquently describes the role of language in culture:

No one was allowed to speak the language—the Dena'ina language. They [the American government] didn't allow it in schools, and a lot of the women had married nonnative men, and the men said, "You're American now so you can't speak the language." So, we became invisible in the community. Invisible to each other. And, then, because we couldn't speak the language—what happens when you can't speak your own language is you have to think with someone else's words, and that's a dreadful kind of isolation. [emphasis added]

Shared language makes people in a culture visible to each other and to the rest of the world. Language helps to bind a cultural identity. Language is also quite personal. We articulate our thoughts, expressions, and dreams in our language; if we lose that ability, we lose a lot of ourselves. Language can reveal much about the way people and cultures view reality. Some African languages have no word or term for the concept of a god. Some Asian languages have no tenses and no system for reporting chronological events, reflecting the lack of cultural distinction between then and now.

Language is so closely tied to culture that language is often found at the heart of cultural conflict and political strife. The province of Quebec has passed several laws that promote the use of the province's distinct version of the French language. In 1974, the Quebec National Assembly passed the Official Language Act (Bill 22), making French the sole language in the province. This was replaced in 1977 by the Charter of the French Language (Bill 101). The Charter made French the official language of education, business, legislation, and commercial signage in the province. It is important to remember, however, that Canada is officially bilingual, as stipulated in the federal Official Languages Act (established in 1969 and substantially amended in 1988), which reflects the colonial division of the country between France and Great Britain. This means that federal government documents, for example, are printed in both English and French. However, most of the country's French speakers live in the province of Quebec.

In recent history, the Québécois have periodically called for more independence for their province within Canada, even voting on secession twice, in the Quebec referendums of 1980 and 1995. Although a majority has never voted for secession,

it continues to be a contentious issue within the province, and in Canada more broadly. As mentioned, Bill 101 compelled all businesses in the province to demonstrate that they functioned in French. When this law came into effect, many businesses and individuals moved out of the province of Quebec into neighbouring Ontario. In 1993, the Quebec government passed a law requiring the use of French in advertising. The law allowed the inclusion of both French and English (or another language) on signage, as long as the French letters were twice the size of the other language's letters.

Not all of Quebec's residents identify with the French language. Within the province, a small proportion of people speak English at home, others speak indigenous languages (Figure 8.21), and still others speak another language altogether—one associated with their country of origin. When the Quebec National Assembly passed laws promoting French during the 1980s and 1990s, members of Canada's First Nations, such as the Cree and Mohawk (who live in Quebec), expressed a desire to remain part of Canada should Quebec secede from the country. During the same period, Quebec experienced an influx of international migrants, many of whom seek residence in the province as a way to enter Canada and North America at large. Under Quebec law, these new immigrants must learn French.

Calls for independence in Quebec are waning as the separatist political party has captured fewer seats in recent parliamentary elections for the province. Nonetheless, the Québécois still feel a connection to France (Figure 8.22), and the province even has a presence in Paris in the *Maison du Québec* (House of Quebec), an embassy-like entity representing the province. As people, ideas, and power flow through the province, change will continue. Yet the province's laws, programs, and presence in France, and the desire of the Québécois to remain loyal to their French language, will at the very least keep the language alive as the province continues to experience change.

FIGURE 8.21 Street Signs in Cree Native Language, English, and French in the Cree Nation of Mistissini, Quebec. Though French dominates in Quebec, other languages are also spoken. (© Megapress/Alamy)

FIGURE 8.22 A Building Displays the Flags of France and Quebec in the Historic District of Quebec City. The Québécois continue to strive to maintain their ties to France and their French language and culture. (© North Wind Picture Archives/Alamy)

MAPPING LANGUAGES

One way we can understand how language is diffused is to examine where certain languages are spoken—mapping languages. The first step in mapping the distribution of world languages is to classify languages. Linguists and linguistic geographers classify languages in terms that are also used in biology because, like species, some languages are related and others are not. At the global scale, we classify languages into language families. Members within a single language family have a shared but fairly distant origin. We break language families into sub-families (divisions within a language family) where the commonalities are more definite and the shared origin is more recent. Completing the categorization are individual languages, covering a smaller extent of territory, and dialects, covering the smallest extent of territory.

The world map of languages in Figure 8.23 maps 15 major **language families**. The Indo-European language family stretches across the greatest extent of territory and also claims the greatest number of speakers. Within the Indo-European language family, English is the most widely spoken language. Speakers of English encircle the world, with 300 million in North America, 64 million in Great Britain and Ireland, and 22 million in Australia and New Zealand. Hundreds of millions of people in India, Europe, and Africa use English as a second language.

> **Language family** Group of languages with a shared but fairly distant origin.

The world map of language families shows several language families spoken by dwindling, often marginally located or isolated groups. The Indo-European languages of European colonizers surround the language families of Southeast Asia. Languages in the Austro-Asiatic language family survive in the interior of eastern India and in Cambodia and Laos. Languages in the Austronesian family are numerous and quite diverse, but

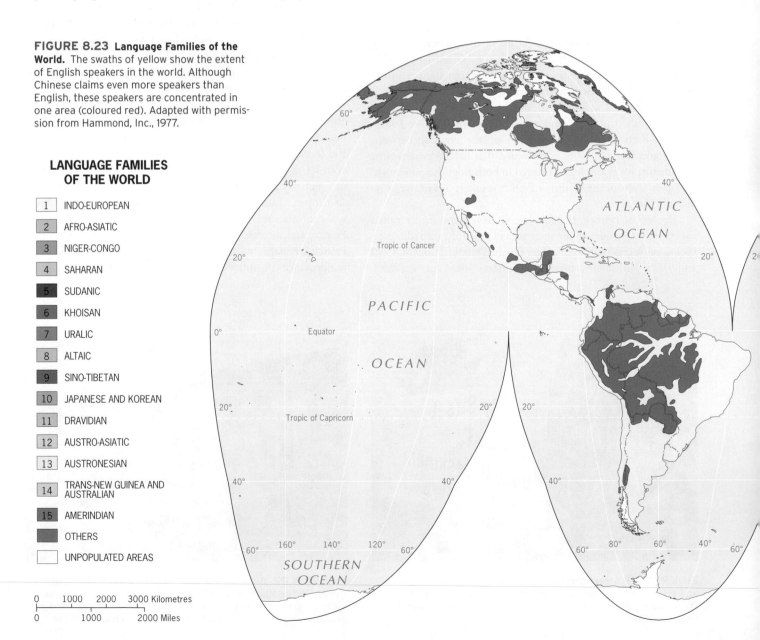

FIGURE 8.23 Language Families of the World. The swaths of yellow show the extent of English speakers in the world. Although Chinese claims even more speakers than English, these speakers are concentrated in one area (coloured red). Adapted with permission from Hammond, Inc., 1977.

LANGUAGE FAMILIES OF THE WORLD

1. INDO-EUROPEAN
2. AFRO-ASIATIC
3. NIGER-CONGO
4. SAHARAN
5. SUDANIC
6. KHOISAN
7. URALIC
8. ALTAIC
9. SINO-TIBETAN
10. JAPANESE AND KOREAN
11. DRAVIDIAN
12. AUSTRO-ASIATIC
13. AUSTRONESIAN
14. TRANS-NEW GUINEA AND AUSTRALIAN
15. AMERINDIAN

OTHERS

UNPOPULATED AREAS

0 1000 2000 3000 Kilometres

0 1000 2000 Miles

many of the individual languages are spoken by fewer than 10 million people. Remoteness helps account for the surviving languages in the Amerindian language family. These languages remain strongest in areas of Middle America, the high Andes, and northern Canada.

Just a few thousand years ago, most habitable parts of the Earth were characterized by a tremendous diversity of languages. However, with the rise of empires under the rule of larger-scale, more technologically sophisticated and literate societies, some languages began to spread over larger areas. By 2,000 years ago, languages such as Chinese and Latin had successfully diffused over large regions. The Han Empire in China and the Roman Empire in Europe and North Africa knit together large swaths of territory, encouraging the diffusion of one language over these regions. The most powerful and wealthiest people were the first to learn Chinese and Latin in these empires, as they had the most to lose by not learning the languages. Local languages and illiteracy continued among the poor in the empires, and some blending of local with regional languages occurred. When the Roman Empire disintegrated, some places within the region discontinued interaction, prompting a round of linguistic divergence.

Johann Gutenberg perfected the movable-type printing press in Germany in 1440. Twelve years later he printed the first Gutenberg Bible (the sacred text for Christians), which brought the scriptures out of churches and monasteries. The Gutenberg press diffused quickly in the century following—throughout Europe and beyond—and allowed for unprecedented production of written texts in languages besides Latin. Gutenberg's press made it possible to print the Bible in one's own language, such as French or German, rather than Latin, which helped to standardize European languages and spread literacy.

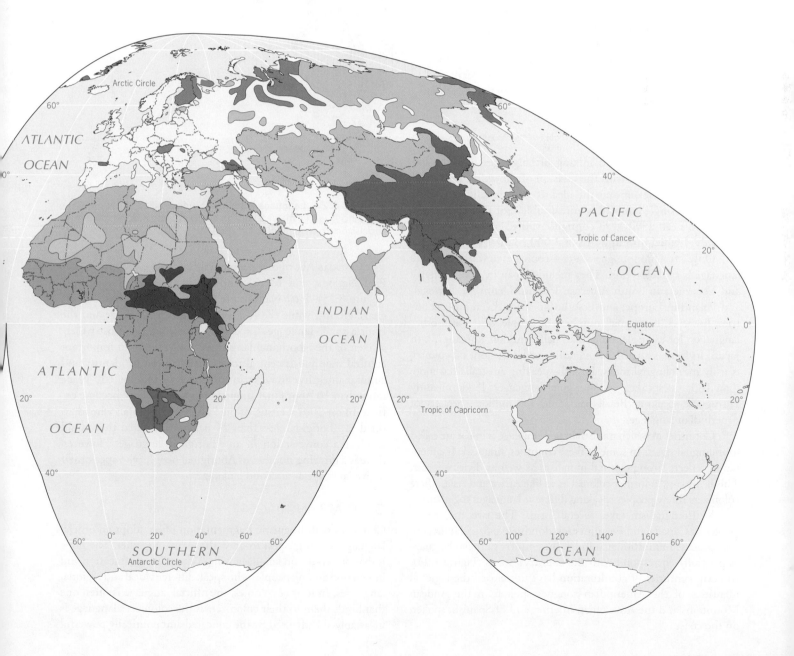

The rise of relatively large nation-states was equally important (see Chapter 3), for these political entities had a strong interest in promoting a common culture, often through a common language (such as French or Dutch). Political elites who were literate and had access to written texts brought peoples together and played a key role in distributing printed texts. Moreover, as the leaders of countries such as England and Spain sought to expand their influence overseas through mercantilism and colonialism, they established networks of communication and interaction, helping to diffuse certain languages over vast portions of the Earth's surface.

Over the last 500 years, the world's people have had innumerable opportunities for spatial interaction and, as a result, contact between and among languages. The increasing contact has encouraged the formation of new languages to bridge linguistic gaps in trade and commerce, has spurred language replacement (in which one language replaces another), and has encouraged language extinction (which occurs when a language no longer has any native speakers). The modern world also provides technology to preserve and stabilize languages and supports institutions that teach languages to large numbers of people.

MULTILINGUALISM

Widespread diffusion and mixing of languages over the last 500 years, combined with the division of the world into more than 200 countries, means the idea of a single language being spoken in a single country is unrealizable. For that to happen, we would need a world of contiguous, discrete languages territorially divided into upwards of 3,000 countries.

Only a few monolingual states—countries in which only one language is spoken—exist. They include Japan in Asia; Uruguay and Venezuela in South America; Iceland, Denmark, Portugal, and Poland in Europe; and Lesotho in Africa. Even these countries, however, have small numbers of people who speak other languages; for example, more than half a million Koreans live in Japan. In fact, as a result of migration and diffusion, no country is truly monolingual today. English-speaking Australia has more than 180,000 speakers of Aboriginal languages. Predominantly Portuguese-speaking Brazil has some 1.5 million speakers of Amerindian languages.

Countries in which more than one language is in use are called multilingual states. In some of these countries, linguistic fragmentation reflects strong cultural pluralism as well as divisive forces. This is the case in former colonial areas like Africa and Asia, where colonizers threw peoples speaking different languages together.

Multilingualism takes several forms. The two major languages in Canada and Belgium each dominate particular areas of the country. In multilingual India, the country's official languages generally correspond with the country's states (Figure 8.24). In Peru, centuries of acculturation have not erased the regional identities of the Amerindian tongues spoken in the Andean Mountains and the Amazonian interior, and of Spanish, spoken on the coast.

FIGURE 8.24 Language Families of India. India's states generally coincide with a major language family or language. Adapted with permission from Hammond, Inc., 1977.

Canada's Aboriginal peoples fall into three groups—Inuit, First Nations, and Métis—and speak a variety of languages (Figure 8.25). First Nations are thought to have over 10 language groups, while the Métis have a mixed language and the Inuit a single language. Cree and Ojibwe are the most widely spoken of the Aboriginal languages. Language is an important cultural trait and is central to the preservation of identity and cultural integrity. Some estimate that over the last 100 years, more than 10 Aboriginal languages in Canada have become extinct. In the 2001 Census, of the 976,300 individuals who identified as Aboriginal, less than 24 percent indicated they could conduct a conversation in an Aboriginal language. However, there is a growing number of Aboriginal people who speak their native language as a second language.

OFFICIAL LANGUAGES

Countries with linguistic fragmentation often adopt an official language (or languages) to draw the people together. The hope is that one common language will promote communication and interaction among peoples who speak different local and regional languages. In former colonies, the official language is often one that binds them to their colonizer, as the colonizer's language is invariably already used by the educated and politically powerful

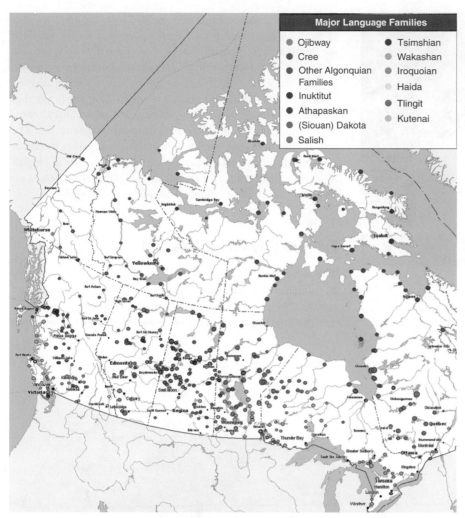

Major Language Families	
● Ojibway	● Tsimshian
● Cree	● Wakashan
● Other Algonquian Families	● Iroquoian
● Inuktitut	● Haida
● Athapaskan	● Tlingit
● (Siouan) Dakota	● Kutenai
● Salish	

FIGURE 8.25 Languages of Canada's Aboriginal Peoples. The main Aboriginal language families of Canada are distributed across the country. Aboriginal Languages by Community, 1996, http://atlas.nrcan.gc.ca/site/english/maps/peopleandsociety/lang/aboriginallanguages/bycommunity. Reproduced with the permission of Natural Resources Canada 2011, courtesy of the Atlas of Canada.

The official languages in a country are a reflection of the country's history. In Peru, Spanish and the Amerindian language Quechuan have official status and are found in distinct regions. In the Philippines, English (spoken primarily in Manila) and a creolized Spanish called Pilipino are both official languages. Tiny Singapore, the city-state at the tip of the Malay Peninsula, has four official languages: English, Chinese, Malay, and Tamil (an Indian tongue). India is the country with the largest number of official languages—22 if we include both official languages listed in the country's constitution and official languages proclaimed by states within India.

The European Union is not a country, but it recognizes 23 official languages, and the United Nations has 6 official languages. In each of these cases, the international organization offers simultaneous translation in all the official languages to any member of the parliament (European Union) or the general assembly (United Nations) who requests it. Each international organization also publishes paper documents and maintains its website in all official languages.

GLOBAL LANGUAGE

What will the global language map look like 50 years from now? More and more people are using English in a variety of contexts. It is now the standard language of international business and travel, much of contemporary popular culture bears its imprint, and the computer and telecommunications revolution relies heavily on the use of English terminology. Does this mean that English is on its way to becoming a global language?

If a global language is the principal language people use around the world in their day-to-day activities, the geographical processes we have examined so far emphatically do not point to the emergence of English as a global tongue. Population growth rates are generally lower in English-speaking areas than they are in other areas, and there is little evidence that people in non-English-speaking areas are willing to abandon their local language in favour of English. Indeed, since language embodies deeply held cultural views and is a basic feature of cultural identity, many people actively resist switching to English.

Yet if a global language is a common language of trade and commerce used around the world, the picture looks rather different. Although not always welcomed, the trend throughout much of the world is to use English as a language of cross-cultural communication—especially in the areas of science, technology, travel, and business. Korean scholars are likely to communicate with their Russian counterparts in English; Japanese scientific journals are increasingly published in English; Danish tourists

elite. Reflecting its colonial heritage, Canada has two official languages. Many former African colonies have adopted English, French, or Portuguese as their official language, even though they have gained independence from former imperial powers. Thus, Portuguese is the official language of Angola, English is the official language of Nigeria and Ghana, and French is the official language of Côte d'Ivoire.

Such a policy is not without risks. In some countries, including India, citizens objected to using a language (English in India) that they associated with colonial repression. Some former colonies chose not just one but two official languages: the European colonial language plus one of the country's own major languages. English and Hindi are official languages of India. Similarly, English and Swahili are official languages of Tanzania. In Mauritania, French and Arabic are official languages. But this solution was not always enough. When India gave Hindi official status, riots and disorder broke out in non-Hindi areas of the country. Kenya, which at first made English and Swahili its official languages, decided to drop English in the face of public opposition to rules requiring candidates for public office to pass a test of their ability to use English.

FIGURE 8.26 Hindu Crematorium, Mombasa, Kenya. In Kenya, the predominant religion is Christianity, which is the faith of some 66 percent of the population, followed by Islam, at about 10 percent. A Hindu temple is an unusual feature in the Kenyan landscape. (© H. J. de Blij)

visiting Italy may use English to get around; and the meetings of most international financial and governmental institutions are dominated by English. Under these circumstances, the role of English as an international language of commerce will grow.

We must be careful in this conclusion, however. Anyone looking at the world 200 years ago would have predicted that French would be the principal language of cross-cultural communication in the future. Times are different now, of course. The role of English in the computer revolution alone makes it hard to imagine a fundamental shift away from the dominance of English in international affairs. Yet economic and political influences on language use are always in flux, and nothing is inevitable.

DIFFUSION OF RELIGION

The cultural landscape is marked by religion—most obviously by churches and mosques, cemeteries and shrines, statues and symbols (Figure 8.26). Other more subtle markers of religion dot the landscape as well. The presence or absence of stores

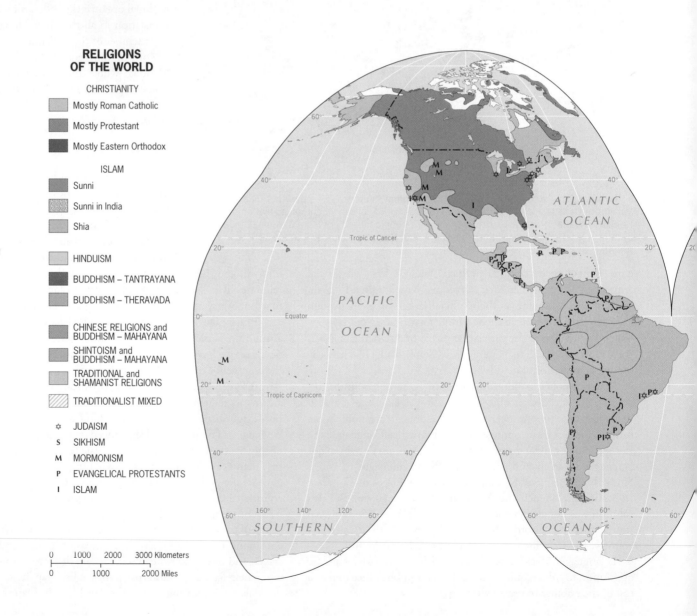

RELIGIONS OF THE WORLD

CHRISTIANITY
- Mostly Roman Catholic
- Mostly Protestant
- Mostly Eastern Orthodox

ISLAM
- Sunni
- Sunni in India
- Shia

- HINDUISM
- BUDDHISM – TANTRAYANA
- BUDDHISM – THERAVADA
- CHINESE RELIGIONS and BUDDHISM – MAHAYANA
- SHINTOISM and BUDDHISM – MAHAYANA
- TRADITIONAL and SHAMANIST RELIGIONS
- TRADITIONALIST MIXED

✡ JUDAISM
S SIKHISM
M MORMONISM
P EVANGELICAL PROTESTANTS
I ISLAM

selling alcohol or of signs depicting the human form in particular ways reflect prevailing religious views. Religion is also proclaimed in modes of dress (e.g., veils, turbans) and personal habits (e.g., beards, ritual scars). The outward display of religious beliefs often reveals the inward structure of a religion. For example, in the Islamic Republic of Pakistan in 1991, the government proclaimed that possessing a beard would be a condition for the appointment of judges. The beard requirement is an outward display of religion, and it also shows the inward structure of Islam in Pakistan, where women are not in a place of power.

Although religious beliefs and prescriptions influence many societies, secularism now prevails in others. In these places, religion, at least in its organized form, has become less significant in the lives of most people. But even in secular societies, religion permeates art, history, customs, and beliefs. Indeed, no matter what society you come from, religion influences what you eat, when you work, when you shop, and what you are allowed to do. In short, organized religion has a powerful effect on human societies. It has been a major force in combating social ills, sustaining the poor, promoting the arts, educating the deprived,

and advancing medical knowledge. However, religion has also blocked scientific study, encouraged the oppression of dissidents, supported colonialism and exploitation, and condemned women to an inferior status in many societies. Religion is, if nothing else, one of the most complex—and often controversial—aspects of the human condition.

THE WORLD MAP OF RELIGIONS TODAY

The map in Figure 8.27 provides an overview of the distribution of the world's major religions. Any map of world religions is a generalization, and we must use caution when drawing conclusions from the map. First, the shadings on the map show the major religion in an area, thereby masking minority religions, many of which have significant numbers of followers. India, for example, is depicted as a Hindu region (except in the northwest), but other religions, such as Islam and Sikhism, attract millions of adherents (e.g., 150 million Muslims live in India). Second, some of the regions shown as belonging to a particular religion are places where faiths have penetrated relatively recently and where

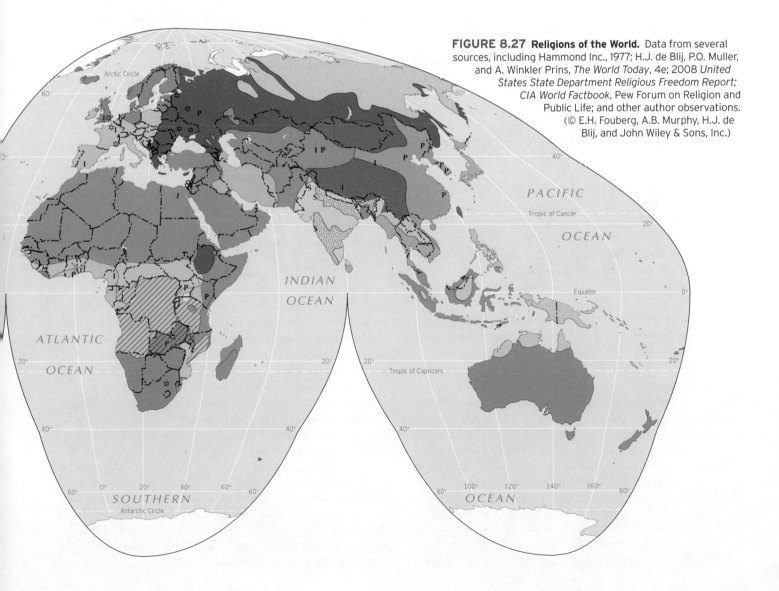

FIGURE 8.27 Religions of the World. Data from several sources, including Hammond Inc., 1977; H.J. de Blij, P.O. Muller, and A. Winkler Prins, *The World Today*, 4e; 2008 *United States State Department Religious Freedom Report; CIA World Factbook*, Pew Forum on Religion and Public Life; and other author observations. (© E.H. Fouberg, A.B. Murphy, H.J. de Blij, and John Wiley & Sons, Inc.)

TABLE 8.1	Adherents to Major World Religions	
Religion	Number of Adherents	Percent of Global Total
Christianity	2.1 billion	33%
Islam	1.3 billion	21%
Hinduism	950 million	14%
Buddhism	347 million	6%
Traditional beliefs	250 million	5%
Sikhism	24 million	0.36%
Judaism	13 million	0.22%

Data from *The Atlas of Religion*, Joanne O'Brien and Martin Palmer, 2007.

traditional religious ideas influence the practice of the dominant faith. Many Christian Africans, for example, continue to believe in traditional powers even as they profess a belief in Christianity. Finally, in a number of areas many people have moved away from organized religion entirely. Thus, France appears on the map as a Roman Catholic country, yet a significant number of French people profess adherence to no particular faith.

Despite these limitations, the map does illustrate how far Christian religions have diffused (2.1 billion adherents worldwide), the extent of the diffusion of Islam (1.3 billion), the connection between Hinduism (950 million adherents) and one of the world's major population concentrations, and the continued importance Buddhism (347 million followers) plays in parts of Asia. Many factors help explain the distributions shown on the map, but one in particular is a characteristic that each of the widespread religions shares: they are all universalizing religions. This means they actively seek converts because they view themselves as offering belief systems of universal appropriateness and appeal. Christianity, Islam, and Buddhism all fall within this category (Table 8.1).

Universalizing religions are relatively few in number and of recent origin. Throughout much of human history, most religions have not actively sought converts. Rather, a given religion has been practised by one particular culture or group. In any religion, adherents are born into the faith and converts are not actively sought. Religions tend to be spatially concentrated—as is the case with traditional religions in Africa and South America (250 million followers). The principle exception is Judaism (13 million adherents), a religion whose adherents are widely scattered as a result of forced and voluntary migrations.

THE RISE OF SECULARISM

The world map of religion might mislead us into assuming that all or even most of the people in areas portrayed as Christian or Buddhist do in fact adhere to these faiths. This is not the case. Even the most careful analysis of worldwide church and religious membership produces a total of about 4 billion adherents—in a world population of over 6 billion. Hundreds of millions of people are not counted in this figure because they practise traditional religions. But even when these people are taken into account, additional hundreds of millions do not practise a religion at all. Moreover, even church membership figures do not accurately reflect the number of active members of a church. When polled about their church-going activities, less than 3 percent

of the population of Scandinavia reported frequent attendance, and in France and Great Britain, less than 10 percent reported attending church at least once a month. The lack of members, active or otherwise, underscores the rise of secularism—indifference to or rejection of organized religious affiliations and ideas.

The level of secularism throughout much of the Christian and Buddhist world varies from country to country and regionally within countries. In North America, for instance, a poll in 2002 asked people whether religion was very important to them. Only 30 percent of Canadians agreed it was very important, whereas 59 percent of Americans felt religion was very important to them. In France, in an effort to assert secularism in government-funded institutions, the government banned the wearing of overt religious symbols in public schools. The French government wanted to remove the "disruption" of Muslim girls wearing *hijab* (head scarves), Jewish boys wearing yarmulke (skullcaps), and Christian students wearing large crosses to school. The French government took the position that banning all religious symbols was the only egalitarian approach.

In some countries, anti-religious ideologies contribute to the decline of organized religion. For example, church membership in the former Soviet Union, which dropped drastically during the 20th century under communist rule, rebounded after the collapse of the Soviet system but to much lower numbers. Maoist China's drive against Confucianism was, in part, an anti-religious effort, and China continues to suppress some organized religious practices.

In many areas labelled Christian on the world map of religions, from Canada to Australia and from the United States to western Europe, the decline of organized religion as a cultural force is evident. In the strongly Catholic regions of southern Europe and Latin America, many people are dissatisfied with the papal teachings on birth control as the desire for larger families wanes. In Latin America, the Catholic Church is being challenged by rapid social change, the diffusion of other evangelical Christian denominations into the region, and sexual abuse scandals similar to those that have occurred in the United States and Canada.

Secularism has become more widespread during the past century. People have abandoned organized religion in growing numbers. Even if they continue to be members of a church, their participation in church activities has declined. Traditions have also weakened. For example, there was a time when almost all shops and businesses were closed on Sundays, preserving the day for sermons, rest, and introspection. Today, shopping centres are mostly open as usual, and Sunday is increasingly devoted to business and personal affairs, not church. We can see the rise of secularism among Christians in Canada first-hand when we explore our neighbourhood on a Sunday morning and compare the number of people wearing casual clothes and hanging out at the coffee shop reading newspapers with the number of people attending church services.

The division between secularism and fervent adherence is not confined to the Christian world. Secularism is growing in South Korea, where half the population does not profess adherence to any particular religion. And although major faiths are experiencing an overall decline in adherence, several smaller religions are growing in importance, including Baha'i, Cao Dai, Jainism, and the Spiritual Church of Brazil.

- Cultural traits can be diffused across a variety of scales, from the local to the global. This diffusion can occur through simple word of mouth and local circulation or through global transportation, marketing, and communication networks. Diffusion can occur quite rapidly or take place over many centuries.

- The major world religions—Buddhism, Christianity, Hinduism, Islam, and Judaism—can be traced from their respective hearths through their global circulation over many centuries. In their travels, religions have been transformed as they were taken up in distinctive ways in specific locations.

- North America, Japan, and Europe dominate popular culture with the rapid diffusion of music, fashion, arts, television shows, literature, and games across the globe. For some local cultures, this raises concerns about cultural homogenization and the loss of particular local customs and traits. Diffusion may be so rapid and ubiquitous that knowledge of the original hearth may be lost.

- Concern over the loss of a traditional culture is also a concern for countries in the global north that are experiencing rapid changes as a result of immigration and secularization. This is evident in the rise of some forms of religious fundamentalism and the implementation of restrictive immigration policies.

8.5 How Is Culture Reflected in the Landscape?

The tension between popular and local culture can be seen in the cultural landscape—the visible imprint of human activity on the physical environment. Cultural landscapes reflect the dominant values, norms, and aesthetics of a culture. On major roadways in North American towns and suburbs, the landscape is a series of big box stores, gas stations, and restaurants that reflect popular culture (Figure 8.28). As you drive down one of these roadways, one town or city looks like the next. You drive past Tim Horton's, KFC, Walmart, Boston Pizza, and McDonald's. Then, several miles down the road, you pass another conglomeration (clustering) of the same stores. Geographer Edward Relph (1976) coined the word **placelessness** to describe the loss of uniqueness of place in the cultural landscape to the point that one place looks like the next.

> **Placelessness** The loss of uniqueness of place in the cultural landscape so that one place looks like the next, as defined by geographer Edward Relph.

Cultural landscapes can contain similar meanings and symbols across a variety of locations, places, and regions. This is usually the result of several factors, including (1) the broad diffusion of particular architectural forms and planning ideas; (2) the widespread visibility of individual businesses and products; and (3) the wholesale borrowing of idealized landscape images in ways that promote a blurring of place distinctiveness.

The global diffusion of the skyscraper provides a clear illustration of the first point—particular architectural forms and planning ideas have diffused around the world (Figure 8.29). In the second half of the 1800s, with advances in steel production and improved costs and efficiencies of steel use, architects and engineers created the first skyscrapers (the Home Insurance Building of Chicago, completed in 1885, is typically pointed to as the very first one). The fundamental difference between a skyscraper and another building is that the outside walls of the skyscraper do not bear the major load or weight of the building; rather, the internal steel structure or skeleton of the building bears most of the load. Once those first skyscrapers appeared in the U.S., commercial centres of

FIGURE 8.28 Tim Hortons, Napanee, Ontario. This photograph was taken in 2009 in Napanee, Ontario, but it could be anywhere in Canada. (© Kathy deWitt/Alamy)

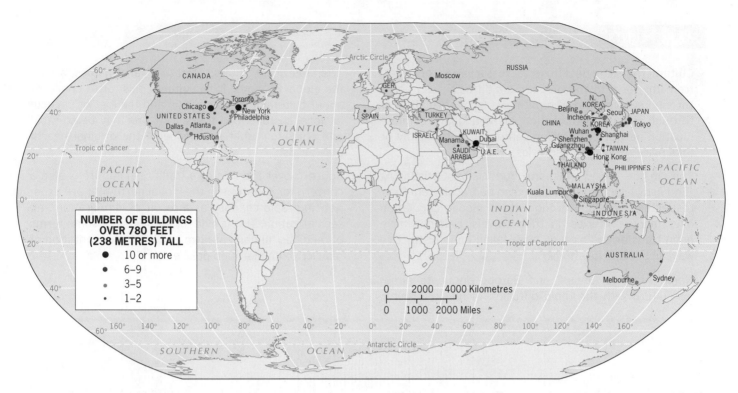

FIGURE 8.29 World Distribution of Skyscrapers. Skyscrapers, buildings taller than 700 feet (213 metres), can be seen in all parts of the world, though this architectural form originated in the United States. Data from Emporis Inc., 2005.

major cities began to be dominated by tall buildings, many of which have been designed by the same architects and engineering firms. From Singapore to Johannesburg and from Caracas to Toronto, the cultural landscape of cities has been profoundly impacted. Skyscrapers require substantial land clearing in the vicinity of individual buildings, the construction of wide, straight streets to promote access, and the reworking of transportation systems around a highly centralized model. The proliferation of skyscrapers in Taiwan, Malaysia, and China in the 1990s marked the arrival of these economies as major players in the world economy. Today, the appearance of skyscrapers in Dubai, United Arab Emirates, signals the world city status of the place.

Reading commercial signs is an easy way to see the second dimension of cultural landscape convergence: the far-flung stamp of global businesses on the landscape. Walking down the streets of Rome, you will see signs for Blockbuster and Pizza Hut. The main tourist shopping street in Prague hosts Dunkin' Donuts and McDonald's. A tourist in Munich, Germany, will wind through streets looking for the famed beer garden, the Hofbrauhaus, and will happen upon the Hard Rock Cafe right next door. Marked landscape similarities such as these can be found everywhere from international airports to shopping centres. The global corporations that develop spaces of commerce have wide-reaching impacts on the cultural landscape.

Architectural firms often specialize in building one kind of space—for example, performing arts centres, medical laboratories, or international airports. Property management companies have worldwide holdings and encourage the Gap, the Cheesecake Factory, Barnes and Noble, and other companies to lease space in all of their properties. As a result, all facilities, such as airports and college food courts, begin to look the same, even though they are separated by thousands of miles.

The third dimension of cultural landscape convergence is the wholesale borrowing of idealized landscape images across the world. As you study the cultural landscape, you may notice landscape features transplanted from one place to another, regardless of whether that feature even "fits."

The strip in Las Vegas, Nevada, represents an extreme case of this tendency, with various structures designed to evoke different parts of the planet. The popular Venetian Hotel and Casino, for example, replicates the Italian city of Venice, including canals. The Las Vegas Sands Corporation, a casino developer and owner, recently built a new Venetian Hotel and Casino across the Pacific in Macao (formerly a Portuguese port that became part of China again in 1999). The Venetian Macao Resort cost $2.4 billion and is three times the size of the largest casino in Las Vegas (Figure 8.30). Gambling is illegal in mainland China, but Macao's special status has allowed gambling to grow on the small island.

(a)

(c)

(b)

FIGURE 8.30 Venice in Italy, Las Vegas, and Macao. (a) Venice, Italy, is an internationally renowned tourist destination. (b) The Venetian Hotel and Casino in Las Vegas is an attempt to create an "authentic" Venetian experience at a casino. (c) The Venetian Macao Resort is another example of cultural borrowing as the global city becomes a local attraction. The diffusion of popular culture through such media as film and television enables us to "read" the Las Vegas and Macao images as Venice, even if we have never actually been in Italy. (Cindy Milter Hopkins/Danita Delimont; © David Noble Photography/Alamy; © Paul Yeung/Reuters/Landov)

> **Global-local continuum** The notion that what happens at the global scale has a direct effect on what happens at the local scale, and vice versa. This idea posits that the world comprises an interconnected series of relationships that extend across space.

In less obvious ways, cultural borrowing and mixing happens all around the world. This borrowing and mixing is behind the concept of the **global-local continuum**, a notion that emphasizes that what happens at one scale is not independent of what happens at other scales. Human geography is not simply about documenting the differences between places; it is also about understanding the processes unfolding at different scales that produce those differences. What happens in an individual place is the product of interaction across scales. People in a local place mediate and alter regional, national, and global processes, in a process called *glocalization* (described in Chapter 2). The character of place ultimately arises from a multitude of dynamic interactions between local distinctiveness and events and influences on a wider scale.

RELIGIOUS LANDSCAPES IN CANADA

One of the most important and visible cultural landscapes are those related to religion. Canada has historically been a Christian country, though this may be gradually changing. Statistics Canada captures information on religious affiliation in the nation usually every 10 years, the last time being the 2001 Census (Table 8.2). Results of this most recent study indicate that Canada remains predominantly Roman Catholic and Protestant, with 7 out of 10 Canadians reporting one of these two affiliations. In 2001, Roman Catholics comprised 43 percent of those reporting religious affiliations; Protestants, 29 percent. Historically, Protestants outnumbered Roman Catholics in Canada. In 1901, for instance, Protestants accounted for well over half of all religious affiliations in Canada (56 percent). However, that changed in the 1971 Census, which reported Roman Catholic affiliation had surpassed Protestant (48 percent and 44 percent respectively). Part of the reason for the shift is immigration patterns. Since the 1960s, Roman Catholic has been the predominant faith of new immigrants to Canada.

TABLE 8.2	Major Religious Denominations, Canada, 1991[1] and 2001				
	2001		1991		Percentage change 1991–2001
	Number	%[3]	Number	%[3]	
Roman Catholic	12,793,125	43.2	12,203,625	45.2	4.8
Protestant	8,654,845	29.2	9,427,675	34.9	-8.2
Christian Orthodox	479,620	1.6	387,395	1.4	23.8
Christian, not included elsewhere[2]	780,450	2.6	353,040	1.3	121.1
Muslim	579,640	2.0	253,265	0.9	128.9
Jewish	329,995	1.1	318,185	1.2	3.7
Buddhist	300,345	1.0	163,415	0.6	83.8
Hindu	297,200	1.0	157,015	0.6	89.3
Sikh	278,415	0.9	147,440	0.5	88.8
No religion	4,796,325	16.2	3,333,245	12.3	43.9

[1] For comparability purposes, 1991 data are presented according to 2001 boundaries.
[2] Includes persons who report "Christian," as well as those who report "Apostolic," "Born-again Christian," and "Evangelical."
[3] Percentages do not add up to 100 due to rounding.
Source: Data from Statistics Canada.

However, these numbers are shrinking. Together, the total reported Roman Catholic and Protestant affiliations fell by 8 percent between 1991 and 2001. They are giving way to increased affiliations with Islam, Hinduism, Sihkism, and Buddhism, among others. Due to the shifts in immigration discussed in Chapter 5, which have led to a more diverse population overall, it stands to reason that religious affiliations are changing as well. There are fewer European-based immigrants, and an increase in those coming from Asia, the Middle East, and other regions. The largest increase was in the number of people who identified as Muslim, which grew 121 percent over the 10-year period and now represents 2 percent of the total population (up from 0.9 percent in 1991). The number who identified as Hindu and Sikh increased by 89 percent each, and the number who identified as Buddhists increased by 84 percent. It is important to note, as well, that there are more people reporting no religious affiliation; over 16 percent of Canadians reported no religious affiliation in 2001, up from 12 percent in 1991.

It is interesting to note the geographical propensity of religious affiliations in Canada. For example, nearly half of the country's Roman Catholic population is located in Quebec, accounting for 83 percent of the total provincial population. Roman Catholics also made up 54 percent of the population of New Brunswick. The lowest proportion of Roman Catholics was found in British Columbia (17 percent of the population). Ontario was home to 73 percent of the Hindu population, 61 percent of the Muslim population, and 38 percent of Sikhs, according to the 2001 Census data. Nearly half of the Sikh population was located in British Columbia. The highest proportion of people reporting no religion was found in the Yukon (37 percent), closely followed by British Columbia (35 percent) and

Alberta (23 percent). The lowest proportion of those reporting no religious affiliation was found in Newfoundland (2 percent), followed by Quebec (6 percent).

Religion marks cultural landscapes with houses of worship (e.g., churches, mosques, synagogues, and temples), with cemeteries dotted with religious symbols and icons, with stores that sell religious goods, and even with services provided to religious adherents who travel to sacred sites—places or spaces people infuse with religious meaning. Members of a religious group may define a space or place as sacred out of either reverence or fear. If a sacred site is held with reverence, adherents may be encouraged to make a pilgrimage to the sacred site for rejuvenation, reflection, healing, or fulfillment of a religious commitment.

Canada demonstrates considerable diversity in its religious cultural landscapes. Sacred places and spaces mark the Canadian landscape in particular ways, rendering visible the cultures of various belief systems. When we pass through cities and towns, we see a variety of churches, cathedrals, synagogues, mosques, and houses of assembly, and we "read" these architectures to get a sense of local populations (Figure 8.31).

Sacred places in Canada are sometimes spaces of controversy and even violence. First Nations land is particularly emblematic of the struggle over land and its cultural meaning. For example, a dispute over the lands of Ipperwash Provincial Park in Ontario goes back to 1942, when the Government of Canada implemented the *War Measures Act* and expropriated lands belonging to the Stony Point band to build a military base, Camp Ipperwash. The Stony Point band fought for years, claiming that the land contained a sacred burial ground destroyed during the making of the military base. In 1993, still with no resolution, Stony Point band members began moving back onto the land, and the military withdrew. However, in 1995, during a confrontation on these sacred lands with the Ontario government, Stony Point band member Dudley George was shot and killed by a member of the Ontario Provincial Police. The lands were returned to the Kettle and Stony Point First Nation in 1998, and a public inquiry into George's death was held in 2007. One of the inquiry reports discusses the difficulty in identifying Aboriginal burial grounds, stating that governments will not accept First Nations' identification of burial grounds, but,

rather, require physical proof, which usually means uncovering remains. Moreover, as these sacred grounds are not marked in ways easily identifiable to non-First Nations people, they are often not discovered until the graves have been disturbed, usually for urban development, archaeological research, or road building. Efforts are being made to establish better connections between local First Nations groups and local and regional governments to ensure sacred places such as burial grounds are found before such places are disturbed.

(a)

(b)

(c)

FIGURE 8.31 Religious Landscapes. (a) Sainte-Anne-du-Beaupré Roman Catholic church, 30 kilometres east of Quebec City, receives more than half a million pilgrims each year. (b) Visitors to the Swaminarayan Mandir Hindu temple in Toronto marvel at its unique and intricately hand-carved marble structure. (c) Congregation Emanu-El in Victoria, British Columbia is the oldest surviving synagogue in Canada, dating back to 1859. Its building is a national historic site. (Andrew Gunners/Photodisc/Getty Images; © Oleksiy Maksymenko/All Canada Photos/Corbis; Congregation Emanu-El, Victoria, B.C.)

- Cultural landscapes reflect the dominant values, norms, and aesthetics of a culture.

- Cultural landscapes can contain similar meanings and symbols across a variety of locations, places, and regions. This is usually a product of (1) the broad diffusion of particular architectural forms and planning ideas; (2) the widespread visibility of individual businesses and products; and/or (3) the wholesale borrowing of

idealized landscape images in ways that promote a blurring of place distinctiveness.

- Cultural landscapes are the product of interaction across scales. People in a local place mediate and alter regional, national, and global processes, in a process called glocalization. The character of place ultimately arises from a multitude of dynamic interactions between local distinctiveness and events and influences on a wider scale.

SUMMARY

Cultural geographers study how culture—a set of shared belief systems, norms, and values practised by a particular group of people—is reflected in landscapes and the built environment. Some geographers regard culture as a "way of life" that becomes visible in building styles, music, food, fashion, and language.

Geographers have approached the study of culture in different ways. The work of Carl Sauer and the Berkeley School dominated geographical enquiry until the 1960s. This intellectual approach saw culture as a unified active agent in creating or determining a cultural landscape that was in a constant state of transition. With the social and political upheavals in the global north during the 1960s and 1970s, geographers began to focus on whether a culture was universally shared by all individuals in a particular place or region. Given that individuals experienced places differently based on race, gender, class, and sexual orientation, geographers began to argue that what was visible in the landscape was in fact the dominant cultural beliefs, norms, and values, and different cultural perspectives were rendered invisible. Geographers such as Don Mitchell went so far as to argue that there is no such thing as culture.

Geographers who accept the view that there is a discernable thing called "culture" that can be studied have

traditionally described cultures as fitting along a continuum from local to popular. Local cultures are groups of people associated with particular locations, places, or regions who understand that they share experiences, customs, and traits, and who work to preserve those traits and customs in order to claim uniqueness and to distinguish themselves from others. Local cultures often have to work hard to preserve their culture and avoid its commodification and appropriation. In contrast, popular culture is dominant and ubiquitous and often changes rapidly. Given that cultures can be subject to appropriation and rapid change, questions are raised about the authenticity of certain places and practices and the potential to "freeze" certain groups in both place and time.

Geographers can trace the diffusion of culture or particular cultural traits, such as language or religion, from their hearths. In the case of religion, scholars can trace the diffusion of the world's major cultures around the globe. Popular culture, particularly from the global north, can diffuse rapidly around the world and, in some cases, raise concerns about the preservation of local cultures. On the other hand, some traditional cultures in the global north express concern at the apparent loss of their cultural values, and we see the rise of religious fundamentalism and more stringent immigration policies in response.

DISCUSSION AND REVIEW QUESTIONS

1. Discuss the story of the Tata Corporation and what it reveals about cultural geography in India and the role of globalization in shaping the experiences of a local cultural group.

2. Though culture is a highly contested concept, geographers and academics recognize that cultural groups can be viewed as displaying varying aspects of folk culture and popular culture. Compare and contrast the aspects

of folk culture with that of popular culture. How are both influenced by, and through, geographic scale? Can you think of any particular aspects of your cultural milieu that are rooted in folk customs or in popular culture?

3. Identify and explain the various means by which Canada has worked to preserve and maintain a distinctive, local, Canadian culture. What have been some of the positive and negative results of the Canadian approach?

4. Who are the Anabaptists and what has been their experience in North America? What influence does geography have on such cultural groups?

5. Geographers accept that cultural landscapes reflect the tensions between popular and local culture. One of the results of the tension, combined with the globalizing forces of the capitalist world economy, is, what Edward Relph called, "placelessness." What is placelessness and what are the factors that lead to it? Can you think of examples in your own context that reflect this placelessness? Conversely, can you identity unique places and what it is about them that makes them "unique"?

GEOGRAPHIC CONCEPTS

assimilation   222
authenticity   227
commodification   226
cultural appropriation   226
cultural landscape   216
cultural trait   231
culture   216
custom   223
folk culture   220
global-local continuum   243

hearth   221
hierarchical diffusion   221
language families   234
local culture   220
material culture   220
nonmaterial culture   220
placelessness   241
popular culture   220
reterritorialization   230

ADDITIONAL RESOURCES ONLINE

About the Hutterites: www.hutterites.org

Merchants of Cool: www.pbs.org/wgbh/pages/frontline/shows/cool

The Way the Music Died: www.pbs.org/wgbh/pages/frontline/shows/music

Last Call at the Gladstone Hotel: http://hotdocslibrary.ca/dsr/#/en/video/11105

Alaska: The Last Frontier? www.learner.org/resources/series85.html

chapter 9

AGRICULTURE

Winds of Change in Farming Communities

DRIVING through the Townships of Ashfield and Colborne in Ontario's Huron County on a sunny summer afternoon, one could clearly see the important role that agricultural activities play in the local economy. However, it is also evident that the individuals who own these farms have witnessed many significant changes in recent decades that have forced them to adapt their operations in order to remain competitive, both with their neighbours and with farm operators in other parts of the world. Indeed, the winds of change are blowing throughout Canada's agricultural sector. What was once the country's most prominent source of employment has become a relatively small part of the job market. There has been a trend to mechanization, replacing human labour with machine labour, along with a shift to industrialization and agribusiness (Figure 9.1). This has created challenges for the family farm, an important part of Canada's agricultural heritage.

Through an in-depth study of farming in Ashfield and Colborne, geographers John Smithers, Paul Johnson, and Alun Joseph found that farm families have adapted in a variety of ways to increasing global competition and other changes. Some have expanded and intensified their operations. By growing the size of their farms, purchasing the most up-to-date and efficient equipment, and specializing in only a few types of crops, these farmers are hoping to achieve the economies of scale needed to compete with large corporate-owned farms and with farmers in other countries, whose costs of production are often lower and are also often heavily subsidized by their governments. Other farmers have opted to diversify their operations by, for example, entering into the world of agri-tourism, in order to increase their incomes. Still others have found off-farm work, using the additional source of income to sustain the family farm through hard economic times, or have chosen to downsize their farms by selling or renting land, reducing the size of their herds, or leaving some of their fields to sit idle for one or more growing seasons. Many farm families have been forced to make a much more painful decision—to exit farming completely, often bringing to an end a lifestyle that had

FIGURE 9.1 Agricultural Activity in Huron County, Ontario.
(Andrew McLachlan/All Canada Photos/Getty Images)

been passed on from one generation to the next over a century or more.

Studies conducted by rural geographers such as Smithers, Johnson, and Joseph highlight the dynamism of family farming and of agriculture generally. They also focus on the ways in which global-scale processes have very local impacts. Indeed, geographical processes, such as the increasing international competition created by economic globalization, have significant impacts at the local scale, including at the level of the family farm.

KEY QUESTIONS FOR CHAPTER 9

1.   What is agriculture, and where did it begin?

2.   How did agriculture change with industrialization?

3.   What imprint does agriculture make on the cultural landscape?

4.   What is the global pattern of agriculture and agribusiness?

9.1 What Is Agriculture, and Where Did It Begin?

Agriculture is the deliberate tending of crops and livestock to produce food, feed, and fibre. As evidenced in the field note above, agriculture in Canada has changed enormously in the last 50 years, as it has in much of the rest of the world. However, this is just the latest episode in a human activity that has been going on for thousands of years. In this chapter we examine the origins of agriculture and trace the geography of change in agriculture across time to the latest movements in agricultural production, such as genetic modification, organic production, and the practice of sustainable agriculture. In the process, we describe the early hearths (source areas) of agriculture, the geography of technological changes in agriculture, global patterns of agricultural production, and the imprint of agriculture on the cultural landscape.

> **Agriculture** The purposeful tending of crops and livestock in order to produce food and fibre.

In this section of the chapter, we discuss how people lived before the origins of agriculture and the circumstances that gave rise to the invention of agriculture many millennia ago.

HUNTING, GATHERING, AND FISHING

Before agriculture, people subsisted on food they obtained through hunting, gathering, and fishing. What people hunted or gathered depended on the region, and the size of hunting and gathering clans varied according to climate and resource availability. Areas of abundance could support larger populations. For example, people living on the margins of forests could gather food in the forest when hunting yielded poor results and then return to hunting when opportunities improved. In contrast, people living in areas with only one source of food were likely to starve—or would be forced to move—if that food source disappeared.

Hunter-gatherers worked to perfect tools, control fire, and adapt environments to their needs. The first tools used in hunting were simple clubs—tree limbs that were thin at one end and thick and heavy at the other. When people began using bone and stone, and developing spears, their hunting technique became far more effective. Fashioning stone into hand axes and, later, handle axes was a crucial innovation that enabled hunters to skin their prey and cut the meat; it also made it possible to cut down trees and build better shelters and tools.

The controlled use of fire was another important early achievement of human communities. The first opportunities to control fire were offered by natural conditions (e.g., lightning strikes or spontaneous combustion of surface-heated coal). Archaeological finds at ancient settlement sites suggest that people would capture fire that was caused accidentally and would work to keep the fire burning continuously. Later, people learned they could generate fire by rapidly rotating a wooden stick in a small hole surrounded by dry tinder. Fire became the focal point of settlements, and the campfire became a symbol of the community. It was a means of making foods digestible and was also used to drive animals into traps or over cliffs.

In addition to hunting game on the land, humans harvested shellfish, trapped fish by cutting off small patches of standing water from the open sea, and invented tools to catch fish, including harpoons for spearing large fish, hooks for catching fish, and baskets to capture fish in streams that had fish runs.

Using tools and fire, human communities altered their environments, establishing more reliable food supplies by combining hunting and fishing with some gathering. They also migrated to take advantage of cyclical movements of fish and animals and to avoid exhausting the supply of edible plants in any one area.

THE FIRST AGRICULTURAL REVOLUTION

Plant domestication Genetic modification of a plant such that its reproductive success depends on human intervention.

Where did **plant domestication** begin? Geographer Carl Sauer believed that the experiments necessary to establish agriculture and settle in one place occurred in lands of plenty. Only in such places could people afford to experiment with raising plants or take the time to capture animals and breed them for domestication.

As part of a lifetime spent studying cultural origins and diffusion, Sauer closely examined the geography of early agricultural practices, focusing particularly on the location of the agriculture hearths and on the kinds of agricultural innovations that took place in those hearths. He suggested that Southeast and South Asia may have been the scene, more than 14,000 years ago, of the first domestication of tropical plants. There, Sauer believed, the combination of human settlements, forest margins, and freshwater streams may have given rise to the earliest planned cultivation of **root crops**—crops that

Root crop Crop that is reproduced by cultivating the roots of or the cuttings from the plants.

are reproduced by cultivating either the roots or cuttings from the plants (such as tubers, including manioc or cassava, yams, and sweet potatoes in the tropics). A similar development may have taken place later in northwestern South America.

The planned cultivation of **seed crops**, plants that are reproduced by cultivating seeds, is a more complex process that

Seed crop Crop that is reproduced by cultivating the seeds of the plants.

First agricultural revolution Dating back 10,000 years, the First Agricultural Revolution achieved plant domestication and animal domestication.

involves seed selection, sowing, watering, and well-timed harvesting. Again, the practice seems to have developed in more than one area at different times. Some scholars believe that the first domestication of seed plants may have occurred in the Nile River Valley in North Africa, but the majority view is that this crucial development took place in a region of southwestern Asia (also called the Fertile Crescent) through which flow the two major rivers of present-day Iraq, the Tigris and the Euphrates (Figure 9.2). Regardless of where it actually began, this period marked the beginning of what has been called the **First Agricultural Revolution**.

Archaeologists note that, as part of the First Agricultural Revolution, a number of changes occurred in southwestern Asia

along with plant domestication. First, the plants themselves changed because people chose seeds from the largest, heartiest plants to save for planting, yielding domesticated plants that grew larger over time than their counterparts in the wild. Archaeologists in southwestern Asia have found preserved seeds, which tell them what plants were being domesticated when. Grain crops, such as wheat and barley, grew well in the warming Asian climate. Soon people found that the river-inundated plains of Mesopotamia provided yet another location suitable for farming. Agriculture provided a reliable food source, and grain surpluses enabled people to store grain for long-term distribution and use and to settle permanently in one place. With a reliable food source and a permanent base, the population of settlements began to increase, an event more fully explored in Chapter 10.

Figure 9.3 depicts the global distribution of plant domestication hearths. In Southeast Asia (Region 1), taro, yams, and bananas were the leading food plants. In southwestern Asia (Region 4), plant domestication centred on wheat, barley, and other grains. In the Mesoamerican region (Region 6), the basic plants were maize (corn), squashes, and several kinds of beans.

Archaeologists continually find new sites to excavate, and as these sites are analyzed, academics revise their assumptions about the timing of the hearths of agriculture. The central China hearth (Region 7) has recently attracted greater attention because new evidence suggests a much earlier development of agriculture in this region—so early, in fact, that Chinese farmers may have been among the world's first. Another agricultural source region lies in West Africa (Region 9). Archaeological research on agriculture in this area is relatively recent, and analysts are not certain whether agriculture developed independently there, but they are certain secondary domestication took place in West Africa.

Table 9.1 may be overwhelming at first glance, but it is worth careful attention. It reveals the enormous range of crops that were cultivated around the world, as well as how, at various times and in different locales, particular groups of crops became the mainstays of life. Soon the knowledge needed to farm such crops diffused outward from these agricultural hearths. For example, both millet and sorghum diffused from the West African region—millet to India and sorghum to China.

In many cases, what we now think of as centres of production of particular crops are not the places where those crops were originally domesticated. The corn (maize) we associate with the Corn Belts of southwestern Ontario and the midwestern United States, for example, diffused from Central America and southern Mexico into North America. Later, the Portuguese took it back across the Atlantic to Europe, and corn became a staple in much of Africa. The white potato that we associate with Ireland, Prince Edward Island, and the American state of Idaho came originally from the Andean highlands but was carried to Europe in the 1600s, where it became a staple all the way from Ireland to the eastern expanses of the north European plain. The banana we associate with Central America came from Southeast Asia, as did a variety of yams. Diffusion of crops and seeds was greatly accelerated by worldwide trade and communications networks established by mercantilism and colonialism.

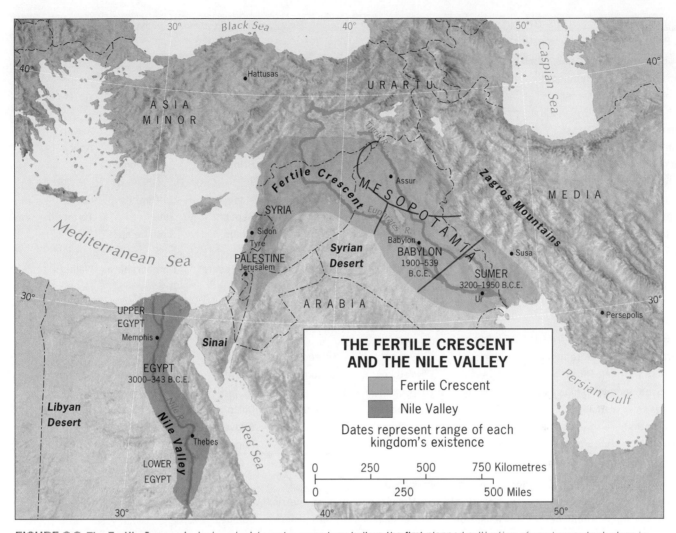

FIGURE 9.2 The Fertile Crescent. Archaeologists and geographers believe the first planned cultivation of seed crops took place in the Fertile Crescent of Mesopotamia (green), between the Tigris and Euphrates Rivers, or possibly in the Nile Valley (grey). Other ancient states and civilizations are shown in different colours. Modern political boundaries are shown for reference. (© E. H. Fouberg, A. B. Murphy, H. J. de Blij, and John Wiley & Sons, Inc.)

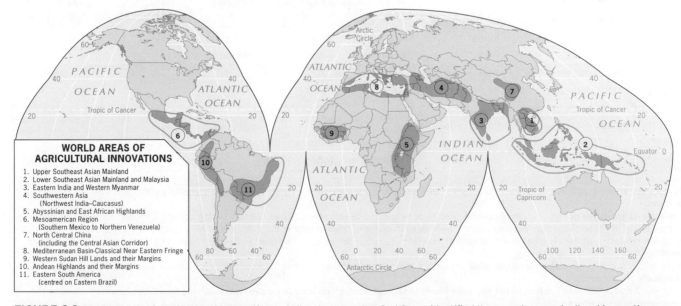

WORLD AREAS OF AGRICULTURAL INNOVATIONS

1. Upper Southeast Asian Mainland
2. Lower Southeast Asian Mainland and Malaysia
3. Eastern India and Western Myanmar
4. Southwestern Asia
   (Northwest India–Caucasus)
5. Abyssinian and East African Highlands
6. Mesoamerican Region
   (Southern Mexico to Northern Venezuela)
7. North Central China
   (including the Central Asian Corridor)
8. Mediterranean Basin–Classical Near Eastern Fringe
9. Western Sudan Hill Lands and their Margins
10. Andean Highlands and their Margins
11. Eastern South America
    (centred on Eastern Brazil)

FIGURE 9.3 World Areas of Agricultural Innovations. Cultural geographer Carl Sauer identified 11 areas where agricultural innovations occurred. Adapted with permission from C. O. Sauer, Agricultural Origins and Dispersals. New York: American Geographical Society, 1952, p. 24.

TABLE 9.1	Chief Source Regions of Important Crop Plant Domestications						
A. Primary Regions of Domestications							
1. Upper Southeast Asian Mainlands							
Citrus fruits*	Bamboos*	Yams*	Rices*	Eugenias*	Lichi	Teas	Ramie
Bananas*	Taros*	Cabbages*	Beans*	Job's tears	Longan	Tung oils	Water chestnut
2. Lower Southeast Asian Mainland and Malaysia (including New Guinea)							
Citrus fruits*	Taros*	Pandanuses	Breadfruits	Lanzones	Vine peppers*	Nutmeg	Areca
Bananas*	Yams*	Cucumbers*	Jackfruits	Durian	Gingers*	Clove	Abaca
Bamboos*	Almonds*	Sugarcanes	Coconuts	Rambutan	Brinjals*	Cardamom	
3. Eastern India and Western Burma							
Bananas*	Beans*	Millets*	Grams	Vine peppers*	Mangoes	Safflower	Lotus
Yams*	Rices*	Sorghums*	Eggplants	Gingers*	Kapok*	Jute	Turmeric
Taros*	Amaranths*	Peas*	Brinjals*	Palms*	Indigo	Sunn hemp	
4. Southwestern Asia (Northwest India-Caucasus)							
Soft wheats*	Peas*	Rye*	Beets*	Hemp	Soft pears*	Pomegranates	Walnuts
Barleys*	Oil seeds*	Onions	Spinach	Apples	Cherries*	Grapes*	Melons
Lentils*	Poppies	Carrots*	Sesames	Almonds*	Plums*	Jujubes*	Tamarind
Beans*	Oats*	Turnips	Flax	Peaches*	Figs	Pistachio	Alfalfa
5. Ethiopian and East African Highlands							
Hard wheats*	Sorghums*	Barleys	Beans*	Oil seeds*	Melons*	Coffees	Okras
Millets*	Rices*	Peas*	Vetches	Cucumbers*	Gourds*	Castor beans	Cottons*
6. Mesoamerican Region (Southern Mexico to Northern Venezuela)							
Maizes	Taros*	Tomatoes*	Avocados	Muskmelons	Cottons*		
Amaranths*	Sweet potatoes	Chili peppers	Sapotes	Palms*	Agaves		
Beans*	Squashes	Custard apples	Plums*	Manioc	Kapok		
B. Secondary Regions of Domestications							
7. North-Central China (including the Central Asian corridor)							
Millets*	Soybeans	Naked oat	Mulberries	Bush cherries*	Peaches*		
Barleys*	Cabbages*	Mustards	Persimmons	Hard pears*	Jujubes*		
Buckwheats	Radishes*	Rhubarb	Plums*	Apricots			
8. Mediterranean Basin–Classical Near Eastern Fringe							
Barleys*	Lentils*	Grapes*	Dates	Parsnips	Lettuces	Carrots*	Sugar beet
Oats*	Peas*	Olives	Carobs	Asparagus	Celeries	Garlic	Leek
9. Western Sudan Hill Lands and Their Margins							
Sorghums*	Rices*	Yams*	Peas*	Melons*	Oil palms	Kola nut	
Millets*	Fonio	Beans*	Oil seeds*	Gourds*	Tamarind*		
10. Andean Highlands and Their Margins							
White potatoes	Tomatoes*	Beans*	Quinoa	Cubio	Ulluco		
Pumpkins	Strawberries	Papayas	Oca	Arrocacha			
11. Eastern South America (centred on eastern Brazil)							
Taros*	Peanuts	Cashew nut	Cacao	Cottons*			
Beans*	Pineapples	Brazil nut	Passion fruits	Tobaccos			

Source: J. E. Spencer and W. L. Thomas, *Introducing Cultural Geography*. New York: Wiley, 1978. Reproduced with permission from John Wiley & Sons, Inc.

*The asterisk indicates domestication of related species or hybridized development of new species during domestication in some other region or regions. Some of these secondary domestications were later than in the original region, but evidence of chronologic priority is seldom clear-cut. The plural rendering of the crop name indicates that several different varieties/species either were involved in initial domestication or followed thereafter.

The term "oil seeds" indicates several varieties or species of small-seeded crop plants grown for the production of edible oils, without further breakdown.

In regions 2 and 3, "brinjals" refers to the spicy members of the eggplant group used in curries, whereas in region 3, "eggplants" refers to the sweet vegetable members.

None of the regional lists attempts a complete listing of all crop plants/species domesticated within the region.

The table has been compiled from a wide variety of sources.

DOMESTICATION OF ANIMALS

Some scholars believe that animal domestication began earlier than plant cultivation, but others argue that animal domestication began as recently as 8,000 years ago—well after crop agriculture. In any case, goats, pigs, and sheep became part of a rapidly growing array of domestic animals.

As with the growing of root crops, the notion of **animal domestication**—adapting wild animals to accept life in intimate association with, and to the advantage of, humans—also emerged in stages over time. The process of domestication began when people became more sedentary. Animals were kept as pets or for other reasons, such as for ceremonial purposes. Animals may also have attached themselves to human settlements as scavengers (foraging through garbage near human settlements) and even for protection against predators, thus reinforcing the idea that they might be tamed and kept. Docile wild animals could have easily been penned up. Goats were domesticated in the Zagros Mountains (in the Fertile Crescent) as early as 10,000 years ago, sheep some 9,500 years ago in Anatolia (Turkey), and pigs and cattle shortly thereafter. The advantages of domesticating animals for use as beasts of burden, companions/protectors, and providers of milk or meat stimulated the rapid diffusion of this idea among interlinked places and gave the sedentary farmers of southwestern Asia and elsewhere a new measure of security.

Once in captivity, animals changed considerably from their wild state. Archaeological research indicates that when animals such as wild cattle were penned in a corral, they underwent physical changes over time. The corral protected them from predators, which meant animals that would have been killed in the wild survived. Our domestic versions of goat, pig, cow, and horse differ considerably from those first kept by our ancestors. In early animal domestication, people chose the more docile,

> **Animal domestication**
> Genetic modification of an animal such that it is rendered more amenable to human control.

often smaller, animals to breed in order to protect themselves from the larger, fiercer, more powerful animals.

Archaeologists discern the beginnings of animal domestication in a region by inspecting the bones of excavated animals. They look for places where bones get smaller over time, as this usually indicates early domestication. As with plant domestication, archaeologists can use the combination of bone fragments and tools to identify general areas where the domestication of particular animals occurred. In southwestern Asia and adjacent parts of northeastern Africa, people domesticated the goat, sheep, and camel. Southeast Asians domesticated several kinds of pigs, the water buffalo, chickens, and some waterfowl (such as ducks and geese). In South Asia, people domesticated cattle, which then came to occupy an important place in the regional culture. In Central Asia, people domesticated the yak, horse, sheep, and some species of goats. In the Mesoamerican region (including the Andes from Peru northward and Central America north to central Mexico), early Americans domesticated the llama and alpaca, along with a species of pig and the turkey.

Some species of animals may have been domesticated almost simultaneously in different places. The water buffalo, for example, was probably domesticated in both Southeast and South Asia during the same period. Camels may have been domesticated in Central Asia as well as in southwestern Asia. The pig was domesticated in numerous areas. Different species of cattle were domesticated in regions other than South Asia. Dogs and cats may, in fact, have been the first animals domesticated, having attached themselves to human settlements very early and in widely separated regions. Single specific hearths can be pinpointed for only a few animals, including the llama and the alpaca, the yak, the turkey, and the reindeer.

Efforts to domesticate animals continue today. Several experimental stations in the African savannas are trying to find ways to breed the continent's wildlife to serve as a source of meat in a region where a stable supply of protein is greatly needed. The farms have had some success domesticating a species of eland (Figure 9.4), a type of antelope, but less success

FIELD NOTE Kenya

Attempts to tame wildlife started in ancient times, and still continue. At Hunter's Lodge on the Nairobi-Mombasa road, we met an agricultural officer who reported that an animal domestication experimental station was located not far into the bush, about 16 kilometres south. On his invitation, we spent the next day observing this work. In some herds, domestic animals (in this case, goats) were combined with wild gazelles, all penned together in a large enclosure. This was not working well; all day the gazelles sought to escape. By comparison, these eland were docile, manageable, and in good health. More important, they were also reproducing in captivity.

FIGURE 9.4 Eland Domestication in Nairobi, Kenya. (© H. J. deBlij)

with various species of gazelles, and they have been unable to domesticate the buffalo. Throughout the world, only about 40 species of higher animals have been domesticated—and most of these were domesticated long ago. Jared Diamond, author of *Guns, Germs, and Steel*, explains that only five domesticated mammals are important throughout the world: cow, sheep, goat, pig, and horse. According to Diamond, if we select only the big (over 50 kilograms), herbivorous, terrestrial animals, we have 148 species that meet these criteria "in the wild." Only 14 of those 148 have been domesticated successfully, and each of these 14 was domesticated at least 4,500 years ago. Modern attempts at animal domestication, even those driven by knowledgeable geneticists, have failed because of problems with the particular animal's diet, growth rate, breeding patterns, disposition, or social structure. Thus, the process of animal domestication, set in motion more than 8,000 (and perhaps as long as 14,000) years ago, continues.

HUNTER-GATHERERS IN THE MODERN WORLD

In the modern world, hunter-gatherers live in the context of a globalized economy and experience pressures to change their livelihoods. In many cases, the state places pressures on hunter-gatherers to settle in one place and farm. Cyclical migration by hunter-gatherers does not mesh well with bounded, territorial states. Some nongovernmental organizations encourage settlement by digging wells or building medical buildings, permanent houses, or schools for hunter-gatherers. Even hunter-gatherers who continue to use their knowledge of seeds, roots, fruits, berries, insects, and animals to gather and trap

the food they need for survival do so in the context of the world economy. The San of southern Africa, the Aboriginals of Australia, the indigenous peoples of Brazil, and several other groups in the Americas, Africa, and Asia have been studied, mapped, recorded, photographed, donated to, defended, and, in many cases, exploited.

SUBSISTENCE AGRICULTURE IN THE MODERN WORLD

Hundreds of millions of farmers around the world are involved in **subsistence agriculture**, growing only enough food to survive. The term "subsistence" can be used in the strictest sense of the word—that is, to refer to farmers who grow food only to sustain themselves and their families, who find building materials and firewood in the natural environment, and who do not enter into the cash economy at all. This definition fits farmers in remote areas throughout South and Central America, Africa, and South and Southeast Asia (Figure 9.5). Many farm families living at the subsistence level will occasionally sell a small quantity of produce (perhaps to pay taxes), and are therefore not subsistence farmers in the strict sense. Nonetheless, the description is surely applicable to societies where farmers with small plots sometimes sell a few kilos of grain on the market but where poverty, indebtedness, and tenancy are ways of life. For the indigenous peoples in the Amazon Basin, the sedentary farmers of Africa's savannas, villagers in much of India, and peasants in

> **Subsistence agriculture**
> Self-sufficient agriculture that is small scale and low technology and emphasizes food production for local consumption, not for trade.

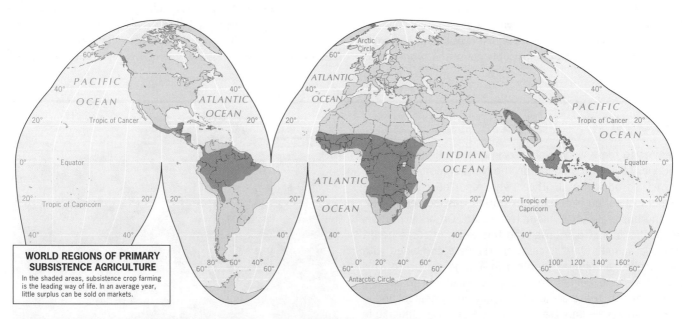

WORLD REGIONS OF PRIMARY SUBSISTENCE AGRICULTURE
In the shaded areas, subsistence crop farming is the leading way of life. In an average year, little surplus can be sold on markets.

FIGURE 9.5 World Regions of Primarily Subsistence Agriculture. Definitions of subsistence farming vary. On this map, India and China are not shaded because farmers sell some produce at markets; in Equatorial Africa and South America, subsistence farming allows little excess, and thus little produce is sold at markets. (© E. H. Fouberg, A. B. Murphy, H. J. de Blij, and John Wiley & Sons, Inc.)

Indonesia, subsistence is not only a way of life but also a state of mind. Experience has taught farmers and their families that subsistence farming is often precarious and that times of comparative plenty will be followed by times of scarcity.

Subsistence farmers often hold land in common. In such cases, surpluses are shared by all the members of the community, accumulation of personal wealth is restricted, and individual advancement at the cost of the group as a whole is limited. As A. H. Bunting wrote in *Change in Agriculture* (1970):

> To allocate the land or manage the seasonal migrations, and to survive through hardship and calamity these societies have to be cohesive, communal and relatively little differentiated socially and economically: the chiefs, elders or elected headmen may be little richer than their fellows—to many of whom they are in addition linked by ties of relationship within the extended family. Mutual dependence, imposed by the environment and the state of the agricultural art, is maintained and reinforced by genetic relationships. The community is enclosed socially and may even tend to be isolated culturally. Landlords and feudal rulers are unknown; the cultivators are poor but free.

Although much has changed for subsistence farmers since Bunting wrote these words in 1970, a strong sense of community remains important to the social fabric of these people.

Some subsistence farmers are sedentary, living in one place throughout the year, but many others move from place to place in search of better land. The latter engage in a form of agriculture known as **shifting cultivation**. This activity is found primarily in tropical and subtropical zones and is still widely practised. In fact, between 150 million and 200 million people sustain themselves today through shifting cultivation in Africa, Central America, tropical South America, and parts of Southeast Asia.

> **Shifting cultivation**
> Cultivation of crops in tropical forest clearings in which the forest vegetation has been removed by cutting and burning. These clearings are usually abandoned after a few years in favour of newly cleared forestland. Also known as slash-and-burn agriculture.

The system of shifting cultivation has changed little over thousands of years. People usually live in a central village surrounded by parcels of land that are worked successively. The farmers first clear vegetation from a parcel of land. Then they plant crops that are native to the region: tubers in the humid, warm, tropical areas; grains in the more humid subtropics; vegetables and fruits in cooler zones. However, when soils in these regions are stripped of their natural vegetative cover and deprived of the constant input of nutrients from decaying vegetative matter on the forest floor, they can quickly lose their nutrients as rain water leaches out organic matter. Faced with these circumstances, farmers move to another parcel of land, clear the vegetation, turn the soil, and try again. In tropical areas, a plot of cleared soil will carry a good crop at least once

and perhaps two or three times. After that, the land is best left alone to regenerate its natural vegetative cover and replenish the soil with nutrients lost during cultivation. Several years later, the plot may yield a good harvest once again.

When the village grows too large and the distance to usable land becomes too great, part of the village's population may establish a new settlement some distance away. Shifting cultivation is possible only in areas where population densities are low.

One specific kind of shifting cultivation is **slash-and-burn agriculture** (also called milpa agriculture or patch agriculture). This name reflects the central role of the controlled use of fire in places where this technique is used. In slash-and-burn, farmers use tools (e.g., machetes and knives) to slash down trees and tall vegetation; then they burn the vegetation on the ground. A layer of ash from the fire settles on the ground and contributes to the soil's fertility.

> **Slash-and-burn agriculture**
> The technique in which tools (e.g., machetes and knives) are used to slash down trees and tall vegetation, which are then burned on the ground, forming a layer of ash that contributes to the soil's fertility.

MARGINALIZATION OF SUBSISTENCE FARMING

During the era of colonialism (ca. 1500 to 1950), European powers sought to "modernize" the economies of the colonies by ending subsistence farming practices and integrating farmers into colonial systems of production and exchange. One way they did this, described by Duckham and Masefield in *Farming Systems of the World* (1970), was by tempting farmers into wanting cash by making desirable consumer goods available. Often their methods were much harsher: by demanding that farmers pay taxes, colonizers forced subsistence farmers to begin selling some of their produce to raise the necessary cash. They also compelled many subsistence farmers to devote some land to a cash crop, such as cotton, thus bringing them into the commercial economy. The colonial powers encouraged commercial farming by conducting soil surveys, building irrigation systems, and establishing lending agencies that provided loans to farmers. In addition, the colonial powers sought to make profits, yet it was difficult to squeeze very much from subsistence-farming areas. Forced cropping schemes were designed to solve this problem. If farmers in a subsistence area cultivated a certain acreage of corn, they were required to grow a specified acreage of a cash crop, such as cotton, as well. Whether this crop would be grown on old land that was formerly used for grain or on newly cleared land was the farmers' decision. If no new lands were available, the farmers would have to give up food crops for the compulsory cash crops. In many areas, severe famines resulted, and local economies were disrupted.

In the interests of "progress" and "modernization," subsistence farmers have been pushed away from their traditional modes of livelihood. Yet many aspects of subsistence farming may be worth preserving. Regions with shifting cultivation do not have neat rows of plants, carefully turned soil, or precisely laid-out fields. Nonetheless, shifting cultivation conserves both forest and soil, its harvests are substantial given the environmental limitations, and it requires better organization than one might assume. It also requires substantially less energy than more modern techniques of farming. Shifting cultivation and specifically slash-and-burn agriculture have been sustainable methods of farming for thousands of years. Shifting cultivation gave ancient farmers opportunities to experiment with various plants, learn the effects of weeding and crop care, cope with environmental vagaries, and discern the decreased fertility of soil after sustained farming.

Nevertheless, in many parts of the world, subsistence land use is giving way to more intensive farming and cash cropping—even to mechanized farming in which equipment does much of the actual work. In the process, societies from South America to Southeast Asia are profoundly affected. Land that was once held communally is being parcelled out to individuals for cash cropping. The system that ensured an equitable distribution of resources is breaking down. Furthermore, the distribution of wealth has become stratified, with poor people at the bottom and rich landowners at the top.

| MAIN POINTS | **9.1**   What Is Agriculture, and Where Did It Begin? |

- Agriculture is the deliberate tending of crops and livestock to produce food, feed, and fibre.

- Geographer Carl Sauer suggested that Southeast and South Asia may have been the scene of the first domestication of tropical plants more than 14,000 years ago, although a similar development may have taken place later in northwestern South America. The first domestication of seed plants, which marked the start of what is now referred to as the First Agricultural Revolution, is believed to have taken place in a region of southwestern Asia known as the Fertile Crescent, although some have argued that this may have occurred in the Nile River Valley in northern Africa.

- The process of animal domestication began when people became more sedentary. The advantages of animal domestication simulated the rapid diffusion of this idea among interlinked places and gave sedentary farmers a new measure of security.

- Hundreds of millions of farmers around the world are involved in subsistence agriculture, growing only enough food to survive. However, many farm families living at the subsistence level are occasionally able to sell a small quantity of produce in order to generate some income.

- Some subsistence farmers are sedentary, living in one place throughout the year, but many others engage in shifting cultivation by moving from place to place in search of better land.

- During the colonial era, European powers sought to "modernize" the economies of their colonies by ending subsistence farming practices and integrating farmers into colonial systems of production and exchange. In some cases, they forced subsistence farmers to begin selling produce in order to raise the cash needed to pay their taxes, while in other instances they compelled subsistence farmers to move into the commercial economy by devoting land to a cash crop, such as cotton or rubber.

9.2 How Did Agriculture Change with Industrialization?

THE SECOND AGRICULTURAL REVOLUTION

For the Industrial Revolution to take root, a **Second Agricultural Revolution** had to take place—one that would move agriculture beyond subsistence to generate the kinds of surpluses needed to feed thousands of people working in factories instead of in agricultural fields. Like the Industrial Revolution, the Second Agricultural Revolution was composed of a series of innovations, improvements, and

> **Second Agricultural Revolution** Dovetailing with and benefiting from the Industrial Revolution, the Second Agricultural Revolution witnessed improved methods of cultivation, harvesting, and storage of farm produce.

techniques, which in this case took place in Great Britain, the Netherlands, Denmark, and neighbouring countries.

By the 17th and 18th centuries, European farming had undergone significant changes. New crops, including corn and potatoes, came into Europe from trade with the Americas. Several of the new crops were well suited for the climate and soils of western Europe, and new lands were brought into cultivation, including many that were previously defined as marginal. The governments of Europe played a role in spurring on the Second Agricultural Revolution by passing laws such as Great Britain's *Enclosure Act,* which encouraged consolidation of fields that had been communally owned into large, single-owner holdings. Farmers increased the size of their farms, pieced together more contiguous parcels of land, fenced in their land, and instituted field rotation. Methods of soil preparation, fertilization, crop care, and harvesting improved.

New technologies improved production as well. The seed drill enabled farmers to avoid wasting seeds and to plant in

FIGURE 9.6 Canadian Pacific Railway (CPR) Advertisement, ca. 1893. The CPR played an essential role in bringing European immigrants into western Canada throughout the late 19th and early 20th centuries. (Library and Archives Canada)

rows, which made it easier to distinguish weeds from crops. Advances in breeding livestock allowed farmers to develop new breeds that were either strong milk producers or good for beef. By the 1830s, farmers were using new fertilizers on crops and giving artificial feeds to livestock. Increased agricultural output made it possible to feed much larger urban populations, permitting the growth of a secondary (industrial) economy.

Innovations in machinery, made possible by the Industrial Revolution in the late 1800s and early 1900s, helped sustain the Second Agricultural Revolution. The railroad moved agriculture into new regions, such as Canada's Prairie provinces and the United States' Great Plains. The railroad companies advertised in Europe (Figure 9.6) to attract immigrants to these regions, and the railroads took the migrants to their new homes, where they would transform prairie grasslands to agricultural fields. Later, the internal combustion engine made possible the invention of tractors, combines, and a multitude of large farm equipment. New banking and lending practices helped farmers afford the new equipment.

UNDERSTANDING THE SPATIAL LAYOUT OF AGRICULTURE

When commercial agriculture is geared to producing food for people who live in a nearby town or city, a clear geography based on perishability of products and cost of transportation

emerges. In the 1800s, Johann Heinrich von Thünen (1783–1850) experienced the Second Agricultural Revolution first-hand: he farmed an estate not far from the town of Rostock, in northeastern Germany. Studying the spatial patterns of farming around towns such as Rostock, von Thünen noted that one commodity or crop gave way to another, in succession, as one moved away from the town. He also noted that this process occurred without any visible change in soil, climate, or terrain. When he mapped this pattern, he found that each town or market centre was surrounded by a set of more-or-less concentric rings within which particular commodities or crops dominated.

Nearest the town, farmers produced commodities that were perishable and commanded high prices, such as dairy products and strawberries. In this zone, von Thünen believed agriculture was practised with a high level of intensity, and much effort went into production, in part because of the value of the land closer to the city. In von Thünen's time, the town was still surrounded by a belt of forest that provided wood for fuel and building; however, immediately beyond the forest, the ring-like pattern of agriculture continued. In the next ring the crops were less perishable and bulkier, including wheat and other grains. Still farther out, livestock began to replace field crops.

Based on his observations, von Thünen built a model of the spatial distribution of agricultural activities. As with all models, he had to make certain assumptions. For example, he assumed that the terrain was flat, that soils and other environmental conditions were the same everywhere, and that there were no barriers to transportation to market. Under such circumstances, he reasoned, the costs of transportation would govern the use of land. He reasoned that the greater the distance to market, the higher the transport costs that had to be added to the cost of producing a crop or commodity. At a given distance to market, then, it would become unprofitable to produce high-cost, perishable commodities, and market gardens would give way to field crops such as grains and potatoes. Still farther away, livestock would replace field agriculture.

The **von Thünen model** (Figure 9.7) is often described as the first effort to analyze the spatial character of economic activity. The Thünian patterns discerned in many parts of the world are not solely the result of the forces modelled by von Thünen. Differences in climate type and soil quality heavily influence the kinds of goods produced in a place. However, even when agricultural production does not conform to the concentric rings of von Thünen's model,

> **von Thünen model** A model that explains the location of agricultural activities in a commercial, profit-making economy. A process of spatial competition allocates various farming activities into rings around a central market city, with profit-earning capability the determining force in how far a crop locates from the market.

his underlying concern with the interplay of land use and transportation costs is frequently still determinative. The fresh flowers grown in South America for sale in Toronto could be viewed as the application of the von Thünen model on a larger scale, for it is less expensive to grow flowers in South American countries,

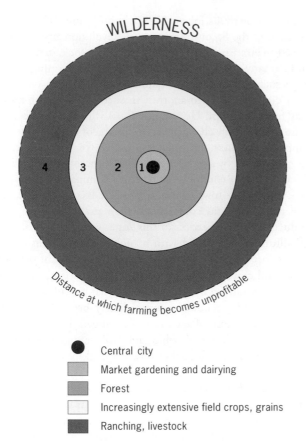

WILDERNESS

4   3   2   1

Distance at which farming becomes unprofitable

- ● Central city
- ▨ Market gardening and dairying
- ▨ Forest
- □ Increasingly extensive field crops, grains
- ▨ Ranching, livestock

FIGURE 9.7 Von Thünen's Model. (© H. J. de Blij, P. O. Muller, and John Wiley & Sons, Inc.)

such as Ecuador and Colombia, and ship them to Toronto than it is to grow them in other locations in North America.

Geographer Lee Liu studied the spatial pattern of agricultural production in one province of China, giving careful consideration to the intensity of the production methods and the amount of land degradation. Liu found that the farmers living in a village would farm lands close to the village and lands far away from the village with high levels of intensity. However, the methods used varied spatially, resulting in land improvements close to the village and land degradation farther from the village. In lands close to the village, farmers improved lands by, for example, putting organic material onto the fields, which made the grasslands close to the village fertile and productive. In lands more remote from the village, farmers tended to use more chemical fertilizer, pesticides, and herbicides and fewer conservation tactics, resulting in land degradation. Liu argued that this pattern of land use in modern China occurred in large part because the farmers lived in the village, not in the remote fields, and therefore put most of their time and energy into the fields closest to them.

THE THIRD AGRICULTURAL REVOLUTION

The **Third Agricultural Revolution**, also called the **Green Revolution**, dates as far back as the 1930s, when agricultural scientists in the midwestern United States began experimenting with

technologically manipulated seed varieties to increase crop yields. In the 1940s, American philanthropists funded research on maize (corn) production in Mexico, trying to find a hybrid seed that would grow better. They did, and by 1960 Mexico was no longer importing corn because production within the country was high enough to meet demand. In the 1960s, the focal point of the Green Revolution shifted to India, where farmers began growing a strain of rice developed by scientists at a research institution in the Philippines. These scientists crossed a variety of Chinese dwarf rice with an Indonesian variety and produced IR8, which, among other desirable properties, developed a bigger head of grain and had a stronger stem that did not collapse under the added weight of the bigger head.

IR8 produced much better yields than either of its parents, but the researchers were not satisfied. In 1982 they produced IR36, bred from 13 parents to achieve genetic resistance against 15 pests. IR36 had a growing cycle of 110 days under warm conditions, which made it possible to grow three crops per year in some places. By 1992, IR36 was the most widely grown crop on Earth, but two years later, scientists had developed a strain of rice that was even more productive. They continue to work on improvements. Researchers at the International Rice Research Institute, for example, are working to breed a genetically modified "super rice" that can be seeded directly in the paddy soil, instead of having to be transplanted as a seedling. It may yield nearly twice as much rice per acre than the average for strains in current use. The charting of the rice genome (the 12 chromosomes that carry all of the plant's characteristics) is underway, which means it may also soon be possible to transform rice genetically so that it will continuously acquire more desirable properties. Not only could yields improve; so could resistance to diseases and pests.

In addition to improving the production of rice, the Green Revolution brought new high-yield varieties of wheat and corn from the United States to other parts of the world, particularly South and Southeast Asia.

Coming at a time of growing concern about global hunger, the successes of the Green Revolution were truly extraordinary. Today, most famines result from political instability rather than failure in production. India became self-sufficient in grain production by the 1980s, and Asia saw a two-thirds increase in rice production between 1970 and 1995. These drastic increases in production stemmed not only from new seed varieties but also, in some places, from the use of fertilizers, pesticides, irrigation, as well as significant capital improvements.

The geographical impact of the Green Revolution has been highly variable. Its traditional focus on rice, wheat, and corn meant that it had only limited impact throughout much of

> **Third Agricultural Revolution** Currently in progress, the Third Agricultural Revolution has as its principal orientation the development of genetically modified organisms (GMOs).
>
> **Green Revolution** The recently successful development of higher-yield, fast-growing varieties of rice and other cereals in certain developing countries, which led to increased production per unit area and a dramatic narrowing of the gap between population growth and food needs.

Africa, where agriculture is based on different crops and where lower soil fertility makes agriculture less attractive to foreign investment. Increasingly, however, researchers are turning their attention to new agricultural products, and this could expand the geographical impact of the Green Revolution. Research has already led to methods for producing high-yield cassava and sorghum, both of which are grown in Africa. And beyond Africa, research on fattening livestock faster and improving the appearance of fruits is having an impact in North and South America.

The promise of increasing food production in a world in which almost a billion people are malnourished has led many people to support genetically engineered foods (see next section). However, many others question whether gene manipulation could create health risks and environmental hazards. Environmentalists have speculated about the impacts of pollen dispersal from genetically modified plants and the potential for disease-resistant plants to spur the evolution of super-pests. Vandana Shiva, a vocal opponent of the Green Revolution in India, argues that

the Green Revolution has been a failure. It has led to reduced genetic diversity, increased vulnerability to pests, soil erosion, water shortages, reduced soil fertility, micronutrient deficiencies, soil contamination, reduced availability of nutritious food crops for the local population, the displacement of vast numbers of small farmers from their land, rural impoverishment and increased tensions and conflicts. The beneficiaries have been the agrochemical industry, large petrochemical companies, manufacturers of agricultural machinery, dam builders and large landowners. (Shiva, 1991)

One difficulty of assessing the present situation is that developments are occurring so fast that it is not easy to keep up with them. However, the Green Revolution today has a large number of detractors concerned that the higher inputs of chemical fertilizers and pesticides can lead to reduced organic matter in the soil and to groundwater pollution. Moreover, many small-scale farmers lack the resources to acquire genetically enhanced seeds and the necessary fertilizers and pesticides. In most of the world that is affected by the Green Revolution, farmers produce on very small acreages. A 2005 report in *Scientific American* explains that in these cases the Green Revolution has done little to alleviate poverty: "The supply-driven strategies of the Green Revolution...may not help subsistence farmers, who must play to their strengths to compete in the global marketplace. The average size of a family farm is less than four acres in India, 1.8 acres in Bangladesh and about half an acre in China." Small-scale farmers are in a poor competitive position, and some are being driven off their lands. In addition, the need for capital from the West to implement Green Revolution technologies has led to a shift away from production for local consumers toward export agriculture. In the process, local places become subject to the ups and downs of the global economy, where a downward fluctuation in the price of a given crop can create enormous problems for farmers dependent on the sale of that crop.

GENETICALLY MODIFIED FOODS

An entire field of biotechnology has sprung up in conjunction with the Third Agricultural Revolution, and the development of genetically engineered (GE) crops, or **genetically modified organisms (GMOs)**, is its principal orientation. Since the origin of agriculture, people have experimented with hybrid crops and crossbreeding animals. Today, some experts estimate that about 60 percent of processed foods and as many as 30,000 items on grocery store shelves in Canada contain genetically modified organisms. The GMO Compass, a website created with the financial support of the European Union to provide users with up-to-date information regarding genetically modified food quality and safety issues, noted that Canada was the world's fifth-highest producer of genetically engineered crops in 2007 (behind only the United States, Argentina, Brazil, and India).

> **Genetically modified organisms (GMOs)** Crops that carry new traits that have been inserted through advanced genetic engineering methods.

Some regions have embraced genetically engineered crops; others have banned them. While many of the poorer countries of the world do not have access to the necessary capital and technology to obtain GM crops, some 46 percent of fields in which such crops are grown are found in developing nations. Moreover, ideological resistance to genetically engineered foods is strong in some places—particularly in western Europe. Agricultural officials in most west European countries have declared genetically modified foods to be safe, but the public has a strong reaction against them based on combined concerns about health and taste. Such concerns have spread to less affluent parts of the world. In many poorer regions, seeds are a cultural commodity, reflecting agricultural lessons learned over generations. In these regions, many resist the invasion of foreign, genetically engineered crops.

REGIONAL AND LOCAL CHANGE

Recent shifts from subsistence agriculture to commercial agriculture have had a dramatic impact on rural life. Land-use patterns, land-ownership arrangements, agricultural labour conditions, and even intra-community relations have all changed as rural residents cope with shifting economic, political, and environmental conditions. In Latin America, huge increases in the production of export crops (also known as "cash crops," such as fruits and coffee) have occurred at the expense of crop production for local consumption. In the process, subsistence farming has been pushed to ever more marginal lands. In Asia, where the Green Revolution has had the greatest impact, the production of cereal crops (i.e., grains such as rice and wheat) has increased for both foreign and domestic markets. Agricultural production in this region remains relatively small in scale and depends on manual labour. In sub-Saharan Africa, total commercialized agriculture has increased, but overall agricultural exports have decreased. As in Asia, farm units in sub-Saharan Africa have remained relatively small and dependent on intensified manual labour.

GUEST FIELD NOTE   Gambia

I am interested in women and rural development in sub-Saharan Africa. In 1983, I went to Gambia to study an irrigated rice project that was being implemented to improve the availability of rice, the dietary staple. What grabbed my attention? The donors' assurance that the project would benefit women, the country's traditional rice growers. Imagine my surprise, a few months after the project was implemented, when I encountered hundreds of angry women refusing to work because they received nothing for their labour from the first harvest.

In registering women's traditional rice plots as "family" land, project officials effectively sabotaged the equity objectives of the donors. Male heads of households held control of "family" land, and they reaped the income produced by female labour. Contemporary economic strategies for Africa depend increasingly upon labour intensification. But whose labour? Human geography provides a way of seeing the significance of gender in the power relations that mediate culture, environment, and economic development.

Judith Carney, University of California, Los Angeles

FIGURE 9.8 Women Cultivating Rice in Gambia. (Judith Carney)

What this regional-scale analysis does not tell us is how these changes have affected local rural communities. These changes can be environmental, economic, and social. For example, a study by Judith Carney in the small West African country of Gambia has shown how changing agricultural practices have altered not only the rural environment and economy but also relations between men and women (Figure 9.8). Over the last 30 years, international developmental assistance in Gambia has funded ambitious projects designed to convert wetlands to irrigated agricultural lands, making possible the production of rice year-round. By the late 1980s, virtually all of the country's suitable wetlands had been converted to year-round rice production. This transformation created tensions within rural households by converting lands women traditionally used for family subsistence into commercialized farming plots. In addition, when rice production was turned into a year-round occupation, women found themselves with less time for other activities crucial for household maintenance.

This situation underscores the fact that in Africa, as in much of the rest of the less-industrialized world, agricultural work is overwhelmingly carried out by women. In sub-Saharan Africa, over 85 percent of all women in the labour force work in agriculture; in China the number is close to 75 percent, and in India 70 percent. A geographical perspective that is sensitive to scale helps shed light on how changes in agricultural practices throughout the world not only alter rural landscapes but also affect family and community relationships.

MAIN POINTS   9.2 How Did Agriculture Change with Industrialization?

- Like the Industrial Revolution, the Second Agricultural Revolution was composed of a series of innovations, improvements, and techniques. The Second Agricultural Revolution moved agriculture beyond subsistence to generate the kinds of surpluses needed to feed thousands of people working in factories instead of in agricultural fields. This phase in the evolution of agriculture involved the introduction of new crops, the expansion of farm sizes, innovations in farm machinery, and improvements in methods of soil preparation, fertilization, crop care, and harvesting.

- The Third Agricultural Revolution, also called the Green Revolution, dates as far back as the 1930s. Over time, this phase was marked by drastic increases in agricultural production that stemmed from the creation of new seed varieties; the use of fertilizers, pesticides, and irrigation in some places; and significant capital improvements.

- The geographical impact of the Green Revolution has been highly variable. While countries such as Mexico and India have experienced large increases in productivity, Africa has seen only a limited impact.

MAIN POINTS *continued* **9.2 How Did Agriculture Change with Industrialization?**

- Concerns about the Green Revolution focus on the higher inputs of chemical fertilizers and pesticides that are typically used in modern-day agricultural production, which can lead to reduced organic matter in the soil and to groundwater pollution. Moreover, small-scale farmers often have not benefited because they lack the resources to acquire genetically enhanced seeds and the necessary fertilizers and pesticides. Another controversial element of the Third Agricultural Revolution has been the creation of genetically modified organisms, which has prompted fears about food quality and safety.

- Recent shifts from subsistence to commercial agriculture have had dramatic impacts on rural life. Land-use patterns, land-ownership arrangements, agricultural labour conditions, and even intra-community relations have all changed as rural residents cope with shifting economic, political, and environmental conditions.

9.3 What Imprint Does Agriculture Make on the Cultural Landscape?

A pilot flying from the west coast of Canada to the east coast will see the imprint agriculture makes on Canada's cultural landscape. The green circles standing out in arid regions of the country, such as those around the town of Rolling Hills, Alberta (Figure 9.9), show where centre-pivot irrigation systems have been in place, providing irrigation to a circle of crops. In turn, the checkerboard pattern on the landscape reflects the cadastral system—the method of land survey by which land ownership and property lines are defined. Cadastral systems were adopted in places where settlement could be regulated by law, and land surveys were crucial to their implementation. The type of survey that prevails throughout much of Canada, and which appears as checkerboards across agricultural fields, is the **rectangular survey system**. The U.S. government adopted the rectangular survey system after the American Revolution as part of a cadastral system known as the **township-and-range system**. This was replicated throughout most of present-day Manitoba, Saskatchewan, and Alberta during the late 1800s and early 1900s. Designed to facilitate the movement of non-Aboriginals across the Canadian prairies, the system

Rectangular survey system Also called the Public Land Survey, the system was used by the U.S. Land Office Survey to parcel land west of the Appalachian Mountains. The system divides land into a series of rectangular parcels.

Township-and-Range System A rectangular land division scheme designed by Thomas Jefferson to disperse settlers evenly across farmlands of the U.S. interior.

FIGURE 9.9 Centre-Pivot Irrigation, Rolling Hills, Alberta. These circles show the unique physical imprint of centre-pivot irrigation. This technique is commonly used where water scarcity or rough terrain necessitate creative approaches to agricultural activity. (© 2011 Google , Imagery © 2011 Cnes/Spot Image, DigitalGlobe, GeoEye, M.D. of Taber)

FIGURE 9.10 Regina, Saskatchewan, and Surrounding Agricultural Area. The imprint of the township-and-range system that was used to survey and subdivide land throughout western North America is clearly evident in images of land taken from space. At the centre of this photo sits the city of Regina, one of the main service centres for Saskatchewan's agricultural industry. (© 2011 Google, Imagery © 2011 TerraMetrics)

imposed a rigid grid-like pattern on the land (Figure 9.10). The basic unit was the 1-square-mile "section"—land was bought and sold in whole, half, or quarter sections. The section's lines were drawn without reference to the terrain; as a result, they imposed a remarkable uniformity across the land.

Different cadastral patterns predominate in other parts of Canada and the United States. These patterns reflect particular notions of how land should be divided and used. Among the

Metes and Bounds Survey System A system of land surveying east of the Appalachian Mountains. It is a system that relies on descriptions of land owner-ship and natural features such as streams or trees. Because of the imprecise nature of metes and bounds surveying, the U.S. Land Office Survey abandoned the technique in favour of the rectangular survey system.

Long-lot Survey System Distinct regional approach to land surveying found in the Canadian Maritimes, parts of Quebec, Louisiana, and Texas whereby land is divided into narrow parcels stretching back from rivers, roads, or canals.

most significant are the **metes and bounds survey system**, adopted along the eastern sea-board, in which natural features are used to demarcate irregular parcels of land. One of the most distinct regional approaches to land division can be found in the Canadian Maritimes and in parts of Quebec, Louisiana, and Texas, where a **long-lot survey system** was implemented. This system divided land into narrow parcels stretching back from rivers, roads, or canals. It reflects a particular approach to survey-ing that was especially common in the French colonies of North America.

A society's norms for property ownership are also reflected in the landscape. Property ownership is symbolized by landscapes in which par-cels of land are divided into neat, clearly demarcated segments. The size and order of those parcels are heavily influenced by

Primogeniture System in which the eldest son in a family—or, in exceptional cases, daughter—inherits all of a parent's land.

rules about property inheri-tance. In systems where one child inherits all of the land—such as the Germanic system of **primogeniture**, in which all land passes to the eldest son—parcels tend to be larger and farmers work a single plot of land. This is the norm in northern Europe and in the principal areas of northern European colonization—the Americas, South Africa, Australia, and New Zealand.

In areas where land is divided among heirs, however, con-siderable fragmentation can occur over time. The latter is the norm throughout much of Asia, Africa, and southern Europe, and it means that farmers living in villages tend a variety of scattered small plots of land. In some places, land reform ini-tiatives have consolidated landholdings to some degree, but fragmentation is still common in many parts of the world.

VILLAGES

Throughout this book we have taken note of various core-periphery contrasts that our world presents. Such contrasts are prominent in rural as well as urban areas. Traditional farm-village life is still common in India, sub-Saharan Africa, China, and Southeast Asia. In India, for example, farming, much of it subsistence farming, still occupies nearly 70 percent of the population. In the world's core areas, however, agriculture has taken on a very different form, and true farm villages—in which farming or providing services for farmers are the dominant

activities—are disappearing. In Canada, where farming once was the leading economic activity, only about 2 percent of the labour force remains engaged in agriculture.

Traditionally, the people who lived in villages either farmed the surrounding land or provided services to those who did the farming. Thus, they were closely connected to the land, and most of their livelihoods depended, directly or indirectly, on the cultivation of nearby farmland. These vil-lages tended to reflect historical and environmental condi-tions. Houses in Japanese farming villages, for example, were so tightly packed together that only the narrowest passage-ways remained between them. This reflected the need to al-locate every possible square foot of land to farming; villages must not use land where crops could grow. On the Canadian prairies, on the other hand, individual farmhouses lay quite far apart in what we call a "dispersed settlement" pattern: the land was intensively cultivated, but by machine rather than by hand. On the populous Indonesian island of Java, villages are still located every kilometre or so along rural roads, and settlement there is defined as nucleated. Land use is just as intense, but the work is done by people and animals. Hence, when we consider the density of human settlement as it re-lates to the intensity of land use, we should keep in mind the way the land is cultivated. "Nucleated settlement" is by far the most prevalent rural residential pattern in agricultural areas (Figure 9.11). When houses are grouped together in tiny clus-ters or hamlets, or in slightly larger clusters we call villages, their spatial arrangement also has significance.

In the hilly regions of Europe, villages were frequently clustered on sloping hillsides, leaving the level land for farm-ing. Often an old castle sat atop the hill, for in earlier times

FIGURE 9.11 Strathclair, Manitoba. The "nucleated settlement," such as that shown in this photo, is by far the most prevalent rural residential pattern in agricultural areas throughout the world. (© Concord Aerial Photo)

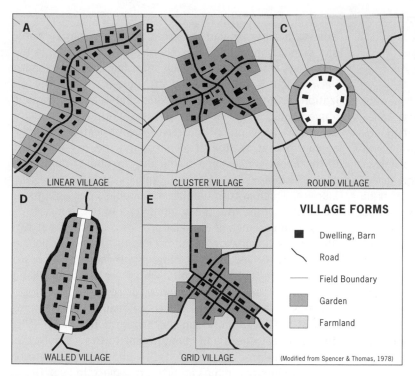

FIGURE 9.12 Village Forms. Examples of five different representative village layouts are shown here. Adapted with permission from J. E. Spencer and W. H. Thomas, *Introducing Cultural Geography.* New York: John Wiley & Sons, Inc., 1978, p. 154.

the site offered protection as well as land conservation. In the low-lying areas of western Europe, many villages were located on dikes and levees, so they often took on linear characteristics (Figure 9.12a). Where there was space, a house and outbuildings would have been surrounded by a small garden; the farms and pasturelands lay just beyond. In other cases, a village took on the characteristics of a cluster (Figure 9.12b). It might have begun as a small hamlet at the intersection of two roads and then developed by accretion. The European version of the East African circular village, with its central cattle corral, was the round village or *rundling* (Figure 9.12c). This layout was first used by Slavic farmer-herdsmen in eastern Europe and was later modified by Germanic settlers.

In many parts of the world, farm villages were fortified to protect their inhabitants from marauders. Ten thousand years ago, the first farmers in the Fertile Crescent faced attacks from the horsemen of Asia's steppes and clustered together to ward off this danger. In Nigeria's Yorubaland, the farmers would go out into the surrounding fields by day but retreat to the protection of walled villages at night. Villages, as well as larger towns and cities in Europe, were frequently walled and surrounded by moats. When the population became so large that people had to build houses outside the original wall, a new wall would be built to protect them. Walled villages (Figure 9.12d) still exist in rural areas of many countries, reminders of a turbulent past.

More modern villages, notably planned rural settlements, may be arranged on a grid pattern (Figure 9.12e). This is not,

however, a 20th-century novelty. Centuries ago the Spanish invaders of Central America laid out grid villages and towns, as did other colonial powers elsewhere in the world. In urban Africa, such imprints of colonization are pervasive.

Although the 20th century has witnessed unprecedented urban growth throughout the world, approximately half of the world's people still reside in villages and rural areas. As total world population increases, total population in rural areas is also increasing in many parts of the world (even though the *proportion* of the total population in rural areas may be stagnant or declining). In China, for instance, some 58 percent of the country's more than 1.35 billion people inhabit villages and hamlets. In India, with a population over 1.15 billion, about 72 percent of the people live in places the government defines as non-urban. Small rural settlements are also home to most of the inhabitants of Indonesia, Bangladesh, Pakistan, and many other countries of the periphery, including those in Africa. Indeed, the agrarian village remains one of the most common forms of settlement on Earth.

In some places, rural villages have changed as the global economy has changed. For example, Mexico has experienced rapid economic change since the North American Free Trade Agreement (NAFTA) was implemented in 1994. Along with major changes in industrial production (see Chapter 13), substantial changes in agricultural production have occurred in Mexico. American geographer Daniel Klooster studied changes in Mexican agriculture and found that, since 1994, U.S. exports of maize (corn) to Mexico have tripled and "now supply a third of Mexican domestic demand " (Klooster, 2005). Agricultural production in Mexico has decreased since NAFTA, but the total rural population in Mexico is growing (along with the total population of the country). Currently, about 24 percent of Mexico's population is defined as rural. How, then, are people in these rural areas making a living? Klooster found that "as agriculture declined, off-farm income from activities such as construction work, petty commerce and craft production increased" and that for rural families in Mexico (as is the case throughout much of rural Canada and the rural United States), off-farm income accounts for "more than half of family income." Decreasing agricultural production has increased the rate at which Mexicans are migrating to the United States, with many jobless people from rural areas moving to the United States to work and sending remittances home. At the same time, migration from Mexico to Canada has increased significantly since NAFTA came into force. Between 1981 and 2001, the number of Mexicans given permanent or temporary residency in Canada increased twofold. Interestingly, many of them have migrated in order to fill labour shortages in some parts of Canada's agricultural sector.

FIELD NOTE
Gravelbourg, Saskatchewan

To many people, the town of Gravelbourg, Saskatchewan, appeared to be at serious risk of disappearing from Canada's prairie landscape in the early 1990s—a victim of changing demographics, a globalizing agricultural economy, and a preference for urban living. But an aggressive program of grassroots-based community development and activism, made all the more possible by the town's rich stock of historical, social, and cultural resources, helped save this community. In recent years, Gravelbourg has experienced economic and population growth at a time when many other prairie agricultural communities are turning into "ghost towns." Gravelbourg's success story has captured the attention of media outlets across Canada, as well as interested professionals, local community organizations, and politicians at all levels of government.

My interest in rural geography reflects my personal experiences. I spent my teenage years on a small hobby farm south of Ottawa and completed my undergraduate studies in Northern Ontario. My first jobs were in the economic development field in Northern Manitoba and Southern Saskatchewan, so it is somewhat natural that my research interests are driven by my personal commitment to rural landscapes. Living in these diverse, rural, and remote settings instilled in me a very strong attachment to the people and places of rural Canada and a passion for rural geography. My recent scholarly activities reflect my commitment to understanding the complex challenges threatening the future viability of many rural and remote Canadian places and the various approaches communities might employ to address these challenges. In my work, I am thinking about whether "community economic development" strategies represent practical means of promoting the long-term viability of rural communities as places to live, work, and play.

The community economic development approach emphasizes the pursuit of a variety of economic, social, cultural, and environmental objectives through the grassroots-based planning and implementation of projects. My applied, community-based research primarily focuses on the experiences of Gravelbourg, Saskatchewan, a small town (population 1,200) in the heart of the Canadian prairies. Gravelbourg's community economic development story, which began in 1998, has been referred to as "hyperactive," with the town experiencing significant population and economic growth in the past few years. This itself is surprising, given its relatively remote location and that many other communities in the same region have shrunk considerably in size. These positive changes include: the retention of residents and the attraction of new ones (including over 250 newcomers between 2006 and 2008 alone); the purchase, expansion, and renovation of several existing businesses and the creation of several new ones; and significant growth in levels of tourism activity. In my interviews with over a dozen key informants in Gravelbourg between 2005 and 2010, many attribute the town's revitalization to the broad range of community-based initiatives implemented over the past decade. Various community economic development initiatives—beautification projects, a Main Street revitalization strategy, the enhancement of local tourism resources, and the hosting of numerous special events—created a high "quality-of-place" in Gravelbourg, which in turn heightened people's perceptions of the quality-of-life that the community had to offer.

Arguably, much of Gravelbourg's success can be attributed to the abundance of "social capital" found within the community. Gravelbourg is replete with citizens who are committed to their community, who are more than willing to volunteer their time and money for community projects and events, and who make efforts to ensure that all members of the community can participate if they wish. This strong cohesiveness and commitment to Gravelbourg has clearly influenced residents' desire and ability to ensure their community remains an attractive place to live.

All this suggests that I now need to explore whether a causal link can truly be established between the quality-of-place and quality-of-life improvements generated through the Gravelbourg's development efforts and the considerable recent population growth and business development activities. Indeed, one of the most important lessons I learned living in different regions of Canada is that the country's rural communities have incredibly diverse human and physical geographies. One cannot assume that what works in one place will always work in another. In Gravelbourg's case, for example, the success of the town's community economic development efforts cannot be considered without also thinking about the multitude of local, "place-based" resources that residents have been able to harness. For instance, tourism has boomed, given the presence of several national and provincially-designated historic sites—many related to its former role as an important centre for the French-Canadian Roman Catholic Church (Figure 9.13)—and culturally themed community events building on Gravelbourg's multicultural diversity. The town's most significant business development, the creation of a new mustard milling and processing facility driven by local and regional financial investments, was a natural choice due to Gravelbourg's location at the centre of the world's largest mustard-growing region. Whether Gravelbourg's remarkable community revitalization story is exceptional, or if it is an approach that can be replicated in other rural places, remains to be seen. Similar research in other rural and remote communities throughout Canada—in different geographical regions and in communities of varying sizes—will provide further insights into community economic development and its potential benefits for such places.

FIGURE 9.13 **Our Lady of the Assumption Cathedral, Gravelbourg.** This majestic church, a National Historic Site, has played a central role in the development of a thriving tourism economy in Gravelbourg. (© Christopher Fullerton)

Engaging in studies such as these has enabled me to contribute to the growing volume of research being conducted by a small but active group of Canadian rural geographers. Sitting with study participants to conduct interviews and in focus groups and public meetings opened my eyes to how passionate rural dwellers are about where they live and how dedicated they are to their communities. Knowing that my research may assist them in their efforts to ensure these places survive also makes this work very rewarding at a personal level.

Christopher Fullerton, Brock University, St. Catharines, Ontario

---

MAIN POINTS   **9.3**   What Imprint Does Agriculture Make on the Cultural Landscape?

- A society's norms for property ownership are reflected in the landscape. Property ownership is symbolized by landscapes in which parcels of land are divided into neat, clearly demarcated segments. The size and order of those parcels are heavily influenced by the cadastral system (the method of land survey by which land ownership and property lines are defined) and by rules about property inheritance in a particular place.

- Although the 20th century saw unprecedented urban growth throughout the world, approximately half of the world's people still reside in villages and rural areas. Indeed, the agrarian village remains one of the most common forms of settlement on Earth.

- Traditional farm-village life remains especially common in much of the world's periphery, where agriculture is often still the most prominent economic activity. In the world's core areas, on the other hand, true farm villages, in which farming or providing services for farmers are the dominant activities, are disappearing.

9.4 What Is the Global Pattern of Agriculture and Agribusiness?

WORLD AGRICULTURE

When looking at patterns of agriculture at the global scale (Figure 9.14), it is important to recognize that von Thünen's concerns regarding the interplay of market location, land use, and transportation costs can reveal only one part of the picture. We must also consider the effects of different climate and soil conditions, variations in farming methods and technology, involvement by governments, and the lasting impacts of history. Decisions made by colonial powers in Europe led to the establishment of plantations from Central America to Malaysia. The plantations grew crops not for local markets but for consumers in Europe; similarly, U.S. companies founded huge plantations in the Americas. Over the past few centuries, the impact of this plantation system transformed the map of world agriculture. And the end of colonial rule did not signal the end of the agricultural practices and systems that had been imposed on the former colonial areas. Long-entrenched agricultural systems and patterns are not quickly or easily transformed, and even food-poor countries must continue to grow commercial crops for export on some of their best soils where their own food should be harvested.

Commercial farming has come to dominate in the world's economic core, as well as in some places in the semi-periphery and periphery. Commercial farming is the agriculture of large-scale grain producers and cattle ranches, mechanized equipment and factory-type labour forces, plantations and profit. As we will see, it is a world apart from the traditional farms of Asia and Africa.

FIGURE 9.14 World Agriculture. Areas where various kinds of agriculture are practised throughout the world are indicated with different colours on this map. Adapted with permission from Hammond, Inc., 1977.

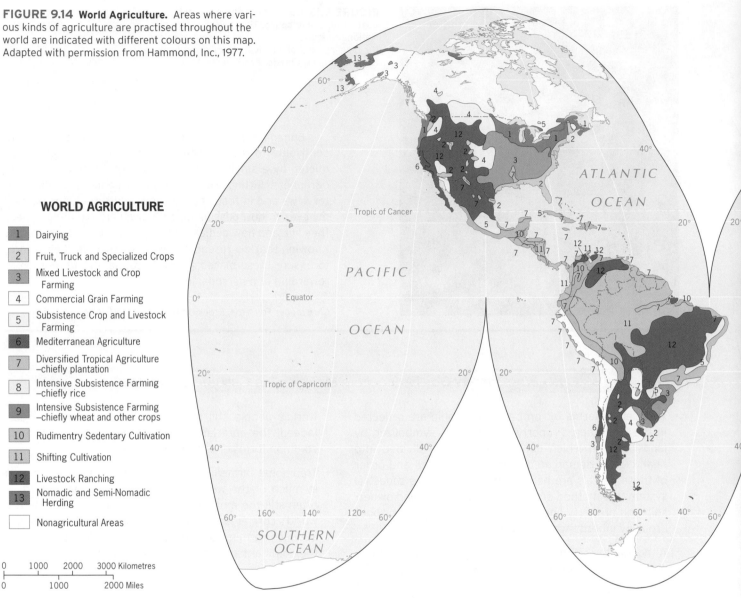

WORLD AGRICULTURE

1 Dairying

2 Fruit, Truck and Specialized Crops

3 Mixed Livestock and Crop Farming

4 Commercial Grain Farming

5 Subsistence Crop and Livestock Farming

6 Mediterranean Agriculture

7 Diversified Tropical Agriculture –chiefly plantation

8 Intensive Subsistence Farming –chiefly rice

9 Intensive Subsistence Farming –chiefly wheat and other crops

10 Rudimentry Sedentary Cultivation

11 Shifting Cultivation

12 Livestock Ranching

13 Nomadic and Semi-Nomadic Herding

☐ Nonagricultural Areas

0   1000   2000   3000 Kilometres
0   1000   2000 Miles

Commercial agriculture
Large-scale farming and ranching operations that employ vast land bases, large mechanized equipment, factory-type labour forces, and the latest technology.

The roots of modern **commercial agriculture** can be traced to the vast colonial empires established by European powers in the 18th and 19th centuries. Europe became a market for agricultural products from around the world, but with an added dimension: European countries manufactured and sold in their colonies the finished products made from imported raw materials. Thus, cotton grown in Egypt, Sudan, India, and other countries colonized by Europe was bought cheaply, imported to European factories, and made into clothes—many of which were then exported and sold, often in the very colonies where the cotton had been grown in the first place. Major changes in transportation and food storage, especially refrigeration (Figure 9.15), have further intertwined agricultural production and food-processing regions around the world. The beef industry of

FIGURE 9.15 Dunedin, New Zealand. The technology of refrigeration has kept pace with the containerization of seaborne freight. Incoming containers are attached to refrigeration units so that meat and other perishables can be kept frozen until they are transferred to a refrigerator ship. (© H. J. de Blij)

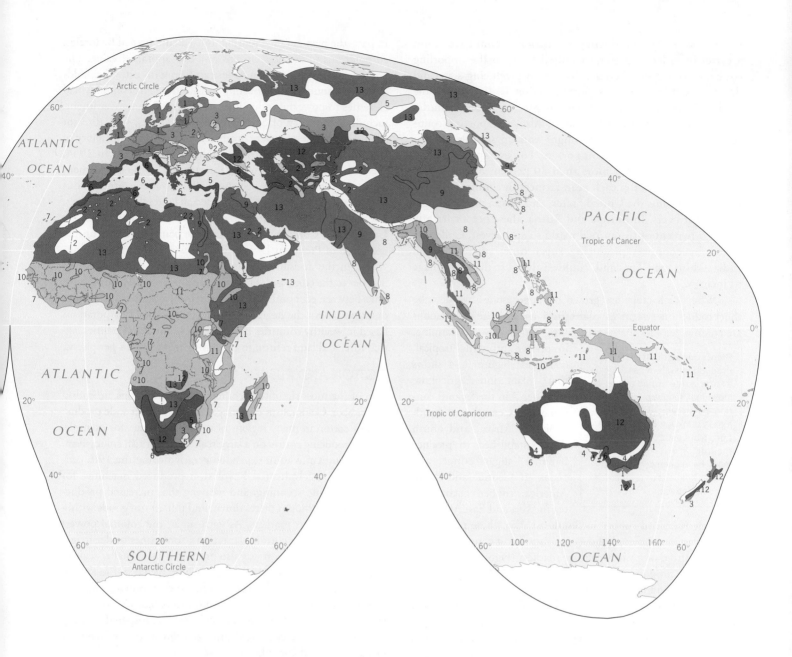

Argentina, for example, secured a world market when the invention of refrigerated ships made it possible to transport a highly perishable commodity over long distances.

European colonial powers also required farmers in their colonies to cultivate specific crops. One major impact of colonial agriculture was the establishment of **monoculture** (dependence on a single agricultural commodity) throughout much of the colonial world. Colonies became known for certain crops, and colonizers came to rely on those crops. Ghanaians still raise cacao, Mozambiquans still grow cotton, and Sri Lankans still produce tea. Poorer countries are often required to continue producing these cash crops today in order to meet loan and aid requirements from lending countries, the World Trade Organization, the International Monetary Fund, and the World Bank (see Chapter 11).

> **Monoculture** Dependence on a single agricultural commodity.

CASH CROPS AND PLANTATION AGRICULTURE

Nonsubsistence farming in many poorer countries is a leftover from colonial times. Colonial powers implemented particular agricultural systems to benefit their needs, a practice that has tended to lock poorer countries into production of one or two "cash" crops. Cash farming continues to provide badly needed money, even if the conditions of sale to the urban-industrial world are unfavourable. In the Caribbean region, for example, whole national economies depend on the export of sugar, which was introduced by the European colonists in the 1600s. These island countries wish to sell the sugar at the highest possible price, but they are not in a position to dictate prices. Sugar is produced by many countries in various parts of the world, as well as by farmers in the core. Governments in the core place quotas on imports of agricultural products and subsidize domestic production of the same commodities.

Occasionally, producing countries attempt to form a cartel in order to present a united front to the importing countries and gain a better price, as oil-producing states did during the 1970s. Such collective action is difficult, as the wealthy importing countries can buy products from countries that are not members of the cartel. Also, if exporting countries withhold produce, they might end up stimulating domestic production among importers. For example, although cane sugar accounts for more than 70 percent of the world's commercial sugar crop each year, farmers in countries such as France, Germany, the United States, and Russia produce sugar from sugar beets. In Europe and Russia, these beets currently yield 25 percent of the annual world sugar harvest. Collective action by countries producing sugar cane, such as Brazil, India, China, and Thailand, could easily cause that percentage to increase.

When cash crops are grown on large estates, we describe the production system as **plantation agriculture**. Plantations are colonial legacies that persist, along with subsistence farming, in poorer, primarily tropical, countries. Figure 9.14 shows that plantation agriculture (number 7 in the legend) continues in Central and South America, Africa, and South Asia. Established to produce bananas, sugar, coffee, and cocoa in Central and South America; rubber, cocoa, and tea in West and East Africa; tea in South Asia; and rubber in Southeast Asia, these plantations have outlasted the period of decolonization and continue to provide specialized crops to wealthier markets (Figure 9.16). Many of the most productive plantations are owned by European or American individuals or corporations.

Multinational corporations have tenaciously protected their economic interests in plantations. In the 1940s and 1950s, the Guatemalan government began an agrarian reform program.

> **Plantation agriculture**
> Production system based on a large estate owned by an individual, family, or corporation and organized to produce a cash crop. Almost all plantations were established within the tropics; in recent decades, many have been divided into smaller holdings or reorganized as cooperatives.

In part, the plan entailed renting unused land owned by foreign corporations to landless citizens at a low appraised value. The United Fruit Company, an American firm with extensive holdings in the country, did not support this idea. The company had close ties to powerful individuals in the American government, including Secretary of State John Foster Dulles, CIA director Allen Dulles (the two were brothers), and Assistant Secretary of State for Inter-American Affairs John Moors Cabot. In 1954, the United States supported the overthrow of the government of Guatemala, ostensibly because the U.S. was concerned about the spread of communism. This ended all land reform initiatives, leading many commentators to question the degree to which the United Fruit Company was behind the coup. Indeed, with the exception of President Dwight Eisenhower, every individual involved in the decision to help topple Guatemala's government had ties to the company. This example illustrates the inextricable links between economics and political motivations—and it raises questions about the degree to which multinational corporations based in wealthy countries influence decisions about politics, agriculture, and land reform in the semi-periphery and periphery.

COTTON AND RUBBER

Two of the most significant contemporary cash crops are cotton and rubber. Colonialism encouraged the plantation-scale production of cotton in many regions of the world. India, for example, began producing cotton on a large scale under British colonialism.

Cotton cultivation expanded greatly during the 19th century, when the Industrial Revolution produced machines for cotton ginning, spinning, and weaving that increased productive capacity, brought prices down, and put cotton goods within the reach of mass markets. As with sugar, the colonial powers laid out large-scale cotton plantations, sometimes under irrigation. Cotton cultivation was also promoted on a smaller scale in numerous other countries: in Egypt's Nile Delta, in the Punjab region shared by Pakistan and India, and in Sudan, Uganda, Mexico, and Brazil. The colonial producers received low prices for their cotton, and the European industries prospered as cheap raw materials were converted into large quantities of items for sale at home and abroad.

Wealthier countries continue to buy cotton, and cotton sales remain important for some former colonies. Today, however, they must also compete with cotton being grown in the United States, northeastern China, and Central Asia. Much of the cotton purchased by Japan, the United Kingdom, and western Europe, for example, comes from the United States. Cotton is now also in competition with synthetic fibres such as nylon and rayon.

Similarly, rubber is now in competition with synthetic rubber. Before the synthetic form was developed, rubber was collected from rubber-producing trees in equatorial rainforests, mainly in the Amazon Basin of northern South America. Around 1900, for example, the town of Manaus on the Amazon River experienced a rubber boom. Rubber companies in the Congo Basin in Africa experienced a similar period of prosperity. The boom in wild rubber was short-lived, however. Rubber-tree plantations were created to make rubber collection easier and more efficient. Seedlings of Brazilian rubber trees were planted elsewhere, and

FIGURE 9.16 A Tea Plantation in Kenya. The tea industry plays an important role in Kenya's economy. Much of the tea is grown on large and often foreign-owned plantations, while the rest is grown by small-scale growers. (© Xu Suhui/Xinhua Press/Corbis)

they did especially well in Southeast Asia. Within two decades, nearly 90 percent of the world's rubber came from new plantations in colonial territories in Malaysia, the Netherlands East Indies (now Indonesia), and neighbouring colonies.

As time went on, manufacturers found more and more uses for rubber, and consumer demand grew continuously. The advent of the automobile was an enormous boost for the industry, and most of the rubber now produced is used to manufacture vehicle tires. World War II created a need for alternative sources of rubber, since Japan had occupied much of Southeast Asia. This stimulated the production of synthetic rubber. In 2007, world rubber production totalled approximately 21.2 million tonnes, more than 12.2 million tonnes synthetic. Of the natural rubber produced that year, almost 70 percent came from the plantations of Southeast Asia.

The development of rubber plantations in Southeast Asia, rather than in the Amazon Basin or the Congo Basin, is due less to environmental factors than to the availability of labour. The colonial powers were aware that Southeast Asia combined conditions of tropical environment and labour availability that neither the Amazon region nor Equatorial Africa could match. Eventually, a large-scale rubber industry developed in Liberia (West Africa), but in the 1990s it was destroyed during the country's disastrous civil war. Lately, efforts have been made to introduce the plantation system along the Amazon River in the heart of northern Brazil.

LUXURY CROPS

A combination of suitable environment and available labour led the European colonial powers to establish huge plantations

Luxury crops Non-subsistence crops such as tea, cacao, coffee, and tobacco.

for the cultivation of **luxury crops** such as tea, cacao, coffee, and tobacco. After petroleum, coffee is now the second-most-valuable traded commodity in the world. It is also one of the best examples of colonialism's impact on present-day agricultural practices. In the early 18th century, coffee was virtually unknown in most of the world. It was first domesticated in the region of present-day Ethiopia, but today it thrives in Central and South America, where approximately 70 percent of the world's annual production is harvested.

It is estimated that 400 billion cups of coffee are consumed each year, equivalent to about 12,000 cups per second. The United States buys more than half of all the coffee sold on world markets annually, and western Europe imports most of the rest. The most familiar image of coffee production in North America is probably that provided by Juan Valdez, who is portrayed as a simple yet proud Colombian peasant who handpicks beans by day and enjoys a cup of his own coffee by night. However, this image is far from the reality of much coffee production in Latin America or elsewhere. In many cases, coffee is produced on enormous, foreign-owned plantations, where it is picked by local labourers who are hired at very low wage rates. Most coffee is sent abroad; if the coffee pickers drink coffee, it is probably of the imported and instant variety.

Coffee production is undergoing changes as more consumers demand fair trade coffee and more coffee producers seek fair

trade certification. CNN reports that "retailers who are certified Fair Traders return up to 40 percent of the retail price of an item to the producer." Once a producer meets the requirements of organic coffee production and a few other criteria, that producer can be registered on the International Fair Trade Coffee Register. Coffee importers then purchase the fair trade coffee directly from the registered producers. Being registered guarantees coffee producers a "fair trade price" of $1.26 per pound of coffee (plus bonuses of $0.20 per pound for organic). Over 500,000 farmers in 20 countries in the periphery and semi-periphery are on the fair trade register. The fair trade campaign pressured Starbucks into selling fair trade coffee, and the coffee chain now purchases more than 10 percent of the global production of fair trade coffee. Major Canadian supermarkets, such as western Canada's Co-op stores and those owned by the Loblaw Companies, also sell fair trade coffee.

Tea is a more recent addition to the Western diet. It was grown in China perhaps 2,000 years ago, but it became popular in Europe only during the 19th century. The colonial powers (mainly the British) established enormous tea plantations in Asia and thus began the full-scale flow of tea into European markets. Tea production, both the fair trade and traditionally traded varieties, is on the rise globally to meet the increasing consumption of the luxury crop. Compared with coffee, tea is consumed in greater quantities in areas where it is grown, including India, China, Sri Lanka, and Japan. Whereas coffee is cultivated and consumed mainly in the Americas, tea is the dominant beverage in significant parts of Eurasia. Tea goes from the Asian-producing areas to the United Kingdom and the rest of Europe and North America.

Today, fair trade production goes far beyond coffee and tea. Dozens of other commodities and products, ranging from bananas and fresh cut flowers to chocolate and soccer balls, can also be certified fair trade. According to Fairtrade Labelling Organizations International, consumers spent more than C$4.5 billion on fair trade certified products in 2008, representing an increase of 22 percent over 2007 consumption levels.

COMMERCIAL LIVESTOCK, FRUIT, AND GRAIN AGRICULTURE

By far the largest areas of commercial agriculture (numbers 1 through 4 on Figure 9.14) lie outside the tropics. Dairying (1) is widespread at the northern margins of the mid-latitudes—particularly in southeastern Canada, the northeastern United States, and northwestern Europe. Fruit, truck, and specialized crops (2), including the market gardens von Thünen observed around Rostock, are found in the eastern and southeastern United States and in widely dispersed small areas where environments are favourable. (Major oases can be seen in the Sahara and in Central Asia.)

Mixed livestock and crop farming (3) is widespread in the more humid parts of the mid-latitudes, including much of the eastern United States, western Europe, and western Russia, but it is also found in smaller areas in Uruguay, Brazil, and South Africa. Commercial grain farming (4) prevails in the drier parts of the mid-latitudes, including the southern Prairie provinces of Canada, in the Dakotas and Montana in the United States, as well as in Nebraska, Kansas, and adjacent areas. Spring wheat (planted in the spring and harvested in the summer) grows in the northern zone, and winter wheat (planted in the autumn and harvested in the spring of the following year) is primarily used in the southern area. An even larger belt of wheat farming extends from Ukraine through Russia into Kazakhstan. The Argentinean and Australian wheat zones are smaller in area, but their exports are an important component of world trade.

Even a cursory glance at Figure 9.14 reveals the wide distribution of **livestock ranching** (12), the raising of domesticated animals for meat and by-products, such as leather and wool. In addition to the large cattle-ranching areas in Canada, the United States, and Mexico, much of eastern Brazil and Argentina are devoted to ranching, along with large tracts of Australia, New Zealand, and South Africa. You may see a Thünian pattern here: livestock ranching on the periphery and consumers in the cities. Refrigeration has overcome the problem of perishability, and high volume has lowered the unit cost of transporting beef, lamb, and other animal products.

> **Livestock Ranching** The raising of domesticated animals for the production of meat and other by-products such as leather and wool.

SUBSISTENCE AGRICULTURE

The map of world agriculture in Figure 9.14 also labels three types of subsistence agriculture: subsistence crop and livestock farming, intensively subsistence farming (chiefly rice), and intensively subsistence farming (chiefly wheat and other crops). In some regions, the "subsistence" label does not tell the whole story. For example, most Southeast Asian farmers are subsistence grain farmers, but the area is also a source of significant rice exports, so subsistence and export production occur side by side. However, the rice is grown on small plots while the grain-growing takes place on a much larger proportion of the land. Accordingly, Southeast Asia appears on the map as primarily a subsistence grain-growing area.

MEDITERRANEAN AGRICULTURE

Only one form of agriculture mentioned in the legend of Figure 9.14 refers to a particular climatic zone: **Mediterranean agriculture** (6). As the map shows, this kind of specialized farming occurs only in areas where the Mediterranean dry summer climate prevails: along the shores of the Mediterranean Sea, in parts of California and Oregon in the United States, in central Chile, at South Africa's Cape, and in parts of southwestern and southern Australia. Farmers here grow a special combination of crops: grapes, olives, citrus fruits, figs, certain vegetables, dates, and others. These areas also produce many wines. These and other commodities are exported to distant markets because Mediterranean products tend to be popular and command high prices.

> **Mediterranean agriculture** Specialized farming that occurs only in areas where the dry summer Mediterranean climate prevails.

ILLEGAL DRUGS

Important cash crops that cannot be easily mapped and do not appear in Figure 9.14 are those that are turned into illegal drugs. Globally, the United Nations Office on Drugs and Crime estimates that between 155 and 250 million people (3.5 to 5.7 percent of the world population aged 15 to 64) used illicit substances at least once in 2008. Because of the high demand for drugs, particularly in the core, farmers in the periphery often find it more profitable to cultivate opium poppies, coca, or marijuana than standard food crops. Cultivation of these plants increased steadily through the 1980s and 1990s. Although cultivation has levelled off in recent years, and even declined in some areas, these crops continue to make up an important source of revenue for parts of the global economic periphery. Coca, the source plant of cocaine, is grown widely in Colombia, Peru, and Bolivia. Over half of the world's cultivation of coca occurs in Colombia alone.

Heroin and opium are derived from opium poppies, grown predominantly in southeastern and southwestern areas of Asia, especially Afghanistan and Myanmar. In the 2010 World Drug Report, the United Nations reported that 90 percent of the world's opium production took place in Afghanistan (Figure 9.17). The United States-led overthrow of the Taliban in Afghanistan in 2001 created a power vacuum in the country and an opportunity for illegal drug production to quickly rebound (the austere Taliban government had virtually eradicated opium production in Afghanistan by 2001). Most opium production in Afghanistan occurs in the country's five unstable southern provinces; however, a major blight (in this case caused by a fungal disease) wiped out about half of Afghanistan's production in 2010.

FIGURE 9.17 Opium Poppy Field in the Nangarhar Province, Afghanistan. Afghan police and provincial security forces destroy poppy fields in the Nangarhar province of Afghanistan. (© Benjamin Lowry/Getty Images)

ENVIRONMENTAL IMPACTS OF COMMERCIAL AGRICULTURE

Commercial agriculture creates significant environmental change. If you travel to Mediterranean Europe today, for example, you will see a landscape that reflects the clearing of forests in ancient times to facilitate agriculture and trade. Look carefully at many hill slopes and you will see evidence of terraces cut into the hills many centuries ago. The industrialization and commercialization of agriculture has accelerated the pace and extent of agriculture's impact on the environment. More land has been cleared, and the land that is under cultivation is used more and more intensively.

Significant changes in the natural environment go far beyond the simple clearing of land. They range from soil erosion to changes in the organic content of soils to the presence of chemicals (e.g., herbicides, pesticides, and even antibiotics and growth hormones from livestock feces) in soils and groundwater. In places where large commercial crop farms dominate, the greatest concern is the introduction of chemical fertilizers and pesticides into the environment—as well as soil erosion. And, as we have seen, the move to genetically modified crops carries with it another set of environmental concerns.

The environmental impacts can be particularly severe when commercial agriculture expands into marginal environments. This has happened, for example, with the expansion of livestock herding into arid or semi-arid areas. The natural vegetation in these areas cannot always sustain the herds, especially during prolonged droughts. This can lead to ecological damage and, in some areas, to desertification (see Chapter 11).

In recent years, the popularity of fast-food chains that serve hamburgers has led to the deforestation of wooded areas in order to open up additional pastures for beef cattle, notably in Central and South America. Livestock ranching is an extremely land-, water-, and energy-intensive process. Significant amounts of land must be turned over to the cultivation of cattle feed, and the animals themselves need extensive grazing areas (Figure 9.18). By stripping away vegetation, the animals exacerbate the erosion of river banks, with implications for everything from water quality to wildlife habitat.

More efficient technologies and the growing demand for protein-rich foods have led to overfishing in many regions of the world. Fish stocks are declining rapidly. From mid-century to the late 1980s, the fish harvest from oceans and seas increased five-fold, and there seemed to be no limit to it. Countries quarrelled over fishing rights, poorer countries leased fishing grounds to richer ones, and fleets of trawlers plied the oceans. International attempts to regulate fishing industries failed. Then in the 1970s and 1980s, overfishing began destroying fish stocks. The cod fisheries on Canada's Grand Banks, off the coast of Newfoundland, collapsed. In 1975, biologists estimated the Atlantic blue-fin tuna population at 250,000; today the western stock is listed as critically endangered, and the stock in the Mediterranean is listed as endangered. From ocean perch and king crabs off Alaska to rock lobsters and roughies off New Zealand, fish and shellfish populations are being depleted. The total annual catch is also declining and may already be beyond

FIGURE 9.18 Ranchers Herd Cattle in a Deforested Patch of the Amazon Rain Forest. The growing global appetite for meat, much of which is being served in fast-food restaurants, has resulted in the extensive deforestation of wooded areas around the world, particularly in Central and South America. (Jack Chang/MCT via Getty Images)

the point of recovery. Much of the damage has been done, with fishing industries in many parts of the world reporting dwindling harvests and missing species.

AGRIBUSINESS AND THE CHANGING GEOGRAPHY OF AGRICULTURE

The commercialization of crop production and the associated development of new agricultural technologies have changed how agricultural goods are grown and have sparked the rapid growth of **agribusiness**—an encompassing term for the businesses that provide a vast array of goods and services to support the agricultural industry. Agribusiness serves to connect local farms to a spatially extensive web of production and exchange. At the same time, it fosters the spatial concentration of agricultural activities.

> **Agribusiness** The businesses that provide the vast array of goods and services that support the agriculture industry.

Agribusiness is shaping the world distribution of commercial agricultural systems and their relationship to subsistence agriculture. Through time, many factors have affected that relationship. History and tradition have played important roles, as have environment and technology. At times, governments have encouraged their citizens to limit family size in an attempt to lift the population above the subsistence level. Some governments upheld the privileges of large landowners, whereas others initiated bold land reform programs. Communist governments, notably those of the former Soviet Union and Maoist China, tried to control agricultural output by creating collective farms and agricultural communes—a giant experiment that resulted in significant displacement of rural peoples and mixed results in terms of output. (Today, both Russia and China are reprivatizing farms.)

The map of global agricultural regions reveals the capacity of markets, above all, to influence the activities of farmers. The range and variety of products on the shelves of grocery stores across Canada are a world away from the constant quest for sufficient, nutritionally balanced food that exists in some places. A global network of farm production is especially oriented to the one-fifth of the world's population that is highly urbanized, wealthy, and powerful. Few farmers in distant lands have real control over land-use decisions because the better-off people in the global economic core continue to decide what will be bought and at what price. The colonial era may have come to an end, but, as the map of agricultural regions reminds us, its imprint remains strong.

LOSS OF PRODUCTIVE FARMLAND

As cities expand outward and agricultural lands are converted into suburbs, some of the most fertile, productive farmlands are lost to housing and retail developments (Figure 9.19). Many cities were established amid productive farmlands that could supply the needs of their inhabitants. Now the cities are absorbing the productive farmlands as they expand. Only about 5 percent of Canada's total land mass is considered to be dependable farland, most of which is concentrated in Manitoba, Saskatchewan, and Alberta. A study by Statistics Canada showed that in 2001 almost half of Canada's urban land area was located on land that had previously served as dependable agricultural land. Not only has this reduced the country's ability to grow its own food, but it has also forced many farming activities onto lower-quality farmland that is less conducive to long-term food production. Figures for other countries in the richer parts of the world (such as Japan), as well as for less affluent countries (such as Egypt), prove that this is a global problem with serious implications for the future.

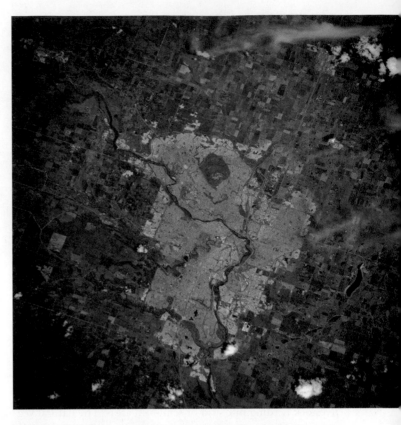

FIGURE 9.19 Calgary, Alberta, and Surrounding Area. Calgary's exponential population growth in the late 20th and early 21st centuries, driven largely by its important role as a headquarters for Alberta's prosperous oil and gas industry, has led to the city's outward growth onto surrounding agricultural lands. Between 1991 and 2001, for example, Calgary's population grew by 24 percent, but its urban land area grew by 43 percent. In other words, for every 100 new residents, Calgary added 6.3 hectares of urban land. (Image courtesy of Earth Sciences and Image Analysis Laboratory, NASA)

MAIN POINTS   9.4   What Is the Global Pattern of Agriculture and Agribusiness?

- Today's global agricultural patterns are influenced by a wide array of factors, including the location and accessibility of markets, land use and transportation costs, climate and soil conditions, variations in farming methods and technology, involvement by governments, and the lasting impacts of history (such as decisions made by colonial powers and historical trade patterns).

- Commercial farming has come to dominate in the world's economic core, as well as in some regions of the semi-periphery and periphery. The roots of modern commercial agriculture can be traced to the vast colonial empires established by European powers in the 18th and 19th centuries.

- Colonial powers implemented particular agricultural systems to benefit their needs, a practice that has tended to lock poorer countries into production of one or two "cash" crops. However, cash farming continues to provide badly needed money for some countries, even if the conditions of sale to the urban-industrial world are unfavourable.

- Commercial agriculture creates significant environmental change that goes beyond the simple clearing of land. Soil erosion, deforestation, desertification, and the infiltration of chemicals from fertilizers and pesticides into soils and groundwater are among the greatest concerns.

- Many cities in Canada and around the world were established amid productive farmlands that could supply the needs of their inhabitants. Today, the processes of urban growth and urban sprawl have resulted in the widespread absorption of productive farmlands. In the case of Canada, this is of particular concern, given that only about 5 percent of the country's total land area is made up of dependable farmland.

SUMMARY

Agricultural production has changed drastically since the First Agricultural Revolution, but not to the same extent in all places around the world. Today, agricultural products, even perishable ones, are routinely shipped thousands of kilometres and from one continent to another. In many parts of the world, agriculture has also industrialized and spurred the growth of agribusiness. At the same time, however, agriculture in the globalized economy is complicated by concerns about new technologies, genetically engineered crops, cultural change, government involvement, and the lasting impacts of history. Furthermore, in many parts of the world, especially in peripheral regions, agricultural practices remain the same as they have been for hundreds of years. Hundreds of millions of farmers around the world are involved in subsistence agriculture, growing only enough food, on small plots of land and through heavily labour-intensive means, to sustain themselves and their families.

DISCUSSION AND REVIEW QUESTIONS

1. The most significant events in the history of humanity are arguably the agricultural and animal domestication revolutions. Where did the first revolutions take place and why did they occur in those locations? What were some of the specific impacts of the revolutions?

2. Since its inception, the agricultural revolution has evolved into a second and third phase. Compare and contrast the so-called second agricultural revolution with the third agricultural revolution. Further, how do the two evolutionary phases compare and contrast spatially?

3. Discuss whether or not the "green revolution" has been a success or a failure, and provide reasons for either case.

4. Beginning with Johann Heinrich von Thünen, identify and discuss the various ways geographers have tried to understand the spatial layout of agricultural systems. Geographers are also interested in the cultural landscapes of agricultural systems. Explain the various systems that have profoundly shaped the North American landscape.

5. Commercial agriculture has come to dominate the world's economic core. Discuss how and where commercial agriculture developed, as well as its various forms. How has commercial agricultural impacted the environment?

GEOGRAPHIC CONCEPTS

agribusiness   271
agriculture   249
animal domestication   253
commercial agriculture   266
First Agricultural Revolution   250
genetically modified organisms (GMOs)   259
Green Revolution   258
livestock ranching   270
long-lot survey system   262
luxury crops   269
Mediterranean agriculture   270
metes and bounds survey system   262
monoculture   267

plant domestication   250
plantation agriculture   268
primogeniture   262
rectangular survey system   261
root crops   250
Second Agricultural Revolution   256
seed crops   250
shifting cultivation   255
slash-and-burn agriculture   255
subsistence agriculture   254
Third Agricultural Revolution   258
township-and-range system   261
von Thünen model   257

ADDITIONAL RESOURCES ONLINE

About agriculture at the global scale: www.fao.org

About the state of farming in Canada:
   www.statcan.gc.ca/ca-ra2006

About genetically modified organisms:
   www.gmo-compass.org/eng/home

About illicit drugs: www.unodc.org

About fair trade and agriculture: transfair.ca

About water quality issues: www.cwn-rce.ca

chapter 10

URBAN GEOGRAPHY

Straddling the Wall

AS A CHILD, I stood in West Berlin, facing the Berlin Wall. I looked at the grey wall and grey city of East Berlin (Figure 10.1) and turned around to see the more vibrant city of West Berlin. Why, I wondered, why is this city divided this way? Why is the East German government working so hard to keep their citizens in East Berlin? My mother interrupted my thoughts, saying, "Look! Look at the guards. Their guns are pointing EAST!" The East German guards along the wall were watching the East Germans to make sure they did not escape to the West.

In 1989, the people of East Berlin and West Berlin took control of the streets, the guard towers, and the wall itself. Berliners occupied the buffer spaces that had divided East Berlin and West Berlin, and they stood on the wall. The guards stood down. As hundreds of millions of people throughout Europe and the rest of the world watched the events unfold live on television, they knew the people who occupied these previously forbidden spaces were not only crushing the wall, but were fundamentally changing the space and the city, starting it down the path of reunification. No one knew what reunification would feel like or look like, and certainly no one knew with any certainty what problems would surface as a result of reunification, but everyone knew on that fateful night in December that Berlin had fundamentally changed.

In the summer of 2001, I took my own children to the place in Berlin where I had stood with my parents 40 years earlier. Instead of looking at the guards, my family looked for the wall. We tried to find traces of the old wall. Along the relict boundary (one that no longer functions) between the cities, we could see differences in architecture, differences in streets, and even a few remnants of the wall itself. It was a difficult task, as it seemed everything was under construction. New buildings had sprung up, city planners were changing street patterns, and cars were travelling freely across what used to be a fervently defended boundary.

Walking past Potsdamer Platz, we spotted a remnant of the old order that no one could miss: an old East German guard tower looming over a cultural landscape being remade before our eyes. My son was the first to point out that on the street next to the guard tower was a heavy machine, helping to recreate and recast the cultural landscape of Berlin.

FIGURE 10.1 West Berlin, West Germany. The Berlin Wall, as it stood when the city was divided. This photo was taken in West Berlin, looking across the wall to East Berlin. (© Alexander B. Murphy)

Berlin is no longer a divided city, and the German government is altering the cultural landscape to prove it. When Berlin was divided, many roads ended at checkpoints, buffers of development traced the outline of the wall, and each city had its own focal point where the roads led to particular buildings that were larger than others. Today, with the removal of the wall, Berlin's street patterns have changed, new buildings stand astride the site of the old wall, and the layout of the eastern and western parts of the cities reflects their different histories.

Urban geographers study cities. Urban geographers also study how states build and rebuild cities, and work to understand the interlinkages between political geography and urban geography. When West Germany and East Germany reunified in 1990, Germans debated the choice of a new capi-

tal. Many favoured Bonn, which served as the capital of West Germany and is located near the country's western border—symbolizing Germany's prominence in western Europe. Many others preferred a return to Berlin, which had served as the capital since Bismarck united the country and formed the first German state in 1870. Still other Germans wanted to put the past and both cities behind them; they argued for a totally new choice, such as Hanover, near the centre of the country. In the end, the German government selected Berlin and began a giant construction program to transform Berlin to symbolize a new era. As geographers, we are interested in tracing the evolution of urbanization in geographic context, in understanding how economic, cultural, and political factors influence the shaping of a city's form and function, and in studying how people live, work, and play in the cities they create.

KEY QUESTIONS FOR CHAPTER 10

1. When and why did people start living in cities?
2. Where are cities located, and why?
3. How are cities organized, and how do they function?
4. How do cities evolve?
5. What is the connection between cities and globalization?

10.1 When and Why Did People Start Living in Cities?

Cities hold a prominent place in our imaginations. Perhaps you hope to travel to one or more of the world's most famous cities, such as Montreal, New York, Paris, or Beijing. You can probably recognize the more well-known city skylines in Figure 10.2 even though you may never have been there. You may live in the suburbs or rural areas surrounding a major Canadian city, such as Ottawa or Calgary, and view a trip into the city centre for shopping or the theatre with a sense of adventure and excitement. Cities are centres of political and economic power, administration and government, technological innovation, and artistic achievement. They are the location of dominant economic markets, centres of specialization and interaction, sources of news and information, suppliers of services, and providers of sports and entertainment. Cities are the anchors of modern culture; urban systems and their spokes form the structural skeleton of society. Former Toronto mayor David Miller summed up the importance of Canadian cities in a 2010 editorial in the *Toronto Star*, stating, "As our large cities go, so goes the nation. When we succeed, the province and the country succeed." Geographical study of cities and urban areas straddles subdisciplinary boundaries, drawing on political and economic geography, social and cultural geographies, and other disciplinary work on humans and the built environment.

We can define a **city** as a conglomeration of people and buildings clustered together to serve as a centre of politics, culture, and economics. As of 2006, over 80 percent of Canadians lived in urban areas, with half of them living in Canada's four major cities. Figure 10.3 illustrates the distribution of Canada's population between urban and rural spaces from 1851 to 2006. In this context, Statistics Canada defines "urban" as a combination of total population (1,000) and density (400 persons per square kilometre). As we can see, in 1851, Canada was a largely rural country, but over the last 150 years it has become mainly urban.

> **City** Conglomeration of people and buildings clustered together to serve as a centre of politics, culture, and economics.

Virtually everywhere in the world we discover the same pattern as the one we see in Canada. People are moving from the countryside to urbanized areas—to towns, cities, and suburbs. Globally, more people live in towns and cities than in rural areas, making the global population predominantly **urban**, a term we use to describe the build-up of the central city and the **suburban realm**, which

> **Urban (area)** The entire built-up, non-rural area and its population, including the most recently constructed suburban appendages. Provides a better picture of the dimensions and population of such an area than the delimited municipality (central city) that forms its heart.
>
> **Suburban realm** The surrounding environs connected to the city.

(a)

(b)

(c)

FIGURE 10.2 Distinctive City Skylines. (a) Toronto, Ontario;
(b) Sydney, Australia; (c) London, England. (© Lester Lefkowitz/Corbis;
© Jose Fuste Raga/Corbis; © Luke Macgregor/Reuters/Corbis)

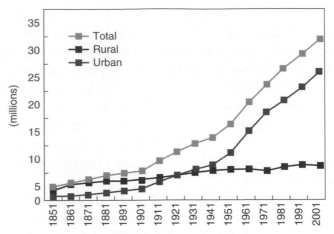

FIGURE 10.3 Urban and Rural Population 1851-2006. The rural popu-
lation for 1981 to 2006 refers to people living outside centres with a population of 1,000 *and* outside areas with 400 people per square kilometre.
Previous to 1981, the definitions differed slightly but consistently referred
to people outside centres of 1,000 population. Source: Industry Canada,
SME Financing Data Initiative - Rural-Based Entrepreneurs, Section -
Population Trends in Rural Canada, Figure 1: Population Trends in Canada's
Rural and Urban Areas, 1851-2001, October 2008, http://www.sme-fdi.
gc.ca/eic/site/sme_fdi-prf_pme.nsf/eng/h_02133.html. Reproduced with the
permission of the Minister of Public Works and Government Services, 2011.
Data source: Statistics Canada, Censuses of Population, 1851-2001.

refers to the surrounding environs connected to the city. An
urban place is distinctively non-rural and non-agricultural.
The movement of people from rural to urban locations reflects the changing global economy and the increasing ease of
movement in our globalized world. Urbanization is happening
everywhere; however, the distribution of urbanization across
the globe is not even. Figure 10.4 illustrates the population
densities of urban areas in the six main regions of the world.
The most densely populated urban areas in the world–those
with over 10 million people–can be found in Latin America
and the Caribbean (14 percent) and Asia (10 percent). The
least densely populated urban areas, with less than 500,000
residents, can be found in Europe (68 percent) and Africa
(58 percent). Oceania does not have any urban centres with
more than 5 million people, which is somewhat similar to
Canada, where only one urban area, the Greater Toronto
Area, has a population of more than 5 million. Other major
urban areas in Canada–Montreal, Vancouver, and Ottawa-
Gatineau–each have a population between 1 and 5 million.

Despite our sense that much of the global population
lives in cities, it is important to remember that over half of
the world's population lives in
cities of fewer than 500,000
people. On the other hand,
some cities in the world are
what we would now term
mega-cities, having populations of over 10 million inhabitants. These are more
properly understood as **urban
agglomerations**, defined by
the United Nations as those

Mega-city A city having a
population of more than 10
million inhabitants.

Urban agglomerations
Defined by the United Nations
as those populations of 1 million or more people "within a
contiguous territory inhabited
at urban levels of residential
density."

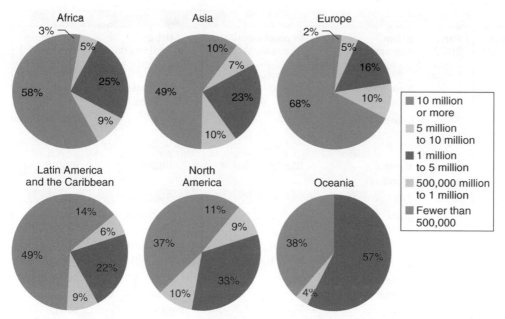

FIGURE 10.4 **Distribution of Urban Populations by Size of Urban Settlement, Major Areas, 2007.** From the United Nations, Department of Economic and Social Affairs, Population Division, Urban Agglomerations, 2007. Retrieved July 27, 2011, from http://www.un.org/esa/population/publications/wup2007/2007_urban_agglomerations_chart.pdf.

populations of 1 million or more people "within a contiguous territory inhabited at urban levels of residential density." In Table 10.1, we see the top 20 urban agglomerations in the world today and the top 20 projected populations in 2025. Note that North American and European cities are no longer the largest, as Latin American, African, and Asian cities are growing rapidly and moving up the list. For example, New York is ranked second in 2007 but is projected to be ranked seventh if current growth rates continue.

In this chapter, we focus on the process of urbanization—how and why people began living in cities, and how cities change over time. We are interested in why cities are located where they are and the reasons for their internal form and function. We also consider how cities evolve and how their relationships with each other vary across a variety of scales—local, regional, national, and global. Urban geographers, with their spatial perspective, focus on the location of cities, their regional interconnections, movements between and within cities, and the sense of place people have about cities and the landscapes they inhabit.

THE HEARTHS OF URBANIZATION

The process of urbanization, which can happen so quickly today, originally took thousands of years to develop; indeed, the rise of the city is a very recent phenomenon in human history. While human communities have existed for over 100,000 years, more than 90,000 years of human existence passed before people began to cluster more densely in villages and towns. Archaeological evidence indicates that people established the first cities about 8,000 years ago. However, it is only in the last 200 years that cities begin to assume their modern size and structure.

Scholars argue that there were essentially two urban revolutions. The first, beginning about 3500 BCE, was driven by shifts in technology associated with agricultural production and changing social relations. The second, occurring in the core region about 500 BCE, resulted from rapid technological and scientific advances related to the Industrial Revolution. Before people could live in cities, they had to switch from a hunting and gathering society to an agricultural one. This switch was the result of improved technologies and new forms of social order and social relations. As we discussed in Chapter 9, agricultural advances, including the domestication of animals and the planting and harvesting of crops, began between 10,000 and 12,000 years ago, allowing people to become more sedentary, staying in one place to tend their fields. People clustered in small **agricultural villages** and towns, living there year round. Agricultural villages were relatively small in size and in population. Everyone living in these villages was involved in agriculture, and people lived at near-subsistence levels, producing just enough to get by. The dwellings in ancient agricultural villages were all about the same size and contained about the same number of possessions, reflecting the egalitarian nature of such societies, in which people shared goods in common. That these villages were permanent is indicated by the fact that the dwellings were built to last longer than the tents used earlier, with plaster floors and other enduring elements. Scholars are fairly certain that these descriptors accurately depict the agricultural villages in Mesopotamia, the area of Southwest Asia called the Fertile Crescent (see Figure 10.5), which was the first agricultural hearth. Additional archaeological evidence suggests that agricultural villages in the Indus River Valley and Mesoamerica, later hearths of agricultural innovation, also fit these descriptors.

Egalitarian societies persisted long after agriculture began. When urban areas of some size and population began to develop, however, the egalitarian social order began to change as well. In cities, people, mainly men, generated material wealth that

> **Agricultural village** A relatively small, egalitarian village, where most of the population was involved in agriculture. Starting over 10,000 years ago, people began to cluster in agricultural villages as they stayed in one place to tend their crops.

TABLE 10.1   World's 20 Largest Urban Agglomerations, 1975, 2007, and 2025 (Projected)

Rank 1975	Urban Agglomeration	Population (thousands)	Rank 2007	Urban Agglomeration	Population (thousands)	Rank 2025	Urban Agglomeration	Population (thousands)
1	Tokyo	26,615	1	Tokyo	36,676	1	Tokyo	36,400
2	New York-Newark	15,880	2	New York-Newark	19,040	2	Mumbai (Bombay)	26,385
3	Ciudad de México (Mexico City)	10,690	3	Ciudad de México (Mexico City)	19,028	3	Delhi	22,498
4	Osaka-Kobe	9,844	4	Mumbai (Bombay)	18,978	4	Dhaka	22,015
5	São Paulo	9,614	5	São Paulo	18,845	5	São Paulo	21,428
6	Los Angeles-Long Beach-Santa Ana	8,926	6	Delhi	15,926	6	Ciudad de México (Mexico City)	21,009
7	Buenos Aires	8,745	7	Shanghai	14,987	7	New York-Newark	20,628
8	Paris	8,558	8	Kolkata (Calcutta)	14,787	8	Kolkata (Calcutta)	20,560
9	Kolkata (Calcutta)	7,888	9	Dhaka	13,485	9	Shanghai	19,412
10	Moskva (Moscow)	7,623	10	Buenos Aires	12,795	10	Karachi	19,095
11	Rio de Janeiro	7,557	11	Los Angeles-Long Beach-Santa Ana	12,500	11	Kinshasa	16,762
12	London	7,546	12	Karachi	12,130	12	Lagos	15,796
13	Shanghai	7,326	13	Al-Qāhira (Cairo)	11,893	13	Al-Qāhira (Cairo)	15,561
14	Chicago	7,160	14	Rio de Janeiro	11,748	14	Manila	14,808
15	Mumbai (Bombay)	7,082	15	Osaka-Kobe	11,294	15	Beijing	14,545
16	Seoul	6,808	16	Beijing	11,106	16	Buenos Aires	13,768
17	Al-Qāhira (Cairo)	6,450	17	Manila	11,100	17	Los Angeles-Long Beach-Santa Ana	13,672
18	Beijing	6,034	18	Moskva (Moscow)	10,452	18	Rio de Janeiro	13,413
19	Manila	4,999	19	Istanbul	10,061	19	Jakarta	12,363
20	Tianjin	4,870	20	Paris	9,904	20	Istanbul	12,102

Source: Data from the United Nations, Department of Economic and Social Affairs, Population Division, Urban Agglomerations, 2007. Retrieved July 27, 2011, from http://www.un.org/esa/population/publications/wup2007/2007_urban_agglomerations_chart.pdf.

Agricultural surplus One of two components, together with social stratification, that enable the formation of cities; agricultural production in excess of that which the producer needs for his or her own sustenance and that of his or her family and which is then sold for consumption by others.

Social stratification One of two components, together with agricultural surplus, that enables the formation of cities; the differentiation of society into classes based on wealth, power, production, and prestige.

was owned by the individual, engaged in trade over long distances, and pursued a diversity of economic activities—not just agriculture—that led to changing social and political structures, including the development of differing social classes and methods of governance.

Archaeologists, anthropologists, and geographers studying the remains and records of the first cities have developed numerous theories on how cities came about. Most agree that some series of events led to the establishment of two main components that allowed early cities to form—**agricultural surplus** and **social stratification**—although which came first varies by theory. The series of events spurring these two components also varies according to the theory proposed. One theory maintains that advances in technology,

Leadership class Group of decision-makers and organizers in early cities who controlled the resources, and often the lives, of others.

such as irrigation, generated an agricultural surplus; then a **leadership class**, largely made up of men, formed to control the surplus as well as the technology that produced it. Another theory holds that a king or priest-king centralized political power and then demanded more labour to generate an agricultural surplus, which would help the ruler retain political power.

Regardless of how the leadership class emerged, we do know that, once established, it helped maintain a surplus and controlled its distribution. The link between the surplus and the leadership class is clear in early cities, where the home of the leaders was often positioned close to the grain storage. The leadership class, or urban elite, consisted of a group of male decision-makers and organizers who controlled the resources, and often the lives, of others. Generating an agricultural surplus allowed some to devote their efforts to pursuits besides agriculture. Members of the male urban elite, for instance, did not work the fields. Rather, they devoted time to pursuits such as religion and philosophy, out of which came the concepts of writing and record keeping. Writing made possible the codification of laws, the keeping of accurate records of trade and commerce, and the preservation of traditions. Urban elites saw to the defence of the city (and the preservation and protection of trade, commerce, and wealth) by constructing walls, controlling access to the city, and maintaining a standing army. The leadership class was also able to collect taxes and tribute from people under their control beyond the city walls in order to pay for a growing administration.

THE FIRST URBAN REVOLUTION

Some cities grew out of agricultural villages; others grew in places previously unoccupied by sedentary people. The innovation of the city is called the **first urban revolution**, and it occurred independently in as many as six separate hearths (Figure 10.5). It is important to note that scholars do not agree on the number of hearths. Those who argue that there are fewer than six hearths attribute more urbanization to diffusion. In each of the urbanization hearths, something triggered the establishment of a leadership class and an agricultural surplus. People became engaged in economic activities beyond agriculture, including specialty crafts, the military, trade, and government.

First urban revolution The innovation of the city, which occurred independently in six separate hearths.

Not surprisingly, the six urban hearths are tied closely to the hearths of agriculture. The first hearth of agriculture, the Fertile Crescent, is the first place we see cities, in about 3500 BCE. This urban hearth is called **Mesopotamia** and is the region of great cities, such as Ur and Babylon, located between the Tigris and Euphrates rivers (Figure 10.6). Studies of the cultural landscape of Mesopotamian cities have found signs of social inequality in the varying sizes and ornamentation of houses. Urban geographers use concepts like **urban morphology**, which refers to the layout

Mesopotamia Region of great cities (e.g., Ur and Babylon) located between the Tigris and Euphrates Rivers; chronologically the first urban hearth, dating to 3500 BCE, which was founded in the Fertile Crescent.
Urban morphology The study of the physical form and structure of urban places.

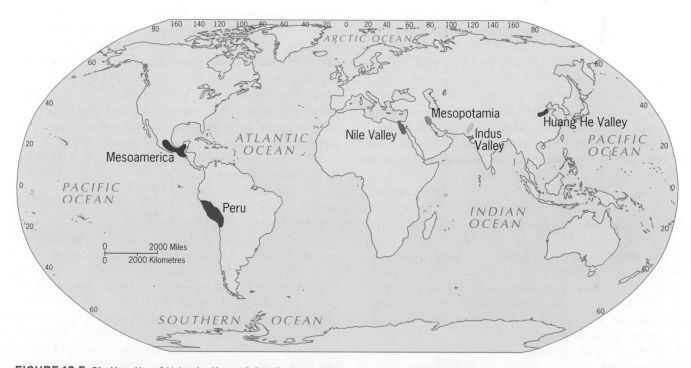

FIGURE 10.5 Six Hearths of Urbanization. (© E.H. Fouberg, A.B. Murphy, H.J. de Blij, and John Wiley & Sons, Inc.)

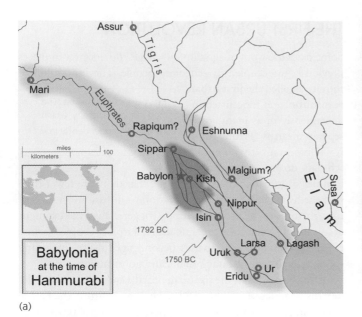

(a)

(b)

FIGURE 10.6 Babylon. (a) The city-state of Babylon was located approximately 85 kilometres south of Baghdad. This map shows the area as it was in the time of Hammurabi, king of Babylon from 1792 BCE to 1750 BCE. (b) In 1983, the ruler of Iraq, Saddam Hussein, began a reconstruction project on the grounds of the ruins of Babylon, visible in this aerial view from Google Earth in 2004. (Wikimedia Commons, MapMaster, Hammurabi's Babylonia, http://en.wikipedia.org/wiki/File:Hammurabi%27s_Babylonia_1.svg; © 2011 Google, Image © 2011 DigitalGlobe, © 2011 ORION-ME)

(physical form and structure) of a city, when they study urban areas in order to understand how states build and rebuild cities, and to recognize the linkages between political geography and urban geography.

In Mesopotamia, male urban elites erected palaces, protected themselves with walls, and employed countless artisans to beautify their spaces. They also established a priest-king class and developed a religious-political ideology to support the priest-kings. Rulers in the cities were both priests and kings, and they levied taxes and demanded tribute from the harvest brought by the agricultural labourers. The ancient Mesopotamian city was usually protected by a mud wall surrounding the entire community. Sometimes there was a cluster of temples and shrines at the city centre. Temples dominated the urban landscape, not only because they were the largest structures in town but also because they were built on artificial mounds that were often over 30 metres high. Male priests and other authorities resided in substantial buildings, many of which might be called palaces. Ordinary citizens lived in mud-walled houses packed closely together and separated only by narrow lanes. The poorest inhabitants lived in tiny huts, often with mud-smeared reed walls, on the outskirts of the city. The leadership class held slaves in prison-like accommodations that were sometimes outside the city wall. Lacking waste-disposal or sewage facilities, ancient cities were far from sanitary. Mesopotamians threw their garbage and refuse into the streets and other open spaces, and in some places layers of this waste accumulated to a depth of several metres. As a result, disease kept the populations of ancient cities small. Archaeologists have been able to sift through the garbage for clues to life in the ancient city.

The second hearth of urbanization, dating back to 3200 BCE, is the **Nile River Valley**. Some scholars contend that this region is not a hearth but, rather, a case of diffusion from Mesopotamia, although other evidence strongly supports the claim that there was independent invention of urbanization in the Nile River Valley. At the very least, the interrelationship between urbanization and irrigation in this region distinguishes it from other urban hearths. Unlike residents of other early cities, the people of the Nile River Valley did not build walls around their cities. From early on, power along the river was concentrated in the hands of the men who controlled the irrigation systems. The absence of walls around individual cities reflects the singular control of the region. The might of the rulers of the Nile River Valley is reflected in the feats of architecture such as the pyramids, tombs, and sphinx that were built by thousands of slaves.

The third urban hearth, dating to 2200 BCE, is the **Indus River Valley**, another place where agriculture likely diffused from the Fertile Crescent. Unable to decipher ancient Indus writing, scholars are puzzled by the characteristics of Harappa and Mohenjo-Daro, the first cities of this hearth (Figure 10.7). The intricate planning of the cities points to the existence of a leadership class, but the houses continued to be equal in size, with no palaces or monuments appearing in the cities. In addition, all the dwellings in the cities had access to the same infrastructure—including wastewater drains and carefully maintained stone-lined wells. The cities had thick walls, and the discovery of coins from as far away

> **Nile River Valley**
> Chronologically, the second urban hearth, dating to 3200 BCE.

> **Indus River Valley**
> Chronologically, the third urban hearth, dating to 2200 BCE.

Huang He (Yellow) and Wei (Yangtze) river valleys Chronologically, the fourth urban hearth, established around 1500 BCE, at the confluence of the Huang He and Wei rivers in present-day China.

as the Mediterranean at the gateways in these walls points to significant trade over long distances.

The fourth urban hearth arose around the confluence of the **Huang He (Yellow) and Wei (Yangtze) river valleys** of present-day China, dating to 1500 BCE. The Chinese purposefully planned their ancient cities to centre on a vertical structure in the middle of the city and then built an inner wall around it. Within the inner wall, the people of this hearth typically placed temples and palaces for the leadership class. The urban elite of the Huang He and Wei region, like the urban elite of the Nile River Valley, demonstrated their power by building enormous, elaborate structures. Around 200 BCE, the Emperor Qin Xi Huang directed the building of the Great Wall of China. Like the Egyptians, he also had an elaborate mausoleum built for himself. An estimated 700,000 slaves worked for over 40 years to craft the intricate faces and weapons, horses, and chariots of an army of over 7,000 terracotta warriors who stand guard over his burial place (Figure 10.8).

Chronologically, the fifth urban hearth is **Mesoamerica**, dating to 200 BCE. The male urban elite in Mesoamerica augmented their authority with priests, tem-

Mesoamerica Chronologically, the fifth urban hearth, dating to 200 BCE.

ples, and shrines, and many ancient cities in the region were religious centres where rulers were deemed to have divine authority and were, in effect, god-kings. Examples of these theocratic centres include the great structures of Yucatan, Guatemala, and Honduras built by the Maya Indians (including Tikal, Chichén-Itza, Uxmal, and Copán in Figure 10.9).

The most recent archaeological evidence establishes Peru as the sixth urban hearth, chronologically. The Chavín built cities in Peru dating to 900 BCE. The largest settlement, Chavín, was sited at an elevation of 10,530 feet (3,200 metres) in the Andean highlands. How large were the ancient cities? We have only estimates, given that it is nearly impossible to judge the dimensions of a city at its height, or the number of people who might have occupied each residential unit, from excavated ruins. By modern standards, the ancient cities were not particularly large. The cities of Mesopotamia and the Nile River Valley are thought to have had between 10,000 and 15,000 inhabitants after nearly 2,000 years of growth and development. That number of people

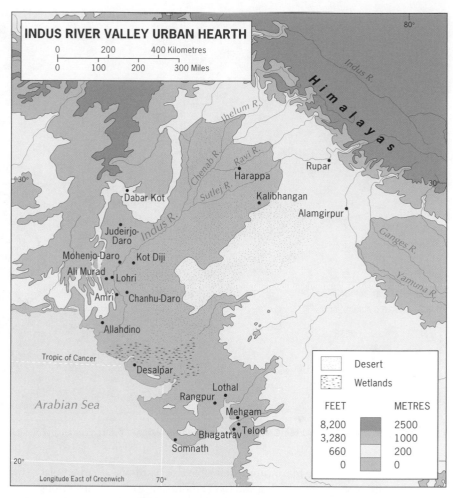

FIGURE 10.7 The Urban Hearth in the Indus River Valley. (© H.J. de Blij, P.O. Muller, and John Wiley & Sons, Inc.)

FIGURE 10.8 Terracotta Warriors Guarding the Tomb of the Chinese Emperor Qin Xi Huang. An estimated 700,000 slaves worked for over 40 years, around 200 BCE, to craft more than 7,000 terracotta warriors who stand guard over the emperor's tomb. (© O. Louis Mazzatenta/National Geographic Society/Getty Images)

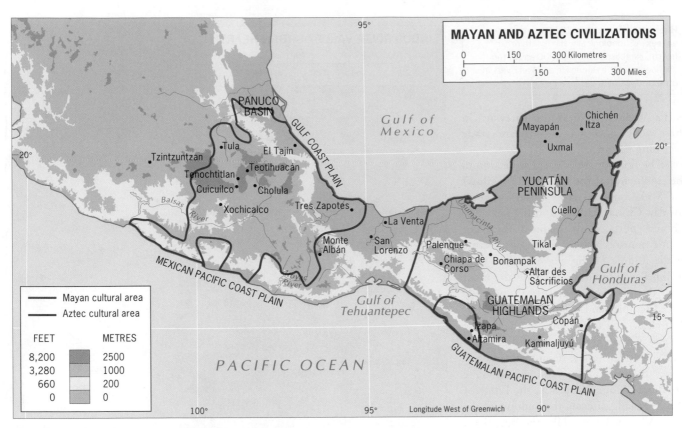

FIGURE 10.9 Mayan and Aztec Civilizations in Mesoamerica. (© E.H. Fouberg, A.B. Murphy, H.J. de Blij, and John Wiley & Sons, Inc.)

is thought to be about the maximum sustainable size based on existing systems of social organization and food production, gathering, and distribution. These urban places were geographical exceptions in an overwhelmingly rural world.

DIFFUSION OF URBANIZATION

Urbanization diffused from Mesopotamia in several directions. Populations in Mesopotamia grew with the steady food supply and a sedentary lifestyle. People migrated out from the hearth, diffusing their knowledge of agriculture and urbanization. Diffusion from Mesopotamia happened quite early in the process and mainly before agriculture developed independently in some other hearths. In fact, urbanization diffused to the Mediterranean from Mesopotamia (and perhaps from the Nile River Valley) more than 3,500 years ago, at about the same time cities were developing in the hearth of the Huang He, and long before cities emerged in Mesoamerica.

GREEK CITIES

More than 3,500 years ago, the city of Knossos, on what is now the Greek island of Crete, was the cornerstone of a system of towns in the Minoan civilization. By 500 BCE, Greece had become one of the most highly urbanized areas on Earth, and the urbanization of ancient Greece ushered in a new stage in the evolution of cities. At its height, ancient Greece encompassed a network of more than 500 cities and towns, not only on the mainland but also on the many Greek islands. Seafarers connected these

urban places with trade routes and carried the notion of urban life throughout the Mediterranean region. Athens and Sparta soon became Greece's leading cities, often vying with each other for power. Athens may have been the largest city in the world at the time, with an estimated 250,000 inhabitants.

Given the hilly topography of Greece, the people had no need to build earthen mounds on which to perch temples; these were provided by nature. Every city had its **acropolis** (acro = high point, polis = city), on which the people built the most impressive structures—usually religious buildings (Figure 10.10). The Parthenon of Athens remains the most famous of all, surviving to this day despite nearly 2,500 years of war, earth tremors, vandalism, and environmental wear and tear. Construction of this magnificent structure, designed by the Athenian architect-engineer Phidias, began in 447 BCE, and its rows of tapering columns have inspired architects ever since.

> **Acropolis** Literally "high point of the city." The upper fortified part of an ancient Greek city, usually devoted to religious purposes.

Public spaces in Greece were similar to those found in older Southwest Asian cities, though the Asian versions seem to have been rather cramped, crowded, and bustling with activity. In Ancient Greece, public spaces were designed to be more open and spacious. They were often in a low part of town, with steps leading down to them. On these steps, the men in Greek society debated, lectured, judged each other, planned military campaigns, and socialized. As time went on, this public space, called

FIGURE 10.10 Ancient Athens. The Parthenon of Athens sits atop the acropolis. (John Elk III/Lonely Planet Images/Getty Images)

> **Agora** In ancient Greece, public spaces where citizens debated, lectured, judged each other, planned military campaigns, socialized, and traded.

the **agora** (meaning "market"), also became the focus of commercial activity.

Although Greece was not a hearth of urbanization, the Greek city had global, rather than regional, impact. Urbanization diffused from Greece to the Roman Empire, which in turn diffused its urbanization and urban culture through western Europe. The city declined in Europe for a time after the fall of the Roman Empire, but Europeans eventually carried their notions of city life around the world through colonialism, imperialism, and capitalism. From Washington, DC, to Toronto, the urban landscape shows the imprints of Greco-Roman urban culture (Figure 10.11).

FIGURE 10.11 Union Station, Toronto, Ontario. Opened in 1927, Toronto's Union Station is imprinted with Greco-Roman architectural styles, most noticeably its 12-metre columns, each weighing 75 tonnes, which mark the entrance to this grand building. (G. Brown)

ROMAN CITIES

Most of Greece's cities and towns were located near the Mediterranean Sea on peninsulas and islands and linked by sea routes. When the Romans succeeded the Greeks (and Etruscans) as rulers of the region, their empire incorporated not only the Mediterranean shores but also a large part of interior Europe and North Africa (Figure 10.12). The Roman urban system was the largest yet—much larger than that in ancient Greece. The capital, Rome, served as the apex of a hierarchy of settlements ranging from small villages to large cities. The Romans linked these places with an extensive transportation network that included hundreds of kilometres of roads, well-established sea routes, and trading ports along the roads, sea, and rivers. Roman regional planners displayed a remarkable capacity for choosing the **site** of cities, identifying suitable locales for settlements.

> **Site** The internal physical attributes of a place, including its absolute location, spatial character, and physical setting.

The site of a city is its absolute location, often chosen for its trade location, its defensive advantages, or its appropriateness as a religious location.

Romans were greatly influenced by the Greeks, as is evident in Roman mythology and most visibly in the cultural landscape and urban morphology of Roman cities. Greeks planned their colonial cities in a rectangular grid pattern, and Romans adopted this plan wherever surface conditions made it possible. Romans also took the Greek acropolis and agora and combined them into one zone, the **Forum**, the focal point of Roman public life (Figure 10.13). In Rome, the forum included the world's

> **Forum** The focal point of ancient Roman life combining the functions of the ancient Greek acropolis and agora.

first great stadium, the Colosseum, which was a much grander version of the Greek theatre. Before crowds of thousands of onlookers, Roman gladiators fought each other or killed wild animals imported from Africa. After Christianity diffused to Rome, but before the Roman Empire adopted Christianity as the state religion, Romans even forced Christians into the Colosseum, where hungry lions attacked and ate them. All Roman cities of any size had an arena like the Colosseum, where competitions, war games, ceremonies, and other public events took place.

Throughout the Roman Empire, cities were places of cultural contrasts. Still standing amid the ruins in many places around the Mediterranean are monumental buildings, impressive villas, spacious avenues, ingenious aqueducts and baths, and sewage systems built of stone and pipe (Figure 10.14). What we can no longer see in the ruins of the empire are the thousands of slaves who built these structures (estimates are between one-third and two-thirds of the population was enslaved) and the wretchedly poor who were crammed into overcrowded tenements and lived in filth. The city of the Roman Empire, like the city of today, was home to both rich and poor and reflected both the greatest achievements and the worst failings of civilization.

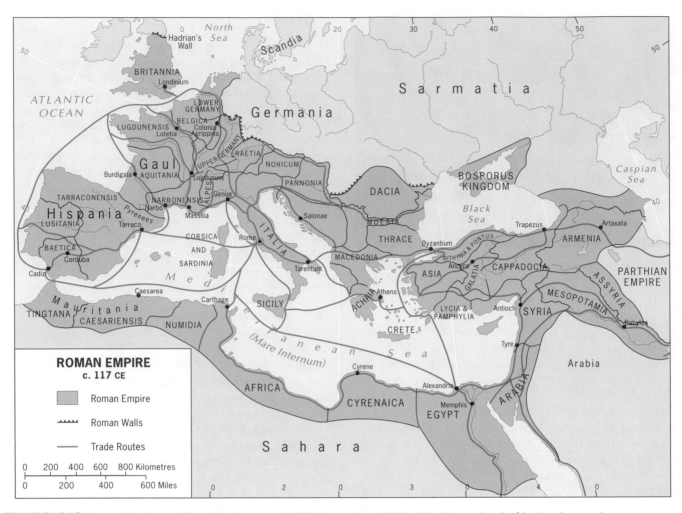

FIGURE 10.12 Roman Empire ca. 117 CE. The Romans established a system of cities linked by a network of land and sea routes. Many of the Roman cities have grown into modern metropolises. (© E.H. Fouberg, A.B. Murphy, H.J. de Blij, and John Wiley & Sons, Inc.)

FIGURE 10.13 The Forum, Rome, Italy. (© Alex Serge/Alamy)

FIGURE 10.14 Aqueducts Outside Nîmes, France. The aqueducts were built during the Roman Empire, about 2,000 years ago. (© Alexander B. Murphy)

FIGURE 10.15 Altun Ha, Belize. Between 300 and 900 CE, Altun Ha served as a thriving trade and distribution centre for the Caribbean merchant canoe traffic. Some of the trails in Altun Ha led all the way to Teotihuacan.
(© H.J. de Blij)

URBAN GROWTH AFTER GREECE AND ROME

After the Roman Empire fell in 495 CE, Europe entered an era historians call the Middle Ages, which ran from about 1,300 to 500 years ago (or later in some parts of Europe). During the first two-thirds of this period, little urban growth occurred in Europe; in fact, urbanism went into sharp decline in some parts of the continent.

Urbanization continued vigorously outside Europe, particularly on the sites of oases and resting places along the Silk Route between Europe and Asia. Many of these settlements grew into towns, and some, such as Bukhara and Samarqand, became major cities. In Asia, Chinese styles of city building diffused into Korea and Japan, with Seoul becoming a full-fledged city by 1200 and Kyoto, Japan's historic capital, growing rapidly after the turn of the ninth century. In West Africa, trading cities developed along the southern margin of the Sahara. By 1350, Timbuktu (part of Mali today) was a major city—a seat of government, a university town, a market, and a religious centre.

The Americas also experienced significant urban growth during Europe's Middle Ages, especially within the Mayan and Aztec empires (Figure 10.15). The largest pre-Columbian city in the Americas was the Aztec capital of Tenochtitlán, on the Mexican Plateau, which had nearly 100,000 inhabitants when many European cities lay in ruins.

THE SECOND URBAN REVOLUTION

During the last decades of the 18th century, the Industrial Revolution began in Great Britain and Europe. None of Europe's cities was prepared for what lay ahead: an avalanche of changes that ripped the fabric of urban life. Around 1800, western Europe was still overwhelmingly rural, but as thousands migrated to the cities as a result of industrialization, cities had to adapt

to the mushrooming population, the proliferation of factories and supply facilities, the expansion of transportation systems, and the construction of tenements for the growing labour force.

The Industrial Revolution marks a moment in human history where rapid advances in technology and science radically altered society. As we noted in Chapter 4, Europe went through a demographic transition at this time. During the late 17th century and into the 18th century, Europeans saw a series of important improvements in agriculture, including development of the seed drill and hybrid seeds, and improved breeding practices for livestock, which ensured an agricultural surplus. No longer needed in the fields, labourers were forced to migrate to cities in hopes of finding work. Scientific advancements in medicine ensured a steady decline in death rates for the young, higher survival rates for infants and young children, and greater longevity for the population as a whole. These improvements in health and medicine contributed to a population explosion supported by improved food production techniques. Urban factories and the growing industrial sector drew workers to cities. Manufacturers tapped into this labour force for the burgeoning manufacturing and resource industries (for a further discussion of industrialization, see Chapter 13).

Not all mercantile cities—that is, those engaged in trade—turned into industrial cities. The primary determinant in the development of early industrial cities was proximity to a power source. For example, textile manufacturers had to be sited near fresh water sources that would power the water loom. In Great Britain, industrial cities involved in textile manufacturing were located in the Pennines, where vast quantities of fresh water rushed down the hillsides. Iron manufacturers were located around Birmingham and Coalbrookdale, which offered easy access to Great Britain's coal and iron ore fields. When industrialization diffused from Great Britain to the European mainland, those areas poised to industrialize had already undergone their own second agricultural revolution and had surplus capital from mercantilism and colonialism (Figure 10.16).

With industrialization, cities became unregulated jumbles of activity. Factories engulfed private homes. Open spaces became garbage dumps. Urban dwellers converted elegant housing into overcrowded slums. Sanitation systems failed, and water supplies were inadequate and often polluted. By the late 1800s, the Industrial Revolution had changed transportation significantly. The steam engine, powered by coal, not only pumped water from mines for coal mining but also powered the railroad and steamship. The diffusion of the railroad gave cities that were not near coal fields the chance to industrialize. The central areas of cities like London, Paris, and Amsterdam retained their pre-industrial shape, but with the diffusion of the railroad, rail tracks knifed through long-stable neighbourhoods.

Living conditions were dreadful for workers in cities, and working conditions were shocking. Children worked 12-hour shifts in textile mills, typically six days a week. In industrial cities, health conditions were worse than they had been in medieval times; the air was polluted and the water contaminated. The grimy, soot-covered cities of the British Midlands were appropriately deemed the "black towns." Few if any safety mechanisms protected the labourers, and injuries were common.

In the mid-1800s, as Karl Marx and Friederich Engels (writing in Germany, Belgium, and England) encouraged "workers of the world" to unite, conditions in European manufacturing cities gradually improved. Industries began to recognize workers' rights, and governments intervened by legislating workers' rights and introducing city planning and zoning. Many manufacturing cities in North America emulated their European predecessors, with working conditions for factory workers (and "blue-collar" workers generally) largely similar to those found in European industrial cities. During the late 19th and early 20th centuries, the North American manufacturing cities grew rapidly, often with inadequate planning and rapid immigration leading to the development of slums.

During the second half of the 20th century, the nature of manufacturing changed, as did its location. Cities moved many factories away from congested, overcrowded, expensive urban areas. Some companies simply abandoned large manufacturing

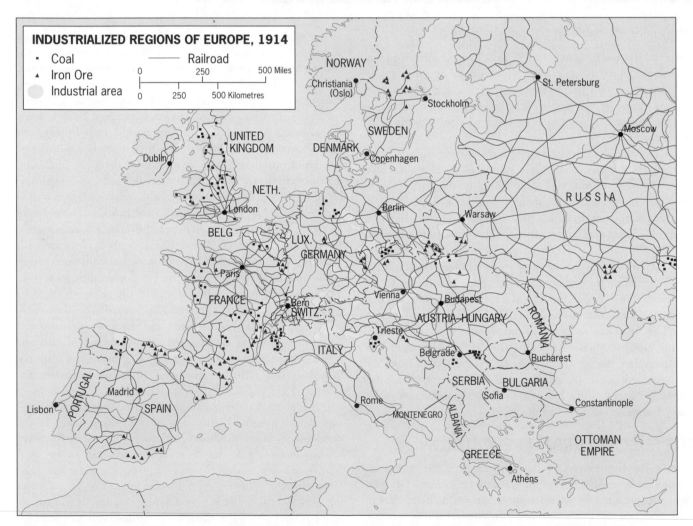

FIGURE 10.16 Industrialized Regions of Europe, 1914. Adapted with permission from Geoffrey Barraclough, ed., *The Times Concise Atlas of World History*, 5th edition, Hammond Incorporated, 1998.

plants, making "rust belts" out of once-thriving industrial districts. Many of these plants still stand today, overgrown by weeds, with broken windows and cracking walls.

Although factories and factory jobs are not permanent, the urbanization that went along with industrialization is still apparent. Today, western Europe is about 80 percent urban. The statistics on urbanization vary by source, as some define urban areas as being over 2,500 people and others over 5,000 people; still others use employment (i.e., the percent that is not agricultural) as the major criterion. By whatever definition, urbanization has become a global phenomenon, with the majority of the world's people living in cities today.

MAIN POINTS 10.1 When and Why Did People Start Living in Cities?

- Canada is truly an urban nation with over 80 percent of the population living in urban centres. Globally, more people live in towns and cities than in urban areas, making the global population predominantly urban as well. The modern city is a centre for economic development, technological innovation, services, and entertainment.

- The first urban revolution began around 3500 BCE, driven by changing technologies that resulted in an agricultural surplus and social stratification, and sprang up in six known hearth regions—Mesopotamia, Nile River Valley, Indus River Valley, Huang He and Wei River Valleys, and Mesoamerica. The diffusion of urbanization occurred throughout the Mediterranean, Central America, and South Asia and is evidenced in the great Greek and Roman cities of the period.

- The second urban revolution began in the last decades of the 18th century as a result of the Industrial Revolution, colonialism, and rapid technological changes. Rapid urbanization occurred throughout Europe and European colonies including North America. Many cities became increasingly crowded, unsanitary, and poorly planned.

10.2 Where Are Cities Located, and Why?

A map in an atlas of the United States or Canada, or a road map of a state or province, shows an array of places of different sizes, with varying distances between them. The map looks like a jumble, yet each place is where it is because of some decision, some perception of the site or its **situation**.

> **Situation** The external locational attributes of a place; its relative location or regional position with reference to other nonlocal places.

Site and situation help explain why certain cities were planned and why cities thrive or fail. To understand why a conglomeration of cities is distributed across space the way it is and why cities are different sizes, it is necessary to examine more than one city at a time and see how those cities fit together in the region, the state, and the globe as a whole—in other words, we need to look at urban systems.

CENTRAL PLACE THEORY

Walter Christaller wrote the classic urban geography study to explain where cities, towns, and villages are likely to be located. He argued that villages, towns, and cities worked together in interlocking and hierarchical urban systems that could be examined on a local, regional, national, or international basis. In his book *The Central Places in Southern Germany* (1933), Christaller laid the groundwork for **central place theory**. He attempted to develop a

> **Central place theory** Theory proposed by Walter Christaller that explains how and where central places in the urban hierarchy should be functionally and spatially distributed with respect to one another.

model to predict how and where central places in the urban hierarchy, as well as their connected hamlets, villages, towns, and cities, would be functionally and spatially distributed. Christaller based his theory on a set of assumptions: the surface of the ideal region would be flat and have no physical barriers; soil fertility would be the same everywhere; population and purchasing power would be evenly distributed; the region would have a uniform transportation network to permit direct travel from each settlement to the other; and, finally, from any given place, a good or service could be sold in all directions out to a certain distance.

Through his studies, Christaller calculated the ideal central place system, then compared his model to real-world situations and tried to explain the variations and exceptions. In the urban hierarchy, the central places would be nested, so the largest central place provided the greatest number of functions to most of the region (see Figure 10.17). Within the **trade area** of the largest central place, a series of large towns would provide functions to several smaller places. The smaller places

> **Trade area** Region adjacent to every town and city within which its influence is dominant.

would then provide fewer central functions to an even smaller service area. To determine the locations of each central place, Christaller needed to define the goods and services provided. He studied the sale of goods and services and calculated the distance people would willingly travel to acquire them. Cities, he postulated, would be regularly spaced, with central places where the same product was sold at the same price located a standard distance apart. Central places were those locations with a larger number of higher-order goods and services. Customers would be prepared to travel greater distances to obtain these consumer goods, which are usually more expensive and purchased less frequently, such as automobiles or household appliances.

Central place theory maintains that each central place has a surrounding complementary region, an exclusive trade area within which the town has a monopoly on the sale of certain goods because it alone can provide such goods at a given price and within a certain range of travel. These are usually goods needed more frequently but not things for which people want to travel very far, such as bread, milk, or newspapers. Farther down the hierarchy are those locations, such as villages or hamlets, that may contain a corner store and a gas station.

Christaller postulated that there was a relationship between urban areas based not only on functional interdependency but also on population size. He argued that there would be a statistical regularity in population, which could be predicted using the **rank-size rule**, which posits that the size of a city has a direct relationship to the size of the largest city. For example, if the largest city in an urban system has 100,000 people, then the nth largest city would have 1/nth the number of people. In other words, the fifth largest city would have one-fifth the population of the largest city, or 20,000 people. In some cases, due to particular historical, political, or cultural circumstances, the population distribution within an urban system is distorted so that the largest city has a disproportionately large number of people. In this urban system, such a city is called a **primate city**. In the current global context, cities such as London

> **Rank-size rule** In a model urban hierarchy, the idea that the population of a city or town will be inversely proportional to its rank in the hierarchy.

> **Primate city** A country's largest city–ranking atop the urban hierarchy–most expressive of the national culture and usually (but not always) the capital city as well.

and Buenos Aires are primate cities in that they are substantially larger than the next largest city in the urban system. However, just because a city has a large population, it is not necessarily a primate city. Primate cities are not only large but also have a primary functional role within a larger urban system. For example, they might be the seat of government or a financial centre. Conversely, some cities may have a relatively small population within an urban system but be very important in terms of administrative, economic, or political significance. This is called **centrality**. Bangkok is an example of such a city; with only 10 percent of Thailand's population, it dominates the economic and political life of the region.

> **Centrality** The strength of an urban centre in its capacity to attract producers and consumers to its facilities; a city's "reach" into the surrounding region.

HEXAGONAL HINTERLANDS

Based on this description of Christaller's theory, we might expect the shape of each central place's trade area to be circular (like a bull's eye, with concentric circles surrounding each place). However, circles either overlap or leave certain areas unserved. Hence, Christaller chose perfectly fitted hexagonal regions as the shape of each trade area (Figure 10.17).

Urban geographers were divided on the relevance or usefulness of Christaller's model. Some saw hexagonal systems everywhere while others saw none at all. Christaller received support from geographers who applied his ideas to regions in Europe, North America, and elsewhere. In China, both the North China Plain and the Sichuan Basin display the seemingly uninterrupted flatness assumed by Christaller's model. When

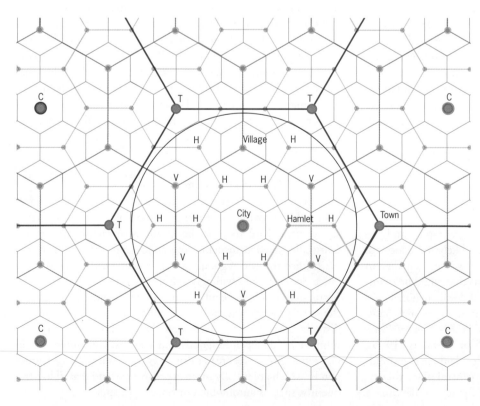

FIGURE 10.17 Christaller's Hierarchy of Settlements and Their Service Areas. Christaller's interlocking model of a hierarchy of settlements and their service areas includes cities (indicated by C), towns (T), villages (V), and hamlets (H).

G. William Skinner examined the distribution of Chinese villages, towns, and cities in these areas in 1964, he found a spatial pattern closely resembling the one predicted by Christaller's model. Studies in the U.S. Midwest suggested that while the square layout of the township-and-range system imposed a different kind of regularity on the landscape, the economic forces at work tended to confirm Christaller's theory. The Canadian urban system, discussed in the next section, follows a similar pattern.

Christaller recognized that not all his assumptions would be met in reality; physical barriers, uneven resource distributions, and other factors all modify his hexagons. Nonetheless, his model yielded a number of practical insights. His studies pointed to a hierarchy of urban places that are spatially balanced and also established that larger cities would be spaced farther from each other than smaller towns or villages. Although Christaller's model of perfectly fitting hexagons is not often realized, his studies confirm that the distribution of cities, towns, and villages in a region is not an accident but is tied to trade areas, population size, consumer buying patterns, and distance.

CENTRAL PLACES TODAY

When Christaller worked on his spatial model and developed central place theory to help explain the distribution of urban areas, the world was a simpler and much less populated place than it is today. As many urban geographers have pointed out during the debate that followed Christaller's publication of his ideas, new factors, forces, and conditions not anticipated by his models and theories (including the Internet and the interstate system) make them less relevant today. However, his model remains useful.

CANADA'S URBAN SYSTEM

Canada's urban system provides a good example of how urban areas are organized into a hierarchical and interlocking relationship. For much of the country's history, Montreal has vied with Toronto to be the largest city in our urban hierarchy, with Vancouver holding that position in the west. Each city is distinctive in its own way due to its specific demographic composition, social and economic history, and political organization, but all are interconnected on the regional, national, and international scale. In turn, each of these cities holds a central place within their region, surrounded by smaller towns, villages, and hamlets. In most cases, their size and location are in keeping with the essential principles of Christaller's model.

However, urban systems are vibrant and constantly in flux, influenced by changing political, social, and economic circumstances, both national and global, and by each city's own local planning and policy decisions. As a result, as geographers Larry Bourne and J. Simmons argue, although the situation has been relatively stable throughout much of Canada's history, it is currently in a state of transition. Bourne and Simmons note that Canada has five mega-urban regions (Figure 10.18) that affect areas far beyond their borders.

These are the Greater Toronto Area, the Greater Montreal Area, Alberta's central urban corridor (Edmonton–Red Deer–Calgary–Lethbridge), Vancouver–Victoria, and Ottawa–Gatineau. These mega-urban regions, also known as census metropolitan areas or CMAs (areas with populations of greater than 100,000 people) grew by 6.2 percent between 1991 and 2006. By contrast, census agglomerations—areas with between 10,000 and 100,000 people, such as Winnipeg, Saskatoon, Quebec City, St. John's, and Halifax—grew by only 1.5 percent. Finally, as Figure 10.18 illustrates, other areas of the country reported zero or declining growth. Whereas in 2006 Canada had some 140 urban centres of more than 10,000 people (with 80 percent of all Canadians living in these centres), Bourne and Simmons argue that Canada now has essentially two types of regions: those few dozen urban areas experiencing rapid growth and a large number of smaller places with declining populations. As a region's population and economic circumstances change, it finds itself occupying a different position within the urban system.

Bourne and Simmons suggest several underlying factors for this uneven population growth. First, they argue that Canada no longer has a rate of natural increase that can sustain population growth, so the country relies on immigration to fill the gap. As we discussed in Chapter 5, over 50 percent of Canada's population growth is due to immigration. As we discussed in Chapter 5, more than 80 percent of all newcomers to Canada settle in Vancouver, Toronto, and Montreal, which is part of the explanation for the rapid growth of these regions.

Second, with economic change, employment opportunities have shifted away from manufacturing and resource industries toward the service sector and information technologies. Businesses in these sectors flourish in urban areas, which offer the concentrations of goods, services, and technologies such businesses need to be competitive. Therefore these businesses are most likely to locate within one of Canada's five mega-regions.

Third, trade and commerce in Canada used to flow in an east-west direction, but with new trade agreements, including the North American Free Trade Agreement (NAFTA), Canadian trade has been reoriented toward the United States, consolidating the continental economy. This new orientation benefits some areas of Canada, such as Ontario and Alberta, but not others. With this change in orientation, a place such as Toronto, a gateway to the United States market, experiences an increase in population and economic growth, rising in importance in the urban hierarchy.

A number of implications arise from these changes in the Canadian urban system. Cities undergoing rapid growth also tend to exhibit an increase in congestion and pollution as well as a rise in costs for housing and social services, such as health care and schooling. Areas losing population or recording zero population growth lack the skilled workers needed to attract industry. Their tax base declines even as their aging population requires increased social services such as health care. These uneven growth patterns may lead to inequalities in wealth and quality of life between regions, which can cause a weakening of the urban system and divisions between regions.

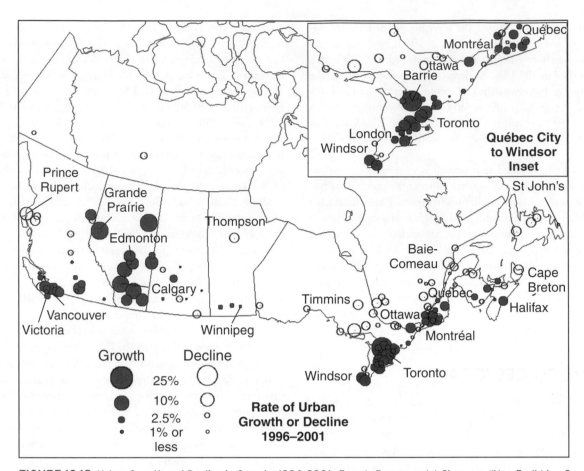

FIGURE 10.18 **Urban Growth and Decline in Canada, 1996-2001.** From L. Bourne and J. Simmons, "New Fault Lines? Recent Trends in the Canadian Urban System and Their Implications for Planning and Policy," *Canadian Journal of Urban Research* 12, 1 (2003): 22–47. Reprinted with permission of the authors, the Canadian Journal of Urban Research, and the Cartography office, Department of Geography, University of Toronto.

MAIN POINTS   10.2   Where Are Cities Located, and Why?

• Cities are interconnected in an urban system at a variety of scales, from the local and regional to the national, continental, and global. Urban geographers are interested in understanding the formation and operation of urban systems, their size, distribution, and organization.

• Central place theory is a model developed by Walter Christaller to predict where central places and their related urban areas would be located and how they would be connected. In the urban hierarchy, central places had the highest order goods and services and were surrounded by lower order places in a predictable way.

• Christaller's rank-size rule works out the statistical relationship between population size for various urban areas in an urban system. When the size of the largest city is distorted, in that it has a disproportionate population, it is called a primate city.

• The Canadian urban system has five mega-urban regions—Greater Toronto Area, Greater Montreal Area, Alberta's central urban corridor (Edmonton-Red Deer-Calgary-Lethbridge), Vancouver-Victoria, and Ottawa-Gatineau. Smaller urban areas within these urban systems are experiencing either no growth or very slow growth, creating uneven development and regional divisions between areas of rapid growth and those with declining growth.

• Growth in the mega-urban regions is important for economic competitiveness but these areas also tend to have increasing congestion and pollution, and rising social service costs. Areas with declining populations have a declining tax base and an aging population that requires additional services. Policy makers at all levels of government must consider how to address these issues.

10.3 How Are Cities Organized, and How Do They Function?

Within urban systems, each city is unique, with its own internal organization of land uses, transportation systems, and social life. Cities are not simply random collections of buildings and people. Rather, they exhibit functional structure, which means they are spatially organized to perform their functions as places of commerce, production, education, and much more. Certain spaces may be designated and developed as residential, industrial, commercial, or parkland. Needless to say, the internal form and function of a city depends on both its history and its geography. Cities in North America and Europe have evolved in a distinctly different way from cities in Latin America, Africa, or Asia. As urban geographers, we study, chart, and map cities to create models that describe how different parts of cities come together in different regions of the world. We are interested in the historical geography of the built environment; that is, we look at how the urban morphology of the city has changed over time and why those changes occurred.

(a)

(b)

FIGURE 10.19 Condominium Developments in the Central Business District of Canadian Cities, (a) Toronto and (b) Vancouver.
(© Ralph William/Alamy; © Gunter Marx Photography/Corbis)

MODELS OF THE CITY

Each model of the city, regardless of the region, is a study in **functional zonation**—the division of the city into certain zones for certain purposes (functions). For example, cities typically have residential zones, which are separate from industrial zones, which in turn are separate from garbage dumps. By studying the kinds of zones cities have, and by examining where the zones are located with respect to one another, urban geographers draw models of cities. The organization of city spaces has a pattern that is stable but subject to change. Different cities may have similar patterns or land use organization, and these similarities allow us to develop general models describing, very broadly, how cities are laid out.

> **Functional zonation** The division of a city into different regions or zones (e.g., residential or industrial) for certain purposes or functions (e.g., housing or manufacturing).

Before examining the models of urban spaces, we must define some terms commonly used in referring to parts of the city (especially cities in North America). The term **zone** is typically preceded by a descriptor that conveys the purpose of that area of the city, and models describe zones as areas with a relatively uniform land use; for example, an industrial zone or a residential zone. Most models define the key economic zone of the city (if there is one) as the **central business district (CBD)**, where business and

> **Zone** Area of a city with a relatively uniform land use (e.g., an industrial zone, or a residential zone).
>
> **Central business district (CBD)** The downtown heart of a central city, marked by high land values, a concentration of business and commerce, and the clustering of the tallest buildings.

commerce are concentrated, usually in the city's downtown. The Canadian CBD typically has high land values, tall buildings, busy traffic, converging highways, and mass-transit systems. One distinctive feature of the Canadian CBD in contrast to its American counterpart is the substantial residential population living and working in the downtown core and supporting a vibrant social and economic life. In Canadian cities such as Vancouver and Toronto, a number of high-density condominium developments have been built (Figure 10.19). In Toronto, for example, some 12,000 new units were built between the mid-1990s and 2005. While many people support the construction of condominiums and the residential population it brings downtown, others argue some of these condominiums have cut the City of Toronto off from its waterfront and are suitable only for those with the money to afford such accommodation while increasing traffic congestion.

The term **central city** describes the urban area that is not suburban. In effect, the central city is the older

> **Central city** The urban area that is not suburban; generally, the older or original city that is surrounded by newer suburbs.

Suburb A subsidiary urban area surrounding and connected to the central city. Many are exclusively residential; others have their own commercial centres or shopping malls.

city as opposed to the newer suburbs. A **suburb** is an outlying, functionally uniform part of an urban area that is often (but not always) adjacent to the central city. Most suburbs are residential, but some have other land uses, including schools, shopping malls, and office and industrial parks.

Suburbanization is the process by which lands that were previously outside the urban environment become urbanized,

Suburbanization The process by which lands that were previously outside the urban environment become urbanized, as people and businesses from the city and other areas move to these spaces.

as people and businesses from the city and other areas move to these spaces. The process of suburbanization holds special interest for human geographers because it involves the transformation of large areas of land from rural to urban uses and affects large numbers of people who can afford to move to larger and more expensive suburban homes. The aesthetic of the suburb reveals the occupants' idealized living patterns because the suburban layout can be planned in response to choice and demand. Ideals of suburban living can also change. For example, in the 1970s and 1980s, many subdivision communities banned the use of clotheslines, arguing that hanging laundry was an "eyesore." However, as people became more concerned about the environment and conserving energy, the Ontario government passed legislation in 2008 that prohibited municipalities from implementing such bans. Elsewhere, municipalities have banned the time-honoured sport of street hockey, arguing that it is too noisy, an inconvenience to drivers, and unsafe for children (Figure 10.20). In Canada, the residential subdivision as we know it is largely a post-World War II

phenomenon. As noted earlier, some 80 percent of Canadians now live in urban areas, but the vast majority of them live in suburban areas. All Canadian cities have suburbs, which have their own history and geography, influenced by changing demographics, economic and social phenomena, and the changing political landscape.

By using such terms as "residential area" and "central business district," people acknowledge the existence of a regional structure within cities. When we refer to the downtown, the airport, or the city zoo, we are in fact referring to urban regions where certain functions prevail (i.e., business activity, transportation, and recreation in the three just mentioned). These urban regions or zones lie near or adjacent to each other and together make up the metropolis. But how are they arranged? Is there any regularity or recurrent pattern in the location of the various zones, perhaps reflecting certain prevailing growth processes? In other words, can we create a model of the zones of a city that can then be recognized in every city, perhaps with modifications related to a city's particular site, size, shape, and relief? This is indeed one of the objectives of urban geographers.

MODELLING THE NORTH AMERICAN CITY

Urban geographers have constructed a succession of models that reflect change and growth in the geographic layout of North American cities. The first model, the **concentric zone model** (Figure 10.21a), was the result of sociologist Ernest Burgess's study of Chicago in the 1920s. Burgess's model divides the city into five concentric zones, defined by their function. As the city grew,

Concentric zone model A structural model of the American central city that suggests the existence of five concentric land-use rings arranged around a common centre.

land was converted in zones around the outside of the city, and the concentric zone model emerged. At the centre is the CBD (1), itself subdivided into several subdistricts (e.g., financial, retail, theatre).

The zone of transition (2) is characterized by residential deterioration and encroachment by business and light manufacturing. Zone 3 is a ring of closely spaced but adequate homes occupied by the blue-collar labour force. Zone 4 consists of middle-class residences, and zone 5 is the suburban ring. Burgess described his model as dynamic: as the city grew, inner zones encroached on outer ones, so that CBD functions invaded zone 2 and the problems of zone 2 affected the inner margins of zone 3.

In the late 1930s, Homer Hoyt published his sector model (Figure 10.21b), partly as a response to the limitations of the Burgess model. Hoyt focused on residential patterns, explaining where in a city the wealthy chose to live. Hoyt argued that the city grows outward from the centre, so a low-rent area could extend all the way from the CBD to the city's outer edge, creating zones shaped like pieces of pie. Hoyt found that the pie-shaped pieces describe the high-rent residential, intermediate-rent residential, low-rent residential, education and recreation, transportation, and industrial sectors.

FIGURE 10.20 Street hockey in Enfield, Nova Scotia. In April 2010, an RCMP officer responding to a noise complaint made kids stop their road hockey game. Similarly, in Dollard-des-Ormeaux, Quebec, a bylaw prohibits street sports. In March 2010, a father there was fined $75 for playing street hockey with his son. (CBC Still Photo Collection)

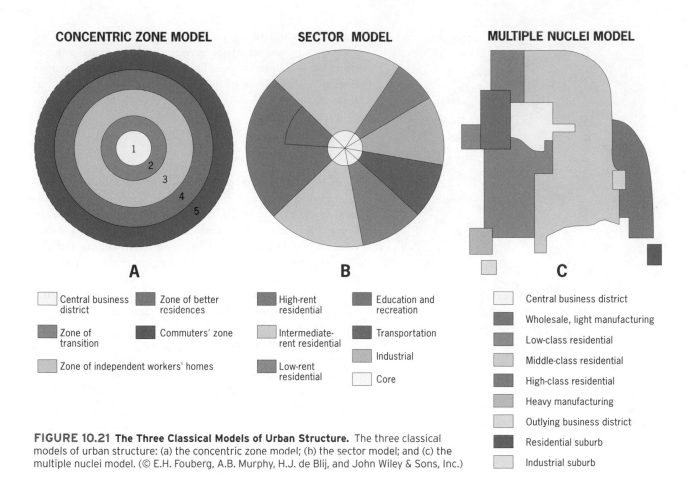

CONCENTRIC ZONE MODEL　　**SECTOR MODEL**　　**MULTIPLE NUCLEI MODEL**

A　　B　　C

Central business district
Zone of better residences
Zone of transition
Commuters' zone
Zone of independent workers' homes

High-rent residential
Intermediate-rent residential
Low-rent residential
Education and recreation
Transportation
Industrial
Core

Central business district
Wholesale, light manufacturing
Low-class residential
Middle-class residential
High-class residential
Heavy manufacturing
Outlying business district
Residential suburb
Industrial suburb

FIGURE 10.21 The Three Classical Models of Urban Structure. The three classical models of urban structure: (a) the concentric zone model; (b) the sector model; and (c) the multiple nuclei model. (© E.H. Fouberg, A.B. Murphy, H.J. de Blij, and John Wiley & Sons, Inc.)

Researchers studied both theories of city form and function, and many argued that neither the concentric rings model nor the sector model adequately reflected city structure by the mid-20th century. As a result, the multiple nuclei model was developed (Figure 10.21c), and many geographers claimed it more clearly reflected the form of urban cities. This model recognized that the CBD was losing its dominant position as the single nucleus of the urban area as several urban regions developed their own nuclei.

Although Canadian cities display great diversity in their form and function, certain commonalities or similarities exist. Geographer Peter Smith argues that most Canadian cities and their suburbs, "whatever their size or growth history, conform to the pattern shown" in Figure 10.22. In this model, we can see the older inner-city core and its older residential subdivisions and areas of industry and manufacturing. Surrounding those districts are new subdivisions and newer town centres. Beyond that we can see the suburbanization of adjacent rural towns and villages within commuting distance of the city. Finally, there are rural residential developments for people who want a more rural lifestyle but want to be within commuting distance of the city.

Today, most urban geographers think these models are too simplistic to describe the modern city. With the availability of personal automobiles and the construction of ring roads and other arteries around cities in the 1970s and 1980s, suburbanization

exploded. The outer city grew rapidly and became more functionally independent of the central city, and new suburban downtowns emerged to serve their local economies. Often located near key freeway intersections, these suburban downtowns developed mainly around big regional shopping centres and attracted industrial parks, office complexes, hotels, restaurants, entertainment facilities, and even sports stadiums. They became **edge cities**, attracting tens of thousands of suburbanites living nearby, offering workplaces, shopping, leisure activities, and all the other elements of a complete urban environment—thereby loosening remaining ties not only to the central city but to other suburban areas as well. As a result, many suburbs have experienced their own form of urbanization and provide yet another example of the continuously changing city landscape. Richmond, British Columbia, and Mississauga, Ontario, are examples of suburbs that started out as "bedroom" communities but have become increasingly independent, with their own city centre, local economy, and community services.

Edge cities A term introduced by American journalist Joel Garreau in order to describe the shifting focus of urbanization in the United States away from the central business district (CBD) toward new loci of economic activity at the urban fringe. These cities are characterized by extensive amounts of office and retail space, few residential areas, and modern buildings (less than 30 years old).

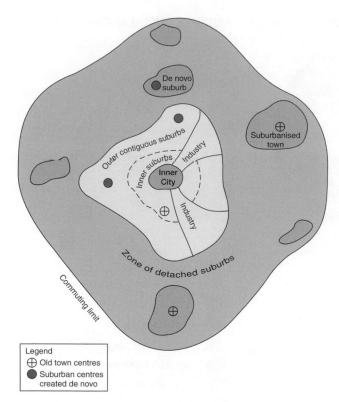

Legend
⊕ Old town centres
● Suburban centres
created de novo

FIGURE 10.22 Suburbs in Generalized Structure of a Typical Canadian City. Adapted from Peter. J. Smith, "Suburbs," in *Canadian Cities in Transition: Local through Global Perspectives*, 3rd edition, Figure 12.1, page 214, Trudi Bunting and Pierre Filion, eds; © Oxford University Press Canada 2006. Adapted by permission of the publisher.

MODELLING THE CITIES OF THE GLOBAL PERIPHERY AND SEMI-PERIPHERY

While certain models may help us understand how North American cities have evolved, these models are often not applicable elsewhere around the globe. Cities in other places, including Europe, can trace their function and internal organization to different circumstances.

In the 1960s, researchers classified "colonial" cities as urban areas where European administrators dictated the form the city took and laid it out according to the needs of the colonizing country, using mainly Western architecture and styles. South American cities, for example, have been endowed with strong Iberian cultural imprints that define a certain common social-spatial geography. Researchers have also developed distinctive models based on those indigenous cities that remained remote from globalizing influences.

Today, colonial cities that have grown as a result of massive migration defy generalization. Mexico City (Mexico) and São Paulo (Brazil) are examples of the kinds of mega-cities that are difficult to analyze and model. Even indigenous cities deep in continental interiors (such as those in West Africa's Sahel and in Central Asia) have been transformed by the processes of

globalization and immigration. However, some former colonial cities in sub-Saharan Africa have retained the spatial components lost in enormous cities like Lagos (Nigeria) and Kinshasa (Democratic Republic of the Congo), and some middle-sized cities in Southeast Asia continue to exhibit a fairly consistent pattern.

THE LATIN AMERICAN CITY

Cities around the world developed in their own distinctive style as a result of local and national political, economic, and cultural forces as well as the city's position within global urban systems. Scholars studying Latin American cities argue that they reflect a blend of traditional Latin American culture and elements driven by the forces of globalization that have reshaped the urban scene.

In 1980, geographers Ernst Griffin and Larry Ford developed the **Griffin-Ford model** as a result of their study of Latin American cities (Figure 10.23). Their early models noted a thriving CBD that contained the primary business, employment, and entertainment focus of these cities. The CBD is usually divided into a traditional market

> **Griffin-Ford model** Developed by geographers Ernst Griffin and Larry Ford, a model of the Latin American city showing a blend of traditional elements of Latin American culture with the forces of globalization that are reshaping the urban scene.

sector and a more modern high-rise sector. The most successful cities have adequate public transit systems and nearby affluent residential areas that assure the continuing dominance of the CBD. Emanating outward from the urban core along the city's most prestigious axis is the commercial spine, which is surrounded by the elite residential sector. This widening corridor is essentially an extension of the CBD and features offices, shopping, high-quality housing for the upper and upper-middle classes, restaurants, theatres, and such amenities as parks, zoos, and golf courses.

At the end of this commercial/elite spine is an incipient edge city, shown as "mall" in Figure 10.23, and flanked by high-priced residences. This reflects the emergence of suburban nodes in South American cities. The remaining concentric zones are home to less well-off residents, who compose the great majority of the urban population. Socio-economic levels and housing quality decrease markedly the farther one goes from the city centre. The zone of maturity in the inner city contains the best housing outside the spine sector and attracts the middle classes, who invest sufficiently to keep their solidly built but aging dwellings from deteriorating. The adjacent zone of *in situ* accretion is one of much more modest housing. Interspersed with the more modest areas are densely populated unkempt areas, which represent a transition from inner-ring affluence to outer-ring poverty. The outermost zone of peripheral squatter settlements is home to the impoverished and recent migrants. Although this ring consists mainly of teeming, high-density shantytowns, residents here are surprisingly optimistic about finding work and improving their living conditions.

A NEW AND IMPROVED MODEL OF LATIN AMERICAN CITY STRUCTURE

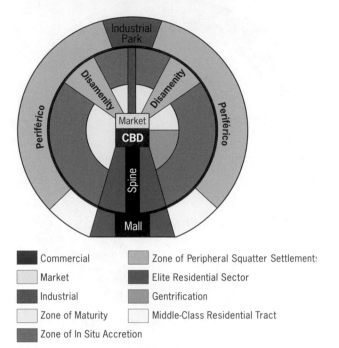

Commercial

Market

Industrial

Zone of Maturity

Zone of In Situ Accretion

Zone of Peripheral Squatter Settlement

Elite Residential Sector

Gentrification

Middle-Class Residential Tract

FIGURE 10.23 A Model of the Latin American City Structure. In a 1996 journal article, Larry Ford updated the model he originally developed with Ernst Griffin, adding a ring highway (periférico) around the outskirts of the city, dividing the downtown business district into a CBD and a market, adding a mall near the elite space, and leaving room for suburban industrial parks. Adapted with permission from L. Ford, "A New and Improved Model of Latin American City Structure," *The Geographical Review* 86 (1996), p. 438.

A structural element of many Latin American cities is the **disamenity sector**, the very poorest sector, which in extreme cases is not connected to regular city services and is controlled by gangs and drug lords. The disamenity sectors in Latin American cities contain relatively unchanging slums known as *barrios* or *favelas*. The worst of these poverty-stricken areas are often inhabited by large numbers of people who are so poor they are forced to live in the streets. There is little in the way of regular law enforcement within such communities, and drug lords often run the show—or battle with other drug lords for dominance. Such conditions also prevail in places beyond the ring highway or *periférico*, which is now a feature of most South American cities.

In Figure 10.23, we also see two smaller sectors: an industrial park, reflecting the ongoing concentration of industrial activity in the city; and a gentrification zone, where historic buildings are preserved. Gentrification remains much less common in South American cities than in North America, but it is an emerging phenomenon. The model reflects the enormous differences between the spaces of privilege and the spaces of abject poverty within the Latin American city. It also describes elements of sector

Disamenity sector The very poorest parts of cities that in extreme cases are not even connected to regular city services and are controlled by gangs or drug lords.

development evident in many large South American cities, but the concentricity suggested by the model seems to be breaking down.

THE SOUTHEAST ASIAN CITY

Some of the most populated cities in the world are in Southeast Asia. The city of Kuala Lumpur, Malaysia, is a complex of high-rise development, including the 450-metre-tall Petronas Towers, which until recently was the world's tallest building. The city of Jakarta, Indonesia, called Jabotabek by the locals, is an enormous conurbation of Bogor, Tangerang, and Bekasi.

Scholars studying the medium-sized cities of Southeast Asia found that they exhibited similar land-use patterns, which could be modelled (Figure 10.24). The focal point of the city is the old colonial port zone, which combines with the largely commercial district that surrounds it. There is often no formal central business district, although elements of the CBD are present as separate clusters surrounding the old colonial port zone. There is a government zone; the Western commercial zone (practically a CBD by itself); an ethnic commercial zone, dominated by Chinese merchants whose residences are attached to their places of business; and the mixed land-use zone that contains miscellaneous economic activities, including light industry. The other non-residential areas are the market-gardening zone at the outskirts of the urban area and, still farther from the city, a recently built industrial park or "estate."

A GENERALIZED MODEL OF LAND USE AREAS IN THE LARGE SOUTHEAST ASIAN CITY

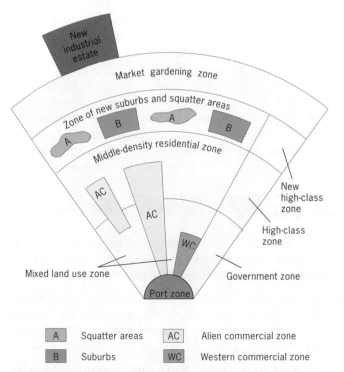

A Squatter areas

B Suburbs

AC Alien commercial zone

WC Western commercial zone

FIGURE 10.24 Model of the Large Southeast Asian City. A model of land use in a Southeast Asian city includes sectors and zones within each sector. Adapted with permission from T.G. McGee, *The Southeast Asian City*, London: Bell, 1967, p. 128.

The residential zones in these models are similar to those in the models of the Latin American city. Other similarities are the hybrid structure of sectors and zones, an elite residential sector that includes new suburbs, an inner-city zone of middle-income housing, and peripheral low-income squatter settlements. One main difference is that the Latin American model includes middle-income housing in a suburban zone, reflecting the larger middle class in these cities of the global semi-periphery and the small middle class in Latin American cities. Regardless of the region or city, we recognize that models do not explain how or why cities are organized the way they are. A model of a city shows us an end product, whether planned or not, and suggests the forces that created that end product.

THE AFRICAN CITY

Farmers make up a majority of the population in the tropical region of Africa; as a result, most countries in the tropics remain under 40 percent urbanized. Outside the tropics, sub-Saharan Africa is about 57 percent urban. At the beginning of this century, some countries in sub-Saharan Africa recorded the world's lowest levels of urbanization. Despite these statistics, Africa now has the world's fastest-growing cities, followed by those in South Asia, mainland East Asia, and South and Central America. In contrast, the cities of North America, southern South America, and Australia are growing more slowly, and those of western Europe are barely growing at all.

The imprint of European colonialism can be seen in many African cities. During colonialism, Europeans laid out prominent urban centres such as Kinshasa (Democratic Republic of the Congo), Nairobi (Kenya), and Harare (Zimbabwe) in the interior, and Dakar (Senegal), Abidjan (Ivory Coast), Luanda (Angola), Maputo (Mozambique), and other ports along the coast. Other African cities are neither traditional nor colonial. South Africa's major urban centres (Johannesburg, Cape Town, and Durban) are essentially Western, with elements of European as well as American models, including high-rise CBDs and sprawling suburbs.

As a result of this diversity, it is difficult to formulate a model African city. Studies of African cities indicate that the central city often consists of not one but three CBDs (Figure 10.25): a remnant of the colonial CBD, an informal and sometimes periodic

A MODEL SUB-SAHARAN AFRICAN CITY

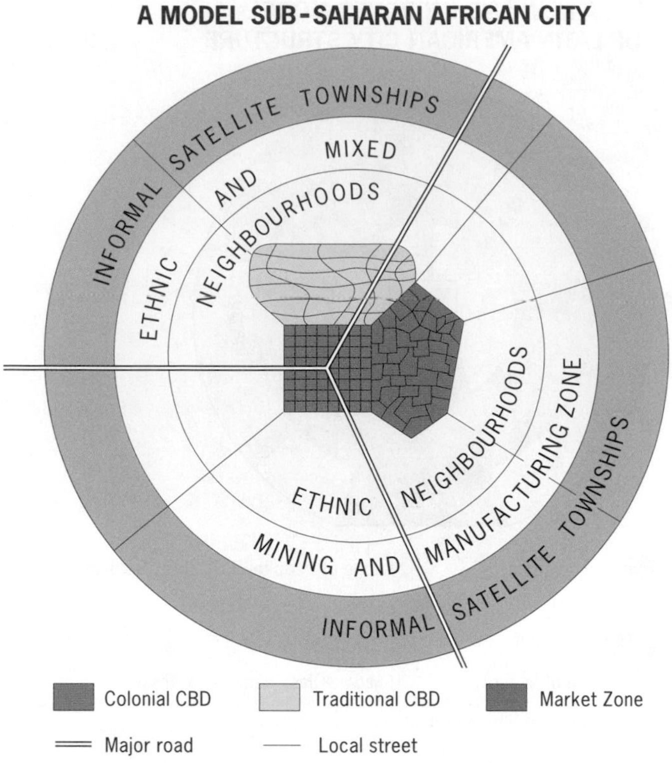

FIGURE 10.25 **Model of the Sub-Saharan African City.** One model of the African city includes a colonial CBD, traditional CBD, and market zone. (© E.H. Fouberg, A.B. Murphy, H.J. de Blij, and John Wiley & Sons, Inc.)

market zone, and a transitional business centre where commerce is conducted from curbside stalls or storefronts. Vertical development occurs mainly in the former colonial CBD; the traditional business centre is usually a zone of single-storey buildings with some traditional architecture; and the market zone tends to be open-air, informal, yet still important. Sector development occurs in the encircling zone of ethnic and mixed neighbourhoods (often characterized by strong ethnic identities); manufacturing or mining operations are found next to some parts of this zone. Finally, many African cities are ringed by satellite townships that are squatter settlements.

MAIN POINTS 10.3 How Are Cities Organized, and How Do They Function?

- All cities have their own internal structure, which arises as a result of their history and geography, and their functions, as well as city planning and policy.

- Urban geographers develop models of urban spaces to map out various functional zones. These zones include a central business district, inner-city residential and industrial/manufacturing areas, suburban zones, and rural countryside.

- There are three classic North American urban models—concentric zone model, sector model, and multiple nuclei model. While these are accurate to a point, the modern

urban city is far more complicated than these early models suggest, particularly when we consider recent complex developments on the city's outer edge.

- Cities in the periphery and semi-periphery have developed very different internal structures. Colonial cities developed form and function for the benefit of the colonial or imperial power. Other cities around the globe, from South America to South Asia, develop their own distinctive style in response to national political and economic forces and their distinctive cultural and social development.

10.4 How Do Cities Evolve?

Numerous economic, social, political, technological, and cultural processes are in play in the ever-evolving form and function of cities. The roles individual people, governments, corporations, developers, financial lenders, and realtors play in the transformation of cities vary. In some parts of the world, governments pass strict laws limiting urban structures and enforce them, while in other parts of the world, governments either do not pass laws or do not enforce them.

Powerful social and cultural preferences shape the character of particular parts of the city and influence who lives where. Indicators of these preferences and of historical processes are embedded in urban landscapes (see Chapters 7 and 8) and are visible to passers-by in various elements. These might include the presence of single-family or multifamily homes, particular styles of construction and building materials, the distance between houses, the nature and style of vegetation around houses, the distance between the houses and the streets, and even the amount of space devoted to automobile movement and storage. Cities take shape around their CBDs, and the form of the city is governed by planning and transportation decisions, immigration and settlement patterns, shifting economic circumstances, and the way these many factors play out within broader local, regional, national, and global processes.

CITIES IN THE GLOBAL CORE

Developers and governments are important actors in the making of cities, and they have had different goals over time. In the 1960s and 1970s, many North American and European cities experienced de-industrialization and a loss of manufacturing businesses as a result of changing global economic circumstances. Many businesses deserted the downtown core, leaving behind abandoned buildings, factories, and warehouses as they moved into new industrial and residential subdivisions on the city's outskirts. In cities experiencing high levels of suburbanization, people left the central city for the suburbs for a number of reasons, including the need for work and the desire for single-family homes, yards, better schools, and safety. With suburbanization, city governments lost tax revenue as middle- and upper-class taxpayers left the central city and began paying taxes in the suburbs instead. In order to counter the suburbanization trend, city governments are encouraging commercialization of the central city and gentrification of the central city's neighbourhoods.

One way people make cities is by remaking them, reinventing neighbourhoods or changing layouts to reflect current goals and aesthetics. The plans that city governments draft to revive central cities usually involve cleaning streets, sidewalks, and buildings; tearing down old, abandoned buildings; and building up commercial offerings and residences. In the CBD, city governments have often created programs to encourage **commercialization**, which entails transforming

Commercialization The transformation of an area of a city into an area attractive to residents and tourists alike in terms of economic activity.

FIGURE 10.26 Locke Street, Hamilton, Ontario. The Locke Street area of Hamilton, Ontario—a city known for its industrial sector and steel mills—is developing into a bustling area of festivals, boutiques, and upscale restaurants. (Copyright © 2011, John Ellin CC SA BY)

the central city into an area attractive to residents and tourists alike (Figure 10.26). Several cities—for example, Toronto and Halifax or Boston and New York—have created waterfront "theme" areas that include festival marketplaces, parks with exotic sculptures and play areas, and amusement zones occupying former industrial sites. Such ventures have been successful in attracting tourists and in generating business, but they cannot revive downtowns on their own because they cannot attract what the core of the city needs most: permanent residents with a stake in its future. The newly commercialized downtowns often stand apart from the rest of the central city.

Since the 1960s, some people have moved back into central cities—often in conjunction with a process known as **gentrification** (Figure 10.27). Gentrification occurs when individuals buy up and rehabilitate the houses in a previously abandoned or rundown neighbourhood, raising the housing value in the neighbourhood and changing the neighbourhood itself. Gentrification began in cities with a tight housing market and defined central city neighbourhoods, such as Toronto, Chicago, and Paris. Gentrification slowed in the 1990s but is occurring again, as governments encourage beautification programs and offer significant tax breaks to people who buy abandoned or dilapidated buildings and convert them to new residential and commercial uses. The growing interest in central city housing has resulted, in part, from the changing character of North American society: the proportion of childless couples and single people in the population is

Gentrification The rehabilitation of deteriorated, often abandoned, housing of low-income inner-city residents.

FIGURE 10.27 Osborne Village, Winnipeg, Manitoba. Osborne Village, previously known as one of Winnipeg's more poverty-stricken neighbourhoods, has recently been gentrified. The influx of stores such as American Apparel, along with an emerging "hipster" culture, has increased rents, pushing the poor out of the area. (Janelle Lagasse Photography)

growing, and for these urbanites, the suburbs do not look very attractive. Living within walking distance of the workplace and being near cultural and recreational amenities attracts more residents to central city neighbourhoods every year. However, there have been some negative consequences to these developments. For example, rising housing costs associated with gentrification have played a key role in the growing problem of homelessness.

The suburb is not immune to gentrification. Rampant in many North American suburbs (especially those close to the city)

is the **tear-down** phenomenon, in which individuals buy a house with the intention of tearing it down and building a much larger home. The new houses, sometimes referred to as "monster homes" because of their size, often stretch to the outer limits of the lot (Figure 10.28). Like gentrification, tear-downs change the landscape and increase the neighbourhood's average housing values and average household income. Unlike gentrification, tear-downs destroy the original houses instead of preserving them. Those in favour of tear-downs argue that the phenomenon slows urban sprawl (see the next section) by replacing existing homes with new homes, rather than converting farmland to residential lots. Those opposed to tear-downs say the process destroys the character of a place by demolishing older homes and replacing them with houses that are too large for their lots and that dwarf the neighbouring houses.

> **Tear-downs** Homes bought in many North American suburbs with the intent of tearing them down and replacing them with much larger homes, often referred to as "monster homes."

URBAN SPRAWL AND NEW URBANISM

As populations have grown, urban areas in many parts of the world, including Canada, have experienced **urban sprawl**—the unrestricted growth of housing, commercial developments, and roads over large expanses of land, with little concern for urban planning. Urban sprawl, a phenomenon of the automobile era, is characterized by the razing of farmland and old industrial sites; the building or widening of roads; and the proliferation of strip malls, big-box stores, chain restaurants, huge intersections, and numerous housing developments, spread out over many acres along major roadways in any urbanized part of the

> **Urban sprawl** Unrestricted growth in many North American urban areas of housing, commercial development, and roads over large expanses of land, with little concern for urban planning.

(a)

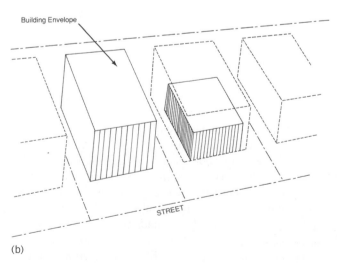

(b)

FIGURE 10.28 Examples of Monster Homes. (a) New "monster homes" often dwarf older neighbouring dwellings, even though they are built within the same zoning regulations. (b) The new houses take advantage of the entire building envelope. From Hodge, Gerald and Gordon, David. *Planning Canadian Communities: An Introduction to the Principles, Practice, and Participants.* 5th ed. p. 335. © 2008 Nelson Education Ltd. Reproduced by permission. www.cengage.com/permissions.

country. Does population growth explain which cities experience the most urban sprawl? Scholars studying North American urbanized areas found that urban sprawl happened even in urban areas without significant population growth.

To counter urban sprawl, a group of architects, urban planners, and developers outlined an urban design vision they call **new urbanism**. The Congress for the New Urbanism, established in 1993, defines this as a philosophy of development, urban revitalization, and suburban reforms that create walkable neighbourhoods with a diversity of housing and jobs. The Congress for the New Urbanism website explains that "New Urbanists support regional planning for open space, appropriate architecture and planning, and the balanced development of jobs and housing. They believe these strategies are the best way to reduce how long people spend in traffic, to increase the supply of affordable housing, and to rein in urban sprawl." New urbanists want to create neighbourhoods that promote a sense of community and a sense of place, and they often use neo-traditional housing designs, with front porches, sidewalks, and mixed-use town centres.

> **New urbanism** Outlined by a group of architects, urban planners, and developers from over 20 countries, an urban design that calls for development, urban revitalization, and suburban reforms that create walkable neighbourhoods with a diversity of housing and jobs.

New urbanism surfaced in Canadian planning policy in the 1980s, along with ideas of smart growth and sustainability. According to Canadian urban planner Jill Grant, these ideas are now intertwined in Canadian planning policies at all levels of government. Sustainability, Grant argues, is concerned with ensuring "compact form, transportation options, healthy living environments, affordable housing, and environmental responsibility." The ideas behind smart growth developed in the United States in response to anti-growth movements and sought to reduce the negative impacts of growth and encourage development and regional planning that struck a balance between jobs and housing. According to Canadian planners Andrejs Skaburskis and Diana Mok, the City of Markham is considered to have the highest concentration of "new-urbanist subdivisions in North America with Cornell as its flagship." As Figure 10.29 illustrates, communities such as Cornell feature higher densities as well as sidewalks and more public transit, which encourage greater community interaction.

While many communities, planners, politicians, and developers may agree with the philosophy behind new urbanism, smart growth, and sustainability, researchers have found many of the ideas are not put into practice. Jill Grant asserts that political, economic, and social barriers operate to varying degrees to foil full implementation of these ideals. While planners may press for development that achieves the goals of new urbanism, smart growth, and sustainability, politicians may override their recommendations based on objections from developers, engineers, and traffic planners who find the new standards difficult to implement. Developers often claim that economic markets do not support innovative changes in community design and that consumers are more interested in larger lots and privacy than in compact city living.

Canadian cities also attempt to regulate growth at the urban fringe through the use of "greenbelts," rural reserves, or urban growth boundaries that are meant to protect agricultural land, land with considerable environmental diversity, or land needed to preserve water (e.g., watersheds, lakes, and rivers). The province of Ontario implemented a greenbelt plan in 2005 to continue protecting environmentally sensitive areas, such as the Niagara Escarpment and the Oak Ridges Moraine (Figure 10.30). Central to this legislation was the creation of a greenbelt to contain and manage development around the Greater Toronto Area by ensuring varying degrees of protection depending on the nature, features, and functions of the natural landscape. Greenbelt plans,

FIGURE 10.29 Cornell, Markham, Ontario. This subdivision is an example of new urbanism and neo-traditional design that encourages community interaction and sustainability. (Peter Power/GetStock.com)

FIGURE 10.30 Encroaching Development on the Oak Ridges Moraine, 2004. Heavy machinery work on new development on the Oak Ridges Moraine in 2004. Environmentalists, some urban planners, and local activists have lobbied for greater protection of greenbelt areas, such as the Oak Ridges Moraine and the Niagara Escarpment, against encroaching development. (Tony Bock/Toronto Star)

together with other growth management strategies, are being implemented in a number of jurisdictions in Canada in order to regulate growth beyond various cities' current development areas and to encourage increasing densities in the built-up area.

Some geographers are critical of new urbanism because it seems to redefine certain kinds of urban spaces. For example, new urbanism's ideas often mean that public spaces become privatized for the enjoyment of the residents of the neighbourhood to the exclusion of others. Geographers Stuart Aitken, Don Mitchell, and Lynn Staeheli note that as new urbanism strives to turn neighbourhoods back in time, "spaces and social functions historically deemed public (such as parks, neighbourhood centres, shopping districts)" are privatized. The houses with porches that encourage neighbours to talk, and the parks that are within walking distance for the residents, create "mythic landscapes that are ingratiating for those who can afford them and exclusionary for those who cannot."

Noted geographer David Harvey offers one of the strongest critiques of new urbanism, explaining that most new urbanist designs are "greenfield" projects—that is, projects built on previously undeveloped land—designed for the affluent with the aim of making the suburbs more livable. Harvey argues that the new urbanism movement is a kind of "spatial determinism" that does not recognize that "the fundamental difficulty with modernism was its persistent habit of privileging spatial forms over social processes." Harvey, and others who critique new urbanism, claim that new urbanism does nothing to break down the social conditions that privilege some while disadvantaging others. The new urbanist projects arguably do take away much of the grittiness and character of the city, and they often create exclusionary communities that further the racial and class segregation of cities. Despite the critiques, however, developments in the new urbanist tradition are attracting a growing number of people, and when these developments are situated within cities, they can work against urban sprawl.

CITIES IN THE GLOBAL PERIPHERY AND SEMI-PERIPHERY

As we saw in Table 10.1, many of the world's most populous cities are located in the less prosperous parts of the world, including São Paulo (Brazil), Mexico City (Mexico), Mumbai (India), Dhaka (Bangladesh), and Delhi (India). Across the world, people continue to migrate to cities in response to "pull and push" factors of immigration (discussed in Chapter 5). Particularly in the economic periphery, new arrivals (as well as many long-term residents) are crowded together in overpopulated apartment buildings, dismal tenements, and teeming slums. New arrivals come from other cities and towns and from the rural countryside, often as large families, adding to the cities' rate of natural growth. Housing cannot keep up with this massive inflow. As a result, huge **shantytowns**—unplanned developments of crude dwellings and shelters made largely of scrap wood, iron, and pieces of

> **Shantytown** Unplanned slum development on the margins of cities, dominated by crude dwellings and shelters made mostly of scrap wood, iron, and even pieces of cardboard.

cardboard—develop around these cities. The overcrowding and dismal conditions do not deter additional urban migration, and the result is that millions of people spend their entire lives in urban housing of wretched quality.

Cities in poorer parts of the world generally lack enforceable **zoning laws**, which evolved in most cities in North America over the last century. These laws are meant to ensure space is used in ways that the society at large would deem culturally and environmentally acceptable. If, for example, a city had zoned all the lots in a suburban block exclusively for single-family homes, a fast-food franchise could not occupy a corner lot in that block. Zoning laws do not exist, nor are they equally enforced, everywhere in the global north. In Europe, for example, most cities have loose land-use plans but few have zoning laws. In the United States, Houston, Texas, is the only large city that does not have zoning laws on the books, and citizens in the city have voted against the creation of zoning laws three different times (most recently in 1993). All jurisdictions in Canada have some form of planning authority and legislation designed to guide development.

> **Zoning laws** Legal restrictions on land use that determine what types of building and economic activities are allowed to take place in certain areas. In North America, areas are most commonly divided into separate zones of residential, retail, or industrial use.

Without zoning laws, cities in the periphery will have mixed land use throughout the city. For example, in cities such as Madras, India (and in other cities in India), open space between high-rise buildings is often occupied by squatter settlements (Figure 10.31). In Bangkok, Thailand, elementary schools and noisy, polluting factories stand side by side. In Nairobi, Kenya, hillside villas overlook some of Africa's worst slums. Over time, such incongruities may disappear, as is happening in many cities in East Asia, where rising land values and greater demand for enforced zoning regulations are transforming the central cities. But in South Asia, sub-Saharan Africa, Southwest Asia, North Africa, and Central and South America, unregulated growth continues.

FIGURE 10.31 Squatter Settlements, Hyderabad, India. Temporary shelters, built to withstand the summer monsoon, protect the migrants who work on the new construction in the background. (© Erin H. Fouberg)

(a)

(b)

FIGURE 10.32   Cairo, Egypt. (a) The modern high-rises and free-ways of central Cairo are in stark contrast to (b) the rundown buildings and roadways outside the downtown core. (© Alexander B. Murphy)

Across the periphery and semi-periphery, one trait all major cities display is the stark contrast between the wealthy and the poor—for example, homeless people can be seen sleeping on heating grates half a block from the Parliament Buildings in Ottawa–Gatineau. Yet the intensity and scale of the contrast are greater in cities of the periphery. The central area of Cairo, Egypt, appears to be a modern, Mediterranean metropolis, but this impression fades as one nears the city's outskirts: paved streets give way to dusty alleys, apartment buildings to tenements, and sidewalk coffee shops to broken doors and windows (Figure 10.32). Traffic-choked, garbage-strewn, polluted Cairo is home to an estimated 12.5 million people, more than one-fifth of Egypt's population. The city is bursting at the seams, yet people continue to arrive, seeking the better life that pulls countless migrants from the countryside year after year.

IMMIGRANT NEIGHBOURHOODS IN THE GLOBAL PERIPHERY AND SEMI-PERIPHERY CITY

In cities of the periphery and semi-periphery, a sea of slum development typically begins where the permanent buildings end, in some cases engulfing and dwarfing the central city. From a hill outside Lima (Peru) or overlooking the Cape Flats near Cape Town (South Africa), one sees a conglomeration of make-shift shacks built of every conceivable material, vying for every metre of space, extending to the horizon. There are few trees, and narrow footpaths wind through the shacks, leading to a few unpaved streets that go into the central city.

Millions of migrants travel to such environments every year. The total number of people living in these places is uncertain because government control is impossible and enumeration impractical. In Rio de Janeiro (Brazil), the migrants build their dwellings on dangerous, landslide-prone slopes; in Port Moresby (Papua New Guinea), the migrants sink stilts in the mud and build out over the water, risking wind and waves. In Calcutta (India), thousands of migrants do not even try to erect shelters; there and in many other cities they live in the streets, under bridges, even in storm drains. City governments do not have the resources to adequately educate, medicate, or police the burgeoning populations, let alone provide even minimal housing for most.

The vast slums of cities in poorer parts of the world are typically ethnically delineated, with new arrivals precariously accommodated. For example, Kibera, the large slum area in Nairobi, Kenya, is one of the worst in sub-Saharan Africa in terms of amenities (Figure 10.33). Much of the land on which Kibera is situated is owned by Nubians, who are of Sudanese descent. They settled in the area during the colonial era, and many have become businesspeople in the city of Nairobi. The modern tenants of the shanty settlements in Kibera are largely Luo from western Kenya and Luhya from northwestern Kenya. During the fall of 2001, some of the Kiberian tenants were unable to pay the latest increase in rents. The Nubian landowners came to evict them; in the fighting that followed, a number of people were killed. Groups of Luo, Luhya, and others even began fighting among themselves. The government intervened to stabilize the situation, and the rent increases were withdrawn, but the fundamental problems—crowding, unemployment, unsanitary conditions, hunger, and lack of education—remain, and the ethnic groups living in Kibera will likely experience fighting again.

FIGURE 10.33 Kibera, Kenya. Kibera, located within 5 kilometres of Kenya's capital city, Nairobi, is considered one of the most crowded places on earth. (© Nigel Pavitt/JAI/Corbis)

How do the many millions of urban immigrants living in the slum-ridden rings and pockets of the cities of the global periphery and semi-periphery survive? Extended families share the money they manage to earn; when one member of the family has a salaried job, his or her income supports a dozen or more relatives. When a family member (or several members of a larger community) emigrates to a core country or an island of development and makes good money there, part of that income is sent back home and becomes the mainstay for those left behind. Hundreds of millions of dollars are transferred this way every year; these "remittances" make a critical difference in the poorer countries of the world (see Chapter 5).

In the vast slums, *barrios*, and *favelas*, those who are jobless or unsalaried are not idle. They work inside or in front of their modest homes, fixing things, repairing broken items for sale, sorting through small piles of waste for salvageable items, trading and selling goods from makeshift stands. What prevails here is referred to as the **informal economy**—the economy that is not taxed and is not counted toward a country's national income. What is generated in the informal economy can

add up to a huge total in unrecorded monetary value. This is of concern to governments, because no taxes are paid on this income. Similarly, remittances are usually delivered in cash, not via Western Union or a bank, and are also unrecorded and untaxed. Typically, a trusted community member (who might pay a comparatively small bribe at the airport when passing through immigration) carries remittances to family members.

Even as the informal economy thrives among the millions in the shantytowns, the new era of globalization is having a major impact in the major cities founded or fostered by the colonial powers. In 2002, geographers Richard Grant and Jan Nijman documented this transformation in former colonial port cities, including Mumbai, India (formerly Bombay), where colonial rule produced an urban landscape marked by strong segregation of foreign and local activities, commercial as well as residential (Figure 10.34), and high levels of functional specialization and

> **Informal economy** Economic activity that is neither taxed nor monitored by a government and is not included in that government's gross national product (GNP); as opposed to a formal economy.

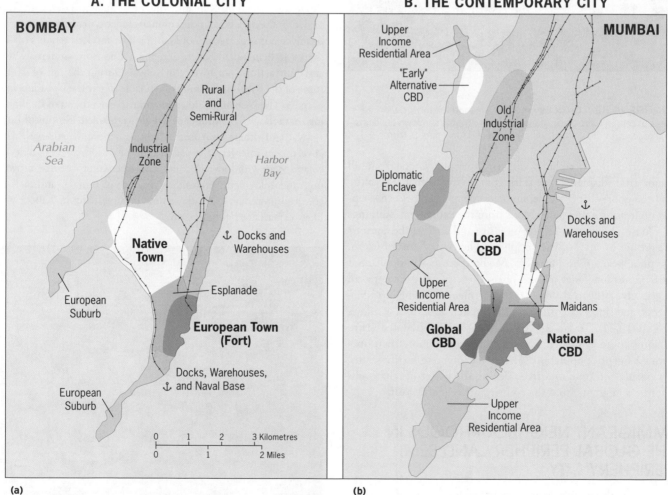

FIGURE 10.34 The Changing Character of Mumbai, India. (a) The colonial city and **(b)** the contemporary city. Adapted with permission from Richard Grant and Jan Nijman, "Globalization and the Corporate Geography of Cities in the Less-Developed World," *Annals of the Association of American Geographers*, 92, 2 (2002).

concentration. Adjacent to the port area was a well-demarcated European business district containing foreign (mostly British) companies. Economic activities in this European commercial area involved trade, transport, banking, distribution, and insurance. Zoning and building codes were strictly enforced. Physically separated from this European district were the traditional markets and bazaars of the so-called Native Town, a densely populated mix of commercial and residential land uses.

In the era of globalization, a new spatially demarcated foreign presence has arisen in Mumbai. The city now has a busy CBD at the heart of the original colonial city, housing mostly foreign corporations and multinational companies and linked mainly to the global economy. The former European Town has a large presence of big domestic companies and a pronounced orientation to the national (Indian) economy. The Native Town has a high concentration of small domestic company headquarters and the strongest orientation to the immediate urban area.

IMMIGRANT NEIGHBOURHOODS IN THE EUROPEAN CITY

Ethnic neighbourhoods in European cities are typically affiliated with migrants from former colonies. For example, Algeria was a colony of France, and now Paris and other French cities have distinct Algerian neighbourhoods. Similarly, London (United Kingdom) has a Jamaican neighbourhood, and Madrid (Spain) has a distinct Moroccan neighbourhood, reflecting their colonial ties with these now sovereign countries. Other European countries cultivated relationships with countries outside Europe after the colonial era. For example, after World War II, Germany invited young men from Turkey to migrate to Germany as guest workers, and German cities, such as Frankfurt, now have distinct Turkish neighbourhoods. Current immigration to countries in Europe typically focuses on the cities. And most of the migrants to European cities come from the global periphery or from eastern Europe, not from other countries in western Europe.

Migration to Europe is constrained by government policies and laws. Many western European cities have public housing zones that were built following the devastation of World War II. Governments in Europe are typically very involved in the social rights of people, such as health care and housing. European cities are also much older than North American cities and were laid out for foot and horse traffic, not automobiles. Thus, European cities are generally more compact, densely populated, and pedestrian friendly. Much of the city's history took place in the city centre, which has been preserved and which attracts tourists today. Whereas skyscrapers are typically the focal point of downtown in North American cities, a historic city centre is the focal point of downtown in European cities, and skyscrapers are reserved for developments on the outskirts of town. Housing in the European city is often combined with places of work, with work spaces on the bottom floors of buildings and housing above. Large zones of housing in Europe typically begin in a ring around the city centre, in what Ernest Burgess called the zone of transition. After the war, many European governments built public housing structures in the spaces around the city centre that had been levelled by bombing (Figure 10.35).

Immigration is changing the spatial-cultural geography of European cities. As immigrants settled in large numbers in the zone of transition, locals relocated to other neighbourhoods. Walking from the city centre of Paris out through immigrant neighbourhoods, one can see the cultural landscape change to reflect the significant number of immigrants from the "Maghreb" of Africa, the region of North Africa around Algeria and Morocco. In these tenement-lined, littered streets, the elegant avenues of historic Paris seem remote indeed—but they are only a short subway ride away.

(a)

(b)

FIGURE 10.35 (a) Paris, France and (b) Munich, Germany. (© Radius Images/Corbis; © Radius Images/Getty Images)

Whether a public housing zone is divided into ethnic neighbourhoods in a European city depends in large part on government policy. Urban geographers Christian Kesteloot and Cees Cortie studied housing policies and zones in Brussels (Belgium) and Amsterdam (The Netherlands). They found that there is very little public housing in Brussels and that immigrants live in privately owned rentals throughout the city. Kesteloot and Cortie also found that immigrant groups in Brussels who came from a distinct region of their home country, especially rural regions, tended to cluster in ethnic neighbourhoods. In contrast, immigrant groups who came from cities chose rental units scattered throughout the city and, therefore, did not establish ethnic neighbourhoods in Brussels.

In contrast, Amsterdam has a great deal of public housing and few ethnic neighbourhoods within the public housing units. When immigration to Amsterdam from former colonies (Indonesia, Suriname) and non-colonies (Morocco and Turkey) increased in the 1960s, Amsterdammers moved from the transition zone of public housing to neighbouring towns such as Almere (Figure 10.36). The Dutch government then implemented a policy in the public housing zone that slowed the creation of ethnic neighbourhoods. The Dutch government allots public housing to legal immigrants by assigning homes on a sequential basis in the city's zone of transition, where some 80 percent of the housing stock is public housing. As a result of government assignment of housing, a family from Suriname in public housing may live next to an Indonesian family and a Moroccan family rather than other Surinamese families. The housing and neighbourhoods are multicultural, and the ethnic groups maintain their traditions through religious and cultural organizations rather than residential segregation. In Amsterdam, the call to prayer for Muslims rings out all over the immigrant areas, as Muslims from various countries are spread throughout the city.

VISIBLE MINORITY NEIGHBOURHOODS IN CANADA

North American cities have varying degrees of segregated or concentrated minority communities in inner-city and suburban neighbourhoods. Certainly, it is difficult to compare the Canadian and American situation given each country's distinctive history and geography. American cities remain deeply divided along racial lines. In major Canadian cities there are some spatial concentrations of Aboriginal people, visible minorities, and newcomers, but most scholars conclude that Canadian cities do not have urban ghettos of the type generally associated with American cities.

Geographers Alan Walks and Lawrence Bourne argue that there has also been a change in how planners, sociologists, and others understand urban concentrations of visible minorities. In the 1960s and 1970s, scholars and policy makers regarded the formation of ethnic neighbourhoods as a "breakdown in the process of assimilation and integration" and as a form of social exclusion. Yet Canada, with its policy of multiculturalism, is among a number of countries that have come to regard visible minority concentrations in a more positive light. Such neighbourhoods are not only seen as contributing positively to the diversity and cosmopolitanism of a city (e.g., they ensure a diverse and interesting variety of foods, types of music, and fashions) but are also seen as a necessary place for newcomers to find the support and community they need as they learn about Canadian society. Such neighbourhoods are seen as maintaining important cultural ties and group identities in an increasingly global world.

(a)

(b)

FIGURE 10.36 Almere, The Netherlands. (a) Almere is the youngest city in The Netherlands. The first house was completed in 1976, and it became a municipality in 1984. It is now The Netherlands' seventh-largest city, with a population of approximately 350,000, and its ambition is to be the fifth-largest city by 2030. (b) It has become known for its vibrant, diverse population and unique architectural approach. (© OpenStreetMap contributors, CC-BY-SA. www.openstreetmap.org, www.creativecommons.org; © Henry George Beeker/Alamy)

Given their research, Walks and Bourne argue that Canada's visible minority populations are not forming ghettos in the sense that term is usually understood—i.e., involuntarily segregated neighbourhoods that give residents little opportunity for advancement beyond those locations. As well, while there is some suggestion in a few cases of a link between visible minority neighbourhoods and a lower income level or poverty, there is no discernible connection between poverty and visible minority concentrations. As we noted in Chapter 5, most newcomers to Canada settle in the country's largest CMAs, including Toronto, Vancouver, Montreal, and Ottawa–Gatineau. The majority of Canadian cities do have some segregation and concentration of visible minorities but

at levels lower than are seen in countries such as Britain and Australia. However, in the four most segregated CMAs— Toronto, Vancouver, Winnipeg, and Montreal—levels of polarization are higher. Given Canada's social history, Walks and Bourne suggest that it is difficult to predict whether we are going to see greater spatial assimilation or more social exclusion. What we can say, they argue, is that "for certain groups a new pattern of cultural pluralism" is developing, "marked by the emergence of ethnic communities." How these new patterns develop in various cities will depend on numerous factors, including immigration policy, global and political economic processes, government policy, and the specific directions taken by different visible minority groups.

MAIN POINTS 10.4 How Do Cities Evolve?

- Cities are constantly changing as a result of economic, social, technological, political, and cultural processes at the local, regional, national, and global level.

- Cities in the core region have developed within the broader context of globalization and deindustrialization, which has influenced the development of downtown cores. Processes such as gentrification and redevelopment play a role in the changing shape of central city residential neighbourhoods, while shifting immigration policies influence the emergence of particularly racialized and ethnic neighbourhoods.

- In core regions, new planning and development policies— such as New Urbanism, smart growth, and sustainability—attempt to ameliorate the negative impacts of rapid

urbanization, such as urban sprawl and the loss of agricultural land and environmentally sensitive ecosystems. These new concepts are only partially successful, given political and economic circumstances and consumer tastes.

- Cities in the periphery and semi-periphery often have fewer regulatory controls of development, which allow for makeshift communities to spring up at the city's edge. Suburban development in many cities reflects instances of formal and informal segregation and concentrations of various groups along ethnic and racial lines. While some may see these neighbourhoods as a failure of certain groups to assimilate, others argue they reflect the positive aspects of multiculturalism and diversity.

10.5 What Is the Connection between Cities and Globalization?

Globalization, as we defined the term in the second chapter, is a set of processes and outcomes that occur on the global scale, circumventing and leaping over state boundaries and making new connections between places. In the context of globalization, cities are playing an integral role that was not anticipated. Most statistics about economic activity at the global scale are gathered and disseminated by states. However, many of the most important processes occur among and between cities, not states as a whole. **World cities** function at the global scale, transcending state borders and functioning as the service centres of the world economy.

World city Dominant city in terms of its role in the global political economy. Not the world's biggest city in terms of population or industrial output, but rather centres of strategic control of the world economy.

In this newly emerging system, models of cities and hierarchies of cities within states (such as Christaller's model) no longer represent what is happening with the city. Geographers Taylor and Lang maintain that the city has become something other than a simple CBD tied in to a hierarchy of other cities within the state. The world city is a node in globalization—a place through which action and interaction occur. As a node, a world city is connected to other cities at the global level, and the forces shaping globalization pulse across these connections and through the cities—a phenomenon geographer Manuel Castells calls the "space of flows." Most lists of world cities provide a hierarchy of the most important world cities, then the next most important, and so forth. Virtually all agree that New York, London, and Tokyo are the most important world cities, but beyond that point the definition of what makes a world city, and the list of world cities, changes depending on the perspective of the researcher. For example, one of the most recent assessments of which cities can be considered "global," and the criteria for assessment, is from the Institute for Urban Strategies at the Mori Memorial Foundation in Tokyo. The

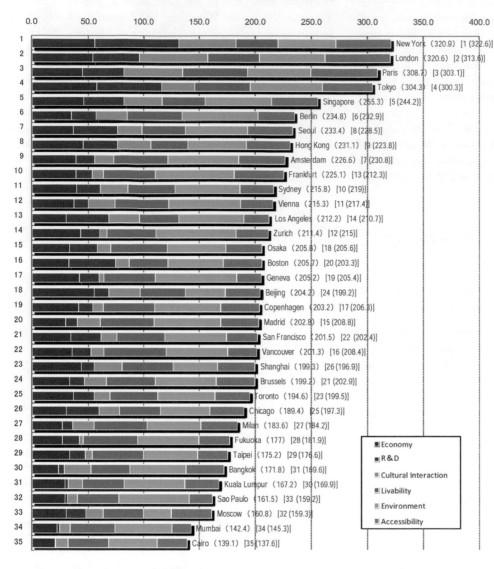

【GPCI-2011】Total score and rank by Functions

FIGURE 10.37 Global Power City Index, Total Score and Rank by Functions, 2011. From Figure 2-1 Comprehensive Ranking in *Global Power City Index, 2011*, Institute for Urban Strategies, The Mori Memorial Foundation: Tokyo, Japan, p. 8. Available at http://www.mori-m-foundation.or.jp/english/research/project/6/pdf/GPCI2011_English.pdf. Copyright © The Mori Memorial Foundation.

Note: The number in [] is ranking of GPCI-2010

institute has developed a Global Power City Index (GPCI) that evaluates six main city functions to determine the strength of individuals cities. The six functions are economy, research and development, cultural interaction, livability, ecology and natural environment, and accessibility.

Figure 10.37 illustrates the ranking of the top 35 world cities and a breakdown of where each city ranks for each of the functions. Note, for example, that New York and London top the list but rank poorly with respect to livability and environment. On the other hand, Paris is ranked third overall but is positioned at the top in terms of accessibility and is second in terms of livability. Two Canadian cities make the list, Vancouver (22nd) and Toronto (25th); Vancouver ranks second overall, behind Paris, in terms of livability. Overall, Asian cities rank quite highly in economic function, whereas cities in Europe are highly ranked for cultural interaction, livability, and environment. While such rankings are important in terms of understanding the characteristics of cities, their functions, and their position in the global urban system, there is some disagreement about which functions

are the most important criteria for evaluating a world city. As the *Guest Field Note* from Robert Oliver suggests, cities vie for such high-profile events as the Olympics or the World University Games, although not everyone agrees that hosting such events is in a city's best interests.

World cities do not exist merely to service players in the global economy. Major world cities such as London and Paris are also capital cities. Even though London and Paris are a short distance apart, both function as world cities, in part because of the role they play within their respective states: each became a magnet for economic and political activity within its state and then the globe. States often focus development in one particular city, such as the capital city, and encourage interconnectedness between that city and the rest of the world, thereby bolstering that city above the rest of the cities in the state. As we noted earlier, a primate city is one that is disproportionately large within a regional or national urban system. Primate cities tend to be the largest and most economically influential within the state, with the next largest city in the state being much smaller and much less influential.

GUEST FIELD NOTE
A Sporting Chance for Cities

More than a century ago, French nobleman Pierre Coubertin restored the Olympic Games as a mechanism to internationalize the benefits of sport. Coubertin believed that through participation or spectatorship, the Olympic spectacle had the capacity to reduce the social distance between various nations, regions, or societies of the world. As a researcher, and as someone with a life-long passion for sports, I am interested in the role that sport plays in modern life. From our recreational pursuits (e.g., sport leagues) to decisions regarding spectatorship (should I cheer for the Toronto Maple Leafs or the Montreal Canadiens?), sport assists many citizens to deliberate and assert their "right to the city."

One of the most visible opportunities to witness the symbolic power of sport is during the Olympic bidding process. Cites vie aggressively for what many see as the privilege of hosting the Olympic Games. Success means a city may gain recognition on the international stage and the construction of new sports and recreational facilities that enhance the quality of life for inhabitants while contributing, many argue, to the overall economic, political, and social life of the city.

It is the interplay between being a sporting spectacle and its socially educative potential that has made the Olympics a very powerful symbol, capable of catering to numerous agendas and interests across a range of spatial scales. Many cities competing in an economic climate characterized by globalization and deindustrialization have been forced to adopt more entrepreneurial models of urban growth. The competition for talented workers and wealthy tourists has produced fierce place wars, with numerous cities seeking to demonstrate their competitive advantages. With the capability of mixing sport, cultural consumption, and entertainment, the Olympic Games provide a seductive new form of urban development. The pursuit of the Olympic Games can be an occasion to leverage funds from senior levels of government, to address the city building desires of the citizenry, and to trumpet the physical and social benefits of sport, physical education, and recreation across a range of skill levels and ages. At a time when cuts to physical education programs, the cancelling of after-school sports programs, increased municipal user fees for swimming pools and skating rinks, and skyrocketing rates of obesity dominate urban itineraries, winning the right to host the Olympics can offer a reprieve. Without question, sport and leisure, as budget items, simply do not rank as high as health and social services.

The Olympics offer city managers, corporate stakeholders, and local residents an occasion to address questions concerning both image and infrastructure. Thinking about the Olympics allows our imaginations to soar. It is exciting to imagine thousands of the world's fastest and strongest athletes convening in one place. At the same time, the construction of multiple sporting venues and their supporting infrastructure, the demands on the transportation network,

FIGURE 10.38 Rio de Janeiro Prepares to Host the 2016 Olympic Games. From left, Carlos Fernando Carvalho, Rio de Janeiro's Mayor Eduardo Paes, International Olympic Committee President Jacques Rogge, head of the IOC Evaluation Commission Nawal El Moutawakel, and Brazil Olympic Committee President Carlos Arthur Nuzman view a model of Rio's Olympic village. (Buda Mendes/LatinContent/Getty Images)

and the refashioning of the city to meet the communicative and consumptive demands of tourists, often overshadows the fact that people actually live in the host city (Figure 10.38). Not surprisingly, residents' understanding of what an Olympic city is does not always mesh with those of growth-minded visionaries. Residents work and play in the Olympic city long after the crowds have dissipated. While the Olympics are often presented as a politically saleable commodity, cities often struggle with very difficult questions about the benefits and drawbacks of hosting the Games. Concerns over massive operating and capital costs, exorbitant security expenses, corporate greed, and other local inconveniences and injustices make hosting seem a risky proposition. For local-area residents, concerns over inflation, housing prices, and increased policing are just as important as the issues of job creation, urban regeneration, and city image. Social justice groups argue that instead of sinking critical resources into new sport installations, we should invest in social programs.

Exploring how the various claims to urban space rendered visible during the Olympic planning and hosting process provides geographers with a prime opportunity to examine myriad social and political conflicts around urban space. What are the risks of trying to appease global markets, develop international contacts, and open our borders to the world? These and other questions continue to attract the interest of geographers seeking to understand the implications of the globe's premier sporting event on the fabric of our local communities. By examining the manner by which claims to urban space are negotiated and represented, we have a prime opportunity to examine the "conflicting geographies of democracy." Do the Olympics represent a modern version of bread and circuses—the subjugation of democracy—or can they be utilized to create an urban culture that is both socially and spatially accessible?

Robert Oliver, Virginia Polytechnic Institute and State University

There are primate cities in many former colonies, as the colonial powers often ruled from a single dominant city, where economic and political activities were concentrated. In the non-colonial context, London and Paris each serve as examples of primate cities and world cities today, but some countries, such as the United States and Germany, have two or more world cities within their state borders. They thus do not have a single, distinct primate city. To understand the role of cities in globalization, we must also consider the services cities provide to places and peoples around the world, as well as the interconnectedness among cities. Geographers are now working to uncover the globalized flows and processes occurring across world cities, bringing them closer together.

CITIES AS SPACES OF CONSUMPTION

In addition to being nodes in globalization, cities are also products of globalization. Major changes in cities, such as the redevelopment of New York's Times Square and the remaking of Berlin's Potsdamer Platz, are the result of global processes. Frank Roost has found that "the global media industry is becoming the driving force in the reshaping of cities" such as New York and Berlin, transforming city centres into **spaces of consumption**. Media companies are investing heavily in urban centres in order to create major entertainment districts, places where tourists can go to consume their products.

> **Spaces of consumption** Areas of a city, the main purpose of which is to encourage people to consume goods and services; driven primarily by the global media industry.

For example, in New York City—ranked first on the 2011 GPCI—government entities began to redevelop Times Square in the early 1980s. At that time, this area of the city was known for its neon lights, pornographic movie houses, prostitution, and other illicit economic activities. The city sought to push these businesses out of Times Square and bring back the conglomeration of restaurants, hotels, bars, and entertainment spaces that had filled the business district before World War II. Over the next decade the city closed hundreds of small businesses in Times Square, and in 1995, Mayor Rudolph Giuliani reached a deal with Michael Eisner, CEO of Walt Disney Company. The mayor promised to remove the remaining sex shops, and Eisner committed to renovating the New Amsterdam Theater, a focal point in Times Square (Figure 10.39). Secured with a $26-million low-interest loan from the state of New York, Disney set the course for a new family-friendly entertainment district in New York. The restored New Amsterdam Theater now hosts Disney musicals such as *The Lion King* and *Beauty and the Beast* (both based on Disney movies), and the area around Times Square has become a space of consumption and a variation on a theme park with themed restaurants (e.g., Hard Rock Café, ESPN Zone), cross-promoting themed stores (e.g., Warner Brothers Store, Disney Store), and retail stores that cater to families (for example, an enormous Toys R Us with a Ferris wheel inside).

Potsdamer Platz in Berlin is also becoming a new space of consumption in the city centre. Prior to the bombing of Berlin

(a)

(b)

FIGURE 10.39 New Amsterdam Theater, Times Square, New York City. (a) The New Amsterdam Theater in Times Square as it appeared in 1947. Note the signs around the building advertising arcade games and a flea circus. (b) During the 1980s and 1990s, Times Square was "cleaned up" and reinvigorated. The Walt Disney Company renovated the New Amsterdam Theater and now shows productions of musicals such as *Beauty and the Beast* and *The Lion King*. (Corbis-Bettmann)

FIGURE 10.40 The Sony Center, Potsdamer Platz, Berlin. (© Guido Cozzi/Atlantide Phototravel/Corbis)

during World War II, Potsdamer Platz was a centre of entertainment for Berlin's middle class. After the war, little was left of the area. By the 1960s a 460-metre border zone and the Berlin Wall occupied the formerly vibrant area of the city. After reunification, the city divided Potsdamer Platz and sold the land. The two largest owners are the German company Daimler-Benz and the Japanese company Sony. Sony built a huge entertainment structure called the Sony Center (Figure 10.40) for cross-promotion. According to Roost, much of the Daimler-Benz

structure, known as Daimler City, is a space of consumption, with entertainment venues, restaurants, bars, and hotels.

Although tourists will be focused on the theme park atmosphere of these spaces of consumption, the renovations in both cities have also brought spaces of media production to the cities. Sony has placed its European headquarters in Berlin, Warner Brothers moved its offices to Times Square, and new office towers around Times Square house many other media companies.

MAIN POINTS 10.5 What Is the Connection between Cities and Globalization?

- The processes of globalization have repositioned certain cities within economic and political contexts that are beyond the reach of the nation-state. Cities that function in this global context are called world cities.

- World cities operate within a global urban system, forming important nodes in the global flow of people, technologies, finances, and goods and services. New York, London, and Tokyo are the most important world cities.

- There are various ranking systems for determining where a city fits in the world system. The Institute for Urban Strategies at the Mori Memorial Foundation in

Tokyo, Japan, has developed a Global Cities Power Index (GCPI), which uses six main city functions to determine a city's strength. These functions are economy, research and development, cultural interaction, liveability, ecology and natural environment, and accessibility.

- Cities are also spaces of consumption when they are marketed as places tourists can experience and consume as entertainment. World cities market themselves as unique locations with distinctive features—e.g., buildings and structures that everyone recognizes even though they may never have been there.

SUMMARY

Today much of the world's population resides in cities; indeed, in Canada 80 percent of the population resides in urban areas. Human beings initially began living in urban areas some 3,500 years ago, and the development of cities can be traced to six urban hearths. The modern city emerged at the time of the Industrial Revolution, during the era of colonialism and imperialism. With more efficient agricultural practices, a food surplus, and the development of mass manufacturing, rural people flocked to cities for the opportunities they offered. The growth of city planning and development helped organize the city into distinctive land uses, and various models were created to map the various areas of a city–the CBD, inner residential and industrial zones, suburban zones, and the rural hinterland. The form a city takes varies, and individual political, economic, and cultural histories determine the evolving structure of core, peripheral, and semi-peripheral cities. While models give us some sense of how cities are structured, each city is unique and must be studied for its own particularities.

Cities are also interconnected to each other, and models such as Central Place Theory and the rank-size rule seek to make sense of the patterns found in various urban systems.

Urban systems develop at a variety of scales, from the local and the regional to the national. As a result of the processes of globalization, certain cities have become world cities, functioning as nodes for the global flow of people, technologies, finances, and goods and services.

The city is an ever-changing cultural landscape, its layers reflecting grand plans by governments, impassioned pursuits by individuals, economic decisions by corporations, and processes of globalization. In North America, planning concepts such as New Urbanism, smart growth, and sustainability were developed to try to deal with some of the more negative aspects of city growth and development, including congestion, sprawl, loss of agricultural land, and environmental damage. Geographers who study cities have a multitude of topics to examine. From gentrification to tear-downs, from *favelas* to monster homes, from spaces of production to spaces of consumption, from ancient walls to gated communities, cities have so much in common, yet each has its own pulse, its own feel, its own spatial structure, its own set of realities. The pulse of the city is undoubtedly created by the peoples and cultures who live there.

DISCUSSION AND REVIEW QUESTIONS

1. The process of urbanization took thousands of years to develop. What were the key innovations and technologies that lead to the first urban revolution? Where were the hearths of humanity's urban revolution and when did they initially develop?

2. Similar to the agricultural revolution, the urban revolution occurred in phases. What precipitated the second urban revolution and what were the spatial changes associated with the second wave?

3. Urban geographers are interested in where cities form, how they develop (urban morphology), and how cities act as organizing centres for a collection of

settlements. Walter Christaller was one of the first to develop models and a theory of city formation. Discuss Christaller's contribution to our understanding of urban geography. What was his key theory?

4. Discuss the spatial characteristics of Canada's urban history and the evolution of a Canadian urban system. What are the primary factors that have led to its unique spatial pattern?

5. One of the major challenges in modern cities is urban sprawl. What is urban sprawl? What has caused it? What, if anything, is being done to counteract it? What has been your experience with urban sprawl?

GEOGRAPHIC CONCEPTS

ADDITIONAL RESOURCES ONLINE

About the Congress for the New Urbanism: www.cnu.org

About globalization and world cities: www.lut.ac.uk/gawc/index.html

About opposition to urban sprawl: www.sierraclub.org/sprawl

About Berlin: www.learner.org/resources/series180.html#program_descriptions

Click on Video On Demand for "Berlin: United We Stand" www.learner.org/resources/series85.html#program_descriptions

Click on Video On Demand for "Berlin: Changing Centre of a Changing Europe"

About sprawl in Chicago: www.learner.org/resources/series180.html

Click on Video On Demand for "Chicago: Farming on the Edge"

chapter 11

DEVELOPMENT

Geography, Trade, and Development

WALKING DOWN ONE of the major streets of Timbuktu, Mali (Figure 11.1), one could hardly believe they were in the renowned intellectual, spiritual, and economic centre of the 13th to 16th centuries–a place with such a great reputation for wealth that it spurred the first European explorations along the African coast. What survives is a relatively impoverished town of some 35,000 people that functions as the central place for the surrounding area and seeks to attract some tourist business based on its legendary name.

What happened to Timbuktu? Many centuries ago the city derived its wealth from its ability to control the trans-Sahara trade in gold, salt, ivory, kola nuts, and slaves. However, when trade patterns shifted with the development of maritime routes along the west coast of Africa, Timbuktu lost its strategic position, and a long period of decline set in. Timbuktu's story serves as a reminder that *where* a place is located in relation to patterns of economic development and exchange can be as important as, or even more important than, the commodities found in that place.

Indeed, there are many examples of places where the presence of a valuable commodity does not translate into an improved economy for those living nearby. The people working on the oil wells in Gabon or chopping down rare hardwood trees in Thailand, for example, are not the ones who most benefit from the wealth associated with demand for the goods they help produce. Instead, international corporations or the wealthiest families in a place, those who own the industry, tend to be the principal beneficiaries.

To understand how the production of an item creates wealth for some and not for others, we must understand the concept of the commodity chain. A commodity chain is a series of links connecting the many places of production and distribution that produce a commodity that is then exchanged on the market and, ultimately, consumed (see Chapter 2). Each link along the chain adds a certain value to the commodity, generating different levels of wealth for the places and the people where production occurs.

What Timbuktu had to offer was the ability to coordinate and facilitate an overland trade based on its geographic situation

FIGURE 11.1 Timbuktu, Mali. The dirt streets found throughout much of the town reflect the impoverishment of this once celebrated place. (© Alexander B. Murphy)

near the Niger River, the last major water source for those crossing the Sahara from south to north across what is now Mali and Algeria. When the trade that was essential to the commodity chain shifted westward, Timbuktu's economic foundation crumbled. In modern times, commodity chains include miners and agriculturalists, manufacturers, exporters and importers, wholesalers and retailers, advertisers and designers, and, of course, consumers. Places positioned strategically along a commodity chain can benefit, but they benefit in different ways. Furthermore, the structure and geographical characteristics of a commodity chain can always shift in response to changing conditions, in many cases quite quickly.

The amount of wealth generated at each step of production (that is, at each link in the commodity chain) depends on how production occurs at that step. In Chapter 2, we introduced the concepts of core and periphery. Sophisticated technology, high skill levels, extensive research and development, and high salaries tend to be associated with segments of global commodity chains located in the core. The segments located in the periphery, by contrast, tend to be associated with basic technology, less

education, little research and development, and lower wages. Since the people with the highest salaries own the businesses or work in advertising, and the people with the lowest salaries work in the mines or fields, global commodity chains often reinforce sharp divisions between core and peripheral regions.

One challenge of development is transforming peripheral processes into core ones, or redirecting the profit generated through core processes to improve peripheral processes. As the 21st century unfolds, countless governments, academics, non-governmental organizations, and international financial institutions will offer ideas about how to lift up the peripheral and semi-peripheral parts of the world. The theories, methods, and recommendations vary, but they are all focused on the elusive concept of development.

In this chapter, we review how development is defined and measured, and look at some of the theories of development. We examine how geography affects development, considering the structures of the world economy. We also look at the barriers to and costs of development within countries and ask why uneven development occurs *within* the state.

KEY QUESTIONS FOR CHAPTER 11

1. How is development defined and measured?

2. How does geographical situation affect development?

3. What are the barriers to, and the costs of, development?

4. How do political and economic institutions influence uneven development within states?

11.1 How Is Development Defined and Measured?

The economic and social geography of the contemporary world is a patchwork of almost inconceivable contrasts. On their shifting fields carved out of equatorial American and African forests, farmers grow root crops using ancient methods and rudimentary tools (Figure 11.2). On the Great Plains of North America, in the Ukraine, and in eastern Australia, farmers use expensive, modern machines to plough the land, seed the grain, and harvest the wheat. Toolmakers in the villages of Papua New Guinea still fashion their implements by hand, as they did many centuries ago, whereas factory workers in Ontario use

FIGURE 11.2 Practising Traditional Agricultural in Niger, Africa.
(© Finbarr O'Reilly/Reuters)

FIGURE 11.3 Honda Plant in Alliston, Ontario. (Dick Loek/
GetStock.com)

cutting-edge robotics to produce automobiles by the shipload
for distribution throughout the world (Figure 11.3). Between
these extremes, the variety of productive activities and the
means of production are virtually endless.

These contrasts point to a major issue in understanding development: wealth does not depend solely on *what* is produced
but also depends in large part on *how* and *where* it is produced.
People can grow agricultural commodities with rudimentary
tools or with expensive combines. Is one or the other necessary
for development to occur? The idea of development is everywhere, but rarely do we pause to ask exactly what development
means or how we can measure it.

Development implies progress. In the modern world, progress is typically understood to mean improvements in technology
and production, as well as improvements in the social and economic welfare of people. To say a country is **developing**, then,
is to say that progress is being
made in technology, production, and socio-economic welfare. Our modern notion of
development dates back to the
time of the Industrial Revolution and the idea that technology
can improve the lot of humans. Indeed, it is through advances
in technology that people can produce more food, create new
products, and accrue material wealth. In more recent years,
however, there has been growing recognition that these things
do not necessarily bring happiness, social stability, or environmental sustainability. This near-exclusive focus on economic

> **Developing** With respect to
> a country, making progress in
> technology, production, and
> socio-economic welfare.

considerations has made the notion of development, as it is currently understood, a narrow and sometimes controversial indicator of the human condition.

GROSS NATIONAL INCOME

Methods of measuring development typically fit into three
major areas of concern: development in economic welfare, development in technology and production, and development
in social welfare. Over the past six decades, the most common
way to compare development in economic welfare was to use
the index economists created to compare countries, the gross
national product. **Gross na-
tional product (GNP)** is a
measure of the total value of
the officially recorded goods
and services produced by the
citizens and corporations of a
country in a given year. It includes things produced both
inside and *outside* the country's
territory, and it is therefore
broader than **gross domestic
product (GDP)**, which measures only goods and services
produced *within* a country's
borders during a given year.

In recent years, econo-
mists have turned to **gross
national income (GNI)** as a
more accurate way of measuring a country's wealth in the
context of a global economy. GNI measures the total value of
all goods and services produced within a country plus income
received from investments outside the country. In order to compare GNI across countries, however, economists must standardize the data. The most common way to standardize GNI data is
to divide it by the population
of the country, yielding the
per capita GNI. For example,
according to the World Bank,
Norway's per capita gross national income in U.S. dollars
in 2010 was $85,380. That
same year, the United States'
was $47,140. Canada's GNI for 2009 (2010 data not being
available) was $41,950. But in Pakistan, the world's sixth most
populous country, it was only $1,050, in Mali (where Timbuktu
is located) it was $600, and in Togo the per capita GNI in 2010
was a mere $440. This enormous range across the globe in per
capita GNI reflects the often-searing contrasts between rich and
poor.

Although the table of per capita GNI in 2010 (Table
11.1) clearly shows the startling differences between rich and
poor in the world, the use of this statistic as an indicator of
development has several shortcomings. Most critically, GNI

> **Gross national product
> (GNP)** The total value of all
> goods and services produced
> by a country's economy in
> a given year. It includes all
> goods and services produced
> by corporations and individu-
> als of a country, whether or
> not they are located within the
> country.
>
> **Gross domestic product
> (GDP)** The total value of all
> goods and services produced
> within a country during a given
> year.
>
> **Gross national income
> (GNI)** The total value of all
> goods and services produced
> within a country plus income
> received from investments
> outside the country.

> **Per capita GNI** The total
> value of all goods and services
> produced within a country plus
> income received from invest-
> ments outside the country,
> divided by the population of
> the country.

TABLE 11.1	Per Capita World GNI, 2010				
Ranking	Economy	Atlas methodology (U.S. dollars)	Ranking	Economy	Atlas methodology (U.S. dollars)
1	Monaco	197,460 a	183	Tajikistan	780
2	Liechtenstein	136,540 a	185	Cambodia	760
3	Bermuda	.. a	186	Benin	750
4	Norway	85,380	187	Haiti	650
5	Qatar	.. a	188	Bangladesh	640
6	Luxembourg	79,510	189	Chad	600
7	Switzerland	70,350	189	Mali	600
8	Cayman Islands	.. a	192	Burkina Faso	550
9	Isle of Man	.. a	193	Guinea-Bissau	540
10	Denmark	58,980	193	Rwanda	540
11	Channel Islands	.. a	195	Tanzania	530 b
12	United Arab Emirates	.. a	196	Nepal	490
13	Kuwait	.. a	196	Uganda	490
14	Sweden	49,930	198	Central African Republic	460
15	Netherlands	49,720	198	Zimbabwe	460
16	San Marino	50,670 a	200	Afghanistan	330 a
17	Finland	47,170	201	Gambia, The	440
18	United States	47,140	201	Madagascar	440
19	Austria	46,710	201	Mozambique	440
20	Faeroe Islands	.. a	201	Togo	440
21	Belgium	45,420	206	Ethiopia	380
22	Andorra	41,130 a	206	Guinea	380
23	Australia	43,740 a	208	Niger	360
24	Germany	43,330	209	Eritrea	340
26	France	42,390	209	Sierra Leone	340
27	Canada	41,950 a	211	Malawi	330
28	Japan	42,150	213	Liberia	190
29	Ireland	40,990	214	Congo, Democratic Rep.	180
30	Singapore	40,920	215	Burundi	160

Note: Rankings include all 215 World Bank Atlas economies, but only those with confirmed GNI per capita estimates or those that rank among the top twenty for the Atlas method are shown in rank order.
Figures in italics are for 2009 or 2008; .. = not available
a = 2010 data not available and ranking is approximate; b = covers mainland Tanzania only
Source: Data from the World Bank; accessed October 17, 2011 at http://siteresources.worldbank.org/DATASTATISTICS/Resources/GNIPC.pdf.

Formal economy The legal economy that is taxed and monitored by a government and is included in a government's gross national product (GNP); as opposed to an informal economy.

Informal economy Economic activity that is neither taxed nor monitored by a government and is not included in that government's gross national product (GNP); as opposed to a formal economy.

is a limited measure because it includes only transactions made in the **formal economy**, the legal economy that governments tax and monitor. Many of the countries have a per capita GNI of less than $1,000 per year—a figure so low it seems impossible that people could survive on it. However, a key component of survival in these countries is the **informal economy**, the illegal or uncounted economy that governments do not tax or keep track of, which can include everything from a garden plot in a yard to the black market or the illegal drug trade. For example, the Swedish International Development Cooperation Agency reported in 2004 that the size of the informal labour force in Africa is almost 80 percent, and this sector accounts for over 90 percent of the new jobs that are created on that continent. The informal economy is clearly a significant element in the economies of many countries, but GNI statistics omit it entirely.

Another limitation of using GNI per capita as a development indicator is that it masks the extremes in the distribution of wealth *within* a country. In Table 11.1, the Middle Eastern oil countries of Kuwait and the United Arab Emirates (UAE) have per capita GNIs higher than that of several European countries. However, these figures give us no hint of the degree of overall participation in the country's economy, of the average citizen's material standard of living, or of development gaps between genders or among regions. We know from other indicators that economic production and the wealth it generates are not distributed evenly across the seven emirates that make up the United Arab Emirates. For example, Abu Dhabi, the emirate that dominates the petroleum industry, generated over half of the country's GNI in 2007. Dubai, the next largest emirate, generated about a quarter of the GNI. The Qaywayn emirate, on the other hand, generated less than one percent of the country's gross GNI.

At first glance, Canada's relatively high per capita GNI would also seem to indicate that it is a prosperous core country. Much like the United Arab Emirates, however, significant developmental disparities exist across different regions of Canada and among the country's various population subgroups. Unemployment rates, for example, vary considerably across Canada. In December 2010, Newfoundland and Labrador's unemployment rate was 13.7 percent and 11.9 percent of Prince Edward Island's active labour force was out of work. Saskatchewan's unemployment rate, on the other hand, was only 5.5 percent, and Manitoba had the lowest provincial unemployment rate in the country, at 5.2 percent. Unemployment rates also vary among men and women in Canada and are sometimes much higher for particular age groups. In December 2010, for example, the national unemployment rate for women over the age of 25 was only 6.2 percent, while it was 6.6 percent for men aged 25 and over. However, for youth aged 15 to 24 years, the unemployment rate that month was more than twice as high, 13.8 percent. Unemployment rates must be used cautiously as indicators of economic development, as they only take into account people who are actively working or looking for work, but these interprovincial and demographic variations certainly confirm the need to consider geographical circumstances and differences within the country or region being analyzed when assessing levels of development.

Yet another limitation of the GNI per capita indicator is that it measures only outputs (i.e., production). It does not account for the costs of production, which may take a toll on the environment by depleting resources or polluting air and water. Per capita GNI may even treat such externalities as a good thing. For example, the sale of cigarettes augments GNI—and if the cigarettes cause sickness that requires hospitalization, the GNI is boosted further. Conversely, the use of energy-efficient devices can lower GNI.

Another useful example of how the GNI per capita indicator may fail to adequately consider the negative costs of production is provided by looking at the Athabasca tar sands. Industrial development of these bituminous sands, which are located in northeastern Alberta and are believed to be one of the world's largest oil reserves, began in the late 1960s and has accelerated dramatically since the late 1990s. In 2006 some 1.3 million barrels of oil were being produced each day, and this is projected to increase to as much as 3.3 million barrels of oil per day (or more) by 2020. The province of Alberta, the Canadian government, the various corporations doing business in the region, and the many individuals and families who

have moved here in search of work have certainly enjoyed numerous economic benefits as a result of this growing production. Indeed, oil sands production contributes significantly to Canada's GNI each year. However, criticism of some of the practices associated with oil extraction and processing in the tar sands has been mounting in recent years. Areas of concern include the incredibly high levels of water consumption required to extract the oil from the sand (two to five barrels of water per barrel of oil), the toxicity of the waste water created by this extraction process, and the harm this water has done to fish and other aquatic life as it seeps into the area's water bodies. The extent to which these and other problems exist in the oil sands region, and the question of how long such practices can be sustained environmentally, are hotly contested topics. David Schindler of the University of Alberta has noted that "environmental groups and the handful of aboriginal communities living in towns near the oil sands have repeatedly warned that the rapid development has come at too high a cost to the environment."

Together, the various deficiencies of the GNI per capita indicator underscore the importance of reading and interpreting development indicators with caution.

The clear need to measure and compare levels of development more accurately has prompted many analysts to create indices of the advancement and integration of technology, on improvements in productivity, or on the development of social welfare as alternative measures of economic development.

For example, to gain a sense of the role of technology in the economy, analysts can measure the Occupational Structure of the Labour Force, using the percentage of workers employed in various sectors of the economy. A high percentage of labourers engaged in the production of food staples (i.e., agriculture) signals a low overall level of development, as conventionally defined, while a high percentage of workers involved in high-tech industries and services implies a high level of development.

Productivity per Worker is examined by summing production over the course of a year and dividing it by the total number of people in the labour force. A more productive workforce points to a higher level of mechanization in production.

To measure access to technology, some analysts measure Transportation and Communications Facilities per Person, which reduces railway, road, airline connections, telephone, radio, television, and so forth to a per capita index—and reflects the amount of infrastructure that exists to facilitate economic activity. Table 11.2 highlights some of the extraordinary disparities in access to communications around the world.

Other analysts focus on social welfare to measure development. One tool in this regard is the Dependency Ratio, a measure of the number of dependents, young and old, that each 100 employed people must support (Figure 11.4). A high dependency ratio can result in significant economic and social strain. Yet, as discussed in Chapter 4, the aging countries of

Country	Phone mainlines per 1,000	Cellular subscribers per 1,000	Internet users per 1,000
Norway	423.6	1,105.0	850.0
Australia	470.5	1,024.9	539.9
Canada	554.8	616.8	730.0
Democratic Republic of Congo	0.1	105.2	3.7
Zimbabwe	25.8	91.8	101.2
World Average	191.0	504.1	208.6

TABLE 11.2 Differences in Communications Connectivity, 2007

Source: Data from Earthtrends, World Resources Institute.

Europe have high dependency ratios and also very high per capita GNIs.

We can employ countless other statistics to measure social welfare, including literacy rates, infant mortality, life expectancy, caloric intake per person, percentage of family income spent on food, and amount of savings per capita. Looking through all of these, we quickly gain a sense that many countries come out in approximately the same position no matter which measures are used. Each indicator shares one limit with per capita GNI, however; they do not capture differences in development *within* countries, an issue discussed further at the end of this chapter.

One of the most widely referenced measurements of development today is the Human Development Index, a tool that was first employed by the United Nations in 1990. According to the United Nations, the Human Development Index was designed in the interest of going beyond economics by incorporating the "three basic dimensions of human development: a long and healthy life, knowledge and a decent standard of living." Several statistics—including life expectancy at birth, literacy rates and school enrolment rates, and per capita GDP—factor into the calculation of the Human Development Index. The 2010 *Human Development Report*, which presented the Human Development Index for countries based on 2008 data, once again demonstrated the stark disparities that exist among world regions and, as part of this, between the core and periphery (see Figure 11.5 on page 320).

DEVELOPMENT MODELS

This discussion of ways of measuring development takes us back to the problem with terminology. The word "developing" suggests that all countries are consistently making progress as it pertains to each of these indicators by, for example, increasing literacy, improving communications, or raising levels of worker productivity. The central concern here is that current conceptualizations of development suggest that all countries have moved or will move through the same process of development, as if travelling from the bottom to the top of a scale or ladder, but this does not take geographical differences very

seriously. Just because Japan moved from a rural, agrarian state to an urbanized, industrial one, for example, does not mean that Sudan will, or that it might do so in the same way. Another criticism is that today's prevailing conceptualization of development has a Western bias. Critics argue that some of the measures taken in poorer countries that the West views as progress, such as attracting industry and mechanizing agriculture, can actually lead to worsened social and environmental conditions for many people in the poorer countries. Still others criticize the development model because it treats countries as autonomous units moving through a process of development at different speeds. The model does not consider geography or interrelations across scales, and does not account for the fact that actions at one scale influence socio-economic changes at other scales.

Many theories of development grew out of the major decolonization movements of the 1960s. The classic development model, one that is certainly subject to each of the criticisms identified above, is economist Walter Rostow's **modernization model**. Economists like Rostow, questioning how dozens of newly independent countries in Africa and Asia would survive economically, looked to how the economically powerful countries had arrived where they were. The result was a model that assumed all countries follow a similar path to development or modernization, one that involves advancing through five stages of development.

> **Modernization model** A model of economic development most closely associated with the work of economist Walter Rostow. The modernization model (sometimes referred to as modernization theory) maintains that all countries go through five interrelated stages of development, which culminate in an economic state of self-sustained economic growth and high levels of mass consumption.

The first stage is "traditional": the society's dominant activity is subsistence farming, its social structure is rigid, and technology is slow to change. The second stage brings "preconditions for takeoff": new and more active leadership deliberately pushes the country toward greater flexibility, openness, and economic diversification. This, in turn, leads to the third stage, "takeoff," during which the country experiences

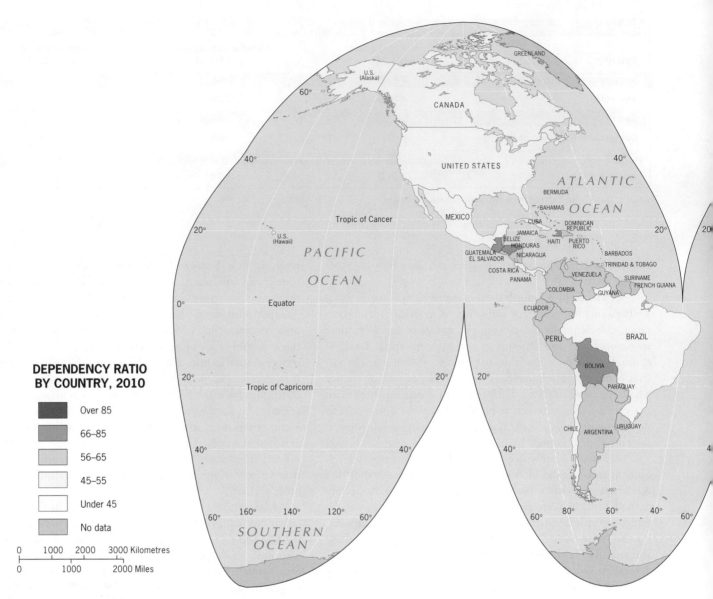

FIGURE 11.4 Dependency Ratio by Country, 2010 (% of Working-Age Population). The dependency ratio is the ratio of the number of children (younger than 15 years old) and older persons (65 years old and over) in the population to the number of people in the working-age groups (15 to 64 years old). The working-age adults in the formal economy contribute to a country's tax base, thereby supporting the young and old in the country. The higher the number, the more "dependents" (under 15 or over 65) each working-age adult supports through taxes. Data from the World Bank, 2011; available at http://data.worldbank.org/indicator/SP.POP.DPND.

something akin to an industrial revolution. Breakthroughs in technology and mass-production occur, industrialization proceeds, urbanization increases, and sustained growth takes hold. Next, the economy enters the fourth stage, the "drive to maturity," in which technologies diffuse, industrial specialization occurs, and international trade volumes expand. Modernization is evident in key areas of the country and population growth slows. In Rostow's model, some countries reach the final stage, "high mass consumption," which is

marked by high incomes and widespread domestic production of many goods and services. During this stage, a majority of workers enter the service sector of the economy.

Another name for Rostow's model (and other models derived from it) is the Ladder of Development. Visually, we can see his five stages of development as rungs on a ladder (Figure 11.6), with each country climbing the ladder one rung at a time. In addition to the general criticisms of development models, the major problem with Rostow's model is that it provides no

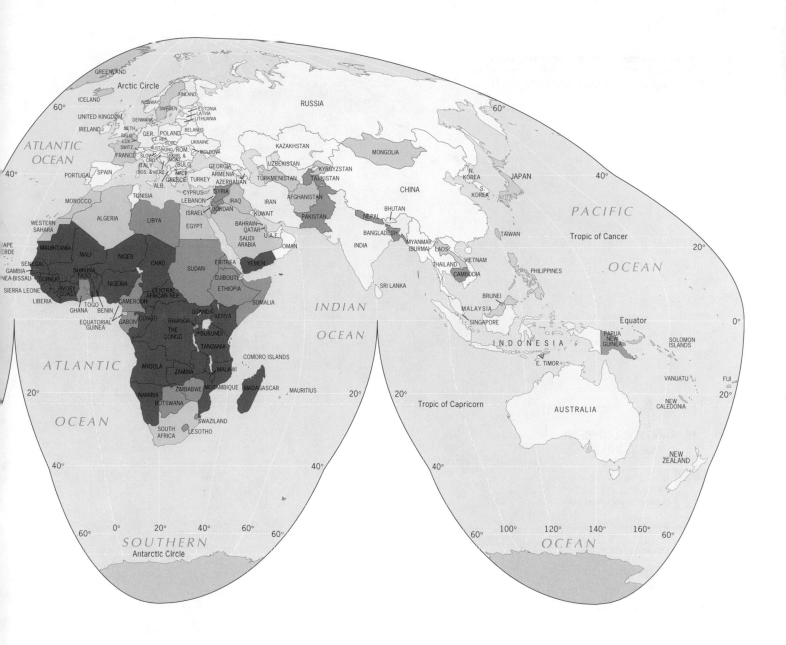

larger context to development. Is a climb up the ladder truly dependent only on what happens within one country? Or do we need to take into account all other countries, their relative positions on the ladder, and how those countries' actions, as well as global forces, affect an individual country's movement on the ladder? The theory also ignores the context within an individual country, leaving us to wonder where regional or cultural differences fit into the picture. Even the notion of calling wealthy countries "industrialized" and saying poor countries

need to "industrialize" implies that economic development can only be achieved by following the same trajectory as that taken by today's wealthy countries. Yet if a poor country quickly industrialized today through foreign investment, it might not reap much economic benefit and could experience severe environmental damage at the same time. Nonetheless, and despite all of these criticisms, Rostow's model has still been very influential because it is descriptive of the experiences of *some* countries.

FIGURE 11.5 Human Development Index, 2010.
Data from United Nations Human Development Report, at http://hdr.undp.org/en/media/HDR_2010_EN_Table1_reprint.pdf.

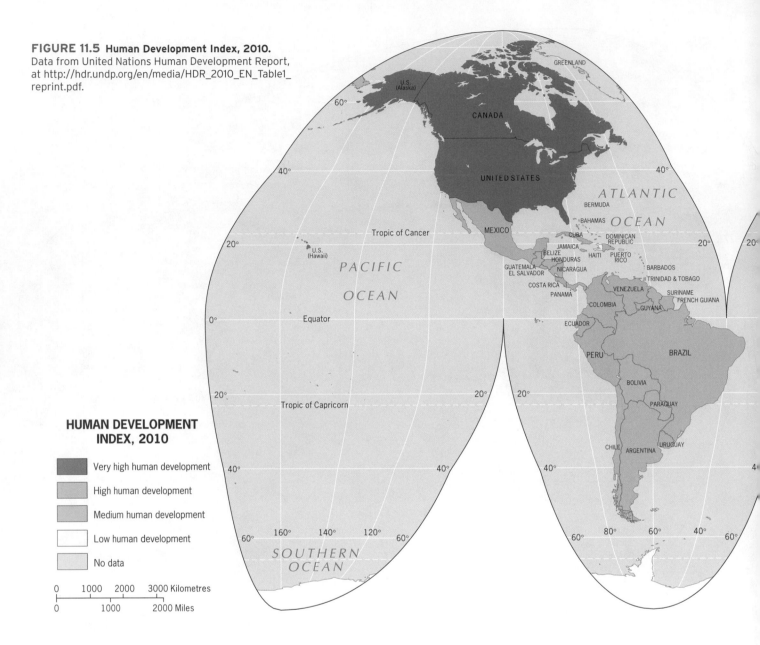

HUMAN DEVELOPMENT
INDEX, 2010

Very high human development

High human development

Medium human development

Low human development

No data

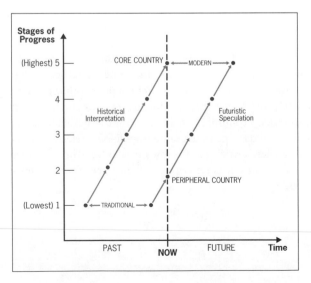

FIGURE 11.6 Rostow's Ladder of Development. Rostow's model assumes that all countries can reach the same level of development and that all will follow a similar path. Adapted with permission from P.J. Taylor, "Understanding Global Inequalities: A World-Systems Approach," *Geography* 77 (1992): 10-21.

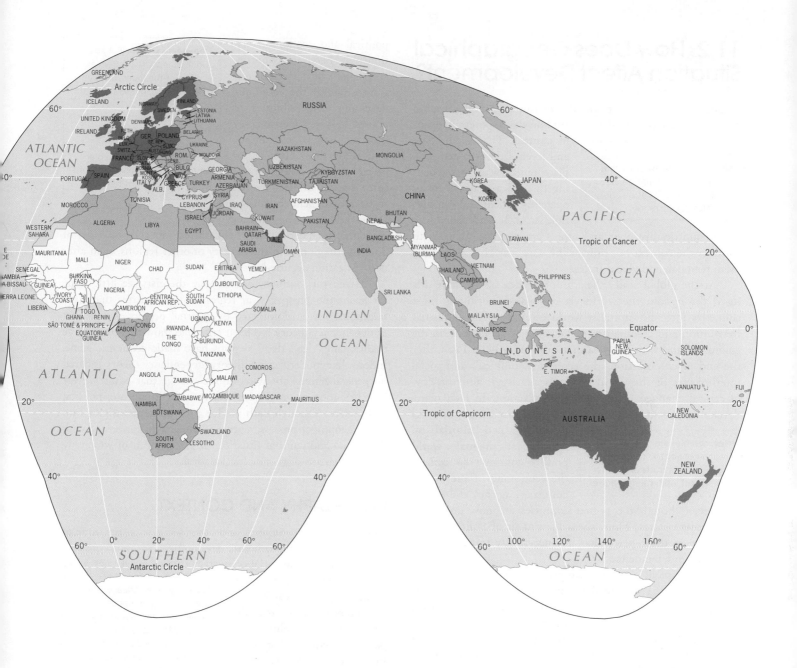

- A major issue in understanding development is that wealth does not depend solely on *what* is produced, but also depends in large part on *how* and *where* it is produced.

- A near-exclusive focus on economic considerations makes the notion of development, as it is currently understood, a narrow and sometimes controversial indicator of the human condition.

- Some development models, such as Walter Rostow's modernization model, have been criticized for their assumption that all countries will follow the same path to development. A major weakness of such models is that they fail to consider the *context* in which development takes place.

11.2 How Does Geographical Situation Affect Development?

As noted earlier, a major criticism of Rostow's modernization model is its lack of consideration for how development happens in **context**. That is, the type and level of development in a place reflect what is happening there as a result of forces operating concurrently at multiple scales. To understand why some countries are poor and others are wealthy, we need to consider the context not only at the state scale, but also at the local, regional, and global scales.

> **Context** The geographical situation in which something occurs; the combination of what is happening at a variety of scales concurrently.

At the global scale, the European idea of the state diffused throughout the world via colonialism, bringing most countries into the capitalist world economy. The Industrial Revolution and colonialism made colonies dependent on the colonizers and brought wealth to the colonizers. Even after the end of colonization, the economic, political, and social interlinkages of the world economy persisted, and the flow of capital changed little after decolonization. In fact, many development scholars argue that the poor are simply now experiencing **neo-colonialism**, which means the major world powers continue to control the economies of the poorer countries, as they did in the past, even though the poorer countries are now politically independent states. Thus, the achievement of political independence in these places has not necessarily translated into economic independence.

> **Neo-colonialism** The entrenchment of the colonial order, such as trade and investment, under a new guise.

Development scholars have produced a number of theories that take into account the context of neo-colonialism. One example of these **structuralist theories** holds that large-scale, difficult-to-change economic arrangements shape what can happen in fundamental ways. The development of the global economy brought into being, and firmly entrenched, a set of structural circumstances—such as the concentration of wealth in certain areas and unequal relations among places—that make it very difficult for poorer regions to improve their economic situation. Structuralists argue that these countries face a different set of development circumstances than those faced by the small number of western European countries on which Rostow based his modernization model.

> **Structuralist theory** A model of economic development that treats economic disparities among countries or regions as the result of historically derived power relations within the global economic system.

DEPENDENCY THEORY

Structuralists have developed a major body of development theory called **dependency theory**, which suggests that the political and economic relationships between countries and regions of the world control and limit the economic development possibilities of poorer areas. Dependency theorists note, for example, that colonialism created political and economic structures that caused the colonies to become dependent on the colonial powers. They further argue that such dependency helped to sustain the prosperity of dominant regions and the poverty of other regions, even after decolonization occurred.

> **Dependency theory** A structuralist theory that offers a critique of the modernization model of development. Based on the idea that certain types of political and economic relations (especially colonialism) between countries and regions of the world have created arrangements that both control and limit the extent to which regions can develop.

Given this outlook, dependency theorists see little hope for economic prosperity in regions and countries that have traditionally been dominated by external powers. This aspect of dependency theory has been criticized, however, since some traditionally "dependent" regions have made economic gains. Indeed, like modernization theory, dependency theory is based on generalizations about economic change that pay relatively little attention to geographical differences in culture, politics, and society. Although both models provide some insights into the development process, neither is adequately concerned with the spatial and cultural situation of places, both of which are central elements of geographical analysis.

GEOGRAPHY AND CONTEXT

As geographers, economists, and other social scientists came to realize that studying economic development without considering the political and social contexts within which it takes place does not reflect reality, geographers began to search for a development theory that did encompass geography, scale, place, and culture. For many, Immanuel Wallerstein's **world-systems theory**, first introduced in Chapter 2, has provided a useful framework.

> **World-systems theory** Theory originated by Immanuel Wallerstein and illuminated by his three-tier structure, proposing that social change in the developing world is inextricably linked to the economic activities of the developed world.

World-systems theorists hold that to understand any levels of development within any state or region, we must also understand its spatial and functional relationships within the world economy. To simplify their research, we can study the three basic tenets of world-systems theory, as Wallerstein defines them:

1. The world economy has one market and a global division of labour.
2. Although the world has multiple states, almost everything takes place within the context of the world economy.
3. The world economy has a three-tiered structure.

Regarding the first tenet, Wallerstein explains that the development of a world economy began with capitalist exchange around 1450 and encompassed the globe by 1900. Under the current system of **capitalism**, people, corporations, and states produce goods and exchange them on the world market, with the goal of achieving profit. To generate a profit, producers seek the cheapest labour from around the globe, which means a corporation can move production of a good from southern Ontario to Mexico and then to China, simply to take advantage of cheaper labour. In addition to the world labour supply, producers gain profit by commodifying whatever they can. **Commodification** is the process of placing a price on a good and then buying, selling, and trading the good. Companies create new products, generate new twists on old products, and create demand for the products through marketing. When the authors of this book were children, none of them could have imagined buying a bottle of water; now we do it all the time.

According to Wallerstein's second tenet, despite the existence of approximately 200 states, everything takes place within the context of the world economy (and has done so since 1900). Colonialism set up this system, exporting the concept of the politically independent state and also constructing an interdependent global economy. During the first wave of colonialism (which happened during mercantilism), colonizers extracted goods from the Americas and the Caribbean and exploited Africa for slave labour, amassing wealth through sugar, coffee, fruit, and cotton production. During the second wave of colonialism (which happened after the Industrial Revolution), colonizers set their sights on cheap industrial labour, cheap raw materials, and large-scale agricultural plantations. Gaining the legal status of sovereign states was relatively easy for most colonies when they became independent; the United Nations Charter even set up a committee to help colonies do so after World War II. But gaining economic independence is proving to be a difficult task for many former colonies. The economies of the world are tied together, generating intended and unintended consequences that fundamentally change places.

Finally, as we first outlined in Chapter 2, a world-systems approach presents the world economy as a **three-tier structure** with a core, periphery, and semi-periphery. **Core** processes incorporate higher levels of education, higher salaries, and more technology; core processes generate more wealth in the world economy. **Periphery** processes incorporate lower levels of education, lower salaries, and less technology; peripheral processes generate less wealth in the world economy. Wallerstein defined the **semi-periphery** as places where core and periphery processes are occurring simultaneously—places that are exploited by the core but in turn exploit the periphery. By taking advantage of its cheap labour or lax environmental standards, the core exploits the periphery. The semi-periphery acts as a buffer between the core and periphery, preventing the polarization of the world into two extremes.

The core and periphery are processes, but these processes happen in places. Some geographers stress the processes and try to avoid labelling places as core or periphery because processes in places are not static and they are not confined by state borders. Other geographers, however, are drawn to the world-systems theory because it is sensitive to geographical differences and the relationships among development processes that occur in different places. As a result, some of these geographers have defined certain places as core and others as peripheral in the world economy (Figure 11.7).

Wallerstein's division of the world into a three-tier structure helps explain the interconnections between places in the global economy. As discussed in more detail in Chapter 2, core processes generate wealth in a place because they require higher levels of education, more sophisticated technologies, and higher wages and benefits. When core processes are embedded in a place (such as the Technology Triangle in southwestern Ontario's Waterloo region, for example), wealth is generated for the people in that place. Core regions are those that have achieved high levels of socio-economic prosperity and are dominant players in the global economic game. Peripheral processes, on the other hand, require little education, lower technologies, and lower wages and benefits. When peripheral processes are embedded in a place (such as the growing of bananas in Ecuador), the processes often generate little wealth for the people in that place. Peripheral regions are poor regions that are dependent in significant ways on the core and do not have as much control over their own affairs, economically or politically. The semi-periphery supports both core and peripheral processes, and semi-peripheral places serve as a buffer between core and periphery in the world economy. Countries of the semi-periphery exert more power than peripheral regions but nonetheless remain heavily influenced by core regions.

Capitalism Economic model wherein people, corporations, and states produce goods and exchange them on the world market, with the goal of achieving profit.

Commodification The process through which something is given monetary value. Commodification occurs when a good or idea that previously was not regarded as an object to be bought and sold is turned into something that has a particular price and that can be traded in a market economy.

Three-tier structure With reference to Immanuel Wallerstein's world-systems theory, the division of the world into the core, the periphery, and the semi-periphery as a means to help explain the interconnections between places in the global economy.

Core Processes that incorporate higher levels of education, higher salaries, and more technology; generate more wealth than periphery processes in the world economy.

Periphery Processes that incorporate lower levels of education, lower salaries, and less technology; and generate less wealth than core processes in the world economy.

Semi-periphery Places where core and periphery processes are both occurring; places that are exploited by the core but in turn exploit the periphery.

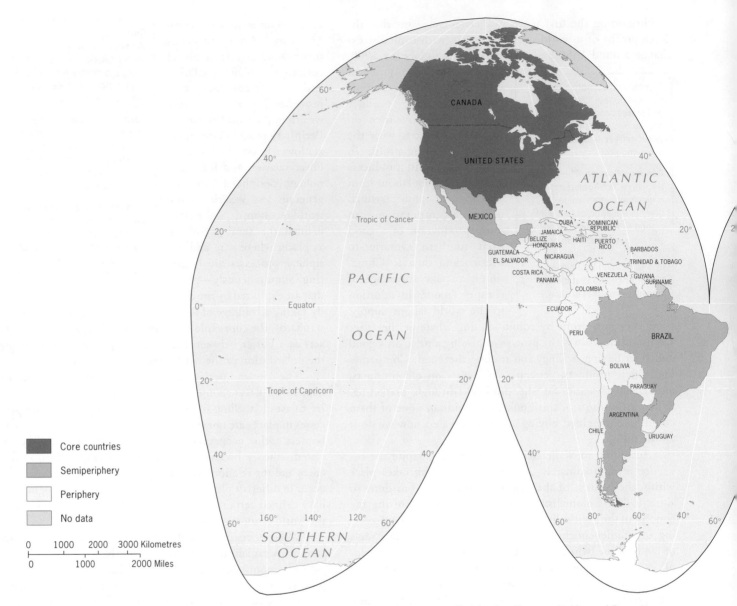

FIGURE 11.7 Countries' Status within the World-System, 2000. Data from Chase-Dunn, Christopher, Kawano, Yukio, and Brewer, Benjamin D. (2000). "Trade globalization since 1795: Waves of integration in the world-system," *American Sociological Review* 65 (1), pp. 77-95, Table A2. Accessed May 20, 2011 at http://www.irows.ucr.edu/cd/appendices/asr00/asr00app.htm.

Dividing the world into cores, semi-peripheries, and peripheries might seem to do little more than replace "developed—developing—underdeveloped" with a new set of terms. But the core-periphery model is fundamentally different from the modernization model because it holds that not all places can be equally wealthy in the capitalist world economy.

World-systems theory also makes the power relations among places explicit and does not assume that socio-economic change will occur in the same way in all places. It is thus more sensitive to geographical context than dependency theory and the modernization model, at least in economic terms. Geographer Peter J. Taylor uses the analogy of a school of tadpoles to demonstrate these ideas. He envisions different places

in the world as tadpoles and explains that not all tadpoles can survive to develop into toads. Rather, those who dominate survive; the others perish. World systems theorists see such domination (i.e., exploitation) as a function of the capitalist drive for profit in the global economy. Thus, capitalists can move production quickly from one place to another around the globe to enhance profits, but places that lose a production facility can suffer. Moreover, their coping capacity can be small if, as is often the case, they abandoned traditional ways and shifted to an export economy when external investment first came in.

Economic geographers, political geographers, and other academics continue to debate world-systems approaches. Some

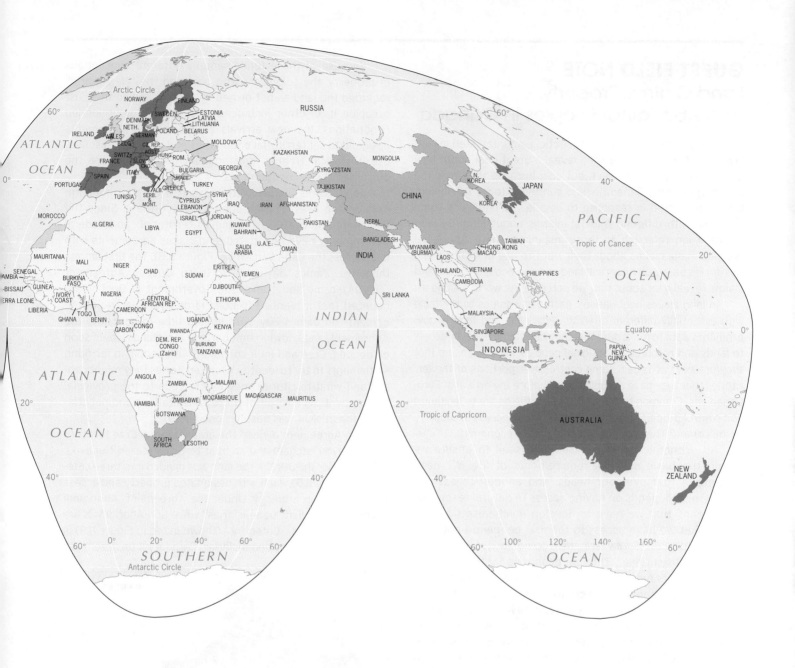

argue that this approach overemphasizes economic factors in the development process (rather than cultural or technological factors, for example) and that it is very state-centric in that it does not focus enough attention on processes operating at micro or macro scales. Nonetheless, Wallerstein's work has encouraged many to see the world map as a system of interlinking parts that needs to be understood in relation to one another, as well as a whole. As such, a world-systems approach has a considerable impact on human geography (particularly the economic and political aspects of human geography), and it is increasingly commonplace for geographers to refer to the kinds of core-periphery distinctions suggested by world-systems approaches.

It is important to note that world-systems theory is also very much applicable at scales beyond the state. A core-periphery relationship can exist within a region, a state (country), or a local area. For example, the Johannesburg area can be described as the core of the South African state, the Greater Golden Horseshoe can be described as the core of the province of Ontario, and the Central Business District can be described as the core of São Paulo, Brazil. Yet another example of how the core-periphery relationship can exist *within* a country is provided in the following *Guest Field Note*, where geographer Nicole Gombay discusses the lasting legacy of, and challenges created by, the colonization of Canada's Arctic and sub-Arctic regions.

GUEST FIELD NOTE
Land Claims, Property, and Aboriginal Peoples in Canada

As a geographer working in the Arctic, I am interested in land claims, not only because they reveal a great deal about how peoples and lands intersect, but also because they help me to recognize how Canada is and continues to be fundamentally constructed in response to people's struggles to come to terms with differing understandings about land. By land claims, I am referring to those instances where Aboriginal peoples make claims about their right to use or hold certain territories based on historical land use and occupancy. So land claims reveal a lot about how we perceive the world around us.

In land claims negotiations, each party comes to the table with essentially different interests. Provincial and federal governments want to make sure that they have legal rights of access to lands and resources. Aboriginal peoples want to ensure that they preserve or regain some control over portions of the territories that they have occupied since before the arrival of Euro-Canadians. Common to both, however, is the desire to legitimize and control property rights. So why is having access to property so important? The answer, at least in part, is economics.

All economic systems essentially seek to ensure we obtain the basic material requirements of life. We need clothing, a roof over our heads, and enough to eat and drink, which depends on having access to natural resources. This means that we have to develop mechanisms for ensuring that we have access to them. If people do not have rights to property, how are they going to get the things they need to survive? Thus all economic systems rely on property rights being set up and preserved, and in order to make sure this happens, we create various laws and regulations. The trouble is that people can have widely differing perspectives about what property is and how it should be used, and so correspondingly, they create quite different laws. Much of the history of conflict among human beings revolves around struggles to have power over property.

In Canada, these struggles have been especially acute for Aboriginal peoples. With the arrival of colonizers, Aboriginal peoples increasingly lost control over, and access to, property and resources. The Europeans had quite different ideas about property and how to negotiate access to land than did the original inhabitants. As far as Euro-Canadians are concerned, the land and its resources may be turned into private property, and the laws of the state are designed to protect that property. Land that is not privately owned is called "Crown land" and is commonly viewed as belonging to nobody. From the perspective of many of the Aboriginal peoples in Canada, the idea that land and resources can be privately owned makes no sense. Aboriginal peoples have their own complex laws that have traditionally governed people's access to land and resources. For Aboriginals, property is understood as owned commonly by a limited number of people via laws that control their access to, and use of, it.

Because of these fundamentally different conceptions of property, the colonizers who occupied the "New World" regarded the land as not owned by anyone and so they just occupied it. In other instances, after battles or prolonged negotiations, the new arrivals set up legal arrangements designed to set territorial boundaries and delineate resource use. Historical treaties and ongoing land claims are the outcomes of such negotiations.

Land claims in the Arctic have had an enormous impact on the lives of the people who live there. Since the mid-twentieth century, provincial, territorial, and federal governments have negotiated land claims agreements with Inuit across the Canadian Arctic (Figure 11.8). The first among them—the James Bay and Northern Quebec Agreement (JBNQA)—came about after the Government of Quebec announced that it planned to build large hydroelectric developments on James Bay. With limited time to negotiate the Agreement, and knowing that parts of their lands would soon be flooded, Cree and Inuit consulted with people in far-flung settlements to try to identify what territories they might control and what territories they had to cede to the provincial government. As a result of these consultations and negotiations, the JBNQA was hastily signed in 1975.

The Agreement divided the area up into a Cree territory (called Eeyou Istchee) and an Inuit territory (called Nunavik). In turn, under the JBNQA the land was divided into three categories (Figure 11.9), each with designated property and access rights based on ethnicity. Under the Agreement, Aboriginal residents are called "beneficiaries" while non-Aboriginals are "non-beneficiaries." Category I (shown in red in Figure 11.9) is exclusively for use by beneficiaries. Category II (in green) are

FIGURE 11.8 Inuit Land Claims Settlement Regions of Canada. From Makivik Corporation, Nunavik Research Centre-Cartographic Services.

Crown lands in which hunting, fishing, and trapping rights are reserved for beneficiaries, while activities such as forestry, mining, and tourism development are subject to shared authority with the state. Category III (in white) are Crown lands that are subject to a joint regulatory scheme, though non-beneficiaries may harvest resources from these lands as long as they respect provincial regulations.

Figure 11.9 might lead us to think that the categories of land and rights of resource use have been tidily sorted out. But in fact this is far from the case. The white spaces on the map make the land appear empty. All its cultural content is erased. The traditional laws of the Inuit, which up to the signing of the Agreement had defined how the land was used, are simply invisible, and indigenous presence is instead neatly located and contained in small coloured pockets. So the map silently suppresses one set of laws and replaces them with another, and in the process state control of a huge area of property is legitimized. Yet, a careful look at the map reveals two settlements—Puvirnituq and Ivujivik—whose residents refused to sign the Agreement. They have come to be called "dissident communities" because they did not agree to relinquish their land and resources to the state.

Most people in Nunavik *did* sign the Agreement, though, and as a result, they have essentially lost control over how their local resources are to be used. Instead, the state has taken over that power. This is a source of profound unease for many Inuit whose own rules governing people's access to resources are being challenged by Euro-Canadian laws. So, for example, Inuit are now being told that they are not allowed to harvest certain animals, like belugas, in the ways they had been accustomed to doing for millennia. This has caused great distress among many Inuit in Nunavik. As one person from one of the dissident settlements put it, "[The JBNQA] opened the door for the *Qallunaat* [non-Inuit] to do as they wished. The people were fooled. They were taken for a ride. They thought that they were given land to say, 'Hey, this is mine! Keep off! I'll do what I want.' When we already were <u>doing</u> that!" For many, it appears that rather than retaining control over the land and its resources, the Inuit lost that control, and can no longer govern themselves according to their own laws of property and access to resources.

Nicole Gombay, University of Canterbury, New Zealand

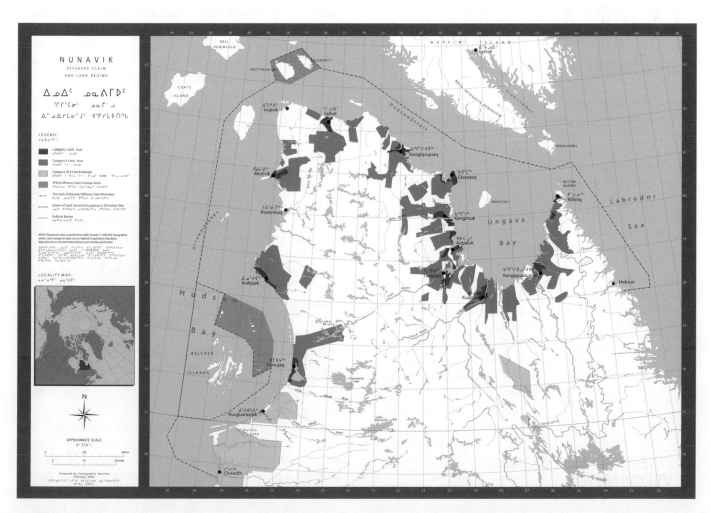

FIGURE 11.9 Nunavik Offshore Claims and Land Regime. Valid as of 2003. From Makivik Corporation, Nunavik Research Centre-Cartographic Services

- Development happens in context. The type and level of development in a place reflects what is happening there as a result of forces operating concurrently at multiple scales, from the local to the regional, and from the national to global.

- Development scholars have produced a number of theories, referred to as structuralist theories, that take into account the context of neo-colonialism and its influences on the development prospects of peripheral regions. For example, one structuralist theory holds that large-scale, difficult-to-change economic arrangements shape what can happen in fundamental ways.

- Structuralists have developed a major body of development theory, called dependency theory, that sees little hope for economic prosperity in regions and countries that have traditionally been dominated by external powers. Like modernization theory, however, dependency

theory has been criticized for not considering the importance of context; indeed, it is based on generalizations about economic change that pay inadequate attention to geographical differences in culture, politics, and society.

- A world-systems approach, developed by Wallerstein, argues that states find themselves organized in a hierarchical relationship as core, periphery, or semi-peripheral participants in the global economy. This means that some states gain greater benefits through their position in the global economy over others.

- World-systems theory helps us understand the geography of development. It is sensitive to geographical differences and the relationships among development processes that occur in different places. World-systems theory divides the world into a three-tier structure, with a core, periphery, and semi-periphery, that helps explain the interconnections between places in the global economy.

11.3 What Are the Barriers to, and the Costs of, Development?

International organizations and governments measure individual countries' progress in development and then create programs that they hope will break down barriers to development and help improve the condition of people around the world, especially in the poorest countries.

In 2000, 189 world leaders at a high-profile United Nations summit adopted the UN Millennium Declaration, which stated their goal of improving conditions for people in the countries with the lowest standards of human development. At the summit, the leaders recognized the principal barriers to economic development and identified eight key development goals to be achieved by the year 2015, each of which would be realized by reaching a corresponding set of targets (Table 11.3). These **Millennium Development Goals** represent a high degree of consensus about the conditions that must be changed if economic development is to be attained.

> **Millennium Development Goals** A set of eight human development-related goals for the world's most impoverished countries, which were adopted at the United Nations Millennium Summit in 2000 with the intention of achieving all of these goals by the year 2015.

BARRIERS TO ECONOMIC DEVELOPMENT

As described earlier in this chapter, the structures and geography of the world economy have created numerous obstacles and barriers that inhibit economic development in the

periphery. In Chapter 4, we discussed the causes of malnutrition and examined how AIDS has ravaged sub-Saharan Africa. In Chapter 6, we discussed the natural hazards found in many peripheral countries and the lack of infrastructure to cope with those hazards. It is clear that the world economic system often works to the disadvantage of the periphery, but it is also clear that the system is not the only obstacle that peripheral countries face.

Conditions within the periphery, such as high population growth rates, lack of education, high foreign debt, political instability, and widespread disease, can seriously hamper development efforts. There is a conundrum here: did the structures of the world economy create these conditions or did these conditions help create the structures of the world economy? Many think that neither argument can stand alone, as it seems that both factors have combined to create a cycle that will be difficult to interrupt. Indeed, regardless of which came first, the fact remains that millions of people throughout the periphery are burdened with familial, economic, cultural, and political upheavals. In this section of the chapter, we will discuss several of the conditions that affect the economic development prospects of people in the poorest countries of the world, including many factors outlined in the UN Millennium Development Goals.

SOCIAL CONDITIONS

Countries in the periphery face numerous demographic, economic, and social problems. As noted in Chapter 4, most of the less well-off countries have high birth rates, along with a relatively low life expectancy at birth. Across the global periphery, as much as half the population is 15 years old or younger, making the supply of adult, tax-paying labourers low relative to the number of dependents. Low life expectancies and high infant and child mortality rates stem largely from inadequate nutrition.

TABLE 11.3	Millennium Development Goals and Corresponding Targets
Goal 1: Eradicate extreme poverty and hunger	
Target 1.A: Halve, between 1990 and 2015, the proportion of people whose income is less than $1 a day	
Target 1.B: Achieve full and productive employment and decent work for all, including women and young people	
Target 1.C: Halve, between 1990 and 2015, the proportion of people who suffer from hunger	
Goal 2: Achieve universal primary education	
Target 2.A: Ensure that, by 2015, children everywhere, boys and girls alike, will be able to complete a full course of primary schooling	
Goal 3: Promote gender equality and empower women	
Target 3.A: Eliminate gender disparity in primary and secondary education, preferably by 2005, and in all levels of education no later than 2015	
Goal 4: Reduce child mortality	
Target 4.A: Reduce by two-thirds, between 1990 and 2015, the under-five mortality rate	
Goal 5: Improve maternal health	
Target 5.A: Reduce by three-quarters, between 1990 and 2015, the maternal mortality ratio	
Target 5.B: Achieve, by 2015, universal access to reproductive health	
Goal 6: Combat HIV/AIDS, malaria, and other diseases	
Target 6.A: Have halted by 2015 and begun to reverse the spread of HIV/AIDS	
Target 6.B: Achieve, by 2010, universal access to treatment for HIV/AIDS for all those who need it	
Target 6.C: Have halted by 2015 and begun to reverse the incidence of malaria and other major diseases	
Goal 7: Ensure environmental sustainability	
Target 7.A: Integrate the principles of sustainable development into country policies and programmes and reverse the loss of environmental resources	
Target 7.B: Reduce biodiversity loss, achieving, by 2010, a significant reduction in the rate of loss	
Target 7.C: Halve, by 2015, the proportion of people without sustainable access to safe drinking water and basic sanitation	
Target 7.D: By 2020, to have achieved a significant improvement in the lives of at least 100 million slum dwellers	
Goal 8: Develop a global partnership for development	
Target 8.A: Develop further an open, rule-based, predictable, non-discriminatory trading and financial system	
Target 8.B: Address the special needs of the least developed countries	
Target 8.C: Address the special needs of landlocked developing countries and small island developing states	
Target 8.D: Deal comprehensively with the debt problems of developing countries through national and international measures in order to make debt sustainable in the long term	
Target 8.E: In co-operation with pharmaceutical companies, provide access to affordable, essential drugs in developing countries	
Target 8.F: In co-operation with the private sector, make available the benefits of new technologies, especially information and communications	

From Millenium Development Goals, United Nations Development Programme website at http://www.un.org/millenniumgoals/.

For example, protein deficiency is a common problem in many places. Many in the global economic periphery also lack public sewage systems, clean drinking water, and access to health care, making economic development all the more difficult.

Lack of access to education is also a major problem in the periphery. In some places, even the poorest families must pay for their children to attend school. As a result, large numbers of school-age children do not go to school, and illiteracy rates are high. Moreover, access to education in the periphery is often gendered, with boys attending school longer than girls. Girls often stop attending school in order to work to earn the money needed to pay for their brothers' school fees.

Lack of education for girls is founded on, and compounded by, the widespread assumption (not just in the periphery, but in most of the world) that girls will leave their homes (and communities) when they marry, no longer bringing income to the family. In parts of the periphery, trafficking in children, especially girls, is common. Mike Dottridge, a modern anti-slavery activist, explains that **trafficking** happens when "adults and children fleeing poverty or seeking better prospects are manipulated, deceived, and bullied into working in conditions that they would not choose." This phenomenon is not considered slavery because the family does not sell a child; instead, the child is sent away with a recruiter in the hopes that the recruiter will send money and the child will earn money to send home. The trafficked children are often taken to neighbouring or nearby countries that are wealthier and in need of domestic servants. Others are trafficked across the world, again typically to work as domestic

> **Trafficking** When a family sends a child or an adult to a labour recruiter in hopes that the labour recruiter will send money, and the family member will earn money to send home.

servants. Dottridge explains that the majority of trafficked children are girls, and that the majority of girls are "employed as domestic servants or street vendors," although some girls are "trafficked into prostitution." The extent of this problem is well illustrated in statistics compiled by the United Nations' Global Initiative to Fight Human Trafficking, which showed that some 2.5 million people were in forced labour at any given time in 2007 as a result of trafficking, and that almost 90 percent of these people were found in peripheral countries. It also noted that the majority of trafficking victims were between the ages of 18 and 24 years old and that some 43 percent of victims were used for forced sexual exploitation.

Some countries are working to improve access to primary education in order to make education universally available. In 2000, the Millennium Development Report prompted the government of Rwanda to improve access to education. In 2003, fees for primary education were eliminated, and two years later, schools started receiving revenues based on the number of students they were educating. Rwanda set the goal of making primary education available to all by 2010. By 2009, more than 2 million children were enrolled in primary school, up significantly from about 1.4 million students in 1998–99. But access and completion are two different things; thus far, only about half the children in Rwanda reach the sixth year of school. Moreover, without adequate funding to support the growing student population, Rwanda's students are often required to meet under trees and in overcrowded classrooms. Aid is flowing in from outside, but sustaining support for the country's educational sector remains an ongoing challenge.

FOREIGN DEBT

Complicating the picture further is the foreign debt crisis that many peripheral and semi-peripheral countries face. Shortly

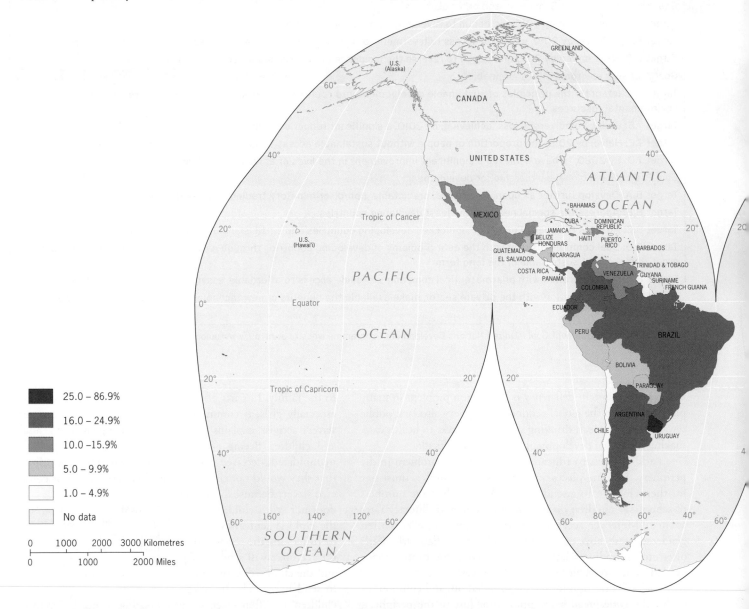

FIGURE 11.10 External Debt Service as a Percentage of Exports of Goods and Services for Low- and Middle-Income Economies, 2006. Data from the World Bank, Millennium Development Goals Atlas. Washington, D.C.: The World Bank. Data available at http://devdata. worldbank.org/atlas-mdg/.

after the decolonization wave of the 1960s, banks and other international financial institutions began lending large sums of money to the newly independent states, money earmarked for development projects. By the 1980s and 1990s, the World Bank and the International Monetary Fund (IMF) were lending massive amounts of money to peripheral and semi-peripheral countries, but with strings attached. To secure these **structural adjustment loans**, as they were known, countries had to agree to implement economic or governmental reforms, such as privatizing government entities, opening the country to foreign trade, reducing tariffs,

> **Structural adjustment loans**
> Loans granted by international financial institutions such as the World Bank and the International Monetary Fund to countries in the periphery and the semi-periphery in exchange for certain economic and governmental reforms in that country (e.g., privatization of certain government entities and opening the country to foreign trade and investment).

and encouraging foreign direct investment. (These loans provide one example of how political independence has not translated into economic independence for many countries.)

The IMF, which is managed, traditionally, by a European, lends money to peripheral countries in an effort to head off major economic problems. Once peripheral countries owe money to the IMF, the World Bank, and private banks and lending institutions, they need to repay their debts. Spending a large part of the country's budget on debt repayment makes it difficult for that country to invest in more development projects. In many cases, the cost of servicing the debt (that is, the cost of repayments plus interest) has exceeded the country's revenues from the export of goods and services (Figure 11.10). Meanwhile, in many countries, the returns on development projects have been much lower than anticipated. These factors have created a global debt crisis for the poorest countries in the world.

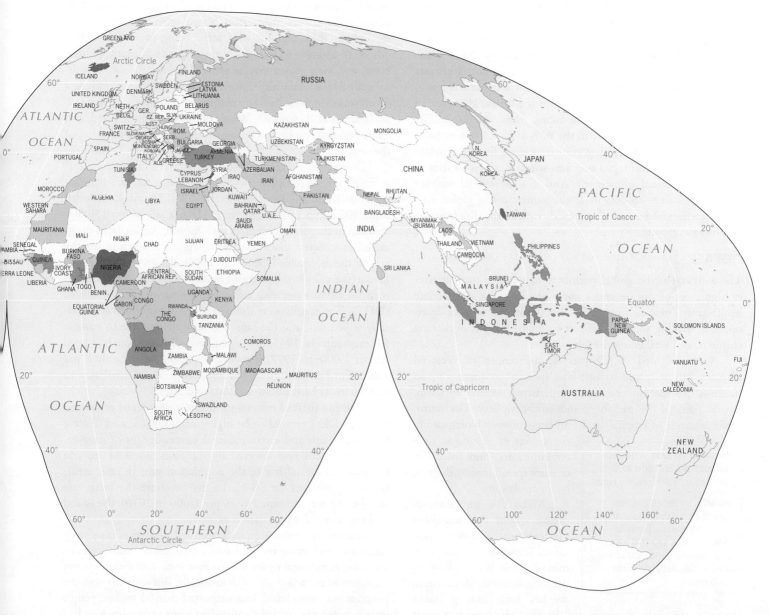

Structural adjustment loans were part of a larger trend toward neo-liberalism in the late 20th century. Neo-liberalism derives from the neo-classical economic idea that government intervention in markets is inefficient and undesirable, and should be resisted wherever possible. These ideas were at the heart of the conditions that were attached to loans and refinancing programs, but neo-liberal ideas also spurred a general shift toward the transfer of economic control from states to the private sector. This, in turn, fostered economic globalization while shrinking the size of the public sector in a number of countries. The result was the expansion of corporate control and the erosion of the ability of regions and states to control their economic destinies. Hence, the "neo-liberal turn" has been highly contentious.

High debt obligations and related neo-liberal reforms arguably contributed to the economic and political crisis in Argentina at the end of 2001. This led to overreliance on a privatized export sector that left the country vulnerable when shifts in the global economy weakened the competitiveness of Argentinian exports. Government spending was also unsustainably high, and corruption was rampant. By 2005, internal economic growth and aid from Venezuela put Argentina in a position to work out a complex debt-restructuring plan that has pulled the country back from the brink. However, in other cases where countries are facing imminent economic, political, and social meltdown, the only alternative may be to default on loans. Defaulting countries then find themselves in a severely disadvantaged position when it comes to attracting future external investment. And if a substantial number of countries were to default at the same time, a global economic crisis could ensue that would work to the disadvantage of almost everyone.

DISEASE

Those living in the global periphery experience comparatively high rates of disease and a corresponding lack of adequate health care. These circumstances directly affect economic development, making survival difficult for many people, orphaning children, and weakening the labour force.

As highlighted in Chapter 4, a number of **vectored diseases**—those spread by one host (person) to another by an intermediate host or vector—are a particular scourge in warm, humid parts of the periphery and semi-periphery. The warm, moist climates of tropical environments enhance biological activity. Vectors abound in such environments, and infectious diseases spread rapidly through host populations.

Malaria is an infectious disease spread by mosquitoes that carry the parasite in their saliva. Scientists did not determine the role of mosquitoes in the diffusion of the disease until the late 18th century. Today, the sequence of the disease is well known. The mosquito stings an infected host and sucks up some of the disease agents. In the mosquito's stomach, the parasites reproduce and multiply, eventually reaching its saliva. When the mosquito stings the next person, some of the parasites are injected into that person's bloodstream. The person who has been stung develops malaria and becomes a host. The disease manifests itself through recurrent fever and chills, with associated symptoms such as anemia and an enlarged spleen.

Malaria is a major factor in infant and child mortality, as most of the victims are children age five or younger. If a person survives the disease, he or she will develop a certain degree of immunity. However, many infected by malaria are weak, lack energy, and face an increased risk of other diseases taking hold in their weakened body.

Malaria occurs throughout the world, except at higher latitudes and altitudes, and in drier environments (Figure 11.11). Although people in the tropical portions of Africa suffer most from this disease, malaria also prevails in India, Southeast Asia, China, and the tropical Americas. Several types of malaria spread throughout these regions, with some being more severe than others. In addition to humans, various species of monkeys, rats, birds, and even snakes can be affected by the disease. In sub-Saharan Africa, malaria's virulence results from the effectiveness of its vectors—three African mosquitoes (*Anopheles gambiae*, *A. arabiensis*, and *A. funestus*). Whole populations are afflicted, and entire regions have been abandoned because of the prevalence of the disease.

Development experts look at malaria as a "silent tsunami" in the periphery, comparing its death toll to the tsunami that ravaged South and Southeast Asia in late 2004. That tsunami killed some 300,000 people at one time. Malaria kills about 150,000 children in the global periphery each month. Antimalarial drugs exist, but to defeat malaria, afflicted regions must eliminate the vector: the mosquito. During the 1940s, the government of Sri Lanka (then Ceylon) launched a massive attack on the mosquito with the aid of a pesticide called *dichlorodiphenyltrichloroethane* (DDT). The results were dramatic. The mosquito was practically wiped out, and the rate of deaths attributable to malaria fell markedly. In 1945, Sri Lanka's overall death rate had been 22 per 1,000; in 1972, it reported a death rate of only 8 per 1,000. Furthermore, there was not a single death attributed to malaria in Sri Lanka between 2005 and 2008.

The conquest of malaria produced a new set of problems, however. DDT proved to be highly carcinogenic and to have negative health and environmental consequences of its own. Also, the death rate lowered by the eradication of malaria led to a substantial rise in the population growth rate, creating new problems for Sri Lanka. By the time the birth rate dropped (it was estimated at 16 per 1,000 in 2010), the island had experienced a population explosion.

Success in combating major vectored diseases is often only temporary. Following the Sri Lankan experiment, India initiated a massive assault against the malaria mosquito, and the number of new cases of malaria declined dramatically. But ten years after the program was introduced, India reported that 60 million people were infected with malaria, more than half the number who had

> **Vectored disease** A disease carried from one host to another by an intermediate host.
>
> **Malaria** Vectored disease spread by mosquitoes that carry the malaria parasite in their saliva and that kills approximately 150,000 children in the global periphery each month.

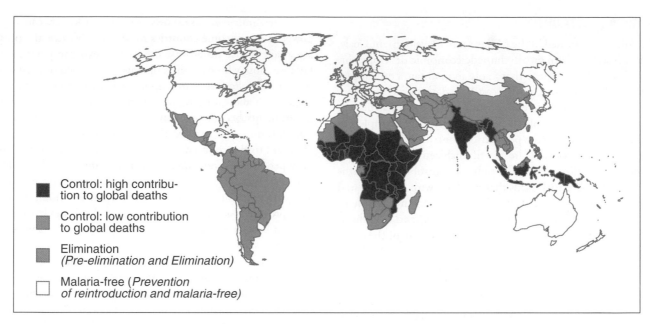

FIGURE 11.11 Malaria Endemic Countries and Level of Control, 2008. From Global Malaria Action Plan 2008/Roll Back Malaria Partnership, World Health Organization. Accessed October 28, 2011 at http://www.rollbackmalaria.org/endemiccountries.html.

the disease before the antimalarial campaign began. This example proved the mosquito population's ability to rebound quickly after even the most intensive application of pesticides.

Today the war against malaria is taking a new tack in the form of genetic interference with the mosquito so that its capacity to transmit the malaria parasite, *Plasmodium*, is destroyed. By introducing "engineered" mosquitoes into the general population, health experts hope that the number of non-virulent mosquitoes will rise significantly. A number of programs also focus on distributing insecticide-laden mosquito nets to surround sleeping quarters

and protect people from the mosquitoes, which are most active at night (Figure 11.12). One such program, the "Spread the Net" campaign, was co-founded by two Canadians, television personality Rick Mercer and Member of Parliament Belinda Stronach, in 2006 (Figure 11.13). The project's initial goal of raising enough money to buy 500,000 bed nets was achieved in 2010, with half of the nets being shipped to Liberia and the other half to Rwanda. Efforts such as this one are having some dramatic impacts in parts of Africa, but malaria remains a scourge of the poorer peoples of the world—and a major impediment to economic development.

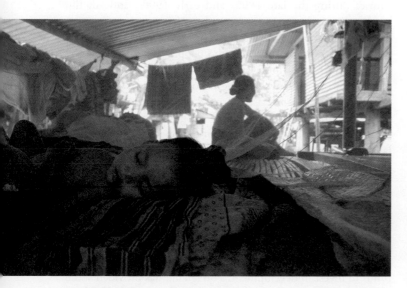

FIGURE 11.12 Tamalu, India. Tamalu is on the Car Nicobar islands off the coast of India. After the 2004 tsunami, the wetlands became breeding grounds for the mosquitoes that carry malaria. This baby sleeps under a mosquito net distributed to villagers by United Nations Children's Fund (UNICEF) workers. (© Pallava Bagla/Corbis)

FIGURE 11.13 Rick Mercer's "Spread the Net" Campaign. Former Liberal Member of Parliament Belinda Stronach (left) and Canadian comedian Rick Mercer are part of the "Spread the Net" Campaign, an initiative designed to reduce malaria outbreaks by ensuring that bed netting is available to protect children when they are sleeping. (© Christinne Muschi/Reuters/Corbis)

POLITICAL INSTABILITY

Although not addressed in the Millennium Development Goals, political instability can greatly impede economic development. Establishing a government that's able to maintain control over and lead a low-income country can be a daunting task. In peripheral countries, a wide divide often exists between the very wealthy and the poorest of the poor. In Kenya, for example, the wealthiest 10 percent of the population controls over 40 percent of the country's income. The disenfranchisement of the poor and the competition among the rich for control of the government (and the potential spoils that go along with that) can lead to extreme political instability within a state. An example of this is provided by Kenya, where, in 2007–8, two months of violence followed the controversy-laden re-election of the country's incumbent president, Mwai Kibaki (Figure 11.14). Many felt that the election had been rigged in favour of Kibaki and against another candidate, Raila Odinga, leader of the Orange Democratic Movement (ODM), which was formed in response to continued dissatisfaction with the imbalanced allocation of wealth and resources in the country.

Add to these factors involvement from outside the country (especially by powerful countries), and the political instability escalates, yielding horrid conditions in which military dictators, selfish megalomaniacs, and corrupt governments can come to power. In places where poverty is rampant, politicians often become corrupt, misusing aid and exacerbating the plight of the poor. In Zimbabwe in 2002, many people were starving after poor weather conditions created a meagre harvest. The country's ruling party, ZANU-PF, headed by Robert Mugabe, demanded that Zimbabweans who registered for the "food for work" program produce cards demonstrating their membership in the ZANU-PF political party. As conditions worsened in subsequent years, the Mugabe government faced increasing resistance from Zimbabweans. A potential challenger emerged in 2008, but after he was harassed and members of his opposition party were killed, he pulled out, and Mugabe was once again elected on an uncontested ballot.

FIGURE 11.14 Civil Unrest in Kenya Following 2007 Election. The controversial re-election of Kenya's incumbent president, Mwai Kibaki, led to mass violence throughout the country, leaving some 1,300 people dead. (Boniface Mwangi/AFP/Getty Images)

The Zimbabwe case shows that corrupt leaders can stay in power in low-income countries for decades because the people are afraid to rise up against the leader's extreme power, often because those who have risen up have been killed or harmed by the leader's followers. Circumstances and timing need to work together to allow a new government to come to power. When governments become excessively corrupt, other countries and non-governmental organizations sometimes cut off development aid to the country. Yet when this happens, it is the ordinary people who most often bear the brunt of hardship. Even when the global community cuts off the corrupt government's aid, core countries and non-governmental organizations typically provide food aid to the people, but this is rarely sufficient to meet basic needs or reverse the trajectory of hardship in the country.

Political stability is difficult to achieve and maintain in a poorer country. Countries of the core have established liberal democracies for themselves; since World War II, all of them have held regularly scheduled democratic elections. But countries in the periphery and semi-periphery have had a much harder time establishing and maintaining democracies. In the process of decolonization, the colonizing countries typically left governments that reflected political and social hierarchies during the colonial period. Some failed, some were overthrown by military coups, and some saw the consolidation of power around a dictatorial strongman. Many countries in the periphery and semi-periphery have alternated repeatedly between quasi-democratic and military governments.

Yet another cause of political instability in many peripheral and semi-peripheral countries has been what Jeffrey Herbst has referred to as the "haphazard and arbitrary" way in which colonizing nations such as Great Britain, France, Belgium, and Germany subdivided their claims to African territories during the late 1800s and early 1900s. Indeed, the borders separating many present-day African countries were delineated without any consideration for the cultural or social characteristics or the needs of the people living there at the time. In this regard, John Ravenhill has noted, "The arbitrary division of the continent by the European powers, with little or no respect for pre-existing social and political groupings or even, sometimes, for "natural" geographical features, has immensely complicated the tasks of nation and state building faced by African governments."

Opening the homepage of any major newspaper on any given day will reveal a story somewhere in the world that demonstrates the link between economic stability and political stability. In post-Taliban Afghanistan, for example, economic woes represent one of the greatest threats to the stability of the NATO-supported government in Kabul. More than half of the population is impoverished, and the government lacks the funds to invest in development. Foreign aid has provided some help, but the flow of aid has been variable and its amount insufficient to address the country's searing economic problems. Many analysts see this as a key impediment to achieving stability in Afghanistan. As the *Economist* put it in 2006, "poverty helps the Taliban."

COSTS OF ECONOMIC DEVELOPMENT

Economic development changes a place. In order to increase productivity, whether industrial or agricultural, people transform the environment. When a country goes through intensification of industrial production, air and surface water are often polluted. When a country goes through intensification of agricultural production, the introduction of pesticides and herbicides can have deleterious impacts on the soil and groundwater. Tourism can be just as hard on the environment and can tax the existing infrastructure beyond its capacities, often to the detriment of the country's permanent residents. The costs of tourism often stretch far beyond the environment, affecting ways of life and fundamentally altering the cultural landscape.

INDUSTRIALIZATION

In their efforts to attract new industries, the governments of many countries in the global periphery and semi-periphery have set up special manufacturing zones called **export processing zones (EPZs)**, which offer favourable tax, regulatory, and trade arrangements to foreign firms. In 2007 there were more than 2,700 EPZs around the world, many of which have become major manufacturing centres (Figure 11.15). It is estimated that as many as 63 million people are employed in these areas, about 40 million of them in China alone. The vast majority of EPZs are located in peripheral regions, although they are increasingly used to stimulate development in core countries as well. For example, Canada now has two such zones—the

> **Export processing zones (EPZs)** Zones established by many countries in the periphery and semi-periphery where they offer favourable tax, regulatory, and trade arrangements to attract foreign trade and investment.

Gander Foreign Trade Zone in Newfoundland and CentrePort Canada in Winnipeg, Manitoba.

Two of the best known EPZs are the **special economic zones** of China (discussed in Chapter 10) and Mexico's **maquiladoras**. Governments site such zones in places with easy access to export markets. Thus, the maquiladora zone in Mexico is located directly across the border from the United States, while the special economic zones of China are sited near major ports. These zones typically attract a mix of manufacturing operations, depending on the skill levels of the labour force and the available infrastructure.

The maquiladoras started in 1965 when the Mexican government designated northern Mexico as a district where manufactured products could be sent to the United States free of import tariffs. In response, many U.S. corporations established manufacturing plants in the area, where Mexican workers assembled a collection of components and raw materials into finished industrial products, tax-free. The corporations then exported at least 80 percent of these goods to the United States.

Although the maquiladora phenomenon started in the mid-1960s, it did not really take off until the 1980s. This was when American companies recognized the growing wage gap between U.S. and Mexican workers and began relocating to the maquiladora district. Although competition from other parts of the world has led to the closing of some plants, today some 3,000 maquiladoras continue to function, employing 1 million

> **Special economic zone** Specific area within a country in which tax incentives and less stringent environmental regulations are implemented to attract foreign business and investment.
>
> **Maquiladora** Zones in northern Mexico with factories supplying manufactured goods to the U.S. market. The low-wage workers in the primarily foreign-owned factories assemble imported components and/ or raw materials and then export finished goods.

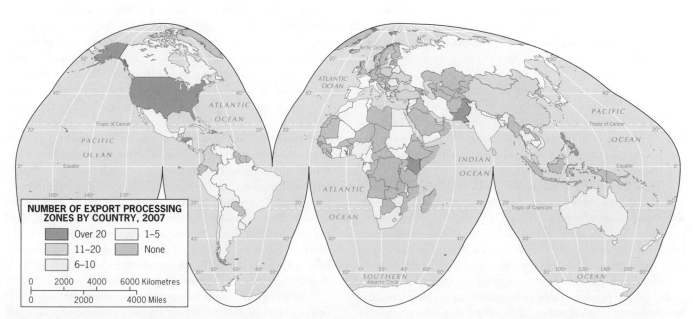

FIGURE 11.15 Export Processing Zones. Number of export processing zones by country. Data from International Labour Organization.

workers and accounting for 45 percent of Mexico's exports. The maquiladora plants produce such goods as electronic equipment, electrical appliances, automobiles, textiles, plastics, and furniture. The plants are controversial both in Mexico and the United States, as corporations that have relocated there avoid the employment and environmental regulations that are in force just a few kilometres to the north. Many maquiladora factories hire young women and men for low pay and few, if any, benefits, putting them to work in repetitive jobs, often in environmentally questionable conditions.

In 1992, Canada, the United States, and Mexico ratified the **North American Free Trade Agreement (NAFTA)**, which

> **North American Free Trade Agreement (NAFTA)** Agreement entered into by Canada, Mexico, and the United States in December 1992 that took effect on January 1, 1994, to eliminate the barriers to trade in, and facilitate the cross-border movement of, goods and services between the countries.

took effect January 1, 1994, and prompted further industrialization of the border region. In addition to manufacturing plants, NAFTA has facilitated the movement of service industries, including data-processing operations, from the United States to Mexico. Most of the new plants are located in two districts: Tijuana on the Pacific coast, linked to San Diego across the border, and Ciudad Juarez on the Rio Grande across from El Paso, Texas.

AGRICULTURE

As discussed in Chapter 9, agricultural activities in peripheral countries typically focus on personal consumption (i.e., subsistence farming) or on production for a large agricultural conglomerate. Where zones of larger-scale, modernized agriculture have developed in the periphery, foodstuffs are produced for the foreign market and often have minimal impact on the impoverished conditions of the surrounding lands. Little is produced for the local marketplace because distribution systems are poorly organized and because the local population is typically unable to pay for foodstuffs. If the local population owns land, their landholdings are usually fragmented, creating small plots of land that are difficult to farm in a manner that produces much income. Even if farmers have larger plots of land, they are generally equipped with outdated, inefficient tools and equipment. The main crops tend to be grains and roots; farmers produce little protein because high-protein crops typically have lower yields than grain crops. On the farms in the periphery, yields per unit area are low, subsistence modes of life prevail, and many families are constantly in debt.

Impoverished farmers can ill afford such luxuries as fertilizers, and educational levels are typically too low to achieve widespread soil conservation efforts. As a result, soil erosion is commonplace in most peripheral areas. Severe soil erosion in desert-bordering areas with dry or semi-dry climates results in extreme degradation of the land and the spread of the desert into these lands. Although the expansion and contraction of deserts can occur naturally and cyclically, the process of **desertification** is more often caused by humans destroying vegetation and eroding soils through the overuse of lands for livestock grazing or crop production.

Desertification has hit Africa harder than any other continent, although portions of Europe and Asia have also been greatly affected by this process (Figure 11.16). More than half of Africa is arid or semi-arid, and many people farm the marginal, dry lands of the continent. Land ownership patterns, the need for crops

> **Desertification** The encroachment of desert conditions on moister zones along the desert margins, where plant cover and soils are threatened by desiccation–through overuse, in part by humans and their domestic animals, and, possibly, in part because of inexorable shifts in the Earth's environmental zones.

and protein sources (both for local consumption and for export), and power differences among groups of people lead some farmers and ranchers to turn marginal, semi-arid lands into farms and ranches. Lands that are available for farming or ranching may be used more intensively in order to increase agricultural production (see Chapter 9). In semi-arid regions, the decision to farm more intensively and increase agricultural production has the unintended consequences of eroding the land, causing migration flow and creating conflict.

In sub-Saharan Africa over the last 50 years, more than 700,000 square kilometres of farming and grazing land have become desert, extending the Sahara Desert to the south. Some of the African desertification may be caused by climatic fluctuations, but overgrazing, woodcutting, soil exhaustion, and misuse have undoubtedly accelerated the process.

TOURISM

All development strategies have pros and cons, something that is well illustrated by the case of tourism. Peripheral countries in the Caribbean region of Central America and in other parts of the world have become leading destinations for millions of tourists from richer states. Among the countries that earn substantial income from tourism are Thailand, Kenya, Barbados, and Fiji. Tourism brings some wealth and employment to these and other countries (see Chapter 13), but the industry's contributions are often narrow in scope and time. Tourism may also have serious negative effects on cultures and environments in the periphery.

In economic terms, the "host" country must make a substantial investment to support tourism development. Sometimes imports of building materials and equipment strain the country's supply system, and funds are diverted to the construction of hotels, airports, cruise-ports, and other tourism-supportive infrastructure that could have been spent on internal needs, such as education or housing for citizens. Moreover, many hotels and other tourist facilities are owned not by the host country but by large multinational corporations. These corporations earn enormous profits, most of which are sent back to their headquarters in their home country. At the same time, tourism-generated income does not always benefit local economies (Figure 11.17). Tourism can create local jobs, but they are often low-paying and offer little job security. In tourist zones, many employees work two or three jobs in order to break even.

In social terms, tourism frequently strains the fabric of local communities as well. Wealthier visitors' invasion of poor communities can foster antipathy and resentment. Tourism can also

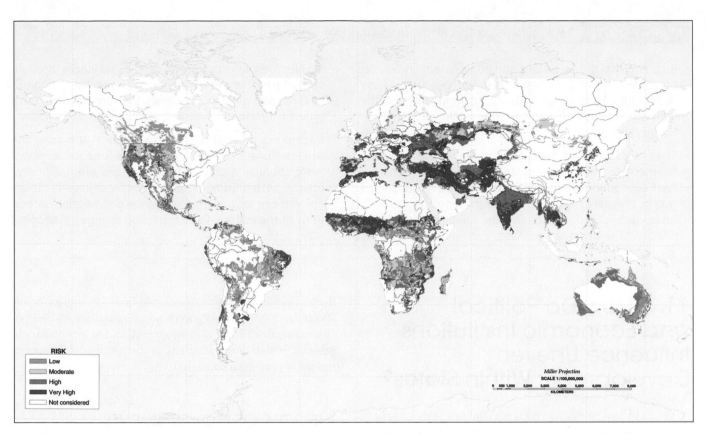

FIGURE 11.16 **Areas at Risk of Human Induced Desertification.** Deserts expand and contract cyclically, but nature's cycles can be distorted by human intervention. This map shows areas threatened or affected by human induced desertification. Source: Global Desertification Vulnerability map, US Department of Agriculture, Natural Resources Conservation Service. Soil Survey Division and World Soil Resources, 1998. Accessed November 8, 2011 at http://soils.usda.gov/use/worldsoils/mapindex/dsrtrisk.html.

debase local culture, which is adapted to suit the visitors' tastes. In many instances, tourism fosters a "demonstration effect" among locals, encouraging them to behave in ways that may please or interest the visitors but that is disdained by the larger local community. Some tourism workers consider employment in the tourist industry dehumanizing because it demands displays of friendliness and servitude that locals find insulting.

FIGURE 11.17 **Cruise Ship, Labadee, Haiti.** Vessels such as this one often dock in poor countries, but passengers are often strictly segregated from local residents and contribute little to the region's economy through their visits. (Lynne Sladky/Associated Press)

The idea of a flood of affluent tourists may be appealing to the government of a poor country (whose elite may have a financial stake in the hotels where they can share the pleasures of the wealthy), but local entrepreneurs often take a different view. Indeed, powerful multinational corporations and national governments may intervene to limit the opportunities of local, small-scale operators in favour of mass, prearranged tourist destinations (e.g., "exclusive" resorts) that isolate the tourist from local society. Overreliance on tourism can also leave an economy vulnerable if changing economic circumstances cause a sharp decline in the number of tourists or if natural disasters hit. Because many tourist destinations in poorer countries are beach attractions, natural hazards such as the 2004 tsunami in Southeast Asia can destroy the lynchpin of a country's economy. Locals must suffer the loss of thousands of people; deal with the after-effects of sewage, homelessness, orphans, and the destitute; and rebuild the tourist destinations, all while the flow of tourist-related income has stopped.

The cultural landscape of tourism is frequently a study in harsh contrasts: gleaming hotels tower over modest, often poor, housing; luxury liners glide past poverty-stricken villages; opulent meals are served in hotels, while children suffer from malnutrition just down the street. If the tourist industry offered real prospects for economic progress in low-income countries, such circumstances might be viewed as temporary, unfortunate by-products. However, the evidence too often indicates that tourism does not produce development.

- International organizations and governments have created a variety of programs and initiatives, such as the Millennium Development Goals, to help improve the condition of humans around the world, especially in the periphery.

- The structures and geography of the world economy have created numerous obstacles and barriers that inhibit economic development in the periphery. Conditions within the periphery, such as high population growth rates, lack of education, foreign debt, political instability, and widespread disease, can seriously hamper

development efforts. Indeed, people and places throughout the periphery are burdened with familial, economic, cultural, and political upheavals that prevent long-term progress in the improvement of people's quality of life.

- Regardless of whether it takes place in the core, the semi-periphery, or the periphery, economic development changes a place. These changes are not always for the better. Some negative consequences of development can include environmental degradation, alterations to the cultural landscape, and changes in people's ways of life.

11.4 How Do Political and Economic Institutions Influence Uneven Development Within States?

In our globalized world, poverty is not confined to the periphery. Core countries, including Canada, have regions and peoples that are markedly poorer than others, or regions where people's economic lives do not improve when the country's economy grows. In Europe, areas of isolation and stagnation persist—particularly in the east. At the same time, some places in peripheral countries are experiencing rapid economic growth. The local conditions in these places differ sharply from those prevailing in surrounding areas. Recent economic growth on the Pacific Rim of East Asia has created huge regional disparities in economic conditions between some coastal provinces of China and distant interior provinces. Such regional economic contrasts have significant political, as well as social, consequences.

As noted at the beginning of this chapter, regional contrasts in wealth are a reminder that per capita GNI does not accurately represent the economic development of individual places. Any statistic that is derived for an entire country hides the variety of economic situations within that country. Peripheral countries are notoriously marked by severe regional disparities. In Chapter 10, we discussed the stark contrasts between wealthy and poor citizens in Latin American and African cities. When viewed at the scale of the state, however, major cities (particularly capitals) and their surroundings often look like islands of prosperity, with modern buildings, factories on the outskirts, and modern farms nearby. In some cases, roads and rails lead to a bustling port, where luxury automobiles are unloaded for use by the privileged elite, and raw materials or agricultural products from the country are exported to points around the world. In these core areas of countries, the rush of "progress" may be evident. If you travel a few kilometres into the countryside or even into a different neighbourhood in the city, however, you will likely see a very different picture. In

this section of the chapter, we discuss how government policy affects development, how governments collaborate with corporations to create islands of development, and how people try to generate growth in the periphery of the periphery (the poorest regions of peripheral countries).

THE ROLE OF GOVERNMENTS

Governments play a critical role in determining whether, how, and where wealth is produced. This is because the distribution of wealth is influenced by tariffs, trade agreements, taxation structures, land ownership rules, environmental regulations, and many other manifestations of governmental authority. Government policies play an important role at the international level, but they also shape patterns of development *within* states—not just between urban and rural areas, but also within each of these sectors.

Of course, governments alone do not determine patterns of wealth and poverty, but they are almost always part of the picture. Consider the case of the Lower Ninth Ward in New Orleans, which was devastated by Hurricane Katrina in 2005. On its surface, what happened to the Lower Ninth Ward was the result of a natural disaster. But the flooding of that part of New Orleans was also the result of government decisions, made decades earlier, to build levies and settle flood-prone areas. The concentration of people living there was also the product of innumerable policies affecting housing, the construction of businesses, and the like. Once the hurricane hit, many looked to government to rebuild this devastated section of the city. The limited nature of the governmental response, however, is clearly evident in the landscape today (Figure 11.18).

An examination of commodity chains can also help us understand the role of governments in uneven distribution of wealth and development, both within and between states. In her 2005 book *The Travels of a T-Shirt in the Global Economy*, economist Pietra Rivoli described grabbing a T-shirt out of a bin at a Walgreens in Florida, buying it, and then tracing its production back through the commodity chain to see how it

FIELD NOTE
New Orleans After Katrina

Walking through New Orleans' Lower Ninth Ward in late 2007, more than two years after Hurricane Katrina, it seemed as if the natural disaster had only just happened. Street after street of devastated, vacant buildings was all the eye could behold—many still bore the markings made by the emergency crews that had moved through the neighbourhood in the wake of the hurricane, showing whether anyone had died inside. It struck the observer that reconstruction of this primarily African-American, working-class community would require a public commitment on the order of what occurred in Europe after World War II, when cities reduced to rubble by bombing were rebuilt almost from scratch.

Today, it is fair to ask whether a comparable commitment has ever existed to rebuild the Lower Ninth Ward. Such a sentiment was expressed in a *Time Magazine* headline on the five-year anniversary of Katrina: "New Orleans' Lower Ninth: Katrina's Forgotten Victim?" In the article, author Tim Padgett noted that "homeowners in predominantly black communities like the Lower Ninth Ward have received substantially lower house-reconstruction grants from local, state and federal agencies than white Katrina victims have,

FIGURE 11.18 Destroyed House in the Lower Ninth Ward, New Orleans. (© Alexander B. Murphy)

even though it usually costs as much to rebuild a house in the Lower Ninth as it does in more upscale districts." At the same time, Padgett noted that many of the Lower Ninth's parks, schools, and community centres have also not yet been re-established, despite the passage of five years since Katrina devastated New Orleans.

ended up in her hands. The cotton for her T-shirt was grown in West Texas, where the cotton lobby (the political arm of America's cotton producers) has effectively pressed for governmental labour programs and price supports that help the lobby grow cotton and sell it at predictable prices. From West Texas, the cotton bale travelled to China by ship. There, it was spun into thread and woven into fabric. Women from rural China worked in state-owned factories set up in regions slated for economic development; they cut and sewed T-shirts and kept the textile machines in good repair. The women were considered cheap labour at the global scale, earning about $100 per month. Rivoli reports that over 40,000 garment factories operate in China alone.

The T-shirts were then shipped to the United States for sale. In an attempt to protect T-shirts produced in America with higher labour costs from those produced in China, the U.S. government has established quotas on how many items from various clothing categories can be imported into the United States from China and other countries. An unintended consequence of the quota system has been a "quota market," in which countries buy and sell their U.S. quota numbers to producers in other countries (an illegal but rampant practice). Instead of trading in quotas, some production facilities have moved to places where quotas and cheap labour are available—places such as Sri Lanka, Poland, and Lesotho. Rivoli describes how one producer of cotton shirts has moved around the world:

The Esquel Corporation, today the world's largest producer of cotton shirts, started in Hong Kong in the late 1970s, but, unable to obtain quota to sell to the United States, shifted production to mainland China. When the United States tightened Chinese shirt quotas in the early 1980s, Esquel moved production to Malaysia. When Malaysian quota also became difficult to obtain, Esquel moved yet again, this time to Sri Lanka. The globe hopping continued, with the Chinese shirt producer setting up operations in Mauritius and Maldives.

The point is that quota laws, like other policies made by governments, regional trade organizations, and international political regimes (such as the World Trade Organization and the International Labour Organization), affect whether and how regions can produce and exchange goods on the world market.

ISLANDS OF DEVELOPMENT

In both core and periphery, governments often prioritize the creation of wealth in the capital city, which is the seat of governmental authority. In most states, the capital city is the political nerve centre of the country, home to government buildings and jobs, and often to universities, museums, heritage centres, convention centres, and the headquarters of large corporations as well. After gaining independence, many former colonial states spent lavishly on their capitals, not because this was essential

FIGURE 11.19 Putrajaya, Malaysia. Putrajaya is the capital of Malaysia, replacing Kuala Lumpur. (© Bazuki Muhammad/ Reuters/Corbis)

to political or economic success but because the states wanted to showcase their independence and their futures, and create a national treasure. They were following the example of their European colonizers, who focused their wealth and treasures on such capital cities as Great Britain's London, France's Paris, and the Netherlands' Amsterdam.

In many countries of the global economic periphery, the capital cities are by far the largest and most economically influential cities in the state (i.e., primate cities). Some newly independent states have built new capital cities, away from the colonial headquarters, in order to either separate themselves from their colonizers, bring together diverse groups into one state with a city built to reflect their common culture, or extend economic development into the interior of the state.

Nigeria, for example, moved its capital from Yoruba-dominated Lagos, on the coast, to Abuja, an ethnically neutral territory in the centre of the state. Malawi moved its capital from Zomba, deep in the south, to a more central location, Lilongwe. Pakistan moved the capital from the colonial headquarters of Karachi to Islamabad in the far north to symbolize the country's reorientation toward its historically important interior and north. Brazil moved its capital from coastal Rio de Janeiro to centrally located Brasília in order to direct attention to the huge, sparsely populated, yet poorly integrated, interior. More recently, Malaysia has moved its capital from the colonial capital of Kuala Lumpur to a completely new centre called Putrajaya, about 40 kilometres to the south. In this case, the Malaysian government decided to build a new, ultramodern seat of government to symbolize the country's rapid economic growth (Figure 11.19).

Corporations can also make cities focal points of development by concentrating corporate activities in a particular place. Often, corporations build up the cities near the resources they are extracting or near manufacturing centres they have built. Multinational oil companies create subsidiaries in peripheral and semi-peripheral countries, creating or expanding cities near oil reserves. For example, in the African country of Gabon, Elf and Shell, two oil companies based in Europe, run Elf Gabon and Shell Gabon. The oil companies took the small colonial town of Port Gentil in Gabon and turned it into a city that the locals call

"oil city." The oil companies built housing, roads, and stores and provide much of the employment in the town (Figure 11.20).

When a government or corporation builds up and concentrates economic development in a certain city or small region, geographers call that place an **island of development**. In Chapter 5, we identified islands of development in the periphery and semi-periphery and discussed why people migrate to these cities from rural areas and other poorer cities. The hope for a job drives many migrants to move to these islands of comparative prosperity.

> **Island of development** Place built up by a government or corporation to attract foreign investment and that has relatively high concentrations of paying jobs and infrastructure.

CREATING GROWTH IN THE PERIPHERY OF THE PERIPHERY

One of the greatest challenges is creating opportunities outside the islands of development. In the most rural, impoverished regions of developing countries, some non-governmental organizations try to improve the plight of residents. **Non-governmental organizations (NGOs)** are not run by state or local governments. Rather, NGOs operate independently, and the term is usually reserved for entities that operate as non-profits. Thousands of NGOs operate in the world today, from churches to charities such as Doctors without Borders, the Aga Khan Foundation, and World Vision. Each NGO has its own set of goals, depending on the primary concerns outlined by its founders.

> **Non-governmental organizations (NGOs)** International organizations that operate outside of the formal political arena but that are nevertheless influential in spearheading international initiatives on social, economic, and environmental issues.

In some countries, so many NGOs are operating that they serve as what the *Economist* calls "a parallel state, financed by foreigners and accountable to nobody." For example, more than 20,000 NGOs operate within the country of Bangladesh at any time, focusing mainly on the rural areas and villages of the state.

FIELD NOTE
Economic Growth in Gabon

Before the 1970s, Gabon's principal exports were manganese, hardwoods, and uranium ores. The discovery of oil off the Gabonese coast changed all that. This oil storage tank at the edge of Port Gentil is but one reminder of a development that has transformed Gabon's major port city—and the economy of the country as a whole. Oil now accounts for 80 percent of Gabon's export earnings, and that figure is climbing as oil prices rise and new discoveries are made. But how much the average citizen of Gabon is benefiting from the oil economy remains an open question. Even as health care and infrastructure needs remain unmet, the French publication *L'Autre Afrique* lists Gabon's ruler as the African leader with the largest real estate holdings in Paris.

FIGURE 11.20 Port Gentil, Gabon. (© Alexander B. Murphy)

One particular kind of NGO venture that has been successful in South Asia and South America is the **microcredit program**. The idea behind these programs is simple: give loans to poor people, particularly women, to encourage them to develop small businesses. Finance the program by having borrowers in the village guarantee each other's credit, or make future lending to others contingent on repayment by the first borrowers. With repayment rates hovering at 98 percent, microcredit programs can be self-sufficient, and many NGOs offer them (Figure 11.21).

By providing microcredit to women, NGOs can alter the gender balance in a region, giving more fiscal power to women who are otherwise often left out of economic development activities. Some microcredit programs are believed to have helped lower birth rates in parts of developing countries and have altered the social fabric of cultures by diminishing men's positions of power. Successful microcredit programs also help alleviate malnourishment, as women with income can feed themselves and their children.

Microcredit programs have been less successful in regions with high mortality rates from diseases such as AIDS. If borrowers are unable to work, or if their families have medical and funeral bills, borrowers are much more likely to default on the microcredit loan. When people in the periphery of the periphery experience a multitude of problems, such as disease, corrupt governments, high mortality rates, high fertility rates, and disruptions from natural hazards, the goal of economic development takes a backseat to daily survival.

> **Microcredit program** Program that provides small loans to poor people, especially women, to encourage development of small businesses.

FIGURE 11.21 Bwindi, Uganda. Women walk by a microcredit agency that has facilitated economic development in the town. (© Alexander B. Murphy)

| MAIN POINTS | 11.4 How Do Political and Economic Institutions Influence Uneven Development within States? |

- The distribution of wealth is greatly influenced by tariffs, quotas, trade agreements, taxation structures, land ownership rules, and environmental regulations. Accordingly, the actions of governments, regional trade organizations, and international political regimes play a critical role in determining whether, how, and where wealth is produced.

- In both core and periphery, governments often prioritize the creation of wealth in the seat of governmental authority, the capital city. Corporations can also make cities focal points of development by concentrating corporate activities in a particular place. When a government or corporation builds up and concentrates economic development in a certain city or small region, geographers call that place an island of development.

- In the most rural, impoverished regions of developing countries, some non-governmental organizations (NGOs) try to improve the plight of the people. Non-governmental organizations are not run by state or local governments, but instead operate independently and usually as non-profit agencies.

SUMMARY

The idea of economic development is relatively new; it implies a sense of progressively improving a country's economic situation. The idea took hold in the wake of the Industrial Revolution. Geographers focus on the spatial structure of the economy, assessing how that structure influences the ability of states and regions to reach the same level of economic development. Geographers also recognize that economic development in a single place is based on a multitude of factors, including its historical ties to other countries, its situation within the contemporary global economy, its place in commodity chains, the efficacy of its government and the success or failure of its policies, the health and welfare of its people, the amount of foreign debt it owes, and the influence of non-governmental programs. Geographers realize that all of these processes operate concurrently across scales, making a country's journey toward economic development much more complicated than climbing a metaphorical ladder. Finally, geographers are also active in building our understanding of barriers to economic development, as well as the impacts of development on people and places.

DISCUSSION AND REVIEW QUESTIONS

1. What happened to Timbuktu? What does its story reveal about the fickle nature of geography, trade, and development?

2. Development is not a straightforward or uncontested process. What are some of the issues and critiques of how development is conceptualized and measured?

3. What is the world-systems theory and how does it assist economic geographers to contextualize development? How is it different from the modernization model?

4. Much attention, effort, and resources have been devoted to promoting development across the globe. The UN Millennium Development goals represent a high degree of consensus about the conditions that must be changed if progress is to be attained. However, there still exist many barriers to development. Identify and briefly explain these barriers. In your view, which barrier is the most challenging to overcome?

5. What are NGOs? What role do they play in development? Can you think of a specific example of how an NGO acted as a positive force for development? Are NGOs an inherently positive force in the promotion of development?

GEOGRAPHIC CONCEPTS

capitalism   323
commodification   323
context   322
core   323
dependency theory   322
desertification   336
developing   314
export processing zone (EPZ)   335
formal economy   315
gross domestic product (GDP)   314
gross national income (GNI)   314
gross national product (GNP)   314
informal economy   315
island of development   340
malaria   332
maquiladoras   335

microcredit program   341
Millennium Development Goals   328
modernization model   317
neo-colonialism   322
non-governmental organizations (NGOs)   340
North American Free Trade Agreement (NAFTA)   336
per capita GNI   314
periphery   323
semi-periphery   323
special economic zones   335
structural adjustment loans   331
structuralist theory   322
three-tier structure   323
trafficking   329
vectored diseases   332
world-systems theory   322

ADDITIONAL RESOURCES ONLINE

About the Millenium Development Goals:
www.un.org/millenniumgoals
http://mdgs.un.org/unsd/mdg/Default.aspx
www.mdgmonitor.org/Index.cfm

About the Human Development Reports and Human Development Index: http://hdr.undp.org/en

About Global Poverty: http://data.worldbank.org/topic/poverty

About the "Spread the Net" Program: www.spreadthenet.org

About the International Monetary Fund (IMF):

www.imf.org/external/index.htm

About the World Bank:
www.worldbank.org

About the Canadian International Development Agency (CIDA): www.acdi-cida.gc.ca/home

About the Maquila Solidarity Network:
http://en.maquilasolidarity.org

About the World Tourism Organization:
http://unwto.org/en/home

chapter 12

TRANSPORTATION

FIGURE 12.1 **Brock University, St. Catharines, Ontario.** Transit ridership among students skyrocketed following the introduction of a universal bus pass program at the school in 2003. (St. Catharines Transit Commission)

Get on the Bus

IT WAS FOUR O'CLOCK on a Tuesday afternoon and I was standing at a bus stop at Brock University in St. Catharines, Ontario. I couldn't help but notice that each of the many bus stops was teeming with undergraduate and graduate students and that as a steady flow of buses pulled up to their designated stops, another steady flow of students boarded each one (Figure 12.1). Almost every bus leaving the campus was filled with as many students as could be safely accommodated. "How much things have changed," I thought to myself. When I first started commuting to Brock University a few years earlier, only a very small proportion of students travelled by public transit. Instead, the poor availability of transit service, marked by long waits between buses and limited hours of operation, prompted most students to commute to the school's isolated suburban location atop the Niagara Escarpment by car, either as a driver or passenger.

As a strong proponent of sustainable transportation, I was pleased to witness this growth in the popularity of public transit among Brock's young adult population. I knew this change in transportation behaviour was largely an outcome of the introduction of a universal bus pass (or "U-Pass") program by the school's student union in September 2003. I also knew that this program, in exchange for a modest ancillary fee added to their tuition, allowed most of Brock's 17,000 students to ride public transit for free simply by showing their student card to the driver. As a transportation geographer, however, I couldn't help asking a number of questions as I watched the flurry of activity at the bus stop that day. First, just how many Brock students were actually commuting by public transit and how did this compare to the proportion travelling by car? Second, what were some of the benefits of public transit's relatively new popularity at Brock University? Also, was this U-Pass program something that students wanted to see continued beyond its initial three-year trial period?

I set out to answer my questions by conducting a survey of Brock students and by interviewing representatives of the three public transit agencies serving the university as part of the U-Pass program. Some of the results amazed me. Data from over 400 completed survey questionnaires showed that over half the students (56.0 percent) regularly commuted to and from Brock by public transit, while only 36.1 percent travelled as car drivers and 5.0 percent rode as car passengers. When considering only those students who lived in St. Catharines or Thorold, the two cities on whose border Brock is located, the proportion of students travelling by public transit rose to 72.6 percent. No wonder the buses were so busy!

I was also curious about the types of benefits that came from Brock University's implementation of a U-Pass program. From the students' perspective, some of these included an overall lower cost of attending university, due to the lower transportation costs, and greatly enhanced levels of accessibility to affordable student housing, employment opportunities, and shopping and recreational facilities. For the participating transit agencies—St. Catharines Transit, Welland Transit, and Niagara Falls Transit—benefits included the additional revenue brought in through the program, ridership increases that qualified each agency for extra provincial government funding, and, more generally, a higher profile for public transit in each city. Research participants also identified broader environmental, social, and economic benefits, such as reductions in air pollution and fuel consumption, better transit service on some routes, the creation of new routes that were also available to non-students, as well as more students travelling off-campus to shop at local businesses.

In asking the participants if they felt the U-Pass program should continue beyond its initial three-year trial period, I assumed that transit riders would be in favour of such a move. I also predicted that students who continued to travel by car after the program's introduction would be opposed to extending the program, given that they were required (with few exceptions) to pay for something they didn't use. I was wrong. Both groups—a total of 82 percent of those surveyed—were in favour of continuing the program. Why this surprising result? Beyond all the positive outcomes noted earlier, it turned out that even those who drove to school were benefiting from the program. For example, they had less trouble finding parking spaces on campus, they could use public transit for free when their cars weren't available or when they were going out on the town with friends and didn't want to drive, and some even used their U-Passes to shuttle by bus between Brock's more peripheral parking lots and the school's main entrance.

Today, U-Pass programs are in place at dozens of post-secondary institutions throughout Canada and the United States. In every case, they provide students with a low-cost alternative to travelling by car while providing affordable transportation to those who do not have the option to drive. U-Pass programs have captured the interest of transportation researchers, including transportation geographers, because they serve as an effective example of how people's transportation behaviour can adapt to changing conditions. Before the U-Pass program was introduced at Brock University, public transit service was both expensive and inadequate in the eyes of most students. As a result, most travelled to school by car. By reducing the cost of using public transit and enhancing the level of service, however, a dramatic shift took place that saw public transit become the most used mode of travel to school among the university's students. The success of U-Pass programs like Brock University's also demonstrates that there is a place for non-automobile modes of transportation within cities, despite the high and growing levels of automobile use that we currently see throughout many of the world's core regions.

Transportation issues, such as this effort to promote public transit use on university campuses, have been described by geographer David Keeling as being "quintessentially geographic" (2007, p. 218). In this chapter, we review the question of why transportation matters in the study of human geography, and we examine the ways in which transportation relates to some of the discipline's central concerns or themes. We then look at how transportation innovations have had an enormous influence on the growth and morphology of cities in Canada and other core countries. We consider the ways in which automobile-dependent transportation patterns found in many countries today have become matters of serious concern due to their negative consequences for people and places, and we look at some of the ways these issues might be resolved over the short and long term. In the latter sections of the chapter we review the roles that transportation has played in the long-standing but rapidly accelerating globalization process, the transportation circumstances of peripheral regions, and the important roles that transportation must play in helping to improve the quality of life for people living in those places.

KEY QUESTIONS FOR CHAPTER 12

1. What is transportation geography, and why does it matter?

2. How has transportation helped to shape the growth of cities?

3. What are some consequences of contemporary transportation patterns?

4. What are the key roles of transportation?

5. Why is transportation an important concern in the development of peripheral regions?

12.1 What Is Transportation Geography, and Why Does It Matter?

Given geographers' inherent interest in such processes as spatial interaction and economic development, and in such issues as human-environment relations and quality-of-life differences among world regions, transportation constitutes a logical and important focus of concern within the study of human geography. Indeed, as transportation geographer Richard Knowles has stated, "The significance of transport and travel in geographical inquiry is undiminished" (2009, p. 449). As we will show throughout this chapter, there is a significant two-way relationship between transportation and geography: The geographical characteristics of places influence the characteristics of the transportation systems and the travel behaviours of people in those places. At the same time, the characteristics of the transportation system in a particular place will also influence that place's human and physical geographies.

Transportation geography is defined in *The Dictionary of Human Geography* (2009, p. 773) as the study of "the movement of people and goods, the transportation systems designed to facilitate such movement, and the relationship of transportation to other facets of human geography such as economic development, energy, land use, sprawl, environmental degradation, values and culture." This means that transportation geographers are interested in building our understanding of everything from who and what is travelling from point A to point B; where, how, and why they are moving between these locations; and what are the implications of such patterns of movement.

> **Transportation geography**
> The study of the movement of people and goods, the transportation systems designed to facilitate such movement, and the relationship of transportation to other facets of human geography such as economic development, energy, land use, sprawl, environmental degradation, values, and culture.

Until recently, transportation had been neglected by geographers. This is primarily because transportation was seen as a relatively insignificant or taken-for-granted aspect of most geographical phenomena or processes, such as the spatial relationship between home and work or the expansion of the global economy. Over time, however, geographers have come to appreciate the significance of transportation as a critical factor in shaping the nature and extent of such concerns. They also recognize that transportation patterns, such as levels of public or private transportation use or the patterns of spatial interaction created by the availability and accessibility of different modes, are influenced by a wide range of geographical factors. As a result, the work of contemporary transportation geographers has increased our understanding of many issues that have historically been of interest within the discipline of human geography.

Transportation systems greatly influence the character of places, whether through their aesthetic qualities, the levels of noise they generate, or the routes they offer users. The degree to which different modes of transportation are available also plays a crucial role in shaping the connectedness of people and places, be it between different parts of the city, between rural and urban areas, across regions, or even across continents. The existence of an effective transportation system is essential for numerous ends: for example, it will provide access to natural resources or sources of energy, enable the establishment of industry, provide people with the ability to move between their homes and necessary facilities and services, and make leisure travel possible, among many other uses.

In some parts of the world today, primarily within core regions, transportation systems are well developed and provide unprecedented levels of access to people and places. Numerous innovations in transportation technology over the past century have dramatically increased the ease and speed of passenger and freight travel over both short and long distances, as many places have witnessed a shift from the era of the steamship, steam locomotive, and horse and buggy to that of the automobile, airplane, high-speed train, and container ship (Figure 12.2). Indeed, the high levels of mobility enjoyed by many people in the world's core regions have become so firmly entrenched that they are often taken for granted.

The diffusion of transportation technologies has not spread across the entire globe, however. In many parts of the world, particularly within peripheral regions, transport systems are much less technologically advanced. For example, in many places walking is still the only mode of transport people can rely on every day. This limitation, combined with the lack of proximity to necessary goods and services, such as safe drinking

FIGURE 12.2 Beijing Capital International Airport, Beijing, China. More than 73 million passengers travelled through Beijing Capital International Airport in 2010, making it one of the world's busiest airports. To keep up with the increase in air travel the city has announced plans to build another airport by 2017. (AFP/Getty images)

water and educational facilities, often has the effect of stifling development because it forces people to devote a great deal of their time to walking long distances to meet their daily needs, or it prevents them from making such trips and satisfying their needs at all.

Transportation geography's importance as a subject of study is reflected in the ways it relates to the five themes of geography first introduced in Chapter 1: location, region, place, landscape, and movement. In the case of geographers' concern with location, for example, the availability of **transport networks** and the levels of accessibility they provide can greatly influence the locational distribution of people or things. Patterns of retail activity in the modern-day urban environment are shaped by a number of factors, for instance, but one of the most significant is the accessibility of local and regional road networks. Big-box stores and power centres are typically located at interchanges along major highways or arterial roadways so they are easy for car drivers to access from numerous directions.

> **Transport networks** The complete system of the routes pertaining to all means of transport available in a particular area.

In relation to the second theme, regions, transportation also contributes to the creation of functional regions. Roads, aviation, shipping, and other transportation networks tend to converge at particular nodes, such as cities, airports, ports, or rail junctions. The spatial distribution of transportation infrastructure emanating from these focal points influences the form, extent, and frequency of spatial interaction within the areas covered by these facilities. For example, we noted in Chapter 1 how all highways in Eastern Ontario converge on Ottawa. Thus, Ottawa serves as the key node of a functional region that encompasses several urban and rural communities.

The third theme of geography, place, relates to human geographers' concern with the characteristics of places and concepts such as sense of place and place attachment. As we noted above, the transportation infrastructure in a place and the extent to which it is used both have a bearing on the characteristics of that place and how attractive it is to people. Compare, for example, the feelings one would have for a congested street filled with exhaust fumes and the honking of car horns to an individual's reactions to a quieter, tree-lined boulevard.

We noted in Chapter 1 that a fourth theme in human geography is landscape. More specifically, we pointed out that human geographers generally understand landscapes to be the visible imprint of human activity on the physical environment. As transportation technologies have evolved over time they have also come to require vast amounts of land to accommodate their related infrastructures—for example, for roads, airports, rail yards, ports, or parking lots. In the cities of many core countries, including Canada, and increasingly in many cities of the periphery, we have witnessed the creation of automobile-dependent landscapes. Urban transportation researchers Peter Newman and Jeff Kenworthy have defined **automobile dependence** as "a situation in which a city develops on the assumption that automobile use will predominate so that it is given priority in infrastructure and in the form of urban development" (1999, p. 60). The high levels of automobile dependence in many countries have had a number of negative environmental impacts and, as we will demonstrate later in this chapter, transportation geographers have been among the most active researchers in the quest to build an understanding of those impacts and, of course, to propose viable solutions.

> **Automobile dependence** A situation in which a city develops on the assumption that automobile use will predominate so that it is given priority in infrastructure and in the form of urban development.

Finally, and perhaps most important, transportation lies at the core of the fifth theme of geography, movement. In Chapter 1 we noted that movement refers to the mobility of people, goods, and ideas across the surface of the planet. Terms such as spatial interaction, accessibility, and connectivity all have special importance in transportation geography, as it is by using different modes of transportation (and, of course, communication) that these movements take place.

The scales of analysis at which transportation geographers work vary considerably. Some focus on the movement of people or goods at the international level (i.e., between countries), while others examine movement between regions (i.e., inter-regional analyses, such as urban-to-rural flows or vice-versa), between urban areas (inter-urban movements), or within urban areas (intra-urban movements). Similarly, transportation geography uses both aggregate and disaggregate data to study particular phenomena (Hanson, 2004). Aggregate-level data are used especially to examine large groups of travellers and the trips they are making, with more concern about the origins and destinations of these trips than with who exactly is travelling. On the other hand, disaggregate (or individual-level) data allow for the analysis of travel flows at a much smaller scale (i.e., the individual or household level). It is through the use of disaggregate data that transportation geographers have also come to understand that many issues affect different groups of people in different ways, and that some groups are more greatly affected by particular transportation problems than others. Accordingly, many current studies conducted by transportation geographers focus on specific population subgroups, such as seniors, persons with disabilities, low-income earners, or children and youth. By doing so, they have been able to build much deeper understandings of the two-way relationship between transportation and geography.

MAIN POINTS   **12.1**   What Is Transportation Geography, and Why Does It Matter?

- Whether it is to provide access to natural resources or sources of energy, to enable the establishment of industry, to provide people with the ability to move between their homes and necessary facilities and services, or to make leisure travel possible, the presence of an effective transportation system is essential. In some parts of the world today, primarily within core regions, transportation systems are well developed and technologically advanced, providing unprecedented levels of access to people and places.

- The diffusion of transportation technologies has not spread across the entire globe, however. In many parts of the world, particularly within peripheral regions, much more rudimentary transport systems are still in place.

- Transportation geography's importance as a subject of study is reflected in the ways it relates to the five themes of geography: location, human-environment interactions, regions, place, and movement.

12.2 How Has Transportation Helped to Shape the Growth of Cities?

Transportation systems have always had a strong influence on urban morphology, which, as first introduced in Chapter 10, refers to the physical form and structure of the city. Numerous transportation innovations have been introduced in cities over the past two centuries. Each time this has happened, the increased speed of travel typically associated with these innovations has dramatically affected the urban morphology by expanding the area of development.

Up to the late 19th century, walking was the predominant mode of travel in cities. This necessitated the efficient distribution and mixing of different land use activities and resulted in a compact city, laid out in a roughly circular shape. The advent of public transportation in the latter half of the 19th century led to the significant outward expansion of cities along streetcar lines. The size and shape of the city continued to evolve with the introduction of the private automobile in the first half of the 20th century. Over the past 60 years the car has come to be the most dominant mode of transportation in cities, to a point where most urban areas in Canada, the United States, Australia, and a growing number of other countries can accurately be described as "automobile dependent."

In their book *Sustainability and Cities: Overcoming Automobile Dependence*, Peter Newman and Jeff Kenworthy have suggested that automobile-dependent cities share three interrelated characteristics. First, they have automobile-oriented land use patterns, including an abundance of road infrastructure and parking facilities, low development densities, and rigidly segregated land use activities. Second, automobile-dependent cities often have poor non-automobile transportation choices, meaning that modes such as walking, cycling, and public transit are not always viable due to a lack of appropriate infrastructure or inadequate levels of service. This in turn often makes it inconvenient, or even impossible, for a person to travel without a car. The third characteristic of an automobile-dependent city is a high level of per capita automobile travel, which means that the number of trips taken by car is fairly high when averaged across the city's population. As Newman and Kenworthy note, these high rates of automobile usage typically prompt governments to invest further in the provision of automobile-oriented transportation infrastructure and to make fewer investments in non-automobile modes.

Over the years, automobile dependence has created numerous environmental, social, and economic consequences. These have prompted an increasing number of transportation geographers and other researchers to advocate a transition toward the development of more sustainable transportation systems. While this may seem an impossible task, it is important to remember that automobile dependence, as pervasive as it is in so many places today, is a relatively recent phenomenon. Most cities have at one time or another in their history been more "walkable" and more transit-friendly. Given that urban areas have not always been automobile dependent, it is conceivable that one day the automobile will again play a less dominant role. Certainly, many believe that walking, cycling, and public transit can return to their former levels of importance within the urban transportation system. They simply require greater priority, and less discrimination, in urban transportation policy-making and planning processes.

THE "WALKING CITY" AND THE INTRODUCTION OF PUBLIC TRANSPORTATION

Up to the latter half of the 19th century, city dwellers relied primarily on walking for any intra-urban travel. At the same time, industrial firms relied heavily on railways and waterways to acquire raw materials and ship their finished products to market. Commercial and retail enterprises also obtained most of their goods by train or boat. These transportation constraints led to the development of a compact urban form in which industrial, commercial, and residential land uses were, out of necessity, located in close proximity to one another and heavily interspersed. A reliance on walking also restricted the outward expansion of Canadian cities. As Peter Newman and Jeff Kenworthy have noted, "One characteristic people have shown that has been important in shaping the nature of our cities is that they do not like to commute, on average, more than half an hour to major urban destinations" (1999, p. 27). Thus, with walking being the predominant mode of travel throughout the 19th century, most Canadian cities tended not to grow beyond a radius of about two kilometres during that period.

The first form of public transportation to be widely introduced in Canadian cities and elsewhere was the horse-drawn omnibus, a wheel-based conveyance that held about seven to ten passengers (Figure 12.3). This innovation did little to enhance the mobility of urban dwellers, however, and had a minimal influence on urban expansion. This was due primarily to two factors. First, most city streets in the mid-1800s were composed of dirt, and rainy weather often created muddy conditions in which the horse-drawn vehicles would get stuck. Similar problems emerged in many places during winter months, when heavy snowfalls hampered the efficient movement of the omnibus along its route. Second, the omnibus only reached a maximum speed of about eight kilometres per hour, even in the most favourable weather conditions. As a result, riding the omnibus was often more time-consuming than travelling on foot.

The deficiencies of the horse-drawn omnibus were largely absent from the electric streetcar, introduced in the late 1880s. These vehicles had a much higher passenger capacity, ran along steel rails instead of on wheels, and could travel at much higher speeds than the omnibus, up to 25 kilometres per hour. This allowed individuals to remain within a reasonable commuting time (i.e., no more than 30 minutes) and distance even while living much farther away from the city's centre than they had done in the past. Middle- and upper-class families were attracted to the idea of residing farther from the central city and its problems of overcrowding and industrial pollution. The ensuing impact on urban morphology was a sizeable outward expansion, with streetcar lines in some cases stretching 10 kilometres or more from the city's centre. Public transit operators simply extended their lines out from the city centre and through the "streetcar suburbs" that were constructed adjacent to these routes.

While the creation of the electric streetcar and the streetcar suburbs encouraged considerable urban growth on the city's

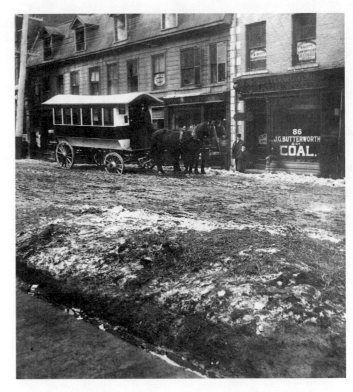

FIGURE 12.3 Horse-Drawn Omnibus in Ottawa, Ontario, ca. 1877. The introduction of this vehicle marked the start of public transportation in many cities, but its effectiveness was greatly limited by its slow travel speed and poor road conditions. (City of Ottawa Archives)

periphery, it was a relatively efficient form of development compared to much of the low-density sprawl evident in many places today. These older neighbourhoods were generally built at medium-to-high densities and with an efficient grid-pattern road layout because individuals residing in streetcar suburbs wanted only a short walk to the streetcar stop and because the higher development densities enabled developers to maximize the return on their investments. Moreover, many businesses selling goods and services were located in commercial areas near the streetcar stops. As a result, people could satisfy many of their daily needs by walking to a store near where they lived, while any needs requiring access to the city centre could be fulfilled by taking the electric streetcar, which followed direct routes and often operated at high frequencies throughout the day.

By the turn of the 20th century, most Canadian cities had electric streetcar services, and public transit became the dominant mode of urban transportation (Figure 12.4). Around the same time, however, the automobile began to appear on city streets. Due to its high cost, the automobile started off primarily as a "toy" for the wealthy through the first few decades of the century and was most commonly used for recreational purposes, such as weekend drives in the countryside, rather than for more utilitarian purposes such as commuting to work or shopping. Throughout the 1920s, automobile ownership became increasingly common among wealthier segments of Canadian society, but there was little increase in this regard through the lean years of the Great Depression and World War II.

FIGURE 12.4 A Streetcar Travels along Portage Avenue, Winnipeg, Manitoba, 1904. By the turn of the 20th century electric streetcars were a prominent part of Canada's urban transportation landscape. The development of "streetcar suburbs" around this time also represented the first major phase of suburbanization across the country. (Notman & Son/Library and Archives Canada/C-006132)

URBAN TRANSPORTATION AFTER WORLD WAR II

Although there were numerous technological innovations in transportation during the period extending from the mid-1800s to the mid-1900s, urban morphology generally remained compact and efficient in places like Canada and the United States throughout this period. A diverse mix of land uses, combined with pedestrian- and transit-oriented streetscapes, enabled most urban dwellers to reach their destinations on foot or by using public transportation. The second half of the 20th century, however, was marked by two interrelated trends—dramatic growth in automobile ownership and increasing suburbanization—that prompted considerable change not only in the spatial relationship between different land use activities, but also in terms of the priority accorded to various modes of transportation in the urban planning process.

After World War II ended in 1945, several trends produced a dramatic increase in private automobile ownership. These included unprecedented levels of economic prosperity, low unemployment, lower car prices resulting from innovations in mass production technologies, and lower fuel costs. The cumulative impact of these trends was to increase significantly the proportion of households that could afford to purchase an automobile.

This increasing demand for automobiles was accompanied by an unprecedented demand for new housing. The poor economic conditions of the Great Depression and the economic restraint accompanying World War II had prevented many families from buying a new home, which created a pent-up demand for housing throughout the 1930s and early 1940s. The post-war baby boom (which lasted from the mid-1940s to the mid-1960s) and massive waves of immigration from Europe to Canadian cities increased the demand for housing even further. Most families searching for

new housing were the same ones who could now also afford the purchase of an automobile. This stimulated a massive outflow of households from the central city and streetcar suburbs to more distant and newly constructed suburbs that were often only accessible by car.

Before World War II, development activities were largely governed by the market forces of supply and demand, with little in the way of formal planning or government intervention. After 1945, however, the incredibly fast pace of suburban growth (Figure 12.5), and the subsequent increase in demand for community services and infrastructure, prompted governments to take a much more active role in the urban development process. Most post-war suburban housing developments were still designed and built primarily by private developers. However, as first discussed in Chapter 10, they were now more often required to adhere to municipally driven master plans and zoning by-laws that regulated what land uses were allowed in a given area and at what densities such development could occur. Of utmost importance to planners and politicians in formulating their policies was the desire to avoid two perceived shortcomings of the pre-World War II city: overcrowding and the mixing of incompatible land use activities, such as housing and industry. In response to these concerns, master plans and zoning regulations typically sought to impose low-density, functionally segregated land use patterns on the urban landscape.

TRANSPORTATION IN POST-WORLD WAR II NEIGHBOURHOOD DESIGN

One important difference between pre-war and post-war urban development was the influence of the automobile in shaping the physical design of residential communities after 1945. Most designers of post-war suburban housing developments in Canada and the United States adopted principles first articulated in the **neighbourhood unit** concept and the **Radburn Idea**, two planning innovations introduced in the United States during the late 1920s. The neighbourhood unit was conceived by American planner Clarence Perry as an attempt to adapt residential areas to the increasing presence of the automobile (Figure 12.6). Alarmed by the number of people, especially young children, being killed or injured by motor vehicles driving through residential districts, Perry sought to design a neighbourhood in which "the automobile menace" could be reconciled with public safety objectives (Perry, 1929, p. 31). A distinguishing feature of the neighbourhood unit concept was abandonment of the grid-pattern street layout typical of the pre-war city. In its place, Perry's design located main thoroughfares on the neighbourhood's perimeter, while

> **Neighbourhood unit** A planning concept developed by Clarence Perry as a means of reconciling the problems of automobile traffic with public safety objectives, most notably those aimed at the safety of children.

> **Radburn Idea** A highly influential community planning concept incorporating a hierarchy of roadways, the deliberate segregation of pedestrian and automobile traffic, and the residential "superblock."

(a)

(b)

FIGURE 12.5 Scarborough, Ontario, In (a) 1954 and (b) 1969. Canadian cities grew quickly after World War II, thanks largely to the widespread adoption of automobiles as the primary means of intra-urban travel. The influence of the neighbourhood unit model is also evident in the street layout of the residential areas in the 1969 photo. From Donald Boyce Kirkup, *Boomtown: Metropolitan Toronto. A Photographic Record of Two Decades of Growth.* Toronto: Lockwood Survey Corporation, 1969. Photos courtesy Scarborough Archives.

FIGURE 12.6 The "Automobile Menace," New York ca. 1924. The growing presence of the automobile and the number of people being killed or injured by motor vehicles in residential areas prompted American planner Clarence Perry to design a "neighbourhood unit" plan in which "the automobile menace" could be reconciled with public safety. (© Bettmann/Corbis)

internal roadways took the form of winding crescents and cul-de-sacs. This latter feature was intended to prevent vehicles from using neighbourhood streets as through-routes and also to discourage drivers from travelling at excessive speeds. Furthermore, vehicular access into the neighbourhood was limited to only a few streets. As yet another way of promoting residential safety, Perry's model also situated public facilities, such as libraries and elementary schools, at the centre of the neighbourhood unit. This was meant to ensure that no child living within the neighbourhood would have to walk more than half a kilometre to these destinations and that he or she could do so without having to cross any busy streets along the way. The central location of these facilities was intended to provide a focal point for neighbourhood life, with the aim of building a strong sense of community among local residents.

Another important and significant influence on the design of post-war suburban housing developments was the Radburn Idea (Figure 12.7), devised by Americans Clarence Stein and Henry Wright. The planned community of Radburn, New Jersey, was built in a rural setting just outside New York City between 1926 and 1929. The initial plan for Radburn was to create a community composed of three distinct yet interconnected neighbourhoods (Stein, 1969). Like its precursor, the neighbourhood unit, the intention was to accommodate the private automobile while at the same time ensuring public safety. The end result, the Radburn Idea, included three especially innovative elements: the incorporation of a hierarchy of roadways, the deliberate segregation of pedestrian and automobile traffic, and the creation of the residential "superblock."

FIGURE 12.7 Plan of Radburn, New Jersey, 1929. Although the community was never fully built, Clarence Stein and Henry Wright's "Radburn Idea" stands to this day as one of history's most influential planning ideas. The principles embodied in the original plan for Radburn have been incorporated into the design of suburban communities around the world, including Canada. From Clarence S. Stein, *Toward New Towns for America*, Figure 21, p. 43, 1969. Published by The MIT Press.

A matter of considerable importance to Stein and Wright was, once again, how to mitigate the negative impacts of automobile traffic on residential streets. Their solution to this dilemma was to further refine Clarence Perry's ideas by physically isolating the community from the rest of the city and introducing a hierarchy of specialized roads and pathways within its boundaries. Smaller roads, including service lanes and cul-de-sacs, were built for specialized uses, such as providing automobile and delivery access to houses (Figure 12.8). As a result, the only vehicles passing directly in front of houses were those destined specifically for those dwellings. The small roads led to secondary collector roads, which in turn led to main thoroughfares that served two purposes: linking adjoining neighbourhoods and providing access to the expressways that connected Radburn to the outside world.

As yet another means of reducing the risk of pedestrian–motor vehicle collisions, walkways and pathways were built throughout the community. By incorporating overpasses and underpasses, designers ensured the pedestrian network was completely segregated from the road network, thus providing residents with the ability to traverse the community on foot without once having to cross the street. A third innovation in

FIGURE 12.8 Cul-de-Sac, Radburn, New Jersey, 2008. An example of the smaller roads that limited traffic in front of houses to vehicles that were destined for those addresses. (Wikimedia Commons)

Radburn was the introduction of the "superblock," a long, rectangular block of housing that was devoid of any through roads, except on its outside perimeter.

Although the entire community plan for Radburn was never fully implemented due to the onset of the Great Depression in 1929, the underlying ideas of the Radburn Idea and the neighbourhood unit concepts had considerable influence on the design of post-war suburban developments throughout the United States and Canada. As urban planning scholar Gerald Hodge has stated in his book, *Planning Canadian Communities,* "The neighbourhood unit became probably one of the strongest physical organizing principles in modern community plans. Its outcome is readily seen when one flies over almost any Canadian city" (2003, p. 53).

Along with the increasing suburbanization of households after 1945 came a substantial amount of road and highway building on the part of local and provincial governments. Although this did not occur in Canada to anywhere near the same extent as it did in the United States, several expressways were built in Canadian cities to help move suburban residents between their homes and their jobs, which were typically found in the core of the central city. For example, the Gardiner Expressway in Toronto (Figure 12.9) was Canada's first urban expressway, followed soon after by the Décarie Expressway in Montreal and Ottawa's Queensway.

Suburban development in the immediate post-war period was primarily residential in nature. However, employment functions soon began to decentralize as well, with retailing and manufacturing activities leading the way. Prior to World War II, most retail businesses were found in the central business district (or CBD, as described in detail in Chapter 10) and along streetcar lines. After 1945, however, people running shops and services found a growing proportion of their clientele moving to suburban neighbourhoods, so it was logical for them to decide to locate

FIGURE 12.9 Gardiner Expressway Under Construction, Toronto, 1962. The mass wave of suburban expansion that began after World War II was accompanied by the construction of new highways in several Canadian cities. The Gardiner Expressway was built to carry people between Toronto's western suburbs and its central business district. (Frank Grant/Toronto Star)

closer to these residential developments. The movement of retailing and other commercial functions to suburban areas generally led to the construction of small neighbourhood shopping plazas in the 1950s. This gave shoppers easy access to stores, and allowed retail employees to reside close to their workplaces.

As suburban development and growth in automobile ownership accelerated through the 1960s, developers also began to build much larger community shopping centres replete with massive parking lots. This was followed in the 1980s and early 1990s by the development of regional-scale shopping centres intended to serve huge market areas. These were typically located near freeway interchanges in order to provide high levels of accessibility for car drivers. Today, suburban retail activities tend to be concentrated in "big-box" stores and "power centres" (i.e., planned agglomerations of big-box stores), which are also commonly located along arterial roads or adjacent to highway interchanges. According to Brian Lorch, a Canadian geographer who specializes in the changing geography of urban retail activities, "the power centre format has all but replaced the enclosed shopping centre as the preferred choice of developers" since the early 1990s (2004, p.1). At the same time, he notes, "power centres are more conveniently accessed by automobile" than by non-automobile modes, such as walking, cycling, or public transit (2004, p. 2).

Manufacturers also began to locate in the suburbs after World War II. As noted earlier in this chapter, manufacturing industries in the 19th and early 20th centuries relied heavily upon railways and waterways for the receipt of raw materials and the shipment of finished products. Furthermore, their workforce's primary mode of commuting was walking. As a result, the manufacturers' location

within the city was largely dictated by the distribution of railway lines and waterways, and by the need to be located within a reasonable walking distance of their workforce. Since these facilities and households tended to be located at or near the centre of the city, the pre-World War II urban core was characterized by the presence of not only commercial activities but also industrial activity. However, growing use of transport trucks in the second half of the 20th century greatly diminished manufacturers' dependence on rail- and water-based modes of transportation. Just as the automobile freed households from transport-related locational constraints, the transport truck did the same for manufacturing firms. So long as a given tract of land was accessible by road and connected to the inter-urban highway network, virtually any location within or outside the city was suitable for the location of a factory.

Yet another important innovation that influenced the suburbanization of manufacturing industries was the horizontal assembly line. Before World War II, many manufacturing enterprises were located in multi-storey buildings, but the adoption of the assembly line frequently compelled their relocation to a more appropriate facility. This need for horizontal space also made suburban settings more attractive to manufacturing firms, because the cost of land there tended to be far lower than it was in the CBD and the central city. As a result, firms were able to buy large tracts of land at relatively low cost on the urban periphery. In response to these trends, many suburban municipalities that were hungry to increase the size of their commercial tax base began to zone large tracts of land exclusively for industrial uses. They also frequently built industrial parks that contained various forms of supporting infrastructure, such as roads, electricity, and water supplies, in the hopes of making their communities more attractive to manufacturing firms. These industrial parks were usually segregated from other sites of urban activity, often by considerable distance, under the assumption that anyone working there would have access to an automobile. Over the past several decades, suburban industrial parks and other settings on the urban periphery have become the location of choice for most urban manufacturing activities (Figure 12.10).

FIGURE 12.10 An Industrial Park in Calais, France. (© Hemis/Alamy)

Institutional land uses also began to decentralize in the post-World War II period as universities, hospitals, and other community facilities were drawn to suburban areas, due primarily to the availability of large and relatively inexpensive tracts of land in such settings. For example, in Canada during the 1950s and 1960s several newly established post-secondary institutions, such as Simon Fraser University (Burnaby, British Columbia), University of Calgary (Alberta), Brock University (St. Catharines, Ontario), Trent University (Peterborough, Ontario), Nipissing University (North Bay, Ontario), and York University (Toronto, Ontario), were built on suburban sites (Figure 12.11). This was in contrast to the location of longer-standing post-secondary institutions, such as the University of Toronto (Ontario), Queen's University (Kingston, Ontario), and the University of British Columbia (Vancouver), which were mostly located in the centre of their respective cities.

FIGURE 12.12 An Office Park in Silicon Valley, California.
(© Harris Shiffman/iStock)

More recently, a great deal of office employment has relocated from the central city to suburban settings. In many cases this has involved the relocation of "back-office" functions, activities that do not require face-to-face contact with clients, from high-cost CBD locations to suburban office parks (Figure 12.12). The primary motivations for such a move have, once again, been the availability of less expensive land and the opportunity to build large parking lots for workers and visitors.

TRENDS AND PATTERNS AROUND THE WORLD: INTERNATIONAL COMPARISONS

There are very clear geographical variations in the levels of automobile dependence in cities around the world. Jeff Kenworthy and Felix Laube (1999) have compiled and compared an extensive body of transportation data from different urban regions. Their findings show that the most automobile-dependent cities are in the United States, followed (in order) by Australia, Canada, Europe, and Asia. Kenworthy and Laube, along with many transportation geographers and other researchers, have sought to understand the reasons for these variations. The list of factors is extensive, and some of the most significant are discussed below.

SUPPORT FOR PUBLIC TRANSIT

According to Todd Litman of the Victoria Transport Policy Institute (Litman, 2011), **public transit** includes various services that provide mobility to the general public in shared vehicles, ranging from shared taxis and shuttle vans, to local and intercity buses and passenger rail. The cost of providing public transit services is subsidized by governments

(a)

(b)

FIGURE 12.11 Two Examples of Suburban Universities. Simon Fraser University (a) in Burnaby, British Columbia, was built on a mountaintop in the suburban community in the late 1960s. Brock University (b) was established in St. Catharines, Ontario, in 1964. The first buildings on its current campus, located atop the Niagara Escarpment, opened in 1966. (Simon Fraser University; Brock University)

> **Public transit** Various services that provide mobility to the general public in shared vehicles, ranging from shared taxis and shuttle vans, to local and intercity buses and passenger rail.

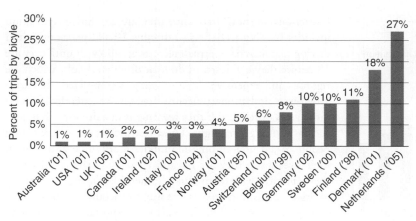

FIGURE 12.13 Bicycle Share of Trips in Europe, North America, and Australia (Percentage of Total Trips by Bicycle). The dramatic international differences in bicycle usage are largely a result of differences in urban development densities and in the provision of bicycle-friendly transportation infrastructure. In countries such as Denmark and The Netherlands, bicycles are an integral part of day-to-day travel and are planned for accordingly, while in automobile-dependent places like Canada and the United States, a lack of attention to the needs of cyclists makes the bicycle a much less attractive mode of transportation. Adapted from John Pucher and Ralph Buehler, "Making Cycling Irresistible: Lessons from The Netherlands, Denmark and Germany." *Transport Reviews* 28, 4 (2008), pp. 495-528.

just about everywhere. An important difference between and within countries, however, is the *extent* to which such services are subsidized. Transit systems in European cities have been subsidized for much longer than those in North American cities, for example—a reality that transportation scholars David Banister, John Pucher, and Martin Lee-Gosselin (2007) have attributed to international differences regarding how the citizens of each country value public transit. Based on their comparative research of Canada, the United States, and several European countries, they argue that people in European cities tend to place a greater value on the societal benefits of public transit than do people in North American cities, and they are therefore more willing to support government expenditures on such services. As a result, there has been significant public investment in the construction of extensive public transit systems that often also serve as the framework around which urban development takes place.

POLICIES FOR CYCLING AND WALKING

Levels of automobile dependence within cities also vary considerably from country to country due to differences in the extent to which walking and cycling are promoted (Figure 12.13). In many, but certainly not all, European countries, far more attention has been devoted to the provision and maintenance of pedestrian and cycling infrastructure. For example, several cities are crisscrossed by extensive and coordinated bicycle networks that provide cyclists with convenient access to popular destinations (Pucher and Buehler, 2008). Many such networks include bicycle lanes that are separated from vehicular and pedestrian traffic and that are given traffic priority over automobiles.

Byron Miller, a geographer at the University of Calgary, has studied European cities with the aim of understanding why some urban areas are more pedestrian- and bicycle-friendly than others. He found, for example, that the city of Groningen in The Netherlands has the highest rate of bicycle usage in Europe, with 57 percent of all trips there being made by bicycle. He attributes this to planning and policy decisions that included the creation of zones within the city centre that were open to pedestrians and cyclists only (Figure 12.14), and the construction of bicycle lanes that are separated from motor vehicle traffic, often with raised curbs or lines of trees serving as a buffer

FIGURE 12.14 Car-Free Zone in Groningen, The Netherlands. This city's incredibly high rate of bicycle use has been nurtured through a series of proactive planning measures, such as closing off particular areas to automobile traffic and providing cyclists with separate off-street pathways. (Zachary Shahan/EcoLocalizer)

to protect cyclists. As Miller has argued, "If you plan a city so the only easy way to get around is by car, bicycling won't be a viable option. Successful promotion of bicycling depends on the extent to which infrastructure investment makes bicycling convenient and safe" (quoted in Myers, 2010).

AUTOMOBILE TAXATION

Governments in Europe have also maintained relatively low levels of automobile use by imposing heavy taxes on the two main costs associated with driving a car. First, the cost of buying an automobile is made more expensive by the addition of a sales or registration tax that in some cases can amount to more than the cost of the vehicle itself. For example, the sales tax on the purchase of a car in Ireland is as much as 30 percent, while in Denmark the registration tax can be up to 180 percent, depending on the vehicle's purchase price and its fuel efficiency. Bigger and more expensive cars are charged

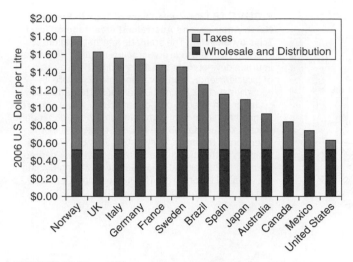

FIGURE 12.15 Vehicle Fuel Retail Prices, 2006. While wholesale and distribution costs are fairly consistent from one country to another, levels of fuel taxation vary considerably. Much higher fuel taxes in Norway, for example, resulted in a 2006 retail price that was more than double what Canadian drivers paid. Data from Victoria Transport Policy Institute website, http://www.vtpi.org/tdm/tdm17.htm. Accessed June 3, 2011.

higher registration taxes. The tax on fuel is also much higher in European countries than it is in automobile-dependent countries like Canada and the United States—in many cases up to eight times higher (Figure 12.15).

PARKING AND DRIVER LICENSING POLICIES

The limited availability of parking in most European cities, caused mainly by the relatively high development densities found there, makes it very expensive to park in such places. This, in turn, creates a disincentive to driving and, at the same time, encourages people to walk, cycle, or use public transit instead. Those wishing to become drivers in European countries must also wait longer than most prospective Canadian and American drivers. The minimum driving age in most European countries is 18 years, while, in most of Canada and the United States, it is 16 years.

Furthermore, it is much more difficult to obtain a driver's licence in Europe, and it costs a lot more. In Denmark, for example, teens can't get a learner's permit until they're 17 and a half. At 18 they can obtain a probationary licence, but all

restrictions are not lifted until they are 21. Driver education includes training in defensive driving, hazard perception, and driving manoeuvres. German teens must also wait until they are 18 before they can learn to drive at driving schools, which are rigorous and expensive. After training is completed, they earn a two-year probationary licence that can be extended for two more years or revoked if they are caught in a driving infraction, such as running a red light. These restrictions encourage young people to use non-automobile modes more often at a time in their lives when they are beginning to build the travel habits they will carry with them into adulthood. Delaying their ability to drive a car is thus seen as one way to encourage young adults to adopt less automobile-dependent transportation behaviours.

LAND USE POLICIES

Other government policies that seem to have little to do with transportation can also have a strong influence on levels of automobile dependence. Land use policies, for example, can affect how much people travel in cars, as opposed to using other modes of transportation. Such policies dictate how far apart different activity sites will be (e.g., the distance between homes and workplaces or shopping areas) and at what densities development may take place. As noted earlier in this chapter, suburban planning in Canada and the United States since the end of World War II has typically involved the extensive segregation of land uses and the low-density development of activity sites. This has done much to encourage automobile use—because of the resulting long travel distances—for even the most routine or basic trip, such as travelling to work or going to a grocery or convenience store. In many European countries, on the other hand, more rigid land use planning policies have been in place over the past several decades. This has limited sprawl and enabled patterns of development that are conducive to walking, cycling, and public transit use. Sweden and Denmark are often cited as good examples of countries where land use planning policies have effectively controlled automobile usage. In both cases, governments have adopted and adhered to policies that promote compact and well-coordinated urban development. They also use public transportation networks as the root of their community planning exercises by focusing the bulk of urban development along rail lines and near transit stations (Pucher and Buehler, 2008).

MAIN POINTS   12.2   How Has Transportation Helped to Shape the Growth of Cities?

- Transportation systems have always had a strong influence on urban morphology, the physical form and structure of the city.

- The car has come to be by far the most dominant mode of transportation in cities over the past 60 years, to a point where most urban areas in Canada, the United States, Australia, and a growing number of

other countries can accurately be described as being "automobile dependent."

- There are very clear geographical variations in the levels of automobile dependence in cities around the world. Most automobile-dependent cities are in the United States, followed (in order) by Australia, Canada, and Europe.

12.3 What Are Some Consequences of Contemporary Transportation Patterns?

Clearly, transportation plays an integral role in our day-to-day lives. However, the increasingly high levels of automobile dependence seen in many countries today, including Canada, have resulted in a number of environmental, economic, and social consequences that range from the local to the global in their impact.

ENVIRONMENTAL CONSEQUENCES

Transportation contributes to all types of pollution and also consumes non-renewable resources and agricultural land. As a result, current patterns of urban transportation place considerable strain on the carrying capacities of ecosystems.

POLLUTION

As we noted in Chapter 6, the environmental impact of each innovation in transportation technology has been greater and greater. This is particularly true with regard to the generation of pollution, especially as it relates to automobile dependence in urban areas. Indeed, the automobile is a major contributor to air, water, and noise pollution, each of which is discussed in turn below.

Air Pollution. **Air pollution** is perhaps the biggest problem emanating from dependence on the automobile, as its effects

> **Air pollution** Pollution of the atmosphere.

range from local to global in scope. The airborne emissions from automobile transportation include a wide range of environmentally harmful chemicals and compounds, such as carbon monoxide, particulates, nitrogen oxides, volatile organic compounds, sulphur oxides, carbon dioxide, methane, road dust, and toxic gases such as benzene. While many of these pollutants may degrade relatively quickly, others have been found to penetrate and remain within the atmosphere for hundreds of years, thus presenting long-term environmental threats. This is why there has been growing concern about the negative long-term *global* impact of automobile emissions. Carbon dioxide (CO_2) is one of the main emissions from fossil fuel combustion in road vehicles (Figure 12.16), and while CO_2 itself is not a pollutant, it has been identified as the primary contributor to recent global warming and climate change trends. This is especially true in core countries and, increasingly, in semi-peripheral countries like China and India.

As the automobile became more important as a mode of transportation in developed countries, automobile manufacturers modified their car designs and their sales and marketing practices to reflect consumer preferences and government policies in different places. In Japan and Europe, for example, the high cost of heavily taxed fuel and the low amount of road space available in cities have resulted in a marked consumer preference

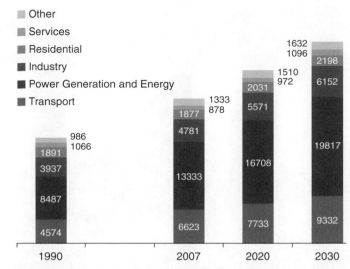

FIGURE 12.16 Global Greenhouse Gas Emissions, 1990, 2007, and Estimated Increases 2020, 2030 (in Metric Tonnes). Carbon dioxide emissions from transportation make up a large proportion of all greenhouse gas emissions, second only to that emitted through the generation of power (such as from coal-burning power plants). From *World Energy Outlook*, © OECD/IEA, 2009, table 4.4, page 185, as modified by the OECD International Transport Forum. Accessed July 28, 2011 at http://www.internationaltransportforum.org/statistics/GlobalTrends/CO2emissions.pdf.

for small and mid-sized vehicles. In the United States, on the other hand, the lower cost of fuel and an abundance of road space have resulted in much higher sales of larger vehicles, such as SUVs, minivans, and pickup trucks, that emit relatively high amounts of carbon dioxide. In fact, more than half the vehicles U.S.-based automobile manufacturers sell are large ones such as these (Austin and Sauer, 2003).

When considering the ways in which motor vehicles add to global carbon dioxide emissions, it is also important to note that these contributions extend far beyond those generated during the actual use of the vehicle. In fact, carbon dioxide emissions are released throughout the life of a motor vehicle, from the initial extraction of raw materials to be used in the manufacture of the vehicle and of thousands of automotive parts, through to the vehicle's distribution to dealerships that can be thousands of kilometres away from the location where it was assembled.

Motor vehicle traffic is also a substantial contributor to the formation of **smog**, a combination of ground-level ozone, airborne particles, and

> **Smog** A combination of ground-level ozone, airborne particles, and other air pollutants.

other air pollutants (Figure 12.17). Smog's impact on humans ranges from the simple irritation of one's eyes, nose, and throat through to the reduction of lung capacity and the aggravation of respiratory diseases. On a global scale, the suspended particulate matter emanating from motor vehicles has been estimated to account for some 460,000 premature deaths each year. Smog can also have economic and environmental impacts, such as inhibiting plant and forest growth and reducing crop yields.

FIGURE 12.17 Smog in Montreal, Quebec, July 2010. Smog, a combination of ground-level ozone, airborne particles, and other air pollutants, is largely caused by motor vehicle emissions. (Mario Beauregard/The Canadian Press)

Acid rain is another environmental consequence of a heavy dependence on motorized vehicles, particularly the use of automobiles in urban areas, although the biggest culprit in the formation of acid rain is industrial activity. Acid rain is caused by the emission of pollutants such as sulphur dioxide and nitrogen oxide as a by-product of fuel combustion. These are converted to sulphuric and nitric acids that, when mixed with falling precipitation, can acidify soils and water bodies, erode building materials, and contribute to human respiratory problems. In Canada, approximately 60 percent of all nitrous oxide emissions come from transportation, as do about 4 percent of sulphur dioxide emissions.

Water Pollution.   Contemporary transportation patterns are responsible for a great deal of the world's problems with **water pollution**. Automobile-oriented cities devote large proportions of their land to road transportation infrastructure, such as highways and parking lots. In the cities of core nations, it is not uncommon for road transportation infrastructure to take

> **Water pollution** Pollution caused when discharges of energy or materials degrade water for other users.

up 30 percent to 60 percent of developed land. In the extreme case of Los Angeles, this figure is closer to 75 percent. This infrastructure prevents rainwater from reaching the subsoil, and the resulting runoff carries various surface pollutants—such as motor oil and other automotive fluids, road salt and sand, and litter—into nearby streams and rivers. This leads to a greater volume of storm water pollution than would be found in higher-density areas, where less land is paved and more land remains in its natural state.

The extraction of oil from underwater wells and its subsequent transportation on ships has also created significant

water pollution problems. For example, the *Exxon Valdez* disaster in Alaska in 1989 and, more recently, the massive oil spill in the Gulf of Mexico that lasted for close to three months before finally being contained serve as blunt reminders of the dangers associated with a heavy dependence on oil. Although these two incidents were highly publicized due to the amount of oil that contaminated water bodies, Transport Canada has noted that there are approximately 14,000 reported oil spills around the world every year (Transport Canada, 2009).

Noise Pollution.   **Noise pollution** is yet another negative environmental consequence of excessive automobile transportation. As the Organisation for Economic Cooperation and Development (OECD) has stated, "transport is by far the major source of noise, ahead of building or industry, with road traffic the chief offend-

> **Noise pollution** A type of pollution in which distracting, irritating, or damaging sounds are freely audible.

er" (OECD, 1990). Furthermore, the OECD noted in 1997 that 66 percent of the population in its member countries, including Canada, was exposed to unsatisfactory noise levels from transportation. This is problematic because noise pollution has been shown to have a variety of negative impacts: it reduces residential property values (especially near urban expressways), contributes to hearing loss, increases stress caused by lack of sleep, and disrupts wildlife habitats. Constructing noise barriers along busy highways is one method being used to minimize noise pollution in urban and suburban areas (Figure 12.18).

FIGURE 12.18 Construction of Noise Barrier in Windsor, Ontario, 2010. This two-kilometre-long, five-metre-tall noise barrier was installed at the request of local residents alongside the new Windsor-Essex Parkway. The parkway was constructed to accommodate heavy volumes of traffic expected to travel between Highway 401, Canada's busiest freeway, and a proposed new international bridge that will connect Windsor with Detroit, Michigan. (Photo courtesy Windsor Border Initiatives Implementation Group, Ontario Ministry of Transportation.)

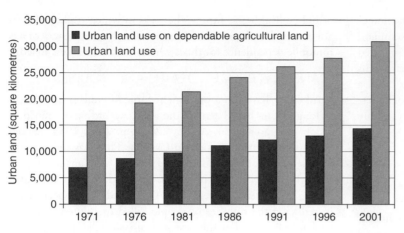

FIGURE 12.19 **Urban Land Use on Dependable Agricultural Land in Canada, 1971–2001.** The amount of land converted from agricultural use to urban development during this 30-year period was equivalent to the size of Prince Edward Island. Adapted from "Urban Land Use on Dependable Agricultural Land in Canada, 1972-2001," adapted from Rural and Small Town Canada Analysis Bulletin, The Loss of Dependable Agricultural Land in Canada, Catalogue 21-006-XIE2005001, Vol. 6, No. 1, Figure 3, p. 7, http://www.statcan.gc.ca/pub/21-006-x/21-006-x2005001-eng.pdf.

CONSUMPTION OF NON-RENEWABLE ENERGY RESOURCES

In their report "Energy and Transport Futures" (2005), Canadian transportation researchers Richard Gilbert and Anthony Perl noted that oil products fuel more than 97 percent of all motorized transport activity in Canada, and that road transportation is responsible for almost 80 percent of this consumption. At the same time, about 71 percent of all oil consumption in Canada is used for transportation purposes, while most of the remainder is used by industry and for electricity generation. Such high levels of fossil fuel consumption, which many see as egregiously wasteful, have concerned researchers and governments for several decades. For example, the energy crisis of the early 1970s brought into the public purview the finite nature of the world's fossil fuel stocks. Since that time, governments have encouraged and supported research and development activities that sought to increase the efficiency of the internal combustion engine. They have also put forward various promotional campaigns to encourage urban dwellers to purchase more fuel-efficient vehicles and/or to use alternative and renewable transportation fuels, such as electricity, natural gas, hydrogen, propane, or solar power. Despite these efforts, however, the consumption of non-renewable energy resources by core nations continues to rise, primarily because of the increasing numbers of cars on the road.

CONSUMPTION OF AGRICULTURAL LAND

The patterns of urban sprawl associated with automobile dependence are also responsible for the widespread consumption of agricultural lands on the edges of cities in Canada, the United States, and other countries. Most of Canada's major urban areas are located amid the country's very small stock of prime agricultural land. According to a study released by Statistics Canada in 2005, some 12,000 square kilometres of these lands were converted to urban uses between 1971 and 2001 alone (Figure 12.19). This represents an area equivalent to the size of Prince Edward Island. This issue is made all the more alarming when one considers, for example, that over 18 percent of Ontario's best farmland—indeed, some of *Canada's* most fertile farmland—has been removed from agricultural production in order to accommodate urban development.

ECONOMIC CONSEQUENCES

The economic costs that individuals, firms, and governments incur in supporting automobile-oriented development have become a matter of concern and debate in recent years. Transportation places considerable strain on financial resources as roads and highways are built and maintained, individuals buy and maintain their automobiles, and businesses cope with the effects of traffic congestion on their employees.

COST OF BUILDING AND MAINTAINING ROADS AND HIGHWAYS

The massive expense of building and maintaining highways is a major economic concern (Figure 12.20). The cost of building a new highway can vary considerably from place to place, and depends in part on the type of terrain over which the road will pass, the type of road to be built, and whether it is to be located in a rural or urban area. The Government of Nova Scotia has noted that in 2009 the cost of building a new two-lane highway,

FIGURE 12.20 **Highway 404/407 Interchange, Toronto, Ontario.** While engineering projects such as this do much to reduce traffic congestion and maintain the flow of traffic, at least temporarily (i.e., until traffic volumes increase beyond the road's capacity), their financial cost can be enormous. (Peter A. Lusztyk/First Light/Getty Images)

including bridges, was approximately $3.5 million per kilometre, while a new four-lane highway would cost about $6 million per kilometre. Ontario's Ministry of Transportation has stated that, on average, it costs about $10 million per kilometre, plus an additional $8 to $12 million per interchange, to build a four-lane highway in Northern Ontario, where the rocky terrain of the Canadian Shield makes road construction a more complicated process.

HOUSEHOLD COST OF TRANSPORTATION

Transportation costs also make up a significant proportion of many household budgets. Surveys conducted by Statistics Canada in cities across Canada routinely show that households spend anywhere from 13 to 20 percent of their annual budget (after taxes) on transportation. This is second only to shelter costs as the biggest household expense. Later in this chapter we will discuss how the cost of transportation in many cities is especially prohibitive for low-income earners and can create a number of financial and social hardships for these individuals.

COSTS TO BUSINESSES

Transportation geographers and other researchers have drawn attention to several additional economic consequences as automobiles have come to dominate personal travel and trucks have done the same for shipping and commercial purposes. In places where traffic congestion has become a routine part of daily life, for example, research shows that businesses incur costs of millions of dollars each year—sometimes even billions of dollars—as a result of reduced productivity due to employees' late arrival at work or lost production time when necessary components are late reaching factories by truck because of traffic jams. The Toronto Board of Trade has estimated that the combined total of such costs may be more than $2 billion per year in the Greater Toronto and Hamilton areas alone.

Researchers have also begun to identify further consequences of traffic congestion and automobile dependence on businesses and their workers. For example, Richard Wener, Gary Evans, and their colleagues (2006) have found that workers who engage in longer and more traffic-filled commutes tend to suffer greater levels of stress and job dissatisfaction, which in turn lead to greater levels of employee turnover, as workers seek out more commuter-friendly places of employment. Some businesses also appear to have difficulty hiring employees for similar reasons or because prospective employees cannot reach the workplace without the use of a car.

SOCIAL CONSEQUENCES

Since the late 1960s, transportation geographers and other researchers have worked to build a better understanding of the social consequences of automobile dependence. As a result, much of their attention has focused on such issues as road safety, the effects of different modes of transportation on levels of public health and fitness, the ways in which traffic volumes affect neighbourhood interaction, and the consequences of automobile dependence for those who do not have access to a car.

TRANSPORT-RELATED DEATHS AND INJURIES

Road safety has been a prominent topic of concern for almost as long as cars have been on the road. According to transportation geographer Jean Andrey (2010, p. 248), 1973 marked an important turning point in Canada. That was the year the number of people killed in road crashes in Canada reached its highest level ever, with 6,706 people killed on Canadian roads. Since then, Andrey notes, great strides have been made in reducing the number of people killed or injured in motor vehicle collisions. For the past several years, the death toll has been reduced to less than 3,000 people per year, even though Canada's population has increased dramatically over this period, and Canadians are driving more than ever before. Similar declines have been experienced in many other Western countries during the same time. Andrey points to a number of factors that have contributed to this decline and a concurrent decline in the number of people injured in motor vehicle collisions. These include roadway and automobile safety improvements, improvements in emergency medicine, socio-demographic shifts, and evolving driving norms (e.g., higher rates of seat belt use and a greater social stigma associated with impaired driving).

As with so many other aspects of people's lives, however, there are notable geographical differences within and between places. Much of this has to do with place-based differences in transportation policy, such as the minimum driving ages and differences in vehicle types discussed earlier in this chapter. Another important variation is the way in which deaths and injuries from motor vehicle collisions vary demographically—that is, by age group.

In terms of place-based differences, collision rates can vary due to a number of factors, such as the climate of a region or the level of car use in a place. With respect to the latter, it has been shown that most motor vehicle collisions in Canada (60 percent of the total in 2001–2) take place within urban areas, a fact that is not surprising given that over two-thirds of Canadians lived within the country's 33 largest urban areas in 2006. Researchers have also found that the motor vehicle collisions most likely to result in death or injury are those that take place in low-density suburban environments. It is in these settings that automobiles tend especially to dominate the transportation landscape, and the needs of pedestrians, cyclists, and transit users are far less likely to be adequately served by the provision of infrastructure, such as safe road crossings, sidewalks, and bike lanes.

Although, in general, countries like Canada have seen substantial road safety improvements, motor vehicle collisions remain a leading cause of death and injury for users of all major transport modes. In 1999 and 2000, 48 percent of all reported severe injuries in Canada were caused by motor vehicle collisions. Furthermore, some 2,767 people were killed and a further 13,723 people were seriously injured in motor vehicle collisions across Canada in 2007 (Table 12.1). The continued danger of today's busy transportation environment is particularly evident among two demographic cohorts: children and

TABLE 12.1	Fatalities and Serious Injuries in Canada as a Result of Vehicle Collisions, 2007			
Mode	Fatalities	Fatalities (as % of total)	Serious Injuries	Serious Injuries (as % of total)
Drivers	1,444	52.2	6,573	47.9
Passengers	609	22.0	3,362	24.5
Pedestrians	377	13.6	1,674	12.2
Bicyclists	65	2.3	426	3.1
Motorcyclists	220	8.0	1,386	10.1
Not stated	52	1.9	302	2.2
Total	2,767	100.0	13,723	100.0

Source: Data from *2007 Canadian Motor Vehicle Traffic Collision Statistics*. Ottawa: Transport Canada. Accessed July 10, 2010 at http://www.tc.gc.ca/eng/roadsafety/tp-tp3322-2007-1039.htm.

young adults. Indeed, motor vehicle collisions remain the most common cause of *injury-related* deaths among Canadian children aged 1 to 14, while they are also the most common cause of death *overall* among people aged 15 to 24.

Social Costs of Motor Vehicle Collisions.
As noted earlier in this textbook, policy makers have a predilection for quantitative (especially economic) indicators when dealing with public interest issues. Accordingly, experts have attempted over the years to build further evidence of the negative consequences of automobile dependence by estimating the social cost of motor vehicle collisions. One such study, prepared for Ontario's Ministry of Transportation (Vodden, et al., 2007), concluded that motor vehicle collisions generated $18 billion in social costs in 2004. Of this, fatalities and injuries were estimated to cost about $15 billion (e.g., through life insurance claims and lost earnings potential) and damage to public and private property was estimated to cost $2 billion; the remaining

FIELD NOTE   Dangerous Streets

The month of January 2010 was a dangerous time to be a pedestrian in the Greater Toronto Area, Canada's most populated metropolitan region. Fourteen people were killed by motor vehicles while walking in the City of Toronto or one of its surrounding municipalities during the first 25 days of that month, with three such incidents happening on the same day. After the tenth fatality in a span of nine days, a headline in the *Toronto Star* asked "Why So Many Pedestrian Deaths?" Mathematicians were quick to point to this frightening trend as a statistical anomaly, but people also wondered if there were any commonalities among the incidents that could offer further explanation. There were few. The victims ranged from teenagers and young adults to the middle-aged and senior citizens, while the motor vehicles involved were cars, trucks, buses, streetcars, and passenger trains. Several of the incidents occurred in densely developed inner-city and downtown neighbourhoods, while others occurred in sprawling suburban settings. In some cases the accidents were attributed to driver error, while in others it was the pedestrian who was seen to be at fault.

This disturbing story of a brief and tragic wave of pedestrian fatalities in the Greater Toronto Area demonstrates in a number of ways why the analysis of transportation-related issues is an important part of human geography. In order to address their many needs—for example, to buy food, visit friends, earn an income, or attend school—individuals have to travel to a variety of destinations on a regular, often daily, basis. At the same time, the ability to reach people and places is also essential for running a business and providing community services. For many people, this everyday need for mobility is well met, and such movements are such a routine part of life that they are often taken for granted and rarely given much critical thought. As this example illustrates all too well, however, the movement and interaction of different modes can be dangerous and can have tragic consequences if each does not have a balanced role.

FIGURE 12.21 Mixed Traffic at Queen's Quay, Toronto. Over time, as cities have grown and new transportation modes have been introduced into urban environments, there has been a growing competition for space among users of different modes. The priority accorded to the car and other motorized vehicles in these settings has often created dangerous travel environments for pedestrians, cyclists, and transit users, as evidenced by a spate of deaths in the Greater Toronto Area in January 2010, when 14 pedestrians were killed over the course of only 25 days. (Rick Eglinton/*Toronto Star*)

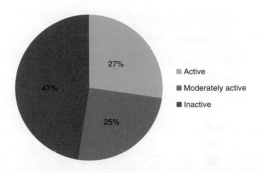

FIGURE 12.22 Levels of Leisure-Time Physical Activity among Canadians, 2005 (Percent). (Statistics Canada, CANSIM Table 105-0433).

$1 billion was attributed to the cost of hospital and health care; tow trucks; and police, fire, and ambulance services, as well as productivity losses resulting from post-accident traffic jams. The study also calculated the average social cost of a single collision in 2004 to be $74,000.

IMPACTS ON PUBLIC HEALTH AND WELL-BEING

Beyond the heavy toll of transportation-related deaths and injuries, yet another social cost that has been attributed to our dependence on the automobile is the detrimental effect on physical health and fitness. One Statistics Canada study found that close to one-half of Canadians were physically inactive in 2005 (Figure 12.22), and thus at greater risk of long-term negative health repercussions. Although television, the Internet, and other technological tools have also been blamed for reducing the amount of time people devote to physical activity, transportation geographers and other researchers have identified automobile-dependent landscapes and automobile-dependent lifestyles as further deterrents. Evidence of the growing dependence on automobiles is seen in the findings of the *Transportation Tomorrow Survey*, a comprehensive travel survey conducted in the Greater Toronto Area and the City of Hamilton

every five years (Figure 12.23). Transportation geographer Reihane Marzoughi's analysis of the survey found that teens in both the 13-to-15- and 16-to-19-year-old cohorts travelled more frequently as automobile passengers in 2006 than they did in 1986, usually at the expense of public transit (Marzoughi, 2011). In a similar study, geographers Ron Buliung and Raktim Mitra, along with their University of Toronto colleague Guy Faulkner, discovered a sizeable decrease in the proportion of teenagers travelling to school on foot or by bicycle in the Greater Toronto Area between 1986 and 2006, particularly within the more suburban reaches of this metropolitan region (Buliung, et al., 2009).

IMPACTS ON NEIGHBOURHOOD INTERACTION

Just as automobile-oriented streetscapes have been shown to reduce people's willingness to walk, cycle, or use public transit, researchers have found that heavier volumes of motor vehicle traffic can decrease levels of neighbourhood interaction. What is perhaps the best-known study of this type was conducted several decades ago by Donald Appleyard in San Francisco, California, and chronicled in his book *Livable Streets* (Appleyard, 1981). Like many researchers, Appleyard was interested in the ways that traffic in urban areas affected the lives of local residents. In the late 1960s, Appleyard identified three streets with differing traffic volumes, which he labelled Light Street (on which 2,000 vehicles travelled per day), Medium Street (8,000 vehicles per day), and Heavy Street (16,000 vehicles per day). He found that people living on Light Street demonstrated much greater levels of interaction with their neighbours and a much stronger sense of community than those living on Heavy Street. In fact, compared to those on Heavy Street, the residents of Light Street had three more friends and twice as many acquaintances on their street. Appleyard also found that the amount of space people considered part of their "community" shrank as traffic volumes increased. This study served as an important reminder of the social implications of automobile-oriented transportation policies. It also prompted planners to take into account more than just engineering-related concerns when dealing with traffic and transportation issues.

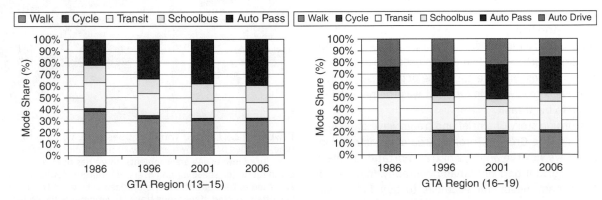

FIGURE 12.23 Mode of Travel among Teens Aged 13-15 and 16-19 in the Greater Toronto Area, 1986-2006. Reihane Marzoughi's research found that the proportion of trips as car passengers rose among teenagers in the Greater Toronto Area between 1986 and 2006 and also that the proportion of walking and transit trips made by 13- to 15-year olds declined. From Reihane Marzoughi, "Teen Travel in the Greater Toronto Area: A Descriptive Analysis of Trends from 1986 to 2006 and the Policy Implications." *Transport Policy* 18 (2011): pp. 623–630.

SOCIAL EXCLUSION

Over the past several decades, researchers have sought to better understand the various accessibility constraints that automobile-oriented development has imposed upon those people—such as persons with disabilities and low-income earners—who do not have automobile access to employment, shopping, child care, and other required facilities and services. By seeking primarily to accommodate demands for automobile transportation, transportation planners and policy makers have failed to adequately serve the accessibility needs of individuals who do not have the use of an automobile, contributing to the **social exclusion** of these individuals. Social exclusion can be defined as "the loss in the ability (by people or households) to fully participate in activities and society and connect with many of the

> **Social exclusion** The inability of people or households to fully participate in society, engage in activities, or access jobs, services, and facilities.

jobs, services, and facilities" (Hine 2009, p. 429). Todd Litman of the Victoria Transport Policy Institute has estimated that about 20 percent of Canadian households do not own an automobile, and that about a third or more of households have at least one member who has been disadvantaged by the creation of automobile-oriented transportation systems (Litman, 2003).

In their study of transportation-related social exclusion in Edmonton, geographers Joseph Mensah and Geoff Ironside (1993) found that many inner-city residents suffered from limited job opportunities due to a lack of adequate public transit service to job sites, especially as more employment was moving from Edmonton's central city to its outer suburbs. They argued that in order to promote social equity, it was necessary to modify routes, schedules, and fares to make transit more accessible to low-income earners. Mensah and Ironside stated, "The need to restructure the city's transportation system to cater for the shopping and employment needs of the city's poor cannot be overemphasized."

MAIN POINTS **12.3** **What Are Some Consequences of Contemporary Transportation Patterns?**

- The increasingly high levels of automobile dependence seen in many countries today have resulted in a number of environmental, economic, and social consequences that range from the local to the global in their impact.

- Environmental consequences include air, water, and noise pollution, as well as the excessive consumption of non-renewable energy resources and of agricultural land.

- Economic costs of automobile dependence include the high cost of building and maintaining roads, the drain on household expenses, and the impacts on the cost of doing business in urban areas.

- Social consequences of automobile dependence range from the social cost of motor vehicle collisions to the social exclusion of people who cannot drive or do not have access to a car.

12.4 What Are the Key Roles of Transportation?

Although transportation geographers are interested in examining issues at a variety of scales, two of the most prominent scales of analysis are the local and global levels. In the case of local level analysis, transportation geographers have been among the most active participants in the quest for solutions to the problem of automobile dependence. At the global level, transportation geographers have contributed much to our understanding of how transportation innovations have played, and will continue to play, a key role in the globalization process.

THE ROLE OF TRANSPORTATION IN SUSTAINABLE URBAN DEVELOPMENT

In light of the enormous consequences associated with growing levels of automobile dependence in developed countries, as well as the fears that these trends will expand into the world's developing nations, geographers have become more active in

calling for the adoption of **sustainable transportation** policies. The idea of sustainable transportation, which is derived directly from the concept of sustainable development, represents a much more holistic approach to urban transportation planning and investment than what is seen in many cities today. Most importantly, building sustainable transportation systems involves simultaneous consideration of environmental, economic, and social objectives in the provision of transportation infrastructure and services. It recognizes that land use patterns influence transportation behaviour, while also acknowledging that the transportation infrastructure in place has a strong influence on decisions about land use. Canada's Centre for Sustainable Transportation (CST) has played a leading role in the global effort to promote sustainable transportation. In fact, CST's definition of the concept and its components has been adopted throughout the world since its formulation in the year 2000. Here is how the CST defines sustainable transportation:

> **Sustainable transportation** An approach to the provision of transportation infrastructure and services that involves simultaneous consideration of environmental, economic, and social objectives.

A sustainable transportation system is one that...

- allows the basic access needs of individuals and societies to be met safely, and in a manner consistent with human and ecosystem health, and with equity within and between generations.
- is affordable, operates efficiently, offers choice of transport mode, and supports a vibrant economy.
- limits emissions and waste within the planet's ability to absorb them, minimizes consumption of non-renewable resources, reuses and recycles its components, minimizes the use of land, and minimizes the production of noise (CST, 1998).

Clearly, in the CST's conceptualization, sustainable transportation seeks to tackle the multitude of problems associated with automobile dependence described earlier in this chapter.

Beyond the various funding and infrastructural concerns outlined in *A New Vision for Urban Transportation* (see the *Field Note*), there are also a number of psychological obstacles to overcome in the pursuit of more sustainable urban transportation systems. Researchers have come to understand that many people have more than simply utilitarian motives for using particular modes of transportation, especially the private motor car (Hiscock, et al., 2002). For example, driving a car has been shown to have symbolic value for many individuals. In this case, the vehicle they

FIELD NOTE   A New Vision for Urban Transportation

The elements necessary for a sustainable urban transportation system "on the ground" are presented in *A New Vision for Urban Transportation*. This document, written by the Transportation Association of Canada (TAC) (1993), has been widely cited as an innovative, comprehensive, and thought-provoking agenda for the role of transportation in cities. The purpose of *A New Vision for Urban Transportation* is to provide a template upon which local and regional governments can develop their own unique and place-specific sustainable transportation visions, plans, and policies. It includes a set of 13 land use and transportation planning principles that have the potential to create more balanced roles for various modes of transportation, including the private automobile, within cities. The principles are as follows:

1. *Plan for increased densities and more mixed land use.*
2. *Promote walking as the preferred mode for person trips.*
3. *Increase opportunities for cycling as an optional mode of travel.* (Figure 12.24)
4. *Provide higher-quality transit service to increase its attractiveness relative to the private automobile.*
5. *Create an environment in which automobiles can play a more balanced role.*
6. *Plan parking supply and price to be in balance with walking, cycling, transit, and auto priorities.*
7. *Improve the efficiency of the urban goods distribution system.*
8. *Promote inter-modal and inter-line connections.*
9. *Promote new technologies that improve urban mobility and help protect the environment.*
10. *Optimize the use of existing transportation systems to move people and goods.*
11. *Design and operate transportation systems that can be used by the physically challenged.*
12. *Ensure that urban transportation decisions protect and enhance the environment.*
13. *Create better ways to pay for future urban transportation systems.*

Although the *New Vision for Urban Transportation* is now close to 20 years old and some progress has been made in building cities where these principles are given consideration in day-to-day land use and transportation planning decisions, it is clear that much more needs to be done to fully achieve the notion of sustainable transportation. Given the success of many European cities in building places where pedestrians, cyclists, and transit riders enjoy high levels of accessibility, there is little reason to believe that the same cannot be achieved in Canada's urban settings. As Susan Hanson and Genevieve Giuliano are quoted as saying elsewhere in this chapter, however, urban transportation systems represent the cumulative outcome of choices made by individuals and institutions in deciding matters such as where to live, how to get around, and at what densities to build. Documents like *A New Vision for Urban Transportation* go a long way in informing those decisions.

FIGURE 12.24 Creating Balanced Roles for Various Modes of Transportation. This parked delivery vehicle blocks a bike lane. Increasing opportunities for cycling as an optional mode of travel is one principle of *A New Vision for Urban Transportation*. (Vince Talotta/*Toronto Star*)

drive might serve an important role in expressing their identity or communicating their social position. Transportation researchers Jillian Anable, Birgitta Gatersleben, and Linda Steg, among others, have also found that people display what are referred to as "affective motives" for using, or not using, certain modes of transportation (Anable and Gatersleben, 2005; Steg, 2005). In these cases, the emotions evoked when travelling are important to the individual's choice of transport mode. For example, driving a car might make one feel powerful, excited, independent, or relaxed, while using public transport may make one feel inferior, powerless, and stressed. It is important to note, however, that driving a car does not always produce positive emotions, and using a non-automobile mode is not always a negative experience. For example, a car driver caught in a traffic jam can feel frustrated and powerless, or commuter train users might find their mode of travel relaxing because it liberates them from having to drive themselves between places.

Susan Hanson and Genevieve Giuliano, two prominent transportation geographers, have rightly pointed out that "it is important to recognize that the urban transportation system we now experience is the result of choices made by individuals and institutions; it is not the outcome of some relentless natural or necessary process" (2004, p. 383). These decisions were made over several decades and will therefore not be reversed easily, and certainly not overnight. However, as the work of transportation geographers and other transportation researchers continues to further our understanding of the benefits and costs associated with different modes of travel, there are opportunities to mitigate some of the negative consequences described earlier in this chapter. The example of the universal bus pass program introduced at Brock University, discussed at the beginning of this chapter, shows that it is sometimes just a matter of creating conditions that favour the use of non-automobile modes where they previously did not exist.

THE ROLE OF TRANSPORTATION IN GLOBALIZATION

As we first noted in Section 1.1 of Chapter 1, globalization refers to "a set of processes that reflect increasing interactions and heightening interdependence among and between places, without regard for national borders." Most of these interactions, relationships, and interdependencies would not be possible, however, without transportation.

MARINE TRAVEL

Perhaps the single most important transportation mode in the globalization of the world economy has been the ship. As Marc Levinson, author of *The Box: How the Shipping Container Made the World Smaller and the World Economy Bigger*, has stated, "Attributing the vast changes in the world economy to a single cause would be foolhardy, but the possibility should not be dismissed that the sharp drop in freight costs from the introduction of container shipping played a major role in increasing the integration of the global economy" (2006, p. 12). Over the past few decades, innovations in the construction of ships have enabled the building of much larger bulk carriers

and container ships than ever before (Figure 12.25). These larger vessels, combined with the enhancement of port facilities that have made it quicker and easier to transfer containers directly from ships onto trains, airplanes, and trucks, have greatly increased the attractiveness of international trade for many firms. The availability of large bulk carriers has enabled the global sourcing of raw materials, while the availability of massive container ships has made it more cost-effective to situate manufacturing operations in peripheral and semi-peripheral regions, where dramatically lower wage rates prevail.

Transportation geographers Robert McCalla, Brian Slack, and Claude Comtois have studied the growth of **containerization** in Canada and at the global scale. They have observed that the location of, and level of traffic at, the world's largest container ports serve as excellent indicators of the spread of economic globalization. McCalla, Slack, and Comtois noted that, historically, the world's biggest ports were generally located within core regions, such as the United States, Europe,

> **Containerization** The use of containers to unitize cargo for transportation, supply, and storage.
>
> **Break-of-bulk point** A location along a transport route where goods must be transferred from one carrier to another. In a port, the cargoes of oceangoing ships are unloaded and put on trains, trucks, or perhaps smaller riverboats for inland distribution.

and Australia. Ports such as those in New York and London once served as major **break-of-bulk points**, places where cargo is transferred from one mode of transportation (for example, a ship) to another mode of transportation (e.g., a truck or train). By 2003, however, the geographic distribution of major world ports had changed considerably, with Hong Kong and Singapore having the two largest facilities, and China having three of the world's four largest ports. China's importance in global container shipping patterns is a testament to its emergence as one of the world's main manufacturing export countries and also highlights the critical role its special economic

FIGURE 12.25 Container Ships. Marine vessels such as this one carry most of the manufactured products that move between continents. (© Hamburger Hafen und Logistik AG)

(a)

(b)

FIGURE 12.26 Intermodal Shipment. Intermodal shipment of containers accounts for a large portion of business for railway companies such as CN. (a) A crane loads a container onto a train at CN's Montreal intermodal terminal at Taschereau. (b) A crane loads a container onto a truck at CN's Montreal intermodal terminal at Taschereau. (Photos by Pascale Simard, Alpha Presse; courtesy of Canadian National Railway)

zones (discussed in Chapter 11) have played in China's integration into the global economy.

AIR TRAVEL

A close counterpart to shipping in the globalization process has been air travel. According to Timothy Vowles, a transportation geographer specializing in air travel, aircraft carry goods worth about 40 percent of the value of all products traded in the world today. Vowles also points out that the air travel industry has been an important source of economic development benefits for many places, as it employs over 4 million people around the world and generates over $ 400 billion in economic output. However, as is the case with so many other geographical processes and phenomena, there are huge discrepancies between core and peripheral regions when it comes to the importance and accessibility of air travel. The vast majority of air passenger and cargo traffic moves within or between three regions: North America, Europe, and East Asia. The world's leading airlines are also headquartered in these regions. Air travel is particularly significant in the United States; for example, the U.S. domestic market makes up about one-third of all passenger air travel in the world.

The important roles that marine and air transport modes have played in shaping globalization processes have also made those industries vulnerable to outside forces. During the economic crisis of 2009, for example, world container traffic fell by 26 percent, and world air freight tonnage fell by 10 percent (International Transport Forum, 2010). This led to widespread job losses and problems of overcapacity.

LAND TRAVEL

While marine and air travel have clearly played key roles in the globalization process, particularly at the inter-continental scale, they are far from being the only important forms of travel influencing the geographical characteristics of this process. Indeed, rail- and truck-based modes of transportation have also contributed greatly to the expansion of global, international, and regional trade over the past several decades. This has been particularly the case in North America, where growth in the use of rail and road transport has coincided with the growing use of containerized shipping to move goods. According to American geographer Andrew Goetz (2009), the transformation of these industries began in the 1980s, when many North American railroads began to carry double-stacked containers from coastal ports, particularly along the Pacific coast, to inland terminals, where the containers were often transferred directly onto trucks for the trip to their final destination. Goetz has also noted that the use of railroads to move containers for this purpose created a form of "land bridge" between Asia and the east coast of North America. Finally, he has pointed out that this **intermodal transportation** of containers accounts for a large segment of business for each of the five North American railroads, including Canadian National Railway (CN), and also for some of the continent's largest trucking firms (Figure 12.26).

> **Intermodal transportation**
> The transportation of a person or a load from its origin to its destination by a sequence of at least two transportation modes, the transfer from one mode to the next being performed at an intermodal terminal.

- Transportation geographers have become more active in calling for the adoption of sustainable transportation policies.

- Building sustainable transportation systems involves simultaneous consideration of environmental, economic, and social objectives in the provision of transportation infrastructure and services.

- The elements necessary for a sustainable urban transportation system "on the ground" are nicely collected in *A New Vision for Urban Transportation*, which includes a set of 13 land use and transportation planning principles that have the potential to create more balanced roles for various modes of transportation—including the private automobile—within cities.

- Decisions that have led to the creation of automobile-dependent cities were made over the course of several decades. Therefore, they will not be reversed easily, and certainly not overnight.

- Many of the interactions, relationships, and interdependencies between places that have been created as part of globalization would not be possible were it not for the transportation innovations that the world has witnessed over the past several decades.

- Perhaps the single most important transportation mode in the globalization of the world economy has been the ship. Over the past few decades, innovations in the construction of ships have enabled the building of much larger bulk carriers and container ships than ever before.

- The vast majority of air passenger and cargo traffic moves within or between three regions: North America, Europe, and East Asia.

- Rail and road transport provide important means of conveying containers between ocean ports and the final destination of the goods being shipped, particularly in North America.

12.5 Why Is Transportation an Important Concern in the Development of Peripheral Regions?

While automobile dependence is a concern in many core countries, a different set of transportation-related problems prevails in peripheral countries. First, the economic development of many places has been limited by a lack of adequate transportation infrastructure. Second, a large proportion of the world's population suffers from inadequate access to even the most basic day-to-day needs due to transportation constraints.

TRANSPORTATION AND ECONOMIC DEVELOPMENT IN THE PERIPHERY

The availability of transportation infrastructure is widely viewed as a critical factor in the economic development of a country. Ports, railways, and roads all contribute to the economy by ensuring access to raw materials and providing a means of exporting products to their ultimate markets. In his modernization theory (discussed in Chapter 11), Walter Rostow recognized the development of transportation networks as an important part of a country's movement along the "ladder of development." However, many countries today suffer from a lack of such infrastructure, which, in turn, has seriously hampered their economic development efforts and limited their integration into the global economy.

The country of Laos, located in southeastern Asia, provides one example of a place where a lack of good transportation infrastructure has limited economic development. The country is

FIGURE 12.27 Highway Construction in Sri Lanka, 2009. Projects such as this can stimulate economic development in countries of the periphery by improving accessibility. However, researchers warn that for those in rural areas, new roads do little to improve accessibility to basic needs, such as clean water, food, employment, or schools. In those areas, infrastructure enhancements that enable the use of non-motorized transportation modes, such as walking or cycling, can do far more good. (Ishara S. Kodikara/AFP/Getty Images)

already somewhat isolated from global trade activity due to its status as a landlocked nation. Much of Laos's road network is rather primitive, a problem that is exacerbated by the country's mountainous terrain. Almost half of Laos's roads are rural roads, and only a fraction of these are in decent condition. Many of the roads are impassable during the rainy season, effectively cutting some communities off from the outside world for extended periods each year.

Governments and international development organizations have invested heavily to provide transportation infrastructure in many countries over the past several decades (Figure 12.27).

For example, improving the national transportation network has been a high priority in the African country of Malawi; in some years, transportation has received over 30 percent of public sector investment. One of the problems with such investment, however, is that it tends to be focused primarily on the urban areas and often neglects to serve the needs of those residing in peripheral regions of the country, thus inhibiting rural development. In Malawi, most road investments have gone to construct and maintain primary highways, despite the fact that over 80 percent of the country's rural population relies more heavily on footpaths, tracks, and bridges than on any formal road network. The ensuing problems are discussed in the following section.

TRANSPORTATION AND QUALITY OF LIFE IN THE PERIPHERY

Given the pervasiveness of globalization processes, it would be easy to assume that transportation innovations have diffused throughout the world and that this has provided a fairly universal level of access to modern means of transportation, including automobiles. However, throughout much of the world, especially in Africa and parts of Asia and South America, the automobile is a luxury beyond the reach of most people. Instead, the primary means of travel is on foot. If one can afford it, transport may sometimes include a bicycle or public transportation, if it is available locally.

As mentioned previously, investments in transportation have done little to improve accessibility for rural dwellers in many peripheral countries. This has resulted in serious quality-of-life concerns. The majority of people living in rural areas spend much of their time walking to access such things as health care, education, and even clean drinking water, which are often taken for granted or which do not even require travel in core countries. They must also walk to procure firewood for cooking and to access grinding mills. Like Malawi, the African country of Zimbabwe suffers from an acute shortage of rural transportation infrastructure. In the late 1990s, Zimbabwe's government examined the travel needs of its rural citizens. It found that an average rural household spent between 60 and

70 hours per week gaining access to water, firewood, grinding mills, markets, clinics, and schools. Furthermore, it was women who did most of this walking (about 77 percent), often carrying loads on their heads (a technique called "headloading," illustrated in Figure 12.28). An important conclusion of this study was that improving the proximity of these services would be a much more significant development initiative than building new roads. It was the inconvenient location of services that was most problematic, and this could be remedied by providing such services locally, or by ensuring that footpaths, bridges, and other necessary walking infrastructure were in place and well maintained. Similar studies in other parts of Africa and other peripheral regions have come to comparable conclusions (Reily et al. 2000; Wynd 1995). One study showed that children in rural Zambia often missed school during the rainy season because they could not safely cross bridges along their walking route (Musonda, 2006).

FIGURE 12.28 Headloading. These women in India, like those in many peripheral and semi-peripheral countries, bear much of the burden when it comes to walking with heavy loads, a consequence of inadequate transportation alternatives. (©Neil McAllister/Alamy).

| MAIN POINTS | **12.5** Why Is Transportation an Important Concern in the Development of Peripheral Regions? |

- A different set of transportation-related problems prevails in peripheral countries. First, the economic development of many places has been limited by a lack of adequate transportation infrastructure. Second, a large proportion of the world's population suffers from inadequate access to even the most basic day-to-day needs due to transportation constraints.

- Transportation-related development efforts in many peripheral countries have focused primarily on the provision of road infrastructure in metropolitan regions. Little attention has been paid to the enhancement of accessibility in rural settings. This is particularly problematic because a high proportion of rural dwellers must walk to fulfill even their most basic needs.

SUMMARY

Transportation is an inherently geographical subject, bringing together geography's focus on spatial interaction, regional differences, human-environment relations, and economic development. In light of their overriding interest in helping to improve people's quality of life, transportation geographers have actively worked to identify transport-related problems, within both the core and the periphery, and to propose solutions for these problems. The solutions are often rooted in the notion of sustainable development, and frequently the same remedy may be applied to different problems. For example, a common initiative advocated by transportation geographers and others has been to bring destinations closer together so that they can be reached more easily on foot. This is effective whether the aim is to enable those in peripheral regions to meet their daily needs with less time devoted to travel, thus advancing the social sustainability agenda, or to enable those in core regions to reduce their levels of automobile dependence by making walking more attractive relative to travelling by car, thus helping achieve environmental sustainability objectives. Given its impact on so many aspects of our lives and on the places we live, transportation is clearly an important issue and growing even more so in our globalized world. It is becoming increasingly evident that transportation issues are worthy of much more detailed examination and, as we have shown throughout this chapter, transportation geographers are leading the way in identifying and addressing these issues.

DISCUSSION AND REVIEW QUESTIONS

1. What is the situation at Brock University with transportation? Does Brock University have a successful sustainable transportation program? Why? Think about your own university or college: would you consider its student transportation system adequate?

2. Until recently, transportation had been neglected by geographers. What is transportation geography and why has it recently emerged as an important sub-discipline of geography?

3. Discuss the themes and arguments presented by Peter Newman and Jeff Kenworthy in their book *Sustainability and Cities—Overcoming Automobile Dependence*. Does the city you live in reflect the ideas presented in their book? Identify any specific things your city is doing to address its transportation situation as it relates to the 13 principles laid out in *A New Vision for Urban Transportation*, published by the Transportation Association of Canada.

4. There are clear geographical variations in transportation systems across the globe—with some dominated by the automobile and others with high rates of non-motorized modes, such as walking and cycling. The most automobile-dependent cities in the world are found in the United States, Australia, and Canada. Describe the factors that explain these variations in transportation systems.

5. Transportation is an integral part of any place and there are inevitable consequences based on the type of transportation systems that predominate. Identify and briefly explain the major consequences of contemporary transportation patterns. Which consequence most aptly fits your city or town?

GEOGRAPHIC CONCEPTS

air pollution   357
automobile dependence   347
break-of-bulk point   365
containerization   365
intermodal transportation   366
neighbourhood unit   350
noise pollution   358
public transit   354

Radburn Idea   350
smog   357
social exclusion   363
sustainable transportation   363
transportation geography   346
transport networks   347
water pollution   358

ADDITIONAL RESOURCES ONLINE

About air transportation: www.iata.org

About air transportation in Canada: www.atac.ca

About railway transportation: www.uic.org

About railway transportation in Canada: www.railcan.ca

About ship transportation and containerization:
   www.worldshipping.org

About ship transportation and containerization in Canada:
   www.shipfed.ca/new

About automobile dependence: www.vtpi.org/tdm/tdm100.htm

About transportation in Canada:
   www.tac-atc.ca
   www.tc.gc.ca

About public transit in Canada: www.cutaactu.ca/en/index.asp

About transportation issues in peripheral regions:
   www.worldbank.org/projects/sector?lang=en

chapter 13

INDUSTRY AND SERVICES

Branding the Backboard

WALKING THROUGH a relatively poor neighbourhood in Skopje, Macedonia, with the midday Muslim call to prayer ringing in my ears, the last thing I expected to see was something from my home state of Oregon. But there it was—the unmistakable Nike swoosh replicated on the backboard of a basketball hoop where the local kids play pickup games (Figure 13.1).

As ubiquitous as the Nike brand of athletic shoes and the company's trademark swoosh are on the physical landscape, it is difficult to examine the cultural landscape and pinpoint where Nikes are produced given the processes of globalization discussed in Chapter 2. Nike was founded in Oregon in 1961 by a former competitive runner (its first-year sales were $8,000), and it has grown to be one of the giants of the shoe and apparel business, with sales of $16.3 billion in 2007. Although its headquarters are in Beaverton, Oregon, a suburb of Portland, the company is far more than a Beaverton concern, and despite a Beaverton workforce of over 6,000 people, not a single individual in Oregon is directly involved in the process of putting a shoe together. Worldwide, 30,000 people work directly for Nike today, and according to Nike, upwards of 800,000 workers are employed by the almost 700 Nike contract factories in 52 countries. Nike began production in the 1960s by contracting with an Asian firm to manufacture its shoes. In 1974, Nike set up its first domestic shoe-manufacturing facility in the small town of Exeter, New Hampshire. By the end of that year, Nike's workforce was still modest in number, but the Oregon contingent focused on running the company and expanding sales, whereas the New Hampshire and Asian contingents focused primarily on the production of athletic shoes.

As Nike grew to become the world's leading manufacturer of athletic shoes (with almost 40 percent of the market), its employment numbers skyrocketed and many new manufacturing plants were established in Asia and beyond (Figure 13.2). Indeed, in Vietnam, Nike is now the largest employer. This transformation did not translate into manufacturing jobs in Beaverton, Oregon, however. The employment opportunities

FIGURE 13.1 Skopje, Macedonia. The Nike "swoosh" is every-where—even on the backboard of a basketball hoop in this relatively poor neighbourhood of Skopje, Macedonia. (Alexander B. Murphy)

at Nike's world headquarters are for the financial administrators, marketing and sales specialists, information technology directors, computer technicians, lawyers, and support personnel needed to run an international company with billions, in annual revenues. The local social and economic geography of Beaverton bears little resemblance to what one might have expected in a town housing an important shoe company 80 years ago.

Today, the production and marketing of Nike shoes and apparel involves an elaborate global network of international manufacturing and sales. The global processes have local outcomes and realities, as each node of the Nike network is functionally specialized, dependent on other nodes, and influenced by the niche it occupies in the network.

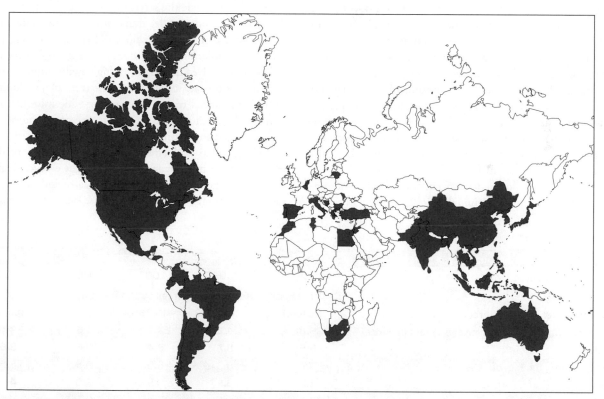

FIGURE 13.2 Nike around the World. The regions coloured orange have a Nike presence: 612 contract factories; 819,990 workers; and 46 manufacturing countries. Data from www.nikeinc.com.

KEY QUESTIONS FOR CHAPTER 13

1. What are industrial and service economies?

2. Where did the Industrial Revolution begin, and how did it diffuse?

3. How do location theories explain historical patterns of industrialization?

4. What are the spatial implications of changes in industrial production?

5. What is the service economy, and where are services concentrated?

13.1 What Are Industrial and Service Economies?

When we look closely at the landscapes around us, we see people engaged in numerous and diverse economic activities. In our own neighbourhood, we drop into the local convenience store to buy gas, pick up milk, or take a chance on a lottery ticket. The nearby neighbourhood strip mall might have a drycleaners, a liquor store, a barber shop and hair salon, or a veterinarian, providing us with the services we use on a regular basis. As we make our daily commute to work, we travel past offices and industrial parks, manufacturing plants, and local factories employing neighbours and friends. From the hotdog vendor in the city park to the high-tech manufacturer, the industrial, manufacturing, and service sectors are major contributors to local and global economies. Driven by the processes of globalization detailed in Chapter 2, these economic activities are fully integrated into continental and worldwide networks and flows of knowledge, goods, services, and technologies. As geographers, we are interested in the spatial organization of industrial and service economies as well as questions of location, regional organization, and movement of goods, services, and labour. In this chapter we will consider the locational aspects of economic activities—more specifically, the locational characteristics of industrial and service sector entities.

The types of employment associated with different economic activities are illustrated in Table 13.1. *Primary activities*,

such as agriculture, logging, and mining, involve the extraction or production of raw materials. *Secondary activities* make something from those raw materials and include such activities as food processing (e.g., cheese, soups, or pasta), the production of lumber or furniture, the manufacturing of granite countertops, building construction, or the making of diamond rings. Note that in Table 13.1, primary and secondary activities are grouped together under the heading "Good-producing sector."

Tertiary activities are those service industries connecting the manufacturing and industrial processes to consumers, as well as services that facilitate trade and commerce. Businesses rely on services provided by bankers, salespeople, insurance brokers, lawyers, accountants, and secretaries. Workers need services that sustain them, including restaurants, clothing stores, doctors, and dentists. In the 21st century, services have become more complicated. We can divide the service-producing sector into a *tertiary* sector that includes trade, transportation, and warehousing; a *quaternary* sector, which includes individuals working with the exchange of information or money; and a *quinary* sector, with individuals involved in research or higher education. Universities and colleges educate individuals to use technologies (quinary) or to broker financial transactions and provide information (quaternary) that, in turn, are integral to the operation of a strong agricultural, manufacturing, and service sector.

Geographers and others use the term "stages of development" to describe how an economy might evolve. Regions are described as going through three stages of industrial development as emerging technologies diffuse across landscapes. The

TABLE 13.1	Employment by Industry in Canada				
Canadian Labour Force	2005	2006	2007	2008	2009
	All Industries (total labour forces by thousands)				
All industries (total labour force)	16, 169.7	16,484.3	16,866.4	17,125.8	16,848.9
Good-producing sector (percentage of labour force)	**25.8**	**24.2**	**23.7**	**23.6**	**22%**
Agriculture	8.5	8.7	8.4	8.1	8.6
Forestry, fishing, mining, oil, gas	7.7	8.3	8.5	8.5	8.5
Utilities	3.1	3.1	3.5	3.8	4
Construction	25.5	26.8	28.4	30.6	31
Manufacturing	55.1	53.1	51.2	49.0	48
Service-producing sector (percentage of labour force)	**74.2**	**75.8**	**76.3**	**76.4**	**78%**
Trade	21.2	21.1	21.0	20.3	20.1
Transportation and warehousing	6.5	6.4	6.4	6.2	6.3
Finance, insurance, real estate, leasing	8.1	8.3	8.2	8.1	8.3
Professional, scientific, technical	8.6	8.7	8.8	9.1	9.2
Business, building, other support services	5.4	5.5	5.5	5.0	5.0
Educational services	9.1	9.3	9.2	9.2	9.1
Health care and social assistance	14.3	14.3	14.3	15.7	15
Information, culture, recreation	6.0	6.0	6.0	5.7	5.9
Accommodation and food services	8.3	8.1	8.3	8.1	8.0
Other services	5.7	5.6	5.6	5.5	6.0
Public administration	6.8	6.7	6.7	7.1	7.1

Source: Adapted from Statistics Canada, CANSIM, table 282-0008 and catalogue no. 71f0004XCB.

first stage is the pre-industrial stage, when primary activities form the backbone of an economy. They mostly take the form of agriculture but may also include lumber production, fishing, and some resource extraction, such as quarrying stone and gravel. A region is understood to have reached the second, or industrial, stage when it develops a manufacturing economy with an output greater than that of the primary sector. In an industrial economy, a substantial portion of the labour force is engaged in secondary activities, which include processing raw materials and producing new goods. The third and last stage is the post-industrial stage, in which most of the labour force is engaged in tertiary, quaternary, and quinary activities. The world's core countries have entered the post-industrial stage.

Canada is a country with bountiful natural resources. From its colonial past to its contemporary present, the Canadian economy has relied on the primary activities of logging, resource extraction, fishing, and, later, agriculture. As geographer Ian Wallace notes, "Canada entered the capitalist world economy, on the undeveloped global periphery, [transporting] crude natural resource products … to the European core." The pressures of World War II drove Canada to increase its industrial capacity, mainly in southern Ontario and Quebec. This continued into the 1950s and 1960s with the expansion of American branch plants into Canada, most notably in the automobile sector. At the same time, oil and gas became an increasingly important staple, particularly in Alberta, with the seemingly insatiable demand for petroleum products from both Canada and the United States. Asian development in the 1980s and 1990s increased the demand for Canadian resources such as copper and coal, especially on the west coast. Today, demand for Canadian natural resources from countries such as China has reinvigorated natural resource extraction and production. Increased demand for uranium and the discovery of diamonds in Nunavut and the Northwest Territories sparked the opening of a number of uranium and diamond mines (Figure 13.3).

As Table 13.1 illustrates, in 2005, over 25 percent of the Canadian workforce was involved in the good-producing sector, which is composed of both primary and secondary activities. Only a little over 16 percent of the Canadian workforce was employed in primary activities such as agriculture, forestry, fishing, mining, oil, and gas. The remainder of the labour force in this sector was involved in secondary activities, including construction and manufacturing. The service-producing sector, which encompasses the tertiary, quaternary, and quinary sectors, employs the remainder of the Canadian workforce, or over 75 percent. By definition, this makes Canada a post-industrial economy. When we look at the service-producing sector, we can see that some 14.3 percent of the workforce is engaged in providing health care and social assistance. Taken together with those involved in public administration (6.8 percent) and educational services (9.1 percent), governments (federal, provincial, and local) employ 30 percent of the service sector labour force. By contrast, Canada has quite modest employment in manufacturing and construction, which employs only about 20 percent of the total workforce. Again, by definition, this means Canada is a post-industrial economy.

Table 13.1 indicates that by 2009, employment in primary and secondary industries had declined from 25.8 percent to a little over 22 percent, with a corresponding increase—from 74.2 percent to about 78 percent—in tertiary, quaternary, and quinary employment. Note the gains in this area were spread across the service-producing sector but are more prominent in professional, scientific, and technical services and in health care and social assistance as well as public administration. Compared to 2005, employment in government-related services increased from 30 percent to about 32 percent. On the other hand, employment in construction and manufacturing declined from about 20 percent of the total labour force to about 17.5 percent. These figures demonstrate the slow shift of the Canadian economy away from a resource- or staples-based economy to a service-producing economy.

FIGURE 13.3 Diavik Diamond Mine, Northwest Territories. Contained within a 20-square-kilometre island at Lac de Gras, roughly 300 kilometres north of Yellowknife, Diavik Diamond Mine, a joint venture between Rio Tinto and Harry Winston, has been mining diamonds in the remote Canadian north since 2003. (Diavik Diamond Mine)

- Economies are classified by what is produced. Primary activities involve the extraction and production of resources. Secondary activities involve manufacturing goods from those raw materials. Tertiary activities are service industries connecting the manufacturing and industrial processes to consumers, while quaternary and quinary sectors involve knowledge and higher education, respectively.

- Economies go through three stages of development, from pre-industrial to manufacturing to post-industrial, where the majority of the workforce is engaged in tertiary, quaternary, and quinary activities. The world's core countries have entered the post-industrial stage.

- Canada is a post-industrial country. Nevertheless, with the increasing demand for raw materials from countries such as China, Canadian resource-based industries extracting coal, lumber, uranium, and diamonds have shown considerable growth in the last decade.

13.2 Where Did the Industrial Revolution Begin, and How Did It Diffuse?

The **Industrial Revolution**, beginning in the 1700s and 1800s, was clearly a watershed event in human history. Technological changes in agriculture led to the second agricultural revolution with its improved farming techniques and resulting food surplus (see Chapter 9). Advances in medicine and in the sciences greatly improved human health, resulting in a rise in birth rates, a decline in death rates, and overall greater life expectancy leading to a population explosion (see Chapter 4). Cities grew rapidly and the need for raw materials for manufacturing grew exponentially. Urban areas expanded as these growing populations sought employment in the manufacturing and industrial sectors developing in and around urban areas and transportation centres (Chapter 10). With improved technologies in ship construction and the growth in knowledge about navigation, European countries entered the age of exploration, colonialism, and imperialism, and the discoveries they made—from spices and precious metals to new civilizations and technologies—in turn fed the development of new ideas and technologies (Chapter 3).

> **Industrial Revolution** The term applied to the social and economic changes in agriculture, commerce, and manufacturing that resulted from technological innovations and specialization in late-18th-century Europe.

What we think of as "industrial production" began long before the Industrial Revolution. Europeans travelled the "Silk Routes" between India, China, and the Mediterranean for some 3,000 years, ensuring an exchange of goods and technologies (Figure 13.4). China and Japan possessed a substantial industrial base long before the European Industrial Revolution. From the 11th century, cottage industries and community workshops were located throughout the world, and trade in the goods produced was widespread even before colonial and imperial exploration. For example, from the time of Marco Polo's travels across Asia some 700 years ago, goods have moved between Asia and Europe. In the towns and villages of India, workshops produced items made from iron, gold, silver, and brass. India's carpenters were artists as well as artisans, and their work was in demand wherever it could be bought. India's textiles, made on individual spinning wheels

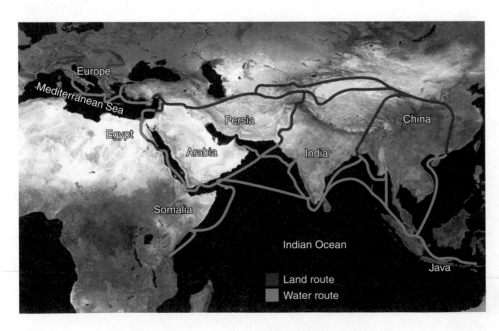

FIGURE 13.4 The Silk Road and Related Trade Routes. The historical Silk Road, which gets its name from the Chinese silk trade and is some 6,400 kilometres in length, is composed of a series of land and sea trade routes that crisscrossed Eurasia from the first millennium BCE through to the middle of the second millennium CE. (NASA Goddard Space Flight Center Image by Reto Stöckli (land surface, shallow water, clouds). Enhancements by Robert Simmon (ocean color, compositing, 3D globes, animation). Data and technical support: MODIS Land Group; MODIS Science Data Support Team; MODIS Atmosphere Group; MODIS Ocean Group Additional data: USGS EROS Data Center (topography); USGS Terrestrial Remote Sensing Flagstaff Field Center (Antarctica); Defense Meteorological Satellite Program (city lights).)

and hand looms, were considered the best in the world. These industries were sustained both by local aristocrats and by international trade, and some European producers thought the Indian manufacturers had an unfair advantage. In Great Britain, textiles were produced by residents of rural villages within their individual homes where, during the winter months, they would spin thread or weave fabric. The quality of production varied according to place but were generally inferior to India's textiles. As a result, British textile makers rioted in 1721, demanding legislative protection against imports from India. The price and quality of products from many European industries, from the textile makers of Flanders and Britain to the iron smelters of Thüüringen, Germany, could not match those of products from other parts of the world.

THE INDUSTRIAL REVOLUTION

In the era of colonial exploration and colonization, European countries such as England, Spain, and France travelled the globe, claiming "discovered" lands and peoples as their own. Newly established commercial enterprises, such as the Dutch and British East India Companies in Asia and the Hudson's Bay Company in North America, laid the groundwork for Europe's colonial expansion. The companies' traders made contact with previously unknown peoples and slowly gained control over

local industries in India, Indonesia, and elsewhere. Goods from this far-flung colonial empire flowed back to the home countries, providing local communities with the opportunities to purchase a hitherto unknown assortment of exotic and unfamiliar spices, foods, art, and fabrics. By the 18th century, the imported raw materials were being refined and turned into furniture, clothing, and household goods that were increasingly in demand in the colonies, leading to the invention of new machinery and the development of larger workforces to service this new market. New networks and flows of goods and people established new connections and relationships between previously unconnected places, facilitating the exchange of knowledge about peoples and places never before experienced. These networks and locations are the foundation for the current world economic system discussed in chapters 2 and 3.

During the 18th century, a series of inventions and discoveries created new uses for known energy sources, such as coal, and prompted the rapid development of communication technologies, such as the telegraph, to help manage and control the colonies. New machines to improve efficiencies, such as steam engines, enabled other new inventions from water pumps to railroads. Funding inventions and supporting inventors required money, and the 18th century was marked by a flow of capital from the colonies and global trade to Western Europe (Figure 13.5).

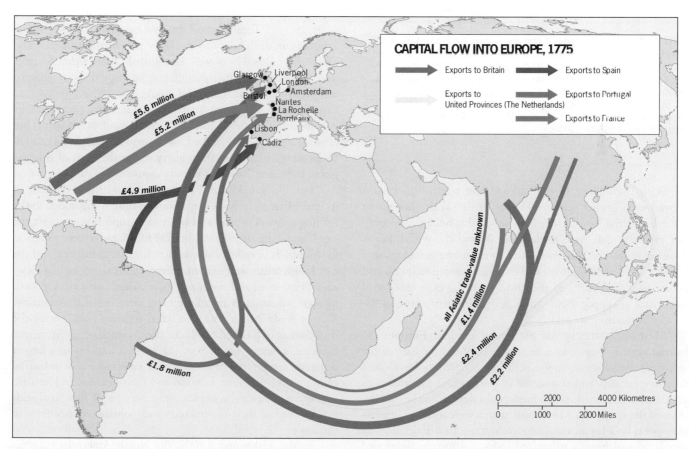

FIGURE 13.5 Capital Flows into Europe during the Era of Colonialism. Major flows of capital entered Europe from European colonies. The capital helped fuel Europe's Industrial Revolution at the end of the 1700s and into the 1800s. Adapted with permission from Geoffrey Barraclough, ed., *The Times Concise Atlas of World History*, 5th ed., Hammond Incorporated, 1998.

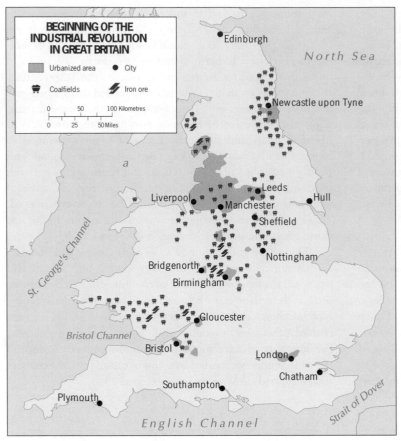

BEGINNING OF THE INDUSTRIAL REVOLUTION IN GREAT BRITAIN

Urbanized area   ● City

Coalfields   Iron ore

0   50   100 Kilometres

0   25   50 Miles

North Sea

Edinburgh

Newcastle upon Tyne

Leeds

Liverpool   Hull

Manchester

Sheffield

Nottingham

Bridgenorth

Birmingham

Gloucester

Bristol Channel

Bristol

London

Chatham

Southampton

Plymouth

English Channel

Strait of Dover

St. George's Channel

FIGURE 13.6 The Origins of the Industrial Revolution. The areas of Great Britain that industrialized earliest were those closest to the resources—coal, iron ore, and capital—needed for industrialization. Large areas of urbanization grew near industrial zones and in the port cities where materials came in and from which industrialized products went out. Adapted with permission from Geoffrey Barraclough, ed., *The Times Concise Atlas of World History*, 5th ed., Hammond Incorporated, 1998.

With the advent of the railroad and steamship, Britain enjoyed even greater advantages than it did at the beginning of the Industrial Revolution. Not only did it hold a monopoly over products that were in demand around the world, but it alone possessed the skills necessary to make the machines that manufactured them. Europe and America wanted railroads and locomotives; England had the know-how, the experience, and the capital to supply them. Soon British influence around the world was reaching its peak.

Meanwhile, the spatial pattern of modern Europe's industrial activity began to take shape. In the early part of the Industrial Revolution, manufacturing needed to be located close to coalfields and connected to ports where raw materials could arrive and finished products could depart. In the first decades of the Industrial Revolution, plants were usually connected to ports by a broad canal or river system. In Britain, densely populated and heavily urbanized industrial regions developed near the coalfields (Figure 13.6). The largest such region was the Midlands of north-central England.

DIFFUSION TO MAINLAND EUROPE

In the early 1800s, as the innovations of Britain's Industrial Revolution diffused into mainland Europe, the same set of locational criteria for industrial zones applied: proximity to coalfields and connection via water to a port. A belt of major coalfields extends from west to east through mainland Europe, roughly along the southern margins of the North European Lowland—across northern France and southern Belgium, the Netherlands, the German Ruhr, western Bohemia in the Czech Republic, and Silesia in Poland. Iron ore is dispersed along a similar belt, and the map showing the pattern of diffusion of the Industrial Revolution into Europe reflects the resulting concentrations of economic activity (Figure 13.7). Industrial developments in one area, such as the Ruhr area of present-day Germany (Germany was not consolidated into a single country until the 1870s), changed the port cities to which they are linked—in this case Rotterdam in the Netherlands. The Rhine River flows through the Ruhr area and enters the sea at Rotterdam. Over the last 200 years, the Dutch radically altered the port of Rotterdam to ease transportation and make it the most important port in Europe and a hub of global commerce.

Technological innovation changed the spatial organization of industry in the latter part of the 18th century. Once the railroad was well established, transportation costs were reduced and some manufacturing moved to or grew in existing urban areas with large markets, such as London and Paris. London was an attractive site for industry because of its port location on the Thames River and, more importantly, because of its major role in the flow of regional and global capital. By locating in London, an industry was at the heart of Britain's global influence. Paris was already continental Europe's greatest city, but, like London, it did not have coal or iron deposits in its immediate vicinity. When a railroad system was added to the existing network of road and waterway connections to Paris, the city became the largest local market for manufactured products for hundreds of miles. Paris attracted major industries, and the city, long a centre for the manufacture of luxury items (e.g., jewellery, perfumes, and fashions), experienced substantial growth in such industries as metallurgy and chemical manufacturing. With a ready labour force, an ideal regional position for the distribution of finished products, the presence of governmental agencies, a nearby ocean port (Le Havre), and France's largest domestic market, the development of Paris as a major industrial centre was no accident. London and Paris became, and remain, important industrial complexes not because of their coalfields but because of their commercial and political connectivity to the rest of the world.

In the 1700s and 1800s, the North American colonies of France and Britain were pre-industrial economies, providing raw materials to the home countries—predominantly

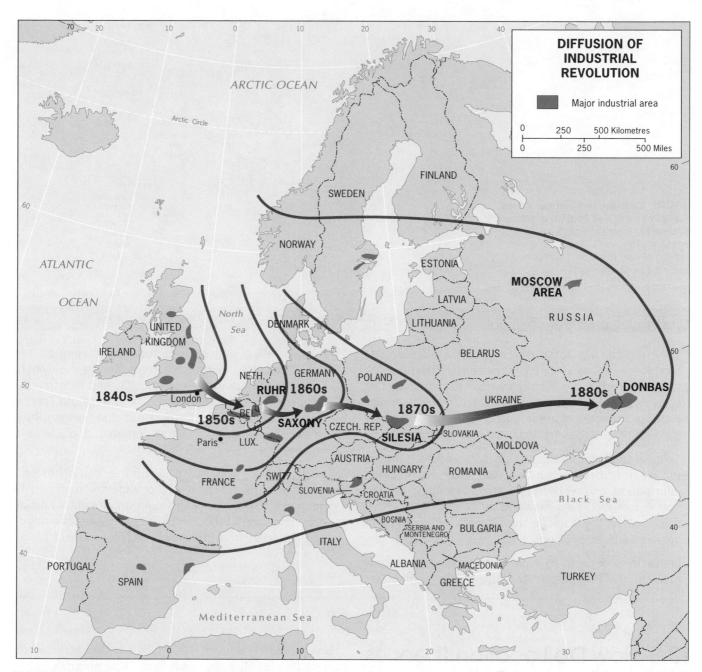

FIGURE 13.7 Diffusion of the Industrial Revolution. The eastward diffusion of the Industrial Revolution occurred during the second half of the 19th century. (© H.J. de Blij, P.O. Muller, and John Wiley & Sons, Inc.)

tobacco, cotton, lumber, animal pelts, and fish—and serving as major markets for finished goods. The imports from North America provided the necessary inputs for the growing industrial regions of Europe and structured the spatial layout and organization of North American hamlets, towns, villages, cities, and ports (Figure 13.8). As in most colonial settlements, transportation systems were established to ensure the smooth flow of goods and materials. Initially, transportation was mainly by the major navigable waterways, and later

it was by railways, as goods were conveyed from the centre of the continent to the eastern coast and the major ports of Montreal, Quebec City, Halifax, and Saint John as well as New York and Boston. Raw materials were processed in the major centres in Europe and imported by the North American colonies as finished goods such as clothing, textiles, books, and furniture. Local manufacturing in North America was modest and included saw and grist mills, blacksmithing, and shipbuilding designed mainly to support the export trade.

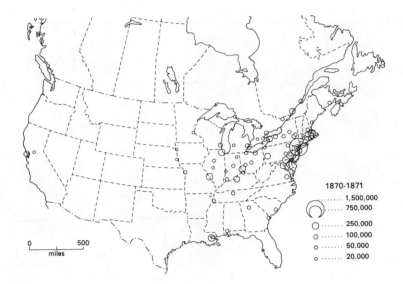

FIGURE 13.8 North American Cities with a Population of 20,000 or More, 1870–1871. From M. Yeats, *The North American City* (1997), Figure 2.7, p. 41. Addison Wesley Publishing Company. Reprinted by permission.

1870-1871
- 1,500,000
- 750,000
- 250,000
- 100,000
- 50,000
- 20,000

0   500
miles

MAIN POINTS   13.2   Where Did the Industrial Revolution Begin, and How Did It Diffuse?

- The Industrial Revolution of the 18th and 19th centuries produced a profound shift in human history from agricultural and resource-based economies to manufacturing economies. It was marked by rapid technological change, increased urbanization, population growth, and global exploration and colonization.

- Colonial and imperial exploration increased trade around the globe and ensured increasing exchanges of goods, information, and technologies among far-flung regions. This established new networks of communication and trade and set the stage for the current interrelationships between different nations.

- Major inventions in Europe, such as improved communications (telegraph) and the steam engine (rail transportation and manufacturing), accelerated the rate of change. Innovations from Britain diffused to mainland Europe in the early 1800s, and industry developed near the major coalfields in northern France, southern Belgium, the Netherlands, the German Ruhr, western Bohemia in the Czech Republic, and Silesia in Poland.

- North America at this time had little industrial development as its main task was to provide raw materials to home countries. North American urban centres developed as transportation nodes began moving raw goods and materials from the centre of the continent to the east coast.

13.3 How Do Location Theories Explain Historical Patterns of Industrialization?

Economic activities have a particular spatial organization that depends on a number of factors as well as historical and cultural circumstances. Primary economic activities are usually located where resources are found—near forests, mineral deposits, or good soils. Secondary industrial and manufacturing activities also depend on obtaining the raw materials they need, and location decisions are often made based on access to those resources as well as the availability of skilled workers and transportation systems that can move their final product to market. However, technological improvements in transportation and communications have created time-space compression (see Chapter 2) in our globalized world, and these secondary industries are much less dependent on resource location than they used to be. Raw materials can be transported to distant locations to be converted into manufactured products—if the resulting profits outweigh the costs. A large body of work in economic geography focuses on **location theory**, which attempts to predict where businesses will or should be located. Clearly this is a very important undertaking given the economic and social advantages that come from having industrial and service businesses located in an area. Urban centres compete to attract companies by offering serviced industrial parks and tax incentives. New companies can offer employment, which, in turn, provides labourers with a wage to spend in the local economy.

> **Location theory** A logical attempt to explain the locational pattern of an economic activity and the manner in which its producing areas are interrelated.

Any attempt to establish a model for the location of secondary industries runs into complications much greater than those confronting J. H. von Thünen (discussed in Chapter 9), who dealt only with primary industries. The location of secondary industries depends to a large extent on human behaviour and decision making; on cultural, political, and economic factors; and even on intuition or whim. Since models must be based on assumptions, geographers have to assume that decision makers are trying to maximize their advantages over competitors and that they want to make as much profit as possible. Decision makers should also take into account the **variable costs** of establishing a manufacturing enterprise in one location over another, such as energy supply, transport expenses, and labour costs.

> **Variable costs** Costs that change directly with the amount of production (e.g., energy supply and labour costs).

In making calculations that are designed to maximize advantages, a key issue is the **friction of distance**, which is defined as the increase in time and cost that usually comes with increasing distance. If a raw material has to be shipped hundreds of miles to a factory, rather than being manufactured right next door, the friction of distance increases. A corollary to the concept of the friction of distance is what geographers call **distance decay**, which assumes that the impact of a function or an activity will decline as one moves away from its point of origin. Distance decay suggests that manufacturing plants will be more concerned with serving the markets of nearby places than more distant places. This basic principle is important in efforts to understand the locational dynamics of a variety of phenomena, including manufacturing. In this section, we consider the location theories or models of Alfred Weber, whose work is prominent in examining the spatial organization of various industries and services at a variety of scales.

> **Friction of distance** The increase in time and cost that usually comes with increasing distance.
>
> **Distance decay** The effects of distance on interaction; generally the greater the distance the less interaction.

WEBER'S MODEL

The German economic geographer Alfred Weber (1868–1958) developed a basic model designed to predict the location of manufacturing plants within a region. Weber was thinking about why a manufacturing plant would pick one place over another to set up shop. He drew from the research of other economic geographers and began with a set of assumptions that enabled him to create his model. In *Theory of the Location of Industries* (1909), Weber calculated the "pulls" exerted on each point of manufacturing in his hypothetical region of analysis. Weber's **least cost theory** accounted for the location (P) of a manufacturing plant in terms of the desire to minimize three categories of costs (Figure 13.9).

> **Least cost theory** Model developed by Alfred Weber according to which the location of manufacturing establishments is determined by the minimization of three critical expenses: labour, transportation, and agglomeration.

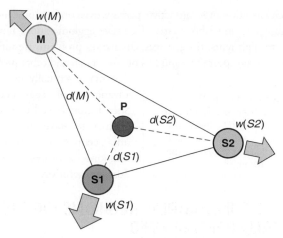

FIGURE 13.9 Weber's Theory of the Location of Industries. Weber's most significant point about transportation was that the site chosen (P) must entail the lowest possible cost of moving raw materials (w(S1) and w(S2)) to the factory and finished products (w(M)) to the market (M). The problem resides in finding an optimal factory location (P) located at the respective distances of d(M), d(S1), and d(S2). (Dr. Jean-Paul Rodrigue, Dept. of Global Studies & Geography, Hofstra University)

The first and most important of these categories was transportation: the site chosen must entail the lowest possible cost of moving raw materials to the factory and finished products to the market. For example, if we are making furniture, we will need to bring wood (lumber) to the factory. We will need other materials, such as screws, glue, paint, and varnish perhaps, although clearly wood is going to be our greatest cost. It could be very expensive to transport these raw materials to our factory if we are located some distance away from the source of wood. The second concern is where we sell our finished tables and chairs. If we have to ship these products great distances to furniture stores and shopping malls, we may not make any money (profit). Weber suggested that the site where transportation costs are lowest is the place where it would be least expensive to bring raw materials to the point of production and distribute finished products to consumers.

The second category of cost was labour. Higher labour costs reduce the margin of profit, so a factory might do better farther from raw materials and markets if cheap labour made up for the added transport costs. We might want to establish our furniture factory nearer to our raw materials and perhaps in an area with higher unemployment, ensuring we have an inexpensive labour pool to draw on.

The third factor in Weber's model was what he called **agglomeration**. When a substantial number of enterprises cluster in the same area, as happens in a large industrial city, they can provide assistance to each other through shared talents, services, and facilities. All manufacturers need office furniture and equipment; the presence of one or more producers in a large city satisfies this need for all. Thus, agglomeration makes a

> **Agglomeration** A process involving the clustering or concentrating of people or activities. The term often refers to manufacturing plants and businesses that benefit from close proximity because they share skilled-labour pools and technological and financial amenities.

big-city location more attractive, perhaps overcoming some increase in transport and labour costs. Excessive agglomeration, however, leads to high rents, rising wages, circulation problems (resulting in increased transport costs and loss of efficiency), and other problems that may eventually negate the advantages of agglomeration. Such factors have led many industries to leave the crowded urban centres and move to other locations—a process known as **deagglomeration**.

> **Deagglomeration** The process of industrial deconcentration in response to technological advances and/or increasing costs due to congestion and competition.

MAJOR INDUSTRIAL REGIONS OF THE WORLD BEFORE 1950

Considering Weber's model helps explain where industries might choose to locate and why. Before 1950, the main locational costs for industries were transportation of raw materials and shipping of finished products. Thus, the first manufacturing belts (i.e., regions of major manufacturing concentration) tended to be close to raw materials and accessible to transportation routes. Yet, at the global scale, several major areas that were sources of raw materials did not industrialize early. The map of major regional-industrial development before 1950 reveals that only a small minority of countries were major industrial economies. Many factors help explain this pattern, including relative location in relation to flows of goods and capital, political circumstances, economic leadership, labour costs, and levels of education and training. The four **primary industrial regions** that stand out on the world map are western and central Europe, eastern North America, Russia and Ukraine, and eastern Asia. Each of these regions consists of one or more core areas of industrial development with subsidiary clusters.

> **Primary industrial regions** Western and Central Europe; Eastern North America; Russia and Ukraine; and Eastern Asia, each of which consists of one or more core areas of industrial development with subsidiary clusters.

WESTERN AND CENTRAL EUROPE

The manufacturing regions of western Europe are largely the regions that experienced industrialization between the late 18th and early 20th centuries. From this region of Europe came the European Coal and Steel Community (ECSC), which initiated the experiment with the integration of Europe's principal coal deposits, lying in a belt across northern France, Belgium, north-central Germany, the northwestern Czech Republic, and southern Poland—and it was along this zone that industrialization expanded in mainland Europe (Figure 13.10). Colonial empires gave France, Britain, Belgium, and the Netherlands, and later Germany, access to the capital necessary to fuel industrialization and, in some cases, the raw materials necessary for production. Three manufacturing districts lay in Germany: the Ruhr, based on the Westphalian coalfield; the Saxony district, near the border of the former Czechoslovakia; and Silesia, now part of Poland. Even though these areas were seriously damaged in World War II, Germany still ranks among the world's leading producers of both coal and steel and remains Europe's leading industrial power (Table 13.2). By the early 20th century, industry began to diffuse far from the original European hearth to such places as northern Italy (now one of Europe's major industrial regions), Catalonia (anchored by Barcelona) and northern Spain, southern Sweden, and southern Finland.

THE MANUFACTURING BELTS OF GERMANY

The Ruhr, named after a small tributary of the Rhine River in Germany, became Europe's greatest industrial complex (Figure 13.11) because it had the combined advantages of high-quality resources, good accessibility, and proximity to large markets. It emerged as a key region during the Industrial Revolution with an industrial base in coal mines and steel mills. When local iron ore reserves became depleted, ores could be brought in from overseas. The Ruhr was already undergoing industrialization in the closing decades of the 19th century, and by the 1930s the river basin had become one of the most important industrial regions in the world,

TABLE 13.2	Top 10 Steel-Producing Countries				
Rank	Country	Percent of World Steel Production, 2010	2010 (Million metric tonnes)	2009 (Million metric tonnes)	Percent change from 2009 to 2010
1	China	44.3	626.7	573.6	9.3
2	Japan	7.8	109.6	87.5	25.2
3	United States	5.7	80.6	58.2	38.5
4	Russia	4.7	67.0	60.0	11.7
5	India	4.7	66.8	62.8	6.4
6	South Korea	4.1	58.5	48.6	20.3
7	Germany	3.1	43.8	32.7	34.1
8	Ukraine	2.4	33.6	29.9	12.4
9	Brazil	2.3	32.8	26.5	23.8
10	Turkey	2.1	29.0	25.3	14.6

World steel production reached 1,414-million metric tonnes in 2010. These leading steel-producing countries accounted for over 80 percent of the world's steel production in 2010. Data retrieved March 29, 2011, from World Steel Association website, http://www.worldsteel.org/?action=newsdetail&id=319.

FIGURE 13.10 Major Industrial Regions of Europe. Western and central Europe was one of the primary industrial regions before 1950, and the major industrial regions of Europe are shown here. (© E.H. Fouberg, A.B. Murphy, H.J. de Blij, and John Wiley & Sons, Inc.)

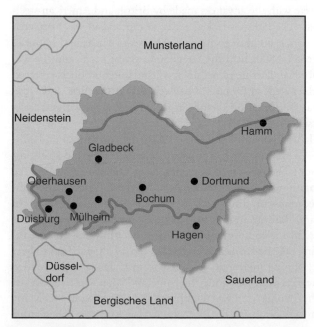

FIGURE 13.11 Ruhr District, Germany.

pouring forth the products of heavy industry, including tanks and other weapons for Hitler's armies.

Saxony (also in present-day Germany), on the other hand, was always oriented toward specialized lighter manufactures. Anchored by Leipzig and Dresden, it became known for such products as optical equipment and cameras, refined textiles, and ceramics. Farther east, the industrial district of Silesia was originally part of Germany but now lies in Poland and extends into the Czech Republic. The development of the Silesian district was based on high-quality coal resources and lesser iron ores that were later supplemented by imports from Ukraine.

The sophistication of European industry ensured that World War II would be the most destructive conflict ever fought, but the war ended up destroying much of the continent's industrial infrastructure in the process. This outcome created considerable challenges in the decade following the war, but from an industrial standpoint it was not altogether a minus. German industry had been reduced to rubble, but with Allied aid, new factories sprang up that incorporated the latest technology. In time, such factories had a competitive edge over older industrial establishments in North America and the parts of Europe that had been hit less hard by the war.

NORTH AMERICA

By the beginning of the 20th century, the only serious rival to Europe was North America, a realm heavily settled by Europeans with particularly close links to Britain, and with links to the capital and innovations that fuelled industrialization there. Manufacturing in North America began in New England as early as late colonial times, but the northeastern states are not especially rich in mineral resources.

Canada, as a colonial country, first developed its primary resources and a strong agrarian base. As the Canadian industrial economy developed in the late 19th century, much of the manufacturing was located in urban areas, contributing to the unique regional organization of the Canadian economy between its rural resource base and its urban manufacturing and service base (Figure 13.12). In the late 1800s, Canada's nascent manufacturing base was protected from foreign competition by a series of tariffs and duties. The policies favoured central Canada—more specifically, Ontario—and established the heartland-hinterland relationship between central Canada and the periphery. The Maritimes had difficulty sending raw materials to the central region due to the friction of distance. Construction of the Canadian Pacific Railway helped to overcome some of the problems and unite the country, but regional disparities continue to

FIGURE 13.12 Massey-Harris Company Farm Implements, Brantford, Ontario. In 1847, Daniel Massey purchased a foundry in Newcastle, Ontario, and opened the Newcastle Foundry and Machine Manufactory, CW. By 1870, with an expanding farm implement export business to Europe, Massey Manufacturing Company was established. In 1891 Massey merged with A. Harris, forming the largest company of its kind in the British Empire, opening plants in the U.S., France, Germany, and Australia. (Canada Science and Technology Museum)

this day. Ontario still has the largest labour force engaged in industrial and service sector employment.

Both Canada and the United States have benefited from the capacity of their companies to acquire needed raw materials from overseas sources. They did not need to go overseas for the raw materials to produce energy, however. Coal was the chief fuel for industries at the time, and there was never any threat of a coal shortage. North American coal reserves are among the world's largest and are widely distributed—from Appalachian Pennsylvania to the northwestern Great Plains through Alberta and Saskatchewan (Figure 13.13). North America still vies with China as the world's largest coal producer.

The steel plants along the northeastern seaboard of the United States were built there largely because they used iron ore shipped from Venezuela, Labrador (Canada), Liberia, and other overseas sources. Instead of transferring the iron ore from ocean-going ships onto trains and transporting it inland, the plants used it where it arrived—practically at the point of unloading at such huge steel-mill complexes as Sparrows Point, near Baltimore, and Fairless, near Philadelphia. So in this case, distant ore deposits affected the location of industry in the United States. In Canada, the majority of the steel fabrication facilities are located in the Saguenay region of Quebec, along the St. Lawrence River, and around the shores of Lake Erie and Lake Ontario (Figure 13.14). These locations provided easy access to transportation networks, including rail, highways, and the Great Lakes–St. Lawrence Seaway system, as well as access to energy production, industrial infrastructure, and raw materials.

Steel played a pivotal role in the emergence of Canada as a player in the global economy in the 1950s and 1960s. From the mid-1700s, Upper Canada relied on iron technology to provide the axes, ploughs, and other iron tools used in harvesting raw materials for export. Rapid technological innovations in smelting iron led to the production of steel between the 1850s and the 1890s. However, the Canadian iron industry was largely unable to compete with the advances made by British and American steelmakers. The industry lacked access to capital and was hampered by the long distance to market. A series of tariffs and bounties in the late 1800s held the fragile industry in place, and the secondary manufacture of nails, screws, and other products emerged in urban areas in Ontario, Quebec, New Brunswick, and Nova Scotia. The Ontario steel industry remained fragile without easily accessible iron ore.

It was not until the early 1900s that provincial and municipal governments began promoting local iron and steel production. The provincial government of Ontario sponsored the exploration of the vast resources of northern Ontario and subsidized transportation, such as the Temiskaming and Northern Ontario Railway, to link the resources to the southern communities. By the end of the 1800s, investment in infrastructure including rail and roads and extraction technologies began to bear fruit. Mining increased, scattered from Calabogie and Madoc in the east to mines along the Seine and Matawin rivers in the north. Algoma Steel was established in 1901 in Sault Ste. Marie to process ore from northern mines, such as the Helen mine

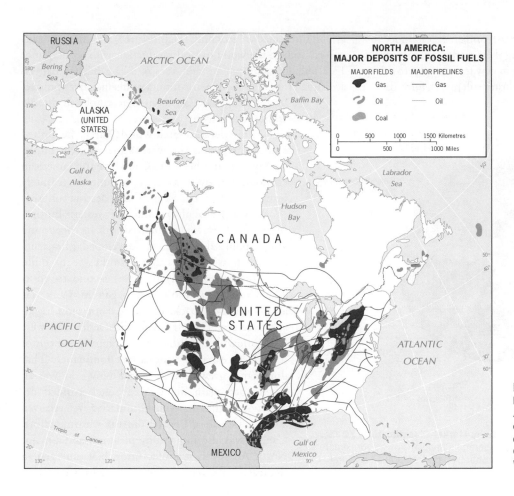

FIGURE 13.13 **Major Deposits of Fossil Fuels in North America.** North America is the world's largest energy consumer, and the realm is also endowed with substantial energy sources. © H.J. de Blij, P.O. Muller, and John Wiley & Sons, Inc.

near Boyer Lake. Much of central Canada's iron and steel industry continued to struggle well into the 20th century despite government intervention and financial support at all levels.

FIGURE 13.14 **Steel Mills, Hamilton Ontario.** The landscape of Hamilton Harbour/Burlington Bay is replete with an array of steel fabrication facilities, including U. S. Steel Canada and Dofasco. (Frank Gunn/The Canadian Press)

By World War II, fortunes in the industry began to change. The pressure of wartime production prompted a restructuring of the iron and steel industry, and the federal government introduced a new set of regulatory frameworks addressing labour, production, distribution, and profits that survived the end of the war and into peace. Post-war prosperity and reconstruction contributed to the growing health of the industry and its competitiveness on the global stage.

The 1970s marked a shift in the steel industry in both Canada and the United States. Several factors precipitated these changes. After an industry-wide strike in 1946, the United Steel Workers of America successfully established a union presence in major mills, thus ending decades of 12-hour workdays and seven-day workweeks under harsh conditions for low pay. Unions established better working conditions for steelworkers, higher pay, and stability. While Dofasco in Hamilton, Ontario, resisted unionization, it nevertheless matched the wages and benefits won by, and paid to, unionized employees at other mills. In the 1970s, competition from low-wage foreign producers began to pose a serious threat to the local industry. Technological innovations and specialized "mini-mills" also led to the shrinking of large mill market share. Moreover, the economic downturn in the 1980s, and the signing of the North American Free Trade Agreement (NAFTA) in 1994, led to more uncertainty in the industry. Through the 1980s and 1990s, companies responded to these pressures by drastically reducing their workforce, introducing flexible work plans, and investing in new technologies to drive industrial change. Today, the steel industry still plays a formidable

role in the Canadian economy (Figure 13.15). In 2010, Canada ranked 16th in the world in steel production with an output of 13.0 million metric tonnes and sales of $13.5 billion. Exports accounted for 6.8 million metric tonnes of the industry's production and 25,000 Canadians were employed directly within the industry.

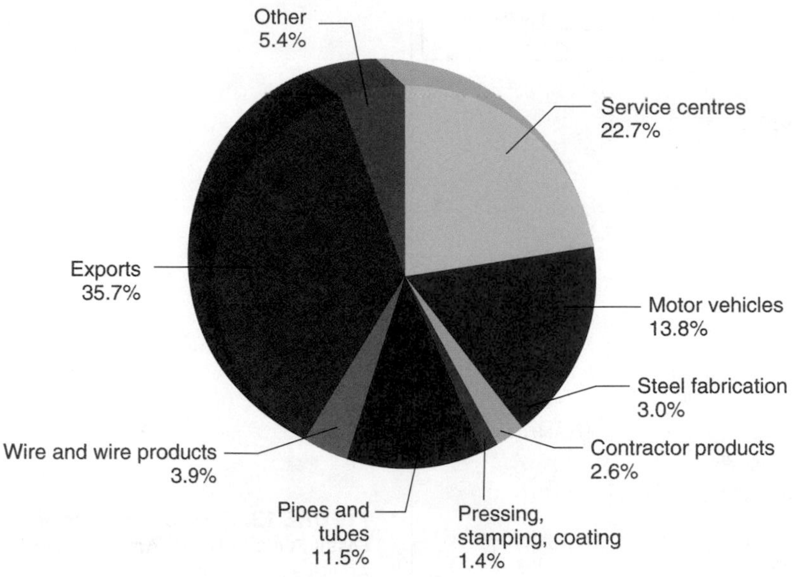

In the decades after World War I, the United States emerged as the world's pre-eminent industrial power, and both the Canadian and American economies thrived as they became increasingly integrated. Having escaped the destruction that World War I brought to much of western Europe, the United States capitalized on its newfound global political stature, its developed infrastructure, and its highly trained workforce to build an industrial economy that was second to none. The Great Depression that began in 1929 was an enormous setback, of course, but only in absolute terms. The effects of the Depression were felt worldwide, and the United States came out of it with an expanded industrial dominance. That dominance grew even greater after World War II, when once again the United States avoided destruction within its own boundaries, yet received a major industrial boost from the wartime effort. Canada was also in a strong position, and a major North American manufacturing belt emerged in the rectangular region shown in Figure 13.16.

FIGURE 13.15 Canadian Steel Shipments by Market Classification, 2010. A variety of products use Canadian steel. On average, Canadians own approximately 1,000 kilograms of steel in a wide array of products. Data from Canadian Steel Producers Association and Statistics Canada.

Pie chart data:
- Other 5.4%
- Service centres 22.7%
- Motor vehicles 13.8%
- Steel fabrication 3.0%
- Contractor products 2.6%
- Pressing, stamping, coating 1.4%
- Pipes and tubes 11.5%
- Wire and wire products 3.9%
- Exports 35.7%

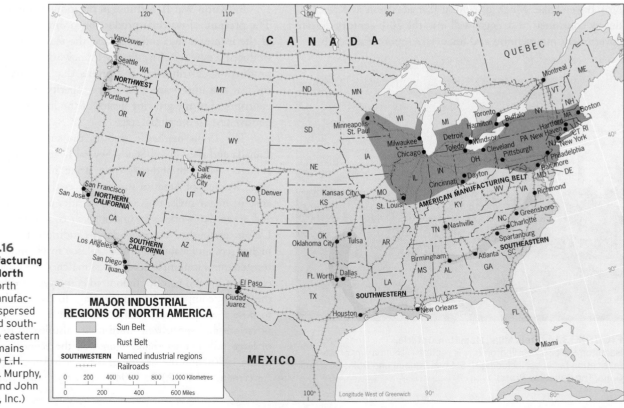

FIGURE 13.16 Major Manufacturing Regions of North America. North American manufacturing has dispersed westward and southward, but the eastern core area remains dominant. (© E.H. Fouberg, A.B. Murphy, H.J. de Blij, and John Wiley & Sons, Inc.)

MAJOR INDUSTRIAL REGIONS OF NORTH AMERICA
- Sun Belt
- Rust Belt
- SOUTHWESTERN Named industrial regions
- Railroads

FIGURE 13.17 Bethlehem Steel, Bethlehem, Pennsylvania. The "Urban Ruins" project of photographer Shaun O'Boyle illustrates the marks left on the North American landscape. Bethlehem Steel, in operation for over 140 years, closed its doors in 1995. Now a "modern ruin," the buildings are a haunting reminder not only of the size, scale, and significance of industrial development, but also of its impact on the environment and landscape. (© Shaun O'Boyle)

The North American Manufacturing Belt. The North American Manufacturing Belt extends from the northeastern seaboard to Iowa and from the St. Lawrence Valley and southern Ontario to the confluence of the Ohio and Mississippi rivers. At the belt's northeastern edge, the light industries of southern Ontario and Quebec and New England and New York give way to heavier manufacturing in the southeast Pennsylvania district (Figure 13.17), centred on metropolitan Philadelphia and encompassing the Baltimore area. Throughout much of the 20th century, iron ores were smelted right on the waterfront in tidewater steel mills. Major chemical industries (notably in northern Delaware), pharmaceutical industries, and lighter manufacturing plants were established there as well.

As part of the North American manufacturing belt, Lambton County, which includes the city of Sarnia, Ontario, its surrounding district, and the adjacent Aamjiwnaang First Nation reserve, has become known as "Chemical Valley" (Figure 13.18). Oil was discovered in the region in the mid-1850s, and when World War II led to the disruption of natural rubber supplies, Sarnia was selected by the Government of Canada to be the site of the development of synthetic, petroleum-based rubbers. Dow Chemical built the Polymer Corporation, a Canadian Crown corporation, in 1942. Polymer was privatized in 1988 and became one of the many chemical plants located in the region. In total, Lambton County is home to a large petrochemical and chemical complex that composes 40 percent of Canada's total chemical industry. There are 62 industrial facilities within a 25-kilometre radius, including oil refineries (e.g., Shell Oil, Imperial Oil, Suncor Energy) and chemical plants (e.g., Nova Chemicals, Bayer, Royal Group). Chemical Valley has been under criticism since the mid-1980s for the environmental effects of heavy industrialization, including a strange

blob at the bottom of the St. Clair River. The "blob," discovered in 1985, was the size of a basketball court and turned out to contain at least 18 hazardous wastes, including dioxins and perchloroethylene. Dow Chemical was fined $16,000 for the blob. According to EcoJustice Canada, Lambton County raises serious concerns about greenhouse gas emissions; air contaminants associated with acid rain, smog, and respiratory diseases; and toxic pollutants associated with environmental contamination and reproductive disorders.

Industrialization began early in New York, which today is at the heart of the American megalopolis and home to tens of thousands of industrial establishments. An early start, large urban growth, and agglomeration played roles in this development. The New York area is not especially endowed with mineral resources, but, like Paris and London, it is a large market. It also has a huge skilled and semi-skilled labour force, is the focus of an intensive transportation network, and has long been one of the world's great ports. Farther west lies the well-defined upstate New York district, extending from Albany, on the Hudson River, to Buffalo, on the shore of Lake Erie. Growth there was originally stimulated by the Erie Canal, which was dug in the early 19th century to connect the East Coast to the Great Lakes. During the mid-20th century, specialty manufacturers developed in this region. Rochester came to be known for cameras and optical products, Schenectady for electrical appliances, and Buffalo for steel.

Canada's southern Ontario district extends from the western end of Lake Ontario to the industrial zone at the western end of Lake Erie. This district links two parts of the U.S. manufacturing belt anchored by Buffalo and Detroit; the most direct route between these two industrial cities is through Ontario (Figure 13.16). Canadian and U.S. manufacturing complexes meet in two great horseshoe-shaped zones around the western ends of Lakes Ontario and Erie. In the northeast is a horseshoe-shaped cluster of industries, which curls from Oshawa through Toronto and Hamilton to Buffalo. Westward, around the western end of Lake Erie, is another horseshoe-shaped cluster of industries, which extends from Windsor in Ontario through Detroit and Toledo to Cleveland. The first of these zones is mainly Canadian, and the second is largely American. The

FIGURE 13.18 Chemical Valley, Sarnia Ontario. (© imac/Alamy)

Montreal area along the upper St. Lawrence River also forms part of the Canadian industrial zone. This area is no match for the Ontario district, but it has one big advantage: cheap hydroelectric power. Aluminum-refining and papermaking industries are located there.

Westward lies the remainder of the U.S. industrial heartland, comprising the interior industrial district, with such nodes as the Pittsburgh–Cleveland area, the Detroit–southeast Michigan area, Chicago–Gary–Milwaukee, and smaller areas centred on Minneapolis, St. Louis, and Cincinnati. Here, industrial power truly transformed the landscape during the 20th century as Appalachian coal and Mesabi iron ore (from Minnesota) were converted into autos, bulldozers, harvesters, armoured cars, and tanks.

THE FORMER SOVIET UNION

The Soviet effort to industrialize focused on manufacturing in the western part of Russia, the region of the Soviet Union that was the base of the Russian culture and the location of the country's capital, Moscow. In Moscow, the city and its surrounding area offered an important local market, converging transport routes, a large labour force, and strong centrality—just like Paris, London, and New York. Light manufacturing could already be found in this district during Tsarist times, but under communist rule heavy industries were added. One of the most famous automobile manufacturers in Russia is Lada (Figure 13.19), and its cars, manufactured since 1970, can be found on every continent on Earth. The success of Lada, whose exports totalled 60 percent of total sales, helped bring much-needed capital to the cash-strapped Soviet Union in the 1980s, in spite of its sometimes suspect reputation. Renault purchased a 25 percent stake in Lada in 2008, and Lada continues to be a prominent manufacturer in Russia.

FIGURE 13.19 The Lada. The Russian Lada 2107, known as the "Classic," was a staple of the Russian economy and a common sight in urban centres around the world from the 1970s through to the 1990s. While other model lines were introduced, the Classic remained relatively unchanged for over 40 years. In July 2011, the manufacturer announced that it would cease production of the iconic vehicle. (© Peter Forsberg/Alamy)

The Soviet Union had an enormous expanse of resources and raw materials within its borders. East of Moscow, the Ural Mountains yield an incredible variety of metallic ores, including iron, copper, nickel, chromite, and bauxite. In the first decades of the 1900s, Russia tapped a large supply of coal and iron ore in Siberia. The country's eastern region afforded a great deal of resources and raw materials for the industrialization of Russia's west. Between the Kuzbas and Lake Baykal lies the Krasnoyarsk–Baykal Corridors. Served by the Trans-Siberian Railroad and several important rivers, this 1,600-kilometre-long region contains impressive resources, including coal, timber, and water (Figure 13.20).

The St. Petersburg area is one of Russia's oldest manufacturing centres. Tsar Peter the Great chose it to serve not only as Russia's capital but also as the country's modern industrial focus. The skills and specializations that Peter the Great nurtured, with the help of western European artisans, still mark the area's key industries: high-quality machine building, optical products, and medical equipment. Industries such as shipbuilding, chemical production, food processing, and textile making were also located there.

The Volga experienced major development beginning in the mid-1930s, when the combination of accessible raw materials and ease of transport facilitated its development. When the Ukraine and Moscow areas were threatened by the German armies in World War II, whole industrial plants were dismantled and reassembled in Volga cities—protected from the war by distance. Samara (formerly Kuibyshev) even served as the Soviet capital for a time during World War II. This was part of a more general eastward shift of industry that occurred during the war, when Russia was invaded from the west.

After the war, the industrialization program continued. A series of dams on the Volga River made electrical power plentiful. Known oil and natural gas reserves were larger there than anywhere else in the former USSR. Canals linked the Volga to both Moscow and the Don River, making it easy to import raw materials. The cities lining the Volga, spaced at remarkably regular intervals, were assigned particular industrial functions in the state-planned economy of the Soviet Union. Samara became an oil refinery centre, Saratov acquired a chemical industry, and Volgograd became known for its metallurgical industries. The Volga was set on a course that has allowed it to remain one of Russia's dominant industrial regions to this day.

EASTERN ASIA

Japan and China were the most significant areas of eastern Asia that avoided direct European colonization—and these are the Asian countries where large-scale industrialization first took root (Figure 13.21). Of the two, Japan was clearly the early dominant player. Less than a century after the beginning of the Industrial Revolution, Japan became one of the world's leading industrial countries. This accomplishment is all the more remarkable when one realizes that Japan has limited natural resources. Much of what Japan manufactures is made from raw materials imported from all over the world. Its transformation into the world's second-largest economy has often been described as a miracle.

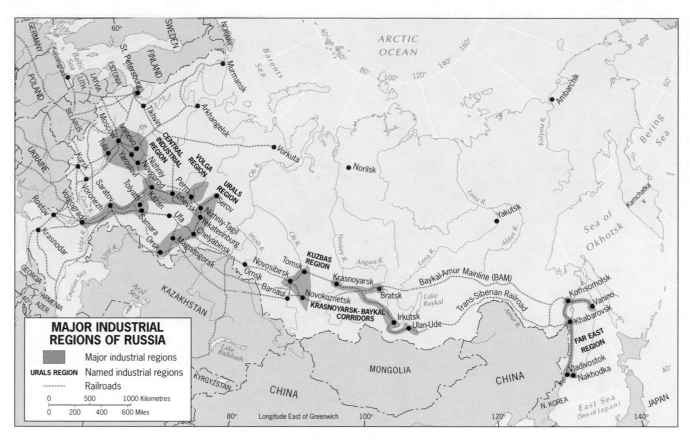

FIGURE 13.20 Major Manufacturing Regions of Russia. The major manufacturing regions of Russia reflect the dominance of the west in the country's economic geography. (© H.J. de Blij, P.O. Muller, and John Wiley & Sons, Inc.)

Yet Japan's economic development was not a miracle. The country's modern economy was built on capital from colonization and on government policies that had the specific goal of industrialization. Its economic development began during the second half of the 19th century, when it embarked on a campaign of industrialization and colonization. Between 1866 and 1869, under the banner of the Meiji Restoration, reformers mechanized Japan's domestic industries, moved the capital from the interior to the coast, organized its armed forces, and obtained advice from British experts on issues ranging from education to transportation (which is why the Japanese drive on the left side of the road). The Japanese also established colonies, and soon raw materials and capital were flowing to Japan from an expanding colonial empire in Korea, Taiwan, and mainland China.

The 1930s and early 1940s brought triumph and disaster—triumph in the form of a military campaign that included vast conquests in the Pacific, East Asia, and Southeast Asia and a surprise attack on Pearl Harbor in Hawaii, and disaster when Japanese forces were driven back with great loss of life. The war ended with the utter destruction of two Japanese cities, Hiroshima and Nagasaki, by American atomic bombs. When U.S. forces took control of Japan in 1945, the nation's economy was in shambles. Yet a few decades later Japan had not only recovered but had become a global economic power.

The Japanese Manufacturing Belt. Japan's dominant region of industrialization and urbanization is the Kanto Plain (see Figure 13.21), which contains about one-third of the nation's population and includes the Tokyo–Yokohama–Kawasaki metropolitan area. The Kanto Plain possesses a fine natural harbour at Yokohama and is centrally located with respect to the country as a whole. It has also benefited from Tokyo's designation as the country's capital. When Japan embarked on its planned course of economic development, many industries and businesses chose Tokyo as their headquarters in order to be near government decision makers. During the mid-20th century, the Tokyo–Yokohama–Kawasaki metropolitan area became Japan's leading manufacturing complex, producing more than 20 percent of the country's annual output.

Japan's second-largest industrial complex extends from the eastern end of the Seto Inland Sea, Japan's pivotal waterway, to the Nagoya area and includes the Kobe–Kyoto–Osaka triangle. This, the Kansai district, comes close to rivalling the Kanto area: it is a vast industrial region with steel mills, a major chemical industry, automobile manufacturing, shipbuilding, textile factories, and many other types of production.

Even after Japan lost its colonial empire with the end of World War II, its industries continued to be sustained by a large, highly skilled labour force (which, before recent wage increases, was relatively cheap). Japanese products dominated

FIGURE 13.21 Major Manufacturing Regions of East Asia. In China, the northeast district was the first to take off. The Chang district followed, and most recently the Guangdong district has been growing. (© E.H. Fouberg, A.B. Murphy, H.J. de Blij, and John Wiley & Sons, Inc.)

markets around the world and allowed Japanese industries to purchase needed raw materials virtually anywhere. Australia, for example, became one of Japan's leading suppliers. The availability of cheap semi-skilled labour has had an immense impact on regional industrial development. Even in an era of automated assembly lines and computerized processing, the prospect of a large, low-wage, trainable labour force continues to attract manufacturers. Japan's postwar success was based in large measure on the skills and the low wages of its labour force, which allowed manufacturers to flood foreign markets with low-priced goods. Into the 1950s, Japanese goods had

little reputation for quality but were known for their afford-ability. However, Japan's factories then began to excel in quality as well. This development in turn led to higher prices, higher wages, and, inevitably, competition from countries where cheaper labour could be found.

EASTERN CHINA

Although some industrial growth occurred in China during the period of European colonial influence, and later during the Japanese occupation, China's major industrial expansion occurred during the communist period. When the communist

FIGURE 13.22 Chang Jiang District, China. A major industrial belt grew along the Chang Jiang (Yangtze) River, from the Chang Jiang district and Shanghai to Chongquing. Adapted from *The World Factbook 2009.* Washington, DC: Central Intelligence Agency, 2009.

planners took over in 1949, one of their first priorities was to develop China's resources and industries as rapidly as possible. China is a vast country and has a substantial resource base. The quality of its coal is good, the quantity enormous, and many of the deposits are near the surface and easily extracted. China's iron ores are not as productive and are generally of rather low grade, but new finds are regularly being made.

Until the early 1960s, Soviet planners helped promote China's communist-era industrial development. China was spatially constrained by the location of raw materials, the developments that had taken place before the 1949 communist takeover, the pattern of long-term urbanization in the country, the existing transportation network, and the eastern clustering of the population. In a manner similar to their erstwhile Soviet allies, China's rulers were determined to speed up the industrialization of the economy, and their decisions created several major and lesser industrial districts.

Under state-planning rules, the Northeast district (formerly known as Manchuria and called Dongbei in China today) became China's industrial heartland, a complex of heavy industries based on the region's coal and iron deposits located in the basin of the Liao River. Shenyang became the "Chinese Pittsburgh," with metallurgical, machine-making, engineering, and other large factories. Anshan, to the south, emerged as China's leading iron- and steel-producing centre. Harbin, China's northernmost large city, with more than 5.4 million inhabitants, produced textiles, farm equipment, and other light manufacturing of many kinds.

The second-largest industrial region in China, the Shanghai and Chang Jiang district, developed in and around the country's biggest city, Shanghai. The communist planners never allowed Shanghai to attain its full potential, often favouring the Beijing–Tianjin complex, but the Chang Jiang district, containing both Shanghai and Wuhan, rose to prominence and, by some measures, exceeded the Northeast as a contributor to the national economy. As Figure 13.22 shows, still another industrial complex developed farther upstream along the Chang Jiang (Yangtze) River, focused on the city of Chongqing. Whether we view the Chang Jiang district as one industrial zone or

more, it became a pacesetter for Chinese industrial growth, if not in terms of iron and steel production, then in terms of its diversified production and local specializations. Railroad cars, ships, books, foods, chemicals—an endless variety of products—come from the thriving Chang Jiang district.

China's enormous labour force and the country's low daily wage have persuaded thousands of companies to move their manufacturing to China, although rather than move the entire company, most typically shift production of component parts to China to lower the cost of the product (Figure 13.23). Thousands of companies take advantage of the lower wages and favourable tax regulations, which have transformed cities and towns in the region.

At the same time, the Northeast has become China's rust belt. Many of its state-run factories have been sold or closed, or are operating below capacity. Unemployment is high, and economic growth has stopped. Eventually, the Northeast is likely to recover because of its resources and its favourable geographic site. But under the new economic policies the dynamic eastern and southern provinces have grown into major manufacturing belts and have changed the map of this part of the Pacific Rim.

FIGURE 13.23 An Employee Works on Circuit Boards at an Electronic Component Factory in Hefei, Anhui province, China. (Jianan Yu/Reuters/Landov)

MAIN POINTS   **13.3**   How Do Location Theories Explain Historical Patterns of Industrialization?

- Location theories, such as those put forward by Weber, attempt to explain the spatial organization of economic activities and the various factors influencing locational choices, such as transportation and labour costs, distance to market, and access to raw materials.

- Canadian manufacturing was initially a protected industrial base located in southern Ontario although distinctly regional variations are evident in the organization of Canada's urban structure. Canadian manufacturing and industrial development is interwoven with the United States in a North American manufacturing belt that runs up the eastern seaboard of the United States and Canada. A variety of industries, from steel to chemicals and appliances to cars, make up this manufacturing belt.

- Prior to 1950, the major locational costs were those associated with transportation of raw materials and shipping goods to market. The four primary industrial regions—western and central Europe, eastern North America, Russia, and eastern Asia—reflect decisions related to these costs as well as the particular social, political, and historical circumstances of each region.

- The manufacturing regions of western Europe are largely the regions that experienced industrialization between the late 18th and early 20th centuries.

- Manufacturing and industrialization in eastern North America is grounded in the region's role as a colonial producer of raw materials for export to the "home" country. Urban patterns and transportation systems reflect this initial responsibility.

- In Russia, industrialization focused on manufacturing in the western part of Russia because this was home to the country's capital, Moscow. That city and its surrounding area offered an important local market, converging transport routes, a large labour force, and strong centrality.

- In eastern Asia, industrialization took root most strongly in Japan and China. While Japan is considered the dominant country in terms of industrialization, with its strong manufacturing belt and industrial development policies, China has also developed a strong industrial base since the communist party took power in 1949.

13.4 What Are the Spatial Implications of Changes In Industrial Production?

After World War II and the boom times of the 1950s, industrial production was restructured on both the local and global scale. Today, the world's major industrial regions still bear the marks of the transportation and communications technologies and skilled labour forces that were in place at that time. When methods of production change (become more efficient) or transportation improves (e.g., shift from water to rail), industries are able to make different locational choices, such as the growth of *maquiladora* or branch plant operations along the Mexican border with the United States. This means that companies such as General Motors, Fisher Price, and Acer Peripherals can take advantage of lower labour costs, fewer environmental regulations, and lower taxes and import–export duties.

The manufacturing boom of the 20th century can be traced to early innovations in the production process. Perhaps the most significant of these innovations was the mass-production assembly line pioneered by Henry Ford, which allowed for the inexpensive production of consumer goods at a single site on a previously unknown scale (Figure 13.24). So significant was Ford's philosophy that the dominant mode of mass production that endured for much of the past century is known as **Fordist**.

Economic geographers also see the Fordist system as including a set of political-economic structures. By this we mean

FIGURE 13.24 Ford Model Ts Ready for Delivery. Henry Ford's assembly line system took hold worldwide and symbolizes the era of mass production. Ford became well known for his production and marketing techniques, as well as for his belief that workers should be paid enough to be able to afford the products they make. (© Bettman/Corbis)

that the government ensures that the laws governing commercial enterprise support the economic system, and the structure of the financial system supports mass production by corporations. For example, the Bretton Woods agreement, put in place as part

> **Fordist** A highly organized and specialized system for organizing industrial production and labour. Named after automobile producer Henry Ford, Fordist production features assembly-line production of standardized components for mass production.

Post-Fordist World economic system characterized by a more flexible set of production practices in which goods are not mass-produced; instead, production has been accelerated and dispersed around the globe by multinational companies that shift production, outsourcing it around the world and bringing places closer together in time and space than would have been imaginable at the beginning of the 20th century.

of the rebuilding effort after World War II, saw core countries adopt the gold standard and agree to peg the values of their currency to gold. This ensured these countries were working within the same monetary and financial systems, which supported their economic development and stability.

Given the rapid changes brought about by the processes of globalization (see Chapter 3), the world economy has transitioned to what most economists and others call a **post-Fordist** system. Under the Fordist system, goods were mass-produced in one place. Raw materials were brought to the factory and the "good" (be it a car, television, or refrigerator) was assembled there. Post-Fordist processes are more flexible: the components of goods are made in different places around the globe and then brought together at different sites as needed to meet local market demand.

Multinational companies play a major role in this system and are in a position to shift production to new sites when a given production site becomes uncompetitive. Post-Fordist production brings places closer together in time and space than would have been imaginable at the beginning of the 20th century.

Geographically, the easiest way to comprehend the dramatic changes in the way we think about time and space in the global economy is through the concept of time-space compression, which suggests that some places in the world are more connected through communication and transportation technologies than ever before (see Chapter 2). Fluctuations in the Tokyo stock market affect New York just hours, if not minutes, later. Overnight, marketing campaigns can turn a product innovation into a fad in far-flung corners of the globe. Kiwi fruit picked in New Zealand yesterday can be in the lunch boxes of boys and girls in Canada tomorrow. And decisions made in London can make or break a fast-developing deal over a transport link between Kenya and Tanzania.

Time-space compression has fundamentally altered the division of labour. When the world was less interconnected, most goods were produced close to the point of consumption. Thus, the major industrial belt in the United States was in the northeast, because coal and other raw materials were readily available there, and also because of the major concentration of the North American population in that region. Now, due to improved transportation and communications technologies, **just-in-time delivery** allows companies to keep just what they need for short-term production, and additional parts are shipped quickly when

Just-in-time delivery Method of inventory management made possible by efficient transportation and communication systems, whereby companies keep on hand just what they need for near-term production, planning that what they need for longer-term production will arrive when needed.

needed. The company no longer has to maintain a large inventory of components or products on site. Corporations can draw from labour around the globe for different components of production, creating a **global division of labour**.

The major global economic players, such as General Motors, Philips, Union Carbide, and Exxon, take advantage of low transportation costs, favourable governmental regulations, and expanding information technology to construct vast economic networks in which different facets of production are carried out in different places, allowing the company to benefit from the advantages of specific locations. This is substantially different from the spatial and structural organization of industries that located near their raw materials and their market and produced all components of the product in one place. Publicly traded companies (companies whose stock you can buy or sell on the stock exchange) are pressured by shareholders to grow their profits annually. One way to grow profits is to cut costs, and labour (i.e., wages, benefits, insurance) makes up a sizable proportion of production costs. As we saw in the opening field note, multinational corporations such as Nike have moved the labour-intensive manufacturing aspects of their business, particularly assembly activities, to countries in the periphery, where labour is relatively inexpensive, regulations are few, and tax rates are low. The manufacturing that remains in the core is usually highly mechanized. Technologically sophisticated manufacturing also tends to be sited in the core, which has both the skilled labour supply and the supporting infrastructure. Research and development activities tend to be concentrated in the core, where high levels of education and access to technology are the norm.

The global division of labour has reshaped the role different economic sectors play within countries. With mechanized, highly efficient agriculture (see Chapter 9) and with the move of manufacturing jobs to the semi-periphery and periphery, core countries now have large labour forces employed in the tertiary sector of the economy. Supporting the global division of labour are elaborate trading networks and financial relations. Trade itself is a tertiary economic activity of considerable importance to the global economy. Regardless of where goods and their components are produced, consumption still takes place in the core and, increasingly, among the wealthy and middle classes of the semi-periphery. The newly industrializing countries of the semi-periphery send manufactured goods to the core (thus the "made in China" labels found on goods throughout North America). Trade flows among countries in the periphery are typically low because, for peripheral countries, the profitable flow is to the core. As the *Guest Field Note* by Heather Maguire suggests, companies that were not able or did not wish to shift their operational organization in light of changing global forces, often were forced out of business, which was the case for Canada's Clairtone Sound Corporation.

Global division of labour Phenomenon whereby corporations and others can draw from labour markets around the world, made possible by the compression of time and space through innovation in communication and transportation systems.

GUEST FIELD NOTE
Clairtone Sound Corporation

Walking through the Design Exchange exhibit in Toronto in 2008, I came face to face with one of Canada's most successful, yet almost entirely forgotten, consumer electronics manufacturers. Clairtone Sound Corporation, founded in 1958 by Peter Munk and David Gilmour, was a Canadian-based manufacturer of consumer electronics, well known for innovative design and high quality. Munk's background in electronics and Gilmour's background in design led to the development of stereo consoles that reflected a European sensibility—Scandinavian-style teak and walnut consoles combined with high-quality sound equipment. Its award-winning design, Project G (Figure 13.25), attained international critical praise and became famous for its globe speakers and sleek image. Project G was also a Hollywood sensation, featured in such films as *The Graduate* and *Marriage on the Rocks*. Frank Sinatra and Hugh Hefner both owned a Clairtone. Oscar Peterson stated that his music sounded as good on a Clairtone as it did in a concert hall. Globally respected, Clairtone quickly became a sign of the times: sleek, modern, sophisticated. In 1966, sales topped $15 million, Clairtone employed nearly 1,000 people, and operations had moved from Toronto to a new plant in Stellarton, Nova Scotia, which produced both stereo units and televisions. The next year, Munk and Gilmour lost

FIGURE 13.25 Clairtone Sound Corporation's Project G.
(clairtone.ca/photo DC Hillier)

control of Clairtone, pushed out by Industrial Estates Limited, an economic development agency of the government of Nova Scotia. Within three years, Clairtone had effectively collapsed, and in 1971, the government of Nova Scotia permanently closed the doors of Clairtone and liquidated the assets. While there are myriad political and economic circumstances that led to the demise of Clairtone, central to its struggle was its Made-in-Canada approach. While other manufacturers of consumer electronics, such as RCA, were by the mid-1960s seeking cheaper offshore manufacturing sites, Clairtone remained steadfast in its Canadian manufacturing philosophy.

Heather Maguire, York University

NEW INFLUENCES ON THE GEOGRAPHY OF MANUFACTURING

Over the last 30 years or so, new influences have been at work reshaping the locational choices of industries and manufacturing. All multinational companies (whether they produce televisions or anything else) are involved in designing products and finding buyers for the products. Many multinationals hire out the other steps in manufacturing, including extraction of raw materials, manufacturing, marketing, and distribution, to outside companies or subsidiaries. In the post-Fordist era, the major influences on industrial location include the low wages we have already discussed, intermodal transportation, regional and world trade agreements, and availability of energy.

IMPORTANCE OF TRANSPORTATION IN INDUSTRIAL LOCATION

One factor we can map is transportation. Efficient transportation systems allow manufacturers to purchase raw materials from distant sources and distribute finished products to a widely dispersed population of consumers. Manufacturers desire maximum transport effectiveness at the lowest possible cost. They will also consider the availability of alternative systems in the event of emergencies (e.g., truck routes when rail service is interrupted).

Since World War II, major developments in transportation have focused on improving **intermodal connections**, places where two or more modes of transportation (including air, road, rail, barge, and ship) meet, in order to ease the flow of goods and reduce the costs of transportation (see Chapter 12).

> **Intermodal connections**
> Places where two or more modes of transportation meet (including air, road, rail, barge, and ship).

The current volume of resources and goods shipped around the globe daily could not be supported without the invention of the container system, in which goods are packed in containers that are picked up by special mechanized cranes from a container ship at an intermodal connection and placed on the back of a semi-trailer truck, on a barge, or on a railroad car. This innovation lowered costs and increased flexibility, permitting many manufacturers to pay less attention to transportation in their location decisions. Refrigerated containers also facilitate the shipment of perishable goods around the globe.

In Canada, one of the most significant systems of transportation that is vital to industrial endeavours is the Great Lakes–St. Lawrence Seaway system (Figure 13.26). The history of this system dates back thousands of years, to First Nations trading routes. Spanning over 3,700 kilometres, Hwy H$_2$O, as it is known, comprises the St. Lawrence Seaway, the St. Lawrence

FIGURE 13.26 A westbound ship goes through the St-Lambert Lock, with the city of Montreal in the background. This lock is the gateway to the Great Lakes St. Lawrence Seaway. (Copyright Air Photo Max Aerial Photography, www.airphotomax.com)

River, and the Great Lakes and is a vital link between international shipping routes and the U.S. and Canadian industrial and agricultural heartlands, reaching approximately 25 percent of both countries' populations. The St. Lawrence Seaway opened in 1959 and moves such products as iron ore, coke, grain, coal, aggregate, and various chemicals, to name but a few. The efficiency of the system cannot be understated. One cargo ship can carry as much as 870 tractor-trailers and requires about 10 to 20 percent of the energy that trucks require.

IMPORTANCE OF REGIONAL AND GLOBAL TRADE AGREEMENTS

The world economic structure and regional and national markets are affected by the movement of goods, services, labour, and money, which could not occur without the negotiation of trade agreements. In the years immediately following World War II, for example, many countries entered into the General Agreement on Tariffs and Trade (GATT), which worked to reduce barriers to trade, starting in 1947. This liberalized the world economy and allowed for the free flow of goods among signatories. Regional trade agreements, such as NAFTA, influence where imported goods (and components of goods) are produced and sold.

In Canada, the Auto Pact, which the country signed with the United States in 1965, served to create a North American market for cars and trucks. At the time, the three major automobile companies had branch plants in Canada where they manufactured automobiles for the Canadian market. The Auto Pact allowed these companies to create a North American market and to compete more effectively with foreign producers. While the Auto Pact came to an end in 2001, it marked the beginning of the integration of the Canadian and American automobile markets. As Figure 13.27 shows, we can understand the development of the automobile manufacturing industry in North America in terms of three distinct periods. The first period, pre-1950, saw the establishment of the Big 3 automakers—Ford, General Motors, and Chrysler—in the U.S. In the second period, from 1950 to 1989, the U.S. auto industry expanded into Canada and Mexico. The third period, from 1990 to 2006, saw the adoption of NAFTA, the extension of *maquiladora* manufacturing in Mexico, and the development of a globalized "corridor" running from north to south. Since 2006, we have witnessed the collapse and subsequent rebuilding of the North American automobile industry. Cities such as Detroit, once famous for its economic power and home to the major auto manufacturers in North America, are now being recast as part of the rust belt of America (Figure 13.28). Windsor, Ontario, known as the Automotive Capital of Canada, has been one of the hardest hit Canadian cities. In 2010, GM closed its last manufacturing plant in Windsor, thereby ending a 90-year relationship between Windsor and Detroit.

With the Free Trade Agreement of 1988, Canada and the United States agreed to develop an integrated North American economy. This agreement was replaced by NAFTA in 1994, which incorporated Mexico into the North American trading block. These agreements had a major impact on the structure and organization of the Canadian economy, including making Canada far more dependent on the United States. Canada is therefore much more susceptible to instability in the American economy, as has been the case in recent years. Canadian trade is increasingly oriented in a north-south direction rather than flowing east-west as it has done historically.

Similarly, governments have individual agreements with each other about production and imports, and most governments (153 states in 2008) are part of the World Trade Organization (WTO), which works to negotiate rules of trade among the member states. The WTO promotes freer trade by negotiating agreements among member states that, typically, dismantle import quota systems and discourage individual countries' protection of their domestically produced goods. Agreements negotiated under the WTO are typically enacted in steps in order to avoid causing a major shock to any state's economy. In 2001, when the European Union (EU) and the

FIGURE 13.27 The North American Auto Plant Corridor. The first auto manufacturing plants in North America were established in the northeast and spread north, south, and west from there. From Richard D. Vogel, *Monthly Review*, 2007.

Year of plant start-up
- ○ Pre-1950
- ◉ 1950–1989
- ● 1990–2006
- ▲ Major parts manufacturing plants in Mexico

FIGURE 13.28 The Abandoned Packard Motors Plant, Detroit. The "Ruins of Detroit" are stark reminders of the effects of global capital movement, and examples of post-industrial landscapes and urban decay. (Eric Thayer/Reuters/Landov)

United States agreed to allow China to become a member of the WTO, they also agreed to remove the quota system that restricts the importation of Chinese goods into Europe and the United States. Soon after these quotas were eliminated, both the United States and the EU issued "safeguard quotas" against Chinese imports. The safeguard quotas were part of the agreement that permitted China's admission to the WTO, and the United States and the EU will not be able to use them in a few years. In the meantime, the safeguards are slowing Chinese imports once again, buffering their impact on domestic producers.

In addition to the growth of the purview of the WTO, the proliferation of regional trade associations in the last two decades is unprecedented, as illustrated by the growing list of acronyms for regional trade associations: EU, NAFTA, MERCOSUR, SAFTA, CARICOM, ANDEAN AFTA, COMESA, to name but a few. The World Trade Organization estimates that there are close to 300 regional trade organizations, which are similar to bilateral agreements on trade between two countries, although they involve more than two countries. Most regional trade agreements encourage movement of production within the trade region and promote trade by diminishing or deleting trade quotas and tariffs among member countries. A regional trade agreement sets up a special free trade agreement among parties to the association, leaving non-member countries to trade through the rules of the WTO or an existing bilateral agreement. Whether regional or global, trade agreements directly affect the location of production and even what is produced in a place.

Canada's economy experienced considerable restructuring as a result of the various trade agreements and the Auto Pact in the 1980s and 1990s. Canada opened its borders to competition from American firms, and Canadian industry and manufacturing, particularly in central Canada, underwent a difficult transition. Canadian companies were forced to reduce the size of their labour force and to move some of their operations offshore to other countries where labour and other costs were lower. Canadian and American relations have been strained as a result of trade disputes over softwood lumber pricing and offshore fishing. Nevertheless, Canada has benefited from access to U.S. markets and from greater participation in the global economy.

IMPORTANCE OF ENERGY IN INDUSTRIAL LOCATION

The role of energy supply as a factor in industrial location decisions has changed over time, in part because sources of energy have changed, but also because of changes in the infrastructure for transporting energy supplies. During the Industrial Revolution, manufacturing plants were often established on or near coalfields because coal was the major source of energy. Through the 20th century, coal increasingly gave way to oil and gas as an energy source for industry, but major industrial complexes are not found near oil fields. Instead, a huge system of pipelines and tankers delivers oil and natural gas to manufacturing regions throughout the world. For some time during and after the global oil supply crises of the 1970s, fears of future increases in oil costs led some industries that require large amounts of electricity to move to sites where the climate is moderate and heating and air-conditioning costs are low. When the crisis waned, national energy-conservation goals were modified, and in the early 2000s the core countries' reliance on foreign energy resources was even greater than it had been in the 1970s.

Energy supply has become a less significant factor in industrial location, but securing an energy supply is an increasingly important national priority. Nowhere is this more true than in the United States. U.S. consumption of petroleum and natural gas today is about 27 percent and 37 percent, respectively, of the annual world total. By 2007, the United States required more than 20.6-million barrels of petroleum per day to keep its power plants, machinery, vehicles, aircraft, and ships functioning. However, U.S. production of oil in recent years has averaged about 10 percent of the world total. Even taking into account the known Alaskan potential, U.S. oil reserves are estimated to be only about 4 percent of the world total. In 2009, the country was the third-largest oil producer

TABLE 13.3	World Oil Production, 2009	
Country	Rank	Total Oil Production (Millions of barrels per day)
Russia	1	9.94
Saudi Arabia	2	9.76
United States	3	9.14
Iran	4	4.17
China	5	3.99
Canada	6	3.31
Mexico	7	3.00
United Arab Emirates	8	2.80
Brazil	9	2.60
Kuwait	10	2.50
Venezuela	11	2.50
Iraq	12	2.40
Norway	13	2.35
Nigeria	14	2.21
Algeria	15	2.08

Data from U.S. Energy Information Administration website. Accessed August 2, 2011 at www.eia. gov/countries.

in the world (Table 13.3), but even with this level of production the United States remains heavily dependent on foreign oil supplies—including Canada's—with all the uncertainties that involves.

Dependence on external fuel supplies affects three of the four principal regions of industrial development: the United States; Europe, which, despite discoveries of oil and gas in the North Sea, still depends on foreign shipments of petroleum; and Japan, which is almost totally dependent on oil from distant sources.

On the other side of the coin, countries with large reserves of oil and natural gas—Saudi Arabia, Kuwait, Iraq, Russia, and others—occupy a special position in the global economy. Of these countries, only Russia is a major industrial power, but they all played a key role in the industrial boom of the 20th century. And while oil has brought wealth to some in the Middle East, it has also ensured that outside powers, such as the United States and Great Britain, are involved and invested in what happens in the region. This has often produced an uneasy relationship at best between countries in the Middle East and the major industrial powers of the West.

TIME-SPACE COMPRESSION AND DEINDUSTRIALIZATION

The sensation that the world is shrinking is so strong that a few commentators have proposed that we are entering an era characterized by the "end of geography," alluding to the idea that distance is no longer an important consideration in terms of the spatial organization of economic systems Some scholars argue that a combination of technological changes and developments in the global economy have reduced the significance of location and place to the point where they matter little. Geographers who study industrial production recognize that the nature and meaning of location and place have changed greatly in recent times, but they also note that these changes do not create an undifferentiated world. New production methods have reshaped the economic geography of the planet profoundly and rapidly. We need a greater understanding of how places have changed as a result of these new production methods and new corporate structures, as well as an examination of the networks and flows between global processes and local places.

Over the last 20 years, many manufacturing regions have experienced **deindustrialization**, a process by which companies move industrial jobs to other regions with relatively inexpensive labour, leaving the newly deindustrialized region to work through a period of high unemployment and, if possible, develop a service economy. At the same time, the places with lower labour costs and the right mix of laws attractive to businesses (often weak environmental laws and pro-free trade laws) become newly industrial regions. The new industrial regions emerge as shifts in politics, laws, capital flow, and labour availability occur.

> **Deindustrialization** Process by which companies move industrial jobs to other regions with cheaper labour, leaving the newly deindustrialized region to switch to a service economy and to work through a period of high unemployment.

Both Europe and the United States have large deindustrialized regions. In the United Kingdom, for example, the major industrial zones of Newcastle, Liverpool, and Manchester lost much of their industrial bases during the 1960s and 1970s. Similarly, the industrial zone of northeastern North America (around the Great Lakes) saw much of its industrial base disappear in the same time period as it lost steel-manufacturing jobs to areas of the world with lower wages. This region of North America, predominantly in the United States, which used to be called the Manufacturing Belt, is now commonly called the Rust Belt, evoking the image of long-abandoned, rusted-out steel factories.

The economic processes leading to deindustrialization in some parts of the world have led to industrialization in other parts of the world. More than two centuries after the onset of the Industrial Revolution, East Asia has become the cauldron of industrialization. Some of the economic policies we discussed in Chapter 11, such as structural adjustments and import quotas, encourage foreign direct investment in a country, and many draw industrial developers seeking to take advantage of economic breaks and inexpensive labour. From Japan to Guangdong and from South Korea to Singapore, the islands, countries, provinces, and cities fronting the Pacific Ocean are caught up in a frenzy of industrialization that has made the geographic term "Pacific Rim" synonymous with manufacturing.

Today, China is pushing industrialization into the interior of the country. A fall 2004 issue of *The Economist* highlighted the growth of China's industrial economy and the drive to spread the wealth into the interior of the country as well as the coastal export-oriented zones. On the coast, Shanghai recently trumped the Netherlands' Rotterdam as the world's busiest port, but the Chinese government's new focus is on generating greater economic activity in the interior.

China is a major recipient of industrial work that is **outsourced** or moved **offshore**. Each of the steps in commodity production that used to take place within the confines of a single factory is now often outsourced to suppliers, which focus their production and offer cost savings. When outsourced work is located outside the originating country, it has gone "offshore." The movement of industry into China's interior will likely occur through the outsourcing of production from China's coasts to the interior.

> **Outsource** With reference to production, to turn over in part or in total to a third party.
>
> **Offshore** With reference to production, to outsource to a third party located outside of the country.

MAIN POINTS   **13.4**   What Are the Spatial Implications of Changes in Industrial Production?

- After World War II and the boom years of the 1950s, changes in transportation and communication technologies altered methods of production as the world's manufacturing industries shifted from Fordist to post-Fordist techniques, changing industries' locational choices.

- Due to time-space compression, industries do not need to be close to their raw materials or their marketplace and can draw on labour from around the globe resulting in a global division of labour. Developments in transportation systems, from container transport to mechanization, has not only increased the flow of goods and services but also altered the location patterns of industry and manufacturing.

- Major industries now tend to locate labour-intensive manufacturing to peripheral countries, where labour is relatively inexpensive—a practice known as outsourcing—and

taxes and costly environmental regulations are relatively low. Conversely, research and development activities remain in core countries where there are high levels of education and access to technology. Major consumption still remains in the core, although the growing middle class in the semi-periphery is increasing consumption there.

- While technological innovation has been key to changing locational choices for industry and manufacturing, new regional and global trade agreements such as NAFTA, the EU, and the World Trade Organization have also had an impact. Reducing trade barriers changes the direction, volume, and flow of goods, to the benefit of some regions over others. Further, access to inexpensive energy in the form of oil, gas, coal, and electricity is also becoming a major factor in manufacturing and industrial locational choices.

13.5 What Is the Service Economy, and Where Are Services Concentrated?

By the end of World War II, the increasing saturation of consumer markets, the tremendous growth in governmental activity, rising labour activism, and declines in the cost of transportation and communication began to challenge the Fordist economic structure. The challenge shifted into high gear in the early 1970s, when a sharp rise in oil prices during a period of international financial instability and inflation produced a dramatic downturn in the global economy. Under these circumstances, it became increasingly difficult for the core industrial regions to sustain their competitive advantage without significant readjustment. That readjustment took the form of mechanization and the development of service and information industries. These changes, along with the need for new markets and the growth of multinational concerns, brought about a post-industrial or post-Fordist economic order in many of the core economies.

Service industries (tertiary industries) do not generate an actual, tangible product; instead, they encompass the range of services that are found in modern societies. So many different types of activities can be thought of as service activities that, as we discussed at the beginning of this chapter, specialized aspects of the service economy were given their own designations: quaternary industries collect, process, and manipulate information and capital (e.g., financial, administrative, insurance, legal, and computer services) and quinary industries facilitate complex decision making and the advancement of human capacities (e.g., scientific research, higher education, high-level management).

Distinguishing among types of services is useful, given the extraordinary growth in the size and complexity of the service sector. In the global economic core, service industries employ more workers than the primary and secondary industries combined, yet these service industries range from small-scale retailing to tourism services to research on the causes of cancer. Placing all these activities in a single category doesn't seem helpful. Specificity in terminology is also useful in highlighting different phases in the development of the service sector. In the early decades of the 20th century, the domestic and quasi-domestic tertiary industries were experiencing rapid growth in the industrialized world. With the approach of World War II, the quaternary sector began expanding rapidly, and this expansion continued after the war. During the last three decades, both the quaternary and quinary sectors have experienced very rapid growth, giving greater meaning to the term "post-industrial."

The expanding service sector in the core economies is only one aspect of the changing global economy. Accompanying, and in some cases driving, this expansion are several other developments that have already been mentioned: the increasing mechanization of production, particularly in manufacturing enterprises operating in the core; the growth of large multinational corporations; and the dispersal of the production process, with components for complex products such as automobiles and consumer electronics coming from factories in many different countries.

GEOGRAPHICAL DIMENSIONS OF THE SERVICE ECONOMY

Deindustrialization and the growth of the service economy unfolded in the context of a world economy that was already characterized by wide socio-economic disparities. Only areas that have industry can deindustrialize, of course, and at the global scale the wealthier industrial regions were the most successful in establishing a post-industrial service economy. Deindustrialization describes a sustained decline in industrial activities, including manufacturing, which has a negative impact on output and employment. What is often left behind are the physical plants and infrastructure such as factories, warehouses, and industrial offices and buildings that are difficult to redevelop. We should not be surprised that deindustrialization did little to change the basic disparities between core and periphery that have long characterized the global economy. Indeed, even in the manufacturing realm, mechanization and innovative production strategies have allowed the core industrial regions to retain their dominance. In the first decade of the 21st century, eastern Asia, western Russia and Ukraine, western Europe, and North America still account for well over 75 percent of the world's total output of manufactured goods.

Despite its continued dominance in the manufacturing arena, the core has experienced some wrenching changes associated with the economic shifts of the past three decades. Anyone who has ever spent time in northern Indiana, the British Midlands, or Silesia (southern Poland and northeastern Czech Republic) knows that there are pockets of significant hardship within the core (Figure 13.29). These examples serve to remind

FIGURE 13.29 Abandoned Street, Liverpool, England. With the deindustrialization of the Liverpool region, the city has lost thousands of jobs and the city's population has decreased by one-third. Abandoned streets, such as this one, are a reflection of the city's industrial decline. (© Philip Wolmuth/Panos Pictures.)

us that not all deindustrialized regions, not even those in the core, are finding their way into the tertiary sector. Location, albeit often defined in new ways, affects where and what kinds of service economies are developed.

Some secondary industrial regions have made the transition to a service economy while retaining their manufacturing base. The **Sunbelt** is the southern region of the United States, stretching from Florida and Georgia through California. The population and economy of the Sunbelt have grown over the last few decades as companies from the service sector choose to locate in areas such as Atlanta and Phoenix, where the climate is warm and the local laws welcome their presence. The eastern part of the Sunbelt served as a secondary industrial region, with Birmingham, Alabama, developing an iron and steel economy, and Atlanta an industrial economy around cotton, tobacco, and furniture. In recent decades, high-tech and financial industries changed the economy and landscape of the Sunbelt, as can be seen in the toponyms of stadiums in the region, such as Alltel Stadium in Jacksonville, Florida, Bank of America Stadium in Charlotte, North Carolina, and Bank One Ballpark in Phoenix, Arizona.

Sunbelt The South and Southwest regions of the United States.

NEW INFLUENCES ON SERVICE INDUSTRY LOCATION

With the striking growth of the service sector and information technologies, new factors have come into play that affect patterns of economic activity. Most service industries are not tied to raw materials and do not need large amounts of energy. Hence, those factors of production are markedly less important for service industries than for traditional manufacturing concerns. Market accessibility is more relevant for the service sector, but advances in telecommunications have rendered even that factor less important for some types of service industries.

To understand the new influences on the location of services, it is useful to go back to our distinction between tertiary, quaternary, and quinary industries. Tertiary services related to transportation and communication are closely tied to population patterns and to the location of primary and secondary industries. As the basic facilitators of interaction, they are strongly linked to the basic geography of production and consumption. Other tertiary services—restaurants, hotels, and retail establishments—are influenced mainly by market considerations. If they are located far from their consumers, they are unlikely to succeed.

Employing technologies such as geographic information systems (GIS) and remote sensing (see Chapter 1), economic geographers working for corporations use this understanding to model the best locations for new businesses, office complexes, government centres, or transportation connections. Major retailers not only shape the landscapes of the places where they choose to put stores, but they also change the landscapes of their hometowns, the location of their headquarters. An extreme example of this is Walmart's headquarters in Bentonville, Arkansas. If producers of consumer products want to sell their goods in Walmart stores, they must travel to Bentonville, Arkansas, to negotiate deals with Walmart. In order to provide low prices to consumers, Walmart negotiates very low prices with major producers. To create lower-priced products, companies have moved production abroad, and to create good relationships with the world's number one retailer (with sales of $374.5 billion in fiscal year 2008), companies have moved into Bentonville, Arkansas.

The locational influences on quaternary services—high-level services that collect, process, and manipulate information and capital—are more diverse. Some of these services are strongly tied to a particular geographical locus of economic activity. Retail banking and various types of administrative services require a high level of interpersonal contact and therefore tend to be located near the businesses they are serving. Other types of quaternary services, however, can operate almost anywhere as long as they have access to digital processing equipment and telecommunications. When you send in your credit card bill, it is unlikely to go to the city where the headquarters of the issuing bank is located. Instead, it will go to North Dakota, South Dakota, Nebraska, or Colorado. Similarly, many "back-office" tasks related to insurance are performed in places such as Des Moines, Iowa, rather than Chicago or Hartford. Many of the call centres for technical help for computers and related industries (e.g., software, hardware) are located in India and the Philippines. With relatively high levels of college attainment, vast numbers of English speakers, and phones routed through the Internet, "help desks" need not be located down the hall or even down the street. These location curiosities occur because technological advances in the telecommunications sector have made it possible for all sorts of quaternary industries to be located far away from either producers or consumers. What matters most is infrastructure, a workforce that is sufficiently skilled but not too expensive, and favourable tax rates.

Those who work in the quinary sector tend to be concentrated around nodes of quinary activity—seats of government, universities, and corporate headquarters. Corporate headquarters tend to be located in large metropolitan areas, whereas seats of government and universities can be found in places that were chosen long ago as appropriate sites for administrative or educational activities based on cultural values or political compromises. The American ideal of the university town (which originated in Germany) led to the establishment of many universities at a distance from major commercial and population centres, in such towns as Champaign-Urbana, Illinois; Norman, Oklahoma; and Eugene, Oregon. Political compromises led to the establishment of major seats of government in small towns. Ottawa and Canberra (in Australia), are examples of this phenomenon. The point is that historical location decisions influence the geography of the quinary sector, and university professors and government officials are not the only ones affected. All sorts of high-level research and development activities are located on the fringes of universities, and a host of specialized consultants are concentrated around governmental centres. These then become major nodes of quinary activity.

HIGH-TECHNOLOGY CORRIDORS

A high-technology corridor is an area designated by local or state government to benefit from lower taxes and high-technology infrastructure with the goal of providing high-technology jobs to the local population. The goal of a high-technology corridor is to attract designers of computers, semiconductors, telecommunications, sophisticated medical equipment, and the like.

California's Silicon Valley is a well-known example of a high-technology corridor. Several decades ago, a number of innovative technology companies located their research and development activities in the area around the University of California, Berkeley, and Stanford University near San Francisco, California. They were attracted by the prospect of developing links with existing research communities and the availability of a highly educated workforce. Once some high-technology businesses located in the Silicon Valley, others were attracted as well. Today, Silicon Valley is home to dozens of computer companies, many of which are familiar to the computer literate (such as Cisco Systems, Adobe, Hewlett-Packard, Intel, IBM, and Netscape) (Figure 13.30). The resulting collection

of high-technology industries produced what Manuel Castells, Peter Hall, and John Hutriyk call a **technopole**. These are locations planned for high technology, where agglomeration built on a synergy among technological companies occurs. A similar sort of technopole developed outside Boston, where the concentration of technology-based businesses close to Harvard and the Massachusetts Institute of Technology gave rise to what is called the Route 128 high-technology corridor. The Route 128 corridor has largely been supported by the federal government rather than the local government, which supports many other technopoles.

> **Technopole** Centres or nodes of high-technology research and activity around which a high-technology corridor is sometimes established.

Technopoles can be found in a number of countries in western Europe and eastern Asia, as well as in North America and Australia. Few are on the scale of Silicon Valley, but they are noticeable elements of the economic landscape. Many of them have sprung up on the edges of good-sized cities, particularly near airports. In Brussels, Belgium, for example, the route into the city from the airport passes an array of buildings occupied by computer, communication, and electronics firms. In Washington, D.C., the route from Dulles International Airport (located in the Virginia suburbs) to the city passes the headquarters of such companies as AOL, MCI, and Orbital Sciences. It's known as the Dulles Corridor. In the Telecom Corridor of Plano-Richardson, just outside Dallas, Texas, telecom companies such as Nortel and Ericsson have taken root, but so too have numerous high-technology companies that are not telecom related. In each of these technopoles, the presence of the major multinational companies attracts other start-up companies hoping to become major companies, provide services to major companies, or be bought by major companies. In Canada, Research In Motion (RIM) Technologies, maker of the BlackBerry, was established in Waterloo, Ontario, in 1984. Since then, the region, comprising the cities of Kitchener-Waterloo, Cambridge, and London, and containing three universities (University of Waterloo, Wilfrid Laurier University, and University of Western Ontario), has become a technology hub, attracting other high-tech companies and related industries.

Many of the technology firms are multinationals. Like their counterparts in other countries, they function in an information environment and market their products all over the world. Being near raw materials or even a particular market is unimportant for these firms; what matters to them is proximity to major networks of transportation and communication. High-technology industries have become such an important symbol of the post-industrial world that local, regional, and national governments often implement aggressive policies to attract firms in this sector. These industries are thought to be pollution free and to offer positive benefits for the communities in which they are located. Bidding wars sometimes develop between localities seeking to attract such industries. Although high-technology industries do indeed bring a variety of economic benefits, they have some drawbacks as well. Communities that have attracted production

FIGURE 13.30 Silicon Valley, California. This map illustrates the concentration of high technology industries in the Silicon Valley region of California. (Silicon Valley Map.)

facilities find that the manufacture of computer chips, semiconductors, and the like requires toxic chemicals and large quantities of water. Even research-oriented establishments sometimes have negative environmental impacts in that land must be cleared and

buildings constructed to house them. Despite these drawbacks, the high-technology sector is clearly here to stay, and areas that can tap into it are likely to find themselves in an advantageous economic position in the coming years.

MAIN POINTS   13.5   What Is the Service Economy, and Where Are Services Concentrated?

- Tertiary or service industries experienced substantial changes in the last 30 years. They now encompass a wide variety of activities (outlined in Table 13.1). As deindustrialization—a decline in industrial activities—has taken place in core countries, many of these economies, including Canada's, are now considered post-industrial. This has meant a substantial loss in manufacturing jobs and a need to develop a service economy as manufacturing processes relocated to peripheral and semi-peripheral nations.

- Service industries include secondary, tertiary, quaternary, and quinary industries. It is important to look at the specifics of each type of industry to understand the factors influencing locational choices.

- Core countries have experienced striking growth in service sector and information technologies, and there

are new factors in play in terms of locational choices. Service industries are not tied to raw materials and do not need large amounts of energy. These industries are more closely tied to the basic geography of production and consumption; that is, they need to be located near their consumers and are strongly influenced by market forces.

- With advanced technologies, not all aspects of service sector industries need to be located near their customers. Many companies place their "back office" activities (e.g., bookkeeping, accounting, and human resources) in the suburbs, where office space, transportation, and parking are less expensive. Further, service sector communications services can be located anywhere in the world.

SUMMARY

Economic activities are classified by what is produced and are generally divided into primary, secondary, tertiary, quaternary, and quinary. Economies are categorized by their stages of development. Pre-industrial economies are largely composed of primary activities, while second-stage economies develop a manufacturing sector that has a greater output than the primary sector. The tertiary or post-industrial stage is an economy with most of the labour force engaged in tertiary, quaternary, and quinary activities. The world's core countries are largely post-industrial.

The Industrial Revolution took place in the 18th and 19th centuries and fundamentally transformed the world geographically, economically, politically, and socially. Industrial production began some 3,000 years before the Industrial Revolution, with trade along the Silk Routes between Europe, China, and India. Rapid technological innovation led to advances in medicine, science, and new energy sources. Colonial and imperial exploration created new networks and flows between people and places and established the foundation of the current world economy. Advances in iron and coal production, and the invention of the steam engine, electricity, and modern manufacturing techniques, created manufacturing economies

in England and at several sites in Europe and North America. Locational choices in this period were largely based on accessibility to raw materials and transportation systems.

Geographers, economists, and others have been particularly interested in developing models that can accurately forecast the spatial organization of manufacturing and industry. The models of Weber, Hotelling, and Losch take into account a variety of factors influencing locational choices, such as labour costs, profitability, distance to market, agglomerations, and competitors' locations. Many of these models were useful for understanding the locational choices of the world's major industrial regions before 1950.

After the end of World War II and the boom years of the 1950s, manufacturing industries underwent substantial changes worldwide. Methods of production evolved from Fordist to post-Fordist as a result of rapid changes in technologies, communications, and transportation. These changes have resulted in time-space compression, which means that some places are more connected, changing the relationship between people, businesses, and places. This has fundamentally altered the global division of labour so that companies can now locate any aspect of their production process in any part of the world with the least expensive labour and production costs. Many labour-intensive industries have located to peripheral and semi-peripheral countries, with research and development remaining in core countries. Advances in transportation (e.g., air transport and container shipping), as well as energy needs, also influence locational choices.

These changing industrial location choices mean that many of the places where industrialization first took hold have since become deindustrialized, through the relocation of manufacturing plants, the outsourcing of steps of the production process domestically and offshore, or both. With changing economies, places change. Some urban centres now look like ghost towns, serving merely as a reminder that industrialization took place there. Others have booming economies and are thriving, having retained industry or successfully cultivated a service economy. Other places are still redefining themselves. (In Chapter 6, we considered another lasting effect of industrialization and deindustrialization: environmental change.)

The service economy has also changed in the post-World War II period. With the shock of the oil crisis in the 1970s and deindustrialization, economic redevelopment fostered growth in the service and information sectors, which encompass a range of employment from part-time retailing and restaurant staff to accounting, engineering, and high technology. In considering the locational choices of the service sector, it is important to focus on the particularities of the business under consideration. Most service industries are not tied to raw materials and do not need large amounts of energy. Accessibility to customers is often more relevant for the service sector, but advances in telecommunications mean that even these businesses can choose to locate aspects of their operations far from the actual marketplace, with back offices in the suburbs and call and help centres located offshore. The spatial organization of economic activities not only varies from place to place and industry to industry, but also has a distinctive historical organization across a variety of scales.

DISCUSSION AND REVIEW QUESTIONS

1. To understand the geography of economic activities, scholars have organized them into a variety of sectors. What are these sectors and with what type of economic activities are they associated? How does this framework apply to Canada's economic organization? Which particular set of economic activities predominate where you live?

2. Alfred Weber's theories and models provided an important means for studying industrial location. Discuss the primary factors of his model and provide a specific regional example that can be explained through Weber's theory.

3. Compare and contrast the Fordist with the post-Fordist industrial model. How have each shaped the processes and geography of industrialization in the last 100 years?

4. What are the "new influences" that are changing the scope and geography of manufacturing? Discuss how each has specifically affected the geography of manufacturing in Canada.

5. The expanding service sector in the core economy is one aspect of the changing global economy. What are the factors that have driven this change? How has the shift to a service economy affected the geography of the core?

GEOGRAPHIC CONCEPTS

agglomeration   379
deagglomeration   380
deindustrialization   396
distance decay   379
Fordist   390
friction of distance   379
global division of labour   391
Industrial Revolution   374
intermodal connections   392
just-in-time delivery   391

least cost theory   379
location theory   378
offshore   396
outsourced   396
post-Fordist   391
primary industrial regions   380
Sunbelt   398
technopole   399
variable costs   379

ADDITIONAL RESOURCES ONLINE

About Eco Justice Canada: www.ecojustice.ca

About the port of Rotterdam: www.portofrotterdam.com

About Nike: www.nikeinc.com

About Walmart's influence on Bentonville, Arkansas: www.pbs.org/wgbh/pages/frontline/shows/walmart

About Canadian Steel Producers Association (CSPA): http://canadiansteel.ca/

About World Steel Association: www.worldsteel.org

About Clairtone Sound Corporation: www.clairtone.ca

About Silicon Valley: www.siliconvalley.com

About the European Union: http://europa.eu/

About the North American Free Trade Agreement: www.international.gc.ca/trade-agreements-accords-commerciaux/agr-acc/nafta-alena/texte/index.aspx

Appendix A

MAPS

The geographer's greatest ally is the map. Maps can present enormous amounts of information very effectively, and can be used to establish theories and solve problems. Furthermore, maps often are fascinating, revealing things no other medium can. It has been said that if a picture is worth a thousand words, then a map is worth a million.

Maps can be fascinating, but they often do not get the attention they deserve. You may spend 20 minutes carefully reading a page of text, but how often have you spent 20 minutes with a page-size map, studying what it reveals? No caption and no paragraph of text can begin to summarize what a map may show;

it is up to the reader to make the best use of it. For example, in Chapter 4 on population issues, we study several maps that depict the human condition by country, in terms of birth rate, infant mortality, and life expectancy. In the text, we can refer only to highlights (and low points) on those maps. But make a point of looking beyond the main issue to get a sense of the global distributions these maps represent. It is part of an intangible but important process: to enhance your mental map of this world.

While on the topic of maps, we should remind ourselves that a map—any map—is an incomplete representation of reality. In the first place, the map is smaller than the real world it represents. Second, it must depict the curved surface of our world on a flat plane; for example, a page of this book. And third, it must contain symbols to convey the information that must be transmitted to the reader. These are the three fundamental properties of all maps: scale, projection, and symbols.

Understanding these basics helps us interpret maps while avoiding their pitfalls. Some maps look so convincing that we may not question them as we would a paragraph of text. Yet maps, by their very nature, to some extent distort reality. Most of the time, such distortion is necessary and does not invalidate the map's message. But some maps are drawn deliberately to mislead. Propaganda maps, for example, may exaggerate or distort reality to promote political aims (Figure A.1). We should be alert to cartographic mistakes when we read maps. The proper use of scale, projection, and symbolization ensures that a map is as accurate as it can be made.

FIGURE A.1 Propaganda Map. Hark! Hark! The Dogs Do Bark! Serio-Comique Map of Europe at War (London, 1914). (Imperial War Museums/CQ 31514)

Map Scale

The scale of a map reveals how much the real world has been reduced to fit on the page or screen on which it appears. It is the ratio between an actual distance on the ground and the length given to that distance on the map, using the same units of measurement. This ratio is often represented as a fraction (e.g., 1:10,000 or 1/10,000). This means that one unit on the map represents 10,000 such units in the real world. One centimetre on the map would actually represent 10,000 cm or 100 m. Such a scale would be useful when mapping a city's downtown area, but it would be much too large for the map of an entire province. As the real-world area we want to map gets larger, we must make our map scale smaller. As small as the fraction 1/10,000 seems, it still is 10 times as large as 1/100,000, and 100 times as large as 1/1,000,000. If the world maps in this book had fractional scales, they would be even smaller. A large-scale map can contain much more detail and be far more representative of the real world than a small-scale map. Look at it this way: when we devote almost a full page of this book to a map of a major city (Figure A.2), we are able to represent the layout of that city in considerable detail. But if the entire continental realm in which that city is located must be represented on a single page, the city becomes just a large dot on that small-scale map, and the detail is lost in favour of larger-area coverage (Figure A.3). So the selection of scale depends on the objective of the map.

But when you examine the maps in this book, you will note that most, if not all, of them have scales that are not given as ratios or fractions, but in graphic form. This method of representing map scale is convenient from several viewpoints. Using the edge of a piece of paper and marking the scale bar's length, the map reader can quickly—without calculation—determine approximate distances. And if a map is enlarged or reduced in reproduction, the scale bar is enlarged or reduced with it and remains accurate. That, of course, is not true of a ratio or fractional scale. Graphic scales, therefore, are preferred in this book.

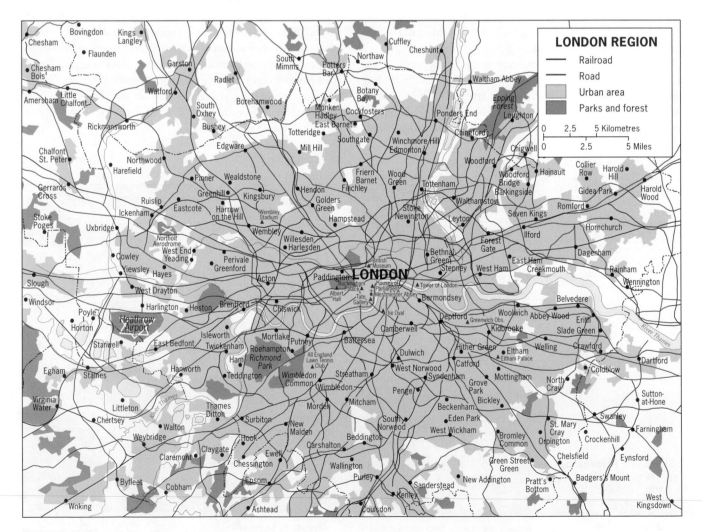

FIGURE A.2 Large-Scale Map. The layout of a major city can be shown in considerable detail at this large scale.

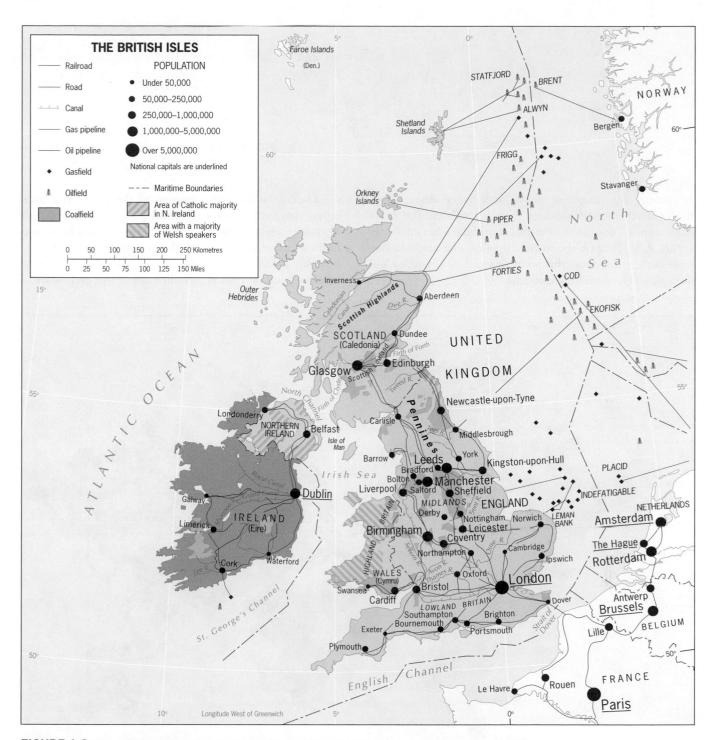

FIGURE A.3 Small-Scale Map. This type of map allows display of a larger area, but with less local detail.

Map Projections

For centuries cartographers have faced the challenge of map projection—the representation of the spherical Earth, or part of it, on a flat surface. To get the job done, there had to be a frame of reference on the globe itself, a grid system that could be transferred to the flat page. Any modern globe shows that system: a set of horizontal lines, usually at 10-degree intervals north and south from

the equator, called parallels, and another set of vertical lines, converging on the poles, often shown at 15-degree intervals and called meridians (see *Numbering the Grid Lines*). On the spherical globe, parallels and meridians intersect at right angles (Figure A.4).

But what happens when these lines of latitude (parallels) and longitude (meridians) are drawn to intersect at right angles on a flat piece of paper? At the equator, the representation of the real world is relatively accurate. But go toward

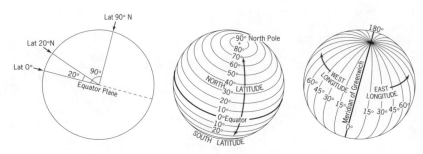

FIGURE A.4 Numbering of Grid Lines. (© H. J. de Blij, P. O. Muller, and John Wiley & Sons, Inc.)

the poles, and distortion grows with every degree until, in the northern and southern higher latitudes, the continents appear not only stretched out but also misshapen (Figure A.5). Because the meridians cannot be made to converge in the polar areas, this projection makes Antarctica look like a giant, globe-girdling landmass.

Looking at this representation of the world, you might believe that it could serve no useful purpose. But in fact, the Mercator projection, invented in 1569 by Gerardus Mercator, a Flemish cartographer, had (and has) a very particular function. Because parallels and meridians cross (as they do on the spherical globe's grid) at right angles, direction is true everywhere on

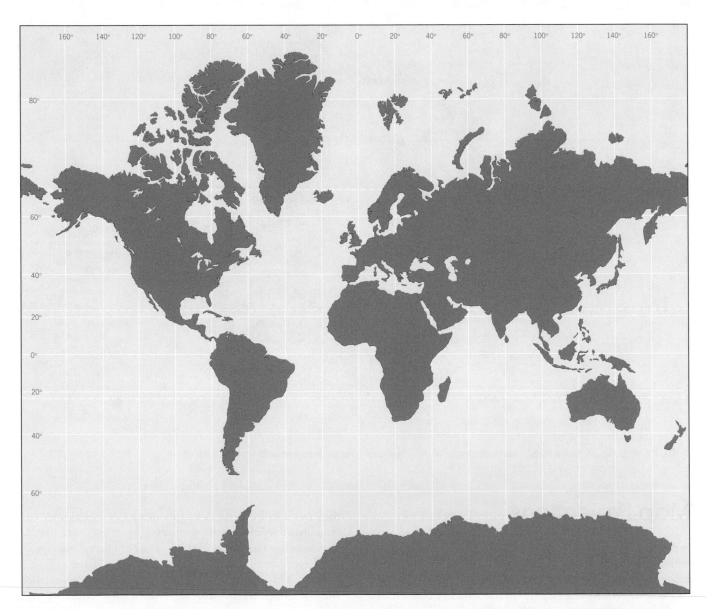

FIGURE A.5 Mercator's Projection. Mercator's projection greatly exaggerates the size and shape of higher-latitude landmasses, but direction is true everywhere on this map.

Numbering the Grid Lines

When cartographers girdled the globe with their imaginary grid lines, they had to identify each line by number; that is, by degree. For the (horizontal) latitude lines, that was easy: the equator, which bisects the Earth midway between the poles, was designated as 0° (zero degree) Latitude, and all parallels north and south of the equator were designated by their angular position (see Figure A.4). The parallel midway between the equator and the pole, thus, is 45° North Latitude in the Northern Hemisphere and 45° South Latitude in the Southern Hemisphere.

But the (vertical) longitude lines presented no such easy solution. Among the parallels, the equator is the only one to divide the Earth into equal halves, but all meridians do this. During the second half of the nineteenth century, maps with conflicting numbers multiplied, and it was clear that a solution was needed. The most powerful country at the time was Britain, and in 1884, an international agreement was reached whereby the meridian drawn through the Royal Observatory in Greenwich, England, would be the prime meridian, 0° (zero degree) Longitude. All meridians east and west of the prime meridian could now be designated by number, from 0° to 180° East and West Longitude. If you go to Greenwich, you can walk up the steep hill to the Observatory, and stand with one foot on either side of the Prime Meridian, a solid red line just like you would see on most maps (Figure A.6).

FIGURE A.6. **The Prime Meridian, Greenwich, England.**
(© deadlyphoto.com/Alamy)

this map. Thus the Mercator projection enabled navigators to maintain an accurate course at sea simply by adhering to compass directions and plotting straight lines. It is used for that purpose to this day.

The spatial distortion of the Mercator projection serves to remind us that scale and projection are interconnected. What scale fraction or graphic scale bar could be used here? A scale that would be accurate at the equator on a Mercator map would be quite inaccurate at higher latitudes. So the distortion that is an inevitable by-product of any map projection also affects map scales.

One might imagine that the spatial (areal) distortion of the Mercator projection is so obvious that no one would use it to represent the world's countries. But in fact, many popular atlas maps (Mercator also introduced the term "atlas" to describe a collection of maps) and wall maps still use a Mercator for such purposes. The American National Geographic Society published its world maps on a Mercator projection until 1988, when it finally abandoned the practice in favour of a projection developed by the American cartographer Arthur Robinson (Figure A.7). During the news conference at which the change was announced, a questioner rose to pursue a point: Why had the Society waited so long to make this change? Was it because the distortion inherent in the Mercator projection made American and European middle-latitude countries large, compared to tropical countries in Africa and elsewhere? Although that was not the goal of the National Geographic Society, the questioner clearly understood the misleading subtleties inherent even in so apparently neutral a device as a map projection.

The Mercator projection is one of a group of projections called cylindrical projections. Imagine the globe's lines of latitude and longitude represented by a wire grid, at the centre of which we place a bright light. Wrap a piece of photographic paper around the wire grid, extending it well beyond the north and south poles, flash the bulb, and the photographic image will be that of a Mercator projection (Figure A.8). We could do the same after placing a cone-shaped piece of paper over each hemisphere, touching the grid, say, at the 40th parallel north and south; the result would be a conic projection (Figure A.9). If we wanted a map of North America or Europe, a form of conic projection would be appropriate. Now the meridians do approach each other toward the poles (unlike the Mercator projection), and there is much less shape and size distortion. And if we needed a map of Arctic and Antarctic regions, we would place the photographic paper as a flat sheet against the North and South Poles. Now the photographic image would show a set of diverging lines, as the meridians do from each pole, and the parallels would appear as circles (Figure A.10). Such a planar projection is a good choice for a map of the Arctic Ocean or the Antarctic continent.

Projections are chosen for various purposes. Just as the Mercator is appropriate for navigation because direction is true, other projections are designed to preserve areal size, keep distances real, or maintain the outlines (shapes) of landmasses and countries. Projections can be manipulated for many needs. In this book, we examine global distributions of various phenomena. The world map that forms the base for these displays is one that is designed to give prominence to land areas at the expense of the oceans. This is achieved by "interrupting" the projection where loss of territory (in this case water area) is not problematic.

When a map is planned, therefore, the choice of projection is an important part of the process. An inappropriate selection may weaken the effectiveness of a map and may lead to erroneous interpretations. Of course, the problem diminishes when the area to be mapped is smaller and the scale larger. We may consider various alternatives when it comes to a map of all of North America, but a map of a single province presents far fewer potential problems of distortion. And for a city map—even of a large city such as Toronto—the projection problem virtually disappears.

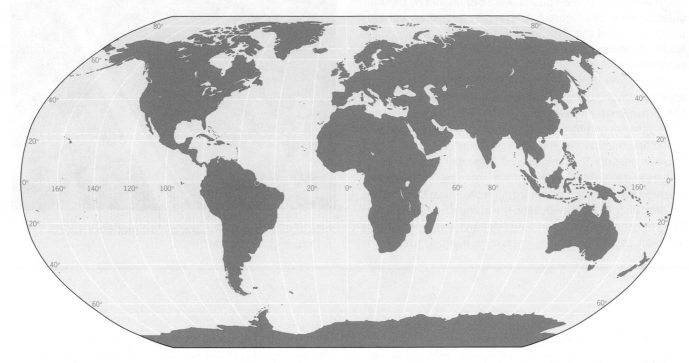

FIGURE A.7 **The Robinson Projection.** The Robinson Projection substantially reduces the exaggerated size of polar landmasses. It better approximates shape, but it lacks the directional utility of the Mercator projection.

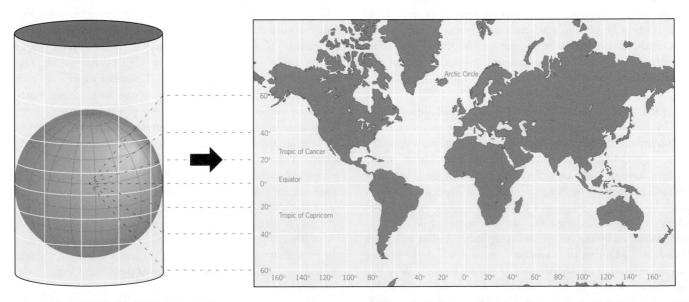

FIGURE A.8 **Cylindrical Projection.** Shadows of the globe's grid lines on wraparound paper: a cylindrical projection results.

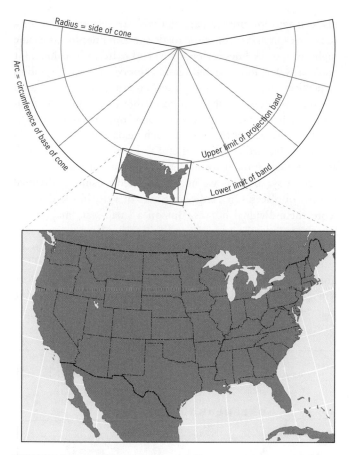

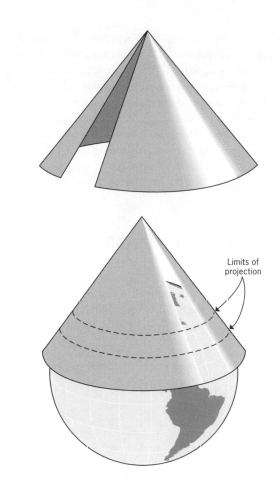

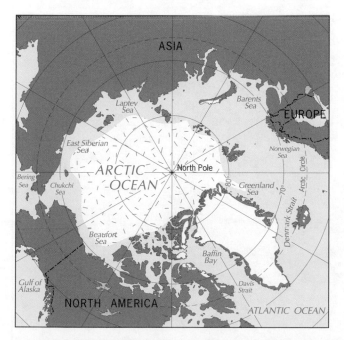

FIGURE A.9 Conic Projection. Construction of a conic projection.

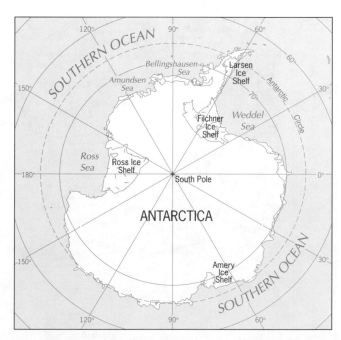

FIGURE A.10 Planar Projection. The light at the centre of the globe projects diverging longitude lines on a flat sheet of paper placed over the North Pole (left) and the South Pole (right). (© H. J. de Blij, P. O. Muller, and John Wiley & Sons, Inc.)

The old problem of how to represent the round Earth on a flat surface has been attacked for centuries, and there is no single best solution. What has been learned in the process, however, will be useful in fields of endeavour other than Earthly geography. As the age of planetary exploration dawns, and our space probes send back images of the surfaces of the Moon, Mars, Jupiter, and other components of our solar system, we will have to agree once again on grids, equators, and prime meridians. What has been learned in our efforts to map and represent the Earth will be useful in depicting the universe beyond.

Symbols on Maps

The third fundamental property of a map is its symbolization. Maps represent the real world, and this can be done only through the use of symbols. Anyone who has used an atlas map is familiar with some of these symbols: prominent dots (perhaps black or red) for cities, a large dot with a circle around it, or a star, for capitals, red lines for roads (double lines for four-lane highways), black lines for railroads, and patterns or colours for areas of water, forest, or farmland. Notice that these symbols respectively represent points, lines, and areas on the ground. For our purposes, we need not go further into map symbolization, which can become a very complex topic when it comes to highly specialized cartography in such fields as geology and meteorology. Nevertheless, it is useful to know why symbols such as those used on the maps in this book were chosen.

Point symbols, as we noted, are used to show individual features or places. On a large-scale map of a city block, dots can represent individual houses. But on a small-scale map, a dot has to represent an entire "city." Still, cities have various sizes and levels of political importance, and those differences can be put in categories and mapped accordingly (Figure A.11). Thus Toronto, Regina, and Fredericton appear as squares on the map, whereas smaller cities are illustrated with dots, such as Medicine Hat, Flin Flon, and Rimouski.

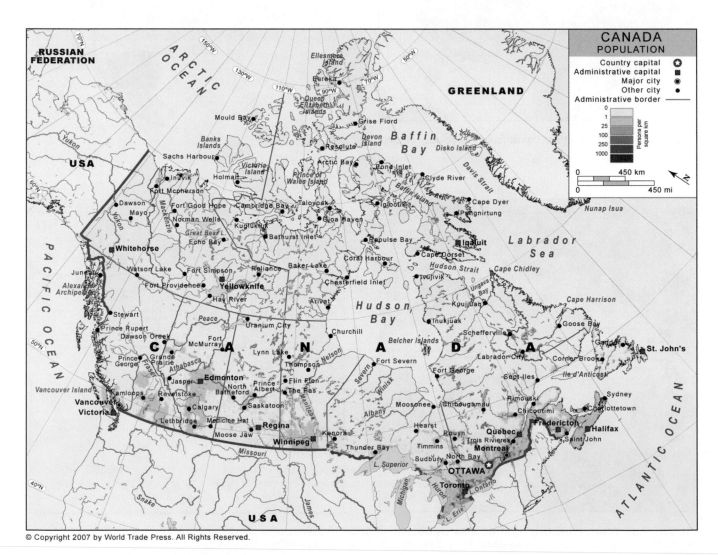

© Copyright 2007 by World Trade Press. All Rights Reserved.

FIGURE A.11 Population Map of Canada. This map uses a series of symbols to denote city size and importance. A circle with a star indicates country capital, a red square indicates administrative capital, a circle with a ring around it indicates a large city, and a circle on its own indicates a smaller city.

Line symbols include not only roads and railroads, but also political and administrative boundaries, rivers, and other linear features. Again, scale plays its crucial role: on a large-scale map, it is possible to represent the fenced boundaries of a single farm, but on a small-scale map, such detail cannot be shown.

Some lines on maps do not actually exist on the ground. When physical geographers do their field work they use contour maps, lines that represent a certain consistent height above mean sea level (Figure A.12). All points on such a contour line thus are at the same elevation. The spacing between contour lines immediately reveals the nature of the local topography (the natural land surface). When the contour lines at a given interval (e.g., 100 feet) are spaced closely together, the slope of the ground is steep. When they are widely separated, the land surface slopes gently. Of course contour lines cannot be found in the real world, and neither can the lines drawn on the weather maps in our daily newspaper. These lines connect points of equal pressure (isobars) and temperature (isotherms) and show the development of weather systems. Note that the letters "iso" (meaning "the same") appear in these terms. Invisible lines of this kind are collectively known as isolines, lines of equal or constant value. These are abstract constructions, but they can be of great value in geographic research and representation.

Area symbols take many forms, and we will see some of them on the maps in this book. Area symbols are used in various ways to represent distributions and magnitudes. Maps showing distributions (of such phenomena as regionally dominant languages or religions in human geography, and climates or soils in physical geography) show the world, or parts of it, divided into areas shaded or coloured in contrasting hues. But be careful: those sharp dividing lines are likely to be transition zones in the real world, and a dominant language or religion does not imply the exclusion of all others. So distribution maps, and there are many in this book, tend to be small-scale generalizations of much more complex patterns than they can reveal. Again, maps showing magnitudes also must be read with care. Here the objective is to reveal how much of a phenomenon prevails in one unit (e.g., country) on the map, compared to others. The maps on population in Chapter 4 are examples of such maps. The important cartographic decision has to do with colour (or black and white, grey tones). Darker should mean more, and lighter implies less. That is relatively easily done when the dominant colour is the same. But on a multicoloured map, the use of reds, greens, and yellows can be confusing, and first impressions may have to be revised upon examination of the key.

Some students who are first drawn to the discipline of geography go on to become professional cartographers, and their work is seen in atlases, foldout magazine maps, books, and many other venues. Although cartographic technology is changing, the world's great atlases and maps are still designed and produced by researchers, compilers, draughts people, and other specialists.

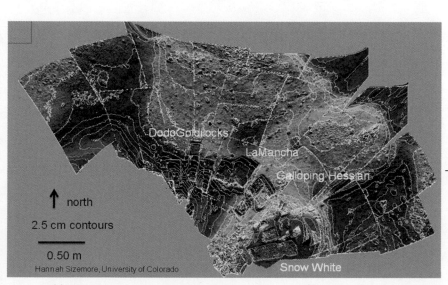

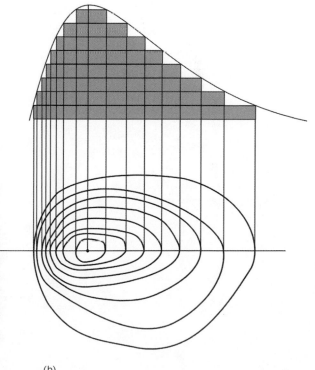

(a) (b)

FIGURE A.12 Contour Lines. (a) Contour map of Mars surface. (b) Elevation lines principle. (NASA/JPL/University of Arizona/University of Colorado; Romary/Wikimedia Commons)

Appendix B

AREA AND DEMOGRAPHIC DATA FOR THE WORLD'S STATES

This data table is a valuable resource, and should be consulted throughout your reading. Like all else in this book, this table is subject to continuous revision and modification. Compared to previous U.S. editions, we have deleted some indices, elaborated others, and introduced new ones. For example, in a world with ever-slower population growth, the so-called Doubling Time index—the number of years it will take for a population to double in size based on its current rate of natural increase—has lost most of its utility. On the other hand, when it comes to

Life Expectancy and Literacy, general averages conceal significant differences between male and female rates, which in turn reflect conditions in individual countries, so we report these by gender. Also in this edition, we continue to use the Corruption Index, not available for all countries but an important reflection of a global problem. The Big Mac Price index, a measure introduced by the journal The Economist, tells you much more than what a hamburger with all the trimmings would cost in real dollars in various countries of the world—it also reflects whether those countries' currencies are overvalued or undervalued. And the final column, in which we formerly used to reported the per-capita GNP (Gross National Product), now reveals the GNI; that is, the Gross National Income per person and what this would buy in each country. In the language of economic geographers, this is called the GNI-PPP, the per-capita Gross National Income in terms of its Purchasing Power Parity.

Indexes that may not be immediately obvious to you include Arithmetic Population Density, the number of people per square kilometre in each country; Physiologic Population Density, the number of people per square kilometre of agriculturally productive land; Birth and Death Rates per thousand in the population, resulting in the national population's rate of Natural Increase; a population's Infant Mortality, the number of deaths per thousand in the first year of life, thus largely reflecting the number of deaths at birth; Child Mortality, the deaths per thousand of children in their first five years; the Corruption Index, based on Transparency International data in which 10.0 is perfect and 0.1 is the worst; the Big Mac Price index, which tells you why Argentina in 2011 was the best place to buy a hamburger in U.S. dollars; and the Per Capita GNI (U.S.$), the GNI-PPP index referred to above, which tells you how spendable income varies around the globe.

Appendix B   Area and Demographic Data for the World's States (Categories explained on page A-11)

	Land Area		Population		Population Density		Birth Rate	Death Rate	Natural Increase %	Infant Mortality per 1,000	Child Mortality per 1,000	Life Expectancy		Percent Urban Pop.	Literacy		Corruption Index	Big Mac Price ($US)	Per Capita GNI ($US)
	Sq. km.	Sq. mi.	2010 (Millions)	2025 (Millions)	Arithmetic	Physiologic						Male (years)	Female (years)		Male %	Female %			
WORLD	134,134,451	51,789,601	6,879.9	8,104.4	51	443	20	8	1.2	33	45	67	71	51	84.0	70.8			$10,030
REALM	5,930,511	2,289,783	594.9	607.1	26	204	11	11	0.0	5	6	72	80	71	99.4	98.4			$25,580
EUROPE																			
Albania	28,749	11,100	3.2	3.3	113	451	10	5	0.5	14	15	72	79	49	95.5	88.0	3.3		$7,950
Austria	83,859	32,378	8.4	8.9	100	556	9	9	0.0	3	4	78	83	67	100.0	100.0	7.9		$37,680
Belarus	207,598	80,154	9.6	9.1	46	150	12	14	-0.3	11	12	65	76	74	99.7	99.2	2.5		$12,150
Belgium	30,528	11,787	10.7	11.8	352	1,408	11	9	0.2	4	5	77	82	99	100.0	100.0	7.1		$34,760
Bosnia	51,129	19,741	3.8	3.7	74	572	9	9	0.0	13	14	72	77	46	96.5	76.6	3.2		$8,620
Bulgaria	110,908	42,822	7.5	6.9	68	165	11	14	-0.4	8	10	70	77	71	99.1	98.0	3.6		$11,950
Croatia	56,539	21,830	4.4	4.3	77	298	10	12	-0.2	5	5	72	79	56	99.4	97.3	4.1		$18,420
Cyprus	9,249	3,571	1.1	1.1	120	751	13	7	0.6	3	4	77	80	62	98.7	95.0	6.3		$24,040
Czech Republic	78,860	30,448	10.4	10.9	132	307	11	10	0.1	3	4	74	80	74	100.0	100.0	4.6	3.43	$22,790
Denmark	43,090	16,637	5.5	5.8	128	229	11	10	0.1	3	4	76	81	72	100.0	100.0	9.3	4.90	$37,280
Estonia	45,099	17,413	1.3	1.3	29	107	12	12	0.0	4	6	69	79	69	99.9	99.6	6.5	2.62	$19,280
Finland	338,149	130,560	5.3	5.8	16	225	11	9	0.2	3	3	77	83	65	100.0	100.0	9.2		$35,660
France	551,497	212,934	62.6	66.1	114	324	13	9	0.4	3	4	78	85	77	98.9	98.7	6.8		$34,400
Germany	356,978	137,830	81.9	79.7	229	655	8	10	-0.2	4	4	77	82	73	100.0	100.0	7.9		$35,940
Greece	131,960	50,950	11.2	11.7	85	283	11	10	0.1	3	3	77	82	73	98.6	96.0	3.5		$28,470
Hungary	93,030	35,919	9.9	9.8	107	194	10	13	-0.3	5	6	70	78	67	99.5	99.3	4.7	3.33	$17,790
Iceland	102,999	39,768	0.3	0.4	3	297	15	6	0.9	2	3	80	83	93	100.0	100.0	8.5		$25,220
Ireland	70,279	27,135	4.6	5.7	65	327	17	6	1.0	4	4	77	82	60	100.0	100.0	8.0		$37,350
Italy	301,267	116,320	59.8	61.9	198	536	10	10	0.0	3	4	79	84	68	98.9	98.1	3.9		$30,250
Kosovo	10,887	4,203	2.3	2.7	208		21	7	1.4	5		67	71	-	96.6	87.5	2.8		-
Latvia	64,599	24,942	2.3	2.1	35	122	10	13	-0.4	7	8	67	78	68	99.8	99.6	4.3	2.80	$16,740
Liechtenstein	161	62	0.1	0.1	874	3,495	10	6	0.4	2	2	79	82	15	100.0	100.0			-
Lithuania	65,200	25,174	3.4	3.1	52	112	11	12	-0.1	5	6	66	78	67	99.7	99.4	5.0	2.71	$18,210
Luxembourg	2,587	999	0.5	0.6	194	778	11	7	0.4	2	3	78	83	83	100.0	100.0	8.5		$64,320
Macedonia	25,711	9,927	2.0	2.0	78	300	12	9	0.2	10	11	71	76	65	94.2	83.8	4.1		$9,950
Malta	321	124	0.4	0.4	1,250	3,678	10	8	0.2	6	7	77	82	94	91.4	92.8	5.6		$22,460
Moldova	33,701	13,012	4.1	4.0	121	184	11	12	0.0	15	17	66	73	41	99.6	98.3	2.9		$3,210
Montenegro	13,812	5,333	0.6	0.6	44	156	13	9	0.4	8	9	71	76	64	100.0	100.0	3.7		$13,920
Netherlands	40,839	15,768	16.5	17.2	404	1,496	11	8	0.3	4	4	78	82	90	100.0	100.0	8.8		$41,670
Norway	323,878	125,050	4.8	5.6	15	497	13	9	0.4	3	3	79	83	80	100.0	100.0	8.6	7.20	$58,500
Poland	323,249	124,807	38.1	37.4	118	251	11	10	0.1	6	7	71	80	61	99.8	99.8	5.3	2.60	$17,310
Portugal	91,981	35,514	10.6	10.9	115	397	9	10	-0.1	3	4	75	82	55	94.8	90.0	6.0		$22,080
Romania	238,388	92,042	21.4	20.6	90	204	10	12	-0.2	10	12	69	76	55	99.1	97.3	3.7		$13,500
Serbia	88,357	34,115	7.3	6.8	83	219	9	14	-0.5	6	7	71	76	58	99.1	100.0	3.5		$11,150
Slovakia	49,010	18,923	5.4	5.4	110	324	11	10	0.2	6	7	71	79	55	100.0	100.0	4.3		$21,300

Continued

	Land Area Sq. km.	Land Area Sq. mi.	Population 2010 (Millions)	Population 2025 (Millions)	Population Density Arithmetic	Population Density Physiologic	Birth Rate	Death Rate	Natural Increase %	Infant Mortality per 1,000	Child Mortality per 1,000	Life Expectancy Male (years)	Life Expectancy Female (years)	Percent Urban Pop.	Literacy Male %	Literacy Female %	Corruption Index	Big Mac Price ($US)	Per Capita GNI ($US)
Slovenia	20,251	7,819	2.0	2.0	99	707	11	9	0.2	2	3	76	82	50	98.6	96.8	6.4		$26,910
Spain	505,988	195,363	46.7	48.4	92	237	11	8	0.3	4	4	78	84	77	100.0	100.0	6.1		$31,130
Sweden	449,959	173,730	9.2	10.2	21	293	12	10	0.2	2	3	79	83	84	100.0	100.0	9.2	6.56	$38,180
Switzerland	41,290	15,942	7.6	8.3	185	1,540	10	8	0.2	4	4	80	84	73	99.5	97.4	8.7	6.19	$46,460
Ukraine	603,698	233,089	45.6	41.9	76	128	11	15	-0.4	13	15	63	74	69	100.0	100.0	2.4	1.84	$7,210
United Kingdom	244,878	94,548	61.8	68.6	252	971	13	9	0.4	5	6	77	82	80	97.6	89.2	7.6	3.48	$36,130
RUSSIAN REALM																			
REALM	**17,261,421**	**6,664,672**	**157.7**	**158.7**	**9**	**123**	**12**	**14**	**-0.2**	**13**	**14**	**62**	**74**	**73**	**99.7**	**99.1**			**$15,531**
Russia	17,075,323	6,592,819	141.0	140.8	8	138	12	14	-0.2	11	12	62	74	73	99.8	99.2	2.1	2.33	$15,630
Armenia	29,800	11,506	3.1	3.3	105	526	15	10	0.6	20	22	68	75	64	99.4	98.1	2.6		$6,310
Azerbaijan	86,599	33,436	8.9	10.3	103	468	17	6	1.1	30	34	70	75	54	98.9	95.9	2.4		$7,770
Georgia	69,699	26,911	4.6	4.3	66	441	13	10	0.3	26	29	69	79	53	99.7	99.4	3.8		$4,850
NORTH AMERICA																			
REALM	**19,941,634**	**7,699,508**	**341.9**	**391.1**	**17**	**139**	**13**	**8**	**0.6**	**7**	**8**	**76**	**81**	**79**	**97.6**	**97.4**			**$45,890**
Canada	9,970,600	3,849,670	33.6	39.7	3	67	11	7	0.4	5	6	78	83	80	95.7	95.3	8.9	4.00	$36,220
United States	9,629,047	3,717,796	308.2	351.4	32	160	14	8	0.6	7	8	75	80	79	99.0	99.0	7.1	3.73	$46,970
MIDDLE AMERICA																			
REALM	**2,714,579**	**1,048,105**	**196.3**	**223.3**	**72**	**447**	**21**	**5**	**1.6**	**19**	**23**	**72**	**78**	**71**	**90.3**	**87.1**			**$11,910**
Antigua and Barbuda	440	170	0.1	0.1	232	1,287	14	6	0.9	11	12	73	77	31					$20,570
Bahamas	13,880	5,359	0.3	0.4	22	2,209	15	6	0.9	9	12	71	77	83	95.4	96.8			–
Barbados	430	166	0.3	0.3	706	1,811	13	8	0.5	10	11	71	76	38	98.0	96.8	7.8		–
Belize	22,960	8,865	0.3	0.4	14	342	27	4	2.3	16	18	71	74	51					$6,040
Costa Rica	51,100	19,730	4.6	5.3	90	1,002	17	4	1.3	10	11	77	82	59	95.5	95.7	5.3	3.83	$10,950
Cuba	110,859	42,803	11.3	11.1	102	248	11	8	0.3	4	6	76	80	75	99.8	99.8	3.7		–
Dominica	751	290	0.1	0.1	135	675	15	8	0.7	8	10	72	78	73			5.2		$8,300
Dominican Republic	48,731	18,815	10.3	11.6	211	679	23	6	1.7	27	32	69	75	67	84.0	83.7	3.0		$7,890
El Salvador	21,041	8,124	7.5	6.9	355	909	20	7	1.4	15	17	67	76	63	81.6	76.1	3.6		$6,670
Grenada	339	131	0.1	0.1	302	943	17	9	0.8	13	15	68	72	31					$8,060
Guadeloupe	1,709	660	0.4	0.5	238	1,585	14	7	0.7	7		76	83	100	89.7	90.5			–
Guatemala	108,888	42,042	14.5	20.0	133	739	34	6	2.8	33	40	66	73	47	76.2	61.1	3.2		$4,690
Haiti	27,749	10,714	9.4	12.2	340	1,030	28	9	1.8	64	87	59	62	48	51.0	46.5	2.2		$1,180
Honduras	112,090	43,278	7.6	9.8	68	378	28	5	2.3	25	30	70	75	50	72.5	72.0	2.4		$3,870
Jamaica	10,989	4,243	2.8	2.9	251	1,005	20	7	1.2	26	31	68	75	52	82.5	90.7	3.3		$7,360
Martinique	1,101	425	0.4	0.4	368	1,839	13	7	0.6	8		77	83	89	96.0	97.1			–
Mexico	1,958,192	756,062	111.0	123.4	57	405	19	5	1.4	15	17	74	79	77	93.1	89.1	3.1	2.50	$14,270
Netherlands Antilles	800	309	0.2	0.2	253	2,534	14	7	0.7	11	26	73	80	92	96.6	96.6			–
Nicaragua	129,999	50,193	5.9	7.5	46	208	23	4	1.8	22	26	69	73	56	64.2	64.4	2.5		$2,620
Panama	75,519	29,158	3.5	4.3	46	516	20	5	1.6	16	23	73	78	64	92.6	91.3	3.6		$11,650

Continued

	Land Area		Population		Population Density		Birth Rate	Death Rate	Natural Increase %	Infant Mortality per 1,000	Child Mortality per 1,000	Life Expectancy		Percent Urban Pop.	Literacy		Corruption Index	Big Mac Price ($US)	Per Capita GNI ($US)
	Sq. km.	Sq. mi.	2010 (Millions)	2025 (Millions)	Arithmetic	Physiologic						Male (years)	Female (years)		Male %	Female %			
Puerto Rico	8,951	3,456	4.0	4.1	450	5,005	12	7	0.4	9	9	75	82	94	93.7	94.0	5.8		–
Saint Lucia	619	239	0.2	0.2	328	1,172	14	7	0.7	19	20	71	76	28		96.0			$9,190
St. Vincent & the Grenadines	391	151	0.1	0.1	260	930	17	8	0.9	18	12	70	74	40	96.0	96.0			$8,770
Trinidad and Tobago	5,131	1,981	1.3	1.4	256	1,068	14	8	0.6	31	35	66	73	12	99.0	97.5	3.6		$23,950
SOUTH AMERICA																			
REALM	**17,867,238**	**6,898,579**	**397.5**	**444.0**	**22**	**356**	**18**	**6**	**1.2**	**17**	**20**	**70**	**77**	**82**	**90.1**	**89.0**			**$10,150**
Argentina	2,780,388	1,073,514	40.6	46.2	15	146	18	8	1.0	13	14	72	79	91	96.9	96.9	2.9	1.78	$14,020
Bolivia	1,098,575	424,162	10.4	13.3	9	474	27	7	2.0	40	51	64	68	65	92.1	79.4	2.8		$4,140
Brazil	8,547,360	3,300,154	200.6	212.4	23	335	17	6	1.0	17	21	69	77	84	85.5	85.4	3.7	4.91	$10,070
Chile	756,626	292,135	17.1	19.1	23	754	15	6	0.9	7	9	76	82	87	95.9	95.5	7.2	3.34	$13,270
Colombia	1,138,906	439,734	45.7	53.5	40	1,002	20	6	1.4	16	19	71	78	75	91.8	91.8	3.5	4.39	$8,510
Ecuador	283,560	109,483	14.4	16.6	51	460	21	5	1.6	20	24	72	78	65	93.6	90.2	2.5		$7,760
French Guiana	89,999	34,749	0.2	0.3	2	235	28	3	2.4	14		75	81	81	83.6	82.3			–
Guyana	214,969	83,000	0.8	0.8	4	191	23	7	1.6	29	35	62	70	28	99.0	98.1	2.7		$2,510
Paraguay	406,747	157,046	6.5	8.1	16	265	25	6	1.9	19	23	70	74	58	94.4	92.2	2.2		$4,820
Peru	1,285,214	496,224	28.7	34.5	22	745	21	6	1.6	19	21	71	76	76	94.7	85.4	3.5	3.54	$7,980
Suriname	163,270	63,039	0.5	0.6	3	312	19	7	1.3	24	26	65	73	67	95.9	92.6			$7,130
Uruguay	177,409	68,498	3.3	3.5	19	268	14	9	0.5	11	13	72	80	94	97.4	98.2	6.9	3.74	$12,540
Venezuela	912,046	352,143	29.1	35.1	32	797	21	5	1.6	15	18	71	77	88	93.3	92.7	2.0		$12,830
SUBSAHARAN AFRICA																			
REALM	**24,292,983**	**9,379,573**	**769.5**	**1,150.7**	**32**	**421**	**40**	**14**	**2.6**	**79**	**127**	**51**	**53**	**34**	**73.1**	**59.9**			**$1,974**
Angola	1,246,693	481,351	17.7	27.4	14	473	42	17	2.5	98	161	45	49	57	55.6	28.5	1.9		$5,020
Benin	112,620	43,483	9.9	13.6	88	548	40	10	3.0	75	118	57	60	41	47.8	23.6	2.8		$1,460
Botswana	581,727	224,606	1.8	2.2	3	316	30	11	1.9	43	57	55	55	60	74.4	79.8	5.8		$13,100
Burkina Faso	274,000	105,792	16.1	25.4	59	490	46	12	3.4	91	166	51	54	23	31.2	13.1	3.1		$1,160
Burundi	27,829	10,745	9.4	11.6	339	789	36	15	2.1	101	166	49	52	10	56.3	40.5	1.8		$380
Cameroon	475,439	183,568	19.4	26.5	41	255	37	14	2.3	95	154	50	52	53	81.8	69.2	2.2		$2,180
Cape Verde	4,030	1,556	0.5	0.7	130	1,185	25	6	2.0	23	28	69	76	61	84.3	65.3	5.1		$3,450
Central African Rep.	622,978	240,533	4.6	6.6	7	244	38	16	2.2	112	171	47	50	38	59.6	34.5	2.1		$730
Chad	1,283,994	495,753	10.7	16.9	8	277	46	17	2.9	124	209	47	50	27	66.9	40.8	1.7		$1,160
Comoros	2,230	861	0.7	0.9	332	626	33	7	2.6	75	104	62	66	28	63.5	49.1	2.1		$1,170
Congo	341,998	132,046	4.0	5.5	12	1165	38	13	2.5	81	128	52	54	60	87.5	74.4	2.1		$3,090
Congo, The	2,344,848	905,351	70.7	101.4	30	754	47	17	2.9	126	199	46	49	33	86.6	67.7	2.0		$290
Djibouti	23,201	8,958	0.8	1.1	36	3,573	29	11	1.8	75	94	54	57	76	65.0	38.4	3.2		$2,330
Equatorial Guinea	28,050	10,830	0.6	1.0	23	252	39	16	2.3	88	145	48	51	39	92.5	74.5	1.9		$21,700
Eritrea	117,598	45,405	5.3	7.4	45	1,128	37	9	2.9	39	55	57	62	21	43.9	33.4	2.6		$630
Ethiopia	1,104,296	426,371	83.1	119.8	75	684	39	12	2.7	67	104	54	57	16	83.7	70.0	2.7		$870

Continued

	Land Area		Population		Population Density		Birth Rate	Death Rate	Natural Increase %	Infant Mortality per 1,000	Child Mortality per 1,000	Life Expectancy		Percent Urban Pop.	Literacy		Corruption Index	Big Mac Price ($US)	Per Capita GNI ($US)
	Sq. km.	Sq. mi.	2010 (Millions)	2025 (Millions)	Arithmetic	Physiologic						Male (years)	Female (years)		Male %	Female %			
Gabon	267,668	103,347	14	2.0	5	269	29	10	1.9	52	69	58	61	84	79.8	62.2	2.8		$12,270
Gambia	11,300	4,363	17	2.5	149	711	38	12	2.7	78	103	54	57	54	43.8	29.6	3.2		$1,280
Ghana	238,538	92,100	25.0	31.8	105	455	31	9	2.2	47	69	58	61	48	79.5	61.2	4.1		$1,430
Guinea	245,860	94,927	10.9	15.9	44	738	41	11	3.0	88	142	55	58	28	55.1	27.0	2.0		$1,190
Guinea-Bissau	36,120	13,946	1.8	2.3	50	385	43	8	2.4	115	193	45	48	30	53.0	21.4	2.1		$530
Ivory Coast	322,459	124,502	21.7	30.8	67	293	37	14	2.4	83	119	51	54	50	54.6	38.5	2.2		$1,580
Kenya	580,367	224,081	40.2	51.3	69	865	37	10	2.7	55	84	56	57	18	89.0	76.0	2.1		$1,580
Lesotho	30,349	11,718	1.8	2.0	60	541	28	19	0.9	61	84	40	43	23	73.6	93.6	3.5		$2,000
Liberia	111,369	43,000	4.2	6.1	37	932	43	11	3.3	80	112	54	57	58	69.9	36.8	3.3		$300
Madagascar	587,036	226,656	20.0	28.6	34	680	37	9	2.7	41	58	59	62	31	87.7	72.9	2.6		$1,040
Malawi	118,479	45,745	14.5	22.9	122	582	44	15	2.9	69	110	48	50	14	74.5	46.7	3.4		$830
Mali	1,240,185	478,838	13.6	22.3	11	273	46	15	3.1	101	191	50	53	33	47.9	33.2	2.7		$1,090
Mauritania	1,025,516	395,954	3.4	4.4	3	328	34	11	2.3	74	117	55	59	40	50.6	29.5	2.3		$2,000
Mauritius	2,041	788	1.3	1.4	646	1,242	12	7	0.5	15	17	69	76	42	87.7	81.0	5.4		$12,480
Mozambique	801,586	309,494	21.3	31.2	27	663	40	15	2.3	96	142	47	49	31	59.9	28.4	2.7		$770
Namibia	824,287	318,259	2.1	2.8	3	260	28	9	1.9	34	48	60	62	35	82.9	81.2	4.4		$6,270
Niger	1,266,994	489,189	15.6	27.4	12	308	52	17	3.5	76	160	48	49	20	23.5	8.3	2.6		$680
Nigeria	923,766	356,668	155.6	217.0	168	495	42	17	2.4	86	138	47	48	47	72.3	56.2	2.4		$1,940
Réunion	2,510	969	0.8	1.0	328	2,185	18	5	1.3			75	82	92	84.8	89.2			—
Rwanda	26,340	10,170	10.1	15.8	384	915	42	14	2.9	70	111	50	53	17	73.7	60.6	4.0		$1,010
São Tomé and Príncipe	961	371	0.2	0.2	220	511	37	7	2.9	52	78	64	69	58	70.2	39.1	3.0		$1,780
Senegal	196,720	75,954	13.4	17.4	68	570	39	11	2.8	51	93	54	57	41	47.2	27.6	2.9		$1,760
Seychelles	451	174	0.1	0.1	227	1,512	18	7	1.0	11	12	68	78	53	82.9	85.7	4.8		$19,770
Sierra Leone	71,740	27,699	5.8	8.1	81	1,007	40	16	2.4	123	192	46	49	36	50.7	22.6	2.4		$750
Somalia	637,658	246,201	9.5	13.9	15	744	46	16	3.0	109	180	48	51	34	85.5	84.5	1.1		—
South Africa	1,221,034	471,444	49.1	54.4	40	309	21	12	0.9	43	62	54	57	52	68.3	46.0	4.5	2.45	$9,780
South Sudan	628,755	242,763	8.5		13.5		45	20	2.5		73	43	46	12	21.0	11.0			$490
Swaziland	17,361	6,703	1.1	1.5	63	576	31	16	1.5	52	73	46	45	22	80.9	78.7	3.2		$5,010
Tanzania	945,087	364,900	42.1	67.4	45	890	42	12	3.0	68	108	55	56	25	84.1	66.6	2.7		$1,230
Togo	56,791	21,927	7.2	9.3	127	294	33	8	2.5	64	98	60	63	40	72.2	42.6	2.4		$820
Uganda	241,040	93,066	31.1	53.4	129	379	47	13	3.4	79	128	52	53	17	77.7	57.1	2.5		$1,140
Zambia	752,607	290,583	12.7	20.3	17	241	45	20	2.5	86	141	41	42	37	85.2	71.2	3.0		$1,230
Zimbabwe	390,759	150,873	13.8	16.8	35	392	30	17	1.3	56	90	41	44	37	95.5	89.9	2.4		—
REALM	**19,318,887**	**7,459,064**	**592.4**	**739.2**	**63**	**687**	**25**	**7**	**1.9**	**33**	**43**	**67**	**71**	**57**	**83.1**	**64.5**			**$8,387**
NORTH AFRICA/SOUTHWEST ASIA																			
Afghanistan	652,086	251,772	34.4	39.4	53	440	39	18	2.1	134	199	44	44	22	51.0	20.8	1.4		—
Algeria	2,381,730	919,591	36.0	43.6	15	503	23	5	1.8	29	32	71	74	63	75.1	51.3	2.9		$7,940
Bahrain	689	266	0.8	1.6	1,201	13,345	15	2	1.3	10	12	73	77	100	91.0	82.7	4.9		—

Continued

	Land Area Sq. km.	Land Area Sq. mi.	Population 2010 (Millions)	Population 2025 (Millions)	Population Density Arithmetic	Population Density Physiologic	Birth Rate	Death Rate	Natural Increase %	Infant Mortality per 1,000	Child Mortality per 1,000	Life Expectancy Male (years)	Life Expectancy Female (years)	Percent Urban Pop.	Literacy Male %	Literacy Female %	Corruption Index	Big Mac Price ($US)	Per Capita GNI ($US)
Egypt	1,001,445	386,660	78.1	103.6	78	2,599	27	6	2.1	18	21	69	75	43	66.6	43.7	3.1	2.28	$5,460
Iran	1,633,182	630,575	74.4	87.1	46	414	19	6	1.3	26	31	70	73	69	70.7	45.0	2.2		$10,840
Iraq	438,319	169,236	30.9	44.7	71	543	32	6	2.6	35	44	64	72	67			1.5		-
Israel	21,059	8,131	7.7	9.4	368	1,751	22	5	1.6	3	4	79	83	92	97.9	94.3	6.1	3.86	$27,450
Jordan	89,210	34,444	6.1	8.5	68	1,363	31	4	2.6	22	25	72	74	83	94.9	84.4	4.7		$5,530
Kazakhstan	2,717,289	1,049,151	16.0	18.4	6	49	23	9	1.4	26	29	63	74	54	99.1	96.1	2.9		$9,690
Kuwait	17,819	6,880	2.8	4.1	157	15,734	22	2	2.0	8	10	76	80	98	84.3	79.9	4.5		$52,610
Kyrgyzstan	198,499	76,641	5.4	6.5	27	387	24	7	1.6	32	37	64	72	35	98.6	95.5	2.0		$2,130
Lebanon	10,399	4,015	4.1	4.7	396	1,276	20	5	1.5	11	12	70	74	87	92.3	80.4	2.5		$10,880
Libya	1,759,532	679,359	6.6	8.1	4	373	23	4	1.9	17	19	72	77	77	90.9	67.6	2.2		$15,630
Morocco	446,548	172,413	32.1	36.6	72	327	21	6	1.5	33	38	69	73	57	61.9	36.0	3.4		$4,330
Oman	212,459	82,031	2.8	4.2	13	1,325	20	3	1.8	9	12	70	74	72	80.4	61.7	5.3		$20,650
Palestinian Territories	6,260	2,417	4.5	6.0	716	35,797	33	4	2.8	25	30	70	73	83	96.3	87.4			-
Qatar	11,000	4,247	0.9	2.1	84	8,429	9	1	0.8	10	11	75	77	100	80.5	83.2	7.7		-
Saudi Arabia	2,149,680	829,996	29.6	35.7	14	688	28	2	2.6	18	21	74	78	81	84.1	67.2	4.7	2.67	$22,950
Sudan (North)	1,877,063	724,735	41.1		16	234	31	10	2.1	69	115	57	60	46	44.0	18.0	1.5		$2,145
Syria	185,179	71,498	20.9	28.6	113	376	28	3	2.5	14	16	72	76	54	88.3	60.4	2.5		$4,350
Tajikistan	143,099	55,251	7.6	9.8	53	761	28	4	2.4	52	61	64	69	26	99.6	98.9	2.1		$1,860
Tunisia	163,610	63,170	10.5	12.1	64	201	18	6	1.2	18	21	72	76	66	81.4	60.1	4.3		$7,070
Turkey	774,816	299,158	76.8	85.0	99	261	18	6	1.2	19	20	69	74	76	93.6	76.7	4.4	3.89	$13,770
Turkmenistan	488,099	188,456	5.4	6.1	11	276	22	8	1.4	42	45	61	69	47	98.8	96.6	1.6		$6,210
United Arab Emirates	83,600	32,278	4.6	7.0	55	5,524	15	2	1.4	7	7	77	79	83	75.5	79.5	6.3	2.99	-
Uzbekistan	447,397	172,741	28.1	34.4	63	524	23	5	1.8	32	36	65	71	36	98.5	96.0	1.6		$2,660
Western Sahara	252,120	97,344	0.5	0.7	2	5	34	9	2.5			58	62	81					-
Yemen	527,966	203,849	23.6	34.5	45	1,493	38	8	3.0	51	66	62	64	29	67.4	25.0	2.2		$2,210

SOUTH ASIA

	Land Area Sq. km.	Land Area Sq. mi.	Population 2010 (Millions)	Population 2025 (Millions)	Population Density Arithmetic	Population Density Physiologic	Birth Rate	Death Rate	Natural Increase %	Infant Mortality per 1,000	Child Mortality per 1,000	Life Expectancy Male (years)	Life Expectancy Female (years)	Percent Urban Pop.	Literacy Male %	Literacy Female %	Corruption Index	Big Mac Price ($US)	Per Capita GNI ($US)
REALM	**4,487,762**	**1,732,734**	**1,569.5**	**1,946.0**	**146**	**291**	**24**	**7**	**1.7**	**51**	**66**	**64**	**66**	**29**	**66.1**	**39.9**			**$2,882**
Bangladesh	143,998	55,598	152.4	195.0	1,058	1,679	22	7	1.5	41	52	65	67	25	51.7	29.5	2.4		$1,440
Bhutan	47,001	18,147	0.7	0.9	16	520	25	8	1.7	52	79	67	68	32	61.1	33.6	5.7		$4,880
India	3,287,576	1,269,340	1,186.4	1,444.5	361	633	23	7	1.5	50	66	63	65	29	68.6	42.1	3.3		$2,960
Maldives	300	116	0.3	0.4	1,029	10,287	22	3	1.9	11	13	72	74	35	96.3	96.4	2.3		$5,280
Nepal	147,179	56,826	28.1	35.7	191	909	28	8	1.9	39	48	64	65	17	59.1	21.8	2.2		$1,120
Pakistan	796,098	307,375	180.8	246.3	227	783	30	7	2.3	71	87	66	67	35	57.6	27.8	2.3	2.46	$2,700
Sri Lanka	65,610	25,332	20.8	23.2	317	1,093	19	7	1.2	13	15	72	76	15	94.5	88.9	3.2	1.86	$4,480

EAST ASIA

	Land Area Sq. km.	Land Area Sq. mi.	Population 2010 (Millions)	Population 2025 (Millions)	Population Density Arithmetic	Population Density Physiologic	Birth Rate	Death Rate	Natural Increase %	Infant Mortality per 1,000	Child Mortality per 1,000	Life Expectancy Male (years)	Life Expectancy Female (years)	Percent Urban Pop.	Literacy Male %	Literacy Female %	Corruption Index	Big Mac Price ($US)	Per Capita GNI ($US)
REALM	**11,774,215**	**4,546,050**	**1,573.4**	**1,703.9**	**134**	**1,083**	**12**	**7**	**0.5**	**16**	**17**	**73**	**77**	**52**	**94.9**	**84.7**			**$9,447**
China	9,572,855	3,696,100	1,338.0	1,484.7	140	998	12	7	0.5	17	19	72	76	47	92.3	77.4	3.5	1.95	$6,020
Japan	377,799	145,869	127.7	119.3	338	2,600	9	9	0.0	2	3	79	86	86	100.0	100.0	7.8	3.67	$35,220

Continued

	Land Area		Population		Population Density		Birth Rate	Death Rate	Natural Increase %	Infant Mortality per 1,000	Child Mortality per 1,000	Life Expectancy		Percent Urban Pop.	Literacy		Corruption Index	Big Mac Price ($US)	Per Capita GNI ($US)
	Sq. km.	Sq. mi.	2010 (Millions)	2025 (Millions)	Arithmetic	Physiologic						Male (years)	Female (years)		Male %	Female %			
Korea, North	120,541	46,541	23.9	23.6	198	1,240	15	10	0.5	26	33	61	66	60	99.0	99.0			–
Korea, South	99,259	38,324	49.1	49.1	495	2,603	9	5	0.4	5	5	77	83	82	99.2	96.4	5.4	2.82	$28,120
Mongolia	1,566,492	604,826	2.8	3.3	2	178	25	6	1.9	24	29	63	70	61	99.2	99.3	2.7		$3,480
Taiwan	36,180	13,969	23.1	23.9	640	2,558	8	6	0.2			75	82	78	97.6	90.2	5.8	2.34	
SOUTHEAST ASIA																			
REALM	**4,494,790**	**1,735,448**	**601.8**	**698.6**	**134**	**642**	**20**	**7**	**1.3**	**28**	**35**	**68**	**72**	**42**	**93.0**	**86.1**			**$4,510**
Brunei	5,770	2,228	0.4	0.5	72	3,578	16	3	1.3	5	7	75	80	72	94.7	88.2	5.5		$50,200
Cambodia	181,040	69,900	15.2	19.0	84	382	25	8	1.6	68	88	59	63	20	79.7	53.4	2.1		$1,820
East Timor	14,869	5,741	1.2	1.9	79	655	41	10	3.1	48	56	60	62	22			2.5		$4,690
Indonesia	1,904,561	735,355	247.2	273.2	130	763	20	5	1.4	30	39	69	73	43	91.9	82.1	2.8	2.51	$3,830
Laos	236,800	91,429	6.2	8.3	26	871	28	7	2.1	46	59	63	66	27	73.6	50.5	2.1		$2,060
Malaysia	329,750	127,317	28.6	34.9	87	361	21	5	1.6	6	6	72	77	63	91.5	83.6	4.4	2.19	$13,740
Myanmar (Burma)	676,577	261,228	50.1	61.7	74	463	20	11	0.9	54	71	56	60	31	89.0	80.6	1.4		$1,290
Philippines	299,998	115,830	94.3	117.6	314	953	26	5	2.1	26	33	70	74	63	95.5	95.2	2.4	2.19	$3,900
Singapore	619	239	4.9	5.7	7,848	392,384	10	4	0.6	2	3	79	84	100	96.4	88.5	9.3	3.08	$47,940
Thailand	513,118	198,116	66.8	72.6	130	325	15	9	0.6	12	14	66	72	31	97.2	94.0	3.5	2.17	$5,990
Vietnam	331,689	128,066	88.3	103.2	266	1,210	17	5	1.2	20	24	72	76	28	95.7	91.0	2.7		$2,700
AUSTRAL REALM																			
REALM	**8,012,942**	**3,093,814**	**26.0**	**31.9**	**3**	**45**	**14**	**6**	**0.8**	**4**	**5**	**79**	**84**	**83**	**100.0**	**100.0**	**8.7**		**$32,850**
Australia	7,741,184	2,988,888	21.6	26.9	3	40	14	6	0.7	4	5	79	84	82	100.0	100.0	8.7	3.84	$34,040
New Zealand	270,529	104,452	4.4	5.0	16	135	14	7	0.8	5	6	78	82	86	100.0	100.0	9.3	3.59	$25,090
PACIFIC REALM																			
REALM	**975,341**	**376,804**	**9.6**	**13.1**	**17**	**806**	**29**	**5**	**2.0**	**42**	**55**	**60**	**65**	**22**	**65.9**	**52.1**			**$2,114**
Federated States of Micronesia	699	270	0.1	0.1	149	286	25	6	1.9	32	39	67	68	22	67.0	87.2			$3,000
Fiji	18,270	7,054	0.9	0.9	51	317	24	7	1.7	15	18	66	71	51	95.0	90.9			$4,270
French Polynesia	3,999	1,544	0.3	0.3	77	964	18	5	1.3			72	77	53	94.9	95.0			–
Guam	549	212	0.2	0.2	375	1,706	19	4	1.5			76	82	93	99.0	99.0			–
Marshall Islands	179	69	0.1	0.1	596	3,506	34	6	2.8	29	35	64	67	68	92.4	90.0			–
New Caledonia	18,581	7,174	0.2	0.3	11	1,105	16	5	1.2			72	80	58	57.4	58.3			–
Papua New Guinea	462,839	178,703	6.8	9.1	15	1,464	31	10	2.2	52	68	57	62	13	63.4	50.9	2.1		$2,000
Samoa	2,841	1,097	0.2	0.2	74	171	26	5	2.0	21	25	72	74	22	100.0	100.0	4.1		$4,340
Solomon Islands	28,899	11,158	0.5	0.8	18	607	33	8	2.5	30	36	62	63	17	62.4	44.9	2.8		$2,580
Vanuatu	12,191	4,707	0.2	0.3	17	172	31	6	2.5	14	16	66	69	24	57.3	47.8	3.6		$3,940

GLOSSARY

Absolute location   The position or place of a certain item on the surface of the Earth as expressed in degrees, minutes, and seconds of latitude, 0° to 90° north or south of the equator, and longitude, 0° to 180° east or west of the Prime Meridian passing through Greenwich, England (a suburb of London).

Accessibility   The degree of ease with which it is possible to reach a certain location from other locations. Accessibility varies from place to place and can be measured.

Acid rain   A growing environmental peril whereby acidified rainwater severely damages plant and animal life; caused by the oxides of sulphur and nitrogen that are released into the atmosphere when coal, oil, and natural gas are burned, especially in major manufacturing zones.

Acropolis   Literally "high point of the city." The upper fortified part of an ancient Greek city, usually devoted to religious purposes.

Agglomeration   A process involving the clustering or concentrating of people or activities. The term often refers to manufacturing plants and businesses that benefit from close proximity because they share skilled-labour pools and technological and financial amenities.

Agora   In ancient Greece, public spaces where citizens debated, lectured, judged each other, planned military campaigns, socialized, and traded.

Agribusiness   The businesses that provide the vast array of goods and services that support the agriculture industry.

Agricultural surplus   Agricultural production in excess of that which the producer needs for his or her own sustenance and that of his or her family and which is then sold for consumption by others; one of two components, together with social stratification, that enable the formation of cities.

Agricultural village   A relatively small, egalitarian village, where most of the population was involved in agriculture. Starting over 10,000 years ago, people began to cluster in agricultural villages as they stayed in one place to tend their crops.

Agriculture   The purposeful tending of crops and livestock in order to produce food and fibre.

AIDS (acquired immune deficiency syndrome)   Immune system disease, caused by the human immunodeficiency virus (HIV), which over a period of years weakens the capacity of the immune system to fight off infection so that weight loss and weakness set in and other afflictions, such as cancer or pneumonia, may hasten an infected person's demise.

Air pollution   Pollution of the atmosphere.

Animal domestication   Genetic modification of an animal such that it is rendered more amenable to human control.

Anthropocentric view   A view in which human interests and perspectives are highlighted.

Aquifers   Subterranean, porous, water-holding rocks that provide millions of wells with steady flows of water.

Arithmetic population density   The population of a country or region expressed as an average per unit area. The figure is derived by dividing the population of the areal unit by the number of square kilometres or miles that make up the unit.

Assimilation   The process through which people lose originally differentiating traits, such as dress, speech particularities, or mannerisms, when they come into contact with another society or culture. Often used to describe immigrant adaptation to new places of residence.

Asylum   Shelter and protection in one state for refugees from another state.

Atmosphere   Blanket of gases surrounding the Earth and located some 600 kilometres above the Earth's surface.

Authenticity   In the context of local cultures or customs, the accuracy with which a single stereotypical or typecast image or experience conveys an otherwise dynamic and complex local culture or its customs.

Automobile dependence   A situation in which a city develops on the assumption that automobile use will predominate so that it is given priority in infrastructure and in the form of urban development.

Barrioization   Defined by geographer James Curtis as the dramatic increase in Hispanic population in a given neighbourhood; referring to *barrio,* the Spanish word for neighbourhood.

Behavioural geography   An approach that seeks to understand and model human behaviour and the decision-making processes implicated in human relationships with place.

Biodiversity   The total variety of plant and animal species in a particular place; biological diversity.

Boundary   Vertical plane between states that cuts through the rocks below (called the subsoil) and the airspace above the surface, dividing one state territory from another.

Break-of-bulk point   A location along a transport route where goods must be transferred from one carrier to another. A port, for example, is a break-of-bulk point where the cargoes of ocean-going ships are unloaded and put on trains, trucks, or perhaps smaller riverboats for inland distribution.

Capitalism   Economic model wherein people, corporations, and states produce goods and exchange them on the world market, with the goal of achieving profit.

Cartography   The art and science of making maps, including data compilation, layout, and design. Also concerned with the interpretation of mapped patterns.

Caste system   The strict social segregation of people—specifically in India's Hindu society—on the basis of ancestry and occupation.

Census   A periodic and official count of a country's population.

Central business district (CBD)   The downtown heart of a central city, marked by high land values, a concentration of business and commerce, and the clustering of the tallest buildings.

Central city   The urban area that is not suburban; generally, the older or original city that is surrounded by newer suburbs.

Central place theory   Theory proposed by Walter Christaller that explains how and where central places in the urban hierarchy should be functionally and spatially distributed with respect to one another.

Centrality   The strength of an urban centre in its capacity to attract producers and consumers to its facilities; a city's "reach" into the surrounding region.

Centrifugal   Forces that tend to divide a country—such as internal religious, linguistic, ethnic, or ideological differences.

Centripetal   Forces that tend to unify a country—such as widespread commitment to a national culture, shared ideological objectives, and a common faith.

Chain migration   Pattern of migration that develops when migrants move along and through kinship links (i.e., one migrant settles in a place and then writes, calls, or communicates through others to describe this place to family and friends, who in turn then migrate there).

Child mortality rate   A figure that describes the number of children who die between the first and fifth years of their lives in a given population.

Chlorofluorocarbons (CFCs)   Synthetic organic compounds first created in the 1950s and used primarily as refrigerants and as propellants. The role of CFCs in the destruction of the ozone layer led to the signing of an international agreement (the Montreal Protocol).

Chronic or degenerative diseases   Generally, long-lasting afflictions that are now more common because of higher life expectancies.

City   Conglomeration of people and buildings clustered together to serve as a centre of politics, culture, and economics.

Colonialism   Rule by an autonomous power over a subordinate and alien people and place. Although often established and maintained through political structures, colonialism also creates unequal cultural and economic relations. Because of the magnitude and impact of the European colonial project of the last few centuries, the term is generally understood to refer to that particular colonial endeavour.

Colonization   Physical process whereby the colonizer takes over another place, putting its own government in charge and either moving its own people into the place or bringing in indentured outsiders to gain control of the people and the land.

Commercial agriculture   Large-scale farming and ranching operations that employ vast land bases, large mechanized equipment, factory-type labour forces, and the latest technology.

Commercialization   The transformation of an area of a city into an area attractive to residents and tourists alike in terms of economic activity.

Commodification   The process through which something is given monetary value. Commodification occurs when a good or an idea that previously was not regarded as an object to be bought and sold is turned into something that has a particular price and that can be traded in a market economy.

Commodity chain   Series of links connecting the many places of production and distribution that result in a commodity, which is then exchanged on the world market.

Complementarity   A condition that exists when two regions, through an exchange of raw materials and/or finished products, can specifically satisfy each other's demands.

Concentric zone model   A structural model of the American central city that suggests the existence of five concentric land-use rings arranged around a common centre.

Connectivity   The degree of direct linkage between one particular location and other locations in a transport network.

Conservationism   A human-centred view of nature that advocates for conservation of resources for future human use.

Contagious diffusion   The distance-controlled spreading of an idea, innovation, or some other item through a local population by contact from person to person—analogous to the communication of a contagious illness.

Containerization   The use of containers to unitize cargo for transportation, supply, and storage.

Context   The geographical situation in which something occurs; the combination of what is happening at a variety of scales concurrently.

Core   Processes that incorporate higher levels of education, higher salaries, and more technology; they generate more wealth than periphery processes in the world economy.

Critical geopolitics   Process by which geopoliticians deconstruct and focus on explaining the underlying spatial assumptions and territorial perspectives of politicians.

Crude birth rate (CBR)   The number of live births yearly per thousand people in a population.

Crude death rate (CDR)   The number of deaths yearly per thousand people in a population.

Cultural appropriation   The process by which cultures adopt customs and knowledge from other cultures and use them for their own benefit.

Cultural barrier   Prevailing cultural attitude rendering certain innovations, ideas, or practices unacceptable or unadoptable in that particular culture.

Cultural diffusion   The expansion and adoption of a cultural element, from its place of origin to a wider area.

Cultural landscape   The visible imprint of human activity and culture on the landscape. The layers of buildings, forms, and artefacts sequentially imprinted on the landscape by the activities of various human occupants.

Cultural trait   A single element of normal practice in a culture, such as the wearing of a turban.

Culture   A set of shared belief systems, norms, and values practised by a particular group of people. According to cultural theorist Raymond Williams, culture is both "ordinary" and a "whole way of life."

Custom   Practice routinely followed by a group of people.

Deforestation   The clearing and destruction of forests to harvest wood for consumption, clear land for agricultural uses, and make way for expanding settlement frontiers.

Deagglomeration   The process of industrial deconcentration in response to technological advances and/or increasing costs due to congestion and competition.

Deindustrialization   Process by which companies move industrial jobs to other regions with cheaper labour, leaving the newly deindustrialized region to switch to a service economy and to work through a period of high unemployment.

Demographic transition   Multistage model, based on Western Europe's experience, of changes in population growth exhibited by countries undergoing industrialization. High birth rates and death rates are followed by plunging death rates, producing a huge net population gain; this is followed by the convergence of birth rates and death rates at a low overall level.

Demography   The study of the characteristics of a population, such as race, age, sex, and ethnicity.

Dependency theory   A structuralist theory that offers a critique of the modernization model of development. Based on the idea that certain types of political and economic relations (especially colonialism) between countries and regions of the world have created arrangements that both control and limit the extent to which regions can develop.

Deportation   The act of a government sending a migrant out of its country and back to the migrant's home country.

Desertification   The encroachment of desert conditions on moister zones along the desert margins, where plant cover and soils are threatened by desiccation—through overuse, in part by humans and their domestic animals, and, possibly, in part because of inexorable shifts in the Earth's environmental zones.

Developing   With respect to a country, making progress in technology, production, and socio-economic welfare.

Devolution   The process whereby regions within a state demand and gain political strength and growing autonomy at the expense of the central government.

Diaspora   From the Greek "to disperse," a term describing forceful or voluntary dispersal of a people from their homeland to a new place. Originally denoting the dispersal of Jews, it is increasingly applied to other population dispersals, such as the involuntary relocation of Black peoples during the slave trade or Chinese peoples outside of Mainland China, Taiwan, and Hong Kong.

Diffusion   The spatial spreading or dissemination of a culture element (such as a technological innovation) or some other phenomenon (e.g., a disease outbreak). See also *contagious*, *expansion*, *hierarchical*, *relocation*, and *stimulus diffusion*.

Disamenity sector   The very poorest parts of cities that in extreme cases are not even connected to regular city services and are controlled by gangs or drug lords.

Distance   Measurement of the physical space between two places.

Distance decay   The effects of distance on interaction; generally the greater the distance, the less interaction.

Dot maps   Maps where one dot represents a certain number of a phenomenon, such as a population.

Doubling time   The time required for a population to double in size.

Dowry death   In the context of arranged marriages in India, the death of a bride arising from a dispute over the price (the dowry) to be paid by the family of the bride to the father of the groom.

Edge cities   A term introduced by American journalist Joel Garreau in order to describe the shifting focus of urbanization in the United States away from the central business district (CBD) toward new loci of economic activity at the urban fringe. These cities are characterized by extensive amounts of office and retail space, few residential areas, and modern buildings (less than 30 years old).

Emigration   The act of leaving one location or place for another, from the perspective of the beginning location.

Endemic   When disease prevails over a particular locality or region.

Environmental determinism   The view that the natural environment has a controlling influence over various aspects of human life, including cultural development.

Environmental stress   The threat to environmental security by human activity such as atmospheric and groundwater pollution, deforestation, oil spills, and ocean dumping.

Epidemic   Regional outbreak of a disease.

Ethnicity   Affiliation or identity within a group of people bound by common ancestry and culture.

Eugenic population policies   Government policies designed to favour one racial sector over others.

Expansion diffusion   The spread of an innovation or an idea through a population in an area in such a way that the number of those influenced grows continuously larger, resulting in an expanding area of dissemination.

Expansive population policies   Government policies that encourage large families and raise the rate of population growth.

Explorer   A person examining a region that is unknown to them.

Export processing zones (EPZs)   Zones established by many countries in the periphery and semi-periphery, where they offer favourable tax, regulatory, and trade arrangements to attract foreign trade and investment.

Federal (state)   A political-territorial system in which a central government represents the various entities within a nation-state where they have common interests—defence, foreign affairs, and the like—but allows these various entities to retain their own identities and to have their own laws, policies, and customs in certain spheres.

First Agricultural Revolution   Dating back 10,000 years, the First Agricultural Revolution achieved plant domestication and animal domestication.

First Urban Revolution   The innovation of the city, which occurred independently in five separate hearths.

Five themes (of geography)   The five themes derived from the spatial perspective of geography are location, region, place, landscape, and movement.

Folk culture   The cultural traits, such as dress modes, dwellings, traditions, and institutions, of usually small, traditional communities.

Forced migration   Human migration flows in which the movers have no choice but to relocate.

Fordist   A highly organized and specialized system for organizing industrial production and labour. Named after automobile producer Henry Ford, Fordist production features assembly-line production of standardized components for mass production.

Formal economy   The legal economy that is taxed and monitored by a government and is included in a government's gross national product (GNP); as opposed to an informal economy.

Formal region   A type of region marked by a certain degree of homogeneity in one or more phenomena; also called uniform region or homogeneous region.

Forum   The focal point of ancient Roman life, combining the functions of the ancient Greek acropolis and agora.

Free trade zones   Areas set aside within countries to make foreign investment and trade easier by reducing or eliminating trade barriers and providing inexpensive labour and raw materials.

Friction of distance   The increase in time and cost that usually comes with increasing distance.

Functional region   A region defined by the particular set of activities or interactions that occur within it.

Functional zonation   The division of a city into different regions or zones (e.g., residential or industrial) for certain purposes or functions (e.g., housing or manufacturing).

Gender   Social differences between men and women, rather than the anatomical, biological differences between the sexes. Notions of gender differences—that is, what is considered "feminine" or "masculine"—vary greatly over time and space.

Gendered   In terms of a place, whether the place is designed for or claimed by men or women.

Genetic or inherited diseases   Diseases caused by variation or mutation of a gene or group of genes in a human.

Genetically modified organisms (GMOs)   Crops that carry new traits that have been inserted through advanced genetic engineering methods.

Genocide   The deliberate and systematic destruction, in whole or in part, of an ethnic, racial, religious, or national group.

Gentrification   The rehabilitation of deteriorated, often abandoned, housing of low-income inner-city residents.

Geocaching   A hunt for a cache, the global positioning system (GPS) coordinates of which are placed on the Internet by other geocachers.

Geographic information system (GIS)   A collection of computer hardware and software that permits spatial data to be collected, recorded, stored, retrieved, manipulated, analyzed, and displayed to the user.

Geomatics technologies   Those processes and tools used in the collection and analysis of spatial data, including remote sensing (RS), geographic information systems (GIS), global positioning systems (GPS), and related forms of earth mapping.

Geometric boundary   Political boundary defined and delimited (and occasionally demarcated) as a straight line or an arc.

Global division of labour   Phenomenon whereby corporations and others can draw from labour markets around the world, made possible by the compression of time and space through innovations in communication and transportation systems.

Global positioning system (GPS)   Satellite-based system for determining the absolute location of places or geographic features.

Global warming   Theory that the Earth is gradually warming as a result of an enhanced greenhouse effect in the Earth's atmosphere caused by ever-increasing amounts of carbon dioxide produced by various human activities.

Global-local continuum   The notion that what happens at the global scale has a direct effect on what happens at the local scale, and vice versa. This idea posits that the world is comprised of an interconnected series of relationships that extend across space.

Globalization   The expansion of economic, political, and cultural processes to the point that they become global in scale and impact. The processes of globalization transcend state boundaries and have outcomes that vary across places and scales.

Glocalization   The process by which people in a local place mediate and alter regional, national, and global processes.

Gravity model   A mathematical prediction of the interaction of places, the interaction being a function of population size of the respective places and the distance between them.

Green Revolution   The recently successful development of higher-yield, fast-growing varieties of rice and other cereals in certain developing countries, which led to increased production per unit area and a dramatic narrowing of the gap between population growth and food needs.

Griffin-Ford model   Developed by geographers Ernst Griffin and Larry Ford, this model of the Latin American city shows a blend of traditional elements of Latin American culture with the forces of globalization that are reshaping the urban scene.

Gross domestic product (GDP)   The total value of all goods and services produced within a country during a given year.

Gross national income (GNI)   The total value of all goods and services produced within a country plus income received from investments outside the country.

Gross national product (GNP)   The total value of all goods and services produced by a country's economy in a given year. It includes all goods and services produced by corporations and individuals of a country, whether or not they are located within the country.

Guest worker   Legal immigrant who has a work visa, usually short term.

Hearth   The area where an idea or cultural trait originates.

Heartland theory   A geopolitical hypothesis, proposed by British geographer Halford Mackinder during the first two decades of the 20th century, that any political power based in the heart of Eurasia could gain sufficient strength to eventually dominate the world. Mackinder further proposed that since eastern Europe controlled access to the Eurasian interior, its ruler would command the vast "heartland" to the east.

Heteronormative   The assumption in research that the "typical" research subject is heterosexual, white, middle-class, and male.

Hierarchical diffusion   A form of diffusion in which an idea or innovation spreads by passing first among the most connected places or peoples. An urban hierarchy is usually involved, encouraging the leapfrogging of innovations over wide areas, with geographic distance a less important influence.

Horizontal integration   Ownership by the same firm of a number of companies that exist at the same point on a commodity chain.

Huang He (Yellow) and **Wei (Yangtze) river valleys**   Chronologically, the fourth urban hearth, established around 1500 BCE, at the confluence of the Huang He and Wei rivers in present-day China.

Human geography   One of the two major divisions of geography; the spatial analysis of human population, its cultures, activities, and landscapes.

Human-environment   The second theme of geography as defined by the Geography Educational National Implementation Project; reciprocal relationship between humans and environment.

Humanistic geography   An approach that focuses on the human aspects of place, including human emotions, values, and desires.

Identifying against   Constructing an identity by first defining the "other" and then defining ourselves as "not the other."

Identity   Defined by geographer Gillian Rose as "how we make sense of ourselves"; how people see themselves at different scales.

Immigration   The act of migrating into a new country or area.

Immigration wave   Phenomenon whereby different patterns of chain migration build upon one another to create a swell in migration from one origin to the same destination.

Indus River Valley   Chronologically, the third urban hearth, dating to 2200 BCE.

Industrial Revolution   The term applied to the social and economic changes in agriculture, commerce, and manufacturing that resulted from technological innovations and specialization in late-18th-century Europe.

Infant mortality rate (IMR)   A figure that describes the number of babies that die within the first year of their lives in a given population.

Infectious diseases   Diseases that are spread by bacteria, viruses, or parasites. Infectious diseases diffuse directly or indirectly from human to human.

Informal economy   Economic activity that is neither taxed nor monitored by a government and is not included in that government's gross national product (GNP); as opposed to a formal economy.

Intermodal (connections)   Places where two or more modes of transportation meet (including air, road, rail, barge, and ship).

Intermodal transportation   The transportation of a person or a load from its origin to its destination by a sequence of at least two transportation modes, the transfer from one mode to the next being performed at an intermodal terminal.

Internal migration   Human movement within a nation-state, such as ongoing westward and southward movements in Canada.

Internally displaced persons (IDPs)   People who have been displaced within their own countries and do not cross international borders as they flee.

International migration   Human movement involving movement across international boundaries.

Intersectionality   The complex connections and relationships between various social categories such as race, class, gender, and sexuality.

Intervening opportunity   The presence of a nearer opportunity that greatly diminishes the attractiveness of sites farther away.

Island of development   Place built up by a government or corporation to attract foreign investment, which has relatively high concentrations of paying jobs and infrastructure.

Just-in-time delivery   Method of inventory management made possible by efficient transportation and communication systems, whereby companies keep on hand just what they need for near-term production, planning that what they need for longer-term production will arrive when needed.

Kinship links   Types of push factors or pull factors that influence a migrant's decision to go where family or friends have already found success.

Landscape   The fourth theme of geography; the overall appearance of an area. Most landscapes are comprised of a combination of natural and human-induced influences.

Language family   Group of languages with a shared but fairly distant origin.

Laws of migration   Developed by British demographer Ernst Ravenstein, five laws that predict the flow of migrants.

Leadership class   Group of decision makers and organizers in early cities who controlled the resources, and often the lives, of others.

Least Cost Theory   Model developed by Alfred Weber according to which the location of manufacturing establishments is determined by the minimization of three critical expenses: labour, transportation, and agglomeration.

Life expectancy   A figure indicating how long, on average, a person may be expected to live. Normally expressed in the context of a particular state.

Livestock ranching   The raising of domesticated animals for the production of meat and other by-products such as leather and wool.

Local culture   Group of people in a particular place who see themselves as a collective or a community, who share experiences, customs, and traits, and who work to preserve those traits and customs in order to claim uniqueness and to distinguish themselves from others.

Local Exchange Trading System (LETS)   A barter system whereby a local currency is created through which members trade services or goods in a local network separated from the formal economy.

Location   The first theme of geography; the geographical situation of people and things.

Location theory   A logical attempt to explain the locational pattern of an economic activity and the manner in which its producing areas are interrelated. The agricultural location theory contained in the von Thünen model is a leading example.

Long-lot survey system   Distinct regional approach to land surveying found in the Canadian Maritimes, parts of Quebec, Louisiana, and Texas whereby land is divided into narrow parcels stretching back from rivers, roads, or canals.

Luxury crops   Non-subsistence crops such as tea, cacao, coffee, and tobacco.

Malaria   Vectored disease, spread by mosquitoes that carry the malaria parasite in their saliva, that kills approximately 150,000 children in the global periphery each month.

Maquiladora   Zones in northern Mexico where factories are established to supply manufactured goods to the U.S. market. The low-wage workers in the primarily foreign-owned factories assemble imported components and/or raw materials and then export finished goods.

Material culture   The art, housing, clothing, sports, dances, foods, and other similar items constructed or created by a group of people.

Mediterranean agriculture   Specialized farming that occurs only in areas where the dry summer Mediterranean climate prevails.

Mega-city   A city having a population of more than 10 million inhabitants.

Megalopolis   Large coalescing supercities that are forming in diverse parts of the world; formerly used specifically with an uppercase "M" to refer to locations such as the Boston–Washington multi-metropolitan corridor on the northeastern seaboard of the United States.

Mental map   Image or picture of the way space is organized as determined by an individual's perception, impression, and knowledge of that space.

Mercantilism   In a general sense, associated with the promotion of commercialism and trade. More specifically, a protectionist policy of European states during the 16th to the 18th centuries that promoted a state's economic position in the contest with other countries. The acquisition of gold and silver and the maintenance of a favourable trade balance (more exports than imports) were central to the policy.

Mesoamerica   Chronologically, the fifth urban hearth, dating to 200 BCE.

Mesopotamia   Region of great cities (e.g., Ur and Babylon) located between the Tigris and Euphrates Rivers; chronologically, the first urban hearth, dating to 3500 BCE, which was founded in the Fertile Crescent.

Metes and bounds system   A system of land surveying east of the Appalachian Mountains that relies on descriptions of land ownership and natural features such as streams or trees. Because of the imprecise nature of metes and bounds surveying, the U.S. Land Office abandoned the technique in favour of the rectangular survey system.

Microcredit program   Program that provides small loans to poor people, especially women, to encourage development of small businesses.

Migrant labour   A common type of periodic movement involving millions of workers in the United States and tens of millions of workers worldwide who cross international borders in search of employment and, in many instances, become immigrants.

Migration   A change in residence intended to be permanent. See also *chain, forced, internal, international, step,* and *voluntary migration.*

Millennium Development Goals   A set of eight human development-related goals for the world's most impoverished countries, which were adopted at the United Nations Millennium Summit in 2000 with the intention of achieving all of these goals by the year 2015.

Modernization model   A model of economic development most closely associated with the work of economist Walter Rostow. The modernization model (sometimes referred to as modernization theory) maintains that all countries go through five interrelated stages of development, which culminate in an economic state of self-sustained economic growth and high levels of mass consumption.

Monoculture   Dependence on a single agricultural commodity.

Montreal Protocol   An international agreement signed in 1987 by 105 countries and the European Community (now European Union). The protocol called for a 50 percent reduction in the production and consumption of chlorofluorocarbons (CFCs) by 2000. Subsequent meetings in London (1990) and Copenhagen (1992) accelerated the timing of CFC phaseout, and a worldwide complete ban has been in effect since 1996.

Movement   The fifth theme of geography; the mobility of people, goods, and ideas across the surface of the planet.

Multinational state   A state with more than one nation within its borders.

Multistate nation   A nation that stretches across borders and across states.

Nation   A tightly knit group of people possessing bonds of language, ethnicity, religion, and other shared cultural attributes. Such homogeneity actually prevails within very few states.

Nation-state   Theoretically, a recognized member of the modern state system possessing formal sovereignty and occupied by a people who see themselves as a single, united nation. Most nations and states aspire to this form, but it is realized almost nowhere. Nonetheless, in common parlance, nation-state is used as a synonym for country or state.

Nationalism   Both an ideology and a political practice that says all nations need their own sovereign government and territory.

Neighbourhood unit   A planning concept developed by Clarence Perry as a means of reconciling the problems of automobile traffic with public safety objectives, most notably those aimed at the safety of children.

Neo-colonialism   The entrenchment of the colonial order, such as trade and investment, under a new guise.

Neo-liberalism   An ideology that emphasizes self-regulating markets, minimal state intervention, and individual choice, as a means of ensuring economic and social well-being.

Networks   A set of interconnected nodes without a centre, as defined by Manuel Castells.

New urbanism   Outlined by a group of architects, urban planners, and developers from over 20 countries, an urban design that calls for development, urban revitalization, and suburban reforms that create walkable neighbourhoods with a diversity of housing and jobs.

Nile River Valley   Chronologically, the second urban hearth, dating to 3200 BCE.

Noise pollution   A type of pollution in which distracting, irritating, or damaging sounds are freely audible.

Nomadism   Movement among a definite set of places—often cyclic movement.

Non-governmental organizations (NGOs)   International organizations that operate outside the formal political arena but are nevertheless influential in spearheading international initiatives on social, economic, and environmental issues.

Nonmaterial culture   The beliefs, practices, aesthetics, and values of a group of people.

Non-renewable resources   Resources that cannot regenerate as they are exploited.

North American Free Trade Agreement (NAFTA)   Agreement entered into by Canada, Mexico, and the United States to eliminate the barriers to trade in, and facilitate the cross-border movement of, goods and services between the countries.

Offshore   With reference to production, to outsource to a third party located outside the country.

One-child policy   A program established by the Chinese government in 1979 to slow population growth in China. Under the policy, families having more than one child were penalized financially and denied educational opportunities and housing privileges.

Outsource   With reference to production, to turn over in part or in total to a third party.

Oxygen cycle   Cycle whereby natural processes and human activity consume atmospheric oxygen and produce carbon dioxide and the Earth's forests and other flora, through photosynthesis, consume carbon dioxide and produce oxygen.

Ozone layer   The layer in the upper atmosphere, located between 30 and 45 kilometres above the Earth's surface, where stratospheric ozone is most densely concentrated. The ozone layer acts as a filter for the Sun's harmful ultraviolet rays.

Pandemic   An outbreak of a disease that spreads worldwide. See also *epidemic.*

Participatory development   The notion that locals should be engaged in deciding what development means for them and how it should be achieved.

Pattern   The design of a spatial distribution (e.g., scattered or concentrated).

Peace of Westphalia   Peace negotiated in 1648 to end the Thirty Years' War, Europe's most destructive internal struggle over religion. The treaties contained new language recognizing statehood and nationhood, clearly defined borders, and guarantees of security.

Per capita GNI   The gross national income (GNI) of a given country (that is, the total value of all goods and services produced within a country, plus income received from investments outside the country) divided by the population of the country.

Perceptual region   A region that exists only as a conceptualization or an idea and not as a physically demarcated entity. For example, the North or the Maritimes.

Periphery   Processes that incorporate lower levels of education, lower salaries, and less technology; and generate less wealth than core processes in the world economy.

Physical geography   One of the two major divisions of systematic geography; the spatial analysis of the structure, processes, and location of the Earth's natural phenomena such as climate, soil, plants, animals, and topography.

Physical-political (natural-political) boundary   A political boundary defined and delimited (and occasionally demarcated) by a prominent physical feature in the natural landscape—such as a river or the crest ridges of a mountain range.

Physiologic population density   The number of people per unit area of arable land.

Place   The third theme of geography; uniqueness of a location.

Placelessness   The loss of uniqueness of place in the cultural landscape so that one place looks like the next, as defined by geographer Edward Relph.

Plant domestication   Genetic modification of a plant such that its reproductive success depends on human intervention.

Plantation agriculture   Production system based on a large estate owned by an individual, family, or corporation and organized to produce a cash crop. Almost all plantations were established within the tropics; in recent decades, many have been divided into smaller holdings or reorganized as cooperatives.

Political geography   A subdivision of human geography focused on the nature and implications of the evolving spatial organization of political governance and formal political practice on the Earth's surface. It is concerned with why political spaces emerge in the places that they do and with how the character of those spaces affects social, political, economic, and environmental understandings and practices.

Popular culture   Cultural traits, such as dress, diet, and music, that identify and are part of today's changeable, urban-based, media-influenced western societies.

Population composition   Structure of a population in terms of age, sex, and other properties such as marital status and education.

Population density   A measurement of the number of people per given unit of land.

Population distribution   Description of locations on the Earth's surface where populations live.

Population explosion   The rapid growth of the world's human population during the past century, attended by ever-shorter doubling times and accelerating rates of increase.

Population geography   The study of why populations have certain characteristics and why they distribute themselves across space in particular ways.

Population pyramids   Visual representations of the age and sex composition of a population in which the percentage of each age group (generally five-year increments) is represented by a horizontal bar, the length of which represents its relationship to the total population. The males in each age group are represented to the left of the centre line of each horizontal bar; the females in each age group are represented to the right of the centre line.

Possibilism   Geographic viewpoint—a response to environmental determinism—that holds that human decision making, not the environment, is the crucial factor in cultural development. Nonetheless, possibilists view the environment as providing a set of broad constraints that limit the possibilities of human choice.

Post-Fordist   World economic system characterized by a more flexible set of production practices in which goods are not mass-produced; instead, production has been accelerated and dispersed around the globe by multinational companies that shift production, outsourcing it around the world and bringing places closer together in time and space than would have been imaginable at the beginning of the 20th century.

Preservationism   A view asserting that nature should be preserved for its own sake, rather than for human use.

Primary industrial regions   Western and central Europe; eastern North America; Russia and Ukraine; and eastern Asia, each of which consists of one or more core areas of industrial development, with subsidiary clusters.

Primate city   A country's largest city—ranking atop the urban hierarchy—most expressive of the national culture and usually (but not always) the capital city as well.

Primogeniture   System in which the eldest son—or, in exceptional cases, the eldest daughter—in a family inherits all of a dying parent's land.

Public transit   Various services that provide mobility to the general public in shared vehicles, ranging from shared taxis and shuttle vans, to local and intercity buses and passenger rail.

Pull factor   Positive conditions and perceptions that effectively attract people to new locales from other areas.

Push factor   Negative conditions and perceptions that induce people to leave their abode and migrate to a new locale.

Quotas   Established limits by governments on the number of immigrants who can enter a country each year.

Race   A categorization of humans based on skin colour and other physical characteristics. Racial categories are social and political constructions because they are based on ideas that some biological differences (especially skin colour) are more important than others (e.g., height, etc.), even though the latter might have more significance in terms of human activity. With its roots in 16th-century England, the term is closely associated with European colonialism because of the impact of that development on global understandings of racial differences.

Racism   An ideology that ascribes (predominantly negative) significance and meaning to culturally, socially, and politically constructed ideas based on visible differences in individuals.

Radburn Idea   A highly influential community planning concept incorporating a hierarchy of roadways, the deliberate segregation of pedestrian and automobile traffic, and the residential "superblock."

Radioactive waste   Hazardous-waste-emitting radiation from nuclear power plants, nuclear weapons factories, and nuclear equipment in hospitals and industry.

Rank-size rule   In a model urban hierarchy, the idea that the population of a city or town will be inversely proportional to its rank in the hierarchy.

Rate of natural increase   An indicator of population change, calculated by subtracting the crude death rate from the crude birth rate.

Rectangular survey system   Also called the Public Land Survey, the system was used by the U.S. Land Office to parcel land west of the Appalachian Mountains. The system divides land into a series of rectangular parcels.

Reference maps   Maps that show the absolute location of places and geographic features determined by a frame of reference, typically latitude and longitude.

Refugees   People who have fled their country because of political persecution and seek asylum in another country.

Region   The second theme of geography; an area on the Earth's surface marked by a degree of formal, functional, or perceptual homogeneity of some phenomenon.

Regional geography   The study of a region's unique characteristics, including its natural and human characteristics, in order to understand how areas differ from each other.

Regional scale   Interactions occurring within a region, in a regional setting.

Relative location   The regional position or situation of a place relative to the position of other places. Distance, accessibility, and connectivity affect relative location.

Relocation diffusion   Sequential diffusion process in which the items being diffused are transmitted by their carrier agents as they evacuate the old areas and relocate to new ones. The most common form of relocation diffusion involves the spreading of innovations by a migrating population.

Remittances   Money migrants send back to family and friends in their home countries, often in cash, forming an important part of the economy in many poorer countries.

Remote sensing   A method of collecting data or information through the use of instruments (e.g., satellites) that are physically distant from the area or object of study.

Renewable resources   Resources that can regenerate as they are exploited.

Repatriation   The process by which a refugee or group of refugees return to their home country, usually with the assistance of government or a non-governmental organization.

Rescale   Involvement of players at other scales to generate support for a position or an initiative (e.g., use of the Internet to generate interest on a national or global scale for a local position or initiative).

Restrictive population policies   Government policies designed to reduce the rate of natural increase.

Reterritorialization   With respect to popular culture, a process where people within a place start to produce an aspect of popular culture themselves, doing so in the context of their local culture and making it their own.

Root crop   Crop that is reproduced by cultivating the roots of or the cuttings from the plants.

Sanitary landfills   Disposal sites for non-hazardous solid waste that is spread in layers and compacted to the smallest practical volume. The sites are typically designed with floors made of materials to treat seeping liquids and are covered by soil as the wastes are compacted and deposited into the landfill.

Scale   Representation of a real-world phenomenon at a certain level of reduction or generalization. In cartography, the ratio of map distance to ground distance; indicated on a map as a bar graph, representative fraction, and/or verbal statement.

Second Agricultural Revolution   Dovetailing with and benefiting from the Industrial Revolution, the Second Agricultural Revolution witnessed improved methods of cultivation, harvesting, and storage of farm produce.

Seed crop   Crop that is reproduced by cultivating the seeds of the plants.

Semi-periphery   Places where core and periphery processes are both occurring; places that are exploited by the core but in turn exploit the periphery.

Sense of place   State of mind derived through the infusion of a place with meaning and emotion by remembering important events that occurred in that place or by labelling a place with a certain character.

Sex/gender/sexuality matrix   The expectation that a person is only one of two biological sexes (male or female); that the proper gender characteristics (masculinity or femininity) will be exhibited by that body and that the normative sexuality is heterosexuality.

Shantytown   Unplanned slum development on the margins of cities, dominated by crude dwellings and shelters made mostly of scrap wood, iron, and even pieces of cardboard.

Shifting cultivation   Cultivation of crops in tropical forest clearings in which the forest vegetation has been removed by cutting and burning. These clearings are usually abandoned after a few years in favour of newly cleared forestland. See also *slash-and-burn agriculture*.

Site   The internal physical attributes of a place, including its absolute location, spatial character, and physical setting.

Situation   The external locational attributes of a place; its relative location or regional position with reference to other non-local places.

Slash-and-burn agriculture   The technique in which tools (e.g., machetes and knives) are used to slash down trees and tall vegetation, which are then burned on the ground, forming a layer of ash that contributes to the soil's fertility. See also shifting cultivation.

Smog   A combination of ground-level ozone, airborne particles, and other air pollutants.

Social exclusion   The inability of individuals or households to fully participate in society, engage in activities, or access jobs, services, and facilities.

Social stratification   One of two components, together with agricultural surplus, that enables the formation of cities; the differentiation of society into classes based on wealth, power, production, and prestige.

Soil erosion   The wearing away of the land surface by wind and moving water.

Solid waste   Non-liquid, non-soluble materials ranging from municipal garbage to sewage sludge, agricultural refuse, and mining residues.

Sovereignty   A principle of international relations that holds that final authority over social, economic, and political matters should rest with the legitimate rulers of independent states.

Space   Defined by Doreen Massey and Pat Jess as "social relations stretched out."

Spaces of consumption   Areas of a city, the main purpose of which is to encourage people to consume goods and services; driven primarily by the global media industry.

Spatial   Pertaining to space on the Earth's surface; sometimes used as a synonym for "geographic."

Spatial analysis   Quantitative procedures used to understand the spatial arrangement of phenomena and the related patterns of connections and flows.

Spatial distribution   Physical location of geographic phenomena across space.

Spatial interaction   The nature and extent of interconnections and linkages. This depends on the distance between places, the accessibility of places, and the transportation and communication connectivity among places.

Spatial perspective   Observing variations in geographic phenomena across space.

Special economic zone   Specific area within a country in which tax incentives and less stringent environmental regulations are implemented to attract foreign business and investment.

Staples thesis   The theory that Canada's economy developed through the export of raw resources to Europe and that, as a result, Canada did not develop a strong manufacturing base, preferring to import finished goods.

State   A politically organized entity that is administered by a sovereign government and is recognized by a significant portion of the international community. A state has a defined territory, a permanent population, and a government and is recognized by other states.

Stateless nation   A nation that does not have a state.

Stationary population level   The level at which a national population ceases to grow.

Step migration   Migration to a distant destination that occurs in stages—for example, from farm to nearby village and later to town and city.

Stimulus diffusion   A form of diffusion in which a cultural adaptation is created as a result of the introduction of a cultural trait from another place.

Structural adjustment loans   Loans granted by international financial institutions, such as the World Bank and the International Monetary Fund, to countries in the periphery and the semi-periphery in exchange for certain economic and governmental reforms in that country (e.g., privatization of certain government entities and opening the country to foreign trade and investment).

Structuralist theory   A model of economic development that treats economic disparities among countries or regions as the result of historically derived power relations within the global economic system.

Subsistence agriculture   Self-sufficient agriculture that is small scale and low technology and emphasizes food production for local consumption, not for trade.

Suburb   A subsidiary urban area surrounding and connected to the central city. Many suburbs are exclusively residential; others have their own commercial centres or shopping malls.

Suburban realm   The surrounding environs connected to the city.

Suburbanization   The process by which lands that were previously outside the urban environment become urbanized, as people and businesses from the city and other areas move to these spaces.

Succession   Process by which new immigrants to a city move to and dominate or take over areas or neighbourhoods occupied by older immigrant groups. For example, in the early 20th century, Puerto Ricans "invaded" the immigrant Jewish neighbourhood of East Harlem and successfully took over the neighbourhood or "succeeded" the immigrant Jewish population as the dominant immigrant group in the neighbourhood.

Sunbelt   The South and Southwest regions of the United States.

Supranational organization   A venture involving three or more nation-states that agree to formal political, economic, and/or cultural cooperation to promote shared objectives. The European Union is one such organization.

Sustainable transportation   An approach to the provision of transportation infrastructure and services that involves simultaneous consideration of environmental, economic, and social objectives.

Synergy   The cross-promotion of vertically integrated goods.

Tear-downs   Homes bought in many North American suburbs with the intent of tearing them down and replacing them with much larger homes, often referred to as "monster homes."

Technopole   Centres or nodes of high-technology research and activity around which a high-technology corridor is sometimes established.

Territorial integrity   The right of a state to defend sovereign territory against incursion from other states.

Territoriality   In political geography, a country's or more local community's sense of property and attachment toward its territory, as expressed by its determination to keep it inviolable and strongly defended.

Thematic maps   Maps that tell stories, typically showing the degree of some attribute or the movement of a geographic phenomenon.

Third Agricultural Revolution   Currently in progress, the Third Agricultural Revolution has as its principal orientation the development of genetically modified organisms (GMOs).

Three-tier structure   With reference to Immanuel Wallerstein's world-systems theory, the division of the world into the core, the periphery, and the semi-periphery as a means to help explain the interconnections between places in the global economy.

Time-space compression   The social and psychological effects of living in a world in which time-space convergence has rapidly reached a high level of intensity; associated with the work of David Harvey.

Total fertility rate   The average number of births per woman of childbearing years, usually considered between 15 and 49 years of age.

Township-and-range system   A rectangular land-division scheme designed by Thomas Jefferson to disperse settlers evenly across farmlands of the U.S. interior. See also *rectangular survey system*.

Toxic waste   Hazardous waste causing danger from chemicals and infectious organisms.

Trade area   A region adjacent to every town and city within which its influence is dominant.

Trafficking   When a family sends a child or an adult to a labour recruiter in hopes that the labour recruiter will send money, and the family member will earn money to send home.

Transport networks   The complete system of the routes pertaining to all means of transport available in a particular area.

Transportation geography   The study of the movement of people and goods, the transportation systems designed to facilitate such movement, and the relationship of transportation to other facets of human geography, such as economic development, energy, land use, sprawl, environmental degradation, values, and culture.

Unilateralism   World order in which one state is in a position of dominance, with allies following rather than joining the political decision-making process.

Unitary (state)   A nation-state that has a centralized government and administration that exercises power equally over all parts of the state.

Urban (area)   The entire built-up, non-rural area and its population, including the most recently constructed suburban appendages. Provides a better picture of the dimensions and population of such an area than the delimited municipality (central city) that forms its heart.

Urban agglomerations   Defined by the United Nations as those populations of 1 million or more people "within a contiguous territory inhabited at urban levels of residential density."

Urban morphology   The study of the physical form and structure of urban places.

Urban sprawl   Unrestricted growth in many North American urban areas of housing, commercial development, and roads over large expanses of land, with little concern for urban planning.

Variable costs   Costs that change directly with the amount of production (e.g., energy supply and labour costs).

Vectored disease   A disease carried from one host to another by an intermediate host.

Vertical integration   Ownership by the same firm of a number of companies that exist along a variety of points on a commodity chain.

Vienna Convention for the Protection of the Ozone Layer   The first international convention aimed at addressing the issue of ozone depletion. Held in 1985, the Vienna Convention was the predecessor to the Montreal Protocol.

Voluntary migration   Movement in which people relocate in response to perceived opportunity, not because they are forced to move.

Von Thünen model   A model that explains the location of agricultural activities in a commercial, profit-making economy. A process of spatial competition allocates various farming activities into rings around a central market city, with profit-earning capability the determining force in how far a crop locates from the market.

Water pollution   Pollution caused when discharges of energy or materials degrade water for other users.

World city   Dominant city in terms of its role in the global political economy. Not the world's biggest city in terms of population or industrial output, but rather a centre of strategic control of the world economy.

World-systems theory   Theory originated by Immanuel Wallerstein and illuminated by his three-tier structure, which proposes that social change in the developing world is inextricably linked to the economic activities of the developed world.

Zone   Area of a city with a relatively uniform land use (e.g., an industrial zone or a residential zone).

Zoning laws   Legal restrictions on land use that determine what types of building and economic activities are allowed to take place in certain areas. In the United States, areas are most commonly divided into separate zones of residential, retail, or industrial use.

REFERENCES

Chapter 1 Introduction to Human Geography

Entrikin, J. N. 1976. Contemporary humanism in geography. *Annals of the Association of American Geographers*, 66.

Hägerstrand, T. 1970. *What about people in regional science?* Papers, Regional Science Association, 24, 7–21.

Hartshorne, R. 1939. *The nature of geography.* Washington, DC: Association of American Geographers.

Huntington, E., & Cushing, S. W. 1940. *Principles of human geography,* 5th ed. New York: John Wiley & Sons.

Johnston, R. J. 1986. *On human geography.* Oxford, New York: Blackwell.

Lawson, V. 2004. *The geographical advantage in development studies.* Keynote Address. Annual Meeting of the Great Plains/Rocky Mountains Division of the Association of American Geographers.

Lewis, P. 1979. Axioms for reading the landscape: Some guides to the American scene. In *The interpretation of ordinary landscapes: Geographical essays,* D. W. Meinig, ed. New York: Oxford University Press, 11–32.

Michener, J. 1970. The mature social studies teacher. *Social Education*, November, 760–766.

Peet, R. 1998. *Modern geographical thought.* Oxford, Malden, MA: Blackwell Publishers.

Relph, E. 1997. Sense of place. In *Ten geographic ideas that changed the world,* S. Hanson, ed. New Brunswick, NJ: Rutgers University Press.

Sauer, C. 1927. Recent developments in cultural geography. In *Recent developments in the social sciences,* C. Λ. Elwood, C. Wissler, and R. H. Gault, eds. Philadelphia: J. B. Lippincott, 154–212.

Sauer, C 1952. *Agricultural origins and dispersals.* American Geographical Society.

Schaefer, F.K. 1953. Exceptionalism in geography: A methodological examination. *Annals of the Association of American Geographers*, 43, 226–245.

Tuan, Y. F. 1976. Humanistic geography. *Annals of the Association of American Geographers*, 66, 266–276.

Chapter 2 Globalization and Geographies

Anderson, B. 1991. Imagined communities: reflections on the origin and spread of nationalism (Revised and extended. ed.). London: Verso.

Castells, M. 2000. Materials for an exploratory theory of the network society. *British Journal of Sociology*, 51(1), 5–24.

Corbridge, S. 1988. The asymmetry of interdependence: The United States and the geopolitics of international financial relations. *Studies in Comparative International Development*, Spring, 3–29.

Dicken, P. 2011. *Global shift: Reshaping the global economic map in the 21st century*, 6th Edition, London: Guilford Press.

Friedman, T.H. 2005. *The world is flat.* New York: Farrar, Straus and Giroux.

Giddens, A. 1990. *The consequences of modernity.* Stanford: Stanford University Press.

Goodman, D. J. & Cohen, M. 2004. *Consumer culture: A reference handbook.* Santa Barbara, CA: ABC–CLIO.

Harvey, D. 1989. *The condition of postmodernity.* Oxford and Cambridge, MA: Basil Blackwell.

Harvey, D. 2005. *A brief history of neoliberalism.* Oxford: Oxford University Press.

Kirby, A. 2004. The global culture factory. In *Globalizaton and its outcomes*, J. O'Loughlin, L. Staeheli, and E. Greenberg, eds. New York: Guilford Press, 133–158.

Kumar, S., & Corbridge, S. 2002. Programmed to fail? Development projects and the politics of participation. *Journal of Development Studies,* 39(2), 73–103.

Maskus, K E. 2004. A system on the brink: Pitfalls in international trade rules on the road to globalization. In *Globalizaton and its outcomes*, J. O'Loughlin, L. Staeheli, and E. Greenberg, eds. New York: Guillford Press, 98–116.

Norcliffe, G. 1992. Canada in a global economy. *Canadian Geographer*, 45, 14–30.

O'Brien, R. 1992. *Global financial integration: The end of geography.* New York: Council on Foreign Relations Press.

O'Loughlin, J., Staeheli, L., & Greenberg, E., eds. 2004. *Globalization and its outcomes.* New York: Guilford Press.

Pacione, M. 1997. Local exchange trading systems as a response to the globalization of capitalism. *Urban Studies,* 34(8), 1179–1199.

Pereira, M., & Mendes. M. 2002. EU competition law, convergence, and the media industry. European Commission, Media and Music Publishing Unit.

Ritzer, G. 2007. Introduction. In *The Blackwell companion to globalization*, G. Ritzer, ed. Malden, MA: Blackwell Publishing, 1–13.

Wallerstein, I. 1983. *Historical capitalism.* London: Verso.

Wallerstein, I. 2001. *The essential Wallerstein.* New York: New Press.

Williams College Museum of Art. 2011. *Julie Mehretu: City sitings.* http://wcma.williams.edu/exhibit/julie-mehretu-city-sitings/. Last accessed December 7, 2011.

Wrigley, N., Coe, N. M., & Currah, A. 2005. Globalizing retail: Conceptualizing the distribution-based transnational corporation (TNC). *Progress in Human Geography,* 29(4), 437–457.

Chapter 3 Political Geography

Anderson, B. 1991. *Imagined communities: Reflections on the origin and spread of nationalism.* London: Verso.

Bush, G. W. 2005. *Address to the Joint Session of Congress.* September 20, 2001. http://www. september11news.com/ PresidentBush-Speech.htm. Last accessed October 2005.

Castells, M. 2000. *The rise of the network society, 2nd ed.* Malden, MA: Blackwell Publishing.

Clinton, W. J. 1998. *Oval Office remarks.* http://usinfo.state. gov/is/Archive_Index/President_Clintons_Oval_Office_ Remarks_on_Antiterrorist_Attacks.htm. Last accessed October 2005.

Cohen, S. B. 1991. Global geopolitical change in the post-cold war era. *Annals of the Association of American Geographers,* 81(4), 551–580.

Flint, C., & Taylor, J. P. 2007. *Political geography: World economy, nation-state and locality, 5th ed.* Harlow, UK: Longman, Scientific and Technical.

Hartshorne, R. 1950. The functional approach in political geography. *Annals of the Association of American Geographers,* 40(2), 95–130.

Jackson, R. H. 1990. *Quasi-states: sovereignty, international relations, and the third world.* New York: Cambridge University Press.

Johnston, R.J., Gregory, D., Pratt, G., & Watts, M., eds. 2000. *Dictionary of human geography, 4th ed.* Malden, MA: Blackwell Publishing Co.

Mackinder, H. J. 1904. The geographical pivot of history. *Geographical Journal,* 23, 421–444.

Mackinder, H. J. 1919. *Democratic ideals and reality: A study in the politics of reconstruction.* New York: H. Holt & Company.

Mackinder, H. J. 1943. The round world and the winning of the peace. *Foreign Affairs.*

Ogborn, M. 1998. *Spaces of modernity: London's geographies 1680–1780.* New York: Guilford Press.

O'Tuathail, G., & Agnew, J. 1992. Geopolitics and discourse: Practical geopolitical reasoning and American foreign policy. *Political Geography,* 11, 155–175.

Ratzel, F. 1969. Laws of the spatial growth of states. In R. E. Kasperson & J. Minghi, eds., *The structure of political geography,* trans. R. L. Bolin. Chicago: Aldine.

Ritzer, G. 2007. *The Blackwell companion to globalization.* Malden, MA: Blackwell Publishing.

Sack, R. D. 1986. *Human territoriality: Its theory and history.* Cambridge: Cambridge University Press.

White, G. 2000. *Nationalism and territory: Constructing group identity in southeastern Europe.* Lanham, MD: Rowman & Littlefield.

Chapter 4 Population

Boserup, E. 1966. *The conditions of agricultural growth: The economics of agrarian change under population pressure.* Chicago: Aldine Publishing Co.

Ehrlich, P. 1983. *The population bomb.* New York: Ballantine Books.

Gould, P. 1993. *The slow plague: A geography of the AIDS pandemic.* New York: Blackwell.

Keil, R., & Ali, S. H. 2006. The avian flu: Some lessons learned from the 2003 SARS outbreak in Toronto. *AREA,* 38(3), 107–109.

Malthus, T. R. 1976. *An essay on the principles of population.* A. Appelman, ed. New York: W.W. Norton.

Population Reference Bureau. *1997 World Population Data Sheet.* Washington, DC: Author.

Robson, E. 2004. Hidden child workers: Young carers in Zimbabwe. *Antipode,* 36(5), 227–248.

Sibley, D. 1995. *Geographies of exclusion: Society and difference in the west.* London: Routledge.

Chapter 5 Migration

Bissoondath, N. 1994. *Selling illusions: The cult of multiculturalism in Canada.* Toronto, ON: Penguin.

Blaut, J. 1993. *A colonizer's model of the world: Geographical diffusionism and Eurocentric history.* New York: Guilford Press.

Boyle, P. 2002. Population geography: Transnational women on the move. *Progress in Human Geography,* 26(4), 531–543.

Castles, S., & Miller, M. 2003. *The age of migration: International population movements in the modern world.* New York: Guilford Press.

Cresswell, T. 2006. *On the move: Mobility in the modern western world.* London and New York: Routledge.

Dallaire, R. 2003. *Shake hands with the devil: The failure of humanity in Rwanda.* Toronto: Random House Canada.

Dittmer, J. 2004. The Soufrière hills volcano and the postmodern landscapes of Mont-Serrat. *FOCUS on Geography,* 1–7.

Hill, L. 2007. *Book of negroes.* Toronto, ON: Harper Collins.

Kobayashi, A. 1993. Multiculturalism: Representing a Canadian institution. In *Place/culture/representation,* J. Duncan and D. Ley, eds. London/New York: Routledge.

Lawson, V. 1998. Hierarchical households and gendered migration in Latin America: Feminist extensions to migration research. *Progress in Human Geography,* 22, 39–53.

Mountz, A. 2004. Embodying the nation state: Canada's response to human smuggling. *Political Geography,* 23, 323–345.

National Commission on Terrorism. 2004. *9/11 commission report.* www.911commission.gov/report/911Report.pdf. Last accessed December 6, 2011.

Ravenstein, E. 1885. The laws of migration. *Journal of the Statistical Society,* 48, 167–235.

Schama, S. 2006. *Rough crossings: Britain, the slaves, and the American Revolution.* New York: Ecco.

Office of the United Nations High Commissioner for Human Rights. 1951. *United Nations Convention relating to the Status of Refugees.* http://www2.ohchr.org/english/law/refugees.htm. Last accessed December 6, 2011.

United Nations High Commissioner for Refugees. 2000. *The state of the world's refugees.* New York: Oxford.

Weiner, E. 2007. *Debunking global migration myths.* National Public Radio website. http://www.npr.org/templates/story/story.php?storyId=10768751. Last accessed December 6, 2011.

Chapter 6 Human–Environment Relations

Brown, L., & Wolf, E. 1984. *Soil erosion: Quiet crisis in the world economy.* Washington, DC, Paper No. 60.

Castree, N. 2005. *Nature.* London: Routledge.

Cosgrove, D., & Daniels, S. 1988. *The iconography of landscape: Essays on the symbolic representation, design, and use of past environment.* Cambridge: Cambridge University Press.

Crosby, A. 1972. *The Columbian Exchange: Biological and cultural consequences of 1492.* Westport, CT: Greenwich Publishing Co.

Energy Information Administration (EIA). 2001. *International Energy Annual 1999.*

Harper, C. L. 2008. Religion and environmentalism, *The Kripke Center Supplement Series.* http://moses.creighton.edu/jrs/2008/2008-11.html. Last accessed December 6, 2011.

Houghton, J. T., ed. 2001. Appendix I—Glossary. In *Climate change 2001: The scientific basis. Contribution of working group I to the third assessment report of the Intergovernmental Panel on Climate Change.* Cambridge: Cambridge University Press.

Intergovernmental Panel on *Climate Change.* 1996. *Climate change 1995: The science of climate change.* J. T. Houghton et al, eds. Cambridge: Cambridge University Press.

Intergovernmental Panel on *Climate Change.* 2001. *Climate change 2001: Impacts, adaptation, and vulnerability; contribution of working group II to the third assessment report,* J. J. McCarthy et al., eds. New York: Cambridge University Press.

Intergovernmental Panel on *Climate Change.* 2001. *Climate change 2001: The scientific basis; Contribution of group I to the third assessment report.* J. T. Houghton et al., eds. New York: Cambridge University Press.

Intergovernmental Panel on Climate Change. 2007. *Climate change 2007: synthesis report. Contribution of working Groups I, II and III to the fourth assessment report of the Intergovernmental Panel on Climate Change* [Core Writing Team, Pachauri, R.K and Reisinger, A., eds.]. Geneva: Author. http://www.ipcc.ch/publications_and_data/ publications_and_data_reports.shtml. Last accessed December 14, 2011.

Kates, R. W. 1994. Sustaining life on the earth. *Scientific American,* 271, 114–122.

Micklin, P., & Aladin, N. 2008. Reclaiming the Aral Sea. *Scientific American Magazine.*

Simmons, I. G. 1996. Humanity's resources. In *The companion encyclopedia of geography: The environment and humankind,* I. Douglas, R. Huggett, & M. Robinson, eds. New York: Routledge.

Smith, N. 1984. *Uneven development: Nature, capital and the production of space.* New York: Blackwell.

United Nations Development Programme. 2004. *Human Development Report.* http://www.undp.org.in/ hdr2004/#HDR2004. Last accessed September 2005.

United Nations Environment Programme. 2005.National carbon dioxide (CO_2) emissions per capita. In *UNEP/ GRID-Arendal Maps and Graphics Library.* http://maps. grida.no/go/graphic/national_carbon_dioxide_co2_ emissions_per_capita. Last accessed December 12, 2010.

United Nations Framework Convention on Climate Change. 1992. *Article 1, Definitions.* http://unfccc.int/essential_ background/convention/background/items/2536.php Last accessed December 7, 2011.

Williams, R. 1988. *Keywords: A vocabulary of culture and society.* Glasgow: Fortana Press.

Chapter 7 Social Geographies— Identities and Place

Anderson, B. 1991. *Imagined communities.* New York: Verso.

Bauder, H., & Sharpe, B. 2002. Residential segregation of visible minorities in Canada's gateway cities. *Canadian Geographer/Le Géographe Canadien,* 46(3), 204–222.

Blaut, J. 1993. *The colonizer's model of the world: Geographical diffusionism and eurocentric history.* New York: Guilford Press.

Boyd, M., Goldmann, G., & White, P. 2000. Race in the Canadian census. In *Race and racism: Canada's challenge,* L. Driedger & S. S. Halli, eds. Montréal, PQ, & Kingston, ON: McGill-Queen's University Press, 33–54.

Curtis, A., Warren Mills, J., & Leitner, M. 2007. Katrina and vulnerability: The geography of stress. *Journal of Health Care for the Poor and Underserved* 18: 315–330.

Curtis, J. R. 2004. Barrio space and place in southeast Los Angeles, California. In *Hispanic spaces, Latino places: Community and cultural diversity in contemporary America,* Daniel D. Arreola, ed. Austin: University of Texas Press.

Domosh, M., & Seager, J. 2001. *Putting women in place: Feminist geographers make sense of the world.* New York: Guilford Press.

Elder, G., Knopp, L., & Nast, H. 2003. Sexuality and space. In G*eography in America at the dawn of the 21st century,* G. L. Gaile and C. J. Willmott, eds. New York: Oxford University Press.

Forest, B. 2002. A new geography of identity? Race, ethnicity and American citizenship. In *American space/American place: Geographies of the United States on the threshold of a new century,* J. Agnew and J. Smith, eds. Edinburgh: University of Edinburgh Press, 231–263.

Gates, G., & J. Ost. 2004. *The gay and lesbian atlas.* Washington, DC: Urban Institute Press.

Hall, S. 1995. New cultures for old. In *A Place in the world? Places, cultures, and globalization,* D. Massey and P. Jess, eds. New York: Oxford University Press.

Hancock, P. 2000. The lived experience of female factory workers in rural West Java. *Labour and Management in Development Journal,* 1(1), 1–18.

Johnson Jr., J. H., Jones, C. K., Farrell, W. C., & Oliver, M. L. 1992. The Los Angeles rebellion: A retrospective in view. *Economic Development Quarterly,* 6(4), 356–372.

Massey, D., & Jess, P. 1995. Places and cultures in an uneven world. In *A place in the world? Places, cultures, and globalization,* D. Massey and P. Jess, eds. New York: Oxford University Press.

Miyares, I. M. 2004. Changing latinization of New York City. In *Hispanic spaces, Latino places: Community and cultural diversity in contemporary America,* D. D. Arreola, ed. Austin: University of Texas Press.

Nash, C. J. 2006. Toronto's gay village (1969 to 1982). Plotting the politics of gay identity. *Canadian Geographer* (March) 50(1), 1–16.

Native Women's Association of Canada. 2010. Sisters in spirit: 2010 research findings. www.nwac.ca/sites/default/files/.../2010_NWAC_SIS_Report_EN.pdf.

Oberhauser, A. M., Rubinoff, D., De Bres, K., Mains, S., & Pope, C. 2003. Geographic perspectives on women. In *Geography in America at the dawn of the 21st century,* G. L. Gaile and C. J. Willmott, eds. New York: Oxford University Press.

Oppong, J. R. 1998. A vulnerability interpretation of the geography of HIV/AIDS in Ghana, 1986–1995. *The Professional Geographer,* 50, 437–448.

Oswin, N. 2008. Critical geographies and the uses of sexuality: Deconstructing queer space. *Progress in Human Geography,* 32(1), 89–103.

Peake, L., & Ray, B. 2001. Racializing the Canadian landscape: Whiteness, uneven geographies and social justice. *Canadian Geographer/Le Géographe Canadien,* 45(1), 180–186.

Rose, G. 1995. Place and identity: A sense of place. In *A place in the world? Places, cultures, and globalization,* D. Massey and P. Jess, eds. New York: Oxford University Press.

Rose, H. M., & McClain, P. D. 1990. *Race, place and risk: Black homicide in urban america.* Albany: State University of New York Press.

Said, E. 1978. *Orientalism.* London: Routledge.

Smith, S.J., Pain, R., Marston, S.A., & Jones III, J.P. 2009. *The SAGE handbook of social geographies.* London: SAGE.

Chapter 8 Local Culture, Popular Culture, and Cultural Landscapes

Bowen, D. 1997. Lookin' for Margaritaville: Place and imagination in Jimmy Buffett's songs. *Journal of Cultural Geography,* 16(2), 99–109.

Bowen, D. 2002. Agricultural expansion in northern Alberta. *Geographical Review,* 92, 503–526.

Florida, R. 2002. *The rise of the creative class: And how it's transforming work, leisure, community and everyday life.* New York: Basic Books.

Harrison, S. 1999. Cultural boundaries. *Anthropology Today,* 15(5), 10–13.

Harvey, D. 1989. *The condition of postmodernity: An enquiry into the origins of cultural change.* Cambridge, MA: Blackwell.

Henderson, S. 2008. Canadian content regulations and the formation of a national scene. *Popular Music,* 27, 307–315.

Merchants of Cool. 2001. www.pbs.org/wgbh/pages/frontline/shows/cool/. Last accessed June 2005.

Mitchell, D. 1995. There's no such thing as culture: Towards a reconceptualization of the idea of culture in geography. *Transactions of the Institute of British geographers,* 20, 102–116.

Relph, E. C. 1976. *Place and placelessness.* New York: Routledge, Kegan and Paul.

Rosati, C. 2005. The image factory: MTV, geography, and the industrial production of culture. Syracuse University, Ph.D. dissertation.

Rosati, C. 2007. MTV: 360 degrees of the industrial production of culture. *Transactions of the Institute of British Geographers,* 32, 556–575.

Sauer, C. 1925. The morphology of landscape. *University of California Publications in Geography,* 2(2).

Williams, R. 1983. *Keywords: A vocabulary of culture and society,* revised edition. New York, NY: Oxford University Press.

Williams, R. 1989. Culture is ordinary. In *Resources of hope: Culture, democracy, socialism,* R. Gale, ed. New York: Verso.

Chapter 9 Agriculture

Bunting, A. H., ed. 1970. *Change in agriculture.* New York: Praeger.

Carney, J. A. 1996. Converting the wetlands, engendering the environment: The intersection of gender with agrarian change in Gambia. In *Liberation ecologies,* R. Peet & M. J. Watts, eds. London: Routledge.

CNN. 2000. Other agricultural reform efforts. http://www.7.cnn.com/SPECIALS/2000yourbusiness/Stones/labor.conditions/

Diamond, J. 1997. *Guns, germs and steel: The fates of human societies.* New York: W.W. Norton & Company.

Duckham, A. N., & Masefield, G. B. 2005. *Farming systems of the world.* New York: Praeger.

Klooster, D. J. 2005. Producing social nature in the Mexican countryside. *Cultural Geographies,* 12, 321–344.

Liu, L. 1999. Labor location, conservation, and land quality: The case of west Jilin, China." *Annals of the Association of American Geographers,* 89(4), 633–657.

Polak, P. 1969. The big potential of small farms. *Scientific American,* September, 84–91.

Sauer, C. O. 1969. *Agricultural origins and dispersals*, 2nd rev. ed. Cambridge, MA: MIT Press.

Shiva, V. 1991. The violence of the green revolution: Ecological degradation and political conflict in Punjab. *The Ecologist*, 21(2), 57–60.

Smithers, J., Johnson, P., & Joseph, A. 2004. The dynamics of family farming in North Huron County; Part II: farm–community interactions. *The Canadian Geographer*, 48(2), 209–224.

Spencer, J. E., & Thomas, W. H. 1969. *Cultural geography: Introduction to our humanized earth.* Artography by R. E. Winter. New York: Wiley.

United Nations Office on Drugs and Crime. 2002. United Nations calls for greater assistance to Afghans in fight against opium cultivation. http://www. unodc.org/unodc/press_release_2002-10-24_1.html. Last accessed November 2005.

Von Thünen, J. H. 1966. *Der isolierte staat.* Trans. C. M. Wartenberg. In *Von Thünen's isolated state*, P. Hall, ed. Elmsford, N.Y.: Pergamon.

Chapter 10 Urban Geography

Aiken, S., Mitchell, D., & Staeheli, L. 2004. Urban geography. In *Geography in America at the dawn of the 21st century*, Gary L. Gaile and Cort J. Willmott, eds. New York: Oxford University Press.

Bourne, L., & Simmons, J. 2002. The dynamics of the Canadian urban system. In *International handbook of urban systems*, H. S. Geyer, ed. Cheltenham UK: E. Elgar. 391–418.

Bourne, L. S., & Ley, D., eds. 1993. *The changing social geography of Canadian cities.* Montreal, PQ: McGill-Queen's University Press.

Burgess, E. 1925. The growth of the city. In *The city*, R. Park et al., eds. Chicago: University of Chicago Press, 47–62.

Castells, M. 2000. *The rise of the network society, 2nd ed.* Malden, MA: Blackwell Publishing.

Christaller, W. 1950. The foundations of spatial organization in Europe. *Frankfurter Geographische Hefte*, 25.

Christaller, W. 1966 [orig. 1933]. *The central places in southern Germany.* Trans. C. Baskin. Englewood Cliffs, NJ: Prentice-Hall.

Congress for New Urbanism. *Charter of the New Urbanism.* http://www.cnu.org/charter. Last accessed December 8, 2011.

Ford, L. R. 1994. *Cities and buildings: Skyscrapers, skid rows, and suburbs.* Baltimore, MD: Johns Hopkins University Press.

Grant, J. 2009. Theory and practice in planning the suburbs: Challenges to implementing new urbanism, smart growth, and sustainability principles. *Planning Theory and Practice*, 10(1), 11–33.

Grant, R., & Nijman, J. 2002. Globalization and the corporate geography of cities in the less-developed world. *Annals of the Association of American Geographers*, 92(2), 320–341.

Griffin, E., & Ford, L. 1980. A model of Latin American city structure. *Geographical Review*, 70(4), 397–422.

Harvey, D. 1997. The new urbanism and the communitarian trap. *Harvard Design Magazine*, 1–3.

Hoyt, H. 1939. *The structure and growth of residential neighborhoods in American cities.* Washington, DC: U.S. Federal Housing Administration.

Kesteloot, C., & Cortie, C. 1988. Housing Turks and Moroccans in Brussels and Amsterdam: The difference between private and public markets. *Urban Studies*, 35(10), 1835–1853.

McGee, T. G. 1967. *The Southeast Asian city: A social geography of the primate cities of Southeast Asia.* New York: Praeger.

Roost, F. 1998. Recreating the city as entertainment center: The media industry's role in transforming Potsdamer Platz and Times Square. *Journal of Urban Technology*, 5(3), 1–21.

Skaburskis, A., & Mok, D. 2006. Cites as land markets. In *Canadian cities in transition*, 3rd ed., T. Bunting and P. Filion, eds. Oxford University Press.

Skinner, G. W. 1964. Marketing and social structure in rural China, part I. *Journal of Asian Studies*, 24, 3–43.

Smith, P. J. 2010. Suburbs. In *Canadian cities in transition: local through global perspectives*, 3rd ed., T. Bunting and P. Filion, eds. Oxford: Oxford University Press.

Taylor, P. J. and Lang, R. E. 2004. The shock of the new: 100 concepts describing recent urban change. *Environment and Planning A*, 36(6), 951–958.

Walks, R. A., & Bourne, L. S. 2006. Ghettos in Canada's cities? Racial segregation, ethnic enclaves and poverty concentration in Canadian urban areas. *Canadian Geographer*, 50(3), 273–297.

Chapter 11 Development

Dottridge, M. 2002. Trafficking in children in West and Central Africa." *Gender and Development*, 10(1), 38–42.

The Economist. 2002. With the wolf at the door. 30 May 2002.

Herbst, J. 1989. The creation and maintenance of national boundaries in Africa. *International Organization*, 43(4), 673–692.

Padgett, T. 2010. New Orleans' lower ninth: forgotten victim? *Time*, August 27.

Ravenhill, J. 1988. Redrawing the map of Africa. In *The precarious balance: State and society in Africa*, D. Rothchild and N. Chazan, eds. Boulder, CO: Westview Press.

Rivoli, P. 2005. *The travels of a t-shirt in the global economy: An economist examines the markets, power, and politics of world trade.* New York: John Wiley & Sons.

Rostow, W. W. 1971. *The stages of economic growth*, 2nd ed. New York: Cambridge University Press.

Schindler, D. 2010. Tar sands need solid science. *Nature*, 468, 499–501.

Taylor, P. J. 1992. Understanding global inequalities: A world-systems approach. *Geography*, 77, 10–21.

Wallerstein, I. 1983. *Historical capitalism.* London: Verso.

Chapter 12 Transportation

Anable, J., & Gatersleben, B. 2005. All work and no play? The role of instrumental and affective factors in work and leisure journeys by different travel modes. *Transportation Research Part A*, 39, 163–181.

Andrey, J. 2010. Long-term trends in weather-related crash risks. *Journal of Transport Geography*, 18(2), 247–258.

Appleyard, D. 1981. *Livable streets.* Berkeley, CA: University of California Press.

Austin, D., & Sauer, A. 2003. *Car companies & climate change: Measuring the carbon intensity of sales and profits.* Washington, DC: World Resources Institute. http://earthtrends.wri.org/pdf_library/feature/ecn_fea_carco.pdf. Last accessed on July 2, 2010.

Banister, D., Pucher, J., & Lee-Gosselin, M. 2007. Making sustainable transport politically and publicly acceptable. In *Institutions and sustainable transport: Regulatory reform in advanced economies*, P. Rietveld and R. Stough, eds. Cheltenham, England: Edward Elgar Publishing, 17–50.

Buliung, R., Mitra, R., & Faulkner, G. 2009. Active school transportation in the Greater Toronto Area, Canada: An exploration of trends in space and time (1986–2006). *Preventive Medicine*, 48(6), 507–512.

Centre for Sustainable Transportation (CST). 1998. *Definition and vision of sustainable transportation.* Toronto, ON: Author.

Gilbert, R., & Perl, A. 2005. *Energy and transport futures.* Report prepared for the National Round Table on the Environment and the Economy. http://www.gttconline.com/files/nrtee_rpt_10.pdf. Last accessed July 21, 2011.

Goetz, A. 2009. Intermodality. In *International encyclopaedia of human geography*, R. Kitchin and N. Thrift, eds. Oxford, UK: Elsevier, 529–535.

Gregory, D., ed. 2009. *The dictionary of human geography.* Malden, MA: Blackwell.

Hanson, S., & Giuliano, G. 2004. *The geography of urban transportation*, 3rd ed. New York: Guilford Press.

Hine, J. 2009. Transport and social exclusion. In *International encyclopedia of human geography*, R. Kitchin and N. Thrift, eds. Oxford, UK: Elsevier, 429–434.

Hiscock, R., Macintyre, S., Kearns, A., & Ellaway, A. 2002. Means of transport and ontological security: Do cars provide psycho-social benefits to their users? *Transportation Research Part D*, 7, 119–135.

Hodge, G. 2003. *Planning Canadian communities: An introduction to the principles, practice and participants.* Toronto, ON: Nelson Thomson Learning.

Hofmann, N., Filoso, G., & Schofield, M. 2005. The loss of dependable agricultural land in Canada. *Rural and Small Town Analysis Bulletin*, 6(1), Ottawa, ON: Statistics Canada.

International Transport Forum (ITF). 2010. New data on major trends in the transport sector. (Press Release), Paris, France, May 19, 2010. http://www.internationaltransportforum.org. Last accessed July 16, 2010.

Keeling, D. J. 2007. Transportation geography: New directions on well-worn trails. *Progress in Human Geography*, 31(2), 217–225.

Kenworthy, J. R., & Laube, F. B. 1999. Patterns of automobile dependence in cities: an international overview of key physical and economic dimensions with some implications for urban policy. *Transportation research part A: policy and practice*, 33(7–8), 691–723.

Knowles, R. D. 2009. Transport geography. In *International encyclopedia of human geography*, R. Kitchin and N. Thrift, eds. Oxford, UK: Elsevier, 441–451.

Levinson, M. 2006. *The box: How the shipping container made the world smaller and the world economy bigger*. Princeton: Princeton University Press.

Levinson, M. 2006. Container shipping and the economy. *Transportation Research News*, 246 (September/October), 10–12. http://onlinepubs.trb.org/onlinepubs/trnews/trnews246.pdf. Last accessed July 22, 2011.

Litman, T. 2002. *The costs of automobile dependency and the benefits of balanced transportation*. Victoria, BC: Victoria Transport Policy Institute.

Litman, T. 2003. Social inclusion as a transport planning issue in Canada. *Contribution to the FIA Foundation G7 Comparison Paper*, presented at the European Transport Conference held in Strassbourg in June, 2003.

Litman, T. 2011. *Evaluating public transit benefits and costs: Best practices guidebook*. Victoria, BC: Victoria Transport Policy Institute. (http://www.vtpi.org/tranben.pdf)

Lorch, B. J. 2004. Big boxes, power centres and the evolving retail landscape of Winnipeg: A geographical perspective. *Research and Working Paper #43*. Winnipeg: University of Winnipeg, MB, Institute of Urban Studies.

Marzoughi, R. 2011. Teen travel in the Greater Toronto Area: A descriptive analysis of trends from 1986 to 2006 and the policy implications. *Transport Policy* 18, no. 4, 623–630.

McCalla, R. J., Slack, B., & Comtois, C. 2004. Dealing with globalisation at the regional and local level: the case of contemporary containerization. *The Canadian Geographer*, 48(4), 473–487.

Mensah, J., & Ironside, R. G. 1993. Employment opportunities of the urban poor: An assessment of spatial constraints and the mismatch hypothesis. In *Public issues: A geographical perspective*, J. Andrey and J. G. Nelson, eds. Waterloo, ON: University of Waterloo, Faculty of Environmental Studies, Department of Geography, 111–131.

Musonda, H. M. 2006. *The rapid assessment of rural transport services in Luapula Province, Zambia: Draft report*. Report prepared for the World Bank's Sub Saharan Africa Transport Policy Program.

Myers, J. n.d. Pedalling to a sustainable future. *U Magazine*, accessed at *http://arts.ucalgary.ca/artsnow/pedalling-sustainable-future* on June 3, 2011

Newman, P., & Kenworthy, J. 1999. *Sustainability and cities: Overcoming automobile dependence*. Washington, DC: Island Press.

Perry, C. A. 1929. The neighborhood unit: A scheme of arrangement for the family-life community. In *Regional study of New York and its environs*, Volume VII. New York: Port of New York Authority, 2–140.

Pucher, J., & Buehler, R. 2008. Making cycling irresistible: Lessons from The Netherlands, Denmark and Germany. *Transport reviews*, 28(4), 495–528.

Reily, K., Craig, H., Poston, M., Saunders, L., & Flynn, A. 2000. *Effective schooling in rural Africa* (Project report 1). UK: Authors.

Steg, L. 2005. Car use: lust and must. Instrumental, symbolic and affective motives for car use. *Transportation Research Part A*, 39, 147–162.

Stein, C. 1969. *Toward new towns for America*. Cambridge, MA: MIT Press.

Toronto Board of Trade, 2003. *A strategy for rail-based transit*. Central Ontario Smart Growth Panel Report. 2003

Transport Canada. 2009. *Marine oil spill preparedness and response regime: Report to Parliament, 2004–2006*. http://www.tc.gc.ca/publications/en/tp14539/pdf/hr/tp14539e.pdf. Last accessed June 13, 2011.

Transport Canada. 2010. *Canadian motor vehicle collision statistics*. Ottawa, ON: Author. Published online at http://www.tc.gc.ca/eng/roadsafety/tp-tp3322-2007-1039.htm, Last accessed July 10, 2010.

Transportation Association of Canada (TAC). 1993. *A new vision for urban transportation*. Ottawa, ON: Author. http://www.tac-atc.ca/english/resourcecentre/readingroom/pdf/urban.pdf

Victoria Transport Policy Institute. 2011. *Fuel taxes: Increasing fuel Taxes and fees*. Victoria, BC: Author. http://www.vtpi.org/tdm/tdm17.htm. Last accessed July 21, 2011.

Vodden, K., Smith, D., Eaton, F., & Mayhew, D. 2007. *Analysis and estimation of the social cost of motor vehicle collisions in Ontario*. Report prepared for Ministry of Transportation. http://www.tc.gc.ca/eng/roadsafety/tp-tp14800-menu-159.htm. Last accessed July 10, 2010.

Vowles, T. M. 2009. Aviation. In *International encyclopedia of human geography*, R. Kitchin and N. Thrift, eds. Oxford, UK: Elsevier, 257–264.

Wener, R., Evans, G. W., & Boately, P. 2005. Commuting stress: Psychophysiological effects of the trip and spillover into the workplace. *Transportation Research Record 1924*, TRB, 112–117.

Chapter 13 Industry and Services

Castells, M., Hall, P., & Hutriyk, J. 1996. Technopoles of the world: The making of 21st century industrial complexes. *The Sociological Review,* 43(4), 895–900.

The Economist. China's economy: Growth spreads inland. 18 November 2004.

Hotelling, H. 1990. *The collected economics articles of Harold Hotelling,* A. Darnell, ed. Springer-Verlag.

Lösch, A. 1967 [1940]. *The economics of location.* Trans. W. Woglom & W. Stolper. New York: Wiley Science Editions.

Wallace, I. 2002. *A geography of the Canadian economy.* Don Mills, ON: Oxford University Press.

Weber, A. 1929 [1909]. *Theory of the location of industries.* Trans. C. Friedrich. Chicago: University of Chicago Press.

World Trade Organization. Regional trade agreements. http://www.wto.org/english/tratop_e/region_e/region_e.htm. Last accessed October 2005.

INDEX

noise barrier, 358f
noise pollution, 358
nomadism, 124
nomads, 14
non-governmental organizations (NGOs), 39, 46,
    163, 185, 340–341
non-renewable fossil fuels, 167
non-renewable resources, 167, 359
non-vectored diseases, 115
nonmaterial culture, 220
Norcliffe, Glen, 32, 34
North Africa
    see also Africa
    and dislocation, 144
    migrant labour from, 127
    refugee numbers, 142
    refugee problems, 144
    unregulated growth, 300
North America
    see also specific countries
    auto plant corridor, 394f
    cities with population of 20,000 or more,
        1870-1871, 378f
    coal reserves, 382
    colonies in, 377
    deindustrialized regions, 396
    fossil fuel deposits, 383f
    global popular culture, influence on, 230
    industrial regions, 382–386
    life expectancy, 111
    major manufacturing regions, 384f
    manufacturing belt, 385–386
    population clusters, 92, 94
    population distribution and density, 94
    population growth, 106, 107
    religion, 240
North American city, 292–293
North American environmentalism, 160–162
North American Free Trade Agreement (NAFTA),
    20, 79, 80, 82, 263, 289, 336, 383, 393
North Atlantic Treaty Organization (NATO),
    76, 80
North Korea
    nuclear capacity, 83, 83f
    UN actions in, 80
North-South Institute, 127
Northern Ireland Assembly, 72
Northwest Passage, 182, 182f
Northwest Territories, 373, 373f
Norway, 98, 314
Nova Chemicals, 385
Nova Scotia, 131, 359
nuclear weapons, 78, 83
"nucleated settlement," 262
Nunavik offshore claims and land regime, 327f
Nunavut, 373

O

Oak Ridges Moraine, 299, 299f
Oberhauser, Ann, 207
obesity, 115–116

O'Brien, Richard, 40
O'Tuathail, Gearoid, 76–77
Occupational Structure of the Labour Force, 316
occupations, and gender, 193, 193f
Occupied Territories, 65
Oceania, 276
"October Crisis," 74
Odinga, Raila, 334
office park, 354f
Official Language Act (Bill 22), 233
official languages, 236–237
Official Languages Act, 233
offshore, 396
oil, 167–168
oil consumption, world, 168f
oil spills, 167f, 358
Oliver, Robert, 306, 307
O'Loughlin, John, 39
Olympic Games, 307
On the Backroad to Heaven (Kraybill and Bow-
    man), 225
one-child policy, 119
100-Mile Diet, 166
One-Tonne Challenge, 162
Ontario
    auto industry, 393
    Huron County, 248–249
    industrial capacity, increase of, 373
    industrial economy, development of, 382
    labour force, size of, 382
    and manufacturing belt, 385–386
    migrant workers, 127, 133
    migratory exchanges, 126
    park lands, 162
    population growth, 102
    religion, 244
    seasonal agricultural workers, 127
    steel industry, 382
Ontario Ministry of Transportation, 360, 361
operational boundary disputes, 60
opium, 270
Oppong, Joseph, 207–208
The Oprah Winfrey Show, 209
Organisation for Economic Cooperation and
    Development (OECD), 358
Organization for European Economic Co-operation
    (OEEC), 81
Osborne Village, Winnipeg, 298f
Ost, Jason, 204
Oswin, Natalie, 204, 218, 219
Ottawa, 12, 12f, 94, 349f
Ottawa–Gatineau, 301
outsource, 396
oxygen cycle, 174
ozone layer, 183–184

P

Pacific Rim, 34
Pacione, Michael, 48
Packard Motors Plant, Detroit, 394f
Pakistan

Afghanistan, migrants from, 144
beards, and appointment of judges, 239
capital, location of, 340
e-waste sites, 176
gross national income, 314
indentured workers, 137
nuclear weapons, 83
population concentration, 93
population growth, 100
Palestinian Arabs, 128
the Palestinians, 65
pandemics, 13, 115
Papua, New Guinea, 301
Paris, 297, 308
Parkdale, Toronto, 226, 226f
parking policies, 356
Parks Canada Agency, 161
Parthenon of Athens, 282, 283f
participatory development, 47
patch agriculture, 255
pattern, 12
patterns of consumption, 165–166
Peace of Westphalia, 62–63, 63f
Peake, Linda, 197
pedestrian deaths, 361
Peet, Richard, 27
Pentagon, 84
People's World Water Forum, 163f
PepsiCo, 44
per capita (GNI), 314–316, 315t
per capita gross national income (GNI), 70f
perceptual region, 7–8, 7f
Pereira, Miguel Mendes, 43
periphery, 323
periphery states, 32, 33f
    barriers to economic development, 328–334
    cities of, 294–296, 300–301
    costs of economic development, 335–337
    downturns, 48
    immigrant neighbourhoods, 301–303
    periphery of the periphery, 340–341
    transportation, 367–368
Perl, Anthony, 359
Perry, Clarence, 350–351
Peru, 126, 237, 281
phenomenology, 26
Philippines
    contraception in, 120
    official language, 237
    women, as domestic servants, 133
Philips, 391
Phuket, Thailand, 156
physical geography, 4
physical-political boundaries, 58
physiologic population density, 89–91
Pier 21, Halifax, 150f
Pinchot, Gifford, 161
Pitt, Brad, 192f
place, 8–9
    authenticity of, 227–228
    commodification, 226–228